The 70-290 Cram Sheet

This Cram Sheet contains the distilled, key facts about the Managing and Maintaining a Microsoft Windows Server 2003 Environment exam. Review this information as the last thing you do before you enter the testing center, paying special attention to those areas where you feel that you need the most review.

HARDWARE DEVICES AND DRIVERS

1. Driver signing is a method for marking or identifying driver files that meet certain specifications or standards. Windows Server 2003 uses a driver-signing process to make sure drivers are certified to work correctly with the Windows Driver Model (WDM) in Windows Server 2003.

2. To restore a device driver back to its previously installed version, open Device Manager, right-click the device you are having trouble with, and select Properties. Click the Driver tab and then click the Roll Back Driver button.

3. You must be logged on as either the local administrator or as a member of the Administrators group to install updated components or to change Automatic Updates settings.

4. If Windows Server 2003 is installed with just one CPU present (a uniprocessor system) and you later want to add one or more additional processors (to create a multiprocessor system), you must use the Hardware Update Wizard to install a new hardware abstraction layer (HAL) to enable support for multiple processors.

5. To configure a hardware profile, copy the default profile and rename it appropriately. Restart the computer and select the profile you want to configure (enable or disable devices or services).

SERVER STORAGE

6. Basic disks use partitions, not volumes, and they can store up to four primary partitions or up to three primary partitions and one extended partition with logical drives.

7. Dynamic disks use volumes, not partitions, that you create from unallocated space. The five types of dynamic volumes are simple, spanned, striped, mirrored, and RAID-5.

8. You can use either the Disk Management console or the diskpart.exe command-line utility to work with disk storage.

9. Only Windows Server 2003, Windows XP Professional, Windows 2000 Professional, and Windows 2000 Server support dynamic volumes.

10. You can convert a basic disk to a dynamic disk and retain all data on the disk. However, you cannot revert a dynamic disk back to a basic disk without first deleting all existing volumes (and data). You must first back up the data on the dynamic disk, and then you can restore the data from backup onto the new basic disk.

11. To convert a FAT to an NTFS filesystem, you use the convert x: /fs:ntfs command where x is the drive letter that you are converting.

12. When moving disks to another Windows Server 2003 computer, choose Rescan from the menu bar in Disk Management. Right-click any disks marked Foreign, click Import Foreign Disks, and then follow the instructions provided by the Disk Management console.

13. Using the diskpart.exe command-line tool, you can extend a basic partition, but it must be formatted as NTFS, it must be adjacent to contiguous unallocated space on the same physical disk, and it can be extended only onto unallocated space that resides on the same physical disk. You cannot use Disk Management for this task.

14. Spanned volumes cannot be mirrored or striped, and spanned volumes are not fault tolerant.

15. Striped volumes cannot be mirrored or extended (spanned), and striped volumes are not fault tolerant.

16. Boot volumes, system volumes, striped volumes, mirrored volumes, and RAID-5 volumes cannot be extended (spanned).

17. The boot partition or volume is the drive letter where the Windows Server 2003 operating system files are stored, such as the c:\windows folder. The system partition or volume is the drive letter where the system's startup files are stored, such as ntldr, ntdetect.com, ntbootdd.sys, and boot.ini. The boot partition or volume and the system partition or volume can be one and the same, such as the c: drive.

18. Mirrored volumes use dynamic volumes stored on two separate physical disks to "mirror" (write) data onto both disks simultaneously and redundantly. This configuration is also referred to as RAID-1.

19. RAID-5 volumes use disk striping with parity information to write data across a minimum of three physical disks and a maximum of 32 physical disks. You effectively lose an amount of storage equivalent to the capacity of one of the disks due to parity information that gets stored across all the

58. From the Remote tab on the System Properties window, make sure that the Turn On Remote Assistance and Allow Invitations To Be Sent From This Computer check box is marked if you want to use RA on the computer.

59. You can actually connect to a Terminal Server's console session by opening the remote desktop session using the `mstsc.exe /console` command. Alternatively, you can use the Remote Desktops MMC snap-in to connect to RDC sessions; connecting to the console session is the default setting for the Remote Desktops snap-in.

60. Internet Information Services (IIS) 6.0 are not automatically installed; you must use the Add or Remove Programs applet in the Control Panel to install the IIS components that you require.

61. If anyone attempts to access a web page hosted by IIS 6.0 that contains a feature that has not yet been installed, such as Active Server pages, server-side includes, or FrontPage server extensions, the user will receive an HTTP Error 404 message.

62. IIS logs typically reside in `%Windir%\System32\Logfiles\W3svc1`.

63. IIS's configuration database file is known as the metabase. The IIS metabase contains all the important configuration data for all the Internet services on the computer. The IIS 6.0 metabase now uses the XML file format. By default, the metabase file is stored in the `%systemroot%\system32\ inetsrv` folder and uses the filename `metabase.xml`.

64. IIS 6.0 automatically creates backups of the metabase on a periodic basis; these backups are called history files, and this feature is enabled by default. The IIS 6.0 `metabase.xml` file has a matching metabase schema file, `mbschema.xml`.

65. You can import an entire IIS 6.0 metabase from one computer into another using the `iisback.vbs` or `iiscnfg.vbs /copy` commands, which will replace all the machine-specific and system-specific settings stored in metabase backup files. To ensure that all new settings have been saved to the metabase file, you can right-click the web server name in the left pane of IIS Manager and select Save Configuration to Disk.

DISASTER RECOVERY

66. If a server does not start after you install a new driver, new software, or a new service, you can use Safe Mode to start the server with a minimal amount of services and drivers so that you can disable or remove the offending driver, software program, or service.

67. If you have difficulty starting a server, you can use the Last Known Good Configuration startup option to restore the server settings that are automatically saved during the most recent successful logon.

68. Use the Recovery Console if a startup disk, Safe Mode, and the Last Known Good Configuration all fail to start the server. You can either preinstall the Recovery Console or run it directly from the Windows Server 2003 CD-ROM.

69. The Recovery Console in Windows Server 2003 gives you a command-prompt–only environment that you can use for enabling and disabling

services, copying files on a local drive, formatting hard disks, and repairing a boot sector. You must log on to the Recovery Console using the local administrator account.

70. Automated System Recovery (ASR) is integrated within the Windows Server 2003 Backup Utility (`NTBackup.exe`), and you can use it to recover a system that does not start. An ASR restore requires the Windows Server 2003 CD-ROM, an ASR backup media set, and the associated ASR floppy disk.

71. If you lose the ASR floppy disk, you can re-create it by restoring the `\windows\repair` folder from the ASR backup media set and copying the `asr.sif` and `asrpnp.sif` files onto a blank floppy disk as a substitute for the ASR floppy disk.

DATA BACKUP

72. The Backup Utility offers you five backup types when you perform a data backup: Normal, Copy, Differential, Incremental, and Daily. Only Normal and Incremental backups reset (or clear) each backed-up file's archive bit.

73. To back up server data, you must be logged on to the computer as a member of the Backup Operators group, a member of the Server Operators group (in a domain environment), or a member of the Administrators group. You can back up both local and network folders and files with the Backup Utility.

74. If an authorized user runs the Backup Utility under the security credentials of a different user with the Run as command, the backup log is saved under the `%username%` folder for the username used with the Run as command. In these instances, the logged-on user cannot view the other username's backup or restore logs. Only the last 10 backup logs are retained; older report logs are overwritten one at a time.

75. You can back up files using `NTBackup.exe` from a command prompt, but you cannot restore files using the command-line options of `NTBackup.exe`.

76. The Verify backup option is turned off by default.

77. You cannot select which components of the system state to back up; all components of the system state are backed up by default with no other options available.

78. You must reboot a DC and select Directory Services Restore Mode from the Windows Advanced Options startup menu to perform a restore of its System State and the DC's Active Directory database. You must log on with the administrator password created for Directory Services Restore Mode when the computer was promoted to a DC.

79. Use the `NTDSUtil.exe` tool to mark restored Active Directory objects as authoritative. This process is known as an authoritative restore.

80. If you have only one DC in the domain, or if you need to rebuild an entire domain from backup when all DCs are lost, you should perform a primary restore.

MCSA/MCSE
70-290

Managing and Maintaining a Microsoft® Windows Server® 2003 Environment

Dan Balter
Patrick Regan

MCSA/MCSE 70-290 Exam Cram: Managing and Maintaining a Microsoft® Windows Server® 2003 Environment

Copyright © 2007 by Que Publishing

All rights reserved. No part of this book shall be reproduced, stored in a retrieval system, or transmitted by any means, electronic, mechanical, photocopying, recording, or otherwise, without written permission from the publisher. No patent liability is assumed with respect to the use of the information contained herein. Although every precaution has been taken in the preparation of this book, the publisher and author assume no responsibility for errors or omissions. Nor is any liability assumed for damages resulting from the use of the information contained herein.

ISBN-10: 0-7897-3617-9

ISBN-13: 978-0-7897-3617-8

Library of Congress Cataloging-in-Publication data is on file.

Printed in the United States of America

First Printing: March 2007

10   4

Trademarks

Warning and Disclaimer

Bulk Sales

Que Publishing offers excellent discounts on this book when ordered in quantity for bulk purchases or special sales. For more information, please contact

U.S. Corporate and Government Sales
1-800-382-3419
corpsales@pearsontechgroup.com

For sales outside the United States, please contact

International Sales
international@pearsoned.com

Publisher
Paul Boger

Associate Publisher
Dave Dusthimer

Acquisitions Editor
Betsy Brown

Development Editors
Todd Brakke
Deadline Driven
Publishing

Managing Editor
Patrick Kanouse

Project Editor
Tonya Simpson

Copy Editor
Rhonda Tinch-Mize

Indexer
Heather McNeill

Proofreader
Leslie Joseph

Technical Editors
Jeff A. Dunkelberger
James Michael
Stewart

Publishing Coordinator
Vanessa Evans

Book Designer
Gary Adair

Page Layout
TnT Design, Inc.

Contents at a Glance

Table of Contents

About the Authors

Dan Balter is the chief technology officer for InfoTechnology Partners, Inc., a Microsoft Certified Partner company. He works as a technology consultant for small- to medium-sized businesses and has worked with several different network operating systems throughout his 22-year career. Dan takes pride in turning complex, technical topics into easy-to-understand concepts. Dan is a Microsoft Certified Desktop Support Technician (MCDST), a Microsoft Certified Systems Administrator (MCSA), and a Microsoft Certified Systems Engineer (MCSE). He specializes in Microsoft networking technologies, firewalls, VPNs, and other security solutions in addition to designing and implementing messaging and business solutions, such as Exchange Server environments. As CTO for InfoTechnology Partners, Inc., Dan has worked to implement an affordable continuous offsite data protection backup system for companies large and small.

Dan is a coauthor for the best-selling books *Exam Cram 2: Windows XP Professional, Exam Cram 2: Supporting Users and Troubleshooting a Windows XP Operating System,* and *Exam Cram 2: Windows 2000 Professional,* published by Que Certification. Dan has been a featured speaker at conferences across North America, including Advisor DevCons and Summits sponsored by Advisor Media and Windows Connections conferences sponsored by *Windows IT Pro Magazine.*

A graduate of USC's School of Business in 1983, Dan has authored more than 300 video-, CD-, and DVD-based computer education courses, including instructional titles on installing, configuring, and administering Windows 95, Windows 98, Windows NT, Windows 2000, Windows XP, and Windows Server 2003. He has also appeared as a featured video trainer for self-paced learning courses on Microsoft Exchange Server, Microsoft Outlook, and Intuit's QuickBooks small business accounting software. Dan is the video instructor for *ExamBlast—Windows XP Professional* and for many of the *QuickBooks Pro* learning series titles on video and DVD from http://www.BlastThroughLearning.com.

Dan and his family live in the Santa Rosa Valley area in Southern California, near the city of Camarillo. Dan lives with his lovely wife, Alison; their 10-year-old daughter, Alexis; their 7-year-old son, Brendan; and their golden retriever, Brandy. When he's not writing, researching, or consulting, Dan enjoys traveling with his family, swimming, playing racquetball and basketball, rooting for the L.A. Lakers and Dodgers, going for long walks, listening to music, and exploring new age spirituality. Dan can be contacted via email at Dan@InfoTech-Partners.com.

Patrick Regan has been a PC technician and network administrator/engineer for the past 15 years after graduating with a bachelor's degree in physics from the University of Akron. He has taught many computer and network classes at Sacramento local colleges (Heald Colleges and MTI Colleges), worked as a product support engineer for the Intel Corporation Customer Service, and participated in and led many projects (Heald Colleges, Intel Corporation, and Miles Consulting Corporation). For his teaching accomplishments, he received the Teacher of the Year award from Heald Colleges. In addition, he received several recognition awards from Intel. Previously, he was a senior network engineer for Virtual Alert support the BioTerrorism Readiness suite. Currently, he is a senior design architect/engineer and training coordinator for Miles Consulting Corp (MCC), a premiere Microsoft Gold partner and consulting firm. He holds many certifications, including the Microsoft MCSE, MCSA, and MCT; CompTIA's A+, Network+, Server+, Linux+, Security+, and CTT+; Cisco CCNA; and Novell's CNE and CWNP Certified Wireless Network Administrator (CWNA). Over the last couple of years, he has written several textbooks for Prentice Hall Publisher, including *Troubleshooting the PC*, *Networking with Windows 2000 and 2003*, *Linux*, *Local Area Networks*, *Wide Area Networks*, and the Acing Series (*Acing the A+*, *Acing the Network+*, *Acing the Security+*, and *Acing the Linux+*).

You can write with questions and comments to the author at Patrick_Regan@hotmail.com. (Because of the high volume of mail, every message might not receive a reply.)

About the Technical Editors

Jeff A. Dunkelberger, MCSE, MCT, is currently a solution architect in the Hewlett-Packard Enterprise Microsoft Services practice, where he works with HP's large federal government and commercial customers, helping them solve their business problems with Windows and Exchange solutions. Most recently, Jeff completed a special assignment as the lab master on the design and delivery team for the HP Windows 2003 Academy series. HP's Windows 2003 Academy program is an intense, practical field-training exercise attended by hundreds of HP's Windows consultants around the world.

Jeff completed his master's degree in business management at the McGregor School of Antioch University and acts as a technical editor for several computer-book publishers. He lives in the Washington, D.C., suburb of Alexandria, Virginia, in a very small house with his attorney wife, two dogs, and three cats, and he can be reached at jeffd@hp.com.

James Michael Stewart has been working with computers and technology for more than 19 years. Michael does business as IMPACT Online d.b.a, a technology focusing writing and training organization. His work focuses on Windows 2003/XP/2000, certification, and security. Recently, Michael has been teaching job skill and certification courses, such as CISSP and CEH.

Michael has coauthored numerous books on Microsoft and security certification and administration. He has written articles for numerous print and online publications. He has developed certification courseware and training materials as well as presented these materials in the classroom. He is also a regular speaker at Interop and COMDEX.

Michael holds the following certifications: CISSP, ISSAP, SSCP, MCT, CEI, CEH, TICSA, CIW SA, Security+, MCSE+Security Windows 2000, MCSA Windows Server 2003, MCDST, MCSE NT & W2K, MCP+I, Network+, and iNet+.

Michael graduated in 1992 from the University of Texas at Austin with a bachelor's degree in philosophy. Despite his degree, his computer knowledge is self-acquired, based on seat-of-the-pants, hands-on experience. You can reach Michael by email at michael@impactonline.com.

Dedication

I dedicate this second edition book to my wonderful, loving parents, Maureen and Herb Balter. Mom and Dad, you're the best!

—*Dan Balter*

Acknowledgments

Endeavoring to author a book is a daunting task at best; accepting the challenge to write a technical guide covering all the ins and outs of a new network server operating system seems near impossible at times, while impending deadlines loom overhead. Of course, it's the family who bears the brunt of the burden with Dad staring at two different computer monitors while tinkering with yet a third one off to the side! My darling wife, Alison, has always encouraged me and supported me: Thank you so much for always being there for me; I love you more than words can convey! To my two beautiful children, Alexis and Brendan: I love you both and I appreciate you both so much. Thanks for being patient with me while I was working on this book!

All our lives seem to be so hectic; where would we be without the help and support from our loved ones, our friends, and our distinguished associates? To Nicole Phelps, our office manager, I really appreciate all that you do for us—thank you so much for helping our company run smoothly and for assisting us in our personal lives as well! To Aaron Brown, our lead technical consultant, what can I say? You've helped our company really grow, and your hard work and technical expertise is just incredible! Thank you very much and keep up the great work!

To Scott Barker, our lead developer/programmer, you're a terrific friend and an invaluable asset to our company and to our clients—we offer you all our gratitude! To Chris Thibedeau, thank you for your continued hard work as one of our talented networking consultants! To Gaby, our priceless residential engineer (a.k.a. housekeeper), thank you for your tireless commitment to keeping our home spotless and organized! Last, but never least, I'm extremely grateful for all the members of my local Thousand Oaks chapter of Business Networking International (BNI); you all make a terrific extended family and you're great for business as well!

To Greggory Peck, thanks for partnering with us on Blast Through Learning (`http://www.BlastThroughLearning.com`) and thanks for being a great friend! A ton of appreciation has to go to Scott McIntyre, Alan Sugano, Dan Holme, Jeremy Moskowitz, Don Jones, and Mark Minasi: I really appreciate all your friendships; you guys all provide me with a lot of inspiration to always keep learning and to be the best author, trainer, and consultant that I can be! To Lisa Champagne of Achievement Resources: Thank you for your guidance, wisdom, and advice that is helping me become a much more effective manager! Also, to Reverend Molly Rockey, her husband, Ed, and everyone associated with Unity Center Church: Thank you for always being my guiding light and assisting me in staying on the spiritual path. There is nothing better, in my view, than always striving to live life in a genuine, heartfelt way—Unity definitely supports me in fulfilling that vision.

We Want to Hear from You!

As the reader of this book, *you* are our most important critic and commentator. We value your opinion and want to know what we're doing right, what we could do better, what areas you'd like to see us publish in, and any other words of wisdom you're willing to pass our way.

As an associate publisher for Que Publishing, I welcome your comments. You can email or write me directly to let me know what you did or didn't like about this book—as well as what we can do to make our books better.

Please note that I cannot help you with technical problems related to the topic of this book. We do have a User Services group, however, where I will forward specific technical questions related to the book.

When you write, please be sure to include this book's title and author as well as your name, email address, and phone number. I will carefully review your comments and share them with the author and editors who worked on the book.

Email: scorehigher@pearsoned.com

Mail: Dave Dusthimer
         Associate Publisher
         Que Publishing
         800 East 96th Street
         Indianapolis, IN 46240 USA

Reader Services

Visit our website and register this book at www.examcram.com/register for convenient access to any updates, downloads, or errata that might be available for this book.

Introduction

Welcome to *MCSA/MCSE Managing and Maintaining a Microsoft Windows Server 2003 Environment Exam Cram*! Whether this book is your first or your fifteenth *Exam Cram* series book, you'll find information here that will help ensure your success as you pursue knowledge, experience, and certification. This book aims to help you get ready to take—and pass—the Microsoft certification exam "Managing and Maintaining a Microsoft Windows Server 2003 Environment" (Exam 70-290). This introduction, along with Chapter 1, explains Microsoft's certification programs in general and talks about how the *Exam Cram* series can help you prepare for Microsoft's latest MCSE and MCSA certification exams. Chapters 2 through 9 are designed to remind you of everything you'll need to know to pass the 70-290 certification exam. The two sample tests at the end of the book should give you a reasonably accurate assessment of your knowledge—and, yes, we've provided the answers and their explanations for these sample tests. Read the book, understand the material, and you'll stand a very good chance of passing the real test.

Exam Cram books help you understand and appreciate the subjects and materials you need to know to pass Microsoft certification exams. *Exam Cram* books are aimed strictly at test preparation and review. They do not teach you everything you need to know about a subject. Instead, the author streamlines and highlights the pertinent information by presenting and dissecting the questions and problems he's discovered that you're likely to encounter on a Microsoft test.

Nevertheless, to completely prepare yourself for any Microsoft test, we recommend that you begin by taking the self assessment that is included in this book, immediately following this introduction. The self-assessment tool will help you evaluate your knowledge base against the requirements for becoming a Microsoft Certified Systems Administrator (MCSA) and a Microsoft Certified Systems Engineer (MCSE) for Windows Server 2003 under both ideal and real circumstances.

Based on what you learn from the self assessment, you might decide to begin your studies with some classroom training or some background reading. On the other hand, you might decide to pick up and read one of the many study guides available from Microsoft or third-party vendors. We also recommend that you supplement your study program with visits to http://www.examcram.com to receive additional practice questions, get advice, and track the Windows Server 2003 MCSA and MCSE programs.

This book also offers you an added bonus of accessing Exam Cram practice tests online. All you need is a connection to the Internet and you can take advantage of these practice exam questions right from your very own web browser! This software simulates the Microsoft testing environment with similar types of questions that you're likely to see on the actual Microsoft exam. We also strongly recommend that you install, configure, and play around with the network operating system software that you'll be tested on: Nothing beats hands-on experience and familiarity when it comes to understanding the questions you're likely to encounter on a certification test. Book learning is essential, but without a doubt, hands-on experience is the best teacher of all!

The Microsoft Certification Program

Microsoft currently offers several certification titles, each of which boasts its own special abbreviation. (As a certification candidate and computer professional, you need to have a high tolerance for acronyms.) Except for the Microsoft Certified Trainer (MCT) and the Microsoft Certified Learning Consultant (MCLC) designations, the current certification credentials that Microsoft offers fall into one of two major categories—*Microsoft Certifications for Application Developers* and *Microsoft Certifications for Information Technology (IT) Professionals*.

> **NOTE**
>
> The MCT credential is offered to qualified instructors whom Microsoft can certify to deliver training classes to *both* IT professionals *and* application developers using Microsoft Official Curriculum (MOC) courseware. MCTs whose job roles have expanded to incorporate a high level of expertise in designing and delivering customized learning solutions for customers can earn the MCLC title.

The Microsoft Certified Professional (MCP) Title

The easiest certification title to earn is the MCP designation. This entry-level certification is designed to provide an individual with the first step on the road to higher levels of Microsoft certification. An MCP candidate needs to pass only one *current* Microsoft certification exam from any current Microsoft certification track. You become an MCP after successfully *passing at least one qualifying exam*—qualifying MCP exams include tests from *both* the application developer certification category *and* from the IT professional certification category.

However, *not all Microsoft exams qualify an individual for MCP status*—for example, passing Exam 70-122, "Designing and Providing Microsoft Volume License

Solutions to Large Organizations," does not certify an individual as a Microsoft Certified Professional (MCP). The list of qualifying certification tracks from which a candidate must successfully pass an exam to achieve MCP status are as follows:

- ▶ MCDST on Windows XP

- ▶ MCSA on Windows 2000

- ▶ MCSA: Security on Windows 2000

- ▶ MCSA on Windows Server 2003

- ▶ MCSE on Windows 2000

- ▶ MCSE: Security on Windows 2000

- ▶ MCSE on Windows Server 2003

- ▶ MCDBA on Microsoft SQL Server 2000

- ▶ MCAD on Microsoft .NET

- ▶ MCSD on Microsoft .NET

- ▶ MCSD on Microsoft Visual Studio 6.0

Microsoft Certifications for Application Developers

The Microsoft certifications for application developers are divided into three basic skill sets—*New Developers*, *Experienced Developers*, and *.NET Development*. The following certification credentials are available to professional application developers:

- ▶ *MCTS (Microsoft Certified Technology Specialist)*—These certification titles reflect a technology professional's in-depth knowledge and expertise in specialized areas of Microsoft technology. An individual receives the designation of MCTS by demonstrating a consistent ability to build, implement, troubleshoot, and debug a specific Microsoft technology by successfully passing the corresponding certification exam. The MCTS certifications include the following areas of specialization:

  - ▶ Technology Specialist: .NET Framework 2.0 Web Applications

  - ▶ Technology Specialist: .NET Framework 2.0 Windows Applications

  - ▶ Technology Specialist: .NET Framework 2.0 Distributed Applications

> ▶ Technology Specialist: SQL Server 2005

> ▶ Technology Specialist: BizTalk Server 2006

▶ *MCSD (Microsoft Certified Solution Developer)*—The MCSD for Microsoft .NET credential reflects the skills required to create multitier, distributed, and Component Object Model (COM)–based solutions, in addition to desktop and Internet applications, using new technologies. To obtain MCSD certification, an individual must demonstrate the ability to analyze and interpret user requirements; select and integrate products, platforms, tools, and technologies; design and implement code; customize applications; and perform necessary software tests and quality assurance operations. To obtain the MCSD for Microsoft .NET credential, an individual must pass a total of five exams: four core exams and one elective exam.

▶ *MCAD (Microsoft Certified Application Developer) for Microsoft .NET*—The MCAD credential provides industry recognition for professional developers who build powerful applications using Microsoft Visual Studio .NET and Web services. MCAD candidates are required to pass two core exams and one elective exam in an area of specialization.

▶ *MCPD (Microsoft Certified Professional Developer)*—The MCPD title does not just share its name with the "Microsoft Campus Police Department." No, not at all. The MCPD credential stands out as the current premier certification for programmers developing applications using Microsoft technology. Individuals who attain the MCPD credential distinguish themselves as experts for building Windows applications, web applications, or enterprise-level applications using the Microsoft .NET Framework 2.0. The MCPD certifications include the following areas of specialization:

> ▶ Professional Developer: Web Developer

> ▶ Professional Developer: Windows Developer

> ▶ Professional Developer: Enterprise Applications Developer

▶ *MCAP (Microsoft Certified Architect Program)*—The Microsoft Certified Architect Program aims to identify and recognize the top experts in the industry who possess the vision and talent to successfully design *both* application-based solutions and infrastructure-based frameworks *and* methodologies across the entire IT life cycle. Microsoft Certified Architects can integrate multiple technologies to solve business problems while providing the necessary metrics and measurements to define the success or failure of each project.

Microsoft Certifications for IT Professionals

The Microsoft certifications for IT professionals provide a series of credentials for individuals to demonstrate their levels of knowledge and proficiency for using Microsoft technology in the realm of computer systems, networking infrastructure, and database infrastructure. The following Microsoft certification titles are available to IT professionals:

- *MCITP (Microsoft Certified IT Professional)*—The MCITP credentials offer technology professionals the opportunity to highlight their particular skills in a specific area of expertise. The MCITP certification titles include such specialized expertise as a database developer, a database administrator, and a business intelligence developer. The current IT Professional certifications include the following designations:

    - IT Professional: Database Developer

    - IT Professional: Database Administrator

    - IT Professional: Business Intelligence Developer

- *MCSA (Microsoft Certified Systems Administrator)*—This certification is for anyone who possesses a high level of networking expertise with Microsoft operating systems and software products. This credential is designed to prepare individuals to manage, maintain, and support information systems, networks, and internetworks built around the Microsoft Windows Server System and Windows XP and Windows 2000 desktop computers. MCSA candidates must pass four exams to become certified. Microsoft currently offers two tracks for the MCSA credential—MCSA on Windows 2000 and MCSA on Windows Server 2003. The exam requirements for attaining each MCSA credential are detailed in Tables I.1 and I.2.

TIP

MCSA on Windows 2000 Specializations—After a candidate successfully passes the three required core exams, he has the options to specialize in the areas of Messaging and/or Security. A candidate earns the specialization title of *MCSA on Windows 2000:Messaging* by passing *one* of the following elective exams as listed in Table I.1—Exam 70-224 covering Exchange 2000 Server or Exam 70-284 covering Exchange Server 2003.

A candidate earns the specialization title of *MCSA on Windows 2000:Security* by passing *two* of the following elective exams also listed in Table I.1—Exam 70-214 covering security in a Windows 2000 network *plus* one of the following three exams:

- Exam 70-227 covering ISA Server 2000
- Exam 70-350 covering ISA Server 2004
- Exam SYO-101: CompTIA Security+

> **NOTE**
>
> Required core exams that are also available as elective exams can only be counted once toward a candidate's certification. An exam may count as fulfilling a core requirement *or* it may count as an elective, but the same exam cannot count as both a core exam and as an elective exam.

> **NOTE**
>
> Once you become an MCSA on Windows Server 2003, you can upgrade your status to the MCSE on Windows Server 2003 credential by passing the remaining exams required for MCSEs. You may take either a Windows Server 2003 networking design exam *or* a Windows 2000 networking design exam to satisfy the MCSE on Windows Server 2003 design skills requirement.

TABLE I.1   MCSA on Windows 2000 Exam Requirements

Exam Number	Exam Title
Client Operating System Exams	
Candidates Must Pass One of the Following Exams	
70-210	Installing, Configuring, and Administering Microsoft Windows 2000 Professional
	OR
70-270	Installing, Configuring, and Administering Microsoft Windows XP Professional
Networking System Exams	
Candidates Must Pass Two of the Following Exams	
70-215	Installing, Configuring, and Administering Microsoft Windows 2000 Server
70-218	Managing a Microsoft Windows 2000 Network Environment
Elective Exams	
Candidates Must Pass One of the Following Elective Exams (or candidates must pass one or two of the qualifying equivalent alternative exams)	
70-028	Administering Microsoft SQL Server 7.0
70-081	Implementing and Supporting Microsoft Exchange Server 5.5
70-089	Designing, Implementing, and Managing a Microsoft Systems Management Server 2003 Infrastructure
70-214	Implementing and Administering Security in a Microsoft Windows 2000 Network
70-216	Implementing and Administering a Microsoft Windows 2000 Network Infrastructure

TABLE I.1 *Continued*

Exam Number	Exam Title

Candidates Must Pass One of the Following Elective Exams (or candidates must pass one or two of the qualifying equivalent alternative exams)

Exam Number	Exam Title
70-224	Installing, Configuring, and Administering Microsoft Exchange 2000 Server
70-227	Installing, Configuring, and Administering Microsoft Internet Security and Acceleration (ISA) Server 2000, Enterprise Edition
70-228	Installing, Configuring, and Administering Microsoft SQL Server 2000 Enterprise Edition
70-244	Supporting and Maintaining a Microsoft Windows NT Server 4.0 Network
70-284	Implementing and Managing Microsoft Exchange Server 2003
70-350	Implementing Microsoft Internet Security and Acceleration (ISA) Server 2004

Qualifying Alternative Exams and Certifications

CompTIA	Security+
CompTIA A+ and CompTIA Network+	Passing both of these alternative exams qualifies as having passed one Microsoft elective exam.
CompTIA A+ and CompTIA Server+	Passing both of these alternative exams qualifies as having passed one Microsoft elective exam.
70-271 and 70-272	Passing both of these exams earns the Microsoft Certified Desktop Support Technician (MCDST) credential and qualifies as having passed one alternative elective exam. *Exam 70-271: Supporting Users and Troubleshooting a Microsoft Windows XP Operating System. 70-272: Supporting Users and Troubleshooting Desktop Applications on a Microsoft Windows XP Operating System.*

TIP

MCSA on Windows Server 2003 Specializations—After a candidate successfully passes the three required core exams, he has the options to specialize in the areas of messaging and/or security. A candidate earns the specialization title of *MCSA on Windows Server 2003:Messaging* by passing the following elective exam as listed in Table I.2—Exam 70-284 covering Exchange Server 2003.

A candidate earns the specialization title of *MCSA on Windows Server 2003:Security* by passing *two* of the following elective exam choices, which are also listed in Table I.2:

► Exam 70-227 covering ISA Server 2000 *or* Exam SYO-101: CompTIA Security+

► Exam 70-350 covering ISA Server 2004

► Exam 70-299 covering security in a Windows Server 2003 Network

Table I.2   MCSA on Windows Server 2003 Exam Requirements

Exam Number	Exam Title
Client Operating System Exams	
Candidates Must Pass One of the Following Exams	
70-210	Installing, Configuring, and Administering Microsoft Windows 2000 Professional
	OR
70-270	Installing, Configuring, and Administering Microsoft Windows XP Professional
Networking System Exams	
Candidates Must Pass Each of the Following Two Exams	
70-290	Managing and Maintaining a Microsoft Windows Server 2003 Environment
70-291	Implementing, Managing, and Maintaining a Microsoft Windows Server 2003 Network Infrastructure
Elective Exams	
Candidates Must Pass One of the Following Elective Exams (or candidates must pass one or two of the qualifying equivalent alternative exams)	
70-086	Implementing and Supporting Microsoft Systems Management Server 2.0
70-089	Designing, Implementing, and Managing a Microsoft Systems Management Server 2003 Infrastructure
70-227	Installing, Configuring, and Administering Microsoft Internet Security and Acceleration (ISA) Server 2000, Enterprise Edition
70-228	Installing, Configuring, and Administering Microsoft SQL Server 2000 Enterprise Edition
70-284	Implementing and Managing Microsoft Exchange Server 2003
70-299	Implementing and Administering Security in a Microsoft Windows Server 2003 Network
70-350	Implementing Microsoft Internet Security and Acceleration (ISA) Server 2004
Qualifying Alternative Exams and Certifications	
CompTIA	Security+ (*satisfies both the MCSA on Windows Server 2003 elective requirement and the MCSA on Windows Server 2003:Security specialization requirement*)
CompTIA A+ and CompTIA Network+	Passing both of these exams qualifies as having passed one Microsoft elective exam.
CompTIA A+ and CompTIA Server+	Passing both of these exams qualifies as having passed one Microsoft elective exam.

TABLE I.2 *Continued*

Exam Number	Exam Title
Qualifying Alternative Exams and Certifications	
70-271 and 70-272	Passing both of these exams earns the Microsoft Certified Desktop Support Technician (MCDST) credential and qualifies as having passed one alternative elective exam. (*Exam 70-271: Supporting Users and Troubleshooting a Microsoft Windows XP Operating System* and *Exam 70-272: Supporting Users and Troubleshooting Desktop Applications on a Microsoft Windows XP Operating System.*)
MCSA on Windows 2000	An individual who holds this certification qualifies as having passed one Microsoft elective exam.
MCSE on Windows 2000	An individual who holds this certification qualifies as having passed one Microsoft elective exam.
MCSE on Windows NT 4.0	An individual who holds this certification qualifies as having passed one Microsoft elective exam.

TIP

If you are already certified as an MCSA on Windows 2000, you can expedite the certification process for becoming an MCSA on Windows Server 2003. Just pass the single upgrade test—Exam 70-292, "Managing and Maintaining a Microsoft Windows Server 2003 Environment for an MCSA Certified on Windows 2000." Once you've passed this one upgrade exam, you're certified as an MCSA on Windows Server 2003.

▶ *MCSE (Microsoft Certified Systems Engineer)*—Anyone who has a current MCSE is recognized as possessing a high level of networking expertise with Microsoft operating systems and networking solutions. This credential is designed to recognize individuals who have the skills to plan, design, implement, maintain, and support information systems, networks, and internetworks built around Microsoft Windows Server 2003, Windows XP, Windows 2000, Windows NT 4.0, Windows 9x, and the Windows Server System family of products. The road to becoming an MCSE can start by attaining MCSA credential. MCSE candidates must pass seven exams to become certified. Microsoft currently offers two tracks for the MCSE credential—MCSE on Windows 2000 and MCSE on Windows Server 2003.

MCSE candidates who are not already certified as MCSEs or MCSAs on Windows 2000 must pass seven tests to meet the MCSE requirements. It's not uncommon for the entire process to take a year or so, and many individuals find that they must take a test more than once to pass. The primary goal of the *Exam Cram* test preparation guides is to make it possible, given proper study and preparation, to pass all Microsoft certification tests on the first try. The exam requirements for attaining each MCSE status are detailed in Tables I.3 and I.4.

> ## TIP
>
> **MCSE on Windows 2000 Specializations**—After a candidate successfully passes the five required core exams, he has the options of specializing in the areas of messaging and/or security. A candidate earns the specialization title of *MCSE on Windows 2000:Messaging* by passing *two* of the following elective exams as listed in Table I.3—Exam 70-224 *and* Exam 70-225 on Exchange 2000 Server *or* Exam 70-284 *and* Exam 70-285 on Exchange Server 2003.
>
> A candidate earns the specialization title of *MCSE on Windows 2000:Security* by passing *three* of the following elective exams also listed in Table I.3—Exam 70-220 covering security design for a Windows 2000 network, Exam 70-214 on security administration for a Windows 2000 network, *plus one* of following exams:
>
> ▶ Exam 70-227 covering ISA Server 2000
>
> ▶ Exam 70-350 covering ISA Server 2004
>
> ▶ Exam SYO-101: CompTIA Security+

TABLE I.3   MCSE on Windows 2000 Exam Requirements

Exam Number	Exam Title
Client Operating System Exams	
Candidates Must Pass One of the Following Two Exams	
70-210	Installing, Configuring, and Administering Microsoft Windows 2000 Professional
OR	
70-270	Installing, Configuring, and Administering Microsoft Windows XP Professional
Networking System Exams	
Candidates Must Pass Each of the Following Three Exams	
70-215	Installing, Configuring, and Administering Microsoft Windows 2000 Server
70-216	Implementing and Administering a Microsoft Windows 2000 Network Infrastructure
70-217	Implementing and Administering a Microsoft Windows 2000 Directory Services Infrastructure
Networking Design Exams	
Candidates Must Pass One of the Following Exams	
70-219	Designing a Microsoft Windows 2000 Directory Services Infrastructure
70-220	Designing Security for a Microsoft Windows 2000 Network
70-221	Designing a Microsoft Windows 2000 Network Infrastructure
70-226	Designing Highly Available Web Solutions with Microsoft Windows 2000 Server Technologies
70-297	Designing a Microsoft Windows Server 2003 Active Directory and Network Infrastructure
70-298	Designing Security for a Microsoft Windows Server 2003 Network

TABLE I.3 *Continued*

Exam Number	Exam Title

Elective Exams

Candidates Must Pass Two of the Following Elective Exams (candidates may also choose from the qualifying equivalent alternative exam listed)

70-219	Designing and Implementing Data Warehouses with Microsoft SQL Server 7.0
70-028	Administering Microsoft SQL Server 7.0
70-029	Designing and Implementing Databases with Microsoft SQL Server 7.0
70-086	Implementing and Supporting Microsoft Systems Management Server 2.0
70-214	Implementing and Administering Security in a Microsoft Windows 2000 Network
70-218	Managing a Microsoft Windows 2000 Network Environment
70-219	Designing a Microsoft Windows 2000 Directory Services Infrastructure
70-220	Designing Security for a Microsoft Windows 2000 Network
70-221	Designing a Microsoft Windows 2000 Network Infrastructure
70-222	Migrating from Microsoft Windows NT 4.0 to Microsoft Windows 2000
70-223	Installing, Configuring, and Administering Microsoft Clustering Services by Using Microsoft Windows 2000 Advanced Server
70-224	Installing, Configuring, and Administering Microsoft Exchange 2000 Server
70-225	Designing and Deploying a Messaging Infrastructure with Microsoft Exchange 2000 Server
70-226	Designing Highly Available Web Solutions with Microsoft Windows 2000 Server Technologies
70-227	Installing, Configuring, and Administering Microsoft Internet Security and Acceleration (ISA) Server 2000 Enterprise Edition
70-228	Installing, Configuring, and Administering Microsoft SQL Server 2000 Enterprise Edition
70-229	Designing and Implementing Databases with Microsoft SQL Server 2000 Enterprise Edition
70-230	Designing and Implementing Solutions with Microsoft BizTalk Server 2000 Enterprise Edition
70-232	Implementing and Maintaining Highly Available Web Solutions with Microsoft Windows 2000 Server Technologies and Microsoft Application Center 2000
70-234	Designing and Implementing Solutions with Microsoft Commerce Server 2000
70-244	Supporting and Maintaining a Microsoft Windows NT Server 4.0 Network
70-284	Implementing and Managing Microsoft Exchange Server 2003

Qualifying Third-Party Alternative Exams

CompTIA	Security+

TIP

If you are already certified as an MCSE on Windows NT 4.0, you do not need to pass an elective exam to attain the MCSE on Window Server 2003 credential. You need to pass only six exams, instead of seven. The core exam requirements are the same for MCSEs on Windows NT 4.0 who want to become certified as MCSEs on Windows Server 2003 as for other candidates; the MCSE on Windows NT 4.0 credential qualifies as an elective exam.

TABLE I.4   MCSE on Windows Server 2003 Exam Requirements

Exam Number	Exam Title
Client Operating System Exams	
Candidates Must Pass One of the Following Two Exams	
70-210	Installing, Configuring, and Administering Microsoft Windows 2000 Professional
	OR
70-270	Installing, Configuring, and Administering Microsoft Windows XP Professional
Networking System Exams	
Candidates Must Pass Each of the Following Four Exams	
70-290	Managing and Maintaining a Microsoft Windows Server 2003 Environment
70-291	Implementing, Managing, and Maintaining a Microsoft Windows Server 2003 Network Infrastructure
70-293	Planning and Maintaining a Microsoft Windows Server 2003 Network Infrastructure
70-294	Planning, Implementing, and Maintaining a Microsoft Windows Server 2003 Active Directory Infrastructure
Networking Design Exams	
Candidates Must Pass One of the Following Exams	
70-297	Designing a Microsoft Windows Server 2003 Active Directory and Network Infrastructure
70-298	Designing Security for a Microsoft Windows Server 2003 Network
Elective Exams	
Candidates Must Pass One of the Following Elective Exams (or one of the qualifying alternative exams)	
70-086	Implementing and Supporting Microsoft Systems Management Server 2.0
70-089	Designing, Implementing, and Managing a Microsoft Systems Management Server 2003 Infrastructure

TABLE I.4 *Continued*

Exam Number	Exam Title

Candidates Must Pass One of the Following Elective Exams (or one of the qualifying alternative exams)

70-227	Installing, Configuring, and Administering Microsoft Internet Security and Acceleration (ISA) Server 2000, Enterprise Edition
70-228	Installing, Configuring, and Administering Microsoft SQL Server 2000 Enterprise Edition
70-229	Installing, Configuring, and Administering Microsoft SQL Server 2000 Enterprise Edition
70-232	Implementing and Maintaining Highly Available Web Solutions with Microsoft Windows 2000 Server Technologies and Microsoft Application Center 2000
70-281	Planning, Deploying, and Managing an Enterprise Project Management Solution
70-282	Designing, Deploying, and Managing a Network Solution for Small- and Medium-Sized Businesses
70-284	Implementing and Managing Microsoft Exchange Server 2003
70-285	Designing a Microsoft Exchange Server 2003 Organization
70-297	Designing a Microsoft Windows Server 2003 Active Directory and Network Infrastructure
70-298	Designing Security for a Microsoft Windows Server 2003 Network
70-299	Implementing and Administering Security in a Microsoft Windows Server 2003 Network
70-301	Managing, Organizing, and Delivering IT Projects by Using Microsoft Solutions Framework 3.0
70-350	Implementing Microsoft Internet Security and Acceleration (ISA) Server 2004

Qualifying Third-Party Alternative Exams

CompTIA	Security+ (*satisfies both the MCSE on Windows Server 2003 elective requirement and the MCSE on Windows Server 2003:Security specialization requirement*)
Unisys UNO-101	Implementing and Supporting Microsoft Windows Server 2003 Solutions in the Data Center

---

TIP

If you are already certified as an MCSE on Windows 2000, you can expedite the certification process for becoming an MCSE on Windows Server 2003. Just pass two exams—70-292, "Managing and Maintaining a Microsoft Windows Server 2003 Environment for an MCSA Certified on Windows 2000," and 70-296, "Planning, Implementing, and Maintaining a Microsoft Windows Server 2003 Environment for an MCSE Certified on Windows 2000." Once you've passed these two upgrade exams, you're certified as an MCSE on Windows Server 2003.

TIP

MCSE on Windows Server 2003 Specializations—After a candidate successfully passes the six required core exams, he has the options of specializing in the areas of messaging and/or security. A candidate earns the specialization title of *MCSE on Windows Server 2003:Messaging* by passing *each* of the following *two* elective exams as listed in Table I.4—Exam 70-284 *and* Exam 70-285 covering Exchange Server 2003.

A candidate earns the specialization title of *MCSE on Windows Server 2003:Security* by passing *three* of the following elective exams also listed in Table I.4—Exam 70-298 covering security design for a Windows Server 2003 network, Exam 70-299 on security administration for a Windows Server 2003 network, *plus one* of following exams:

► Exam 70-227 covering ISA Server 2000
► Exam 70-350 covering ISA Server 2004
► Exam SYO-101: CompTIA Security+

► *MCDBA (Microsoft Certified Database Administrator)*—The MCDBA on Microsoft SQL Server 2000 credential reflects the skills required to implement and administer Microsoft SQL Server databases. To obtain MCDBA certification, an individual must demonstrate the ability to derive physical database designs, develop logical data models, create physical databases, create data services by using Transact-SQL, manage and maintain databases, configure and manage security, monitor and optimize databases, and install and configure Microsoft SQL Server. To become an MCDBA on Microsoft SQL Server 2000, an individual must pass a total of three core exams and one elective exam. Table I.5 outlines the exam requirements for becoming an MCDBA.

NOTE

MCDBA candidates who work with Microsoft SQL Server 2005 might want to become certified as Microsoft Certified Technology Specialists (MCTS) or as Microsoft Certified IT Professionals (MCITP). These newer, more targeted certifications are designed for technology professionals who specialize in managing, developing, programming, and/or analyzing SQL Server 2005 database solutions.

TABLE I.5 MCDBA on Microsoft SQL Server 2000 Exam Requirements

Exam Number	Exam Title
Core Exams: SQL Server Administration	
Candidates Must Pass One of the Following Two Exams	
70-228	Installing, Configuring, and Administering Microsoft SQL Server 2000 Enterprise Edition
70-028*	Administering Microsoft SQL Server 7.0 *(*this exam has been retired)*
Core Exams: SQL Server Design	
Candidates Must Pass One of the Following Two Exams	
70-229	Designing and Implementing Databases with Microsoft SQL Server 2000 Enterprise Edition
70-029*	Designing and Implementing Databases with Microsoft SQL Server 7.0 *(*this exam has been retired)*
Core Exams: Networking Systems	
Candidates Must Pass One of the Following Three Exams	
70-290	Managing and Maintaining a Microsoft Windows Server 2003 Environment
70-291	Implementing, Managing, and Maintaining a Microsoft Windows Server 2003 Network Infrastructure
70-215	Installing, Configuring, and Administering Microsoft Windows 2000 Server
Elective Exams	
Candidates Must Pass One of the Following Elective Exams	
70-216	Implementing and Administering a Microsoft Windows 2000 Network Infrastructure
70-293	Planning and Maintaining a Microsoft Windows Server 2003 Network Infrastructure
70-305	Developing and Implementing Web Applications with Microsoft Visual Basic .NET and Microsoft Visual Studio .NET
70-306	Developing and Implementing Windows-Based Applications with Microsoft Visual Basic .NET and Microsoft Visual Studio .NET
70-310	Developing XML Web Services and Server Components with Microsoft Visual Basic .NET and the Microsoft .NET Framework
70-315	Developing and Implementing Web Applications with Microsoft Visual C# .NET and Microsoft Visual Studio .NET
70-316	Developing and Implementing Windows-Based Applications with Microsoft Visual C# .NET and Microsoft Visual Studio .NET
70-320	Developing XML Web Services and Server Components with Microsoft Visual C# and the Microsoft .NET Framework

TABLE I.5 *Continued*

Exam Number	Exam Title
Elective Exams	
Candidates Must Pass One of the Following Elective Exams	
70-528[1,2]	TS: Microsoft .NET Framework 2.0—Web–based Client Development
70-526[2,3]	TS: Microsoft .NET Framework 2.0—Windows–based Client Development
70-529[4]	TS: Microsoft .NET Framework 2.0—Distributed Application Development

[1] Note: Candidates who have obtained Microsoft Certified Application Developer (MCAD) certification may substitute Exam 70-551: "Upgrade: MCAD Skills to MCPD Web Developer by Using the Microsoft .NET Framework" for Exam 70-528: "TS: Microsoft .NET Framework 2.0—Web-based Client Development."

[2] Note: Candidates who have obtained Microsoft Certified Solutions Developer (MCSD) certification may substitute Exam 70-553: "Upgrade: MCSD Microsoft .NET Skills to MCPD Enterprise Application Developer by using the Microsoft .NET Framework: Part 1" for either of the following exams:

► Exam 70-526: TS: Microsoft .NET Framework 2.0—Windows-based Client Development
► Exam 70-528: TS: Microsoft .NET Framework 2.0—Web-based Client Development

[3] Note: Candidates who have obtained Microsoft Certified Application Developer (MCAD) certification may substitute Exam 70-552: "Upgrade: MCAD Skills to MCPD Windows Developer by Using the Microsoft .NET Framework" for Exam 70-526: "TS: Microsoft .NET Framework 2.0—Windows-based Client Development."

[4] Note: Candidates who have obtained Microsoft Certified Solutions Developer (MCSD) certification may substitute Exam 70-554: "Upgrade: MCSD Microsoft .NET Skills to MCPD Enterprise Application Developer by Using the Microsoft .NET Framework: Part 2" for Exam 70-529: "TS: Microsoft .NET Framework 2.0— Distributed Application Development."

► *MCAP (Microsoft Certified Architect Program)*—The Microsoft Certified Architect Program aims to identify and recognize the top experts in the industry who possess the vision and talent to successfully design *both* application-based solutions *and* infrastructure-based frameworks and methodologies across the entire IT life cycle. Microsoft Certified Architects can integrate multiple technologies to solve business problems while providing the necessary metrics and measurements to define the success or failure of each project.

After a Microsoft product becomes obsolete, MCPs typically have to recertify on current versions. (If individuals do not recertify, their certifications become invalid.) Because technology keeps changing and new products continually supplant old ones, this requirement should come as no surprise. It also explains why Microsoft announced that MCSEs had 12 months past the scheduled retirement date for the Windows NT 4 exams to recertify on Windows 2000 topics.

The best place to keep tabs on the MCP program and its related certifications is on the Web. Currently, the URL for the MCP program is `http://www.microsoft.com/learning/default.mspx`. But Microsoft's website changes often, so if this URL doesn't work, you should use the Search tool on Microsoft's site and type in either `MCP` or the quoted phrase `"Microsoft Certified Professional"` as a search string. This search will help you find the latest and most accurate information about Microsoft's certification programs. If you are already an MCP, you have earned access to the MCP Secured Site, which is open only to skilled technology pros who have passed at least one Microsoft certification exam. MCPs can log on to the MCP Secured Site by visiting `http://www.microsoft.com/learning/mcp/mcpmembersite.asp`. You must use a .NET Passport account to log on to the MCP Secured Site.

Taking a Certification Exam

After you prepare for your exam, you need to register with a testing center. Each computer-based MCP exam costs (U.S.) $125, and if you don't pass, you can take each again for an additional (U.S.) $125 for each attempt. In the United States and Canada, tests are administered by Pearson VUE and by Prometric. Here's how you can contact them:

▶ *Pearson VUE*—You can sign up for a test by calling 800-837-8734 or via the website at `http://www.vue.com/ms`.

▶ *Prometric*—You can sign up for a test through the company's websites, `http://www.2test.com` or `http://www.prometric.com`. Within the United States and Canada, you can register by phone at 800-755-3926. If you live outside this region, you should check the Prometric website for the appropriate phone number.

To sign up for a test, you must possess a valid credit card or contact either Pearson VUE or Prometric for mailing instructions to send a check (in the United States). Only when payment is verified, or a check has cleared, can you actually register for a test.

To schedule an exam, you need to call the appropriate phone number or visit one of the Pearson VUE or Prometric websites at least one day in advance. To cancel or reschedule an exam in the United States or Canada, you must call before 3 p.m. Eastern time the day before the scheduled test time (or you might be charged, even if you don't show up to take the test). When you want to schedule a test, you should have the following information ready:

▶ Your name, organization, and mailing address.

▶ Your Microsoft test ID. (In the United States, this means your Social Security number; citizens of other countries should call ahead to find out what type of identification number is required to register for a test.)

▶ The name and number of the exam you want to take.

▶ A method of payment. (As mentioned previously, a credit card is the most convenient method, but alternate means can be arranged in advance, if necessary.)

After you sign up for a test, you are told when and where the test is scheduled. You should arrive at least 15 minutes early. You must supply two forms of identification—one of which must be a photo ID—to be admitted into the testing room.

All exams are completely closed book. In fact, you are not permitted to take anything with you into the testing area, but you receive a blank sheet of paper and a pen or, in some cases, an erasable plastic sheet and an erasable pen. We suggest that you immediately write down on that sheet of paper all the information you've memorized for the test. In *Exam Cram* books, this information appears on the tear-out sheet (Cram Sheet) inside the front cover of each book. You are given some time to compose yourself, record this information, and take a sample orientation exam before you begin the real thing. We suggest that you take the orientation test before taking your first exam, but because all the certification exams are more or less identical in layout, behavior, and controls, you probably don't need to do so more than once.

When you complete a Microsoft certification exam, the software tells you whether you've passed or failed. If you need to retake an exam, you have to schedule a new test with Pearson VUE or Prometric and pay another (U.S.) $125.

EXAM ALERT

The first time you fail a test, you can retake the test the next day. However, if you fail a second time, you must wait 14 days before retaking that test. The 14-day waiting period remains in effect for all retakes after the second failure. Once you pass an exam, you may not take that exam again. Registration for prerelease (beta) exams is by invitation only, and these exams may be taken only once.

Tracking MCP Status

As soon as you pass a qualified MCP Microsoft exam, you attain MCP status. Microsoft generates transcripts that indicate which exams you have passed. You can view a copy of your transcript at any time by going to the MCP secured site and selecting the Transcript tool. This tool enables you to print a copy of your current transcript and confirm your certification status.

After you pass the necessary set of exams, you are certified. Official certification is normally granted after six to eight weeks, so you shouldn't expect to get your credentials overnight. The package for official certification that arrives includes a welcome kit that contains a number of elements (see Microsoft's website for other benefits of specific certifications):

▶ A certificate that is suitable for framing, along with a wallet card and lapel pin.

▶ A license to use the MCP logo, which means you can use the logo in advertisements, promotions, and documents and on letterhead, business cards, and so on. Along with the license comes an MCP logo sheet, which includes camera-ready artwork. (Note that before you use any of the artwork, you must sign and return a licensing agreement that indicates you'll abide by its terms and conditions.)

▶ Access to the *Microsoft Certified Professional Magazine Online* website, which provides ongoing data about testing and certification activities, requirements, changes to the MCP program, and security-related information on Microsoft products.

Many people believe that the benefits of MCP certification go well beyond the perks that Microsoft provides to newly anointed members of this elite group. We're starting to see more job listings that request or require applicants to have MCP, MCSA, MCSE, and other certifications, and many individuals who complete Microsoft certification programs can qualify for increases in pay and responsibility. As an official recognition of hard work and broad knowledge, an MCP credential is a badge of honor in many IT organizations.

How to Prepare for an Exam

Preparing for any Microsoft certification test (including Exam 70-290) requires that you obtain and study materials designed to provide comprehensive information about the product and its capabilities that will appear on the specific exam for which you are preparing. The following list of materials can help you study and prepare:

▶ The Windows Server 2003 product CD-ROM or DVD-ROM. This disc includes comprehensive online documentation and related materials; it should be one of your primary resources when you are preparing for the test.

▶ The exam preparation materials, practice tests, and self-assessment exams on the Microsoft Training and Certification site, at `http://www.microsoft.com/learning/default.mspx`. The Exam Resources link offers samples of the new question types on the Windows Server 2003 Microsoft Certification track series of exams. You should find the materials, download them, and use them!

▶ The exam preparation advice, practice tests, questions of the day, and discussion groups on `http://www.examcram.com`.

In addition, you might find any or all of the following materials useful in your quest for Windows Server 2003 expertise:

▶ *Microsoft training kits*—Microsoft Learning offers a training kit that specifically targets Exam 70-290. For more information, visit `http://www.microsoft.com/learning/books/`. This training kit contains information that you will find useful in preparing for the test.

▶ *Microsoft TechNet CD or DVD and website*—This monthly CD- or DVD-based publication delivers numerous electronic titles that include coverage of Windows Server 2003 and related topics on the Technical Information (TechNet) series on CD or DVD. Its offerings include product facts, technical notes, tools and utilities, and information on how to access the Seminars Online training materials for Windows Server 2003 and the Windows Server System line of products. Visit http://technet.microsoft.com and check out the information for TechNet subscriptions. You can utilize a large portion of the TechNet website at no charge.

▶ *Study guides*—Several publishers—including Que Publishing—offer Windows Server 2003, Windows Vista, Windows XP, and Windows 2000 titles. Que Publishing offers the following:

  ▶ *The Exam Cram series*—These books give you insights about the material that you need to know to successfully pass the certification tests.

  ▶ *The MCSE Exam Prep series*—These books provide a greater level of detail than the *Exam Cram* books and are designed to teach you everything you need to know about the subject covered by an exam.

  Together, these two series make a perfect pair.

▶ *Classroom training*—CTECs, online partners, and third-party training companies (such as Wave Technologies, New Horizons, and Global Knowledge) all offer classroom training on Windows Server 2003,

Windows Vista, Windows XP, and Windows 2000. These companies aim to help you prepare to pass Exam 70-290 as well as several others. Although this type of training tends to be pricey, most of the individuals lucky enough to attend find this training to be quite worthwhile.

▶ *Other publications*—There's no shortage of materials available about Windows Server 2003. The "Need to Know More?" resource sections at the end of each chapter in this book give you an idea of where we think you should look for further discussion.

This set of required and recommended materials represents an unparalleled collection of sources and resources for Windows Server 2003 and related topics. We anticipate that you'll find this book belongs in this company.

About This Book

Each topical *Exam Cram* chapter follows a regular structure and contains graphical cues about important or useful information. Here's the structure of a typical chapter:

▶ *Opening hotlists*—Each chapter begins with a list of the terms, tools, and techniques that you must learn and understand before you can be fully conversant with that chapter's subject matter. The hotlists are followed with one or two introductory paragraphs to set the stage for the rest of the chapter.

▶ *Topical coverage*—After the opening hotlists and introductory text, each chapter covers a series of topics related to the chapter's subject. Throughout that section, we highlight topics or concepts that are likely to appear on a test, using a special element called an alert:

EXAM ALERT

This is what an alert looks like. Normally, an alert stresses concepts, terms, software, or activities that are likely to relate to one or more certification-test questions. For that reason, we think any information in an alert is worthy of unusual attentiveness on your part.

You should pay close attention to material flagged in Exam Alerts; although all the information in this book pertains to what you need to know to pass the exam, Exam Alerts contain information that is really important. You'll find what appears in the meat of each chapter to be worth knowing, too, when preparing for the test. Because this book's material is very condensed, we recommend that you use this book along with other resources to achieve the maximum benefit.

In addition to the alerts, we provide tips that will help you build a better foundation for Windows Server 2003 knowledge. Although the tip information might not be on the exam, it is certainly related and it will help you become a better-informed test taker.

> **TIP**
>
> This is how tips are formatted. Keep your eyes open for these, and you'll become a Windows Server 2003 guru in no time!

> **NOTE**
>
> This is how notes are formatted. Notes direct your attention to important pieces of information that relate to Windows Server 2003 and Microsoft certification.

▶ *Exam prep questions*—Although we talk about test questions and topics throughout the book, the section at the end of each chapter presents a series of mock test questions and explanations of both correct and incorrect answers.

▶ *Details and resources*—Every chapter ends with a section titled "Need to Know More?" That section provides direct pointers to Microsoft and third-party resources that offer more details on the chapter's subject. In addition, that section tries to rank or at least rate the quality and thoroughness of the topic's coverage by each resource. If you find a resource you like in that collection, you should use it, but you shouldn't feel compelled to use all the resources. On the other hand, we recommend only resources that we use on a regular basis, so none of our recommendations will be a waste of your time or money (but purchasing them all at once probably represents an expense that many network administrators and Microsoft certification candidates might find hard to justify).

The bulk of the book follows this chapter structure, but we'd like to point out a few other elements. Chapters 21 and 23, "Practice Exam 1" and "Practice Exam 2," provide good reviews of the material presented throughout the book to ensure that you're ready for the exam. Chapters 22 and 24, "Answers to Practice Exam 1" and "Answers to Practice Exam 2," offer the correct answers to the questions on the sample tests that appear in Chapters 21 and 23. Appendix A, "Suggested Readings and Resources," offers you several books and websites that contain useful information on Windows Server 2003. Appendix B, "Accessing Your Free MeasureUp Practice Test—Including Networking Simulation!" and Appendix C, "MeasureUp's Product Features," provide helpful information about how to get access to and then take even more practice exams. Finally, you'll find a handy glossary and an index.

Finally, the tear-out Cram Sheet attached next to the inside front cover of this *Exam Cram* book represents a condensed and compiled collection of facts and tips that we think are essential for you to memorize before taking the test. Because you can dump this information out of your head onto a sheet of paper before taking the exam, you can master this information by brute force; you need to remember it only long enough to write it down when you walk into the testing room. You might even want to look at it in the car or in the lobby of the testing center just before you walk in to take the exam.

How to Use This Book

We've structured the topics in this book to build on one another. Therefore, some topics in later chapters make the most sense after you've read earlier chapters. That's why we suggest that you read this book from front to back for your initial test preparation. If you need to brush up on a topic or if you have to bone up for a second try, you can use the index or table of contents to go straight to the topics and questions that you need to study. Beyond helping you prepare for the test, we think you'll find this book useful as a tightly focused reference to some of the most important aspects of Windows Server 2003.

The book uses the following typographical conventions:

▶ Command-line strings that are meant to be typed into the computer are displayed in monospace text, such as

```
net use lpt1: \\print_server_name\printer_share_name
```

▶ *New terms* are introduced in italics.

Given all the book's elements and its specialized focus, we've tried to create a tool that will help you prepare for—and pass—Microsoft Exam 70-290. Please share with us your feedback on the book, especially if you have ideas about how we can improve it for future test takers. Send your questions or comments about this book via email to feedback@quepublishing.com. We'll consider everything you say carefully, and we'll respond to all suggestions. For more information on this book and other Que Certification titles, visit our website at http://www.quepublishing.com. You should also check out the new *Exam Cram* website at http://www.examcram.com, where you'll find information updates, commentary, and certification information.

Thanks for making this *Exam Cram* book a pivotal part of your certification study plan: best of luck on becoming certified!

Self Assessment

The reason we include a self assessment in this *Exam Cram* book is to help you evaluate your readiness to tackle MCSA and MCSE certification. It should also help you to understand what you need to know to master the main topic of this book—namely, Exam 70-290, "Managing and Maintaining a Microsoft Windows Server 2003 Environment." You might also want to check out the Microsoft Skills Assessment Home web page—http://www.microsoft.com/learning/assessment—on the Microsoft Training and Certification website. But, before you tackle this self assessment, let's talk about concerns you might face when pursuing a Microsoft certification credential on Windows 2000 or Windows Server 2003 and what an ideal Microsoft certification candidate might look like.

Microsoft Certified Professionals in the Real World

In the next section, we describe the ideal Microsoft Certified Systems Administrator (MCSA) and Microsoft Certified Systems Engineer (MCSE) candidates, knowing full well that only a few real candidates meet that ideal. In fact, our description of those ideal candidates might seem downright scary, especially with the changes that have been made to the Microsoft Certified Professional program to support Windows Server 2003, Windows XP, and Windows 2000. But take heart: Although the requirements to obtain MCSA and MCSE certification might seem formidable, they are by no means impossible to meet. However, you need to be keenly aware that getting through the process takes time, involves some expense, and requires real effort.

Increasing numbers of people are attaining Microsoft certifications. You can get all the real-world motivation you need from knowing that many others have gone before, so you will be able to follow in their footsteps. If you're willing to tackle the process seriously and do what it takes to obtain the necessary experience and knowledge, you can take—and pass—all the certification tests involved in obtaining the MCSA or MCSE credentials. In fact, at Que Publishing, we've designed the *Exam Cram* series and the *MCSE Exam Prep* series to make it as easy for you as possible to prepare for these exams. We've also greatly expanded our website, http://www.examcram.com, to provide a host of resources to help you prepare for the complexities of Windows Server 2003, Windows XP, and Windows 2000.

The Ideal MCSA or MCSE Candidate

To give you an idea of what an ideal MCSA or MCSE candidate is like, here are some relevant statistics about the background and experience such an individual might have:

> **NOTE**
>
> Don't worry if you don't meet these qualifications or even come very close: This world is far from ideal, and where you fall short is simply where you have more work to do.

- ▶ Academic or professional training in network theory, concepts, and operations. This area includes everything from networking media and transmission techniques through network operating systems, services, and applications.

- ▶ Two or more years of professional networking experience, including experience with Ethernet, Token Ring, modems, and other networking media. This experience must include installation, configuration, upgrading, and troubleshooting experience.

> **NOTE**
>
> The Windows Server 2003 and the Windows 2000 MCSA and MCSE certification testing programs are much more rigorous than the Windows NT 4.0 certification program; you really need some hands-on experience if you want to successfully pass the required exams and become certified. Some of the exams require you to solve real-world case studies and network-design issues, so the more hands-on experience you have, the better off you'll be.

- ▶ Two or more years in a networked environment that includes hands-on experience with Windows Server 2003, Windows 2000 Server, Windows 2000/XP Professional, Windows NT 4.0 Server, Windows NT 4.0 Workstation, and Windows 98. A solid understanding of each system's architecture, installation, configuration, maintenance, and troubleshooting is also essential.

- ▶ Knowledge of the various methods for installing Windows Server 2003, Windows XP, and Windows 2000 operating systems, including manual and unattended installations.

▶ A thorough understanding of key networking protocols, addressing, and name resolution, including Transmission Control Protocol/Internet Protocol (TCP/IP), Novell NetWare's Internetwork Packet eXchange/Sequenced Packet eXchange (IPX/SPX), and Microsoft's NetBIOS Extended User Interface (NetBEUI).

▶ Familiarity with key Windows Server 2003– and Windows 2000 Server–based TCP/IP utilities and services, including Hypertext Transport Protocol (HTTP—used for Web servers), Dynamic Host Configuration Protocol (DHCP), Windows Internet Naming Service (WINS), and Domain Name System (DNS), plus familiarity with one or more of the following: Internet Information Services (IIS), Internet Protocol Security (IPSec), Internet Connection Sharing (ICS), Windows Firewall, Remote Desktop Connections, and Terminal Services.

▶ An understanding of how to implement security for key network data in a Windows 2000 Server or a Windows Server 2003 environment.

▶ Working knowledge of NetWare 3.x and 4.x, including IPX/SPX frame type formats; NetWare file, print, and directory services; and both Novell and Microsoft client software. Working knowledge of Microsoft's Client Service for NetWare (CSNW), the Gateway Service for NetWare (GSNW), the NetWare Migration Tool (NWCONV), and the NetWare Client for Windows (XP, 2000, NT, and 98) is helpful.

▶ A good working understanding of Active Directory. The more you work with Windows Server 2003 or Windows 2000 Server, the more you'll realize that Microsoft's latest server operating systems are quite different from Windows NT Server 4.0. New technologies such as Active Directory have really changed the way Windows is configured and used. We recommend that you find out as much as you can about Active Directory and acquire as much experience using this technology as possible. The time you take learning about Active Directory will be time very well spent!

To meet all of these qualifications, you'd need a bachelor's degree in computer science plus three year's work experience in PC networking design, installation, administration, and troubleshooting. Don't be concerned if you don't have all of these qualifications. Fewer than half of all Microsoft certification candidates meet these requirements. This self-assessment chapter is designed to show you what you already know and to prepare you for the topics that you need to learn.

Put Yourself to the Test

The following series of questions and observations is designed to help you figure out how much work you must do to pursue Microsoft certification and what kinds of resources you can consult on your quest. Be absolutely honest in your answers, or you'll end up wasting money on exams that you're not yet ready to take. There are no right or wrong answers—only steps along the path to certification. Only you can decide where you really belong in the broad spectrum of aspiring candidates. Two things should be clear from the outset, however:

▶ Even a modest background in computer science will be helpful.

▶ Hands-on experience with Microsoft products and technologies is an essential ingredient in certification success.

Educational Background

The following questions concern your level of technical computer experience and training. Depending upon your answers to these questions, you might need to review some additional resources to get your knowledge up to speed for the types of questions that you will encounter on Microsoft certification exams:

1. Have you ever taken any computer-related classes? [Yes or No]

   If Yes, proceed to Question 2; if No, proceed to Question 3.

2. Have you taken any classes on computer operating systems? [Yes or No]

   If Yes, you will probably be able to handle Microsoft's architecture and system component discussions. If you're rusty, you should brush up on basic operating system concepts, especially virtual memory, multitasking regimes, user-mode versus kernel-mode operation, and general computer security topics.

   If No, you should consider doing some basic reading in this area. We strongly recommend a good general operating systems book, such as *Operating System Concepts* by Abraham Silberschatz and Peter Baer Galvin (John Wiley & Sons). If this book doesn't appeal to you, check out reviews for other, similar, books at your favorite online bookstore.

3. Have you taken any networking concepts or technologies classes? [Yes or No]

If Yes, you will probably be able to handle Microsoft's networking terminology, concepts, and technologies. (Brace yourself for frequent departures from normal usage.) If you're rusty, you should brush up on basic networking concepts and terminology, especially networking media, transmission types, the Open System Interconnection (OSI) reference model, and networking technologies, such as Ethernet, Token Ring, Fiber Distributed Data Interface (FDDI), and wide area network (WAN) links.

If No, you might want to read one or two books in this topic area. The two best books that we know are *Computer Networks* by Andrew S. Tanenbaum (Prentice-Hall) and *Computer Networks and Internets* by Douglas E. Comer and Ralph E. Droms (Prentice-Hall).

Hands-On Experience

The most important key to success on all the Microsoft tests is hands-on experience, especially when it comes to Windows Server 2003, Windows XP, Windows 2000, and the many add-on services and components around which so many of the Microsoft certification exams revolve. If we leave you with only one realization after you take this self assessment, it should be that there's no substitute for time spent installing, configuring, and using the various Microsoft products on which you'll be tested. The more in-depth understanding you have of how these software products work, the better your chance in selecting the right answers on the exam:

1. Have you installed, configured, and worked with the following:

   ▶ Windows Server 2003? [Yes or No]

     If Yes, make sure you understand basic concepts as covered in Exam 70-291. You should also study the TCP/IP interfaces, utilities, and services for Exam 70-293, and you should implement security features for Exam 70-298.

     If No, you must obtain one or two machines and a copy of Windows Server 2003. (A trial version is available on the Microsoft website.) Then, you should learn about the operating system and any other software components on which you'll also be tested. In fact, we recommend that you obtain two computers, each with a network interface, and set up a two-node network on which to practice. With decent Windows Server 2003–capable computers selling for about (U.S.) $500 to $600 apiece these days, this setup shouldn't be too much of a financial hardship. You might have to scrounge to come up with the necessary software, but if you scour the Microsoft website, you can usually find low-cost options to obtain evaluation copies of most of the software that you'll need.

▶ Windows 2000 Server? [Yes or No]

If Yes, make sure you understand the concepts covered in Exam 70-215.

If No, you should consider acquiring a copy of Windows 2000 Server and learn how to install, configure, and administer it. Purchase a well-written book to guide your activities and studies (such as *MCSE Windows 2000 Server Exam Cram 2*), or you can work straight from Microsoft's exam objectives.

> **NOTE**
>
> You can download objectives, practice exams, and other data about Microsoft exams from the Training and Certification page at `http://www.microsoft.com/learning`. You can use the "Exams" link to obtain specific exam information.

▶ Windows XP Professional? [Yes or No]

If Yes, make sure you understand the concepts covered in Exam 70-270.

If No, you should obtain a copy of Windows XP Professional and learn how to install, configure, and maintain it. Pick up a well-written book to guide your activities and studies (such as *MCSE Windows XP Professional Exam Cram 2*), or you can work straight from Microsoft's exam objectives, if you prefer.

▶ Windows 2000 Professional? [Yes or No]

If Yes, make sure you understand the concepts covered in Exam 70-210.

If No, you should obtain a copy of Windows 2000 Professional and learn how to install, configure, and maintain it. Pick up a well-written book to guide your activities and studies (such as *MCSE Windows 2000 Professional Exam Cram 2*), or you can work straight from Microsoft's exam objectives, if you prefer.

Use One Computer to Simulate Multiple Machines

If you own a powerful enough computer—one that has plenty of available disk space, a lot of RAM (at least 1GB), and a Pentium 4-compatible processor or better—you should check out the VMware and Virtual PC virtual-machine software products that are on the market. These software programs create an emulated computer environment within separate windows that are hosted by your computer's main operating system—Windows Server 2003, Windows XP, or Windows 2000. So on a single computer, you can have several different operating systems running simultaneously in different windows! You can run everything from DOS to Linux, from Windows 95 to Windows Server 2003. Within a virtual-machine environment, you can "play" with the latest operating systems, including beta versions, without worrying about "blowing up" your main production computer and without having to buy an additional PC. VMware is published by VMware, Inc.; you can get more information from its website at http://www.vmware.com. Virtual PC is available from Microsoft Corporation; you can find more information at http://www.microsoft.com/windows/virtualpc/default.mspx.

TIP

For any and all of these Microsoft operating systems exams, the Resource Kits for the topics involved always make good study resources (see Figure SA.1). You can purchase the Resource Kits from Microsoft Learning (you can search for them at http://www.microsoft.com/learning/books/), but they also appear on the TechNet CDs, DVDs, and website (http://technet.microsoft.com). Along with the *Exam Cram* books, we believe that the Resource Kits are among the best tools you can use to prepare for Microsoft exams. Take a look at the Windows Deployment and Resource Kits web page for additional information: http://www.microsoft.com/windows/reskits/default.asp.

2. For any specific Microsoft product that is not itself an operating system (for example, SQL Server), have you installed, configured, used, and upgraded this software? [Yes or No]

If Yes, skip to the next section, "Testing Your Exam Readiness." If No, you must get some experience. Read on for suggestions about how to do this.

Experience is a must with any Microsoft product exam, be it something as simple as FrontPage 2002 or as challenging as SQL Server 2000. For trial copies of other software, you can search Microsoft's website, using the name of the product as your search term. Also, you can search for bundles such as BackOffice, Enterprise Servers, Windows Server System, or Small Business Server.

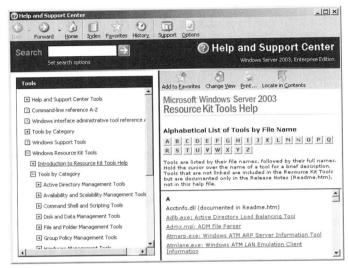

FIGURE SA.1 Viewing the alphabetical list of tools for the Windows Server 2003 Resource Kit.

> **TIP**
>
> If you have the funds, or if your employer will pay your way, you should consider taking a class at a Microsoft Certified Partners for Learning Solutions (CPLS) location. Microsoft CPLS centers were formerly known as Microsoft Certified Technical Education Centers (CTECs). Microsoft CPLS locations deliver official Microsoft Learning products in a classroom setting with Microsoft Certified Trainers (MCTs) as the expert instructors. In addition to classroom exposure on the topic of your choice, you get a copy of the software that is the focus of your course, along with a trial version of whatever operating system it needs, as part of the training materials for that class.

Before you even think about taking any Microsoft exam, you should make sure you've spent enough time with the related software to understand how to install and configure it, how to maintain such an installation, and how to troubleshoot the software when things go wrong. This time will help you in the exam—and in real life!

Testing Your Exam Readiness

Whether you attend a formal class on a specific topic to get ready for an exam or use written materials to study on your own, some preparation for the Microsoft certification exams is essential. At (U.S.) $125 a pop—whether you pass or fail—you'll want to do everything you can to pass your first time. That's where studying comes in.

We include two practice tests in this book (Chapters 21 and 23, "Practice Exam 1," and "Practice Exam 2," respectively), so if you don't score very well on these tests, you can study the practice exams more and then tackle the test again. We also have practice questions that you can sign up for online through `http://www.examcram.com`. The MeasureUP online practice exams have sample questions to quiz you on; you can purchase additional practice questions from `http://www.MeasureUP.com`. If you still don't hit a score of at least 70% after practicing with these tests, you should investigate the other practice test resources that are mentioned in this section.

For any given subject, you should consider taking a class if you've tackled self-study materials, taken the test, and failed anyway. The opportunity to interact with an instructor and fellow students can make all the difference in the world, if you can afford that luxury. For information about Microsoft classes, visit the Training and Certification page at `http://www.microsoft.com/learning/training/find/findcourse.mspx` for locating training courses offered at Microsoft CPLS centers.

If you can't afford to take a class, you can visit the Training and Certification pages anyway because they include pointers to free practice exams and to Microsoft-approved study guides, Microsoft E-Learning courses, and other self-study tools. Even if you can't afford to spend much money at all, you should still invest in some low-cost practice exams from commercial vendors. The Microsoft Training and Certification "Assess Your Readiness" page at `http://www.microsoft.com/learning/assessment` offers several skills-assessment evaluations that you can take online to show you how far along you are in your certification preparation.

The next question deals with your personal testing experience. Microsoft certification exams have their own style and idiosyncrasies. The more acclimated that you become to the Microsoft testing environment, the better your chances will be to score well on the exams:

1. Have you taken a practice exam on your chosen test subject? [Yes or No]

   If Yes, and if you scored 70% or better, you're probably ready to tackle the real thing. If your score isn't above that threshold, you should keep at it until you break that barrier.

   If No, you should obtain all the free and low-budget practice tests you can find and get to work. You should keep at it until you can break the passing threshold comfortably.

> **TIP**
>
> When it comes to assessing your test readiness, there is no better way than to take a good-quality practice exam and pass with a score of 70% or better. When we're preparing ourselves, we shoot for 80% or higher, just to leave room for the "weirdness factor" that sometimes shows up on Microsoft exams.

Assessing Readiness for Exam 70-290

In addition to the general exam-readiness information in the previous section, there are several things you can do to prepare for Exam 70-290. As you're getting ready for the exam, you should visit the *Exam Cram* website at `http://www.examcram.com`. We also suggest that you join an active MCSE/MCSA email list and email newsletter. Some of the best list servers and email newsletters are managed by Sunbelt Software and by Windows IT Pro Magazine. You can sign up at `http://www.sunbelt-software.com` and at `http://www.windowsitpro.com`.

Microsoft exam mavens also recommend that you check the Microsoft Knowledge Base (available on its own CD or DVD as part of the TechNet collection, and on the Microsoft website at `http://support.microsoft.com`) for "meaningful technical support issues" that relate to your exam's topics. Although we're not sure exactly what the quoted phrase means, we have also noticed some overlap between technical-support questions on particular products and troubleshooting questions on the exams for those products.

Go Take on the Challenge!

After you've assessed your readiness, undertaken the right background studies, obtained the hands-on experience that will help you understand the products and technologies involved, and reviewed the many sources of information to help you prepare for a test, you'll be ready to take a round of practice tests. When your scores come back positive enough to get you through the exam, you're ready to go after the real thing. If you follow our assessment regime, you'll not only know what you need to study, but you'll know when you're ready to set a test date at Pearson VUE (`http://www.vue.com`) or Prometric (`http://www.prometric.com`). Go get 'em: Good luck!

CHAPTER ONE

Microsoft Certification Exams

Terms you'll need to understand:

✓ Case study
✓ Multiple-choice question format
✓ Build-list-and-reorder question format
✓ Create-a-tree question format
✓ Drag-and-connect question format
✓ Select-and-place question format
✓ Hot area question format
✓ Active screen question format
✓ Fixed-length test
✓ Simulation
✓ Short-form test

Techniques you'll need to master:

✓ Assessing your exam readiness
✓ Answering Microsoft's various question types
✓ Altering your test strategy depending on the exam format
✓ Practicing to make perfect
✓ Making the best use of the testing software
✓ Budgeting your time
✓ Guessing as a last resort

Exam taking is not something that most people look forward to, no matter how well prepared they might be. In most cases, familiarity helps offset test anxiety. In plain English, this means you probably won't be as nervous when you take your fourth or fifth Microsoft certification exam as you'll be when you take your first one.

Whether it's your first exam or your tenth, understanding the details of taking Microsoft's exams (how much time to spend on questions, the environment you'll be in, and so on) and the new exam software will help you concentrate on the material rather than on the setting. Likewise, mastering a few basic exam-taking skills should help you recognize—and perhaps even outfox—some of the tricks and snares you're bound to encounter on some exam questions.

This chapter, besides explaining the exam environment and software, describes some proven exam-taking strategies that you should be able to use to your advantage.

Assessing Exam Readiness

We strongly recommend that you read through and take the self assessment included with this book. (It appears just before this chapter.) It will help you compare your baseline knowledge to the requirements for obtaining Microsoft certifications, such as the long-standing MCSA and MCSE designations, as well as the newer Microsoft Certified Technology Specialist (MCTS), Microsoft Certified IT Professional (MCITP), and Microsoft Certified Professional Developer (MCPD) titles. The self assessment will also help you identify parts of your background or experience that might be in need of improvement, enhancement, or further learning. If you get the right set of basics under your belt, obtaining Microsoft certification will be that much easier.

After you've gone through the self assessment, you can remedy those topical areas where your background or experience might not measure up to those of an ideal certification candidate. But you can also tackle subject matter for individual tests at the same time, so you can continue making progress while you're catching up in some areas.

After you work through this *Exam Cram* series book, read the supplementary materials, and take the practice tests, you'll have a pretty clear idea of when you should be ready to take the real exam. Although we strongly recommend that you keep practicing until your scores top the 75% mark, 80% is a good goal to give yourself some margin for error in a real exam situation (in which stress will play more of a role than when you practice). After you hit that point, you should be ready to go. But if you get through the practice exam in this book without attaining that score, you should keep taking practice tests and studying the materials until you get there. You'll find more pointers on how to study and prepare in the self assessment. At this point, let's talk about the exam itself.

> **TIP**
>
> In addition, don't forget about this book's bonus practice exam questions that are available online from MeasureUP!

What to Expect at the Testing Center

When you arrive at the testing center where you scheduled your exam, you need to sign in with an exam coordinator. He or she asks you to show two forms of identification, one of which must be a government-issued photo ID. After you sign in and your time slot arrives, you are asked to deposit any books, bags, or other items you brought with you. Then, you are escorted into a closed room.

All exams are computer based and completely closed book. In fact, you are not permitted to take anything with you into the testing area, but you are furnished with a blank sheet of paper and a pen or, in some cases, an erasable plastic sheet and an erasable pen. Before the exam, be sure to carefully review this book's Cram Sheet, located in the very front of the book. You should memorize as much of the important material as you can so you can write that information on the blank sheet as soon as you are seated in front of the computer. You can refer to that piece of paper anytime you like during the test, but you must surrender the sheet when you leave the room.

You are given some time to compose yourself, to record important information, and to take a sample exam before you begin the real thing. We suggest that you take the sample test before taking your first exam, but because all exams are more or less identical in layout, behavior, and controls, you probably don't need to do so more than once.

Typically, the testing room is furnished with anywhere from one to six computers, and each workstation is separated from the others by dividers designed to keep anyone from seeing what's happening on someone else's computer screen. Most testing rooms feature a wall with a large picture window. This layout permits the exam coordinator to monitor the room, to prevent exam takers from talking to one another, and to observe anything out of the ordinary that might go on. The exam coordinator will have preloaded the appropriate Microsoft certification exam—for this book, that's Exam 70-290, Managing and Maintaining a Microsoft Windows Server 2003 Environment—and you are permitted to start as soon as you're seated in front of the computer.

EXAM ALERT

Always remember that the testing center's test coordinator is there to assist you in case you encounter some unusual problems, such as a malfunctioning test computer. If you need some assistance, feel free to notify one of the test coordinators—after all, they are there to make your exam-taking experience as pleasant as possible.

All Microsoft certification exams allow a certain maximum amount of testing time. (This time is indicated on the exam by an onscreen timer clock, so you can check the time remaining whenever you like.) All Microsoft certification exams are computer generated. In addition to multiple choice, most exams contain select–and-place (drag-and-drop), create-a-tree (categorization and prioritization), drag-and-connect, and build-list-and-reorder (list prioritization) types of questions. Although this format might sound quite simple, the questions are constructed not only to check your mastery of basic facts and figures about Windows Server 2003, but also to require you to evaluate one or more sets of circumstances or requirements. Often, you are asked to give more than one answer to a question. Likewise, you might be asked to select the best or most effective solution to a problem from a range of choices—all of which are technically correct. Taking the exam is quite an adventure, and it involves real thinking and concentration. This book shows you what to expect and how to deal with the potential problems, puzzles, and predicaments.

Exam Layout and Design

Historically, there have been six types of question formats on Microsoft certification exams. These types of questions continue to appear on current Microsoft tests, and they are discussed in the following sections:

▶ Multiple-choice, single answer

▶ Multiple-choice, multiple answers

▶ Build-list-and-reorder (list prioritization)

▶ Create-a-tree

▶ Drag-and-connect

▶ Select-and-place (drag-and-drop)

The Single-Answer and Multiple-Answer Multiple-Choice Question Formats

Some exam questions require you to select a single answer, whereas others ask you to select multiple correct answers. The following multiple-choice question requires you to select a single correct answer. Following the question is a brief summary of each potential answer and why it is either right or wrong.

1. You have three domains connected to an empty root domain under one contiguous domain name: `tutu.com`. This organization is formed into a forest arrangement, with a secondary domain called `frog.com`. How many schema masters exist for this arrangement?

    ○ **A.** 1

    ○ **B.** 2

    ○ **C.** 3

    ○ **D.** 4

The correct answer is A because only one schema master is necessary for a forest arrangement. The other answers (B, C, and D) are misleading because they try to make you believe that schema masters might be in each domain or perhaps that you should have one for each contiguous namespace domain.

This sample question format corresponds closely to the Microsoft certification exam format. The only difference is that on the exam, the questions are not followed by answers and their explanations. To select an answer, you position the cursor over the option button next to the answer you want to select. Then, you click the mouse button to select the answer.

Let's examine a question for which one or more answers are possible. This type of question provides check boxes rather than option buttons for marking all appropriate selections.

2. What can you use to seize FSMO roles? (Choose two.)

    ○ **A.** The `ntdsutil.exe` utility

    ○ **B.** The Active Directory Users and Computers console

    ○ **C.** The `secedit.exe` utility

    ○ **D.** The `utilman.exe` utility

Answers A and B are correct. You can seize roles from a server that is still running through the Active Directory Users and Computers console, or in the case of a server failure, you can seize roles with the `ntdsutil.exe` utility. You use the `secedit.exe` utility to force group policies into play; therefore, Answer C is incorrect. The `utilman.exe` tool manages accessibility settings in Windows Server 2003; therefore, Answer D is incorrect.

This particular question requires two answers. Microsoft sometimes gives partial credit for partially correct answers. For Question 2, you have to mark the check boxes next to Answers A and B to obtain credit for a correct answer. Notice that choosing the right answers also means knowing why the other answers are wrong.

The Build-List-and-Reorder Question Format

Questions in the build-list-and-reorder format present two lists of items—one on the left and one on the right. To answer the question, you must move items from the list on the right to the list on the left. The final list must then be reordered into a specific sequence.

These questions generally sound like this: "From the following list of choices, pick the choices that answer the question. Arrange the list in a certain order." Question 3 shows an example of how they appear in this book; for an example of how they appear on the test, see Figure 1.1.

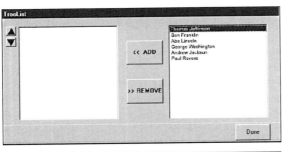

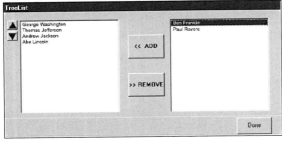

FIGURE 1.1 The format for build-list-and-reorder questions.

3. From the following list of famous people, choose those who have been elected president of the United States. Arrange the list in the order in which the presidents served.

    ○ ▶ Thomas Jefferson

    ○ ▶ Ben Franklin

    ○ ▶ Abe Lincoln

    ○ ▶ George Washington

    ○ ▶ Andrew Jackson

    ○ ▶ Paul Revere

The correct answer is

    1. George Washington

    2. Thomas Jefferson

    3. Andrew Jackson

    4. Abe Lincoln

On an actual exam, the entire list of famous people would initially appear in the list on the right. You would move the four correct answers to the list on the left and then reorder the list on the left. Notice that the answer to Question 3 does not include all the items from the initial list. However, that might not always be the case.

To move an item from the right list to the left list on the exam, you first select the item by clicking it, and then you click the Add button (left arrow). After you move an item from one list to the other, you can move the item back by first selecting the item and then clicking the appropriate button (either the Add button or the Remove button). After you move items to the left list, you can reorder an item by selecting the item and clicking the up or down arrow buttons.

The Create-a-Tree Question Format

Questions in the create-a-tree format also present two lists—one on the left side of the screen and one on the right side of the screen. The list on the right consists of individual items, and the list on the left consists of nodes in a tree. To answer the question, you must move items from the list on the right to the appropriate node in the tree.

These questions can best be characterized as simply a matching exercise. Items from the list on the right are placed under the appropriate category in the list on the left. Question 4 shows an example of how they appear in this book; for an example of how they appear on the test, see Figure 1.2.

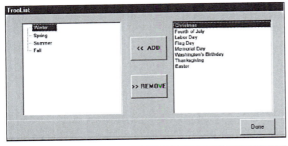

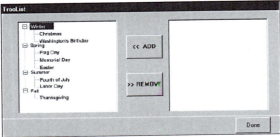

FIGURE 1.2 The create-a-tree question format.

4. The calendar year is divided into four seasons:

1. Winter

2. Spring

3. Summer

4. Fall

Identify the season during which each of the following holidays occurs:

▶ Christmas

▶ Fourth of July

▶ Labor Day

▶ Flag Day

▶ Memorial Day

▶ Washington's Birthday

▶ Thanksgiving

▶ Easter

The correct answers are

1. Winter

   ▶ Christmas

   ▶ Washington's Birthday

2. Spring

   ▶ Flag Day

   ▶ Memorial Day

   ▶ Easter

3. Summer

   ▶ Fourth of July

   ▶ Labor Day

4. Fall

   ▶ Thanksgiving

In this case, you use all the items in the list. However, that might not always be the case.

To move an item from the right list to its appropriate location in the tree, you must first select the appropriate tree node by clicking it. Then, you select the item to be moved and click the Add button. Once you add one or more items to a tree node, the node appears with a + icon to the left of the node name. You can click this icon to expand the node and view the items you have added. If you have added any item to the wrong tree node, you can remove it by selecting it and clicking the Remove button.

The Drag-and-Connect Question Format

Questions in the drag-and-connect format present a group of objects and a list of "connections." To answer the question, you must move the appropriate connections between the objects.

This type of question is best described using graphics. Question 5 shows an example.

5.

The following objects represent the different states of water:

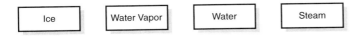

Use items from the following list to connect the objects so that they are scientifically correct:

Sublimates to form

Freezes to form

Evaporates to form

Boils to form

Condenses to form

Melts to form

FIGURE 1.3 The drag-and-connect question format.

The correct answer is

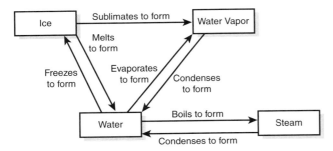

FIGURE 1.4 The answer to a drag-and-connect question format.

For this type of question, it isn't necessary to use every object, and you can use each connection multiple times.

The Select-and-Place Question Format

Questions in the select-and-place (drag-and-drop) format display a diagram with blank boxes and a list of labels that you need to drag to correctly fill in the blank boxes. To answer such a question, you must move the labels to their appropriate positions on the diagram.

This type of question is best described using graphics. Question 6 shows an example.

6.

Place the items in their proper order, by number, on the following flowchart. Some items may be used more than once, and some items may not be used at all.

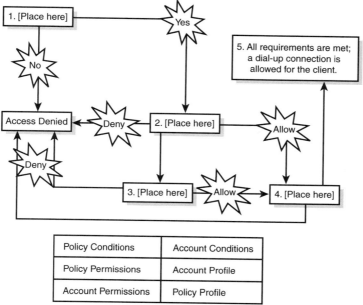

Policy Conditions	Account Conditions
Policy Permissions	Account Profile
Account Permissions	Policy Profile

FIGURE 1.5 The select-and-place question format.

The correct answer is

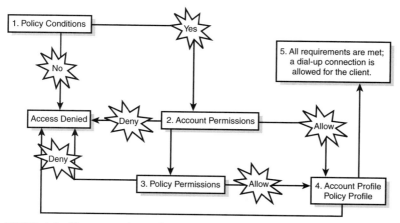

FIGURE 1.6 The answer to a select-and-place question format.

Special Exam Question Formats

Starting with the exams released for the Windows Server 2003 MCSE track, Microsoft introduced several new question types in addition to the more traditional types of questions that are still widely used on all Microsoft exams. These innovative question types have been highly researched and tested by Microsoft before they were chosen to be included in many of the "refreshed" exams for the MCSA/MCSE on the Windows 2000 track and for the new MCSA/MCSE exams on the Windows Server 2003 track. These special question types are as follows:

- Hot area questions

- Active screen questions

- Drag-and-drop–type questions

- Simulation questions

Hot Area Question Types

Hot area questions ask you to indicate the correct answer by selecting one or more elements within a graphic. For example, you might be asked to select multiple objects within a list, as shown in Figure 1.7.

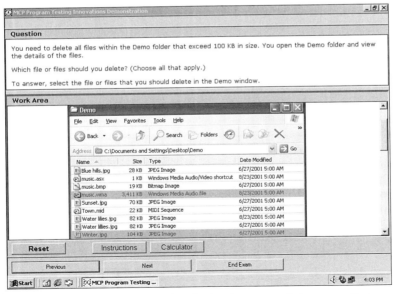

FIGURE 1.7 Selecting objects within a list box to answer a hot area question.

Active Screen Question Types

Active screen questions ask you to configure a dialog box by modifying one or more elements. These types of questions offer a realistic interface in which you must properly configure various settings, just as you would within the actual software product. For example, you might be asked to select the proper option within a drop-down list box, as shown in Figure 1.8.

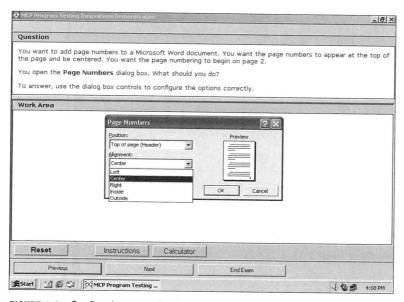

FIGURE 1.8 Configuring an option from a dialog box's drop-down list box to answer an active screen question.

Drag-and-Drop Question Types

New drag-and-drop questions ask you to drag source elements to their appropriate corresponding targets within a work area. These types of questions test your knowledge of specific concepts and their definitions or descriptions. For example, you might be asked to match a description of a computer program to the actual software application, as shown in Figure 1.9.

Simulation Question Types

Simulation questions ask you to indicate the correct answer by performing specific tasks, such as configuring and installing network adapters or drivers, configuring and controlling access to files, or troubleshooting hardware devices. Many of the tasks that systems administrators and systems engineers perform can be presented more accurately in simulations than in most traditional exam question types (see Figure 1.10).

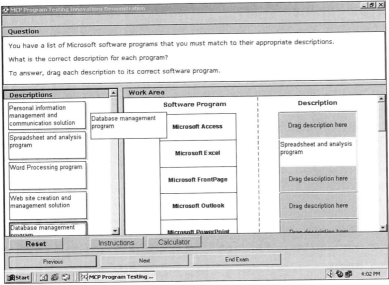

FIGURE 1.9 Using drag and drop to match the correct application description to each software program.

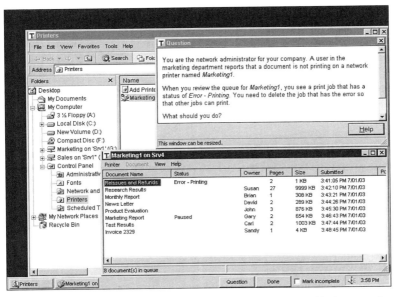

FIGURE 1.10 Answering a simulation question about how to troubleshoot a network printing problem.

Design Exam Question Formats

The Windows 2000 MCSE certification track first introduced Microsoft's design series of exams. For the Windows Server 2003 MCSE track, design exams continue to be a core part of the curriculum. For the design exams, each exam consists entirely of a series of case studies, and the questions can be of six types. The MCSE design exams for the MCSE on Windows Server 2003 track include the following:

- ► 70-229—Designing and Implementing Databases with Microsoft SQL Server 2000 Enterprise Edition

- ► 70-297—Designing a Microsoft Windows Server 2003 Active Directory and Network Infrastructure

- ► 70-298—Designing Security for a Microsoft Windows Server 2003 Network

For design exams, each case study or "testlet" presents a detailed problem that you must read and analyze. Figure 1.11 shows an example of what a case study looks like. You must select the different tabs in the case study to view the entire case.

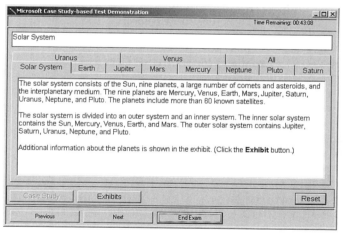

FIGURE 1.11   The format for case-study questions.

Following each case study is a set of questions related to the case study; these questions can be one of six types (which are discussed in the following sections). Careful attention to the details provided in the case study is the key to success. You should be prepared to frequently toggle between the case study and the questions as you work. Some of the case studies include diagrams, which are called *exhibits*, that you'll need to examine closely to understand how to answer the questions.

After you complete a case study, you can review all the questions and your answers. However, after you move on to the next case study, *you might not be able to return to the previous case study to make any changes*.

For the MCSA and MCSE core exams and the upgrade exams, the same six types of questions can appear, but you are not likely to encounter complex multi-question case studies. The MCSA/MCSE core exams and upgrade exams for the Windows Server 2003 track include the following:

- ▶ 70-290—Managing and Maintaining a Microsoft Windows Server 2003 Environment

- ▶ 70-291—Implementing, Managing, and Maintaining a Microsoft Windows Server 2003 Network Infrastructure

- ▶ 70-292—Managing and Maintaining a Microsoft Windows Server 2003 Environment for an MCSA Certified on Windows 2000

- ▶ 70-293—Planning and Maintaining a Microsoft Windows Server 2003 Network Infrastructure

- ▶ 70-294—Planning, Implementing, and Maintaining a Microsoft Windows Server 2003 Active Directory Infrastructure

- ▶ 70-296—Planning, Implementing, and Maintaining a Microsoft Windows Server 2003 Environment for an MCSE Certified on Windows 2000

Microsoft's Testing Formats

Currently, Microsoft uses three different testing formats:

- ▶ Fixed length

- ▶ Short form

- ▶ Case study

Other Microsoft exams employ advanced testing capabilities that might not be immediately apparent. Although the questions that appear are primarily multiple-choice, the logic that drives them is more complex than that in older Microsoft tests, which use a fixed sequence of questions, called a *fixed-length test*. Some questions employ a sophisticated user interface, which Microsoft calls a *simulation*, to test your knowledge of the software and systems under consideration in a more-or-less "live" environment that behaves just like the real thing. You should review the Microsoft Learning, Reference, and Certification web pages at http://www.microsoft.com/learning/default.mspx for more detailed information.

In the future, Microsoft might choose to create exams using a well-known technique called *adaptive testing* to establish a test taker's level of knowledge and product competence. In general, adaptive exams might look the same as fixed-length exams, but they discover the level of difficulty at which an individual test taker can correctly answer questions. Test takers with differing levels of knowledge or ability therefore see different sets of questions; individuals with high levels of knowledge or ability are presented with a smaller set of more difficult questions, whereas individuals with lower levels of knowledge are presented with a larger set of easier questions. Two individuals might answer the same percentage of questions correctly, but the test taker with a higher knowledge or ability level will score higher because his or her questions are worth more. Also, the lower-level test taker will probably answer more questions than his or her more knowledgeable colleague. This explains why adaptive tests use ranges of values to define the number of questions and the amount of time it takes to complete the test.

> **NOTE**
>
> Microsoft does *not* offer adaptive exams at the time that this book was published.

Most adaptive tests work by evaluating the test taker's most recent answer. A correct answer leads to a more difficult question, and the test software's estimate of the test taker's knowledge and ability level is raised. An incorrect answer leads to a less difficult question, and the test software's estimate of the test taker's knowledge and ability level is lowered. This process continues until the test targets the test taker's true ability level. The exam ends when the test taker's level of accuracy meets a statistically acceptable value (in other words, when his or her performance demonstrates an acceptable level of knowledge and ability) or when the maximum number of items has been presented. (In which case, the test taker is almost certain to fail.)

Microsoft has also introduced a short-form test for its most popular tests. This test delivers 25 to 30 questions to its takers, giving them exactly 60 minutes to complete the exam. This type of exam is similar to a fixed-length test in that it allows readers to jump ahead or return to earlier questions and to cycle through the questions until the test is done. Microsoft does not use adaptive logic in short-form tests, but it claims that statistical analysis of the question pool is such that the 25 to 30 questions delivered during a short-form exam conclusively measure a test taker's knowledge of the subject matter in much the same way as an adaptive test. You can think of the short-form test as a kind of "greatest hits exam" (that is, it covers the most important questions) version of an adaptive exam on the same topic.

Because you won't know which form the Microsoft exam might take, you should be prepared for either a fixed-length or short-form exam. The layout is the same for both fixed-length and short-form tests—you are not penalized for guessing the correct answer(s) to questions, no matter how many questions you answer incorrectly.

Strategies for Different Testing Formats

Before you choose a test-taking strategy, you must determine what type of test it is—fixed-length, short form, or case study:

- ▶ Fixed-length tests consist of 50 to 70 questions with a check box for each question. You can mark these questions for review so that you can revisit one or more of the more challenging questions after you finish the rest of the exam (provided that your exam time has not yet expired).

- ▶ Short-form tests have 25 to 30 questions with a check box for each question. You can mark these questions for review so that you can revisit one or more of the more challenging questions after you finish the rest of the exam (provided that your exam time has not yet expired).

- ▶ Case-study tests consist of a tabbed window that allows you to navigate easily through the sections of the case.

Case-Study Exam Strategy

As mentioned earlier, the case-study approach appears in Microsoft's design exams. These exams consist of a set of case studies that you must analyze so that you can answer related questions. Such exams include one or more case studies (tabbed topic areas), each of which is followed by 4 to 10 questions. The question types for design exams and for the four core Windows 2003 exams are multiple-choice, build-list-and-reorder, create-a-tree, drag-and-connect, and select-and-place. Depending on the test topic, some exams are totally case based, whereas others are not.

Most test takers find that the case-study type of test used for the design exams (including Exams 70-229, 70-297, and 70-298) is the most difficult to master. When it comes to studying for a case-study test, your best bet is to approach each case study as a standalone test. The biggest challenge you're likely to encounter with this type of test is that you might feel that you won't have enough time to get through all the cases that are presented.

TIP

Each case study provides a lot of material that you need to read and study before you can effectively answer the questions that follow. The trick to taking a case-study exam is to first scan the case study to get the highlights. You should make sure you read the overview section of the case so that you understand the context of the problem at hand. Then, you should quickly move on to scanning the questions.

As you are scanning the questions, you should make mental notes to yourself so that you'll remember which sections of the case study you should focus on. Some case studies might provide a fair amount of extra information that you don't really need to answer the questions. The goal with this scanning approach is to avoid having to study and analyze material that is not completely relevant because your time allotment to complete the entire exam is limited.

When studying a case, read the tabbed information carefully. It is important to answer every question. You will be able to toggle back and forth from case to questions and from question to question within a case testlet. However, after you leave the case and move on, you might not be able to return to it. We suggest that you take notes while reading useful information to help you when you tackle the test questions. It's hard to go wrong with this strategy when taking any kind of Microsoft certification test.

The Fixed-Length and Short-Form Exam Strategy

One tactic that has worked well for many test takers is to answer each question as well as you can before time expires on the exam. Some questions you will undoubtedly feel better equipped to answer correctly than others; however, you should still select an answer to each question as you proceed through the exam. You should click the Mark for Review check box for any question that you are unsure of. In this way, at least you have answered all the questions in case you run out of time. Unanswered questions are automatically scored as incorrect; answers that are guessed at have at least some chance of being scored as correct. If time permits, once you answer all questions, you can revisit each question that you have marked for review. This strategy also allows you to possibly gain some insight to questions that you are unsure of by picking up some clues from the other questions on the exam.

TIP

Some people prefer to read over the exam completely before answering the trickier questions; sometimes, information supplied in later questions sheds more light on earlier questions. At other times, information you read in later questions might jog your memory about facts, figures, or behavior that helps you answer earlier questions. Either way, you could come out ahead if you answer only those questions on the first pass that you're absolutely confident about. However, be careful not to run out of time if you choose this strategy!

Fortunately, the Microsoft exam software for fixed-length and short-form tests makes the multiple-visit approach easy to implement. At the top-left corner of each question is a check box that permits you to mark that question for a later visit.

Here are some question-handling strategies that apply to fixed-length and short-form tests. Use them if you have the chance:

▶ When returning to a question after your initial read-through, read every word again; otherwise, your mind can miss important details. Sometimes, revisiting a question after turning your attention elsewhere lets you see something you missed, but the strong tendency is to see what you've seen before. Avoid that tendency at all costs.

▶ If you return to a question more than twice, articulate to yourself what you don't understand about the question, why answers don't appear to make sense, or what appears to be missing. If you chew on the subject awhile, your subconscious might provide the missing details, or you might notice a "trick" that points to the right answer.

As you work your way through the exam, another counter that Microsoft provides will come in handy—the number of questions completed and questions outstanding. For fixed-length and short-form tests, it's wise to budget your time by making sure that you've completed one-quarter of the questions one-quarter of the way through the exam period and three-quarters of the questions three-quarters of the way through.

If you're not finished when only five minutes remain, use that time to guess your way through any remaining questions. Remember, guessing is potentially more valuable than not answering. Blank answers are always wrong, but a guess might turn out to be right. If you don't have a clue about any of the remaining questions, pick answers at random or choose all As, Bs, and so on. (Choosing the same answer for a series of question all but guarantees you'll get most of them wrong, but it also means you're more likely to get a small percentage of them correct.)

EXAM ALERT

At the very end of your exam period, you're better off guessing than leaving questions unanswered.

Question-Handling Strategies

For those questions that have only one right answer, usually two or three of the answers will be obviously incorrect and two of the answers will be plausible. Unless the answer leaps out at you (if it does, reread the question to look for a trick; sometimes those are the ones you're most likely to get wrong), begin the process of answering by eliminating those answers that are most obviously wrong.

You can usually immediately eliminate at least one answer out of the possible choices for a question because it matches one of these conditions:

- ▸ The answer does not apply to the situation.

- ▸ The answer describes a nonexistent issue, an invalid option, or an imaginary state.

After you eliminate all answers that are obviously wrong, you can apply your retained knowledge to eliminate further answers. You should look for items that sound correct but refer to actions, commands, or features that are not present or not available in the situation that the question describes.

If you're still faced with a blind guess among two or more potentially correct answers, reread the question. Picture how each of the possible remaining answers would alter the situation. Be especially sensitive to terminology; sometimes the choice of words ("remove" instead of "disable") can make the difference between a right answer and a wrong one.

You should guess at an answer only after you've exhausted your ability to eliminate answers and you are still unclear about which of the remaining possibilities is correct. An unanswered question offers you no points, but guessing gives you at least some chance of getting a question right; just don't be too hasty when making a blind guess.

Numerous questions assume that the default behavior of a particular utility is in effect. If you know the defaults and understand what they mean, this knowledge will help you cut through many of the trickier questions. Simple "final" actions might be critical as well. If you must restart a utility before proposed changes take effect, a correct answer might require this step as well.

Mastering the Test-Taking Mindset

In the final analysis, knowledge breeds confidence, and confidence breeds success. If you study the materials in this book carefully and review all the practice questions at the end of each chapter, you should become aware of the areas where you need additional learning and study.

After you've worked your way through the book, take the practice exams in the back of the book. Taking these tests provides a reality check and helps you identify areas to study further. Make sure you follow up and review materials related to the questions you miss on the practice exams before scheduling a real exam. Don't schedule your exam appointment until after you've thoroughly studied the material and you feel comfortable with the whole scope of the practice exams. You should score 80% or better on the practice exams before proceeding to the real thing. (Otherwise, obtain some additional practice tests so that you can keep trying until you hit this magic number.)

> **TIP**
>
> If you take a practice exam and don't get at least 70% to 80% of the questions correct, keep practicing. Microsoft provides links to practice-exam providers and also self-assessment exams at `http://www.microsoft.com/learning/mcpexams/prepare/default.asp`.

Armed with the information in this book and with the determination to augment your knowledge, you should be able to pass the certification exam. However, you need to work at it, or you'll spend the exam fee more than once before you finally pass. If you prepare seriously, you should do well.

The next section covers other sources that you can use to prepare for Microsoft certification exams.

Additional Resources

A good source of information about Microsoft certification exams comes from Microsoft itself. Because its products and technologies—and the exams that go with them—change frequently, the best place to go for exam-related information is online.

Microsoft offers training, certification, and other learning-related information and links at `http://www.microsoft.com/learning`. If you haven't already visited the Microsoft Training and Certification website, you should do so right now. Microsoft's Training and Certification home page resides at `http://www.microsoft.com/learning/default.mspx` (see Figure 1.12). The Microsoft Windows Server 2003 Resource Kit is another great source for definitive and detailed information on Windows Server 2003 and Exam 70-290. In addition to the Resource Kit, be sure to check out Microsoft's online knowledge base at `http://support.microsoft.com` as well as the Microsoft TechNet site, which you can find at `http://technet.microsoft.com`.

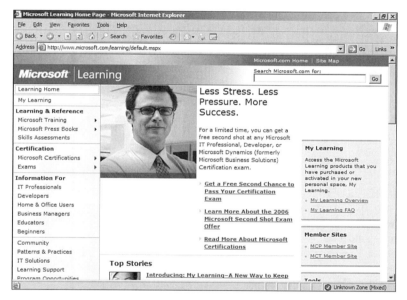

FIGURE 1.12 The Microsoft Learning home page.

Coping with Change on the Web

Sooner or later, all the information we've shared with you about the Microsoft Certified Professional pages and the other Web-based resources mentioned throughout the rest of this book will go stale or be replaced by newer information. In some cases, the URLs you find here might lead you to their replacements; in other cases, the URLs will go nowhere, leaving you with the dreaded "404 File not found" error message. When that happens, don't give up.

(continues)

(continued)

There's always a way to find what you want on the Web if you're willing to invest some time and energy. Most large or complex websites—and Microsoft's qualifies on both counts—offer search engines. All of Microsoft's web pages have a Search button at the top edge of the page. As long as you can get to Microsoft's site (it should stay at `http://www.microsoft.com` for a long time), you can use the Search button to find what you need.

The more focused (or specific) that you can make a search request, the more likely the results will include information you can use. For example, you can search for the string

```
"training and certification"
```

to produce a lot of data about the subject in general, but if you're looking for the preparation guide for Exam 70-290, Managing and Maintaining a Microsoft Windows Server 2003 Environment, you'll be more likely to get there quickly if you use a search string similar to the following:

```
"Exam 70-290" AND "preparation guide"
```

Likewise, if you want to find the Training and Certification downloads, you should try a search string such as this:

```
"training and certification" AND "download page"
```

Finally, you should feel free to use general search tools—such as `http://www.google.com`, `http://www.yahoo.com`, `http://www.excite.com`, and `http://www.ask.com`—to look for related information. You might also want to do some searching at `http://www.google.com/microsoft`—this vendor-specific search page lets you make Microsoft-focused queries using all of Google's indexed Internet-based content.

Although Microsoft offers great information about its certification exams online, there are plenty of third-party sources of information and assistance that need not follow Microsoft's party line. Therefore, if you can't find something where the book says it lives, you should intensify your search.

CHAPTER TWO

Administering Computer Accounts and Resources in Active Directory

Terms you'll need to understand:

✓ Domains

✓ Domain Trees

✓ Domain Forests

✓ Computer accounts

✓ Run As feature

✓ Globally unique identifiers (GUIDs)

✓ Organizational units (OUs)

✓ Microsoft Management Console (MMC) 3.0

✓ Active Directory Users and Computers console

Techniques you'll need to master:

✓ Adding and removing computer accounts

✓ Prestaging computer accounts

✓ Using command-line tools for modifying Active Directory objects

✓ Using the Action Pane in the MMC 3.0

✓ Enabling full functionality for MMC 3.0

✓ Managing resources using the Run As command

Microsoft introduced Active Directory with the debut of Windows 2000 Server in February 2000. Active Directory provides a directory service for Microsoft-based networks in the same way that Novell Directory Services (NDS) provides a directory service for NetWare environments. For Windows Server 2003, Microsoft enhanced and refined Active Directory by making the directory service more flexible, more scalable, and more manageable than its Windows 2000 predecessor. Active Directory is a vital element in Windows Server 2003, and its many benefits can offer a compelling reason to upgrade, especially if you are coming from a Windows NT Server environment.

Understanding how to manage objects within Active Directory is critical for a successful deployment and reliable day-to-day operations of a Windows Server 2003 Active Directory–based network. In this chapter, we introduce you to Active Directory for Windows Server 2003. You'll discover how to add, remove, and manage computer accounts in Active Directory. Unfortunately, network administration doesn't always go smoothly, so you'll also learn about how to troubleshoot computer accounts in Windows Server 2003 and Active Directory.

Microsoft released Windows Server 2003 Service Pack 1 (SP1) on March 2004, as a major update. In December 2005, Microsoft published the R2 (Release 2) Edition of Windows Server 2003, in 32-bit (x86) and 64-bit (x64) versions. This chapter and this book covers all of these different permutations of the Windows Server 2003 operating system—the original Release to Manufacturing (RTM) version, SP1, and R2 in both the 32-bit (x86) and 64-bit (x64) flavors. The functionality and features covered in this book apply to all of these editions, except where noted.

Introduction to Active Directory

The many improvements to Active Directory encompass some of the major feature enhancements of Windows Server 2003. Active Directory is a replicated and distributed database that stores computer-related information such as usernames, passwords, phone numbers, addresses, email addresses, group names, and computer names, to name a few. Active Directory is called a directory service because it provides users and computers with the ability to look up information in a similar way that you look up information using a telephone book directory.

Special servers called domain controllers (DCs) are designated to store a copy of the Active Directory database, and these DCs are responsible for synchronizing the Active Directory database with all of the other DCs that share the database. Server computers, as well as workstation computers that are members of an Active Directory domain, perform several Active Directory queries (or lookups) in their day-to-day operations. For example, Active Directory domain-member computers need to know where nearby DCs are for authentication purposes.

Active Directory is based on open, Internet-related standards, such as the Transmission Control Protocol/Internet Protocol (TCP/IP), the Domain Name System (DNS), the Kerberos authentication protocol, and the Lightweight Directory Access Protocol (LDAP), among many others. In fact, you cannot install Active Directory without TCP/IP and DNS installed and functioning within the network environment. You must name Active Directory domains using a full DNS name such as `examcram2.informit.com`.

Domains, Domain Trees, and Domain Forests

A Windows Server 2003 computer (or a Windows 2000 Server computer) becomes a DC when an administrator runs the Active Directory Installation Wizard. You can run the wizard by clicking Start, Run; typing `dcpromo.exe`; and clicking OK. This process promotes a server to a DC. The wizard makes several changes to the server computer to prepare it to become a DC. One of the major changes is the creation of the Active Directory database file itself. This file is named `ntds.dit`, and it must reside on a hard disk partition or volume that is formatted as NTFS. The default location for the `ntds.dit` file is the `%systemroot%\ ntds` folder (for example, `c:\windows\ntds`).

The very first Windows Server 2003 (or Windows 2000 Server) DC that you promote creates the *root domain*. For example, if you promote a DC and name the domain `examcram2.net`, this domain becomes the root domain within the new Active Directory forest. The basic logical components of Active Directory are as follows:

- ▶ *Domain*—One or more DC servers and a group of users and computers that share the same Active Directory database for authentication and can share common server resources.

- ▶ *Domain Tree*—One or more Active Directory domains that share a common hierarchical DNS namespace (parent-child-grandchild and so on). For example, `examcram2.net` could be the parent domain, `northamerica. examcram2.net` could be the child domain, `us.northamerica. examcram2.net` could be the grandchild domain, and so on.

- ▶ *Domain Forest*—One or more Active Directory domain trees (each tree has its own DNS namespace) that share the same Active Directory database. An Active Directory forest is a logical container for one or more related domains.

No Primary or Backup Domain Controllers

Windows NT Server 3.5x and Windows NT Server 4.0 used the concept of one primary DC (PDC) and backup DCs (BDCs), where only one of the DCs could act as the PDC at any one time. The PDC stores the read/write copy of the security accounts manager (SAM) database, whereas each BDC stores a read-only copy of the SAM database. Instead, Active Directory uses a technique called *multimaster replication* to distribute copies of the Active Directory database to all other DCs that share the same Active Directory namespace. This replication technology means that administrators can make additions, changes, or deletions to the Active Directory database from any DC, and those modifications get synchronized with all of the other DCs within an Active Directory domain and the GCs within the entire AD forest. Active Directory assigns the role of PDC Emulator to the first DC to come online in an Active Directory forest. The DC that has the PDC Emulator role can communicate between Active Directory and down-level PDCs and BDCs running on Windows NT Server 3.5x and Windows NT Server 4.0.

Organizational Units

To improve network administration, Microsoft created organizational units (OUs) to provide for logical groupings of users, groups, computers, and other objects within a single domain. You can delegate administrative authority over each OU to other administrators for distributing network-management chores. The delegated authority can be limited in scope, if necessary, so that you can grant junior administrators just specific administrative powers—not complete administrator-level authority. In addition, you can apply specific group policy object (GPO) settings at the OU level, allowing users and computers to be managed differently according to the OU in which they are placed.

The Microsoft Management Console (MMC)

The MMC is the standard interface for hosting all of the various GUI tools and utilities that administrators use to manage the Windows and Active Directory environments. The MMC is a shell that houses MMC snap-ins—the snap-ins actually provide the functionality. The MMC provides a consistent and standardized *look and feel* for all the snap-in tools. MMC snap-in files use the file extension .msc. You can see several of the default snap-ins if you browse the %systemroot%\system32 folder on a Windows Server 2003 computer.

For example, on a domain controller, you can run the Active Directory Users and Computers (ADUC) snap-in by double-clicking the dsa.msc file in the %systemroot%\system32 folder. Alternatively, you can run the ADUC snap-in by clicking Start, Run, typing in dsa.msc, and clicking OK. You must include the .msc file extension for the snap-in to run. You also have the option of clicking Start, Run, typing in mmc, and clicking OK to display an empty console; you can then click File, Add/Remove Snap-in to load the snap-in(s) of your choice.

MMC 3.0

New to **R2** When you upgrade Windows Server 2003 to the R2 Edition, the MMC gets upgraded to version 3.0 automatically. The MMC 3.0 sports three major improvements over its previous versions:

▶ *The Action pane*—The Action pane is displayed on the right side of the console when it is not hidden. (It is usually hidden by default on most snap-ins.) The *Show/Hide Action Pane* toolbar icon shown in Figure 2.1 is similar to the *Show/Hide Console Tree* toolbar icon. The Action pane displays the actions that can be performed on the currently selected item in the console tree (left pane) or in the results pane (center pane). You can view the same list of actions by right-clicking an item.

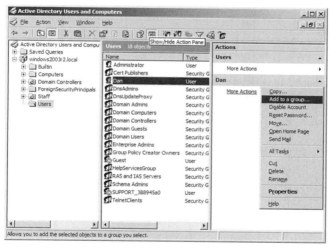

FIGURE 2.1 A view of the Action pane for the ADUC snap-in under MMC 3.0 and Windows Server 2003 R2.

▶ *Enhanced Error Handling*—MMC 3.0 notifies you when errors occur within loaded snap-ins that could cause the MMC shell to stop responding. When the MMC 3.0 detects an error, it offers you some options to deal with the error.

▶ *Improved Add or Remove Snap-in dialog box*—The redesigned Add or Remove Snap-in dialog box for the MMC 3.0 makes it easier to add, remove, and organize snap-ins (see Figure 2.2).

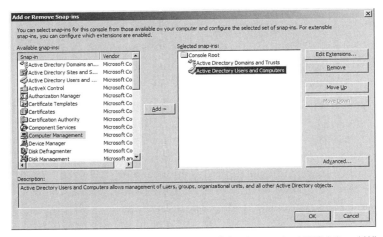

FIGURE 2.2 The Add or Remove Snap-ins dialog box under MMC 3.0 and Windows Server 2003 R2.

EXAM ALERT

To enable MMC 3.0 features such as the new *Add or Remove Snap-in* dialog box, you must add a new subkey to the Windows Registry.

Always have a good, recent backup of your system before you endeavor to make any change to the Registry.

Using `regedit.exe`, the Windows Registry editor tool, navigate to `HKEY_LOCAL_MACHINE\SOFTWARE\Microsoft\MMC`. You must add a new subkey named `UseNewUI` under this existing Registry key to turn on the enhancements to MMC 3.0. No reboot is necessary; the change is effective immediately.

TIP

New to **R2**   MMC 3.0 supports a wider range of functionality than previous versions of the MMC; however, MMC snap-ins must support the new MMC 3.0 features for the enhanced functionality to be available.

Administering Computer Accounts in Active Directory

Computers, such as workstations and member servers, must be authenticated to access Active Directory resources under Windows Server 2003, just as they must be authenticated under Active Directory in Windows 2000 Server. To become a participant in an Active Directory domain, Windows NT, Windows 2000, Windows XP, and other Windows Server 2003 computers must formally join a domain by establishing a computer account within the domain. Windows 95 and Windows 98 (Windows 9x) computers cannot formally join a domain; however, users can log on to a Windows Server 2003 Active Directory domain and access resources as if it were a Windows NT 4.0 domain under both the Windows 2000 mixed and the Windows 2000 native domain functional levels. Windows Server 2003 domain functional levels are discussed in Chapter 5, "Managing Access to Resources."

The Active Directory Client for Windows 9x and Windows NT 4.0

The Windows 2000 mixed domain functional level supports the NTLM (NT LAN Manager) authentication protocol that is used by Windows NT BDCs to authenticate users and computers. The older LM (LAN Manager) authentication protocol and the NTLM protocol are responsible for authenticating Windows 9x– and Windows NT–based computers. Windows 2000 mixed also supports the newer Kerberos authentication protocol that is used by the Windows 2000 native and the Windows Server 2003 domain functional levels. In addition to Kerberos, the Windows 2000 native and the Windows Server 2003 functional levels support the newer NTLM version 2 (NTLM v2) authentication protocol. Windows 9x computers do not natively support NTLM v2, nor do Windows NT 4.0 computers unless they have Service Pack 4 (SP4) or higher installed. Windows 9x and Windows NT 4.0 computers can natively log on to a Windows Server 2003 Active Directory domain in the following circumstances:

- ▶ The Windows Server 2003 domain is set at Windows 2000 mixed and either a PDC emulator or a Windows NT 4.0 BDC is available.

- ▶ The Windows Server 2003 domain is set at Windows 2003 interim and either a PDC emulator or a Windows NT 4.0 BDC is available.

NOTE

When Windows 9x computers log on to a Windows NT 4.0 domain, they can only access Active Directory resources via one-way trust relationships that have been set up by network administrators with Windows Server 2003 Active Directory domains.

To add support for Windows 9x and Windows NT 4.0 computers to access Active Directory resources, you can install the Active Directory client software so that these legacy clients can access resources stored in Windows Server 2003 domains. The Active Directory client software (dsclient.exe) for Windows 9x computers is located on the Windows 2000 Server CD-ROM (it's *not* on the Windows Server 2003 CD-ROM) in the Clients\Win9x folder. The Windows NT 4.0 version of the Active Directory client is available from Microsoft's website at http://www.microsoft.com/windows2000/server/evaluation/news/bulletins/adextension.asp.

Creating Computer Accounts

You can create computer accounts in one of three ways:

▶ Log onto each (Windows NT 4.0, Windows 2000, Windows XP, Windows Vista, or Windows Server 2003) computer and join it to the domain.

▶ Prestage the computer accounts on a DC using the Active Directory Users and Computers (ADUC) MMC snap-in.

▶ Prestage the computer accounts on a DC using the dsadd.exe command-line utility.

▶ Prestage the computer accounts on a DC using some other scripted or command-line utility.

For computers running Windows NT, Windows 2000, Windows XP, Windows Vista, and Windows Server 2003, you create accounts for those computers when you join them to the Windows Server 2003 Active Directory domain, provided that computer accounts for those computers have not been prestaged. For example, on a Windows 2000 (Professional or Server) system, you join the computer to a domain by following these steps:

1. Double-click the System icon in the Control Panel.

2. Click the Network Identification tab from the System Properties window.

3. Click the Properties button.

4. Click the Domain option button, type in the name of the Active Directory domain that you want to join, and click OK.

5. Type in the name and password for a user account in the domain that has administrative-level permission to join computers to this domain and click OK (see Figure 2.3).

6. Click OK for the Welcome message box that confirms you have successfully joined the computer to the domain.

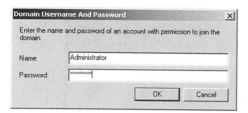

FIGURE 2.3   Joining a Windows 2000 computer to a Windows Server 2003 Active Directory domain.

Troubleshooting Joining a Computer to a Domain

If you have difficulty joining the domain, be sure to check the computer for any physical network connectivity problems. If you verify that the physical network connection is functioning properly, use the TCP/IP `ping` command at a command prompt window to test the connectivity to a domain controller by pinging the DC's IP address. For example, you can type `ping 192.168.0.10` at a command prompt if the DC's IP address is 192.168.0.10. If that works, attempt to ping the DC by its fully qualified domain name (FQDN)—for example, `ping dc1.windows2003.local`.

Using the FQDN for the DC should uncover a DNS name resolution problem, if one exists. If you simply try to ping the server's NetBIOS or hostname by typing `ping DC1`, the name could be resolved by a NetBIOS broadcast, making you think that DNS name resolution is not a problem. If pinging the FQDN does not work, you might very well have a DNS name-resolution problem. You should check the computer's DNS server settings as well as the network's DNS setup. Perhaps the computer is not registered with an appropriate DNS server on your network. If you verify that the computer's DNS server settings are pointed to the appropriate DNS server(s), you can remedy a DNS registration issue on Windows 2000/XP/Vista/2003 computers by performing these steps:

1. Open a command prompt window.

2. Type `ipconfig /flushdns` and press Enter.

3. Type `ipconfig /registerdns` and press Enter.

4. Restart the computer to ensure that these changes take effect.

Prestaging Computer Accounts from the GUI

You can use the ADUC console to view, add, modify, and delete computer accounts, user accounts, and groups from the Windows GUI. On a Windows Server 2003 DC computer, click Start, Administrative Tools, Active Directory Users and Computers to launch the ADUC console. You can also click Start, Run; type `dsa.msc`; and click OK to run the ADUC console. By creating a computer account in Active Directory before the computer joins the domain, you can determine exactly where in the directory the computer account will be placed. The default location for computers joined to a domain without prestaging is the Computers container. In addition, prestaging computer accounts gives administrators more control over Remote Installation Services (RIS) installations. You can specify that only prestaged computer accounts can be installed via RIS.

TIP

You can install the Windows Server 2003 Administration Tools Pack on a Windows XP Professional computer with SP1 or higher or on a Windows Server 2003 member server so that you can manage Active Directory without physically logging on to a DC. You can download the Windows Server 2003 Administration Tools Pack from Microsoft's website at `http://microsoft.com/downloads/details.aspx?familyid=` `c16ae515-c8f4-47ef-a1e4-a8dcbacff8e3&displaylang=en`.

For a new Active Directory domain, the default containers are Built-in, Computers, Domain Controllers, Foreign Security Principals, and Users. If you click the ADUC's View menu and select Advanced Features, you can view the advanced containers that are hidden by default. The advanced containers are LostAndFound, NTDS Quotas, Program Data, and System. To create a new computer account in the ADUC, follow these steps:

1. Open the ADUC MMC snap-in (console).

2. Right-click the container or OU into which you want to place the computer account, select New, and then click Computer.

3. Type in the computer name.

4. Type in the pre-Windows 2000 computer name, if different from the computer name.

5. To change the user or group that has permission to join computers to the domain, click the Change button. The default group is the Domain Admins group: Any member of this group has authority to join computer accounts to the domain.

6. If this computer account is a Windows NT computer, mark the Assign This Computer Account as a Pre-Windows 2000 Computer check box.

7. If this computer account is for a Windows NT BDC computer, mark the Assign This Computer Account as a Backup Domain Controller check box (see Figure 2.4).

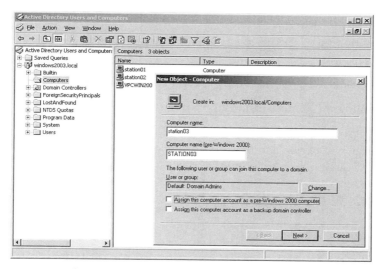

FIGURE 2.4 Creating a new computer account in ADUC.

8. Click Next.

9. If you are prestaging the computer account for later installation via RIS, mark the This Is a Managed Computer check box and type in the computer's unique ID (GUID/UUID), referred to as its globally unique identifier or its universally unique identifier. This extra security measure prevents unauthorized RIS client installations because only computers with matching GUIDs are allowed to be installed via RIS when you follow this procedure. You can find the GUID or UUID in the computer's BIOS or by using a third-party software utility (see Figure 2.5).

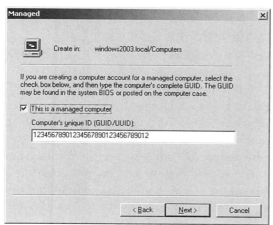

FIGURE 2.5 Specifying a computer's GUID for prestaging a computer account.

10. Click Next.

11. Select an option for specifying the type of RIS server support for this computer account:

   ▶ Any Available Remote Installation Server

   ▶ The Following Remote Installation Server

12. To specify a particular RIS server, select The Following Remote Installation Server option and type in the fully qualified DNS hostname, or click the Search button to locate the server (see Figure 2.6).

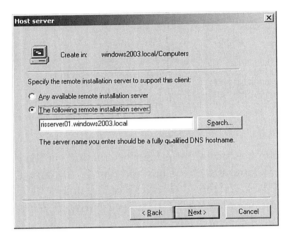

FIGURE 2.6 Specifying the RIS server's name for prestaging a computer account.

13. Click Next.

14. Click Finish for the New Object-Computer summary window.

Prestaging Computer Accounts from the Command Line

Windows Server 2003 offers several new command-line tools for working with Active Directory. For a detailed list of these commands and their functions, see the section "Using Command-Line Utilities for Active Directory Objects" later in this chapter. You can use the dsadd.exe tool to add Active Directory objects such as computer accounts from any Windows Server 2003 command prompt. With dsadd.exe, you can add one computer account at a time from the command line, or you can redirect standard input for dsadd.exe and use a text file that contains the computer account that you want added. For parameters with embedded spaces, such as names of OUs surround the DN with quotes. The following two examples in Table 2.1 and in Figure 2.7 demonstrate some of the possibilities and their associated syntax for adding computer accounts via the command line.

TABLE 2.1 **Examples of the** `dsadd.exe` **Command**

dsadd Command	dsadd Results

`dsadd computer`
`cn=station77,cn=Computers,`
`dc=windows2003,dc=local`
	Adds a computer account named `station77` to Active Directory in the `Computers` container for the domain named `windows2003.local`.

`dsadd computer`
`"cn=station88,ou=west coast,`
`dc=windows2003,dc=local"`
	Adds a computer account named `station88` to Active Directory in the West Coast OU for the domain named `windows2003.local`.

NOTE

Computer account NetBIOS names cannot be longer than 15 characters and these names are resolved by network broadcasts, local LMHOSTS file entries, or by Windows Internet Naming Service (WINS) servers; computer account host names can be up to 63 characters in length and these names are resolved via the Domain Name System (DNS) or local HOSTS file entries. A fully qualified domain name (FQDN) for a computer account can be up to 255 characters in length, such as `server01.sales.northamerica.microsoft.com`.

FIGURE 2.7 Adding computer accounts using the `dsadd.exe` command.

Managing and Troubleshooting Computer Accounts

You can manage problems with computer accounts from the ADUC console. To modify the properties of a computer account, right-click the computer name listed in the ADUC console and select Properties. From the properties sheet, you can make several changes to the account such as trusting the computer for delegation, viewing which operating system the computer is running, adding or removing group memberships, and modifying security permissions and dial-in permissions (see Figure 2.8), among other options.

Administering and Troubleshooting Computer Accounts

You can easily move one or several computer accounts from one container to another container under Windows Server 2003. The ADUC console supports both cut and paste and drag-and-drop functionality by default. You can select one or more computer accounts, right-click the accounts, and select Cut from the right-click menu. Alternatively, you can click and drag one or more selected computer accounts and drop the accounts into a different container. As a third option, you can select one or more computer accounts, right-click the accounts, and select Move. When the Move dialog box appears, select the Active Directory container where you want the accounts moved and click OK.

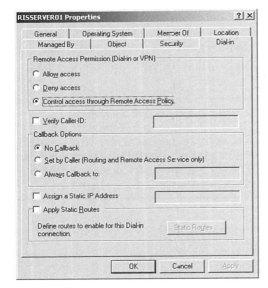

FIGURE 2.8 Working with dial-in properties for a computer account.

EXAM ALERT

New to **SP1**   New to **R2**   Under the SP1 and R2 updates to Windows Server 2003, you now receive a confirmation message box, by default, each time that you drag and drop one or more Active Directory objects within the ADUC console (see Figure 2.9). You can turn off this default message by marking the Don't show this warning while this snap-in is open check box.

An administrator also has the option to *disable* drag and drop functionality within the ADUC under SP1 and R2 by setting the *flags* attribute for the *Display Specifiers* container. You can use the `ADSIedit.msc` MMC snap-in tool to set the flags attribute in Active Directory at the following location: `CN=DisplaySpecifiers,CN=Configuration,DC=<domain name>`. Setting the flags attribute to *any* value disables drag and drop functionality. The default configuration for SP1 and R2 is that the value is *not* set, which enables administrators to drag and drop objects in the ADUC.

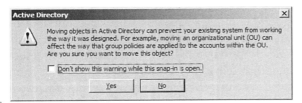

FIGURE 2.9 An Active Directory confirmation message box appears by default whenever you attempt to drag and drop one or more objects in the ADUC under Windows Server 2003 SP1 and R2.

In addition to working with the properties sheet for each computer account, you have several administrative tasks available to you when you right-click a computer account, including the following:

▶ *Name Mappings*—This option maps X.509 security certificates and Kerberos names for the computer account.

▶ *Disable Account*—This option prevents any users from logging on to the domain from the computer account. After you select this option, it toggles to read *Enable Account*, which you can later use for re-enabling the computer account.

▶ *Reset Account*—This option changes the computer account password that is used to authenticate the computer on the domain. If you reset a computer account, you must rejoin the computer to the domain.

▶ *Move*—This option allows you to relocate the computer account to a different container or OU.

▶ *Manage*—This option launches the Computer Management console for remotely administering the selected computer.

▶ *All Tasks, Resultant Set of Policy (Planning)*—This option lets you view simulated policy settings for a selected computer or a selected user.

▶ *All Tasks, Resultant Set of Policy (Logging)*—This option lets you view policy settings for a specific computer on the network.

TIP

Windows 2000, Windows XP Professional, Windows Vista, and Windows Server 2003 computers that are members of an Active Directory domain communicate with a DC using what's known as a secure channel. The secure channel's password is stored with the computer account on the domain controller. For Windows 2000, Windows XP, and Windows Server 2003 computers, the system-generated computer account password is automatically changed every 30 days by default. If, for some reason, the password stored on the domain member computer cannot be validated against the password stored on the DC, the Netlogon service generates one or both of the following errors on the domain member computer:

The session setup from the computer DOMAINMEMBER failed to authenticate. The name of the account referenced in the security database is DOMAINMEMBER$. The following error occurred: Access is denied.

NETLOGON Event ID 3210:

Failed to authenticate with \\DOMAINDC, a Windows NT domain controller for domain DOMAIN.

Either one or both of these errors indicate that you need to reset the computer account.

Using Command-Line Utilities for Active Directory Objects

Microsoft added several useful command-line tools for managing Active Directory and Active Directory objects. In this chapter, you've already learned how to use the dsadd command for adding new computers, but dsadd can do more than just add computers and groups. You can use these new command-line utilities for Active Directory both locally and remotely, provided that you possess the necessary security permissions for the task that you are trying to complete. The following list details the commands that are available and discusses how you can use them:

▶ *DSADD.exe*—This command adds a single computer, contact, group, OU, user, or quota specification to Active Directory. For help with the specific parameters and syntax for each type of object, type dsadd *ObjectType* /? at a command prompt. For example, dsadd user /? displays the available parameters (options) and syntax for adding a user to Active Directory.

▶ *DSGET.exe*—This command displays the properties for computers, contacts, groups, OUs, partitions, quotas, servers (DCs), sites, subnets, and users in Active Directory. For help with the specific parameters and syntax for each type of object, type dsget *ObjectType* /? at a command prompt. For example, dsget server /? displays the available parameters (options) and syntax for viewing the properties of a specific domain controller.

▶ *DSMOD.exe*—This command modifies the properties of a single computer, contact, group, OU, partition, quota, server, or user. For help with the specific parameters and syntax for each type of object, type dsmod *ObjectType* /? at a command prompt. For example, dsmod group /? displays the available parameters (options) and syntax for changing the properties of a specific group, including the ability to change the group type and group scope and adding or removing users.

▶ *DSMOVE.exe*—This command moves or renames a single object within Active Directory. For help with the specific parameters and syntax for this command, type dsmove /? at a command prompt.

▶ *DSQUERY.exe*—This command allows you to perform a search to locate computers, contacts, groups, OUs, partitions, quotas, servers (DCs), sites, subnets, or users within Active Directory. You can specify search criteria for finding Active Directory objects. The dsquery * command can find any type of Active Directory object. For help with the specific parameters and syntax for each type of object, type dsquery *ObjectType* /? at a command prompt. For example, dsquery computer /? displays the available parameters (options) and syntax for finding computers in Active Directory.

▶ *DSRM.exe*—This command removes (deletes) objects within Active Directory. For help with the specific parameters and syntax for this command, type dsrm /? at a command prompt.

▶ *CSVDE.exe*—This command exports data from Active Directory and imports data into Active Directory using the comma-separated values (CSV) file format. Programs such as Microsoft Excel and Microsoft Exchange Server administration utilities can read and write to CSV files. This tool is Microsoft's preferred method for automating the creation of user accounts in Active Directory using a bulk importing procedure. For help with the specific parameters and syntax for this command, type csvde (with no parameters) at a command prompt.

▶ *LDIFDE.exe*—This command exports data from Active Directory and imports data into Active Directory using the Lightweight Directory Access Protocol (LDAP) Data Interchange Format (LDIF) file format. The LDIF files use the .ldf extension, and you can view and edit them using any simple text editor such as Notepad. For help with the specific parameters and syntax for this command, type ldifde (with no parameters) at a command prompt. This tool is not Microsoft's preferred method for automating the creation of user accounts in Active Directory using a bulk importing procedure.

TIP

Although it's been around for a long time, the net command can still prove useful. To view a list of all the available net command options, type net and press Enter at a command prompt. To get help on usage, type net *command_name* /? and press Enter. For example, you can view a list of user accounts for the domain by typing net user and pressing Enter.

Managing Resources Using the Run As Command

The Run As feature gives administrators (and other users) the ability to run programs and system utilities under the security credentials of one user while being logged on to the server as a different user. For example, an administrator named DanB can be logged on to a server or a workstation with an ordinary user account that is only a member of the Domain Users group. While logged on as the ordinary user, DanB, he can right-click any MMC snap-in tool, such as ADUC (dsa.msc), and select Run As from the pop-up menu. The Run As dialog box appears with two options to run this program—Current User (with Restricted Access) and the Following User. By selecting the second option and typing in the appropriate administrative username and password (see Figure 2.10), DanB can log in using the alternate credentials without logging out of the machine.

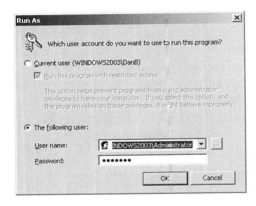

FIGURE 2.10   Running a program as a different user with the Run As right-click menu option.

You can use the Run As command for all types of programs, utilities, and even Control Panel applets. For using Run As on Control Panel tools, hold down the Shift key while you right-click a Control Panel icon to display the Run As option. You might need to hold down the Shift key while you right-click to access the Run As option for other applications as well. Using Run As is a more secure way for accessing security-sensitive utilities rather than always logging on to systems as a user who is a member of the Administrators group.

You can even use the Run As command to launch an instance of the Windows Explorer under the security credentials of a different user. For example, if you are currently logged on as JoeUser, at a command prompt or at the Start, Run box, you can type runas /noprofile /user:domain1\administrator explorer.exe to launch an Explorer window under the security context of Domain1's Administrator account. Any folders or files that you access from *that* Explorer window are subject to the Access Control List (ACL) for the Administrator user account, not the ACL for JoeUser.

EXAM ALERT

Unfortunately, you cannot use the Run As feature for all administrative chores. For instance, if you right-click a network connection icon in the Network Connections folder, Windows Server 2003 does not offer you the Run As option; right-clicking the Printers and Faxes icon in Control Panel does not provide you with the Run As menu option either. So, remember, as convenient as the Run As tool is, you cannot use it in every situation.

Using Run As from the Command Line

You can also use the Run As feature from a command window, both for GUI tools as well as for command-line tools. For example, you can run the Computer Management console as the administrator for the Windows2003.local domain by clicking Start, Run; typing runas /user:windows2003\administrator "mmc %windir%\system32\compmgmt.msc" in the Open box; and clicking OK. From a command prompt, you can type runas /? and press Enter to view the many options and syntax for this command.

You can also open a command-prompt window as a different user—as the administrator for a domain named Windows2003.local, for example—by clicking Start, Run; typing runas /user:windows2003\administrator cmd.exe in the Open box; and clicking OK. In addition, you can create shortcuts to administrative tools that require the administrator's password to run. For an example of how to create such a shortcut, follow these steps:

1. Right-click the Windows desktop and select New, Shortcut.

2. Type a command string such as runas /user:windows2003\administrator "mmc %windir%\system32\compmgmt.msc" in the Type the Location of the Item box.

3. Click Next.

4. Input a name for the shortcut in the Type a Name for This Shortcut box, such as Admin Computer Mgmt.

5. Click Finish.

When you double-click the shortcut, you are prompted for the administrator password. If you do not type in the correct password for the administrator user account, the program (Computer Management, in this example) does not run.

Exam Prep Questions

1. What is the default behavior in Windows Server 2003 RTM (Released to Manufacturing) version (pre-SP1 and pre-R2) when you attempt to drag and drop a computer account from the Computers container into an organizational unit using the Active Directory Users and Computers (ADUC) console? (Choose the best answer.)

   ○ **A.** Drag and drop functionality is not supported in this version.

   ○ **B.** The computer account is moved.

   ○ **C.** You are prompted by a message box to confirm or cancel your action.

   ○ **D.** It depends on whether an administrator has disabled the drag and drop feature.

2. Which of the following methods can you use to create computer accounts in Active Directory under Windows Server 2003? (Choose three.)

   ○ **A.** Log on to a domain from a Windows 98 computer.

   ○ **B.** Join a domain from a Windows NT 4.0 computer.

   ○ **C.** Prestage a computer account from the ADUC console.

   ○ **D.** Prestage a computer account using the `dsget computer` command.

   ○ **E.** Prestage a computer account using the `dsadd computer` command.

   ○ **F.** Join a domain from a Windows 95 computer with the Active Directory client software installed.

3. How can you take advantage of the increased functionality under MMC 3.0? Choose two. Both answers are required for a complete solution.

   ○ **A.** Install SP1 for Windows Server 2003.

   ○ **B.** Install R2 for Windows Server 2003.

   ○ **C.** Download and install MMC 2.0 from Microsoft's website.

   ○ **D.** Add the Value UseNewUI to the Windows Registry key
   HKEY_LOCAL_MACHINE\SOFTWARE\Microsoft\MMC.

   ○ **E.** Enable the new functionality by selecting the Add or Remove Snap-in dialog box from the File menu under MMC 3.0.

   ○ **F.** Add the subkey UseNewUI to the Windows Registry key
   HKEY_LOCAL_MACHINE\SOFTWARE\Microsoft\MMC.

4. As an administrator for the ExamCram.corp domain, how can you run the Active Directory Users and Computers MMC snap-in? (Choose two.)

   ○ **A.** Double-click the file `dsa.mmc` in the %systemroot%\system32 folder from Windows Explorer.

   ○ **B.** Click Start, Run, type `aduc.msc`, and click OK.

   ○ **C.** Double-click the file `dsa.msc` in the %systemroot%\system32 folder from Windows Explorer.

   ○ **D.** Double-click the file `aduc.msc` in the %systemroot%\system32 folder from Windows Explorer.

   ○ **E.** Click Start, Run, type mmc, and click OK. Click File, Add/Remove Snap-in, select Active Directory Users and Computers from the list of available snap-ins, click Add, and then click OK.

5. What happens if you attempt to run an application program using the Run option as a different user than the user who is currently logged on, but you type in an incorrect user name or password? (Choose the best answer.)

   ○ **A.** The program runs using the security credentials of the currently logged-on user.

   ○ **B.** You see a logon failure error message box appear on the screen.

   ○ **C.** The Run As option gives you three more chances to type in the correct password before it logs off the current user.

   ○ **D.** At the Run As dialog box, you must type in the correct username and password for the currently logged-on user if you want to run the program after entering an incorrect username or password.

6. Which of the following features are *not* new in MMC 3.0? (Choose three.)

   ○ **A.** Improved error handling

   ○ **B.** The Results pane

   ○ **C.** Redesigned Add or Remove Snap-in dialog box

   ○ **D.** The Console Tree

   ○ **E.** The Windows Registry key
       `HKEY_LOCAL_MACHINE\SOFTWARE\Microsoft\MMC`

   ○ **F.** The Action Pane

7. How can you perform a bulk import of users into Active Directory to create many user accounts at one time?

   ○ **A.** Use the `dsadd.exe` command.

   ○ **B.** Use the ADUC console.

   ○ **C.** Use the `net user` command.

   ○ **D.** Use the `csvde.exe` command.

   ○ **E.** Use the `dsmod.exe` command.

8. Which of the following commands can perform bulk imports and exports into and out of Active Directory using a file format that is compatible with the Lightweight Directory Access Protocol?

   ○ **A.** The `dsquery.exe` command

   ○ **B.** The `dsrm.exe` command

   ○ **C.** The `net user` command

   ○ **D.** The `ldifde.exe` command

   ○ **E.** The `notepad.exe` utility

9. Which of the following command-line commands can you use to rename an object within Active Directory?

   ○ **A.** `dsadd`

   ○ **B.** `dsquery`

   ○ **C.** `dsmove`

   ○ **D.** `dsrm`

   ○ **E.** `dsget`

   ○ **F.** `net user`

10. While remaining logged on at the console to a Windows Server 2003 computer as Joe User, how can you successfully run the following applets and programs as the domain administrator? (Choose two.)

   ○ **A.** In Control Panel, right-click the Network Connections icon and select Run As. Select the option button for The Following User, type `domain_name\administrator` in the Username box, type the proper password in the Password box, and click OK.

   ○ **B.** Click Start and point to All Programs, right-click the Internet Explorer icon and select Run As. Select the option button for The Following User, type `domain_name\administrator` in the Username box, type the proper password in the Password box, and click OK.

   ○ **C.** In Control Panel, hold down the Shift key, right-click the Printers and Faxes icon and select Run As. Select the option button for The Following User, type `domain_name\administrator` in the Username box, type the proper password in the Password box, and click OK.

   ○ **D.** In Control Panel hold down the Shift key, right-click the Display icon and select Run As. Select the option button for The Following User, type `domain_name'administrator` in the Username box, type the proper password in the Password box, and click OK.

   ○ **E.** Click Start and point to All Programs, Administrative Tools, and click Active Directory Users and Computers. When prompted, select the option button for The Following User, type `domain_name\administrator` in the Username box, type the proper password in the Password box, and click OK.

Answers to Exam Prep Questions

1. **Answer B is correct.** Drag and drop is the default behavior in the ADUC in the RTM version (as well as in SP1 and R2). Answer A is incorrect because drag and drop has always been supported in the ADUC console under Windows Server 2003. Answer C is incorrect because the RTM version does not provide any confirmation message box for dragging and dropping objects within the ADUC console. Answer D is incorrect because there is no Microsoft-supported method for disabling drag and drop functionality under the RTM version. However, turning off the drag and drop feature is supported under SP1 and R2.

2. **Answers B, C, and E are correct.** You can create a computer account when you join a computer to a domain from a Windows NT 4.0, Windows 2000, Windows XP, Windows Vista, or Windows Server 2003 computer. You can prestage a computer account by using either the ADUC console or by using the `dsadd computer` command from a command prompt. Answer A is incorrect because logging on to a domain from a Windows 98 computer does not create a computer account in Active Directory. Answer D is incorrect because the `dsget computer` command displays properties of computers in the directory. Answer F is incorrect because you cannot join a Windows 95 computer to a domain, even with the Active Directory client software installed.

3. **Answers B and F are correct.** MMC 3.0 is automatically installed when you upgrade to Windows Server 2003 R2 Edition. By adding the new subkey `UseNewUI` to the key `HKEY_LOCAL_MACHINE\SOFTWARE\Microsoft\MMC`, you turn on the improved features for MMC 3.0. Answer A is incorrect because MMC 3.0 is not automatically installed when you install SP1. Answer C is incorrect because you cannot enable MMC 3.0 features under MMC 2.0. Answer D is incorrect because adding the *value* `UseNewUI` to the `KEY_LOCAL_MACHINE\SOFTWARE\Microsoft\MMC` Windows Registry key does not enable the enhancements for MMC 3.0. Answer E is incorrect because you cannot enable the new features for MMC 3.0 from the Add or Remove Snap-in dialog box.

4. **Answers C and E are correct.** The file named `dsa.msc` is the MMC snap-in for the Active Directory Users and Computers console. You can add a snap-in from an empty MMC by running the `MMC` command from the Run box and then use the Add/Remove Snap-in dialog box to add the appropriate snap-in. Answer A is incorrect because the default filename for the Active Directory Users and Computers snap-in is `dsa.msc`, not `dsa.mmc`. Answers B and C are incorrect because the default filename for the Active Directory Users and Computers snap-in is `dsa.msc`, not `aduc.msc`.

5. **Answer B is correct.** If you use the Run As option and type the wrong username or password for the different user's security credentials, you receive a message box that states: *Unable to log on: Logon failure: Unknown user name or bad password*. Answer A is incorrect because the program will not run if you type the incorrect username or password for the Run As dialog box. Answer C is incorrect because the Run As option does not limit how many chances you have to type in the correct user credentials after you receive the logon failure message box. Answer D is incorrect because you do not need to type in the username or password to run a program as the currently logged on user; you do not need to use the Run As feature for this purpose.

6. **Answers B, D, and E are correct.** The Results pane, the Console Tree, and the HKEY_LOCAL_MACHINE\SOFTWARE\Microsoft\MMC Windows Registry key are not new features; all of these components existed under the previous MMC version 2.0. Answer A is incorrect because improved error handling is a new feature of MMC 3.0. Answer C is incorrect because the redesigned Add or Remove Snap-in dialog is a new feature of MMC 3.0. Answer F is incorrect because the Action pane is also a new feature of MMC 3.0.

7. **Answer D is correct.** You can use the csvde.exe command from a command prompt to import many users into Active Directory from .csv files. Answer A is incorrect because the dsadd.exe only creates a single user at a time. Answer B is incorrect because the ADUC console can only create one user at a time. Answer C is incorrect because the net user command can only create one user at a time.

8. **Answer D is correct.** You can use the ldifde.exe command from a command prompt to import many users into Active Directory using .ldf files and the LDAP Data Interchange Format (LDIF). Answer A is incorrect because the dsquery.exe utility performs searches for Active Directory objects. Answer B is incorrect because the dsrm.exe command removes objects from Active Directory. Answer C is incorrect because the net user command can only create one user at a time. Answer E is incorrect because notepad.exe cannot import or export objects; it is only a text viewer and editor.

9. **Answer C is correct.** You can use the dsmove command to move and rename objects in Active Directory. Answer A is incorrect because you cannot rename any Active Directory object with the dsadd command; you use it for adding users. Answer B is incorrect because you cannot rename any Active Directory object with the dsquery command; you use it for performing search operations. Answer D is incorrect because you cannot rename any Active Directory object with the dsrm command; you use it for removing objects. Answer E is incorrect because you cannot rename any Active Directory object with the dsget command you use it for displaying an object's properties. Answer F is incorrect because you cannot rename any Active Directory object with the net user command; you use it for adding users and for viewing user information.

10. **Answers B and D are correct.** You can right-click application programs, such as Internet Explorer, to select the Run As option. Certain other tools and utilities, such as most Control Panel applets, require you to hold down the Shift key and then right-click the icon to display the Run As menu option. Answer A is incorrect because the Network Connections system folder is one of the few Control Panel icons that do not support the Run As feature (even if you hold down the Shift key). Answer C is incorrect because the Printers and Faxes system folder is also one of the few Control Panel icons that do not support the Run As feature (even if you hold down the Shift key). Answer E is incorrect because the Active Directory Users and Computers console does not automatically prompt you to use the Run As option (nor does any other built-in utility).

Need to Know More?

1. Stanek, William R. *Microsoft Windows Server 2003 Administrator's Pocket Consultant*. Redmond, Washington: Microsoft Press, 2003.

2. Scales, Lee, and John Michell. *MCSA/MCSE 70-290 Training Guide: Managing and Maintaining a Windows Server 2003 Environment*. Indianapolis, Indiana: Que Publishing, 2003.

3. Lewis, Alex, Morimoto, Rand, Noel, Michael. *Microsoft Windows Server 2003 Unleashed (R2 Edition)*. Indianapolis, Indiana: Sams Publishing, 2006.

4. Search the Microsoft Product Support Services Knowledge Base on the Internet: `http://support.microsoft.com`. You can also search through Microsoft TechNet on the Internet: `http://www.microsoft.com/technet`. Find technical information using keywords from this chapter, such as computer accounts, run as, MMC 3.0, service pack 1 (SP1), R2, active directory, action pane, `dsadd`, and `dsmod`.

CHAPTER THREE

Managing User Accounts in Active Directory

Terms you'll need to understand:

✓ User accounts

✓ User account configuration settings

✓ Option settings for user account passwords

✓ Types of user account names

✓ Active Directory Users and Computers (ADUC) console

Techniques you'll need to master:

✓ Creating user accounts

✓ Modifying user account properties

✓ Enabling and disabling user accounts

✓ Creating and resetting user account passwords

✓ Searching for users in Active Directory

Users are the sole reason why computers exist. Information technology systems empower users to be much more efficient and effective than they would be if they still had to get their jobs done using only pencil and paper. Active Directory, under Windows 2000 Server and Windows Server 2003, provides an efficient way for administrators to manage computer users and enables users to easily access the applications and data they need to get their daily tasks done more effectively. Active Directory scales well—it lets you centrally control just a few users for a small office, while at the same time, it can also help you to manage literally thousands of users for a multinational business entity.

Managing Users in Active Directory

You can manage users in two distinct ways under Windows Server 2003 Active Directory—from the GUI or from the command line. The Active Directory Users and Computers (ADUC) MMC snap-in console provides the graphical method to manage users, whereas command-line tools such as dsadd, dsmod, and dsmove provide the means for adding, changing, and moving users within the directory service. Which method you use for managing users is strictly a preference on your part as the network administrator, or it could be a companywide decision on the part of the IT department that establishes policies for IT administration. The Windows GUI is relatively straightforward, but the command-line tools lend themselves to batch files for a more automated approach.

EXAM ALERT

Remember that Windows computers (except domain controllers) allow two types of user accounts to log on—local user accounts and domain user accounts. Only local accounts exist on standalone and workgroup computers; domain accounts and local accounts exist on Windows computers that are members of a Windows (Active Directory) domain.

Domain-member servers and client computers that are members of a domain allow users to log on as *either* local users (if local accounts have been set up) or as domain users. However, in a domain-based environment, local user accounts are seldom used. Servers that are configured as domain controllers host the Active Directory list (database) of users, computers, and other objects. Domain controllers do not host local user accounts.

Adding New Users

Creating new users in Active Directory is a fairly simple process. You need to assign both a display name and a user logon name for each user. The display name consists of the first name, initials, and last name of the user, by default.

The display name appears in the ADUC console. The display name cannot contain more than 64 characters. The user logon name is used for logging on to the Active Directory domain. The rules for user logon names are as follows:

▶ They must be unique within each Active Directory forest.

▶ They can contain up to 256 characters.

▶ The User Logon Name is actually optional, but you must assign a pre-Windows 2000 User Logon name to each user account.

▶ By default, Active Directory recognizes only the first 20 characters of the logon name, but you can assign a longer name if you want.

▶ User logon names cannot contain the following special characters:

"/ \ [ ] ; | = , + * ? < >

▶ Spaces embedded in user logon names are allowed but not recommended.

NOTE

> You can use either the user logon name or the pre-Windows 2000 user logon name to log on to an Active Directory domain, regardless of the domain functional level in effect.

Types of Domain User Account Names

Active Directory assigns five different types of names to each domain user account. Each name type is required for different functions within Active Directory. The five types of domain user account names are as follows:

▶ *User Logon Name*—As previously mentioned, this name is optional, but if used, it must be unique within the forest and can only be used for logging on to the domain (for example, *JoeUser*, *JUser*, or *Joe.User*).

▶ *Pre-Windows 2000 Logon Name*—This name is mandatory when creating a new user and it *may contain no more than 15 characters*. A user can use this name to log on to a computer running a pre-Windows 2000 operating system, such as Windows 98, by typing this name in the *Domain_Name\User_Name* syntax. This name must be unique within the domain in which it is created. A user or an administrator can use this name when launching an application program with the Runas option.

▶ *User Principal Logon Name (UPN)*—This name is a combination of the User Logon Name, the at sign (@), and the user principal name suffix. For example, *Joe.User@examcram.corp*. The user principal logon name suffix can be the Domain Name System (DNS) name of the Active Directory domain hosting the user account, the DNS name of any

Active Directory domain in the forest, or it could even be a fictitious name created by IT administrators for user logon purposes only. A user or an administrator can also use this name when launching an application program with the Runas option.

▶ *Lightweight Directory Access Protocol (LDAP) Distinguished Name*—This name serves as a unique identifier for every object within an Active Directory forest. Administrators use LDAP distinguished names to programmatically manipulate user accounts via script files or via the command line; users do not use these names. For example, *CN=joe.user,ou=marketing,dc=examcram,dc=corp* would be the LDAP distinguished name for a user named *Joe.User* whose account resides in the *Marketing* organizational unit (OU), within the domain *ExamCram.corp*.

▶ *LDAP Relative Distinguished Name*—This name, as its name suggests, uniquely identifies an Active Directory object *relative to* its parent container. LDAP Relative Distinguished Names need only be unique within the container or OU in which they are stored. For example, *CN=joe.user* would be an LDAP Relative Distinguished Name.

EXAM ALERT

Administrators can reference Active Directory objects by several different names, as just mentioned. Another method for referencing objects is by their *Canonical Names*. An object's Canonical Name uses the same basic naming convention as the LDAP Distinguished Name, but it reverses the sequence of the naming attributes and employs a different syntax. For example, if a user's LDAP Distinguished Name is *CN=joe.user,ou=marketing,dc=examcram,dc=corp*, his Canonical Name would be *examcram.corp/marketing/joe.user*. Canonical names are similar to uniform resource locators (URLs), which are used for accessing websites on the Internet.

Creating New User Objects from the GUI

The initial information required to create a user is minimal. Active Directory can store a vast amount of user information, but you must enter most of those details after a user is created. To create a new user from the ADUC console, follow these steps:

1. Open the ADUC console.

2. Right-click the container or OU where you want to place the new user and select New, User.

3. Type in the first name, initials, and last name of the user.

4. Change the full name, if desired.

5. Type in the user logon name. The user logon name combined with the *@domain.name* drop-down list box compose the user principal name (UPN) that you can use to log on to Active Directory from Windows 2000, Windows XP, and Windows Server 2003 computers.

6. If desired, you can change the pre-Windows 2000 user logon name or else leave it at the default.

7. Click Next to continue.

8. Type in a password for the user in both the Password box and the Confirm Password box. The password must conform to the domain's password policy requirements or else you will receive an error message, as shown in Figure 3.1.

9. To keep the assigned password for the user, clear the User Must Change Password at Next Logon check box.

10. If desired, mark the User Cannot Change Password, Password Never Expires, and Account Is Disabled check boxes.

11. Click Next to review a summary of how the new user will be created. Click Back to make any changes.

12. Click Finish to create the user.

FIGURE 3.1 Viewing an error message for a password that does not meet Active Directory's password-policy requirements.

Creating New Users From a Template Account

You can preconfigure one or more user accounts that you can use as models on which you can base other new user accounts. When you build a template (model or master) account, it then serves as a sample user account whose common properties you can prepopulate to save time when creating new users. To use an existing user account as a template, right-click the model user account in the ADUC console and select Copy. Type in the appropriate names and password to create the new user account and click Finish. Much of the data stored in the existing user account's properties tabs is copied over to the new user:

▶ *Address* tab—All properties for this dialog box are copied over except for the Street Address.

▶ *Account* tab—All properties for this dialog box are copied except for Logon Name.

▶ *Profile* tab—All properties for this dialog box are copied except for Profile Path and Home Folder.

▶ *Organization* tab—All properties for this dialog box are copied except for Title.

▶ *Member of* tab—All properties for this dialog box are copied.

You can see an example of the User Account properties tab later in this chapter, in Figure 3.3.

Creating New User Objects from the Command Line

Using the new `dsadd` command, you can also create users from any command prompt or batch file under Windows Server 2003. The `dsadd user` command offers many options. To get detailed information on the syntax and available parameters, type `dsadd user /?` at a command prompt. In the following step-by-step example, let's create a new user with a display name (CN) of Bill Gates. The user's first name (-FN) is William, his middle initial (-MI) is H, and his last name (-LN) is Gates. The user's user logon name (-UPN) is bgates, his pre-Windows 2000 user logon name (-SAMID) is bgates, and his password (-PWD) is 111-MS$$$, and we will create him within the East Coast OU for the Active Directory domain `windows2003.local`. To create a new user with this minimal amount of detail from the command line, follow these steps:

1. Open a command prompt window.

2. At the command prompt, type the following all on one line and then press Enter (if the length of the command is too long for the command prompt window, it will automatically wrap around to the next line):

```
DSADD USER "CN=Bill Gates,OU=EAST COAST,DC=WINDOWS2003,DC=LOCAL"
-UPN bgates@WINDOWS2003.LOCAL -SAMID bgates -FN William -MI H -LN
Gates -PWD 111-MS$$$
```

3. The `dsadd user` command should process the command and then display `"dsadd succeeded:CN=Bill Gates,OU=EAST COAST, DC=WINDOWS2003,DC=LOCAL"`.

TIP

To import many users into Active Directory at one time, use the `csvde` command-line tool. CSVDE reads and writes using the CSV file format. To import new users from a file named `newusers.csv`, type `csvde -i -f newusers.csv` and press Enter. For help with command-line options and syntax, type `csvde` (with no parameters) and press Enter.

Managing User Password Policies

Computer security has become a focal point the world over due to the tremendous amount of computer viruses and the huge rise in computer hacking incidents. To respond to these security threats, Microsoft pledged to make its new products "secure by design and secure by default." To this end, Active Directory under Windows Server 2003, by default, does not permit blank passwords nor passwords that do not meet its built-in minimum complexity requirements. To view or change these built-in default password settings, perform the following steps:

1. On a DC, click Start, Administrative Tools, Domain Security Policy.

2. From the Default Domain Security Settings console (as shown in Figure 3.2), you can view and edit policy settings for the domain.

3. Expand the Account Policies node and click the Password Policy subnode to view the settings that are currently in effect for the entire domain. The default settings are

   ▶ *Enforce Password History*—24 passwords remembered

   ▶ *Maximum Password Age*—42 days

   ▶ *Minimum Password Age*—1 day

   ▶ *Minimum Password Length*—7 characters

   ▶ *Passwords Must Meet Complexity Requirements*—Enabled

   ▶ *Store Passwords Using Reversible Encryption*—Disabled

4. Double-click each setting that you want to change, and click OK.

5. Exit from the Default Domain Security Settings console.

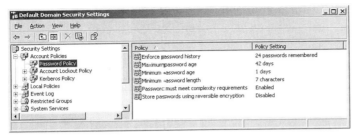

FIGURE 3.2 Working with default password policy settings for an Active Directory domain.

The Password Must Meet Complexity Requirements setting, when enabled, enforces the following rules for all passwords:

▶ Passwords cannot contain all or part of the user's account name.

▶ Passwords must contain at least six characters.

▶ Passwords must contain at least three of the following four different types of characters:

  ▶ Numerals 0 through 9.

  ▶ English lowercase letters a through z.

  ▶ English uppercase letters A through Z.

  ▶ Nonalphanumeric characters such as %, $, #, !, +, and &.

Microsoft considers passwords that meet these standards as strong passwords. Microsoft (and other security experts) recommend that you maintain an overall policy of strong passwords as a best practice. The maximum character length for passwords under Windows Server 2003 is 127; however, Windows 9x computers can only support up to 14-character passwords. A password is considered *weak* if it is blank, if it contains the user's name or company name, if it contains a complete word (or words) that appears in a dictionary, or if any of these examples have numbers appended on the beginning or end of the word. For example, the password *computer* is a weak password, as are the passwords *sunshine1* or *silver2gold*.

NOTE

To reset a user's password from the ADUC console, right-click the user's name and select Reset Password. Read the warning dialog box explaining the implications of changing the password, and then click Proceed. In the Set Password dialog, type the new password in both the New Password box and the Confirm Password box. Mark the User Must Change Password at Next Logon check box to enable this setting. Click OK to change the password.

Modifying and Deleting Users

Active Directory can store a lot of information for each user, as you can see in Figure 3.3. You can double-click a user's name in the ADUC console to view a user's properties sheet. From the properties sheet, you add, change, or delete information for the user. By default, Active Directory can store users' phone numbers, addresses, email addresses, logon information, group memberships, remote control settings, terminal services settings, user dial-in settings, and Active Directory security permission settings, among many other options. By extending the Active Directory schema, Active Directory can store more information, such as Microsoft Exchange Server email settings.

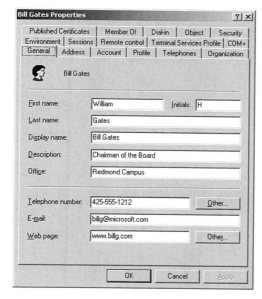

FIGURE 3.3 Viewing a user account's properties sheet in Active Directory.

Modifying User Accounts from the ADUC

When you right-click a user name in the ADUC console, several options are available to you (see Figure 3.4). With the Copy option, you can copy the user's settings to create a new user with the same settings (a user template). You can add the user to an existing group. You can view, add, edit, or remove X.509 certificates and trusted non-Windows Kerberos realms by selecting the Name Mappings option. You can disable or enable a user account and reset the user's password. You can also move the user account to a different container, open the home page for the user (if specified), and send an email message to the selected user. You can run the Resultant Set of Policy (RSoP) Wizard in planning mode by selecting All Tasks, Resultant Set of Policy (Planning). You can run the RSoP Wizard in logging mode by selecting All Tasks, Resultant Set of Policy (Logging).

You can move a user by using the Cut option from the right-click menu, instead of using the Move option and instead of dragging a user account to a different container or OU and dropping it into the other container. You can easily delete a user account by right-clicking it and selecting Delete or by selecting the user account in the ADUC console and then pressing the Delete key on the keyboard. You can rename a user by right-clicking the user account and selecting Rename or by selecting the user account and pressing the F2 key on the keyboard.

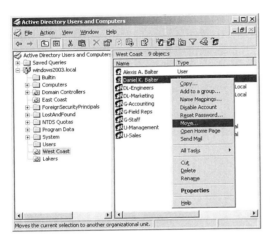

FIGURE 3.4 Viewing the options from right-clicking a user account in the ADUC console.

Modifying User Accounts from the Command Line

You can use the dsmod user command to change user properties from the command prompt. The dsmod user command has several different options. For assistance with using the command, type dsmod user /? at a command prompt. As an example, let's change the last name to Fences, the description to Executive, and the office to Los Angeles for a user account named Bill Gates. This user is located in the East Coast OU in the Active Directory domain windows2003.local. To modify an existing user account from the command line, follow these steps:

1. Open a command prompt window.

2. At the command prompt, type the following all on one line and then press Enter (if the length of the command is too long for the command prompt window, it will automatically wrap around to the next line):

   ```
   DSMOD USER "CN=Bill Gates,OU=EAST COAST,DC=WINDOWS2003,DC=LOCAL" -LN
   Fences -DESC Executive -OFFICE "Los Angeles"
   ```

3. The dsmod user command should process the command and then display

   ```
   dsmod succeeded:CN=Bill Gates,OU=EAST COAST,DC=WINDOWS2003,
   DC=LOCAL
   ```

The *DSMOVE.exe* command moves or renames a single object within Active Directory. For help with the specific parameters and syntax for this command, type dsmove /? at a command prompt.

The *DSQUERY.exe* command allows you to perform a search to locate computers, contacts, groups, OUs, partitions, quotas, servers (DCs), sites, subnets, or users within Active Directory. You can specify search criteria for finding Active Directory objects. The dsquery * command can find any type of Active Directory object. For help with the specific parameters and syntax for each type of object, type dsquery *ObjectType* /? at a command prompt. For example, dsquery computer /? displays the available parameters (options) and syntax for finding computers in Active Directory.

The *DSRM.exe* command removes (deletes) objects within Active Directory. For help with the specific parameters and syntax for this command, type dsrm /? at a command prompt.

To delete a user account from the command line, use the dsrm command. Following the previous example, typing dsrm "CN=Bill Gates,OU=EAST COAST,DC=WINDOWS2003,DC=LOCAL" and pressing Enter will prompt you to confirm that you want to remove the user account from the directory. Type Y to confirm the deletion or type N to cancel the operation. After you confirm the deletion, the user account is removed. The dsrm command then displays dsrm succeeded:CN=Bill Gates,OU=EAST COAST,DC=WINDOWS2003,DC=LOCAL.

To find out which domain groups that a user is a member of, as well as view other pertinent information about a user, type net user *user_logon_name* and press the Enter key, as shown in Figure 3.5.

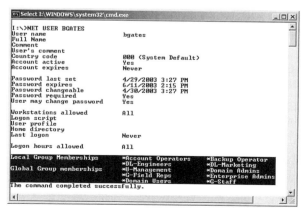

FIGURE 3.5 Using the net user command to find domain groups in which a user is member.

Troubleshooting User Account Problems

A user cannot log on to the domain if his or her user account is either disabled or locked out. An administrator can temporarily or permanently disable a user account by right-clicking the account in the ADUC console and selecting Disable. When you select the Disable option, a message box appears confirming that the user account is now disabled and the user account icon displays with a red X over it, as shown in Figure 3.6. Disabling an account is a good practice for users who take a temporary leave of absence to prevent possible unauthorized access from people who might know those users' logon names and passwords. To re-enable a user account, simply right-click the user account name in the ADUC and select the Enable option.

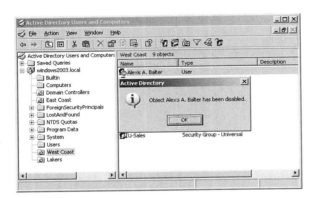

FIGURE 3.6   Disabling a user account in the ADUC console.

Locked-Out User Accounts

If a user attempts to log on to the domain but forgets his or her logon name or password, by default, Windows Server 2003 Active Directory permits an *unlimited* number of logon attempts! The policy settings for the Account Lockout Policy for the domain are configurable from the Default Domain Security Settings console, in the Account Policies, Account Lockout Policy subnode. When you change the default Account Lockout Duration policy setting, you are prompted to configure or accept default settings for the other two domain account lockout policies, as you can see in Figure 3.7. The three domain lockout policies and their available settings are as follows:

- ► *Account Lockout Duration*—This policy defines how long locked-out accounts remain locked out. The default setting is none (or undefined) because you must enable the Account Lockout Threshold policy for this policy to be in effect. The available range is from 0 minutes through 99,999 minutes.

▶ *Account Lockout Threshold*—This policy defines the number of failed logon attempts allowed before the user account is locked out. The default setting is 0, which means that the account lockout feature is disabled. The available range is from 0 attempts through 999 attempts.

▶ *Reset Account Lockout Counter After*—This policy defines the number of minutes that must elapse after one or more failed logon attempts (for each user) before the failed logon attempt counter gets reset to 0 bad logon attempts. The default setting is none (or undefined) because you must enable the Account Lockout Threshold policy for this policy to be in effect. The available range is from 1 minute through 99,999 minutes. This policy setting must be less than or equal to the Account Lockout Duration setting.

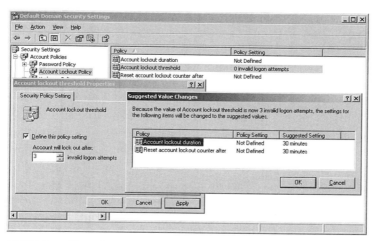

FIGURE 3.7 Managing user account lockout settings from the Default Domain Security Settings console.

NOTE

Once a user account is locked out, it cannot be used for logging the user on to the domain until the account lockout is reset by an administrator or until the lockout duration has expired (see Figure 3.8). By default, the Administrator account *cannot* be locked out; if the Account Lockout Threshold is exceeded for the Administrator account, the Account Is Locked Out check box becomes checked on the Administrator account's properties sheet. However, the Administrator can still log on successfully with the proper username and password from any computer or DC in the domain. For all other user accounts other than the Administrator account, an administrator must clear the Account Is Locked Out check box in the user account's properties sheet or the Account Lockout Duration time must expire before a locked-out user can log on again.

FIGURE 3.8 Viewing the Logon Message box for a user attempting to log on to the domain with a locked-out account.

Troubleshooting User Authentication Problems

By default, Windows Server 2003, Windows XP, Windows 2000, and Windows NT computers all provide the ability for domain user accounts to log on to the computer even if the network connection is down or if there is no DC available to authenticate the user's logon. The user must have logged on to that computer and been authenticated by a DC previously, and the number of users that can log on in such circumstances is limited to 10, by default. Logging on in this manner is referred to as using cached credentials. These cached credentials are stored on the domain-member computer. You can limit or disable the cached-credentials feature by modifying an entry in the Windows Registry for each domain member computer or by configuring a group policy setting for the domain.

Changing Cached Credential Settings Through the Registry

For Windows Server 2003, Windows XP, and Windows 2000 domain-member computers, you can edit the Registry to modify the `cachedlogonscount` value. Remember, however, making any changes to the Windows Registry can render a computer unstable or completely unusable: Always take great care and be sure to have good data backups before editing the Registry. To change the number of cached-credential accounts stored on a computer, follow these steps:

1. On a domain-member computer running Windows Server 2003, Windows XP, or Windows 2000, click Start, Run; type `regedit`; and click OK to run the Windows Registry editor.

2. Starting at the `HKEY_LOCAL_MACHINE` node, expand the Registry keys and subkeys and navigate to `SOFTWARE\Microsoft\Windows NT\ CurrentVersion\Winlogon`.

3. Double-click the `cachedlogonscount` value name to display the Edit String dialog box, as shown in Figure 3.9.

4. Type in a new value data number to reflect how many cached accounts you want the computer to store (0 disables the use of cached credentials on the computer).

5. Click OK to save your new settings and exit from the Registry editor.

6. Restart the computer to ensure that the new settings take effect.

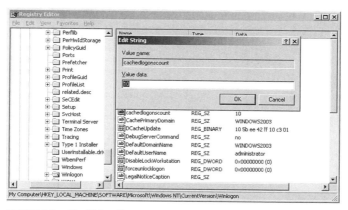

FIGURE 3.9 Modifying the `cachedlogonscount` entry in the Windows Registry.

Changing Cached Credential Settings Through Group Policy

An easier, more efficient, and immensely more manageable method of dealing with the number of available stored cached logon credentials is through a group policy setting. By defining a domainwide policy, you can effectively manage all domain-member computers with just one configuration setting. To change the number of cached-credential accounts stored on each domain-member computer, follow these steps:

1. On a DC, open the Default Domain Security Settings console.

2. Expand the Local Policies node and select the Security Options subnode.

3. Double-click the policy named Interactive Logon: Number of Previous Logons to Cache (in Case Domain Controller Is Not Available) as shown in Figure 3.10.

4. Mark the Define This Policy Setting check box.

5. Type the number of previous logons to store in the Cache: spinner box; the minimum number is 0 (disables cached credentials) and the maximum number is 50.

6. Click OK and exit from the Default Domain Security Settings console.

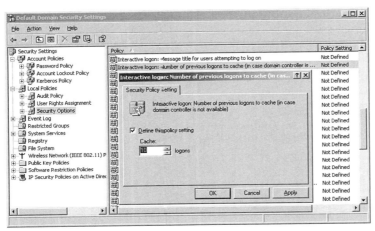

FIGURE 3.10   Defining a Group Policy setting for Interactive Logon: Number of Previous Logons to Cache.

Searching for User Accounts and Other Objects in Active Directory

Because Active Directory scales to support thousands (if not millions) of users, computers, and other objects, Microsoft built a search feature right into the ADUC console. The ability to construct queries and save them for later reuse helps administrators to quickly locate Active Directory objects instead of having to scroll through pages and pages of object listings. You use the Saved Queries container at the top of the Active Directory Users and Computers console tree to create, run, modify, save, and delete Active Directory queries (searches).

All saved queries are stored within the ADUC console and are specific to the domain controller on which they are created. However, you can both import and export stored query definitions so that they may be used on other domain controllers. Query definition files are saved as Extensible Markup Language (.xml) files. These .xml files can be copied and emailed to administrators in other locations just like any other type of file.

Working with Active Directory Queries

You can organize your saved queries in the ADUC console by right-clicking the Saved Queries container, pointing to New, clicking Folder, and typing a name for the folder. You can create subfolders by right-clicking a folder, pointing to New, clicking Folder, and typing a name for the subfolder. To create a new query, perform the following steps:

1. Right-click the folder in which you want to store the query, point to New, and click Query.

2. Type a name for the query in the Name box (see Figure 3.11).

3. Type an optional description in the Description box.

4. Click the Browse button to choose the container that you want to search or accept the default setting to search the entire domain and click OK.

5. Clear the Include subcontainers check box if you do not want to include subcontainers in your search.

6. Click the Define Query button to create the parameters for your search.

7. On the Find dialog box, click the Find drop-down list box to view all the available types of searches that you can choose from, as shown in Figure 3.12. Available searches include Users, Contacts, and Groups; Computers; Printers; Shared Folders; Common Queries.

8. To find disabled user accounts, select Common Queries from the Find drop-down list box, click the Users tab, mark the Disabled accounts check box, and click OK to generate the corresponding LDAP query string.

9. Click OK for the New Query dialog box to perform the search. The search results are displayed in the results pane of the ADUC console (see Figure 3.13). To rerun the query at any time, simply select the saved query and click the Refresh button on the toolbar.

10. You can edit a query definition by right-clicking it and selecting Edit.

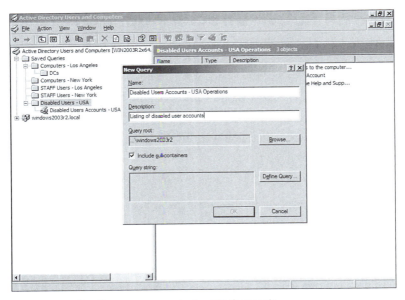

FIGURE 3.11   Creating a new query in the ADUC console.

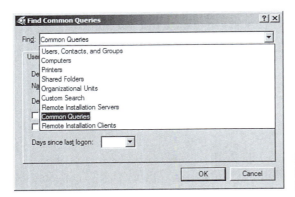

FIGURE 3.12   Selecting the type of search you want to create as a new query in the ADUC console.

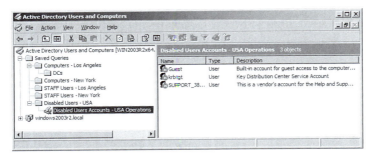

FIGURE 3.13   Viewing the results of a query in the ADUC console.

Exporting and Importing Saved Query Definitions

You can easily export any saved query definition by right-clicking it and choosing the Export Query Definition option. When the Save As dialog box appears, choose a location in which to save the file and then type a name for this query definition file into the File Name box. By default, the query definition is saved as an XML document. Click Save to complete the export procedure.

It's just as easy to import a query definition that you might receive from someone else as it is to export a query definition. Right-click the Saved Queries folder where you want to store the imported definition and select Import Query Definition. When the Open dialog box appears, navigate to the location of the file, select the file, and click the Open button. After you have successfully imported a query definition, you can easily modify its search parameters by right-clicking it and choosing Edit.

Exam Prep Questions

1. Which of the following Windows Server 2003 Active Directory user account names is the User Principal Name (UPN)? (Choose the best answer.)

   ○ **A.** examcram.corp/music/elton.john

   ○ **B.** elton.john.plays.piano.music

   ○ **C.** elton.john@examcram.corp

   ○ **D.** CN=elton.john

2. Which of the following Active Directory object names can exist within the same forest (examcram.corp) at the same time? (Choose the best answer.)

   ○ **A.** CN=DanB stored within the OU named Sales

   ○ **B.** CN=DanB stored within the OU named Marketing

   ○ **C.** CN=DanB,ou=mgmt,dc=examcram,dc=corp

   ○ **D.** examcram.corp/music/DanB

   ○ **E.** None of these

   ○ **F.** All of these

3. What is a user account's Canonical Name if the LDAP Distinguished Name is CN=dan.balter,ou=sales,ou=west,dc=infotech,dc=corp? (Choose the best answer.)

   ○ **A.** CN=dan.balter

   ○ **B.** dan.balter@infotech.corp/west/sales

   ○ **C.** infotech.corp\dan.balter

   ○ **D.** infotech.corp/west/sales/dan.balter

   ○ **E.** infotech.corp/sales/west/dan.balter

   ○ **F.** dan.balter/sales/west/infotech.corp

4. For which of the following user account properties tabs does every property get copied when you create a new user account from a user account template? (Choose the best answer.)

   ○ **A.** Organization

   ○ **B.** Account

   ○ **C.** Member of

   ○ **D.** Address

   ○ **E.** Profile

5. Which of the following statements about object queries in the ADUC console is *not* correct? (Choose the best answer.)

   ○ **A.** Query definitions can be imported.

   ○ **B.** Query definitions can be exported.

   ○ **C.** You can create folders and subfolders within the Saved Queries container.

   ○ **D.** You can select the Active Directory container that you would like to search.

   ○ **E.** You can save query definitions as HTML files.

   ○ **F.** You can choose not to search subcontainers.

6. Where is the Group Policy setting "Interactive Logon: Number of Previous Logons to Cache (in Case Domain Controller Is Not Available)" located within the Default Domain Security Settings console and what is this setting's default value? (Choose the best answer.)

   ○ **A.** It's located under Security Settings\Local Policies\Security Options, and its default value is 50.

   ○ **B.** It's located under Security Settings\Local Policies\Security Options, and its default value is 5.

   ○ **C.** It's located under Security Settings\Local Policies\User Rights Assignment, and its default value is 10.

   ○ **D.** It's located under Security Settings\Local Policies\User Rights Assignment, and its default value is 50.

   ○ **E.** It's located under Security Settings\Local Policies\Security Options, and its default value is 10.

7. How can you perform a bulk import of users into Active Directory to create many user accounts at one time?

   ○ **A.** Use the `dsadd.exe` command.

   ○ **B.** Use the ADUC console.

   ○ **C.** Use the `net user` command.

   ○ **D.** Use the `csvde.exe` command.

   ○ **E.** Use the `dsmod.exe` command.

8. Which of the following requirements do not apply to the default domain security policy setting "Password Must Meet Complexity Requirements" for Active Directory user accounts under Windows Server 2003? (Choose two.)

   ○ **A.** Passwords must contain at least seven characters.

   ○ **B.** Passwords cannot contain all or part of the user's account name.

   ○ **C.** Passwords must contain some nonalphanumeric characters such as %, $, #, !, +, and &.

   ○ **D.** Passwords may contain numerals 0 through 9.

   ○ **E.** Passwords may contain English lowercase letters a through z.

   ○ **F.** Passwords may contain English uppercase letters A through Z.

9. Which of the following command-line commands can you use to rename an object within Active Directory?

   ○ **A.** dsadd

   ○ **B.** dsquery

   ○ **C.** dsmove

   ○ **D.** dsrm

   ○ **E.** dsget

   ○ **F.** net user

10. Which of the following user passwords is acceptable based on the default settings in Active Directory for a user with the logon name of Dan?

   ○ **A.** dan$456

   ○ **B.** zM!993

   ○ **C.** 33#abcd

   ○ **D.** ttrrr789021

Answers to Exam Prep Questions

1. **Answer C is correct.** The User Principal Name (UPN) always includes the at sign (@). Answer A is incorrect because the forward slash (/) format denotes an object's Canonical Name. Answer C is incorrect because the name must be a User Logon Name based on the length of the name and based on its syntax. Answer D is incorrect because a name as simple as CN=elton.john can only be an LDAP Relative Distinguished Name.

2. **Answer F is correct.** LDAP Distinguished names must be unique throughout the Active Directory forest. All the answers represent user accounts with unique LDAP Distinguished Names; therefore, all four of the answers can exist within the same forest at the same time. Answer A is correct because no other user account listed has the same unique LDAP distinguished name because the user DanB resides in the Sales OU. Answer B is correct because no other user account listed has the same unique LDAP distinguished name since the user DanB resides in the Marketing OU. Answer C is correct because no other user account listed has the same unique LDAP distinguished name since the user DanB resides in the Mgmt OU. Answer E is incorrect because each of the listed answers is correct.

3. **Answer D is correct.** Canonical names use forward slashes and reverse the naming sequence of LDAP Distinguished Names. Answer A is incorrect because a name such as CN=dan.balter would be considered an LDAP Relative Distinguished Name. Answer B is incorrect because it is neither a proper User Principal Name (UPN) nor is it a proper Canonical Name. Answer C is incorrect because this name is written in the format for logging on to an Active Directory domain using a pre-Windows 2000 operating system. Answer E is incorrect because a user account's Canonical Names reverses the naming sequence of its equivalent LDAP Distinguished Name—the reverse order of CN=dan.balter,ou=sales,ou=west,dc=infotech,dc=corp is infotech.corp/**west**/**sales**/dan.balter. Answer F is incorrect because even though the basic syntax is correct, the order of the names must be the reverse of the LDAP Distinguished Name.

4. **Answers C is correct.** The Member of tab is the only user account properties tab in which all properties are copied when a new user account is created from a template user account. Answer A is incorrect because the Title property is not copied when you create a new user from a user account template. Answer B is incorrect because the Logon Name property is not copied when you create a new user from a user account template. Answer D is incorrect because the Street Address property is not copied when you create a new user from a user account template. Answer E is incorrect because both the Profile Path and the Home Folder properties are not copied over when you create a new user from a user account template.

5. **Answer E is correct.** When you export a query definition, it gets saved as an XML-formatted file, not as an HTML-formatted file. Answer A is incorrect because query definitions can be imported. Answer B is incorrect because query definitions can be exported. Answer C is incorrect because you can create both folders and subfolders within the Saved Queries container. Answer D is incorrect because you can choose which container to search when you create or edit a query. Answer F is incorrect because you can choose not to search subcontainers when creating or editing a query by unchecking the Include subcontainers check box.

6. **Answer E is correct.** The Group Policy setting "Interactive Logon: Number of Previous Logons to Cache (in Case Domain Controller Is Not Available)" is located under Security Settings\Local Policies\Security Options, and its default value is 10. Answer A is incorrect because the default value is 10, not 50—the maximum value setting is 50.

Answer B is incorrect because its default value is not 5. Answer C is incorrect because the setting is not located under User Rights Assignment. Answer D is incorrect because the setting is not located under User Rights Assignment, nor is its default value 50.

7. **Answer D is correct.** You can use the `csvde.exe` command from a command prompt to import many users into Active Directory from `.csv` files. Answer A is incorrect because the `dsadd.exe` only creates a single user at a time. Answer B is incorrect because the ADUC console can only create one user at a time. Answer C is incorrect because the `net user` command can only create one user at a time.

8. **Answers A and C are correct.** Although the default password policy setting, "Minimum password length," is seven characters, the "Password must meet complexity requirements" setting has a default value of 6; therefore, answer A is correct. Although passwords may contain nonalphanumeric characters, this value is not a requirement; therefore answer C is correct. Answer B is incorrect because it is a requirement that passwords cannot contain all or part of the user's account name. Answer D is incorrect because it is also a requirement of this policy setting that passwords may contain numerals 0 through 9. Answer E is incorrect because this policy does allow passwords to contain English lowercase letters. Answer F is incorrect because this policy does allow passwords to contain English uppercase letters.

9. **Answer C is correct.** You can use the `dsmove` command to move and rename objects in Active Directory. Answer A is incorrect because you cannot rename any Active Directory object with the `dsadd` command; you use it for adding users. Answer B is incorrect because you cannot rename any Active Directory object with the `dsquery` command; you use it for performing search operations. Answer D is incorrect because you cannot rename any Active Directory object with the `dsrm` command; you use it for removing objects. Answer E is incorrect because you cannot rename any Active Directory object with the `csget` command; you use it for displaying an object's properties. Answer F is incorrect because you cannot rename any Active Directory object with the `net user` command you use it for adding users and for viewing user information.

10. **Answer C is correct.** The default settings for user passwords in an Active Directory domain include the following:

   ▶ The minimum password length is seven characters.

   ▶ Passwords must meet complexity requirements; they must contain at least three of the following types of characters: numerals 0 through 9, lowercase letters a to z, uppercase letters A to Z, and special nonalphanumeric characters such as %, $, #, !, and so on.

   Answer A is incorrect. Even though this password contains at least seven characters, it also contains the user's logon name. Answer B is incorrect because it contains all the necessary characters but is not seven or more characters in length. Answer D is incorrect because even though it is more than seven characters in length, it only contains lowercase letters and numerals.

Need to Know More?

1. Scales, Lee, and John Michell. *MCSA/MCSE 70-290 Training Guide: Managing and Maintaining a Windows Server 2003 Environment.* Indianapolis, Indiana: Que Publishing, 2004.

2. Stanek, William R. *Microsoft Windows Server 2003 Administrator's Pocket Consultant.* Redmond, Washington: Microsoft Press, 2003.

3. Lewis, Alex, Morimoto, Rand, and Noel, Michael. *Microsoft Windows Server 2003 Unleashed R2 Edition.* Indianapolis, Indiana: Sams Publishing, 2006.

4. Stanek, William R. *Microsoft Windows Server 2003 Inside Out.* Redmond, Washington: Microsoft Press, 2004.

5. Search the Microsoft Product Support Services Knowledge Base on the Internet: `http://support.microsoft.com`. You can also search through Microsoft TechNet on the Internet: `http://technet.microsoft.com`. Find technical information using keywords from this chapter, such as domain user account names, user accounts, lightweight directory access protocol (LDAP), password policy settings, active directory saved queries, cached credentials, `dsadd`, and `dsmod`.

CHAPTER FOUR

Managing Groups in Active Directory

Terms you'll need to understand:

✓ Security groups

✓ Distribution groups

✓ Local groups

✓ Global groups

✓ Universal groups

✓ Domain local groups

✓ Security principals

✓ Special identity groups

✓ Active Directory Naming Conventions

✓ Domain and forest functional levels

Techniques you'll need to master:

✓ Adding and removing user accounts to groups

✓ Adding, modifying, and deleting groups

✓ How to allocate group membership based on group scope and domain functional level

✓ Using the command line to create new groups

✓ Raising domain and forest functional levels

✓ Adding and removing global and universal groups to other groups

Windows Server 2003 groups play an important role in allowing administrators to grant or deny access to files, folders, printers, and other resources for entire groups of users (or computers) at once instead of individually for every user. Applying security permissions to groups of users instead of to individual users eases the administrative burden of managing control over data and other resources. Under Active Directory, administrators must choose the proper group types and the appropriate group scope for each group that they create and manage. In addition, the current domain functional level dictates the group scope that can be created and the levels of group nesting that you can employ.

Managing Groups in Active Directory

In a non-Active Directory environment, Windows Server 2003 only provides support for local groups. Local groups are created, deleted, and maintained in the Local Users and Groups node of the Computer Management console for nondomain member computers. Local groups are sometimes referred to as machine groups because they apply specifically to the computer that they reside on. Windows Server 2003 supports two types of Active Directory groups:

- *Security*—These groups contain security descriptors that determine access permissions on resources for users who are group members. You can also use security groups as email distribution lists.

- *Distribution*—These groups do not contain security descriptors, and you cannot use them to determine access permissions. Distribution groups are used as email distribution lists only.

> **TIP**
>
> You can change the type of a group from security to distribution or from distribution to security at any time, provided that the domain is set at the Windows 2000 native or the Windows Server 2003 Domain functional level. *You cannot change group types under the Windows 2000 mixed domain functional level.*

Understanding Group Scopes

Groups must take on a specific role, or scope, regarding how they can be used and where they are valid within Active Directory. Each group is assigned one of the following scopes:

- *Domain local*—A group assigned as domain local can only specify permissions on resources within a single domain.

▶ *Built-in local*—These groups are created automatically whenever an Active Directory domain is created, and they have the same scope as domain local groups. You cannot create nor delete built-in local groups, but you can modify their members and their membership within other groups.

▶ *Global*—A global group can contain users, groups, and computers from its own domain as members. Global groups are available under any domain functional level.

▶ *Universal*—A universal group can contain users, groups, and computers from any domain in its forest. These groups are available only when the domain functional level is set at Windows 2000 native or Windows Server 2003. The membership list of universal groups is maintained by global catalog (GC) servers, unlike global groups and domain local groups. Certain DCs must be assigned as GCs so that applications and computers can locate resources within the Active Directory database. When a member is added to or removed from a universal group, global catalog servers must track the change, and each change must be replicated to all the global catalog servers in the forest. The increased overhead and network replication traffic for universal groups is why Microsoft recommends that you use them conservatively.

> **EXAM ALERT**
>
> As a best practice, you should use domain local groups to assign access permissions to non-Active Directory objects, such as files and folders. In a multiple domain environment, if you assign permissions to a domain local group for an Active Directory object (such as a user, a group, a computer, or an organizational unit), an Active Directory domain cannot determine permissions for domain local groups located in different domains. See Microsoft Knowledge Base Article #231273 for more information.

Limiting Group Membership Based on a Group's Scope

Computer accounts, user accounts, and other groups can become members of Windows Server 2003 groups. *Groups that are members of other groups are referred to as group nesting.* However, not all computer accounts, user accounts, and group accounts can join all types of groups; **the ability to join a group depends upon the group's scope**. In turn, a group's scope is affected by the current domain functional level. Table 4.1 summarizes the types of computer and user accounts (accounts) as well as the types of groups that can become members of a group based on the current scope of the group and the current domain functional level.

TABLE 4.1 Group Members Allowed Based on Group Scope

Domain Functional Level	Domain Local Groups Can Contain	Global Groups Can Contain	Universal Groups Can Contain
Windows 2000 mixed	Accounts and global groups from any domain	Accounts from the same domain only	Not available
Windows 2000 native or Windows Server 2003	Domain local groups from the same domain only; Accounts and global and universal groups from any domain	Accounts and other global groups from the same domain only	Accounts from any any domain and all global and universal groups from any domain

---

TIP

For nondomain member computers, the only available groups are called local groups. You can create local groups only on each local computer, and they can only contain local users, not domain user accounts. You can assign permissions only to local groups for the local computer where they reside. You create local users and local groups in the Local Users and Groups node of the Computer Management console. Domain member servers can still create local users and groups using Computer Management; however, you cannot use those users and groups as part of any Active Directory domain. Local users and groups are unavailable for DCs.

Changing a Group's Scope

Administrators can change the scope of domain local groups, global groups, and universal groups. Built-in groups cannot have their scopes changed, and domain local groups cannot be changed to global groups. In addition, global groups cannot be changed to domain local groups. However, you can change all three Active Directory group scopes according to the following guidelines:

▶ *Domain local groups*—You can change these groups to universal groups when the domain functional level is set to Windows 2000 native or higher. No member group of a domain local group may have domain local scope for the scope to change to universal. Domain local groups may be nested inside one another in native or Windows Server 2003 domain functional levels.

▶ *Global groups*—You can also change these groups to universal groups when the domain functional level is set to Windows 2000 native or higher. No member group of a global group may have global scope for the scope to change to universal. Global groups may be nested inside one another in native or Windows Server 2003 domain functional levels.

> ▸ *Universal groups*—You can change these groups to either domain local groups or global groups. Security universal groups are available only when the domain functional level is set to Windows 2000 native or higher. Distribution universal groups are available under any domain functional level. No member group of a universal group may have global scope for the scope to change to global. Universal groups may be nested inside one another in the Windows 2000 native or the Windows Server 2003 domain functional levels.

EXAM ALERT

As a best practice, Microsoft recommends that administrators use the A→G→DL←P group strategy model for Active Directory *single domain* environments. In this model, you place user **A**ccounts (A) into **G**lobal (G) groups; then place **G**lobal (G) groups into **D**omain **L**ocal (DL) groups, and you assign **P**ermissions (P) to resources for the **D**omain **L**ocal (DL) groups.

Maintaining Groups and Group Membership

You manage Active Directory groups from the ADUC console. Default groups are stored within the Built-in container and within the Users container. To change a group's name, you must right-click the group name listed within the ADUC and select Rename. After you change the name, the Rename Group dialog box appears, allowing you to change the pre-Windows 2000 group name as well. Click OK for the Rename Group dialog box when you are done. When you double-click a group, you can view the group's name, the group's pre-Windows 2000 name, the group type, and the group scope from the General tab of the group's Properties window, as shown in Figure 4.1. From the group's properties window, you can

- ▸ Rename the group.

- ▸ Type in a description and an email address.

- ▸ Change the group scope and group type.

- ▸ Add and remove members.

- ▸ Add or remove the group as a member of another group.

- ▸ Specify Managed By information.

- ▸ View the canonical name of the group along with its object class, the date it was created, the date it was modified, and its Update Sequence Numbers (USNs) from the Object tab.

- ▸ View, add, or remove security permissions.

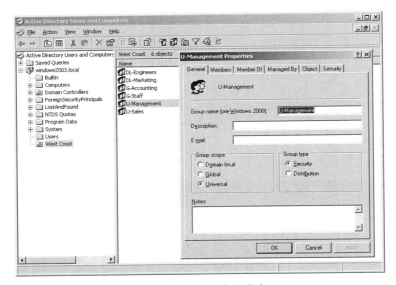

FIGURE 4.1   Working with a group's properties window.

Special Identity Groups

In addition to the default Built-in local groups, Windows Server 2003 supports special identity (SI) built-in groups that the operating system uses internally. No user can change the membership of these groups; membership is situational, and the membership of these groups is determined by what activities users are currently involved in on the server and on the network. Group scopes do not apply to special identity groups. However, you can apply user rights and assign security permissions to SI groups for specific resources. Special identity groups include the following:

- *Anonymous Logon*—This SI group encompasses users and services that access computer resources without supplying an account name, a password, or a domain name. This group is not a member of the everyone group by default.

- *Authenticated Users*—This SI group encompasses all users whose logons have been authenticated. This is a more secure group to assign permissions to than the everyone group.

- *Batch*—This SI group reflects all accounts that are logged on as part of a batch process that is executing.

- *Creator Owner*—This SI group represents the creator and the owner of objects such as files, folders, and print jobs.

- *Dial-up*—This SI group contains all users who are currently accessing the computer using a dial-up connection.

- *Everyone*—This SI group encompasses all current users who are logged on over the network.

- *Interactive*—This SI group contains users who are currently physically logged on to the local computer (console) and accessing local resources. It includes users logged on via remote desktop connections (terminal services).

- *Network*—This SI group encompasses all current network users who are accessing resources remotely (as opposed to a user who is logged on locally accessing local resources).

- *Service*—This SI group identifies any accounts that are currently logged onto the computer as a service that is running.

- *System*—This SI group refers to the operating system itself.

- *Terminal Server User*—This SI group refers to any user accessing the system via terminal services as a remote desktop client.

Security Principals

Windows operating systems in general, and, Windows Server 2003 in particular, use the term *security principal* to describe any object within the operating system that can be authenticated by the operating system. Examples of these objects (or entities) include user accounts, computer accounts, and security groups. A security principal can also be a thread or a process that runs within the security context of a user account or a computer account.

Local user and group accounts are created and exist on a local computer, and they are used to control access to resources stored on that local machine. The Security Accounts Manager (SAM) is the database that maintains the list of local user and group accounts on each local computer. Each time that a user, security group, or computer account is created, these objects become security principals because a security identifier (SID) is automatically assigned to each of these objects at the time they are created. Both local accounts and Active Directory domain accounts become security principals. Security principals (SP) can be granted access to objects created within an Active Directory domain. Adding and removing SPs from an object's access control list (ACL) is the method used to control access to available resources within the domain.

Creating New Groups Using ADUC

You can create new groups from the ADUC console. Members of the account operators group, domain admins group, and the enterprise admins group can create domain local, global, and universal groups from the ADUC console under Windows Server 2003 Active Directory. Other users who are not members of those groups can be delegated the authority to create groups. The ability to create universal groups requires that the domain be set at either the Windows 2000 native or the Windows Server 2003 domain functional level. Group nesting becomes available under these levels as well. To create a new group under any domain functional level, perform these steps:

1. Right-click the container or OU where you want to place the new group and select New, Group.

2. At the New Object—Group dialog box, type in the Group Name and the pre-Windows 2000 Group Name (if different).

3. Select the group scope: domain local, global, or universal (if available).

4. Select the group type: security or distribution.

5. Click OK to create the new group.

Creating New Groups Using the Command Prompt

The same requirements for creating new groups using the ADUC apply for using the `dsadd.exe` command. The only required parameter is that you must specify the new group's DN. If you do not specify any optional parameters, by default, the group is created as a security group with global scope. For example, typing `dsadd` group `"cn=staff,ou=east coast,dc=windows2003,dc=local"` creates a new global security group named `staff` within the OU named `east coast` for the domain named `windows2003.local`. Use quotation marks if any of the parameters have spaces, such as the OU name of `"east coast"`. Type `dsadd group /?` at any command prompt for help with the syntax and parameters for adding a group via the command line. To create a distribution group named `sales managers` with universal scope in the `Users` container, follow these steps:

1. Open a command prompt.

2. Type `dsadd group "cn=sales managers,cn=users,dc=windows2003, dc=local" -secgrp no -scope u`.

3. The `dsadd group` command should process the command and then display `"dsadd succeeded:CN=SALE MANAGERS,CN=USERS,DC=WINDOWS 2003,DC=LOCAL"`.

> **NOTE**
>
> Group names may not be longer than 63 characters in Windows Server 2003 Active Directory.

Active Directory Naming Conventions

Because Active Directory is based on the Lightweight Directory Access Protocol (LDAP), you can reference each object within Active Directory using different types of LDAP naming conventions. Distinguished names (DNs) and relative distinguished names (RDNs) are two of the naming conventions that Active Directory uses for its objects. DNs and RDNs use specific naming components to define the location of the objects that they are identifying. DN and RDN components (or attributes) are the following:

▶ *CN*—Common name

▶ *OU*—Organizational unit name

▶ *DC*—Domain component name

> **NOTE**
>
> The abbreviation CN is not only used for the term *common name*, which is one way used to identify Active Directory objects (such as user objects and group objects). CN also stands for *canonical name*. In Active Directory, a canonical name is a hierarchical method used to describe an object; an object's common name (CN) is one piece of the puzzle that comprises the object's complete canonical name (CN).

Active Directory creates an RDN in addition to a canonical name (CN) for each object based on the available information when the object is created. Every Active Directory object can also be identified by a DN, which is derived from the RDN of the object plus all of its higher-level (parent) container objects. Active Directory uses the following types of names:

▶ The LDAP DN must be unique throughout the forest. For example, the DN of a computer named `station01` located in the `Sales` OU, which is part of the domain named `amazon.com`, would be `CN=station01, OU=sales,DC=amazon,DC=com`.

▶ The LDAP RDN uniquely identifies the object within its parent container. For example, the LDAP RDN of a computer named `station01` is `CN= station01`. The RDNs of objects must be unique within the same OU.

▶ The CN identifies an object as does its DN; however, it uses a different syntax and it reverses the sequence of the name. For example, if the LDAP DN of a computer is `CN=station01,OU=sales,DC=amazon,DC=com`, the CN of the same computer is `amazon.com/sales/station01`.

▶ Security principal names are Active Directory objects, such as users, groups, and computers, that are authenticated by an Active Directory domain. These Security principals are assigned security IDs (SIDs) that uniquely identify these objects during authentication. Users and computers need a SID to log on to an Active Directory domain. You can assign users, computers, and groups security permissions for accessing domain resources. An administrator needs to provide a name that is unique throughout the entire domain for each security principal object when the object is created. Globally unique identifiers (GUIDs) are also used to uniquely identify objects, such as computers, within Active Directory.

Active Directory: The Schema and Functional Levels

The Active Directory database has a default design for the type of data that it stores. For example, Active Directory stores usernames, passwords, and email addresses for each user in the domain; therefore, the database's design must allow for storing this type of information. The Active Directory database structure is referred to as its *schema*. The two components that make up the schema are *attributes* and *classes*. You can extend the Active Directory schema to include other types of information that Active Directory does not store by default. However, for each new element that you add to the schema, that element becomes a permanent part of the schema; added classes and attributes can be disabled, but they can never be removed.

For example, an application such as Microsoft Exchange Server 2003 extends the schema as part of its installation routine by adding new fields and new data types to Active Directory so that the domain can store Exchange Server–related information for users, groups, and other objects. The extended schema allows one or more servers within the domain to operate as Exchange Server computers. In this way, an application such as Microsoft Exchange Server can leverage Active Directory for accessing user and mailbox information, storing directory data, and replicating data across an entire organization.

Exchange Server does not actually store email messages within Active Directory, but it takes advantage of the built-in directory service to store configuration information about each mailbox-enabled user in Active Directory. Examples of Exchange Server data that is stored in Active Directory for mailbox-enabled users include each user's email address, each user's email alias name, and each user's specific home mail server name.

Active Directory Functional Levels

Windows 2000 Active Directory domains offered two modes of functionality— mixed mode (the default) and native mode (enhanced). If you switched a Windows 2000 Active Directory domain to native mode, legacy Windows NT BDCs could no longer be a member of the domain. As a bonus, universal security groups became available when you switched to Active Directory native mode under Windows 2000. *The switch to native mode is a one-time, nonreversible option.* Active Directory under Windows Server 2003 introduces two additional functional levels for domains while offering three new functional levels that operate at the forest level.

Windows Server 2003 Domain Functional Levels

Active Directory under Windows Server 2003 supports four levels of domain functionality. These different levels help ensure backward compatibility with previous versions of Windows and legacy Windows NT Server 4.0 domains. The four domain functional levels for Active Directory are the following (see Figure 4.2):

- *Windows 2000 Mixed*—This domain functional level is the most basic. This level supports Windows NT, Windows 2000, and Windows Server 2003 DCs.

▶ *Windows 2000 Native*—This level supports Windows 2000 DCs and Windows Server 200₹ DCs only. Windows 2000 DCs in native mode *retain* their Windows 2000 native functional level when upgraded to Windows Server 200₹.

▶ *Windows Server 2003 ₹nterim*—This level *applies only to Windows NT Server 4.0 DCs that have been upgraded to Windows Server 2003.* (Formatting over an NT 4.0 installation and installing Windows Server 2003, a *clean install*, is not considered an upgrade.) This level functions in much the same way as the Windows 2000 mixed level; however, it does not support Windows 2000 Server DCs.

▶ *Windows Server 2003*—This level is the highest, and it supports Windows Server 2003 DCs exclusively.

EXAM ALERT

As you switch a domain to an advanced domain functional level, remember that it is a one-time option that cannot be reversed. You can only upgrade (raise) functional levels; you can never downgrade (lower) to previous levels.

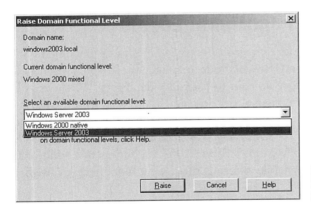

FIGURE 4.2 Raising the domain functional level on a Windows Server 2003 DC.

Windows Server 2003 Forest Functional Levels

New features in Active Directory require Active Directory forests to have their own set of functional levels similar to domains. New support for domain renaming and restructuring, schema class and attribute deactivation, and cross-forest trusts, as well as others, necessitate a higher forest functional level than the basic default setting. The three forest functional levels are

▶ *Windows 2000*—This forest functional level is the most basic. This level supports domains running Windows NT 4.0, Windows 2000, and Windows Server 2003 DCs.

▶ *Windows Server 2003 Interim*—This level supports domains running Windows NT 4.0 and Windows Server 2003 DCs only. It does not support Windows 2000 DCs.

▶ *Windows Server 2003*—This forest functional level is the highest, and it supports domains running Windows Server 2003 DCs exclusively.

EXAM ALERT

Before you can raise the forest functional level of a forest to Windows Server 2003, all DCs within the entire forest must be running the Windows Server 2003 operating system. All domains within the forest must also be operating at either the Windows 2000 native or the Windows Server 2003 domain functional level. *Any DCs operating in domains running at the Windows 2000 native level will be automatically raised to the Windows Server 2003 domain functional level at the time that the forest functional level is raised to Windows Server 2003.*

Exam Prep Questions

1. In which of the following scenarios can you change a group's type or scope? (Choose three.)

    ○ **A.** A domain local group can be changed to a global group when the domain functional level is set to Windows 2000 mixed.

    ○ **B.** A universal group can be changed to a global group when the domain functional level is set to Windows 2000 native.

    ○ **C.** A global security group can be changed to a universal distribution group when the domain functional level is set to Windows 2000 native.

    ○ **D.** A universal distribution group can be changed to a domain local security group when the domain functional level is set to Windows Server 2003.

    ○ **E.** A domain local group can be changed to a global group when the domain functional level is set to Windows 2000 native.

    ○ **F.** A global security group can be changed to a domain local group when the domain functional level is set to Windows Server 2003.

2. Which of the following group types are available in Active Directory under Windows Server 2003? (Choose each correct answer.)

    ○ **A.** Domain local

    ○ **B.** Built-in local

    ○ **C.** Security

    ○ **D.** Universal

    ○ **E.** Global

    ○ **F.** Distribution

3. Which of the following groups are not part of an Active Directory domain? (Choose two.)

    ○ **A.** Local groups

    ○ **B.** Domain local groups

    ○ **C.** Global groups

    ○ **D.** Built-in groups

    ○ **E.** Universal groups

    ○ **F.** Domain global groups

4. For which of the following domain functional levels can administrators nest groups within other groups and change the scope of groups. (Choose two.)

○ **A.** Windows 2000 native

○ **B.** Windows 2000 mixed

○ **C.** Windows Server 2003

○ **D.** Windows Server 2003 interim

○ **E.** Windows Server 2003 mixed

5. Which of the following groups can be members of a universal group for a domain set at the Windows Server 2003 domain functional level? (Choose three.)

○ **A.** Domain local groups

○ **B.** Other universal groups from the same domain only

○ **C.** Global groups from the same domain only

○ **D.** Global groups from any domain

○ **E.** Universal groups from any domain

○ **F.** User accounts from the same domain only

○ **G.** Computer accounts from any domain

6. Which of the following is not a special identity group?

○ **A.** System

○ **B.** Replicator

○ **C.** Everyone

○ **D.** Network

7. Which of the following group strategies does Microsoft recommend for assigning access permissions to users and groups as a best practice in a single domain Active Directory environment? (Choose the best answer.)

○ **A.** Place user accounts into universal groups and assign permissions directly to the universal groups.

○ **B.** Place user accounts into domain local groups, place domain local groups into global groups, and assign permissions directly to the global groups.

○ **C.** Place user accounts into global groups, place the global groups into domain local groups, and assign permissions directly to the domain local groups.

○ **D.** Place user accounts into global groups, place global groups into universal groups, place the universal groups into domain local groups, and assign permissions directly to the domain local groups.

○ **E.** Place user accounts into global groups, place the global groups into local groups, and assign permissions directly to the local groups.

8. Which of the following default built-in groups are considered special identities? (Choose two.)

   ○ **A.** Administrators

   ○ **B.** Guests

   ○ **C.** Remote Desktop Users

   ○ **D.** Terminal Server User

   ○ **E.** Dial-up

   ○ **F.** TelnetClients

9. Which of the following objects are considered security principals?

   ○ **A.** Distribution groups

   ○ **B.** Files

   ○ **C.** Folders

   ○ **D.** Local user accounts

   ○ **E.** NTFS permissions

   ○ **F.** User rights

10. Which of the following is not a characteristic of group accounts in Active Directory?

   ○ **A.** Groups must be created with both a group scope and a group type.

   ○ **B.** Group names may be up to 64 characters in length.

   ○ **C.** Names of group members of universal groups are stored in global catalog servers throughout the Active Directory forest.

   ○ **D.** Group nesting allows global groups to be members of domain local groups, even when the domain functional level is set to Windows 2000 mixed.

Answers to Exam Prep Questions

1. **Answers B, C, and D are correct.** A universal group can be changed to a global group when the domain functional level is set to Windows 2000 native or Windows Server 2003. A global security group can be changed to a universal distribution group when the domain functional level is set to Windows 2000 native or Windows Server 2003. A universal distribution group can be changed to a domain local security group when the domain functional level is set to Windows Server 2003 or Windows 2000 native. Answer A is incorrect because no group can have its scope changed at the Windows 2000 mixed domain functional level. Answer E is incorrect because a domain local group can never be changed to a global group under any domain functional level.

Answer F is incorrect because a global group can never be changed to a domain local group under any domain functional level.

2. **Answers C and F are correct.** Active Directory supports only two *types* of groups—Security groups and Distribution groups. Answer A is incorrect because domain local is a group scope, not a group type. Answer B is incorrect because built-in local is a group scope, not a group type. Answer D is incorrect because universal is a group scope, not a group type. Answer E is incorrect because global is a group scope, not a group type.

3. **Answers A and F are correct.** Local groups are also sometimes referred to as machine groups: They apply on the computer where they are located. Domain global groups do not exist in Active Directory. Answers B, C, D, and E are incorrect because these groups do all exist within an Active Directory domain.

4. **Answers A and C are correct.** Administrators can nest groups and change the scope of groups for the Windows 2000 native and Windows Server 2003 domain functional levels. Answer B is incorrect because administrators cannot nest groups nor change the scope of groups under the Windows 2000 mixed domain functional level. Answer D is incorrect because administrators cannot nest groups nor change the scope of groups under the Windows Server 2003 interim domain functional level. Answer E is incorrect because the Windows Server 2003 mixed level does not exist.

5. **Answers D, E, and G are correct.** Universal groups can contain other universal groups and global groups from any domain. Universal groups can also have computer accounts (and user accounts) from any domain as members. Answer A is incorrect because universal groups cannot have domain local groups as members. Answer B is incorrect because universal groups from any domain can be members of a universal group. Answer F is incorrect because universal groups can contain user and computer accounts from any domain.

6. **Answer B is correct.** The Replicator account in Active Directory is a built-in domain local security group account, not a special identity group. Answer A is incorrect because System is a special identity group. Answer C is incorrect because Everyone is a special identity group. Answer D is incorrect because Network is a special identity group.

7. **Answer C is correct.** The recommended best practice for assigning permissions to users and groups within a single Active Directory domain is the **A→G→DL→P** group strategy model. Place user accounts into global groups, place global groups into domain local groups, and assign permissions to the domain local groups. Answer A is incorrect because universal groups should be used sparingly due to global catalog replication traffic concerns and universal groups are not available at the Windows 2000 mixed domain functional level. Answer B is incorrect because you cannot place domain local groups into global groups. Answer D is incorrect because the **A→G→U→DL→P** group strategy model is not a recommended best practice for a single domain. Answer E is incorrect because local groups apply only to a local computer's resources; therefore, they do not have domainwide use.

8. **Answers D and E are correct.** Terminal Server User and Dial-up are both special identity groups that refer to how a user is accessing the computer, and membership in each special identity group only lasts as long as the user continues to access the computer

in that manner. Answer A is incorrect because the Administrators group is a built-in group, but it is not a special identity. Answer B is incorrect because the Guests group is a built-in group, but it s not a special identity. Answer F is incorrect because the TelnetClients group is a built-in group, but it is not a special identity.

9. **Answer D is correct.** Any operating system object that can be authenticated by the operating system is a security principal—the object can be either a domain-level entity or a local entity. Answer A is incorrect because a distribution group cannot be authenticated by the operating system; however, a security group can be authenticated. Answer B is incorrect because a file cannot be authenticated by the operating system. Answer D is incorrect because a folder cannot be authenticated by the operating system. Answer E is incorrect because even though NTFS permissions contain access control lists and access control entries, NTFS permissions themselves cannot be authenticated by the operating system. Answer F is incorrect because even though user rights define a list of user account privileges, user rights themselves cannot be authenticated by the operating system.

10. **Answer B is correct.** Active Directory group names may only contain up to 63 characters, not 64 characters. Answer A is incorrect. Groups do require both a group scope and a group type. Answer C is incorrect because universal groups do have their membership list maintained by global catalog servers throughout the forest. Answer D is incorrect because group nesting does allow global groups to be members of domain local groups, even when the domain functional level is set to Windows 2000 mixed.

Need to Know More?

1. Holme, Dan, and Orin Thomas. *MCSA/MCSE Self-Paced Training Kit (Exam 70-290): Managing and Maintaining a Microsoft Windows Server 2003 Environment.* Redmond, Washington: Microsoft Press, 2003.

2. Scales, Lee, and John Michell. *MCSA/MCSE 70-290 Training Guide: Managing and Maintaining a Windows Server 2003 Environment.* Indianapolis, Indiana: Que Publishing, 2003.

3. Lewis, Alex, Morimoto, Rand, and Noel, Michael. *Microsoft Windows Server 2003 Unleashed R2 Edition.* Indianapolis, Indiana: Sams Publishing, 2006.

4. Search the Microsoft Product Support Services Knowledge Base on the Internet: http://support.microsoft.com. You can also search through Microsoft TechNet on the Internet: http://technet.microsoft.com. Find technical information using keywords from this chapter, such as domain local groups, group scope, global groups, domain functional levels, forest functional levels, universal groups, security groups, and distribution groups.

CHAPTER FIVE

Managing Access to Resources

Terms you'll need to understand:

✓ Shared folder permissions

✓ Shared Folders snap-in

✓ Offline files

✓ NTFS file and folder permissions

Techniques you'll need to master:

✓ Using the net share command

✓ Using the Create a Folder Wizard

✓ Configuring shared-folder permissions

✓ Working with offline-files settings

✓ Configuring NTFS file and folder permissions

You must manage network resources effectively to meet the changing needs of networked computer users. Setting up shared resources and controlling access to those shared resources are two of the most important jobs that network administrators face. Fortunately, Windows Server 2003 comes well equipped with the tools that administrators require to maintain a secure network infrastructure. Share permissions and NTFS file system permissions enable IT staff members to share and lock down resources. In this chapter, you will discover the benefits, the possible drawbacks, and the many nuances of administering these network services.

Working with Shared Network Folders

You need to set up shared network folders if you want users on remote computers to be able to access files stored on Windows Servers (or files stored on Windows desktop computers). For users who need access to shared data over the network, you can use standard shared folders. For users who need access to shared data over the Internet or over an intranet using a web browser, you can use web folders. To use web folders, you must first install Internet Information Services (IIS) 6.0 on a Windows Server 2003 computer; IIS 6.0 is not installed by default. You install IIS 6.0 with the Add or Remove Programs applet in the Control Panel. Only members of the Administrators group or the Server Operators group have the necessary permissions to create, manage, and remove shared folders under Windows Server 2003.

Creating Shared Folders from Windows Explorer

Sharing folders under Windows Server 2003 is similar to setting up shared folders under Windows XP and Windows 2000. Shared folders are often referred to simply as "shares." From the GUI, you can use the Windows Explorer (or My Computer) to right-click any available folder that you want to share with remote users over the network. To create a shared folder on a Windows Server 2003 computer, follow these steps:

1. Open My Computer or Windows Explorer.

2. Right-click the folder that you want to share and select Sharing and Security.

3. From the Sharing tab, click the Share This Folder button.

4. Type the new shared folder's name in the Share Name box.

5. Optionally, type in a description in the Description box.

6. In the User Limit section, either accept the default setting of Maximum Allowed, or click Allow This Number of Users and type in the number in the spinner box, as shown in Figure 5.1.

7. Click OK to create the shared folder with default share permissions.

EXAM ALERT

Under Windows Server 2003 and Windows XP Professional, the default share permissions are now Everyone: Allow Read as opposed to Everyone: Allow Full Control, which was the case for Windows NT and Windows 2000. Windows XP Professional was Microsoft's first operating system to employ this new default security setting.

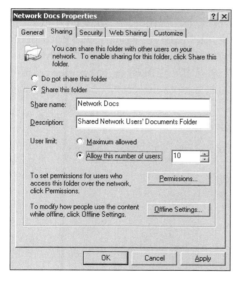

FIGURE 5.1 Creating a new shared folder.

TIP

If you'd like to create multiple shares with different share names that all point to the same physical folder, maybe even with different access permissions on each share, click the New Share button that appears at the bottom of the Sharing tab for an existing shared folder.

Removing Share Names and Shared Folders

To remove a share when you have multiple shares for the same physical folder, select the share from the Share Name drop-down list box and click the Remove Share button at the bottom of the dialog box. To stop sharing the folder entirely, click the Do Not Share This Folder option button at the top of the dialog box; this action removes all shares from the network browse list, and the folder will no longer be accessible by remote users as a network shared folder.

Creating Shared Web Folders

If you installed IIS 6.0 (now known as Application Server), with the World Wide Web Service component, you can create shared web folders. Web folders are accessible from remote computers using a web browser, or you can access them from a program that supports the Web Distributed Authoring and Versioning (WebDAV) protocol, such as Microsoft Word. WebDAV allows users to connect to shared folders through Hypertext Transport Protocol (HTTP) using TCP port 80. This is the same HTTP that you use when browsing websites over the Internet.

To connect to a web folder, a user must possess the appropriate permissions for the folder. By typing the URL for the folder in the Open dialog box for a program such as Microsoft Word, you can access the shared web folder via HTTP instead of accessing it using the usual Server Message Block (SMB) protocol. From the Open dialog box, you can type the URL for the web folder that you want to access in the File Name box and press the Enter key to connect to the shared web folder (see Figure 5.2). You must enable directory browsing for the web folder for users to view the contents of the folder. To set up and configure a shared web folder, perform the following steps:

1. Open My Computer or Windows Explorer.

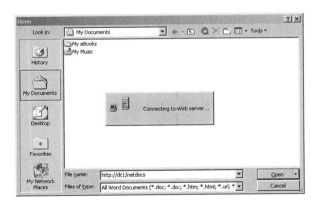

FIGURE 5.2 Connecting to a shared web folder using an application such as Microsoft Word, which supports WebDAV.

2. Right-click the folder that you want to share and select Sharing and Security.

3. From the Web Sharing tab, select the website that will host this shared web folder from the Share On drop-down list box.

4. Click the Share This Folder option button; the Edit Alias dialog box will appear immediately, as shown in Figure 5.3.

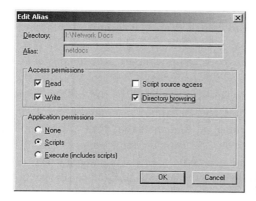

FIGURE 5.3   Setting up a new shared web folder.

5. Type in the Alias (share name) for this web folder (or accept the default). Remote users can only access the web folder by using its alias name.

6. In the Access Permissions section, mark the check box for each permission that you want to assign to this web folder as it applies to remote users. The default permission, Read, is automatically checked. Select from Write, Script Source Access, and Directory Browsing. To use the web folders interface, you must select Read, Write, and Directory Browsing access permissions for each web folder.

7. In the Application Permissions section, click the option button for which level you want to grant: None, Scripts, or Execute (Includes Scripts). The default is Scripts.

8. Click OK to save the settings for the web folder's properties.

9. Click OK to exit from the Properties dialog box and create the web folder.

NOTE

To add more than one alias, click the Add button from the Web Sharing tab of a folder's properties dialog box. To modify an alias's settings, select the alias you want to modify and click the Edit Properties button. Finally, to delete an alias for a web folder, select the alias and click the Remove button. To remove the shared web folder entirely, click the Do Not Share This Folder radio button. Click OK for the folder's properties dialog box when you finish.

Creating Shared Folders from the Command Line

Windows Server 2003 supports an unprecedented degree of command-line functionality compared to previous Windows versions. However, the net series of commands has been around for a number of years, as has the net share command. Using the net share command, you can easily create new shared folders from the command prompt. For help with the syntax and options for the net share command, type net share / ? and press the Enter key at any command prompt. To create a shared folder, type ret share *name_of_share=driveletter:\path* and press Enter. For example, to create a shared folder named companypayroll for the folder C:\Payroll, at a command prompt type net share companypayroll=c:\payroll. To remove the share, type net share companypayroll /delete.

Working with the Shared Folders Snap-In

Another way to work with shared folders is with the Shared Folders Microsoft Management Console (MMC) snap-in. This snap-in is available as a node within the Computer Management console, or you can add it individually from a custom console shell. The Shared Folders snap-in provides a central location for managing all shared folders on a server. To add the fsmgmt.msc file to an MMC shell, follow these steps:

1. Click Start, Run; type mmc; and click OK to open a blank console.

2. At the blank console window, click File, Add/Remove Snap-In.

3. Click the Add button.

4. Select the Shared Folders snap-in from the Available Standalone Snap-Ins list and click Add.

5. Be sure that the Local Computer is selected (if you will be creating shared folders for the local computer), or select Another Computer and click Browse to locate it.

6. Click Finish.

7. Click Close for the Add Standalone Snap-In dialog box and click OK for the Add/Remove Snap-In dialog box. The Shared Folders node appears within the MMC window, as shown in Figure 5.4.

FIGURE 5.4 Viewing shared folders from the Shared Folders MMC snap-in.

Creating Shares from the Shared Folders Snap-In

Microsoft added more functionality to the Shared Folders snap-in for Windows Server 2003. You now use a wizard to create shares from the Shared Folders snap-in. The Share a Folder wizard gives you the ability to customize both share permissions and NTFS folder permissions (if the folder resides on an NTFS drive). To create a new share from the Shared Folders snap-in, follow these steps:

1. Open the Shared Folders node.

2. Right-click the Shares subnode, select New Share, and click Next.

3. Type the drive letter and path for the folder you want to share in the Folder Path box, or click Browse to locate the folder.

4. Click Next.

5. Type an optional description in the Description box.

6. Click the Change button to select an Offline Setting, if you do not want to accept the default—Selected Files and Programs Available Offline. The section "Working with Shared Folder Offline Settings" later in this chapter covers offline settings.

7. Click Next.

8. From the Specify Permissions for the Share dialog box, select one of the following folder access security options, as shown in Figure 5.5:

   ▸ All Users Have Read-Only Access

   ▸ Administrators Have Full Access; Other Users Have Read-Only Access

   ▸ Administrators Have Full Access; Other Users Have Read and Write Access

   ▸ Use Custom Share and Folder Permissions

9. If you select the Use Custom Share and Folder Permissions option, click the Customize button to set both share permissions and security (NTFS) file-system permissions on the folder.

10. Click Finish to create the new share.

EXAM ALERT

Remember that share permissions are quite different from (NTFS) file-system security permissions! Share permissions only affect remote users when they access shared folders over the network. NTFS file-system permissions, on the other hand, are more granular than share permissions, and file-system permissions apply to both folders and files. Share permissions apply only when you are accessing shared folders over a network, not when you are accessing the data from the local computer. File-system permissions also apply to both local users and remote network users; users cannot circumvent file-system permissions by logging on to the local computer where the shared folder resides! Users who log on using Remote Desktop Connections to a Terminal Server are treated as local users. The section "Working with Share Permissions" later in this chapter covers share permissions. The section "NTFS File and Folder Permissions" later in this chapter covers file-system permissions.

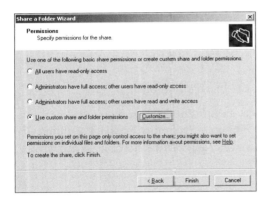

FIGURE 5.5 Specifying folder permissions for a share with the Share a Folder Wizard.

You can publish shares in Active Directory from the Shared Folders snap-in but not from Windows Explorer or My Computer windows. Publishing shares in Active Directory makes it easier for users to locate those shares, and users can search for published shares using different criteria, such as keywords. The Publish tab of a shared folders properties sheet allows you to add a description, the name of an owner, and specific keywords for searches to each share (see Figure 5.6). To publish a share in Active Directory, follow these steps:

1. Open the Computer Management console, expand the Shared Folders node and click the Shares subnode.

2. Right-click the shared folder that you want to publish and select Properties.

3. From the properties sheet, click the Publish tab.

4. Mark the Publish This Share in Active Directory check box.

5. As an option, type a description in the Description box.

6. As an option, type the name of an owner for the share in the Owner box.

7. As an option, click the Edit button to type in appropriate keywords to aid users in searching for this share. Click OK for the Edit Keywords dialog box when you are done.

8. Click OK to save the publish settings for the share.

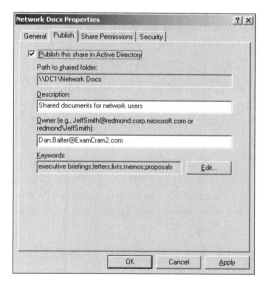

FIGURE 5.6 Publishing a share from the Shared Folders snap-in.

Working with Hidden and Administrative Shares

Windows Server 2003, along with Windows XP, Windows 2000, and Windows NT, automatically creates specific shared folders by default each and every time you start the computer. These default shares are often referred to as *hidden* or *administrative* shares because a dollar sign ($) is appended to their share names, which prevents the shared folder from appearing on the network browse list; users cannot easily discover that these shares exist.

Microsoft Windows networking does not allow hidden shares to appear when someone rummages through My Network Places, for example. The NETLOGON, SYSVOL, and Microsoft UAM volume shares are not hidden; these administrative shares are visible to all users. The default hidden or administrative shares include the following:

- *C$, D$, E$, and so on*—These shares get created for the root of each available drive letter on the local computer.

- *ADMIN$*—This share exposes the `%systemroot%` folder to the network (for example, `C:\Windows`).

- *FAX$*—This share supports shared network faxing.

- *IPC$*—This share is used for interprocess communications (IPCs). IPCs support communications between objects on different computers over a network by manipulating the low-level details of network transport protocols. IPCs enable the use of distributed application programs that combine multiple processes working together to accomplish a single task. The `IPC$` share is on every Windows-based server; it enables you to authenticate using a different set of user credentials to a remote server. For example, if I'm logged on to computer1 as Domain1\DanB, I can use the `net use` command to log on to server1 as the administrator with the command `net use \\server1\share1\ /user:domain1\administrator`.

- *Microsoft UAM volume*—This share is not hidden. This share does not exist unless you install at least one optional Macintosh service. It is used by the File Services for Macintosh service and by the Print Services for Macintosh service for providing Macintosh computers with access to Windows Server 2003 file and print services.

- *NETLOGON*—This share is not hidden. The Net Logon service uses it for processing logon scripts. This share is used for backward compatibility with Windows NT 4.0 and Windows 9x computers that do not have the Active Directory client software installed.

- *PRINT$*—This share holds the printer drivers for the printers installed on the local machine. When a remote computer connects to a printer over the network, it downloads the appropriate printer driver.

- *SYSVOL*—This share is not hidden. It stores Active Directory objects and data, such as group policy objects or user login scripts.

Although you can temporarily disable the default hidden shares or administrative shares, you cannot delete them without modifying the Registry (which is not recommended) because they get re-created each time the computer restarts. You can connect to a hidden share but only if you provide a user account with administrative privileges along with the appropriate password for that user account. Administrators can create their own custom hidden shares simply by adding a dollar sign to the share name of any shared folder. Administrators can view all the hidden shares that exist on a Windows Server 2003 computer from the Shared

Folders MMC snap-in. When you create your own hidden shares, any user can connect to them provided that the user knows the exact uniform naming convention (UNC) path and that the user possesses the necessary permissions for accessing that shared folder.

Working with Shared Folder Offline Settings

Offline access to files by network users is enabled by default for each share that you create under Windows Server 2003. However, you can specify the offline-files setting for each share from its properties sheet. To configure offline settings, follow these steps:

1. Right-click a folder that is already shared in Windows Explorer, My Computer, or the Shared Folders snap-in and select Properties.

2. If you're using the Shared Folders snap-in, click the Offline Settings button from the General tab. If you're using Windows Explorer or My Computer, click the Offline Settings button from the Sharing tab.

3. Select one of the available options for offline files, as shown in Figure 5.7:

   ▶ *Only the Files and Programs That Users Specify Will Be Available Offline*—This default setting is also known as *manual caching*.

   ▶ *All Files and Programs That Users Open from the Share Will Be Automatically Available Offline*—This setting is known as *automatic caching*. This feature automatically caches offline all data files that users open. When you enable this setting, you can mark the Optimized for Performance check box to automatically cache program files on each local computer to reduce network traffic for network-based applications.

   ▶ *Files or Programs from the Share Will Not Be Available Offline*—This setting disables offline files for the share.

4. Click OK for the Offline Settings dialog box and then click OK for the share's properties sheet to save the settings.

TIP

You can also configure offline settings from the command line using the `net share` command. Type `net share /?` and press Enter at a command prompt to view the proper syntax and available options for this command. The `/cache:setting_name` is an optional parameter for this utility. You can type `net share name_of_shared_folder /cache:manual` for manual caching, `net share name_of_shared_folder /cache:programs` for automatic caching of network programs and data files, `net share name_of_shared_folder /cache:documents` for automatic caching of data files only, or `net share name_of_shared_folder /cache:none` to turn off offline files for the share.

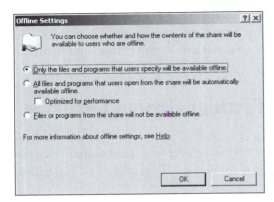

FIGURE 5.7 Configuring a share's offline settings.

Restricting Offline Files Use with Group Policy

You can choose from several different group-policy settings to limit or disable the use of offline files. By default, the Offline Files feature is enabled on Windows 2000 Professional and Windows XP Professional computers, but this feature is disabled on Windows 2000 Server and Windows Server 2003 computers. You can change the default behavior for offline files using group policy for an entire site, domain, or organizational unit (OU).

> **NOTE**
>
> Just after Windows Server 2003 was publicly released, Microsoft officially released the Group Policy Management Console (GPMC). The GPMC provides administrators with a much improved way to manage group policy object (GPO) settings across the enterprise. To download the GPMC, go to `http://www.microsoft.com/downloads`, select Windows Server 2003 from the Product/Technology drop-down list box, and search for the keyword "GPMC." After you download the `GPMC.msi` file, double-click the file to install it on your computer. After you install it, the Group Policy Management icon appears in the Administrative Tools folder off the Start menu. The GPMC runs only on Windows Server 2003 and Windows XP Professional with SP1. However, you can manage Windows 2000 Server DCs as long as those DCs have Windows 2000 SP2 or later installed.

Many settings are available from the GPMC or from the GPO Editor under `Computer Configuration\Administrative Templates\Network\Offline Files`. For example, to enable or disable offline files, double-click the Allow or Disallow Use of the Offline Files Feature policy to specify a setting in the GPO Editor, as shown in Figure 5.8. Several other GPO settings are available under `User Configuration\Administrative Templates\Network\Offline Files`. Just remember that any conflicting GPO settings are always overridden by the GPO setting in the Computer Configuration container.

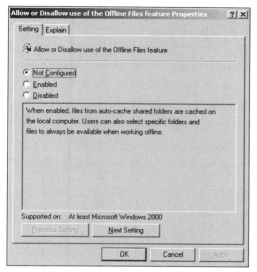

FIGURE 5.8 Configuring a GPO setting for offline files.

NOTE

For a Windows Server 2003 computer, when used as a workstation, the Offline Files feature is not available if the server has Terminal Services installed. This holds true whether you are working directly from the console of the Terminal Server or through a Terminal Services (Remote Desktop Connection) session. However, Windows XP and Windows 2000 computers can still connect to any Terminal Server and make the files stored on that server available offline from their local workstations. In addition, you can use offline files to manually cache files over the network when you connect to any Windows computer that uses the SMB protocol, whether it's running Windows 9x, Windows 2000, Windows XP, or Windows Server 2003. Unfortunately, Novell NetWare servers do not use SMB, so you cannot use offlines files for files stored on NetWare servers.

Working with Share Permissions

When you create a new share under Windows Server 2003 and Windows XP Professional, the default share permissions are Everyone: Allow Read. Share permissions determine the level of access to files and folders stored within the share only for remote users accessing the share over the network; local users accessing local files are not affected by share permissions. For the highest level of security, use NTFS (file system) permissions in addition to share permissions to ensure that local users accessing the files are also subject to any restrictions. You must create a share to allow network access, but you should rely more heavily on the NTFS settings because NTFS permissions apply to both local and network users and NTFS security provides a wider array of permission levels.

Share permissions offer only three levels of security access: Read, Change, or Full Control, as shown in Figure 5.9. Each permission level can be allowed (Allow check box marked), implicitly denied (Allow check box cleared), or explicitly denied (Deny check box marked). The share permissions and their levels of access follow:

▶ *Read*—This default permission lets users view folder names and file-names, view data within files, and execute application program files.

▶ *Change*—This permission allows all Read permissions and lets users add folders and files, change data within files, and delete folders and files.

▶ *Full Control*—This permission grants the same privileges as the Change permission for share permission purposes. (For NTFS file-system permission purposes, Full Control provides more extensive permissions than Change.)

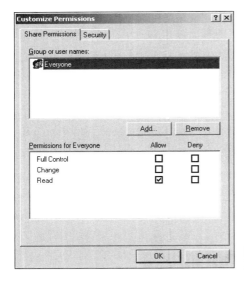

FIGURE 5.9 Configuring share permissions using the Share a Folder Wizard.

Setting Share Permissions

Customizing share permissions is optional when creating a shared folder; the Everyone: Allow Read permission automatically applies to all new shares. You can change the default share permissions for a new share or for an existing share. To modify share permissions, follow these steps:

1. Right-click the shared folder in Windows Explorer or My Computer and select Sharing and Security.

2. Click the Permissions button.

3. Select a user or group name that is listed.

4. Mark the appropriate Allow or Deny check box for the permission that you want to configure: Read, Change, or Full Control.

5. Click the Add button to add a user or group to the list.

6. Select the user or group that you added and mark the appropriate Allow or Deny check box for the permission that you want to configure: Read, Change, or Full Control.

7. To remove a user or group that is listed, select it and click the Remove button.

8. Click OK for the Share Permissions dialog box and then click OK for the folder's properties sheet to save the settings.

NTFS File and Folder Permissions

Windows Server 2003 supports three file systems for disk storage access: the File Allocation Table 16-bit (FAT or FAT16), the File Allocation Table 32-bit (FAT32), and the native Windows Server 2003 NTFS file system. Of these three, only NTFS offers file and folder permissions to protect the files by controlling how they are accessed and by whom. Therefore, if a user logs on to a Windows Server 2003 computer and attempts to access a volume that uses the FAT or FAT32 file system, the user will be able to access all folders and files on those volumes. If a user logs on to a Windows Server 2003 computer and attempts to access a volume that uses the NTFS file system, the user can only access the folders and files that the user has NTFS permissions for.

To individually secure objects such as files and folders, Active Directory objects, registry keys, and printers, as well as devices, ports, services, processes, and threads, you need to use an access control model that enables you to adjust the security of objects to meet the needs of your organization (delegate authority over objects or attributes, and create custom objects or attributes that require unique security protections to be defined).

To keep track of permissions or access rights to objects (NTFS files and folders, processes, events, Active Directory objects, or anything else that has a security descriptor), Microsoft uses access control lists (ACLs). In NTFS, an ACL is made for each file and folder. The ACL will include one or more access control entries (ACEs), and each entry specifies who (a user or group identified by the user's or group's security identifier [SID]) can access the file or folder and the access of the user or group (allowed or denied). Because the permissions are assigned by the discretion cf the file or folder owner, the ACLs used by NTFS are further classified as discretionary access control lists (DACLs).

Another type of access control list is the system access control list (SACL), which controls how access is audited.

You can assign NTFS security permissions to both users and groups and apply them to folders and files. NTFS permissions for Windows Server 2003 can become complex and granular if you use advanced (also known as "special") permissions. Basic permissions are simpler; they enable you to allow or deny access to resources based on six fundamental levels: Read, Read & Execute, List Folder Contents (applies to folders only), Write, Modify, and Full Control. Advanced (special) permissions enable you to fine-tune permission settings for allowing or denying such activities as reading or writing extended object attributes.

Working with Basic NTFS Permissions

Basic NTFS permissions actually consist of predefined advanced NTFS permissions, and you apply them per user and per group. Individual file permissions differ slightly from the permissions that apply to folders. Table 5.1 highlights the basic permissions available for files, whereas Table 5.2 outlines the basic permissions available for folders. In many instances, basic permissions are sufficient for granting or denying fundamental privileges to both users and groups. Best practice dictates that you always assign permissions to groups of users rather than to individual users. It's much easier to manage permissions assigned to groups than having to set and maintain different permissions for each user.

TABLE 5.1   Basic NTFS Security Permissions for Files

Permission Name	Levels of Access
Read	View and list files and folders; view attributes, extended attributes, and permissions of files.
Read & Execute	Run program files; view and list files; view attributes, extended attributes, and permissions of files.
Write	Write data to files; delete file contents; create new files; append data to files; set attributes and extended attributes.
Modify	View and list files; view the contents of files; write data to files; delete files and file contents; view and set attributes and extended attributes.
Full Control	View and list files; view the contents of files; write data to files; delete files and file contents; view and set attributes and extended attributes; change permissions for files; take ownership of files.

TABLE 5.2 *Continued*

Permission Name	Levels of Access
Read	View and list folders and files; view attributes, extended attributes, and permissions of folders.
Read & Execute	Run program files; view and list folders and files; view attributes, extended attributes, and permissions of folders and files.
List Folder Contents	View and list folders and files; run program files.
Write	Add files to a folder.
Modify	View and list folders and files; view the contents of files; write data to files; add folders and files; delete folders, files, and file contents; view and set attributes and extended attributes.
Full Control	View and list folders and files; view the contents of files; write data to files; add folders and files; delete folders, files, and file contents; view and set attributes and extended attributes; change permissions for folders and files; take ownership of folders and files.

NOTE

The List Folder Contents permission is inherited by folders, but not by files, and it appears only when you view folder permissions and drive volume permissions. Read & Execute is inherited by both files and folders and is always present when you view file or folder permissions. By default, NTFS security permissions are inherited from an object's parent. An administrator can manually override the default inheritance and explicitly configure permission settings.

When you create a new NTFS drive volume, Windows Server 2003 automatically assigns default basic NTFS permission settings for five default users and groups. Advanced NTFS permissions are also assigned by the operating system; they are covered in the section "Working with Advanced NTFS Permissions" later in this chapter. The five default groups and their associated default basic permissions follow (see Figure 5.10):

- *Administrators*—Allow Full Control.
- *Creator Owner*—No basic permissions set for the root of the drive volume; all check boxes are cleared.
- *Everyone*—No basic permissions set for the root of the drive volume; all check boxes are cleared.
- *System*—Allow Full Control.
- *Users*—Allow Read, Allow Read & Execute, and Allow List Folder Contents.

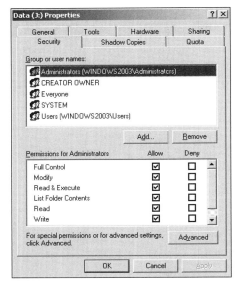

FIGURE 5.10 Viewing default basic NTFS permissions for a new drive volume.

Understanding Inherited Permissions

Each object's NTFS security permissions are automatically inherited from the object's parent container. A file's NTFS permissions are inherited from the folder the file is located in. A subfolder's NTFS permissions are inherited from the folder that the subfolder is located in. Folders stored in the root of a drive volume inherit their NTFS permissions from the drive volume's permissions, which are set by default. Inheritance is the default behavior for NTFS permissions; if you remove inherited permissions, explicit permissions take their place. When you view the Security tab for an object's properties sheet, if the Allow and Deny check boxes for NTFS basic permissions are shaded and not changeable, the file or folder has inherited the permissions from the parent folder.

By clicking the Advanced button at the bottom of the Security tab, you can work with the Advanced Security settings dialog box. From the Advanced Security Settings dialog box, you can clear the Allow Inheritable Permissions from the Parent to Propagate to This Object and All Child Objects. Include These with Entries Explicitly Defined Here check box. By clearing this check box, you can choose to copy the existing inherited permissions and turn them into explicit permissions, or you can remove them entirely and manually establish new explicit permissions. As soon as you clear the check box, the Security message box appears, and you must choose one of the following options (see Figure 5.11):

▶ Copy the existing inherited permissions.

▶ Remove the existing inherited permissions.

▶ Cancel the action and leave the inherited permissions intact.

> **NOTE**
>
> NTFS security permissions are cumulative. Users obtain permissions by having them assigned directly to their user accounts, in addition to obtaining permissions via group memberships. Users retain all permissions as they are assigned. If a user named Brendan has been granted the Allow Read permission for a folder named Contracts, and if Brendan is also a member of the Managers group, which was assigned the Allow Write permission for the same folder, Brendan has both the Allow Read and Allow Write permissions for the Contracts folder. Assigned permissions continue to accumulate; however, Deny entries always override Allow entries for the same permission type (Read, Write, Modify, and so on).

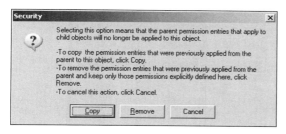

FIGURE 5.11 Choosing to copy or remove NTFS inherited permissions and apply only explicit permissions.

Assigning Basic NTFS Permissions to Users and Groups

Keep in mind that NTFS security permissions apply to all users whether they are local or remote; share permissions apply only to remote users accessing files and folders over the network. However, share permissions can have a major impact on access control to files and folders. If you apply both share permissions and NTFS permissions to a shared folder, the most restrictive permissions apply! This rule is why it is considered a best practice to set either restrictive share permissions or restrictive NTFS permissions, but not both. Microsoft recommends that you use NTFS permissions instead of share permissions. Of course, you must first share a folder before users can access it over the network; you must assign appropriate share permissions to the users or groups who will access the share because the default share permission is Everyone: Read.

To change NTFS security permissions, you must be the owner of the file or folder whose permissions you want to modify, or the owner must grant you permission to make modifications to the object's security settings. Groups or users who are granted Full Control on a folder can delete files and subfolders within that folder regardless of the permissions protecting those files and subfolders. To view or assign basic NTFS permissions on a file or a folder for users and groups, follow these steps:

1. Open Windows Explorer or My Computer, right-click a file or folder stored on an NTFS drive volume, and select Properties.

2. Click the Security tab.

3. To add a user or group to the list of Group or User Names, click the Add button.

4. Type the user or group name in the Enter the Object Names to Select box.

5. To pick from a list of user and group names, click the Advanced button.

   ▶ From advanced Select Users, Computers, or Groups dialog box, verify that the settings for Object Types and Locations are correct; change these settings if necessary.

   ▶ Click the Find Now button to display the names in the Search Results list box, as shown in Figure 5.12.

   ▶ Select one or more names from the Search Results list box and click OK.

6. Click OK for the Select Users, Computers, or Groups dialog box.

7. To remove a user or group, select the name and click Remove.

8. To assign permissions to a user or group, select the name and mark the Allow or Deny check box for each permission that you want to assign.

9. Click OK to save your settings and close the properties window.

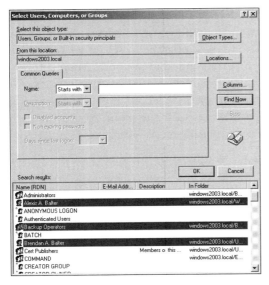

FIGURE 5.12 Choosing users and groups for assigning NTFS permissions from the advanced Select Users, Computers, or Groups dialog box.

Working with Advanced NTFS Permissions

NTFS advanced permissions are called *special* permissions. These special permissions are the building blocks for basic permissions. In Windows Server 2003, special permissions give administrators granular control over exactly what types of security access users can have over files and folders. Special permissions are somewhat hidden from view. They allow administrators to fine-tune ACE security settings. From the Security tab of a file or folder's properties sheet, click the Advanced button to view, add, modify, or remove special NTFS permissions.

When you click the Advanced button, you see the Advanced Security Settings dialog box, which shows each access control entry assigned to every user and group that has permissions on that resource (see Figure 5.13). To remove a permission entry, select the entry and click the Remove button. To view existing individual special permission entries, select one of the users or groups listed and then click the Edit button. When you click the Edit button, the Permission Entry dialog box appears, as shown in Figure 5.14. This dialog gives administrators a fine level of control over the access allowed to individual users and groups on specific resources. For example, this capability gives administrators granular control over the specific permissions users have to manipulate data and program files that are stored on NTFS drive volumes. From the Permission Entry dialog box, you can perform the following tasks for the specified user or group:

▶ Click the Change button to change the user or group listed in the Name box so that this permission entry applies to some other user or group.

▶ Click the Apply Onto drop-down list box to specify exactly where these special permissions should apply.

▶ Change the actual permission entries themselves by marking or clearing the Allow or Deny check box for each permission that you want to assign.

To add a user or a group to the Permission Entries list, click the Add button, select a user or group, and then follow the steps just outlined for editing permission entries. Table 5.3 lists the special NTFS permissions available under Windows Server 2003.

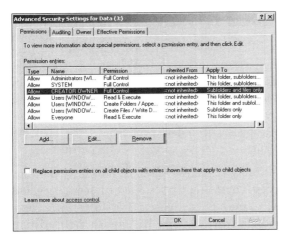

FIGURE 5.13 Viewing default special NTFS permissions for a new drive volume.

TABLE 5.3 Special NTFS Security Permissions for Files and Folders

Permission Name	Levels of Access
Full Control	Assigns the Allow check box entry for all basic and special NTFS security permissions, including the entries for Change Permissions and Take Ownership.
Traverse Folder/Execute File	Moves through folders to reach other files or folders, even if the user has no permissions for the folders being navigated through (applies to folders only). Traverse Folder takes effect only when the group or user is not granted the Bypass Traverse Checking user right in the Group Policy snap-in. The Execute File permission allows or denies running application program files.
List Folder/Read Data	Views filenames and subfolder names within the folder and views data within files.
Read Attributes	Views the attributes—such as read-only, hidden, and archive—for a file or folder.
Read Extended Attributes	Views the extended attributes of a file or folder. Some extended attributes are defined by application programs and can vary by application.
Create Files/Write Data	Creates files within a folder, makes changes to a file, and overwrites the existing data.
Create Folders/Append Data	Creates subfolders within a folder and makes changes to the end of a file; does not include changing, deleting, or overwriting existing data.
Write Attributes	Changes the attributes—such as read-only or hidden—for a file or folder.

TABLE 5.3 *Continued*

Permission Name	Levels of Access
Write Extended Attributes	Changes the extended attributes of a file or folder. Some extended attributes are defined by application programs and can vary by application.
Delete Subfolders and Files	Deletes subfolders and files, even if the Delete permission was not granted on the subfolder or file.
Delete	Deletes files and folders. If you don't have the Delete permission on a file or folder, you can still delete it if you were granted the Delete Subfolders and Files permission on the parent folder.
Read Permissions	Views the permissions that exist on a file or folder.
Change Permissions	Changes permissions on files and folders, such as Full Control, Read, Write, and so on.
Take Ownership	Becomes the owner of a file or folder. The owner of a file or folder can always change permissions on it, even if other permissions were assigned to safeguard the file or folder.

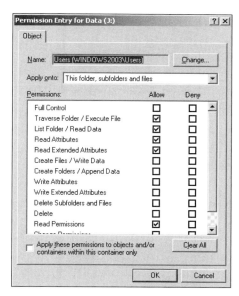

FIGURE 5.14   Viewing default special NTFS permission entries for a group.

Determining NTFS Effective Permissions

Before you assign additional permissions to users or groups for a file or a folder, you should be aware of each user or group's effective permissions based on the current settings. NTFS under Windows Server 2003 provides a way for users and administrators to view current effective permissions from the Advanced Security Settings dialog box for a file or folder. Local administrators logged in to nondomain member computers cannot view NTFS effective permissions for domain users.

The Effective Permissions tab calculates effective permissions based on user permissions, permissions inherited due to group memberships, and permissions inherited from parent folders. It does not use share permissions to calculate effective permissions. To view effective permissions on a file or a folder for a user or group, follow these steps:

1. Open Windows Explorer or My Computer, right-click a file or folder stored on an NTFS drive volume, and select Properties.

2. Click the Security tab.

3. Click the Advanced button to display the Advanced Security Settings dialog box.

4. Click the Effective Permissions tab.

5. Click the Select button, type a user or group name for which you want to view effective permissions, and click OK. (Click the Advanced button and then click Find Now to select from a list of user and group names.)

6. View the effective permissions for the user or group that you selected, as shown in Figure 5.15.

7. Click OK to close the Advanced Security Settings dialog box and then click OK to close the properties sheet.

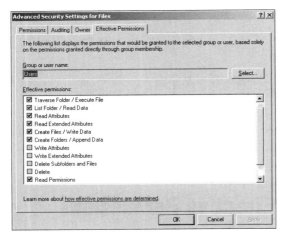

FIGURE 5.15 Viewing NTFS effective permissions for a user or a group from the Advanced Security Settings dialog box.

Understanding Ownership of Files and Folders

Under the NTFS file system in Windows Server 2003, every object, including files and folders, has an owner. The owner of an object has complete control over how permissions are assigned to that object and also over which users or groups can be assigned permissions on the object. The owner of an object retains the power to change permissions on an object at all times, even if the owner's permissions deny him or her access to the object; the role of owner overrides any Deny ACEs on the object. In general, the user who creates a file or folder becomes the owner of that object. However, if the system creates an object, the default owner is the Administrators group, which is the case for files and folders created during the installation of the operating system. One of the following can take ownership over an object:

- ► Users who have been assigned the Restore Files and Directories user right as a local policy or a group policy setting

- ► A user or group who has been assigned the Allow Take Ownership permission for a specific object

- ► Any member of the Administrators group because the Administrators group is granted the Take Ownership of Files or Other Objects user right by default

Changing Ownership of Files and Folders

Windows Server 2003 sports a new feature for NTFS objects—the ability of an owner to transfer ownership of a file or folder to some other user or group. Under previous Windows versions, a user first had to be granted the Take Ownership permission for an object, and then that user could take ownership of it. Now, the owner of an object can assign ownership over that object to another user or group. Ownership over an object can transfer in any one of the following ways:

- ► A member of the Administrators group can take ownership of an object.

- ► The current owner of an object can assign the Allow Take Ownership permission to another user. The user who is assigned Allow Take Ownership permission must actually take ownership of the object to become the new owner.

- ► Any user who is granted the Restore Files and Directories user right can click the Other Users or Groups button at the bottom of the Owner tab for the Advanced Security Settings dialog box (from the object's properties sheet) to assign ownership to some other user or group (see Figure 5.16).

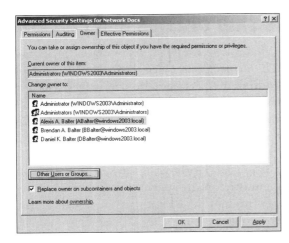

FIGURE 5.16 Changing ownership on a folder from the Owner tab of the Advanced Security Settings dialog box.

NOTE

When you change the ownership of a folder, you can mark the Replace Owner on Subcontainers and Objects check box at the bottom of the Owner tab, as shown in Figure 5.16, to have the new owner take ownership of all files and subfolders stored within the folder. All child objects below the level of the current folder are affected by this setting.

Troubleshooting Access to Files and Shared Folders

When you manage a network environment in which several different factors control access to files and folders, sometimes the user might not be able to access files that he needs. In these instances, it becomes the network administrator's job to diagnose and fix the problem. The major contributing factors for access control issues deal with access permissions:

▶ Shared folder permissions

▶ NTFS file system permissions

If you review these three major factors in the sequence listed, you should be able to solve most access-control issues. Obviously, share permissions do not apply to local users trying to access local folders and files. However, NTFS permissions and EFS encryption apply to both local and network users.

Checking Share Permissions

For remote users attempting to access files over the network, always check the share permissions first. Remember that the most restrictive permissions take precedence between share permissions and NTFS permissions. Also, the default share permissions are Everyone: Allow Read for Windows Server 2003 and Windows XP Professional. If you quickly share a folder without changing the default share permissions, users will be limited to read-only access for all the files accessed through that share, regardless of the NTFS permissions set on the folders and files available through that share.

Checking NTFS Permissions

Share permissions have no effect on local file access by local users; local access includes users interactively logged on to a computer and users logged on to a computer via Terminal Services (Remote Desktop Connections). After you verify the share permissions for a folder, check the NTFS file-system permissions. NTFS permissions apply to all users—whether they are local or network users. Be sure to review all special NTFS permissions, not just the basic NTFS permissions. Right-click the folder or file in question, select Properties, and click the Security tab. Click the Advanced button to view and adjust the special NTFS permissions, if necessary. Also, from the Advanced Security Settings dialog box, click the Effective Permissions tab and check the effective permissions for each user and group that you are investigating. These measures should reveal why users can't access the folders or files that they need.

Exam Prep Questions

1. Which of the following are default hidden shares under Windows Server 2003? (Choose three.)

    ○ **A.** SYSVOL

    ○ **B.** ADMIN$

    ○ **C.** CD$

    ○ **D.** PRINTER$

    ○ **E.** IPC$

    ○ **F.** C$

2. What does the Shared Folders snap-in provide, in terms of setting permissions for a new share, that the Sharing tab of a folder's properties sheet does not offer?

    ○ **A.** Setting share permissions

    ○ **B.** Publishing the share in Active Directory

    ○ **C.** Specifying offine settings

    ○ **D.** Specifying both share permissions and NTFS permissions

    ○ **E.** Specifying Web Sharing access permissions

3. When both share permissions and NTFS permissions exist on the same shared folder, how is access control to the shared folder affected for users trying to access the files stored in the shared folder over the network?

    ○ **A.** NTFS permissions take precedence.

    ○ **B.** Share permissions take precedence.

    ○ **C.** The most liberal permissions take precedence.

    ○ **D.** The most restrictive permissions take precedence.

4. Which of the following characteristics apply to NTFS inherited permissions? (Choose three.)

    ○ **A.** Special permissions are inherited by default.

    ○ **B.** Basic permissions are inherited by default.

    ○ **C.** Explicit permissions are the same as inherited permissions.

    ○ **D.** NTFS permissions are inherited by default.

    ○ **E.** NTFS explicit permissions are not inherited by default.

    ○ **F.** You cannot set explicit permissions on files.

5. The basic NTFS permission, Modify, when set on a folder, consists of which of the following special permissions? (Choose three.)

    ○ **A.** List Folder/Read Data

    ○ **B.** Create Files/Write Data

    ○ **C.** Change Permissions

    ○ **D.** Delete Subfolders and Files

    ○ **E.** Take Ownership

    ○ **F.** Write Extended Attributes

6. When you view NTFS effective permissions for a user or a group, which of the following permissions are displayed?

    ○ **A.** Basic permissions

    ○ **B.** Special permissions

    ○ **C.** Share permissions

    ○ **D.** Not inherited permissions

7. In which of the following ways can ownership of an NTFS file or folder change? (Choose three.)

    ○ **A.** Any user who is a member of the Domain Users group can take ownership of any folder or file whether or not she has permissions to the folder or file.

    ○ **B.** The current owner of a file or folder can assign the Take Ownership permission to another user for the file or folder; the other user must then take ownership of the object.

    ○ **C.** A member of the Administrators group can assign ownership of a file or folder to another user.

    ○ **D.** Any user who is granted the Restore Files and Directories user right can assign ownership of a file or folder to another user.

    ○ **E.** Any member of the Backup Operators group can take ownership of any file or folder at any time.

    ○ **F.** Any member of the Authenticated Users group can assign ownership of files or folders to another user at any time.

8. You have an APP1 folder on a Windows Server 2003 computer. User1 belongs to Group1 and Group2. User has no NTFS permissions assigned. Group1 has Allow Read NTFS permission, and Group2 has Allow Modify NTFS permission. What permission does User1 have for the APP1 folder?

- ○ **A.** Allow Full Control NTFS permission
- ○ **B.** Allow Modify NTFS permission
- ○ **C.** Allow Read NTFS permission
- ○ **D.** No access NTFS permission

9. You have an APP1 folder on a Windows Server 2003 computer. User1 belongs to Group1 and Group2. User has Allow Full Control NTFS permission, and Group2 has Allow Modify NTFS permission. Group1 has Deny Full Control NTFS permission. What permission does User1 have for the APP1 folder?

- ○ **A.** Allow Full Control
- ○ **B.** Allow Modify
- ○ **C.** Allow Read
- ○ **D.** No access

10. On a Windows Server 2003 computer, you have a shared folder called DATA1. You apply the default share permissions and NTFS permissions to DATA1. You then create a folder called DATA2 in DATA1. You apply the default NTFS permissions to DATA2. When GROUP1 tries to add files to DATA2, they get an "Access is denied" error message. What do you need to do so that GROUP1 can create, modify, and delete files in DATA1 and DATA2? All other users must be able to read the files in DATA1 and DATA2?

- ○ **A.** For the DATA1 folder, assign the Change share permission to the Everyone group. For the DATA2 folder, assign the Allow Write NTFS permission for GROUP1 group.
- ○ **B.** For the DATA1 folder, assign the Change share permission to the GROUP1 group and assign the Allow Write NTFS permissions to the GROUP1 group.
- ○ **C.** For the DATA1 folder, assign the Change share permissions to the Everyone group and assign the Allow Modify NTFS permissions to the GROUP1 group.
- ○ **D.** For the DATA1 folder, assign the Change share permissions to the GROUP1 and assign the Allow Modify NTFS permissions to the GROUP1 group.

11. On a Windows Server 2003 computer, you have a shared folder called APP1. At this time, Joe does not belong to the Sales, Marketing, or Executive group. You set the NTFS and APP1 as shown in the following table:

	NTFS permission	Share permission
Everyone	Read	Read
Sales group	Read and Execute	Change
Marketing group	Read/Write	Full Control
Executive group	Read and Execute	Read

You want Joe to be able to make changes to the files in the APP1 folder. What should you do?

- ○ **A.** Assign Joe to the Sales group and assign Allow Write NTFS permission to the Sales group.

- ○ **B.** Assign Joe to the Executive group and assign the Allow Write NTFS permission to the Executive group.

- ○ **C.** Assign Joe to the Executive group and assign the Change share permission to the Executive group.

- ○ **D.** Assign the Full Control share permission to Everyone.

Answers to Exam Prep Questions

1. **Answers B, E, and F are correct.** Default hidden shares include ADMIN$, IPC$, and the root of each available drive letter, such as C$. Answer A is incorrect because although SYSVOL is a default administrative share, it is not hidden. Answer C is incorrect because there is no default share named CD$. Answer D is incorrect because there is no default share named PRINTER$, but there is a default hidden share named PRINT$.

2. **Answer D is correct.** By clicking the Customize button from the permissions window, you can specify both share permissions and NTFS permissions when you create a new share using the Share a Folder Wizard from the Shared Folders snap-in. Answer A is incorrect because both methods allow you to set share permissions. Answer B is incorrect because publishing a share in Active Directory is not a permissions setting. Answer C is incorrect because both methods allow you to specify offline settings. Answer E is incorrect because you can only set Web Sharing access permissions from the Web Sharing tab of a folder's properties sheet.

3. **Answer D is correct.** The most restrictive permissions always override any other permissions, whether they are share permissions or NTFS permissions. Answer A is incorrect because NTFS permissions do not take precedence over share permissions unless they are the most restrictive. Answer B is incorrect because share permissions do not take precedence over NTFS permissions unless they are the most restrictive. Answer C is incorrect because the most restrictive permissions always override more liberal permissions.

4. **Answers A, B, and D are correct.** Special permissions get inherited by child objects, basic permissions get inherited by child objects, and NTFS permissions (in general) all get inherited by default. Answer C is incorrect because explicit permissions are set by users; inherited permissions are set by parent containers. Answer E is incorrect because even explicit permissions set on parent containers (folders) are inherited by child objects (subfolders and files) by default. Answer F is incorrect because you can set explicit permissions on any object or container.

5. **Answers A, B, and F are correct.** When set on a folder, the Modify basic NTFS permission consists of the List Folder/Read Data, Create Files/Write Data, and Write Extended Attributes special permissions, among several others. Answer C is incorrect because the Change Permissions special permissions setting is not part of the Modify permission. Answer D is incorrect because the Delete Subfolders and Files special permission is not part of the Modify permission; however, the Delete special permission is included. Answer E is incorrect because the Take Ownership special permission is not part of the Modify permission.

6. **Answer B is correct.** NTFS special permissions appear in the Effective Permissions dialog box. Answer A is incorrect because basic permissions do not appear in the Effective Permissions dialog box. Answer C is incorrect because share permissions do not appear in the Effective Permissions dialog box. Answer D is incorrect because both inherited and explicit NTFS permissions appear in the Effective Permissions dialog box.

7. **Answers B, C, and D are correct.** A user who is the current owner of an object can assign the Take Ownership permission to another user, a member of the Administrators group can assign ownership, and any user who is assigned the Restore Files and Directories right can transfer ownership to another user. Answer A is incorrect because members of the Domain Users group cannot assign the Take Ownership permission to another user for an object. Answer E is incorrect because members of the Backup Operators group cannot take ownership of files or folders at any time. Answer F is incorrect because members of the Authenticated Users group cannot assign ownership of files to other users at any time.

8. **Answer B is correct.** When combining NTFS permissions on users and groups, you have to look at the least restrictive. In this case, Group2 has the least restrictive NTFS permission, which is the Allow Modify permission.

9. **Answer D is correct.** When combining NTFS permissions on users and groups, you have to look at the least restrictive. However, Deny permissions always take higher precedence. Therefore, since Group1 has Deny Full Control NTFS permission, User1 has no access because the user has been denied Full Control including all permissions.

10. **Answer D is correct.** By default, Everyone is assigned the Read share permission. So for the users to be able to make changes, you have to assign the Change share permission to Group1. In addition, by default, Everyone has Read and Execute NTFS permission to the root of each drive. These permissions are not inherited by folder or file. Therefore, you will also have to assign the Allow Modify NTFS permissions to Group1.

11. **Answer A is correct.** To be able to make changes to the files, Joe will need the Read and Write (or Full Control) NTFS permission and the Change (or Full Control) Share permission. One way would be to add Joe to the Marketing group, but this is not one of the options. Of the options shown, you would assign Joe to the Sales group. This gives the Change Share permission, but not the NTFS permission. Therefore, you would also have to add the Write NTFS permission for the Sales group.

Need to Know More?

1. Honeycutt, Jerry. *Introducing Microsoft Windows Server 2003*. Redmond, Washington: Microsoft Press, 2003.

2. Jones, Don, and Mark Rouse. *Microsoft Windows Server 2003 Delta Guide*. Indianapolis, Indiana: Sams Publishing, 2003.

3. Boswell, William. *Inside Windows Server 2003*. Boston, Massachusetts: Addison-Wesley, 2003.

4. Search the Microsoft Product Support Services Knowledge Base on the Internet: http://support.microsoft.com. You can also search Microsoft TechNet on the Internet: http://www.microsoft.com/technet. Find technical information using keywords from this chapter, such as share permissions, NTFS permissions, offline files, and shadow copies.

5. For more information about NTFS permissions with Windows Server 2003, see the following articles from the Windows Server 2003 Technical Library and Windows Server 2003 Product Help in the Microsoft TechNet website (http://technet.microsoft.com):

   ▶ "Access Control Overview"

   ▶ "Understanding Access Control"

   ▶ "Using Access Control"

6. For more information about Share permissions with Windows Server 2003, see the following articles from the Windows Server 2003 Technical Library and Windows Server 2003 Product Help in the Microsoft TechNet website (http://technet.microsoft.com):

   ▶ "Best Practices for Shared Folders"

   ▶ "Shared Folders How to"

   ▶ "Shared Folder Concepts"

   ▶ "Troubleshooting Shared Folders"

CHAPTER SIX

Implementing Printing

Terms you'll need to understand:

✓ Print device

✓ Printer

✓ Spooler

✓ Print driver

✓ Local printer

✓ Network printer

✓ Print queues

Techniques/concepts you'll need to master:

✓ Understanding the print process on Windows Server 2003 computers

✓ Installing local and network printers on the server

✓ Sharing printers on a Windows Server 2003 computer

✓ Configuring the properties of a printer on a Windows Server 2003 computer

✓ Implementing printer permissions

Users in a home environment mostly print to a local printer directly attached to their home computer. In a business environment, client computers often print to a centralized print server that forwards the print jobs to a print device. Network printing or print sharing allows several people to send documents to a centrally located printer or similar device in an office so that you do not have to connect expensive printers to every single computer in the office. By using a print server, the network administrator can centrally manage all printers and print devices.

Printer Terminology

Microsoft defines the following terms as

▶ *Print device (physical printer)*—The physical print device, such as a printer, copy machine, or plotter.

▶ *Printer (logical printer)*—The printer is the software interface between a print device and the print clients or applications. It is a logical representation of a printer device in Windows that has an assigned printer name and software that controls a printer device. When you print to the printer device, you print to the printer, which then prints to the printer device.

▶ *Spooler*—Often referred to as a queue, the spooler accepts each document being printed, stores it, and sends it to the printer device when the printer device is ready.

▶ *Print driver*—A program designed to enable other programs to work with a particular printer without concerning themselves with the specifics of the printer's hardware and internal language.

EXAM ALERT

Make sure you understand the difference between a printer and a print device when taking the exam. A *printer* is the logical representation and the *printer device* is the physical representation.

You can connect a print device (printer, plotter, copy machine, or similar device) to your Windows Server 2003 computer using a parallel (LPT) port, Universal Serial Bus (USB), or infrared (IR), similar to what you would do on a Windows XP computer. You can then print to the printer when running applications on the Windows Server 2003 computer, or you can share the printer so that other users and network applications can print to the printer over the network using Internet Protocol (IP), IPX, or AppleTalk. You can also connect the printer directly to the network by using a network interface card (such as an HP JetDirect card or similar technology) and use IP, IPX, or AppleTalk to communicate with the network device.

Local Versus Network Printing

As an administrator, you can install two types of printers: a local or a network printer. Both types of printers must be created before sharing them for others to use. Table 6.1 lists the advantages and disadvantages of printing to a local printer or a network printer.

TABLE 6.1   Comparing Local and Network Printers

	Local Printer	Network Printer
Advantages	The print device is usually in close proximity to the user's computer.	Many users can access print devices.
	Plug and Play can detect local printers and automatically install drivers.	Network printers support distributing updated printer drivers to multiple clients.
		The print server manages the printer driver settings.
		A single print queue appears on every computer connected to the printer, enabling each user to see the status of all pending print jobs, including their own jobs.
		All users can see the state of the printer.
		Some processing is passed from the client computer to the print server.
		You can generate a single log for administrators who want to audit the printer events.
Disadvantages	A print device is needed for every computer.	The print device might not be physically close to the user.
	Drivers must be manually installed for every local printer.	Security is physically limited on the print device.
	A local printer takes more processing to print.	

NOTE

Whether you choose to print locally or on a network, make sure that your system has sufficient memory and free disk space to handle your print jobs.

When you print to a local or network printer, you must have a print driver that is compatible with the print device that you are printing to. The print driver is software used by computer programs to communicate with a specific printer or plotter, which translates the print jobs from a certain platform to information that the printer understands. The print driver will also help define the capabilities of the printer to the system.

As with any driver that you load on a Windows system, it is strongly recommended that you use only device drivers with the Designed for Microsoft Windows XP or Designed for Microsoft Windows 2003 Server logos. Installing device drivers that are not digitally signed by Microsoft might disable or impair the operation of the computer or allow viruses on to your computer.

EXAM ALERT

Whenever possible, you should use digital signed device drivers. Having a digital signed device driver means that the driver has been tested, verified, and signed by Microsoft so that it is safe for your computer.

NOTE

A computer running Microsoft Windows XP Professional can also function as a print server. However, it cannot support Macintosh or NetWare services, and it is limited to only 10 network connections.

Printing Process

When users print a document, most know only to click the print icon or select Print from the File menu and go grab their document from the printer. Of course, a lot happens in the background that gets the document out of the printer. The following briefly describes the printer process:

1. If a printer is connected directly to its computer, you must load the appropriate driver so that it knows what commands to send to the printer. If a client computer connects to a printer, the print server downloads a print driver to the client computer automatically.

2. When a user prints from an application such as Microsoft Word, he selects the print option or button, and a print job is created. The application calls up the graphical device interface (GDI), which calls the printer driver associated with the target print device. The GDI renders the print job in the printer language of the print device, such as HP's Printer Control Language or Adobe's Postscript, to create an enhanced metafile (EMF). The application then calls the client side of the spooler (Winspool.drv).

3. After it has been formatted, the print job is sent to the local spooler, which provides background printing.

   ▶ If the print job is being sent to the local print device, it will save it to the local hard drive's spool file. When the printer is available, it will print on the local print device.

   ▶ If the local spooler determines that the job is for a network print device, it sends the job to the print server's spooler. If the local printer is being sent to a shared printer (\\server\printer), the print job goes to the server message block (SMB) redirector on the client. UNIX or other line printer remote (LPR) clients can print to the Windows 2003 line printer daemon (LPD) service. The print server's spooler will save it to the print server's hard drive spool file. When the network print device becomes available, it will print on the network print device.

The print spooler (spoolsv.exe) manages the printing process, which locates the correct print driver, loads the driver, spools (queues) the print job, and schedules the print job.

Adding a Printer to a Windows Server 2003 Computer

If you have the correct permissions to add a local printer or a remote shared printer, use the Add Printer Wizard. The users that have the correct permission are defined by the following:

▶ On domain controllers, members of the Administrators and Print Operators groups can install local printers.

▶ On member servers, members of the Administrators and the local Print Operators groups can install local printers.

▶ On Windows XP Professional or Windows 2000 Professional, only Administrators can install local printers.

▶ Any authenticated user can connect to and submit print jobs to a remote shared printer, assuming that they have the proper printer permissions.

In a small workgroup that has only a few computers, each computer most likely connects to a local printer, a printer connected directly to the computer, or a printer connected directly to the network. They do *not* use a print server. Each user on the network adds the printer to their Printer and Faxes folder without sharing the printer and configures his own driver setting. Unfortunately, there are the following disadvantages when connecting to a local printer.

▶ Users do not know the actual state of the printer, including errors such as paper jams or empty paper trays.

▶ Users can only view their own print queue, which displays their own print jobs.

▶ All the processing of the document being printed is done on that one computer.

Installing a Local Printer

To add a local printer to a Windows Server 2003 computer, perform the following steps:

1. Click the Start button and open Printers and Faxes.

2. To start the Add Printer Wizard, click Add a printer (see Figure 6.1).

3. When the Welcome to the Add Printer Wizard starts, click the Next button.

4. Select the Local Printer Attached to This Computer option (see Figure 6.2). If the printer is a newer Plug and Play printer, select the Automatically Detect and Install my Plug and Play printer check box. Click the Next button.

5. When the Select a Printer Port box appears, as shown in Figure 6.3, specify the port to which the printer is attached. If the port already exists, such as an LPT1 or a network port specified by an IP address, select the port from the Use the Following Port drop-down list. If the port does not exist, click Create a New Port, select Standard TCP/IP Port, and click Next to start the Add Standard TCP/IP Printer Port Wizard. After you enter the IP address or DNS name of the printer, you will need to know the device type that the printer uses to connect to the network, such as HP Jet Direct card. After you add the port, you will return to the Add Printer Wizard.

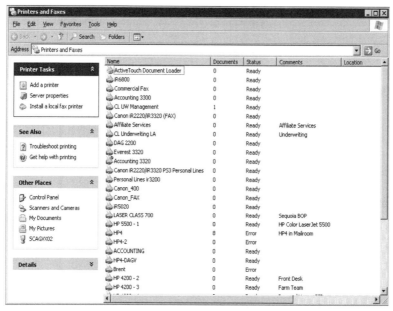

FIGURE 6.1 Adding a printer on a Windows Server 2003 computer.

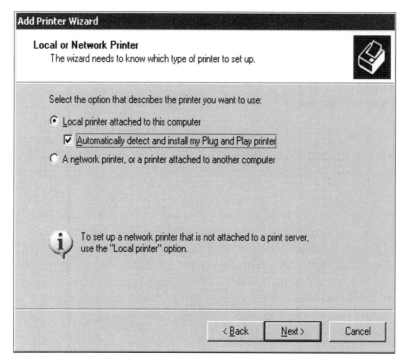

FIGURE 6.2 Choosing between Local and Network printing.

> **NOTE**
>
> The TCP/IP printer port uses host port 9100 to communicate.

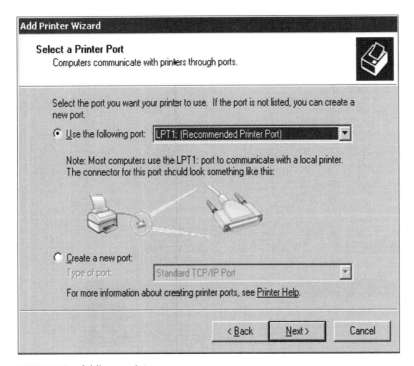

FIGURE 6.3 Adding a printer port.

6. If Plug and Play does not detect and install the correct printer automatically, you can select the print device from the list, or click Have Disk and install the printer from the drivers supplied by the manufacturer (see Figure 6.4).

7. On the Name Your Printer dialog box, you name your printer. Although Windows Server 2003 supports long printer names and share names including spaces and special characters, it is best to keep names short, simple, and descriptive. The entire qualified name, including the server name (for example, \\Server1\HP4100N-1), should be 32 characters or fewer. If you want this to be the default printer for the system you are installing the printer on, select Yes. Click the Next button.

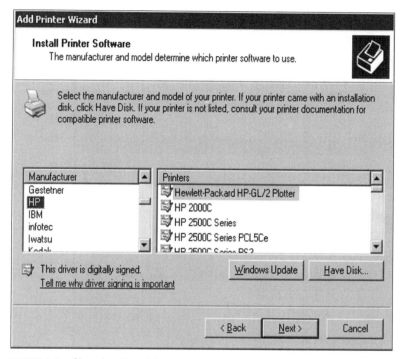

FIGURE 6.4 Choosing the printer.

8. On the Printer Sharing dialog box, if you want the Windows Server 2003 to act as a print server, you can select the ShareName option and type in a sharename. Click the Next button.

9. On the Location and Comment dialog box, you can supply the location and comments to help identify the printer in the future. Click the Next button.

10. On the Print Test Page, you can print the standard Windows test page by selecting the Yes option. Click the Next button.

11. When the Wizard is complete, click the Finish button.

Install a Network Printer

To add a network printer to a Windows Server 2003, perform the following steps:

1. Click the Start button and open Printers and Faxes.

2. To start the Add Printer Wizard, click Add a Printer.

3. When the Welcome to the Add Printer Wizard starts, click the Next button.

4. Select the network printer or a printer attached to another computer option. Click the Next button.

5. On the Specify a Printer dialog box, shown in Figure 6.5, you can find a printer in Active Directory and specify the FQDN (\\servername\ printersharename) or the printer URL. When complete, click the Next button.

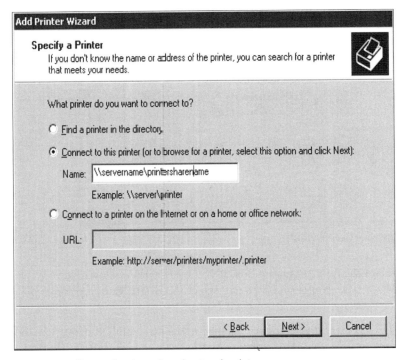

FIGURE 6.5 Connecting to a shared network printer.

6. If you want this to be the default printer for the system you are installing, select Yes. Click the Next button.

7. When the wizard is finished, click the Finish button.

Printer Properties

After installing the logical printer, you can right-click the printer and select Properties to configure numerous settings. The following tabs enable you to configure the settings:

- The General tab (see Figure 6.6) allows you to configure the printer name, location, and comments and to print a test page.

- The Printing Preferences tab, which varies from printer to printer, allows you to configure the default paper size, paper tray, print quality/resolution, pages per sheet, print order (such as front to back or back to front), and number of copies (see Figure 6.7).

- The Finishing tab (see Figure 6.8) defines how many pages appear per sheet, whether the page is to be printed portrait or landscape, and whether the page is to be printed on both sides (assuming your printer supports printing duplex).

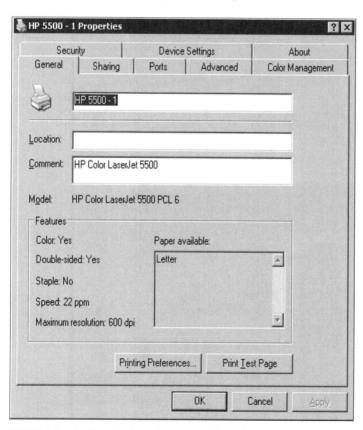

FIGURE 6.6 Configuring the printer properties—General tab.

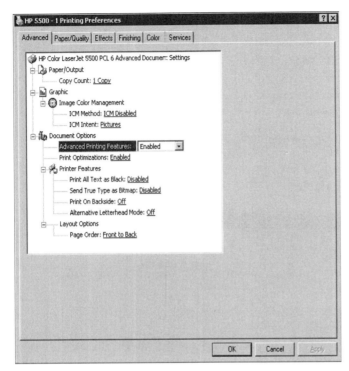

FIGURE 6.7
Configuring printer
preferences—
Advanced tab.

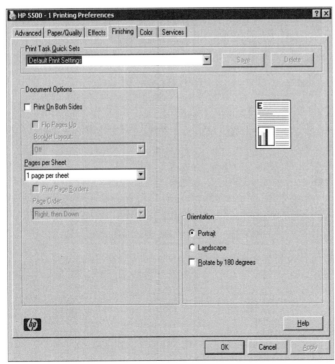

FIGURE 6.8 Printing
preferences—Finishing
tab.

Printer Clients

After you share a printer on a Windows Server 2003 computer, the following clients can access it:

- ▶ 16-bit clients running Windows 3.X and MS-DOS with the appropriate 16-bit driver on each client.

- ▶ 32-bit clients, 64-bit clients, and Itanium PCs such as Windows XP, Windows 2000, and Windows Server 2003.

- ▶ NetWare clients if Microsoft File and Print Services for NetWare is installed on the Windows Server 2003 computer over an IPX/SPX network.

- ▶ Macintosh clients with Microsoft Print Services for Macintosh installed on the Windows Server 2003 computer over AppleTalk.

- ▶ UNIX clients if Microsoft Print Services for UNIX is installed on the print server running Windows Server 2003 using the Line Printer Remote (LPR) and Line Printer Daemon (LPD) services.

- ▶ Clients that support Internet Printer Protocol (IPP) 1.0 using HTTP.

Sharing Options

If you right-click a printer in the Printers and Faxes window and select Sharing, you can access the Printer's sharing tab. The Sharing tab allows you to specify whether the logical printer is shared or not. You can also use it to list the printer in Active Directory or to add print drivers for other Windows operating systems.

> **NOTE**
>
> You can use the Sharing tab to stop sharing a printer, if you take a printer offline to prevent users from accessing the printer.

By default, printers that are added using the Add Printer Wizard are published to Active Directory. If you want to republish a printer, especially after you made changes to its properties, such as the sharename or name of the printer, or if you do not want to have a printer listed in Active Directory, open the printer's Properties dialog box, click the Sharing tab (see Figure 6.9), and select or clear the List In the Directory check box.

If the printer is a shared printer, you can provide additional drivers to the clients so that the users do not have to find print drivers when they connect to the shared printer. By default, Windows Server 2003 includes drivers for x86 Windows 2000, Windows XP, and Windows Server 2003. Additional drivers for other systems include x64, Itanium, Windows 9x (Windows 95, Windows 98, and Windows Millennium), and Windows NT 4.0. The drivers are located on the Windows Server 2003 CD. Print drivers for Microsoft Windows 3.1, MS-DOS, UNIX/Linux, and Macintosh must be installed on each client computer. They cannot be downloaded from the print server.

To add printer drivers for other versions of Windows, follow these steps:

1. In the Printers and Faxes folder, right-click the printer for which you want to install additional drivers, and then click Properties.

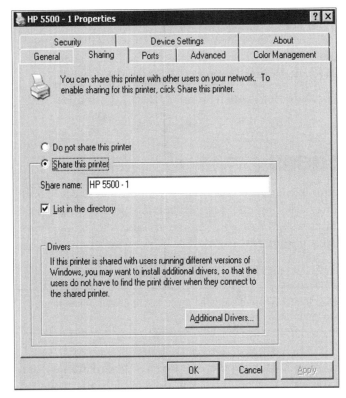

FIGURE 6.9 Printer properties—Sharing tab.

2. In the Properties dialog box, on the Sharing tab, click Additional Drivers.

3. In the Additional Drivers dialog box, select the check boxes for the additional environments and operating systems, and then click OK (see Figure 6.10).

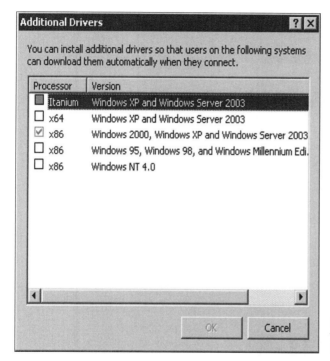

FIGURE 6.10 Adding additional drivers to Windows Server 2003.

Using Paper Trays

If the print device has multiple trays that regularly hold different paper sizes, you can assign a form to a specific tray. A form defines a paper size, such as Letter, Legal, A4, Envelope, and Executive. When a user prints a document to a particular paper size, Windows Server 2003 automatically routes the print jobs to the appropriate paper tray. To assign a form to a paper tray, select the Device Settings tab of the printer's Properties dialog box (see Figure 6.11).

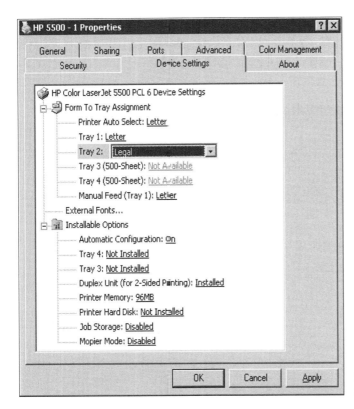

FIGURE 6.11 Printer device settings.

Printer Permissions

To control who can use the printer and who can administer the print jobs and printers, use the Security tab to specify printer permissions for those who are not otherwise administrators. Windows Server 2003 provides three levels of printer permissions:

- *Print*—Allows users to send documents to the printer.

- *Manage Printers*—Allows users to modify printer settings and configuration, including the ACL itself.

- *Manage Documents*—Provides the ability to cancel, pause, resume, or restart a print job.

By default, the Print permission is assigned to the Everyone group. If you need to restrict who can print to the printer, you will need to remove the permission and assign Allow Print permission to other groups or individual users. Much like file permissions, you can deny Print permissions.

The Creator Owner group is allowed Managed Documents permission. This means that when a user sends a print job to the printer, he can manage his own print job. Administrators, print operators, and server operators have the Manage Documents and the Manage Printers permission.

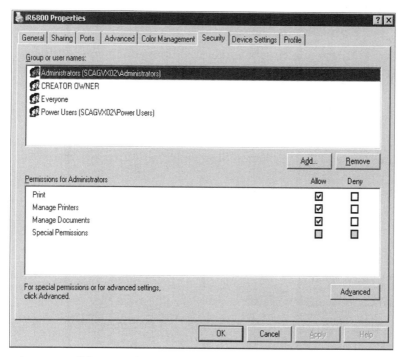

FIGURE 6.12 Printer permissions.

Internet Printing

Another way for a user to print to a printer is to connect to a printer using Internet Print Protocol (IPP), which is transported by being encapsulated in Hypertext Transfer Protocol (HTTP) packets. To make the printer available via Internet Printing, you must first install Internet Information Services (IIS) on the computer running Windows Server 2003.

To install IIS, perform the following steps:

1. Click Start, point to Control Panel, and then click Add or Remove Programs.

2. Click Add/Remove Windows Components.

3. In the Components list of the Windows Components Wizard, double-click Web Application Server, click to select the Internet Information Services (IIS) check box.

4. With the Internet Information Services (IIS) highlighted, click the Details button.

5. Select the Internet Printing option.

6. Click the OK button to close the Internet Information Services IIS dialog box.

7. Click OK to close the Application dialog box.

8. Click the Next button.

9. If necessary, insert the Windows Server 2003 CD or browse to the Windows Server 2003 installation files. Follow the directions that are on the screen.

10. Click Finish, and then click Close.

You must then enable Internet printing using the IIS manager:

1. Start IIS Manager or the IIS snap-in.

2. Expand * server_name.

3. Click Web Service Extensions.

4. On the right pane, click Internet Printing, and then click Allow.

5. Quit IIS Manager.

> **EXAM ALERT**
>
> To print over the Internet using Internet Printing, you must install IIS with Internet printing and enable Internet Printing in Web Service Extensions.

When you use Internet printing, you can print or manage documents using a web browser such as Internet Explorer 4.01 or later. You can then print over the intranet or the Internet by specifying the URL to the print server, such as `http://server1/printers/`.

When a user connects to the printer's web page, the server will bundle the printer drivers and any other necessary files into a `.cab` file so that the files can be downloaded to the user's system. After the files are downloaded and installed, the printer will be displayed in the Printers and Faxes folder.

Exam Prep Questions

1. In Windows Server 2003, the printer is defined as

   ○ **A.** The logical device that represents the print device

   ○ **B.** The physical print device

   ○ **C.** The network IP address located in DNS

   ○ **D.** The print driver

2. Which of the following can install a printer on a server that is part of the domain? (Choose all that apply.)

   ○ **A.** Domain administrators

   ○ **B.** Local administrators

   ○ **C.** Domain Print operators

   ○ **D.** Power users

3. You add a printer directly to the network using a built-in Ethernet card. Now you want to load the printer onto the server. Which of the following is true?

   ○ **A.** The printer is considered a local printer.

   ○ **B.** The printer is considered a network printer.

   ○ **C.** The printer needs to be moved so that it can be plugged directly into the Windows Server 2003 acting as a print server.

   ○ **D.** The printer needs to be assigned a name such as `http://servername/printername`.

4. What do you need to load if you want to print to a Unix computer?

   ○ **A.** LPR and LDP

   ○ **B.** IIS and IPP

   ○ **C.** Appletalk redirector

   ○ **D.** NetWare redirector

5. You are the network administrator for Acme.com. You have a Windows Server 2003 named Server1 with a printer named Printer1. John prints several large print jobs before he is called away from the office. Since these print jobs are so large, they prevent other users from printing important documents. How can you allow Jane, the office manager, to delete those print jobs?

    ○ **A.** Configure the printer permissions to give Jane the Allow Manage Printers permission.

    ○ **B.** Configure the printer permission to assign the Allow Manage Documents permission.

    ○ **C.** Create a new print queue that points to the same print device and assigns full permission to Jane.

    ○ **D.** Configure the Allow Manage Queue permission.

6. What permission do you have to give a user to change the configuration of a printer?

    ○ **A.** Allow Manage Printers

    ○ **B.** Allow Manage Documents

    ○ **C.** Full control for Documents

    ○ **D.** Modify permission for Printers

7. A user sent a large print job to the printer and realized that some changes had to be made. Therefore, the user wants to delete the print job. What do you need to do for that user to delete the print job?

    ○ **A.** Give the user the Allow Manage Printer permission.

    ○ **B.** Give the user the Allow Manage Documents permission.

    ○ **C.** Give the user both Allow Manage Printer permission and Allow Manage Documents permission.

    ○ **D.** Give the Allow Delete Print Jobs permission.

    ○ **E.** You don't have to do anything because the user can already delete his own print job.

8. You are the network administrator for Acme.com. You have a Windows Server 2003 named Server1 with a printer named Printer1. You instruct users to connect to the printer by using the following address: `http://Server1/Printer1`.

   However, users cannot connect to the printer by using HTTP.

   What must you do?

   - ○ **A.** Install IIS on the server and install the Internet Printing component of IIS.

   - ○ **B.** Stop and restart the print spooler.

   - ○ **C.** Make sure that you have sufficient disk space for the print jobs.

   - ○ **D.** Create a virtual directory called Printer1.

Answers to Exam Prep Questions

1. **Answer A is correct.** According to Microsoft, the printer is the logical representation of the points to the physical printer device. Answer B is incorrect because the physical printer is known as a print device. Answer C is incorrect because DNS entries for printers are only for our convenience by assigning a name to an IP address so that we can remember it easier. Answer D is incorrect because the print driver is the component that will be used to translate the documents into a language that is understood by the printer.

2. **Answers A, B, and C are correct.** On domain controllers, members of the Administrators and Print Operators groups can install local printers. On member servers, members of the Administrators and the local Print Operators groups can install local printers. On Windows XP Professional or Windows 2000 Professional, only Administrators can install local printers. Any authenticated user can connect to and submit print jobs to a remote shared printer, assuming that they have the proper printer permissions. Answer D is incorrect because power users are not assigned printer permissions, although the users in power users maybe assigned to other groups that give them permissions for the printer.

3. **Answer A is correct.** When you connect a printer to the network, you install it as a local printer and use the Create a New Port Wizard to create a standard TCP/IP port. Answer B is incorrect because the printer is not connected directly to the server. Answer C is incorrect because you do not have to connect it directly to the printer to use it. Answer D is incorrect because it is not necessary for a printer to use IPP.

4. **Answer A is correct.** Unix and Linux computers use Line Printer Remote (LPR) and Line Printer Daemon (LPD) to print to a print device. Answer B is incorrect because IIS and IPP are necessary for Internet printing. Answer C is incorrect because Appletalk redirector is used for older Apple computers. Answer D is incorrect because Netware redirector is used for printing with Novell NetWare.

5. **Answer B is correct.** By default, a user can delete his own print jobs. To be able to delete any print job, the user must have the Manage Documents permission for the printer. Answer A is incorrect because Allow Manage Printers enables Jane to configure settings on the printer itself and would not allow her to manage the documents being sent to the printer. Answer C is a long-term solution but the question asks how to delete these print jobs. Answer D is incorrect because there is no Allow Manage Queue permission.

6. **Answer A is correct.** To change the printer configuration, the user needs the Allow Manage Printers permission. Answer B is incorrect because if a user has to manage documents, he can only manage documents sent to the print queue. Answer C is incorrect because it would give additional permissions that the question does not ask, including managing the print jobs. Answer D is incorrect because there is no Modify permission for printers.

7. **Answer E is correct.** Users have the ability to delete their print jobs, so no additional permissions must be given. Therefore, answers A, B, C, and D are incorrect.

8. **Answer A is correct.** To make sure that you can print using HTTP, you must have IIS to service the HTTP calls. In addition, you must install the Internet Printing components of IIS. Answer B is incorrect because restarting the print spooler will have no effect. Answer C is incorrect because although you need sufficient disk space to print, it has no bearing on Internet printing. Answer D is incorrect because IIS does not require a virtual directory to print.

Need to Know More?

For more information about printing with Windows Server 2003, see the following articles from the Windows Server 2003 Technical Library and Windows Server 2003 Product Help in the Microsoft TechNet website at `http://technet.microsoft.com`:

▶ "Printer Connectivity Technical Overview"

▶ "Administering Printing"

▶ "Printing Best Practices"

▶ "Printing Concepts"

▶ "Printing Troubleshooting"

7

CHAPTER SEVEN

Managing Printing

Terms you'll need to understand:

✓ Print spooler

✓ Print priority

✓ Print scheduling

✓ Printer pools

Techniques/concepts you'll need to master:

✓ Restarting the print service

✓ Changing the location of the spool file

✓ Changing the priority of printers and print jobs

✓ Creating a printer pool

✓ Managing print jobs

✓ Redirecting print jobs

✓ Enabling and analyzing the printer logs

✓ Monitoring print queue performance

✓ Troubleshooting common printer problems

As an administrator, you will need to plan and implement a networkwide printing strategy that will meet the needs of users. To set up an efficient network of printers, you must know how to troubleshoot installation and configuration problems. Microsoft Windows Server 2003 provides several configuration options to help you perform these tasks efficiently.

Managing the Print Spooler

The print spooler is an executable file that manages the printing process, which includes retrieving the location of the correct print driver, loading the driver, creating the individual print jobs, and scheduling the print jobs for printing.

Typically, the print spooler is loaded during startup and continues to run until the operating system shuts down. You can restart the print spooler by doing the following:

1. Open the Services console located in Administrative Tools.

2. Right-click Print Spooler, and select Restart (see Figure 7.1).

3. You can also stop and start the service.

EXAM ALERT

If the print spooler becomes unresponsive or you have print jobs that you cannot delete, you should try to restart the Print Spooler service.

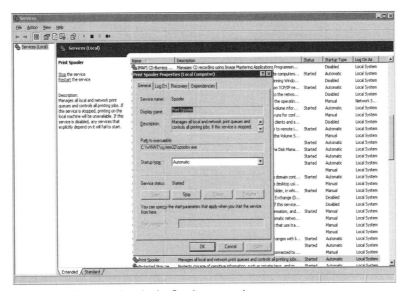

FIGURE 7.1 Print services in the Services console.

After the print jobs are created, they are stored as files on the hard drive. When the print device is available, the spooler retrieves the next print job and sends it to the print device. By default, the spool folder is located at `%SystemRoot%\System32\Spool\Printers`. So on most installations, this will be the `C:\Windows\System32\Spool\Printers` folder. If the system drive becomes full, the performance of the server might slow down dramatically, services and applications running on the server might degrade or not function at all, and the system can become unstable. Because the Print Spooler is on the same volume that holds the Windows system files, the administrator must ensure that spooling print jobs do not accidentally fill up the system volume.

If you have only a couple of printers with low traffic volumes, most likely the default location of the spool folder is sufficient. However, if you have a large number of printers or frequent large print jobs, you should move the spool folder to another location, preferably another volume that is on its own input/output (I/O) controller so that frequent disk reads and writes will not dramatically affect the overall performance of Windows. It is recommended that you use a RAID 1 or 5 volume.

NOTE

When you print a Word document or a PDF file, the actual print job sent to the printer will be many times larger than the original Word or PDF file itself.

To change the location of the spool folder, follow these steps:

1. Open the Printer's and Fax folder.

2. Open the File menu and select Server Properties.

3. Select the Advanced tab.

4. Specify the full local drive letter and path of the new spool folder in the Spool Folder text box (see Figure 7.2).

5. Click OK to save the new settings.

6. Stop the Spooler service and then restart it for the changes to take effect.

NOTE

If you move the location of the spool folder while print jobs are waiting in the queue, those print jobs will not print. Therefore, it is recommended that you wait for documents in the queue to complete before moving the spool folder.

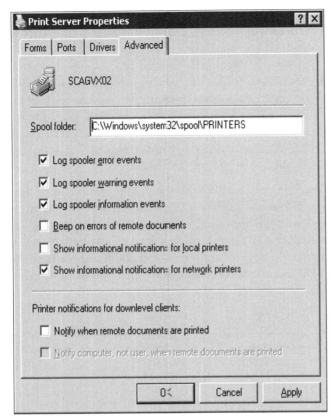

FIGURE 7.2 Specifying the location of the spool folder found within Print Server Properties.

Printers, Print Devices, and Printer Pools

When a user prints something, the user prints to a printer (logical representation), which then sends the print job to the print device (physical representation) after spooling. You can configure several printers to point to a single print device, or you can have a printer print to several print devices, known as a printer pool.

Priorities and Scheduling

By having multiple printers print to a single print device, you can configure a high priority for one printer and a low priority for the other printer. The print jobs sent to the printer with the high priority will print before the printer with the lower priority, even though they are printing to the same print device. The priorities range from 1 to 99. To give some users preference when printing, you can assign some users to one printer that is assigned a low priority and other users to another printer with a high priority. You would use permission to control who can print to which printer.

> **NOTE**
>
> When a printer with a higher priority receives a print job, it does not stop processing a job it is already working on.

To set printer priorities

1. Open Printers and faxes.

2. Right-click the printer and select Properties.

3. Select the Advanced tab.

4. Specify the priority (1–99): the higher the number, the higher the job (see Figure 7.3).

Most printers are configured to print immediately when receiving the print job. In some situations, you might choose to print during certain times, such as at night or when the printer is not being used as much. By configuring a printer's schedule at night, print jobs created during the day are stored in the print queue until night. The jobs print during the night, and the user can pick them up in the morning. Of course, this is assuming that you did not run out of paper during the night.

To configure a printer to print to a printer device at certain times, follow these steps:

1. Open the Printers and Faxes window by clicking Start, and then click Printers and Faxes.

2. Right-click the printer and select Properties.

3. Select the Advanced tab.

4. Select the Available From option and specify the time that the printer will print.

By default, when the print job reaches the spool folder, it will immediately start feeding into the printer. You can configure the print jobs to be spooled entirely in the print queue before being sent to the print device. This comes in handy if you have large print jobs that delay the print device as it waits for the print job being processed on the print queue, minimizing the impact large print jobs have on the performance of the printer. You can do this by going into the Printer properties and selecting the Advanced tab. You can then use the default Start Printing Immediately option, or you can choose the Start Printing After Last Page is Spooled option.

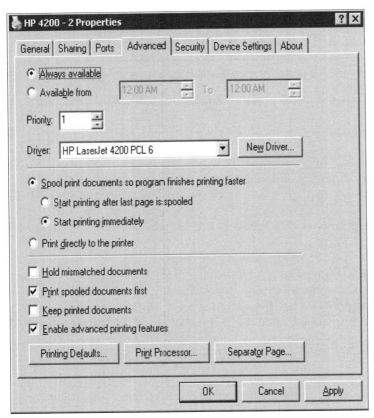

FIGURE 7.3 Specifying printer priority using the Printer Properties—Advanced tab.

Printer Pools

A printer pool associates two or more identical print devices to the same printer. Although this allows for redundancy, it is mostly intended for when you have a high volume of printing that can be evenly distributed between print devices. When a document is sent to the printer pool, the first available printer receives the job and prints it. If one device within a pool stops printing, the current document is still held at that device. Print jobs arriving later are sent to the other print devices.

Although printers can use different ports (parallel, serial, and network), all printers in the pool should be the same model. In addition, it is recommended to have all print devices in the same location so that users don't have to run around the office trying to find their print jobs. Windows Server 2003 places no limit on the number of printers in a pool.

To set up such a pool, first use the Add Printer Wizard and assign the logical printer as many output ports as there are identical printers. Then when you go into the properties of the printer, select the Ports tab and select Enable Printer Pooling. Last, check the various ports that point to the different print devices that you want to include in the printer pool (see Figure 7.4).

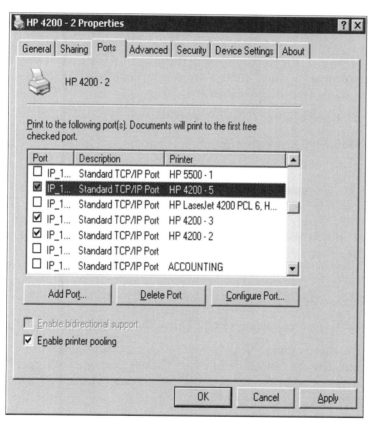

FIGURE 7.4 Create a printer pool.

Managing Print Jobs

As a user or an administrator, at times you might need to manage individual print jobs or documents. To view documents waiting to print, do the following:

1. Open the Printer and Faxes folders.

2. Double-click the printers on which you want to view the print jobs waiting to print.

The print queue shows information about a document such as print status, owner, and number of pages to be printed. From the print queue, you can cancel or pause the printing of a document that you have sent to the printer. You also can open the print queue for the printer on which you are printing by double-clicking the small printer icon in the status area on the taskbar.

To pause a document, perform the following steps:

1. Open the Printer and Faxes folders.

2. Double-click the printer you are using to open the print queue.

3. Right-click on the document you want to pause and select the Pause option.

By default, all users can pause, resume, restart, and cancel their own documents. To manage documents that are printed by other users, however, you must have the Manage Documents permissions.

To cancel a print job, perform the following steps:

1. Open the Printers and Faxes folder.

2. Double-click the printer you are using to open the print queue.

3. Right-click on the document that you want to stop printing and select the Cancel option. You can cancel the printing of more than one document by holding down the Ctrl key and clicking on each document that you want to cancel.

To change the printing priority of documents waiting to print within a print queue, proceed as follows:

1. Open the Printers and Faxes folder.

2. Double-click the printer you are using to open the print queue.

3. Right-click on the document that you want to move in the print order, and click the Properties option.

4. Under the General tab, drag the Priority slider to raise or lower the document priority.

Once a document has started printing, any printing priority change you make will not affect the document.

Redirecting Print Jobs

If a printer fails before printing and cannot be repaired quickly, you might want to transfer the documents to another printer. Follow these steps:

1. Open the Printers and Faxes folder.

2. Double-click the printer that holds the document(s) that you want to redirect.

3. Open the Printer menu and select the Properties option.

4. To send the documents to a different print device on the same print server, click the port to which the other print device is assigned and click OK. To send documents to another printer on a different print server, click the Add Port button, select the Local Port option, and click the New Port button. Type the name of the other print server and the share name using the UNC name. Click OK.

After redirecting the print jobs, the check box of the port of the malfunctioning printer is immediately cleared unless printer pooling is enabled. Because print jobs have already been formatted for a specific printer, the printer on the new port must be compatible with the driver used in the logical printer. It should also be noted that any documents currently printing cannot be redirected.

Looking at the Logs

To look at spooler and printer activity, you can use the logs shown in the Event Viewer to look at the logs that pertain to the printer and spooler activity. By default, the System logs will show printer creation, deletion, and modification (see Figure 7.5). You can also find entries for printer traffic, hard disk space, spooler errors, and other relevant maintenance issues.

To modify the event logging for the spooler:

1. Open the Printers and Faxes folder and choose Server Properties from the File menu.

2. Click the Advanced tab to access the properties.

3. You can then select to log errors, warnings, and information events; beep on errors of remote documents; and show information notifications for local and network printers.

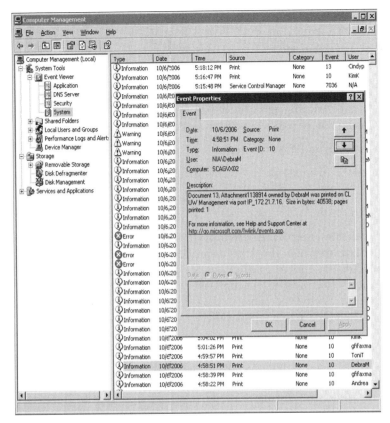

FIGURE 7.5 Looking at the Printer events located in the Event Viewer.

Auditing Printer Access

Similar to file and folder access, you can also audit printers. You can specify which users or groups and which actions to audit for a particular printer.

Before you can do printer auditing, you need to enable Audit Object Access policy, which is done using local or group policies (Computer Configuration\Windows Settings\Security Settings\Local Policies\Audit Policy). After the policy has taken effect, you would then

1. Open the Printer and Faxes folder.

2. Right-click the printer you want to audit and select Properties.

3. Choose the Security tab.

4. Select the Advanced button.

5. Choose the Auditing tab.

6. Select Add, and then choose the groups or users you want to audit.

7. Check the boxes for auditing successful or failed events.

8. Click OK to close the Advanced Security Settings box.

9. Click OK to close the printer Properties box.

You would then look in the Security logs in the Event Viewer for inappropriate or unauthorized printing (see Figure 7.6).

FIGURE 7.6   After enabling auditing, look at the security events in the Event Viewer.

Monitoring Print Queue Performance

If you find that your print jobs are too slow to print or you want to see the overall performance of the printing system, you can monitor the performance of a print server's print queue by using the Performance snap-in. You can monitor real-time statistics using System Monitor, and you can log performance over time using Performance Logs and Alerts. The performance object to specify is Print Queue. The object instances are the printers installed on the local print server computer along with the _Total instance. The available counters include

▶ *Bytes/Printed/sec*—The number of bytes per second printed on a print queue.

▶ *Job errors*—The total number of job errors in a print queue since last restart.

▶ *Jobs*—The current number of jobs in a print queue.

▶ *Job Spooling*—The current number of spooling jobs in a print queue.

▶ *Not Ready Errors (since last restart)*—The total number of printer-not-ready errors in a print queue since the last restart.

▶ *Out of Paper Errors (since last restart)*—The total number of out-of-paper errors in a print queue since the last restart.

▶ *Total Jobs Printed (since last restart)*—The total number of jobs printed on a print queue since the last restart.

▶ *Total Pages Printed (since last restart)*—The total number of pages printed through GDI on a print queue since the last restart.

Troubleshooting Printing Problems

When problems occur, you must be ready to troubleshoot those problems. Of course, when looking at what is causing the problem, you need to look at everything that can cause the problems. When it comes to printing, this includes

▶ The application attempting to print

▶ The logical printer on the local computer

▶ The network connection between the local computer and the print server

▶ The logical printer on the server

▶ The network connection between the print server and the print device

▶ The print device itself, including hardware, configuration, and status

The first step is to identify the scope of the failure; in other words, determine what is working and what is failing. For example, if a user can print from one application but not another on the same computer, the problem is most likely related to the application that is having problems printing. If the user can print to other printers with no problem, you would then try to print from another system in an attempt to duplicate the problem. If the problem occurs on multiple computers, you need to focus on the logical printer on the server or the print device. Of course, one place to give you insight into some problems is the logs in the Event Viewer, specifically if the spooler has written any errors to the event logs.

You can confirm connectivity between the print client and the print server by opening the Printer and Faxes folder and double-clicking the printer to open the printer window. If the printer window opens and it shows documents in the print queue, the client is communicating with the print server. If you cannot open the printer window, the problem is with authentication, security permissions, or a network connectivity problem. You can test connectivity further by trying to ping the print server or by clicking the Start button, selecting run, and typing in *printservername*. Also, make sure that the printer has not been disabled or offline within Windows.

If you suspect that the print server cannot connect to the printer, you should first check to see if the print device is in operation. (Make sure that the printer is on and online, make sure that it is connected to the server or network, and make sure that the printer is not showing any errors.) Next, from the print server, make sure that the print server can access the print device. You can also make sure that the IP address on the logical printer port matches the address of the print device. You could test network connectivity by pinging the address of the print device.

If you suspect a problem with the print server itself, you need to make sure that the Print service and the remote procedure call (RPC) service is running. You might also try to restart the print service and make sure that you have sufficient disk space on the drive where the spool folder is located.

If pages are only partially printed, check that there is sufficient memory on the printer to print the document. If text is missing, verify whether the missing text uses a font that is valid and installed. Of course, another reason might be that you need to replace the printer's toner cartridge.

If your printed documents have garbled data or strange characters, you should verify that you have the correct print driver loaded for the printer. You might also consider reinstalling the drivers since they could be corrupt. Finally, check for bad cables or electromagnetic interference. See Table 7.1 for a list of common printing problems and how to fix them.

EXAM ALERT

Anytime you have garbled data or strange characters, you should always suspect that you have the wrong print driver installed.

TABLE 7.1 Troubleshooting Common Printing Problems

If You Encounter This Problem	Do This
Printer server cannot connect to the printer	Make sure the print device is operational (printer is on and online, printer is connected to the server or network, and printer is not showing any errors).
	Make sure the IP address on the logical printer port matches the address of the print device.
	Try pinging the address of the print device.
Print server is having problems	Make sure that the printer services and remote procedure call (RPC) service is running.
	Restart the print service.
	Make sure you have sufficient disk space on the drive where the spool folder is located.
Pages are partially printed	Check that there is sufficient memory on the printer.
	Check to see whether the printer's toner or ink cartridge needs to be replaced.
Text is missing	Verify whether the missing text uses a font that is valid and installed.
	Check to see whether the printer's toner or ink cartridge needs to be replaced.
Documents have garbled data or strange characters	Verify that the correct print driver is loaded on the printer.
	Reinstall the drivers because they could be corrupt.
	Check for bad cables.
	Check for electromagnetic interference.

Exam Prep Questions

1. You are a network administrator for Acme.com. You have a Windows Server 2003 computer that functions as a print server. You have a couple of groups that print large documents. When they print large documents, the server becomes extremely slow. You decide to use System Monitor to view the performance of the server. You determine that the average disk queue increases and that the hard drive becomes full. What should you do? (Choose the best answer.)

   - ○ **A.** Increase the amount of physical RAM on the server.

   - ○ **B.** Upgrade to a faster processor or install a second processor on the server.

   - ○ **C.** Install an additional hard drive on the server and move the spool folder to the new hard drive.

   - ○ **D.** Configure a printer pool so that you can print faster.

2. You are the administrator for Acme.com. You have a Printer1 connected to a Windows Server 2003 called Server1. You assign the Everyone group the Allow Print permission. When a user tries to print to \\Server1\Printer1, the user is unable to print. You soon discover that a few other users also cannot print to the same printer. You log on to a computer that has been mapped to the share printer and try to print several documents to the printer, but none will print. You soon discover the following message when you try to access the print queue:

   Printer1 on Server1 is unable to connect.

   You are able to ping the server. What do you need to do to ensure that the print jobs will be printed? (Choose the best answer.)

   - ○ **A.** On the domain controller, create a share printer that is published in Active Directory that points to \\Server1\Printer1.

   - ○ **B.** From a command prompt, run the net print \\Server1\printer1.

   - ○ **C.** You restart the Print Spooler service on the local computer.

   - ○ **D.** You restart the Print Spooler service on the print server.

3. You have a Windows Server 2003 sever called Server1. Connected to that printer, you have Printer1 configured with the default settings. You want the accounting department to have exclusive use of the printer between 9:00 a.m. and 3:00 p.m. During the rest of the time, anyone can use the printer. What should you do? (Choose two answers.)

   - ○ **A.** Modify printer 1 to be available only from 3:00 p.m. to 9:00 a.m.

   - ○ **B.** Modify Printer1 to be available only from 9:00 a.m. to 3:00 p.m.

   - ○ **C.** Share and configure a Printer2 to be available from 3:00 p.m. to 9:00 a.m. For the second printer, assign the Everyone group the Deny Print permissions and assign the accounting department to the second printer.

○ **D.** Share and configure a Printer2 to be available from 9:00 a.m. to 3:00 p.m. For the second printer, remove permissions for the Everyone group and assign the accounting department to the second printer. Instruct the users in the accounting group to use the second printer.

○ **E.** Create a printer pool. Assign the Accounting group to the pool.

4. You are a network administrator for Acme.com. You have a Windows Server 2003 named Server1 with a printer named Printer1. You get reports that print jobs for Printer1 are failing. You try to delete the print jobs, but you cannot delete the print jobs. What do you do to overcome this problem?

○ **A.** Increase the priority of Printer1.

○ **B.** Increase the priority of the print jobs.

○ **C.** Delete the files in the `C:\Windows\System32\Spool` folder.

○ **D.** Restart the spooler server on Server1.

○ **E.** Make sure that the printer has the correct driver.

5. You are the network administrator for Acme.com. You have a Windows Server 2003 named Server1 with a printer named Printer1. The president of the company wants his documents to take precedence over documents sent by other users. Of course, if a document is already printing, he wants the document to finish. What do you need to do?

○ **A.** Configure the printer permissions to take ownership of the print jobs.

○ **B.** Give full control to the president of the company.

○ **C.** Create a new printer and configure it to print to the print device. Assign a high priority to that printer. Configure the president's computer to the new printer.

○ **D.** Make the printer into a printer pool. Have the president print to one printer of the pool and everyone else print to the other one.

6. You are the network administrator for Acme.com. You have a Windows Server 2003 named Server1 with a printer named Printer1. When the marketing department prints, they complain that when they print large files that contain multiple complex graphics, the printing of the document is very slow and it pauses for several seconds between each page. How can you minimize the impact that large print jobs with complex graphics have while performing the least administrative effort?

○ **A.** Configure the printer to start printing after the last page is spooled.

○ **B.** Create a printer pool with two or more printers.

○ **C.** Increase the priority of the print job.

○ **D.** Increase the priority of the printer.

7. You are the network administrator for Acme.com. You have a Windows Server 2003 named Server1 with a printer named Printer1. Users report that print jobs being sent to the printer take a long time to print. You want to make sure that the server is performing well. So what would be your next step in identifying the problem?

   ○ **A.** Use task manager to look at the processor and memory usage.

   ○ **B.** Use Windows Explorer to look at the free disk space.

   ○ **C.** Use System Monitor to view the Print Queue\Jobs counter.

   ○ **D.** Use System Monitor to view the Disk\Disk Queue counter.

Answers to Exam Prep Questions

1. **Answer C is correct.** When the large print jobs are being printed, the print jobs stored within the spool folder are filling up the hard drive. As a result, performance of the entire machine slows down. Adding RAM (answer A) or increasing the processor speed (answer B) will not increase the performance of the system when the hard drive fills up. Therefore, you need to move the spool folder to a different hard drive so that the system drive does not fill up. Answer D is incorrect because it is not because the printers cannot keep up, but because the hard drive is full.

2. **Answer D is correct.** If the print spooler stalls, you will need to stop and restart the service. After deleting the queues, the users will need to resubmit their print jobs. Of course, because this affects more than one user, the problem is with one server and not the local computer. Therefore, answer C is incorrect. Answer A is incorrect because creating a share printer and publishing it in Active Directory does not fix the real problem. Answer B is incorrect because running a net command will not fix any printer problems.

3. **Answer D is correct.** You already have a printer that allows everyone to print to it at any time. First, you need to modify the first printer so that it is only available 3:00 p.m. to 9:00 a.m. You then need to create a new printer that is available from 9:00 a.m. to 3:00 p.m. and that only the accountants can print to. You would then have to instruct the accounting department to print to the printer. Answers A and B do not configure a second printer for the accountants to use. Answer C is incorrect because it needs to be available from 9 a.m. to 3 p.m., not 3 p.m. to 9 a.m. Answer E is incorrect because creating a printer pool is used for servicing heavy loads by using two or more printers working together to service a queue.

4. **Answer D is correct.** The print spooler service loads files to memory for printing from the print queue. Sometimes, you need to stop and restart the service to delete the queue. Answers A and B are incorrect because increasing or decreasing priorities will not fix the problem where the print spooler is having problems. Answer C is incorrect because it will not restart the print spooler, which is the main problem. Answer E is incorrect because the incorrect driver will give strange characters and such.

5. **Answer C is correct.** By assigning two different printers that point to the same print device, you can assign different priorities to each one. By assigning different users to the two printers, you can have one group of people with a higher priority than other users. Answer A is incorrect because there is no permission to take ownership of a print job, only a print device. Answer B is incorrect because giving full control will allow him to manage print devices and print jobs but would not give a higher priority. Of course, with those permissions, he could assign himself a higher priority, but that's something you typically don't want to give any of your users. Answer D is incorrect because it would require two printers. Printer pools are used to split a busy print queue among multiple printers.

6. **Answer A is correct.** When you configure spooling options, you specify whether print jobs are spooled or sent directly to the printer. Spooling means that the print jobs are saved to disk in a queue before they are sent to the printer. In the Advanced tab, you can keep the Start Printing Immediately option selected or you can choose the Start Printing After Last Page is Spooled option. If you choose the latter option, a smaller print job that finishes spooling first will print before the large print job. Answer B is not the best answer because multiple large print jobs would also cause problems on multiple printer pools. It is also not cost effective. Answer C is incorrect because increasing the priority of a print job would not help on every print job in the future. Answer D is incorrect because you cannot increase the priority of the printer.

7. **Answer C is correct.** The Print Queue\Jobs counter specifies the current number of print jobs that are pending in the print queue. If processor, memory or disk usage is high, your entire system would be slow, not just printing. You will only have to look at the free disk space if the performance is slow or print jobs are having problems. Answer A is incorrect because processor and memory usage only gives overall performance, not performance measures specific to printing. Answer B is incorrect because although lack of free disk space may cause problems, it is not the best indicator for performance. Answer D is incorrect because these settings will only give you disk performance.

Need to Know More?

For more information about printing with Windows Server 2003, see the following articles from the Windows Server 2003 Technical Library and Windows Server 2003 Product Help at the Microsoft TechNet website (`http://technet.microsoft.com`):

▶ "Printer Connectivity Technical Overview"

▶ "Administering Printing"

▶ "Printing Best Practices"

▶ "Printing Concepts"

▶ "Printing Troubleshooting"

CHAPTER EIGHT

Managing Access to Objects in Organizational Units

Terms you'll need to understand:

✓ Permission

✓ Access control list

✓ Standard permission

✓ Explicit permission

✓ Effective permission

✓ Inheritance

✓ Owner

✓ Delegate administrative control

Techniques/concepts you'll need to master:

✓ Differentiate rights and permissions.

✓ Using the Active Directory Users and Computer console, modify the permissions of an Active Directory object.

✓ Using the Active Directory Users and Computer console, view the effective permissions of an Active Directory object.

✓ Given a scenario of permissions assigned to Active Directory objects, calculate the effective permissions.

✓ Use the Delegate Control wizard to assign permissions to an Active Directory container.

✓ Move an Active Directory to another container.

✓ Explain the permissions of an object when the object is moved from one container to another container.

Because Active Directory is used to organize your resources, including all the users, and Active Directory is a key component in authentication and authorization, you need to know how to manage the objects within Active Directory. By properly managing Active Directory, you will make sure that a user has the proper rights and permissions to do his or her job without having too many rights or permissions that would cause problems with the network resources or become a security breach.

Active Directory Permissions

A permission defines the type of access granted to an object or object attribute. Users, printers, and organizational units are examples of objects in Active Directory. Every object in Active Directory has an owner who controls how permissions are set on an object and to whom permissions are assigned. To keep track of these permissions, each object has an access control list (ACL), which lists each user who has access to the object and the type of access he has to the object. The list of user access permissions is called the discretionary access control list (DACL).

Standard permissions are the most common and frequently assigned permissions that apply to an entire object. Assigning standard permissions is sufficient for most day-to-day administrative tasks (see Table 8.1). The standard permissions are divided into special permissions, which provide a finer degree of control.

TABLE 8.1 Active Directory Standard Permissions

Object Permission	Description
Full Control	Contains all permissions for the object, including changing permissions and take ownership.
Read	Users can view objects and object attributes, including the object owner and the Active Directory permissions.
Write	Enables users to change all object attributes.
Create All Child Objects	Enables users to add any child object to an OU.
Delete All Child Objects	Enables users to delete any child object from an OU.

Explicit permissions are those specifically given to the object when the object is created or assigned by another user. By default, when you assign explicit permissions to a container such as a domain or organizational unit that holds other objects, permissions flow down to its child objects. Those permissions that flow down are known as *inherited* permissions. By using inherited permissions, you can manage objects more easily and can ensure consistency of permissions among all objects within a given container.

To add or change permissions for an object, do the following:

1. Using the Active Directory Users and Computers console, enable the Advanced Features option. **Note: To see the Security tab, you have to enable Advanced Features.** To do this, right-click the object, select the Properties option, and click on the Security tab.

2. To add a new permission, click the Add button, click the user account or group to which you want to assign permissions, and then click Add. Click on the OK button.

3. In the permission box, click on the Allow or Deny check box for each permission that you want to add or remove. See Figure 8.1.

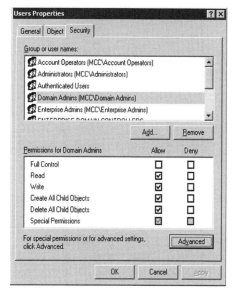

FIGURE 8.1 If you have enabled Advanced Features in Active Directory Users and Computers console, you can modify the DACL of an Active Directory object.

To view special permissions, do the following:

1. Right-click the object, click on the Security tab, and click on the Advanced button.

2. In the Access Control Settings dialog box on the Permission tab, click the entries that you want to view, and click on the View/Edit button.

3. In the Apply Onto: box, select where the permissions are to be applied.

4. Select or deselect the desired permissions (see Figure 8.2).

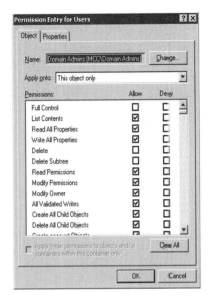

FIGURE 8.2 Special permissions of an Active Directory object.

The permission can be allowed or denied for each user or group. To explicitly allow or deny the permission, click the appropriate check box. If a check box is shaded, the permission was granted to the user or group for a container that the object is in and the permission was inherited in the container you are viewing. If the allow or deny box is not checked for a permission, the permission may still be granted for a user or group. To verify this, you would have to check which groups the user or group is a member of to determine if the rights are granted or denied.

When permission has not been granted (explicitly allowed or inherited), it is implicitly denied. For example, if a Sales group is the only identity that is assigned the Read permission, everyone who is not part of the Sales group is implicitly denied.

Explicit or inherited Deny permissions override the same level of inherited permissions that are assigned to a user or group, even Full Control. So a user might be a member of several groups that have been assigned all permissions including Full Control to an Active Directory object (and possibly the user himself is also assigned Full Control), but if the user or one of the groups that the user is a member of is assigned a deny permission, the deny permission will overwrite the assigned permissions.

EXAM ALERT

You should use the Deny permission only when it is necessary to remove a permission that a user is granted by being a member of a group.

In general, when permissions are set on a parent object, new objects inherit the permissions of the parent. You can remove inherited permissions. To turn off inherited permissions from flowing from the parent object, follow these steps:

1. Right-click the object and select Properties.

2. Select the Security tab.

3. Deselect the Allow inheritable permissions from the parent to propagate to this object and all child objects option (see Figure 8.3).

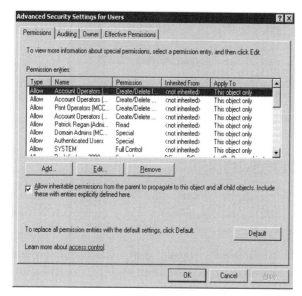

FIGURE 8.3 By going into advanced security, you can select if an object can inherit permissions from the parent object.

You then have the option to copy or remove the permission. If you copy the permission, all permissions from above will be copied and explicitly assigned to the object. If you remove the permissions, only the permissions that are explicitly defined at that level will be applied (see Figure 8.4).

To reenable inheritance, select the Allow inheritable permissions from the parent to propagate to this object and all child objects option.

If you manually assign a standard permission on an organizational unit, the permission applies only to the organizational unit, not to the objects in the organizational unit. The two exceptions to the rule are the Create All Child Objects and Delete All Child Objects permissions. If you would like to modify whether permissions are inherit or not, use the Advanced Security settings at the organizational unit level to modify the permissions granted to This object and all child objects. The default selection is This object and all child objects when you assign permission by using the Delegation of Control Wizard. The Delegation of Control Wizard is covered later in this chapter.

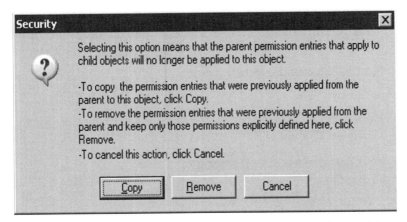

FIGURE 8.4 If you deselect the Allow inheritable permission from the parent to propagate to this object option, you will then have the option to copy the permissions from the parent or remove the permissions.

Effective Permissions

When a user is a member of a group, he or she will also get the permissions assigned to that group. When configuring permissions, it is preferable to assign permissions to groups rather than to individual users.

Because a user can be a member of multiple groups, it is possible that a user can be assigned permissions that are assigned to the user and also permissions assigned to the groups that the user is a member of for the same Active Directory object or objects. If they are permissions that have been allowed, the permissions are cumulative.

You can use the Effective Permissions tool to determine what the cumulative permissions for an Active Directory object are. To retrieve information about effective permissions in Active Directory, you must have permission to read membership information. Domain administrators have permission to read membership information on all objects. Local accounts, including local administrators, on a workstation or a standalone server cannot read the membership permission for a domain user. Authenticated domain users can read membership information only when the domain is in pre-Windows 2000 functional level.

To view the effective permission for an Active Directory object, follow these steps:

1. Right-click the object and select Properties.

2. Select the Security tab.

3. Click the Advanced button.

4. Select the Effective Permissions tab.

5. Click the Select button to specify the user or group that you are checking (see Figure 8.5).

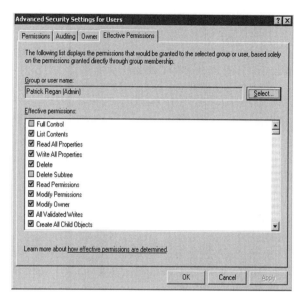

FIGURE 8.5 By selecting the Effective Permissions tab in Advanced Security, you can view a group or user's effective permissions for an Active Directory object.

Ownership

The person who creates the object automatically becomes the owner by default and has full control over the object, even if the ACL does not grant the owner access. If a member of the Administrator group creates an object or takes ownership of an object, the Administrators group becomes the object group. A member of the Domain Administrator group has the ability to take ownership of any object in the domain and then change permissions.

Ownership can be transferred in the following ways:

▶ The current owner can grant to take ownership permission to other users, allowing those users to take ownership at any time.

▶ An administrator can take ownership of any object under his or her administrative control. For example, if an employee leaves the company suddenly, the administrator can take control of the employee's files.

Although administrators can take ownership, they cannot transfer ownership to others. This restriction keeps administrators accountable for their actions.

To take ownership of an object, do the following:

1. Right-click the object, select Properties option, and click on the Security tab.

2. Click on the Advanced button, click the Owner tab, and click your user account.

3. Click on the OK button to close the Access Control Settings dialog box, and click on the OK button to close the object window.

Delegating Control of Organizational Units

The best way to give sufficient permission to an organizational unit is to delegate administrative control to the container (decentralized administration) so that the user or group will have administrative control for the OU and the objects in it. To delegate control to an OU, run the Delegation of Control Wizard. To start the Wizard, right-click the desired OU and select Delegate Control (see Figure 8.6). You can then select the user or group to which you want to delegate control, the organizational units and objects you want to grant those users the right to control, and the permissions to access and modify objects. For example, a user can be given the right to modify the Owner of Accounts property, without being granted the right to delete accounts in that OU. Another example is the ability to reset passwords for users within the organizational unit.

Because you use the Delegation of Control Wizards to assign permissions for a user or group to manage an organizational unit, you must then give the users a way to manage their organizational unit. Unless you want to give users access to the domain controller, you would most likely install the Active Directory administrative tools on a user's workstation and create a custom MMC console that only shows the organizational unit that the user is managing.

The domain administrator can create a custom management console for Active Directory administration by starting a MMC and adding the Active Directory Users and Computers snap-in. The domain administrator would then right-click the organizational unit and select New window from here.

The domain administrators can also create taskpads by right-clicking an organizational unit and then selecting the option to create a New taskpad view. After the wizard is executed, the administrator can run the New Task Wizard to create icons that the user can click to perform tasks.

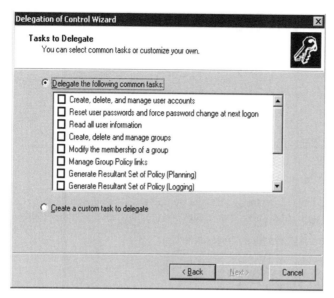

FIGURE 8.6 Use the Delegation of Control Wizard to assign permissions to an Active Directory container.

Moving Active Directory Objects

From time to time, you might need to move objects between organizational units, such as when someone moves to a different department. To move an object in an Active Directory domain, right-click the object and select Move. Then specify the new location and click OK.

When you move an object, permissions that have been explicitly assigned to the object will remain the same. However, when an object is moved, it will inherit the permissions from the new organizational unit and will not inherit the permissions from the old organizational unit. This is because the permissions are assigned explicitly to a container, which inherits down to the objects in the container.

Exam Prep Questions

1. Which of the following are not Active Directory standard permissions?

    ○ **A.** Full control

    ○ **B.** Read

    ○ **C.** Write

    ○ **D.** Modify all child objects

2. To modify permissions on an Active Directory object, what do you have to do?

    ○ **A.** Within the Active Directory Users and Computers console, you have to enable Advanced Features. Then right-click the object and select Properties.

    ○ **B.** Use the Active Directory permissions editor.

    ○ **C.** In regedit, select the Advanced Features option.

    ○ **D.** All three of the above.

3. You are the administrator of the Acme Corporation domain. Jack is a member of the Sales and Executive group. You have assigned the following permissions to the NY Organizational unit:

Jack	No permissions assigned
Sales group	Allow Read permission
Executive group	Allow Read and Write permission

    When Jack logs in, what is Jack's effective permission for the John account, which is located in the NY organizational unit?

    ○ **A.** Jack has no permissions to the John account.

    ○ **B.** Jack has Allow Read permission.

    ○ **C.** Jack has Allow Read and Write permission.

    ○ **D.** Jack has full control.

4. You are the administrator of the Acme Corporation domain. Jack is a member of the Sales and Executive group. You have assigned the following permissions to the NY Organizational unit:

Jack	Deny Read and Write permission
Sales group	Allow Read permission
Executive group	Allow Full Control

When Jack logs in, what is Jack's effective permission for the John account, which is located in the NY organizational unit?

- ○ **A.** Jack has no permissions to the John account.
- ○ **B.** Jack has Allow Read permission.
- ○ **C.** Jack has Allow Read and Write permission.
- ○ **D.** Jack has full control.

5. Who is the initial owner when a user account is created in Active Directory?

- ○ **A.** The administrator
- ○ **B.** The domain administrator
- ○ **C.** The user who creates the account
- ○ **D.** The actual user being created

6. Who can take ownership of an Active Directory account? (Choose all that apply.)

- ○ **A.** Any user who has the Take ownership permission
- ○ **B.** Any user who has Full Control of an object
- ○ **C.** Domain administrators
- ○ **D.** The De Facto user

7. In your domain, you have a Sales organizational unit. You want your sales manager to have the ability to change passwords for all users within the Sales organizational unit. What should you do without giving too many rights or permissions?

- ○ **A.** Right-click the Sales organization and enable the Change password option on the security tab.
- ○ **B.** Right-click the Sales organizational unit and run the Delegation of Control Wizard.
- ○ **C.** Assign the sales manager to the Domain Admin group.
- ○ **D.** Assign the sales manager to the Account Operator group.

8. You are the administrator of the Acme Corporation domain. John has the Allow Read and Write permissions for the Sales organizational unit and Allow Read permission to the Executive organizational units. If you move Jack's user account from the Sales organizational unit to the Executive organizational unit, what is John's permission to Jack's account?

- ○ **A.** No permissions
- ○ **B.** Read permission

    ○ **C.** Read and write permission

    ○ **D.** Full control permission

9. You are the administrator of the Acme Corporation domain. The Jack account is located in the Sales organizational unit. John has the Allow Read and Write permissions for the Sales organizational unit and Allow Read permission to the Executive organizational units. John has also been assigned the implicit Allow Full Control assigned to the Jack account. If you move Jack's user account from the Sales organizational unit to the Executive organization un t, what is John's permission to Jack's account?

    ○ **A.** No permissions

    ○ **B.** Read permission

    ○ **C.** Read and write permission

    ○ **D.** Full control permission

Answers to Exam Prep Questions

1. **Answer D is correct.** The standard permissions include Full Control (answer A), Read (answer B), Write (answer C), Create All Child Objects, and Delete All Child Objects. Therefore, the Modify all child objects is not a standard permission.

2. **Answer A is correct.** To see the Security tab, you have to enable Advanced Features. Then when you right-click the object and select properties, you can modify the security permissions. Answer B is incorrect because there is no such thing as an Active Directory permissions ed tor. Answer C is incorrect because you do not use the Registry editor (regedit) to modify Active Directory permissions. Because B and C are not correct, Answer D is not correct.

3. **Answer C is correct.** Because a user can be a member of multiple groups, it is possible that a user can be assigned permissions that are assigned to the user and permissions assigned to the groups that the user is a member of for the same Active Directory object or objects. If they are permissions that have been allowed, the permissions are cumulative. Because Jack is a member of the Sales and Executive group, you can combine all of the permissions. Because they are cumulative, Jack will have Read and Write permission. Answers A and B are not correct because they do not include both the Read and Write permission. Answer D is not correct because they will not have additional permissions beyond read and write.

4. **Answer A is correct.** Because a user can be a member of multiple groups, it is possible that a user can be assigned permissions that are assigned to the user and permissions assigned to the groups that the user is a member of for the same Active Directory object or objects. If they are permissions that have been allowed, the permissions are cumulative. If the user or one of the groups that the user is a member of is assigned a

deny permission, the deny permission will overwrite the assigned permissions. Because Jack has been assigned Deny read and write permission, Jack has no permissions. Answers B, C, and D are incorrect because they show him having permissions.

5. **Answer C is correct.** The user who creates an object is the owner. Although the administrator and domain administrators have the ability to take ownership of an object, he or she is not the initial owner. In addition, the user is not the owner of his own account, although he does have full permissions.

6. **Answers A, B, and C are correct.** Anyone who has Take Ownership permission of an object can take ownership of an object. Full Control includes Take Ownership. Domain administrators also can take ownership of any object because they have the take ownership right. Answer D is incorrect because the user does not necessarily have the take ownership permissions.

7. **Answer B is correct.** The easiest way to assign permission to an organizational unit is to use the Delegation of Control Wizard. When you run the Wizard, you can assign only the change password permission. This way, the user will not have any additional permissions. Answer A is incorrect because there is no change password option on the Security tab. If you assign the users to the domain admin or account operator groups, they will have additional permissions besides the change password permission.

8. **Answer B is correct.** If you move an object, it will inherit the permissions from the new organizational unit and will not inherit the permissions from the old organizational unit. Therefore, because John has the Read permission to the new organizational unit, the Read permission will flow down to the object, giving John read permission to the object also. Answer A is incorrect because the user does have Read permission. Answers C and D are incorrect because they do not have Write or Full Control permissions.

9. **Answer D is correct.** When you move an object, permissions that have been explicitly assigned to the object will remain the same. Therefore, John has Full Control permission. Therefore, answers A, B, and C are wrong.

Need to Know More?

1. For more information about printing with Windows Server 2003, see the following articles from the Windows Server 2003 Technical Library and Windows Server 2003 Product Help in the Microsoft TechNet website at http://technet.microsoft.com:

   ▶ "Active Directory Users, Computers, and Groups"

   ▶ "Active Directory Object Permissions"

   ▶ "Delegate Control of an Organizational Unit"

   ▶ "Access Control"

CHAPTER NINE

Implementing Group Policy

Terms you'll need to understand:

✓ Group policy objects (GPOs)

✓ Group Policy Object Editor

✓ Group Policy Management Console (GPMC)

Techniques/concepts you'll need to master:

✓ Creating and linking GPOs to a container (site, domain, or organizational unit)

✓ Configuring the No Override and Block inheritance

✓ Modifying GPOs in a domain

✓ Modifying GPO permissions

One of the most powerful features of Active Directory is group policies. Group policies enable IT administrators to automate one-to-many management of users and computers, simplifying administrative tasks and reducing IT costs. Administrators can efficiently implement security settings, enforce IT policies, and distribute software consistently across a given site, domain, or range of organizational units.

Introduction to Group Policies

Group policies objects (GPOs) are collections of user and computer configuration settings that specify how programs, network resources, and the operating system work for users and computers in an organization. Settings include the following:

- *System settings*—Application settings, desktop appearance, and behavior of system services

- *Security settings*—Local computer, domain, and network security settings

- *Software installation settings*—Management of software installation, updates, and removal

- *Script settings*—Scripts for when a computer starts or shuts down and when a user logs on and off

- *Folder redirection settings*—Storage for users' folders on the network

Group policies can be set locally on the workstation (Windows 2000 Professional or Windows XP) or a member server (Windows 2000 or Windows Server 2003), or they can be set at different levels (site, domain, or organizational unit) within Active Directory. The group policies at the site, domain, or organizational unit level are often referred collectively as nonlocal. Group policies are not supported on Microsoft Windows 95, Windows 98, Windows Millennium Edition (Windows Me), or Microsoft Windows NT.

You can also create a GPO and link the GPO to multiple containers, such as organizational units. Because the GPO is its own object, you can also delete a link without deleting the GPO.

Because the Active Directory is a structured hierarchy, there are different levels of policies that enable you to customize your configuration. The different levels of policies are applied in the following order:

1. Local policy object

2. Site Group policy objects, in administratively specified order

3. Domain group policy objects, in administratively specified order

4. Organizational unit group policy objects, from the highest to lowest organizational unit and in administratively specified order

> **EXAM ALERT**
>
> To help remember the order, you can use the LSDOU acronym to remember the order that group policies are applied, which stands for
>
> **L**ocal
>
> **S**ite
>
> **D**omain
>
> **O**rganization Unit

Each computer that is running Windows 2000, Windows XP, or Windows Server 2003 (member server) has one local policy object, which can be stored on individual computers regardless of whether they are part of an Active Directory environment or a networked environment. These settings can be overwritten by any nonlocal group policies (sites, domains, and organizational unit). The local group policy can be accessed using the Group Policy Object Editor MMC snap-in or by running the Local Security Policy program in the Administrative Tools group. The disadvantage of using a local group policy appears if you need to specify settings for multiple computers. To do this using a local group policy, you must configure each computer's local group policy individually.

The group policy settings implemented using Active Directory, on the other hand, are inherited, cumulative, and affect all computers and user accounts in the Active Directory container (domains and organizational units) with which the group policy is associated. If you have settings that conflict with each other, the later policies will generally overwrite the earlier policies. Therefore, because GPOs are processed in the site, domain, and OU order, settings in the OU group policy will overwrite any settings in the other policies. For example, say that you have a site group policy, two domain group policies, one parent organizational unit, and three child organizational unit group policies that are executed in the following order:

1. Site group policy

2. First-listed domain group policy (if any settings from the first domain group policy are in conflict with the next listed domain group policy, the last domain policy to be applied will overwrite the settings from any earlier ones)

3. Parent organizational unit group policy

4. Each child organizational unit group policies in the order in which they are listed

As each group policy is executed, it overwrites any previous settings that are in conflict. If you do not want settings to be overwritten, you must block policy inheritance or enable no override, which is discussed later in this chapter.

By default, two nonlocal GPOs are created in Active Directory:

▶ *Default Domain Policy*—Linked to the domain and affects all users and computers in the domain, including the domain controllers through group policy inheritance.

▶ *Default Domain Controller Policy*—Linked to the Domain Controllers OU. It generally affects only domain controllers because computer accounts for domain controllers are kept in the Domain Controllers OU.

The Default Domain Policy Object contains Account Policies (Password, Account Lockout, and Kerberos policies), which are defined on a domain basis only. This is a very important consideration because GPOs for account settings defined for lower-level OUs will not work for domain users. Settings at lower-level OUs take effect if users log on locally (using a local account) to a computer, but not if logging on to the domain. In addition, because domain controllers do not have local accounts as member servers and workstations do, account policies that are defined in the default domain controllers organizational unit have no effect.

Domain controllers pull some security settings only from the Domain container. Because domain controllers share the same account database for the domain, certain security settings must be set uniformly on all domain controllers, whether the domain controller is in the domain controller organizational unit or not. This ensures that all members of the domain have a consistent experience regardless of which domain controller they use to log on.

Modifying Policy Settings

To organize and manage the group policy settings in each GPO, you use the Group Policy Object Editor. To open the Group Policy Object Editor for the local computer policy, perform the following steps:

1. Open the Microsoft Management Console (MMC) by clicking on the Start button, selecting the Run option, and executing MMC.

2. Open the File menu and select Add/Remove Snap-in.

3. In the Add/Remove Snap-in dialog box, in the Standalone tab, click Add.

4. In the Add Standalone Snap-in dialog box, click the Group Policy Object Editor, and then click Add.

5. In the Group Policy Object, make sure that Local Computer is selected. Click the Finish button.

6. For the Add Standalone Snap-in box, click the Close button.

7. In the Add/Remove Snap-in dialog box, click OK.

Figure 9.1 shows the local policy with the Group Policy Object Editor.

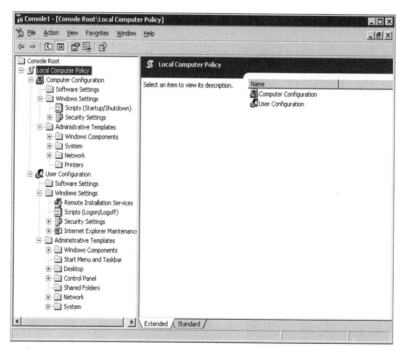

FIGURE 9.1 Local policy with the Group Policy Object Editor.

To open a Group Policy Object Editor for a site, perform the following steps:

1. Click Start, point to Administrative Tools, and then click Active Directory Sites and Services.

2. In the console tree, right-click the site you want to set group policy for, and then click Properties.

3. Click the Group Policy tab, click an entry in the Group Policy Object Links list to select an existing GPO, and then click Edit. (Or, click New to create a new GPO, and then click Edit.)

To open the Group Policy Object Editor for a domain or organizational unit, complete the following steps:

1. Click Start, point to Administrative Tools, and then click Active Directory Users and Computers.

2. In the console tree, right-click the domain or OU you want to set group policy for, and then click Properties.

3. Click the Group Policy tab, click an entry in the Group Policy Object Links list to select an existing GPO, and then click Edit (see Figure 9.2). (Or, click New to create a new GPO, and then click Edit.)

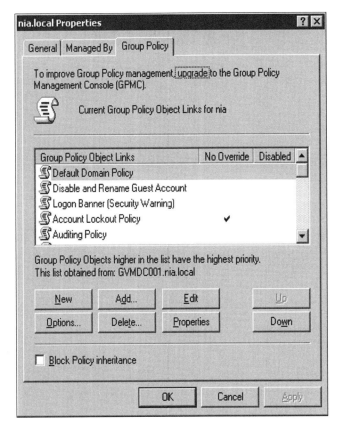

FIGURE 9.2 When you right-click a container in Active Directory Users and Computers and select Properties, you can use the Group Policy tab to view all group policies assigned to the container.

Figure 9.3 shows a nonlocal group policy with the Group Policy Object Editor.

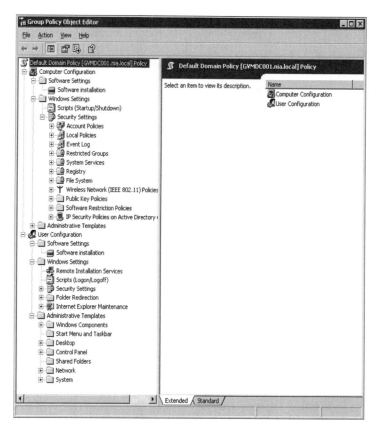

FIGURE 9.3   The Default Domain Policy (nonlocal) with the Group Policy Object Editor.

Another way to manage all nonlocal group policies is to load the Group Policy Management Console (GPMC), which can be downloaded and installed from Microsoft at `http://www.microsoft.com/windowsserver2003/gpmc/gpmcintro.mspx`.

After installing the Group Policy Management Console, you can then open Administrative Tools to see all nonlocal GPOs and where they are applied (see Figure 9.4). You can then see what the settings are for each group policy by using the GUI interface (see Figure 9.5), and you can open the GPO Editor by right-clicking the GPO and selecting Edit.

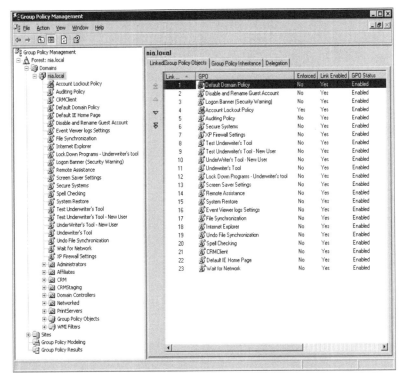

FIGURE 9.4   Using the Group Policy Management Console to organize all nonlocal group policies within an Active Directory Forest.

NOTE

The GPMC can be used to manage group policy in a Windows 2000 domain, but it cannot be installed on a Windows 2000 computer. It can be installed on a Windows XP Professional computer if .NET Framework 1.1 (or better) is installed.

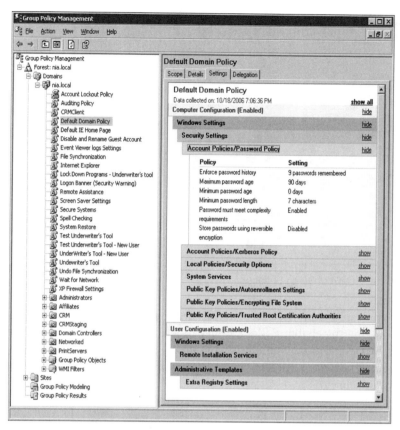

FIGURE 9.5 Using the Group Policy Management Console to see current settings for GPO.

Controlling Inheritance

Sometimes, you might want to enforce a policy so that an earlier executed policy is not overwritten by the policies executed later. To maintain these settings, open the Properties of the GPO, click the Options button, and select No Override (see Figure 9.6). You typically use this in one of the higher levels such as the site or domain GPO to make sure that the administrators of the OUs do not overwrite settings that you want to assign to everyone.

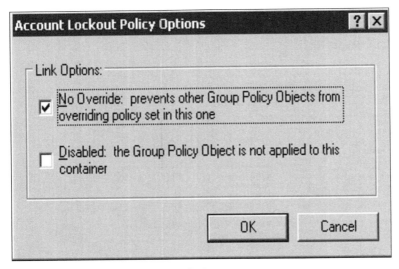

FIGURE 9.6 Account Lockout Policy Options.

In addition, you can prevent a child container from inheriting any GPOs from the parent container by enabling Block Policy inheritance on the child container. This will then stop the group policies from flowing into the lower OUs. This is set by opening the properties of the group policy and selecting the Block Policy Inheritance option.

EXAM ALERT

Block inheritance does not prevent policy that has the no override option applied to it. Enforced GPOs are always applied and cannot be blocked.

User and Computer Configuration Settings

group policy settings are divided into two main areas—User Configuration and Computer Configuration. The user configuration settings modify the HKEY_CURRENT_USER hive of the registry. Group policy settings for users include software settings, Windows settings, desktop settings, security settings, application settings, folder redirection options, and user logon and logoff scripts.

The computer configuration settings modify the HKEY_LOCAL_MACHINE hive of the registry. Group policy settings control how the operating system behaves, security settings, computer startup and shutdown scripts, configuration of Windows components, computer-assigned application options, and application settings.

NOTE

> Active Directory updates changes to group policies to domain controllers every five minutes and to all Windows XP, 2000, and 2003 computers that are not domain controllers every 90 minutes (+/– 30 minutes). These updates are requested by the computer, and administrators can modify the intervals. Security settings are refreshed at least every 16 hours, whether they have changed or not.

Attributes of a GPO Link

You can enable, disable, enforce, and group GPO links. Typically after a GPO is linked and enabled, you might want to disable the GPO link so that you can troubleshoot a GPO. To disable a link, open the properties of the group policy. Then click the Options button. Then select the Disabled option. For example, you can temporarily disable link if you suspect a conflict from one GPO with another GPO.

Group Policy Permissions

By default, once you link a GPO to an Active Directory container, every user and computer object within that container will receive the settings configured in that GPO. This is because, just like Active Directory objects, group policies also have an Access Control List (ACL) that specifies who is affected by the group policy and who can make changes to the group policy (see Figure 9.7).

By default, only members of Domain Administrators, Enterprise Administrators, and Group Policy Creator Owners groups can create new group policy objects. If the Domain Administrator wants a non-administrator or group to be able to create group policy objects, that user or group can be added to the Group Policy Creator Owners security group. When a non-administrator who is a member of the Group Policy Creator Owners group creates a group policy object, that user becomes the creator and owner of the group policy object and can edit the object.

For a group policy to apply to a person, the person must have Apply Group Policy and Read Permission for the policy. By default, Authenticated Users have read access and apply group policy. If you have a special need for a group policy to apply to certain users and not others, you can remove authenticated users and add the group or users you want it to apply to. You can also use the Deny Apply Group Policy permission so that it will not apply to that individual.

NOTE

> The process of managing GPO application via user/group permissions is called *filtering*.

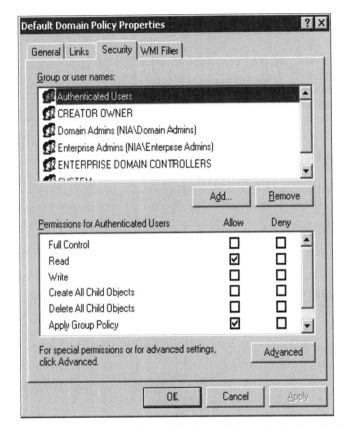

FIGURE 9.7 The permissions of the Default Domain Policy (nonlocal).

Back Up, Restore, and Import GPO

You can use the GPMC to back up and restore GPOs. As with any backup, it would be used in case of corruption of the GPOs. To back up an individual GPO, right-click and select Backup and provide a location. To back up all policies, right-click the Group Policy Objects folder, select Back Up All Policies, and provide a location.

If you delete a GPO by mistake or you want to restore settings that were previously set, you can use the Group Policy Management console to restore the GPO.

Follow these steps to restore a previous version of an existing GPO:

1. Open Group Policy Management.

2. In the console tree, locate Group Policy Objects in the forest and domain containing the GPO that you want to restore.

3. Double-click Group Policy Objects, right-click the GPO you want to restore, and then click Restore from Backup.

4. When the Restore Group Policy Object Wizard appears, follow the instructions and provide the appropriate information about the GPO that you want to restore, and then click Finish.

5. After the Restore Group Policy Object Wizard completes the restore operation, click OK.

To restore a deleted GPO:

1. Open Group Policy Management.

2. In the console tree, locate Group Policy Objects in the forest and domain containing the GPO that you want to restore.

3. Right-click Group Policy Objects, and then choose Manage Backups.

4. In the Manage Backups dialog box, type the path to the backup folder in the Backup Location box. You can also use Browse to locate the backup folder.

5. In the Backed Up GPOs box, select the GPO that you want to restore from the list of GPO backups shown, and then click Restore.

6. When prompted to confirm the restore operation, click OK.

NOTE

When you back up the System State on a domain controller, you are also backing up Group Policies.

If you have several organizational units with similar requirements, you can import settings into a GPO from another GPO and then customize the new GPO as needed. When you run the Import Settings Wizard, you will have a chance to review the settings during the import operation so that if you need to make adjustments to UNC paths or Windows Security groups because of different destination GPOs, you have the opportunity. To start the Import Settings Wizard, open the Group Policy Management console. In the console tree, double-click Group Policy Objects in the forest and domain containing the group policy object (GPO) into which you want to import settings. Then Right-click the target GPO and select Import Settings.

EXAM ALERT

Importing settings into an existing GPO will overwrite all current settings.

Exam Prep Questions

1. GPOs cannot be linked to which of the following?

   ○ **A.** Site

   ○ **B.** Domain

   ○ **C.** First Level Organizational units

   ○ **D.** Second Level Organizational Units

   ○ **E.** Groups

2. When you want to make sure that a domain GPO is not overwritten by an organizational unit GPO, what should you do?

   ○ **A.** Make sure that the organizational unit GPO is listed before the domain GPO

   ○ **B.** Make sure to disable the organizational unit

   ○ **C.** Make sure that the No Override option is selected for the domain GPO

   ○ **D.** Enable block nheritance at the organizational unit

3. What permissions must a user have for a GPO to be linked? (Choose two.)

   ○ **A.** Read

   ○ **B.** Write

   ○ **C.** Apply group policy

   ○ **D.** Administrative

4. If you do not want one user to be affected by a group policy, what can you do?

   ○ **A.** Create a new GPO that is assigned to the one user.

   ○ **B.** Modify the GPO group policy.

   ○ **C.** Add the user to the administrators group.

   ○ **D.** Modify the GPO permissions so that the user is denied the Apply Group Policy permission to the GPO.

5. Which of the following can be affected by Group Policies?

   ○ **A.** Windows Me

   ○ **B.** Windows NT

   ○ **C.** Windows XP

   ○ **D.** Windows 98

6. By default, if a group policy is in conflict with another group policy, what happens?

    ○ **A.** The first group policy stays in effect.

    ○ **B.** The second GPO overwrites any settings from the first group policy.

    ○ **C.** If the user is an administrator, the first group policy stays in effect.

    ○ **D.** The domain level group policy stays in effect.

Answers to Exam Prep Questions

1. **Answer E is correct.** GPOs can be linked to site, domain, or organizational unit (any level). Although a group lists users, it does not contain users; therefore, it is not a container, and it cannot be used to link GPOs.

2. **Answer C is correct.** To make sure that a GPO is not overwritten by GPOs being executed later, you have to use the No Override option.

3. **Answers A and C are correct.** To execute a GPO, a user must have Read and Apply group permission.

4. **Answer D is correct.** To execute a GPO, a user must have Read and Apply group policy. However, if you deny Apply Group policy, the group policy will not execute for the user even if that user has the Read and Apply Group policy permissions because the deny takes precedence.

5. **Answer C is correct.** Group policies can affect Windows 2000, Windows Server 2003, and Windows XP machines. It does not affect Windows 95, Windows 98, Windows Millennium, and Windows NT machines.

6. **Answer B is correct.** When a group policy is executed that conflicts with a group policy that was executed earlier, the settings would be overwritten. The exception would be if you selected the No Override option.

Need to Know More?

For more information about using Group Policies, see the following articles from the Windows Server 2003 Technical Library and Windows Server 2003 Product Help in the Microsoft TechNet website (`http://technet.microsoft.com`):

▶ "Administering Group Policy with Group Policy Management Console Abstract"

▶ "Administering Group Policy with Group Policy Management Console"

CHAPTER TEN

Managing the User Environment by Using Group Policy

Terms you'll need to understand:

✓ Logon script

✓ Logoff script

✓ Restricted groups

✓ Folder redirection

✓ Administrative templates

✓ Resultant Set of Policy

Techniques/concepts you'll need to master:

✓ After a group policy is enabled, disable the group policy.

✓ Assign a script using group policy.

✓ Restrict group membership using group policies.

✓ Enable or disable access to software using group policies.

✓ Enable folder redirection using group policies.

✓ Use Administrative templates to define the end-user experience.

✓ Use gpupdate to refresh group policies.

✓ Use gpresults and the Group Policy Management console to view the Resultant Set of Policy.

As mentioned in Chapter 9, "Implementing Group Policy," group policies can be used to manage the user environment. If you want to lock down the interface so that it is more secure or create a standard look and feel to the desktop, you would use group policies. If you want to run certain applications during bootup or change the default location for My Documents, you would use group policies.

Enabling and Disabling Group Policy Settings

After you enable group policies, you may decide that a group policy causes some network or application problem. Therefore, you may decide to disable or reverse the group policy that you set.

If you enable a policy setting, you are enabling the action of the policy setting. If you disable a policy setting, you reverse the action of the policy setting. If you delete the link or delete a group policy, the action of the policy setting is still in affect for the systems that received the group policy. To reverse the action of the policy setting, you will have to actually establish and apply a group policy that configures a disabled or "Not Configured" option for the setting that you are trying to reverse. For example, if you enable the Prohibit access to the Control Panel settings policy, and you want to reverse the setting, you first need to disable the link or delete the group policy. Second, to cancel the effect from the first group policy, you have to create and apply another group policy that is set to disable for the Prohibit access to the Control Panel.

Assigning Scripts with Group Policy

You can use group policies for users' logon and logoff scripts and computers' startup and shutdown scripts. A script is a batch file or a Microsoft Visual Basic script that can execute code or perform management tasks. When you create a batch file, you use any command that you can execute at the command prompt—including the NET.EXE command—to map drives and printers. Scripts can be located anywhere on the network, as long as the user or computer has network access and has the Read permission to the script. It is recommended to place the scripts in the SYSVOL folder because this folder is replicated to all domain controllers within the domain (see Figure 10.1).

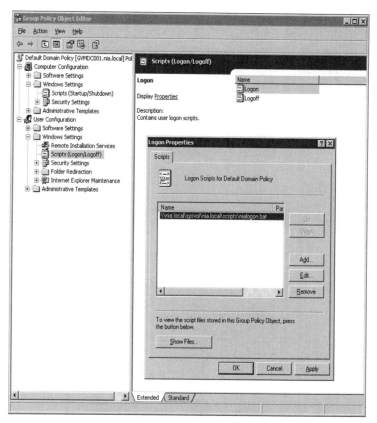

FIGURE 10.1 Loading logon scripts using group policies.

Restricting Group Membership

Built-in groups within the domain, the workstations, and member servers have inherent rights to perform system tasks. Unfortunately, controlling the membership of these groups can be difficult. For example, because the local administrator has full administrative permission for the computer, you might not want your domain users to be the administrator on their own PCs, which would prevent them from installing software and changing system settings.

You use the Restricted Groups policy to control group membership by specifying what members are placed in a group (see Figure 10.2). If a Restricted Groups policy is defined, every time it is refreshed on the system, any current member who is not part of the Restricted Groups policy member list is removed. The Restricted Groups policy setting does not add to the list of users.

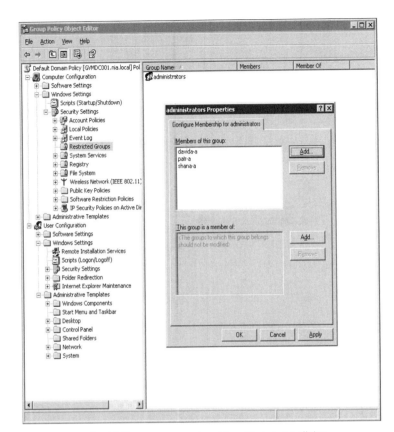

FIGURE 10.2   Restricting group membership with group policies.

Access to Software

To increase security, use group policies to restrict which software can run a computer. Software restriction policy can be used to

▶ Fight viruses and other forms of malware.

▶ Regulate which ActiveX controls can be downloaded.

▶ Run only digitally signed scripts.

▶ Ensure that only approved software is installed on system computers.

▶ Lock down the computer.

To restrict software, you must first create a software restriction policy that consists of security levels, rules, and settings. A policy consists of a default rule about whether programs are allowed to run (unrestricted), as well as exceptions to that rule (disallowed). The default rule can be set to Unrestricted or Disallowed. When you use the unrestricted rule as the default, you then specify which programs are not allowed to run as exceptions. When you use the restricted rule as the default, you then specify which programs are allowed to run as exceptions.

To identify which software can or cannot be allowed to run, create rules (see Figure 10.3) based on the following criteria:

- *Hash*—A cryptographic fingerprint based on a mathematical calculation of the file that uniquely identifies a file regardless of where it is accessed or what it is named

- *Certificate*—A software publisher certificate used to digitally sign a file

- *Path*—The local or universal naming convention (UNC) path of where the file is stored

- *Zone*—Internet Explorer security zone

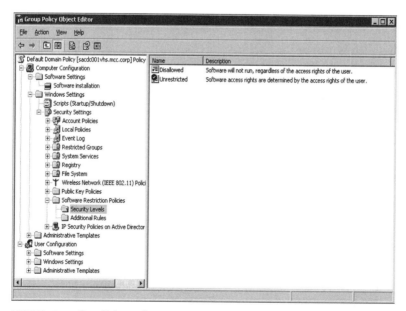

FIGURE 10.3   Specifying software restrictions using group policies.

You can also use group policies to install software—specifically, you can install Windows Installer packages (.MSI files), Transform Files (.MST files), and patch files (.MSP files).

When you deploy an application, you can either publish the application to users or you can assign the application to either users or computers. Publishing does not actually install the application; instead, it makes the application available to users so that they can open the Control Panel, double-click Add/Remove programs, and install the application. Assigning an application to a user makes the application appear in the Start menu and/or appear on the desktop. When the user attempts to start the program, it will install the application at that time. It can also perform a check. If an application is damaged (files missing or Registry settings are missing), it will automatically be replaced. Assigning an application to a computer works similar to assigning an application to a user, except that it actually installs the application without the user first having to execute it.

To publish or assign an application using Group Policy Editor, follow these steps:

1. Navigate through the group policy console to User Configuration, Software Settings, and Software Installation.

2. Right-click on the Software Installation node.

3. Select New, and then select Package.

4. Select the appropriate MSI file and click Open.

5. Select publish or assign the application.

6. Click OK.

The process for assigning an application to a computer is almost identical. The only real difference is that you use the Software Settings | Software Installation container beneath the Computer Configuration container rather than beneath the User Configuration container.

Folder Redirection

When you redirect folders, you change the storage location of folders (My Documents, Desktop, Application Data, and Start Menu) from the local hard disk on the user's computer to a shared folder on a network file server. Moving these folders to a central server allows for increased availability and a central backup point. In addition, when combined with offline files technology, it gives a user access to these key folders even when the user is not connected to the network. If the user makes changes to a document, either on the local computer or through the network, the files will be synchronized when the computer is connected to the network.

Three settings are available for Folder Redirection: none, basic, and advanced. Basic folder redirection is for users who must redirect their folders to a common area or users who need their data to be private. Advanced redirection allows you to specify the different network locations for various Windows user groups. When you specify None for folder redirection, it disables the folder redirection.

For Basic redirection, you have the following options:

▶ *Redirect folder to the following location*—Used for information that does not have to be kept private and can be found in a common area. The Root Path field allows you to specify the UNC path where the folder will be redirected.

▶ *Create a folder*—Used if redirected folders are to be private. The Root Path field allows you to specify the UNC path where the folder will be redirected. You only need to put in the server name and the share name, and Group Policy will append the `%username%` variable to automatically create a subfolder named for the user and move the redirected folder into it.

▶ *Redirect to the local userprofile location*—This setting will redirect the folder back into the default location of the user's profile on the local hard drive.

▶ *Redirect to the user's home directory*—This setting is only available for the My Documents folder. Use this option only if you have already deployed home folders.

For Advanced redirection, you specify the location for various user groups. Folders are then redirected to different locations based on the security group member of the users. After you specify the group whose folders you want to have redirected, you will see the same options that are provided for basic redirection.

The Settings tab allows you to specify whether the user will be granted exclusive rights to the redirected folder and whether the current contents of the folder will be moved to the new location. You can also specify whether the folder should remain in the network location or be moved back to the local user's profile if the group policy is removed.

Administrative Templates

Administrative templates provide the primary means of administering the user environment and defining the end-user computing experience. You can define most options found in the GUI when configuring the Start menu, taskbar,

Desktop, Control Panel, printers, network options, system settings, and Internet Explorer. For example, you can configure the default screen saver and whether it requires a password when the screen saver activates. You can also define the default wallpaper or if the command prompt or control panel will be available to a user. You can also create custom administrative templates to make changes to the Registry that are not included in the defined administrative templates (see Figures 10.4 and 10.5).

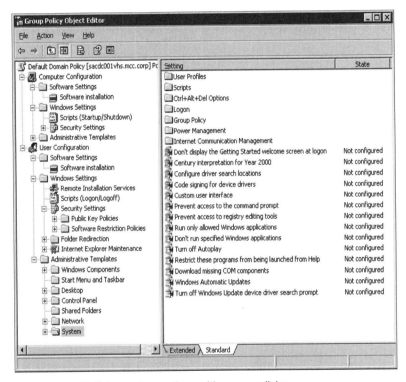

FIGURE 10.4 Defining system options with group policies.

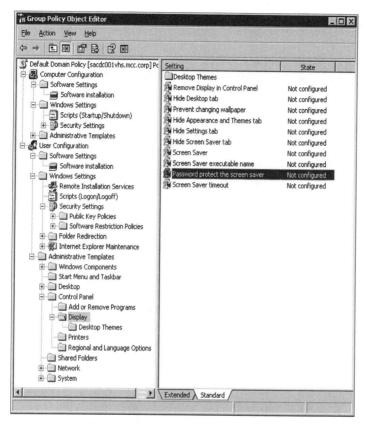

FIGURE 10.5 Defining display options with group policies.

gpupdate

By default, group policies are refreshed every 90 minutes, plus or minus 30 minutes on a workstation or every 5 minutes on a domain controller. You can run the gpupdate command to manually refresh group policies settings.

For example, if you want to update only the computer policy settings, you execute the following command:

```
gpupdate /target:computer
```

To update all group policy settings even if they have not been changed, you would execute the following command:

```
gpupdate /force
```

Table 10.1 shows the gpupdate command parameters.

TABLE 10.1   gpupdate Command Parameters

Value	Description
/Target: {Computer | User}	Specifies that only user or only computer policy settings are refreshed. By default, both user and computer policy settings are refreshed.
/Force	Reapplies all policy settings. By default, only policy settings that have changed are reapplied.
/Wait:{Value}	Sets the number of seconds to wait for policy processing to finish. The default is 600 seconds. The value .0. means not to wait. The value .-1. means to wait indefinitely.
/Logoff	Causes a logoff after the group policy settings are refreshed. This is required for those group policy client-side extensions that do not process policy settings during a background refresh cycle but do process policy settings when a user logs on. Examples include user-targeted software installation and folder redirection. This option has no effect if no extensions are called that require a logoff.
/Boot	Causes the computer to restart after the group policy settings are refreshed. This is required for those group policy client-side extensions that do not process policy during a background refresh cycle but do process policy when the computer starts. Examples include computer-targeted software installation. This option has no effect if no extensions are called that require the computer to restart.
/Sync	Causes the next foreground policy setting to be applied synchronously. Foreground policy settings are applied when the computer starts and when the user logs on. You can specify this for the user, computer, or both by using the /Target parameter. The /Force and /Wait parameters are ignored.

Resultant Set of Policy (RSoP)

If you are using group policies and someone is getting an extra privilege or setting that you did not expect, or someone is being incorrectly denied something, you can use the Resultant Set of Policy (RSoP) tool to help troubleshoot the problem. One way to get this information is to use the gpresult tool (see Figure 10.6). Table 10.2 shows the gpresult command parameters.

TABLE 10.2 `gpresult` **Command Parameters**

Value	Description
`/s computer`	Specifies the name or IP address of a remote computer. The default is the local computer.
`/u domain/user`	Runs the command with the account permissions of the user who is specified by User or Domain/User. The default is the permissions of the user who is currently logged on to the computer that issues the command.
`/p password`	Specifies the password of the user account that is specified in the `/u` parameter.
`/user targetusername`	Specifies the username of the user whose RSoP data is to be displayed.
`/scope {user│computer}`	Displays either user or computer policy settings. Valid values for the `/scope` parameter are `user` or `computer`. If you omit the `/scope` parameter, `gpresult` displays both user and computer policy settings.
`/v`	Specifies that the output will display verbose policy information. Use this switch when you want to see the settings applied.
`/z`	Specifies that the output will display all available information about group policy. Because this parameter produces more information than the `/v` parameter, redirect output to a text file when you use this parameter (for example, you can type `gpresult /z >policy.txt`).
`/?`	Displays help in the command prompt window.

If you installed Group Policy Management Console, you can also use a more comprehensive tool by running the Group Policy Management Wizard. To start the Wizard, right-click the Group Policy Results folder, and click the Group Policy Results Wizard (see Figure 10.7).

```
C:\Documents and Settings\preganadm>gpresult

Microsoft (R) Windows (R) Operating System Group Policy Result tool v2.0
Copyright (C) Microsoft Corp. 1981-2001

Created On 10/21/2006 at 6:08:21 PM

RSOP data for MCC\preganadm on SACMAN001UMS : Logging Mode

OS Type:                        Microsoft(R) Windows(R) Server 2003, Enterprise Edition
OS Configuration:               Member Server
OS Version:                     5.2.3790
Terminal Server Mode:           Remote Administration
Site Name:                      Sacramento-Datacenter
Roaming Profile:
Local Profile:                  C:\Documents and Settings\preganadm
Connected over a slow link?: No

COMPUTER SETTINGS

    CN=SACMAN001UMS,OU=MCC,OU=Servers,OU=Administration,DC=ncc,DC=corp
    Last time Group Policy was applied: 10/21/2006 at 6:05:09 PM
    Group Policy was applied from:    sacd001vhs.ncc.corp
    Group Policy slow link threshold: 500 Kbps
    Domain Name:                      MCC
    Domain Type:                      Windows 2000

    Applied Group Policy Objects
    ----------------------------
        Auditing

    The following GPOs were not applied because they were filtered out
    ------------------------------------------------------------------
        Default Domain Policy
            Filtering:  Denied (Security)

        Set VirtualServer Account Settings
            Filtering:  Not Applied (Empty)

        Local Group Policy
            Filtering:  Not Applied (Empty)

    The computer is a part of the following security groups
    -------------------------------------------------------
        BUILTIN\Administrators
        Everyone
        IIS_WPG
        BUILTIN\Users
        NT AUTHORITY\NETWORK
        NT AUTHORITY\Authenticated Users
        This Organization
        SACMAN001UMS$
        Domain Computers
        CERTSVC_DCOM_ACCESS

USER SETTINGS

    CN=Patrick Regan (Admin),OU=Administrators,OU=Administration,DC=ncc,DC=corp
    Last time Group Policy was applied: 10/21/2006 at 5:45:46 PM
    Group Policy was applied from:    sacd001vhs.ncc.corp
    Group Policy slow link threshold: 500 Kbps
    Domain Name:                      MCC
    Domain Type:                      Windows 2000

    Applied Group Policy Objects
    ----------------------------
        N/A

    The following GPOs were not applied because they were filtered out
    ------------------------------------------------------------------
        Auditing
            Filtering:  Not Applied (Empty)
```

FIGURE 10.6 Using the gpresult command to view the RSoP.

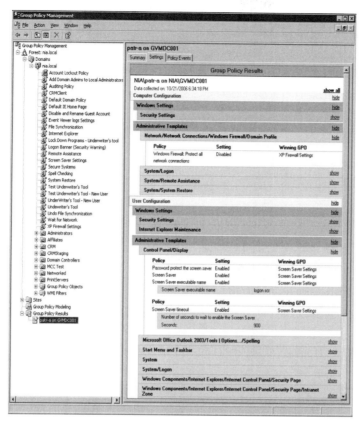

FIGURE 10.7 Using the Group Policy Management Wizard to view the RSoP.

Exam Prep Questions

1. When you set up a group policy to restrict what software can run on a computer, which of the following is rot a parameter that can be used to identify the software?

   ○ **A.** Name and date of the executable

   ○ **B.** Path of where the file is located

   ○ **C.** A digital certificate

   ○ **D.** A hash value

   ○ **E.** A zone defined within Internet Explorer

2. If you need to make a folder redirection based on groups, what do you have to do?

   ○ **A.** Configure basic redirection using group policy.

   ○ **B.** Configure advanced redirection using group policy.

   ○ **C.** Configure basic redirection using user's profile.

   ○ **D.** Configure advanced redirection using user's profile.

3. You want to change the wallpaper to one that includes a company logo. What do you do?

   ○ **A.** Configure an administrative template using group policy.

   ○ **B.** Configure an administrative template using the Registry import function.

   ○ **C.** Create a login script that copies the logo onto the Registry.

   ○ **D.** Modify the Boot.ini file to point to the new company logo.

4. If you make a change to the group policy and you want the group policy to go into effect immediately, what do you have to do on a Windows Server 2003?

   ○ **A.** gpresult /Force

   ○ **B.** secedit /Update

   ○ **C.** gpupdate /Force

   ○ **D.** gpupdate /Sync

5. If you want to see all group policies so that you can figure out where certain settings have come into play, what can you do?

   ○ **A.** gpshow

   ○ **B.** secedit /show

   ○ **C.** gpresult

   ○ **D.** gpdupate /showall

6. Which folder is replicated between domain controllers?

   ○ **A.** Windows

   ○ **B.** Windows\System32

   ○ **C.** Windows\System

   ○ **D.** SYSVOL

7. Where in the group policy settings would you configure computer startup and shut-down scripts?

   ○ **A.** Client configuration

   ○ **B.** User configuration

   ○ **C.** Startup configuration

   ○ **D.** computer configuration

Answers to Exam Prep Questions

1. **Answer A is correct.** The rules that restrict software are based on a hash value, certificate, path, and Internet Explorer security zone. Therefore, Name and date of the executable is not a parameter.

2. **Answer B is correct.** Basic folder redirection is for users who must redirect their folders to a common area or users who need their data to be private. Advanced redirection allows you to specify the different network location for various Windows user groups. Answers C and D are incorrect because folder redirection is done using group policies, not user profiles.

3. **Answer A is correct.** Administrative templates are used to modify the look and feel of Windows. Answer B is incorrect because you do not use the Registry import function with administrative templates. Answer C is incorrect because you also do not change the Registry with login scripts. Answer D is incorrect because the boot.ini file is used to provide the boot menu and specifies which volume to boot from. The boot.ini file does not load logos.

4. **Answer C is correct.** For a group policy to go in effect immediately, you have to use the gpupdate /force command. The /force option pushes out the group policy even if no changes have been made. Answer A is incorrect because the gpresult command is used to view the resultant policy settings. Answer B is incorrect because secedit is the command you would use with Windows 2000 machines. Answer D is incorrect because the Sync option specifies how the group policies are processed.

5. **Answer C is correct.** To show you all group policies that are running and their settings, you would use the gpresult command or the Group Policy Results Wizard. Answer A is incorrect because the gpshow command does not exist. Answer B is incorrect because secedit is used for Windows 2000 machines. Answer D is incorrect because the /showall option does not exist.

6. **Answer D is correct.** SYSVOL is a folder that is replicated between domain controllers. Answers A, B, and C are incorrect because the Windows, System, and System32 folders are not replicated.

7. **Answer D is correct.** Startup and shutdown scripts are found in computer configuration, and logon and logoff scripts are found in user configuration.

Need to Know More?

For more information about using group policies, see the following articles from the Windows Server 2003 Technical Library and Windows Server 2003 Product Help in the Microsoft TechNet website (http://technet.microsoft.com):

► "Administering Group Policy with Group Policy Management Console Abstract"

► "Administering Group Policy with Group Policy Management Console"

CHAPTER ELEVEN

Implementing Administrative Templates and Audit Policy

Terms you'll need to understand:

✓ Permissions
✓ User rights
✓ Security policy
✓ Password policy
✓ Account lockout policy
✓ Strong password
✓ Security templates
✓ Security Configuration and Analysis tool
✓ Auditing
✓ Event viewer
✓ Security logs

Techniques/concepts you'll need to master

✓ Differentiating between permissions and rights
✓ Forcing a group policy to take effect immediately after making changes to it
✓ Configuring user rights
✓ Configuring security policies, including account policies and account lockout policies
✓ Using security templates to secure a system
✓ Using the Security Configuration and Analysis tool to analyze and secure a system
✓ Enabling and configuring auditing on a Windows machine
✓ Using the event viewer to identify security problems

One of the most powerful features of group policies is that they can be used to secure the domain and individual machines on the domain. You also can use group policies to configure auditing so that if there is a security breach, you can look at the security logs to identify where the security breach originated—this provides accountability. Finally, there are tools that can analyze and verify your network security settings to help manage your domain and its security settings.

Permissions Versus Rights

A *permission* defines the type of access that is granted to an object or object attributes. The permissions that are available for an object depend on the type of object. For example, a user has different permissions from a printer. When a user or service tries to access an object, its access is granted or denied by an object manager. See Table 11.1 for common object types.

TABLE 11.1 Common Object Types

Object Type	Object Manager	Management Tool
Files and Folders	NTFS	Windows Explorer
Shares	Server service	Windows Explorer
Active Directory Objects	Active Directory	Active Directory Users and Computers console or snap-in
Registry Keys	The Registry	Registry Editor
Services	Service controllers	Security Templates, Security Configuration and Analysis
Printer	Print spooler	Printer and Faxes folder

A *right* authorizes a user to perform certain actions on a computer, such as logging on to a system interactively or backing up files and directories. Administrators can assign specific rights to individual user accounts or group accounts. Rights can be managed by group policies, specifically by opening Computer Configuration, opening Windows Settings, opening Security Settings, opening Local Policies, and then opening User Rights Assignments using any of the available GPO editing tools.

User Rights

Although rights can be assigned in any group policy (site, domain, or organizational unit), default rights are usually assigned at the default domain controller group policy (see Table 11.2 and Figure 11.1). For example, the domain controller group policy has the Allow Log On Locally right, which is used to log on interactively to the computer and is assigned to account operators, backup operators, print operators, sever operators, and administrators. Yet the Take Ownership of Files or Other Objects right is assigned only to the administrators. Of course, if you assigned rights to a user or group and you want the rights effective immediately, you have to use the `gpupdate /force` command.

> **NOTE**
>
> For quick and easy access, Windows Server 2003 has a domain controller security policy console available in Administrative Tools.

To simplify management, user rights are best administered by using groups. If a user is a member of multiple groups, the user's rights are cumulative, which means that the user has more than one set of rights. The only time when rights assigned to one group might conflict with those assigned to another is in the case of certain logon rights. In general, however, user rights assigned to one group do not conflict with those assigned to another group. To remove rights from a user, the administrator simply removes the user from the group. After the user logs off and back on again, he no longer has the rights assigned to that group.

TABLE 11.2   Default User Rights

Right	Description	Default Groups Assigned to Right
Access this computer from the network	Allows the user to connect to the computer over the network.	Administrators, Everyone, and Power Users
Add workstations to domain	Allows the user to add a computer to a specific domain through an administrative user interface on the computer being added, creating an object in the Computer container in Active Directory.	Authenticated Users
Allow logon locally	Allows a user to log on at the computer's keyboard. Because most protection can be bypassed by being able to log on directly to a machine without going through the network, this right should be given only to a few people.	Administrators, Account Operators, Backup Operators, Print Operators, and Server Operators

(continues)

TABLE 11.2 *Continued*

Right	Description	Default Groups Assigned to Right
Back up files and directories	Allows the user to circumvent file and directory permissions to back up the system. Specifically, the privilege is granting the following permission on all files and folders on the local computer: Traverse Folder/Execute File, List Folder/Read Data Read Attributes, Read Extended Attributes, and Read Permissions. See also Restore files and directories.	Administrators and Backup Operators
Change the system time	Allows the user to set the time for the internal clock of the computer.	Administrators and Power Users
Create a page file	Allows the user to create and change the size of the page file.	Administrators
Force shutdown from a remote system	Allows a user to shut down a computer from a remote location on the network.	Administrators
Load and unload device drivers	Allows a user to install and uninstall plug-and-play device drivers. Device drivers that are not plug-and-play are not affected by this privilege and can be installed only by administrators. Because device drivers run as trusted (highly privileged) programs, these privileges can be misused to install hostile programs and give these programs destructive access to resources.	Administrators
Manage auditing and security log	Allows a user to specify the object access auditing options for individual resources such as files, Active Directory objects, and Registry keys. Object access auditing is not actually performed unless you have enabled it in the computerwide audit policy.	Administrators
Restore files and directories	Allows a user to circumvent file and directory permissions when restoring backed up files and directories, as well as to set any valid security principal as the owner of the object. See also the Back up files and directories privilege.	Administrators and Backup Operators

TABLE 11.2 *Continued*

Right	Description	Default Groups Assigned to Right
Shut down the system Backup	Allows a user to shut down the local computer.	Administrators, Operators, Everyone, Power Users, and Users
Take ownership of files or other objects	Allows a user to take ownership of any securable object in the system, including Active Directory objects, files and folders, printers, Registry keys, processes, and threads.	Administrators

Specific user rights are assigned to the following local groups:

▶ *Administrators*—Gives full rights to the local computer. Rights include Access This Computer from the Network, Adjust Memory Quotas for a Process, Allow Log On Locally, Allow Log on Through Terminal Services, Back Up Files and Directories, Bypass Traverse Checking, Change the System Time, Create a Pagefile, Debug Programs, Force Shutdown from a Remote System, Increase Scheduling Priority, Load and Unload Device Drivers, and Manage Auditing and Security Log.

▶ *Backup Operators*—Gives the ability to back up and restore files. Rights include Access This Computer from the Network, Allow Log On Locally, Back Up Files and Directories, Bypass Traverse Checking, Restore Files and Directories, and Shut Down the System.

▶ *Power Users*—Has the ability to create user accounts, modify and delete accounts they create. Rights include Access This Computer from the Network, Allow Log On Locally, Bypass Traverse Checking, Change the System Time, Profile Single Process, Remove Computer from Docking Station, and Shut Down the System.

▶ *Remote Desktop Users*—Allows access to a computer using terminal services. Rights include Allow Log On Through Terminal Services.

▶ *Users*—Allows remote access to computers. Rights include Access This Computer from the Network; Allow Log On Locally and Bypass Traverse Checking.

Specific user rights are assigned to the groups in the Built-in container (see Figure 11.1):

▶ *Account Operators*—Allows administration of user and computer accounts. Rights include Allow Log On Locally and Shut Down the System.

FIGURE 11.1 Using group policies to define user rights.

▶ *Administrators*—Allows full control over computers within the domain. Rights include Access This Computer from the Network, Adjust Memory Quotas for a Process, Allow Log On Locally, Back Up Files and Directories, Bypass Traverse Checking, Change the System Time, Create a Pagefile, Debug Programs, Enable Computer and User Accounts to be Trusted for Delegation, Force a Shutdown from a Remote System, Increase Scheduling Priority, Load and Unload Device Drivers, and Manage Auditing and Security Log.

▶ *Backup Operators*—This group has the ability to back up and restore files on the domain. Allow Log On Locally, Back Up Files and Directories, Restore Files and Directories, and Shut Down the System Rights.

▶ *Pre-Windows 2000 Compatible Access*—This group allows old machines to access the server. This group has the Access This Computer from the Network and Bypass Traverse Checking Rights.

- ▶ *Print Operators*—This group has the ability to manage printers. This group has the Allow Log On Locally and Shut Down the System Rights.

- ▶ *Server Operators*—This group has the ability to manage the server. This group has the Allow Log On Locally, Back Up Files and Directories, Change the System Time, Force Shutdown from a Remote System, Restore Files and Directories, and Shut Down the System Rights.

- ▶ *Domain Admins*—This group can perform administrative tasks on any computer within the domain. Rights include Access This Computer from the Network, Adjust Memory Quotas for a Process, Allow Log On Locally, Back Up Files and Directories, Bypass Traverse Checking, Change the System Time, Create a Pagefile, Debug Programs, Enable Computer and User Accounts to be Trusted for Delegation, Force a Shutdown from a Remote System, Increase Scheduling Priority, Load and Unload Device Drivers, and Manage Auditing and Security Log.

- ▶ *Enterprise Admins*—This group has administrative control over the entire network (all domains). Rights include Access This Computer from the Network, Adjust Memory Quotas for a Process, Allow Log On Locally, Back Up Files and Directories, Bypass Traverse Checking, Change the System Time, Create a Pagefile, Debug Programs, Enable Computer and User Accounts to be Trusted for Delegation, Force Shutdown from a Remote System, Increase Scheduling Priority, Load and Unload Device Drivers, and Manage Auditing and Security Log.

Security Policies

A *security policy* is a combination of security settings that affect the security on a computer or domain. With a local security policy, you can control

- ▶ Account policies
- ▶ Local policies
- ▶ The Public Key policy
- ▶ The Software Restriction policy
- ▶ IP Security policies

If your network does not use Active Directory, you can configure a security policy by using the Local Security Policy, which is found on the Administrative Tools menu (on computers running Windows XP or Windows Server 2003).

Security policies in Active Directory have the same settings as the security policy on local computers, plus extra settings to deal with domain configurations. You can edit or import security settings in a GPO for any site, domain, or organizational unit, and the security settings are automatically deployed to the computers when the computers start. When editing a GPO, expand Computer Configuration or User Configuration and then expand Windows Settings to find the security policy settings.

Password Policy

The password policy determines the password settings for domain and local user accounts. It can be found by opening the Computer Configuration, opening the Windows Settings, opening Account Policies, and clicking on Password Policies. The most commonly used password settings are as follows:

▶ *Enforce Password history*—Remembers a specific number of passwords. Therefore, when a user changes a password, you cannot use the same password. For example, if Enforce Password History is set to 3, users would have to change the password three times before using the same password again.

▶ *Maximum password age*—Specifies how often the password must be changed.

▶ *Minimum password age*—Specifies how long a user has to wait before changing a password. This prevents users from changing passwords back to the original one immediately.

▶ *Minimum password length*—Specifies the minimum number of characters for a password.

▶ *Complexity requirements*—When enabled, the password must be a strong password that contains at least six characters and must contain characters from at least three of the following four classes:

  ▶ English uppercase letters (A, B, C,..., Z)

  ▶ English lowercase letters (a, b, c,..., z)

  ▶ Westernized Arabic numerals (0, 1, 2,..., 9)

  ▶ Nonalphanumeric ("special characters"), such as punctuation symbols

For a secure network, try setting Enforce Password History to 5 or more, set the maximum password age to between 30 and 45 days, and set the minimum password length to 8 characters. Enable passwords to meet complexity requirements.

Account Lockout Policy

The Account Lockout Policy determines when and for whom an account will be locked out of the system. It can be found by opening the Computer Configuration, opening the Windows Settings, opening Account Policies, and clicking on Account Lockout Policies. The account lockout policy has the following settings:

▶ *Account Lockout Duration*—When an account is locked out, it specifies the duration of the lockout. If you set the account lockout duration to 0, the account will be locked out until an administrator explicitly unlocks it.

▶ *Account Lockout Threshold*—The number of invalid logins within the time specified in Reset Account Lockout Counter After before the account is locked. This setting will eliminate hackers from trying passwords until one works.

▶ *Reset Account Lockout Counter After*—The time that the number of invalid logins are counted before the invalid login counter is reset.

For a secure network, set Account Lockout Duration to 0, set Account Lockout Threshold to 5, and reset Account Lockout and Account Lockout Counter After to 30 minutes.

Security Options

Security options, found under local policies, allow you to secure a system or network. Some of these options include

▶ Enforce digital signing of drivers

▶ Rename administrator or guest accounts

▶ Restrict floppy or CD-ROM disk access

▶ Encrypt data between systems

▶ Clear the page file during shutdown

For example, one security setting—Network security: Force Logoff When Logon Hours Expire—determines whether to disconnect users who are connected to the local computer outside the user account's valid logon hours. When this policy is enabled, which is the default option, it causes client sessions with the SMB server (Microsoft file and print shares server) to be forcibly disconnected when the client's logon hours expire. If this policy is disabled, an established client session is allowed to be maintained after the client's logon hours have expired.

> **NOTE**
>
> The account policy must be defined in the Default Domain Policy, and it is enforced by the domain controllers that make up the domain.

Using Security Templates to Secure Computers

In Windows Server 2003, User Rights assignments have been integrated with group policies. While it is possible to change security settings for a local machine in a group policy object, a better approach is to use a security template. A security template provides a single place in which all system security can be viewed, analyzed, changed, and applied to a single machine or to a group policy object. Security templates do not introduce new security parameters; they simply organize all existing security attributes into one place to ease security administration. Security templates can also be used as a base configuration for security analysis, when used with the Security Configuration and Analysis MMC snap-in. Last, as security needs change, you need to change only the template and reapply it to the computers to get the desired results.

Windows comes with preconfigured security templates for common machine configurations, such as workstations, secure servers, and domain controllers, as shown in Table 11.3. The security templates simplify security administration and help to eliminate gaps in security for servers deployed on the Internet, rather than laboriously going through a checklist to make sure that the server is secure. This results in a substantial savings of administrators' time.

TABLE 11.3   Predefined Templates

Security Template	Description
Basic (`basic*.inf`)	The basic configurations apply the Windows Server 2003 default security settings to all security areas, except those pertaining to user rights.

TABLE 11.3 *Continued*

Security Template	Description
Compatible (`compat*.inf`)	The default Windows Server 2003 security configuration gives members of the local Users group strict security settings, whereas members of the local Power Users group have security settings that are compatible with Windows NT 4.0 user assignments so that the local Users group can use legacy programs. It is not considered a secure environment.
Secure (`secure*.inf`)	The secure templates implement recommended security settings for all security areas, except files, folders, and Registry keys. Besides increasing security settings for account policy and auditing, it also removes all members from the Power Users group. These are not modified because file system and Registry permissions are configured securely by default.
Highly Secure (`hisec*.inf`)	The highly secure templates define security settings for Windows Server 2003 network communications. The security areas are set to require maximum protection for network traffic and protocols used between computers running Windows 2000 or Windows Server 2003. As a result, computers configured with a highly secure template can communicate only with other Windows 2000 or Windows Server 2003 computers. They will not be capable of communicating with computers running older versions of Windows (Windows 9X, Windows Me, and Windows NT).

Follow these steps to import a security template to a group policy object:

1. Click Start, point to Run, type **mmc**, and click OK.

2. On the File menu, click Add/Remove snap-in.

3. In Add/Remove Snap-in, click Add. In Add Standalone Snap-in, double-click Group Policy Object Editor.

4. In Select Group Policy Object, click Browse, select the policy object you would like to modify, click OK, and then click Finish.

5. Click Close, and then click OK.

6. In the Group Policy console tree, right-click Security Settings.

7. Click Import Policy, click the security template you want to import, and then click Open. If you want to clear the database of any previously stored security templates, select the Clear This Database Before Importing check box.

To customize a predefined security template, follow these steps:

1. In the Security Templates snap-in, double-click Security Templates.

2. Double-click the default path folder (`Systemroot\Security\Templates`), and right-click the predefined template you want to modify.

3. Click Save As and specify the filename for the security template.

4. Double-click the new security template to display the security policy (such as Account Policies) and double-click the security policy you want to modify.

5. Click the security area you want to customize (such as Password Policy), and then double-click the security attribute to modify (such as Minimum Password Length).

6. Check Define This Policy Settings in the template check box in order to allow editing.

Security Configuration and Analysis Tool

A popular tool that you can use to analyze computer security is the Security Configuration and Analysis tool. The Security Configuration and Analysis tool compares the security configuration of a local computer with a separate database (`*.sdb`) template file. The database file can be one that you retrieve from a website or one that you create. You can then browse the security settings in the console tree to see the results. Discrepancies are marked with a red x, and consistencies are marked with a green check mark. You can then eliminate the discrepancies by configuring the settings in the database to match the current computer settings, or you can import another template file, merging its settings and overwriting settings in which a conflict exists. You can also export the current database settings to a template file.

To open the Security Configuration and Analysis Tool, follow these steps:

1. Open the MMC console by clicking the Start button and running the MMC with the Run option.

2. Open the file menu and select the Add/Remove Snap-in.

3. Click the Add button and select the Security Configuration and Analysis. Click Add button.

4. Click the Close button to close the Add Standalone Snap-in.

5. Click OK to close the Add/Remove Snap-in dialog box.

Follow these steps to open an existing database:

1. Right-click the Security Configuration and Analysis scope item.

2. Click Open Database.

3. Select a database, and then click Open.

Follow these steps to create a new database:

1. Right-click the Security Configuration and Analysis scope item.

2. Click Open Database.

3. Type a new database name, and then click Open.

4. Select a security template to import, and then click Open.

Follow these steps to configure your computer:

1. Right-click the Security Configuration and Analysis scope item.

2. Select Configure Computer Now.

3. In the dialog, type the name of the log file you want to view, and then click OK.

After you have a database file, you can then compare the security of other systems by comparing or analyzing your system with the Security Configuration and Analysis console. Follow these steps to analyze your computer security settings:

1. Right-click the Security Configuration and Analysis scope item.

2. Select Analyze Computer Now.

3. In the dialog, type the log file path, and then click OK.

Setting Up Auditing

Auditing is a feature of Windows Server 2003 that tracks and records various security-related events so that you can detect intruders and attempts to compromise data on the system. Therefore, you want to set up an audit policy for a computer to

▶ Track the success and failures of events, such as attempts to log on, attempts by a particular user to read a specific file, changes to user accounts, or changes to security settings.

▶ Minimize the risk of unauthorized use of resources.

▶ Maintain a record of user and administrator activity.

Some events that you can monitor are access to an object such as a folder or file, management of user and group accounts, and logging on and off a system. The security events are provided in the Event Viewer, specifically the security logs. The Event Viewer contains

▶ The action that was performed

▶ The user who performed the action

▶ The success or failure of the event and when the event occurred

▶ Additional information, such as the computer where the event occurred

Auditing is one way to find security holes in your network and to ensure accountability for people's actions.

Events are not audited by default. If you have Administrator permissions, you can specify what types of system events to audit using group policies (Computer Configuration\Windows Settings\Security Settings\Local Policies\Audit Policy). The amount of auditing that needs to be done depends on the needs of the organization. A minimum-security network might only audit failed logon attempts so that brute-force attacks can be detected. A high security network will most likely audit both successful and failed logon to track who successfully gains access to the network.

The first step in implementing an audit policy is to select the types of events that you want Windows Server 2003 to audit. Table 11.4 describes the events that Windows Server 2003 can audit (see Figure 11.2).

TABLE 11.4   Audit Events

Event	Example
Account Logon	When a user logs on to the local computer, the computer records the Account Logon event. When a user logs on to a domain, the authenticating domain controller records the Account Logon event.
Account Management	An administrator creates, changes, or deletes a user account or group; a user account is renamed, disabled, or enabled; or a password is set or changed.
Directory Service Access	A user accesses an Active Directory object. Note: You must then configure specific Active Directory objects for auditing.
Logon	A user logs on to or off a local computer, or a user makes or cancels a network connection to the computer; the event is recorded on the computer that the user accesses, regardless of whether a local account or a domain account is used.

TABLE 11.4 *Continued*

Event	Example
Object Access	A user accesses a file, folder, or printer. Note: You must then configure specific files, folders, or printers to be audited, the users or groups that are being audited, and the actions that they will be audited for.
Policy Change	A change is made to the user security options (for example, password options or account logon settings), user rights, or audit policies.
Privilege Use	A user exercises a user right (not related to logging on or off), such as changing the system time or taking ownership of a file.
Process Tracking	An application performs an action. This is generally used only for programmers and can be very intensive.
System	A user restarts or shuts down the computer, or an event occurs that affects Windows Server 2003 security or the security log.

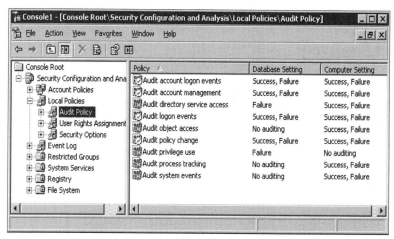

FIGURE 11.2   Using Security Configuration and Analysis to check security settings.

To audit files and folders, you can only audit those volumes that are formatted with NTFS. In addition, you must first enable Object Access auditing using group policies. After the group policy has been applied, you can set, view, or change auditing a file or folder by doing the following:

1. Using a group policy, enable object access auditing.

2. Open Windows Explorer and locate the file or folder that you want to audit.

3. Right-click the file or folder and select the Properties option.

4. Click the Security tab, click on the Advanced button, and click on the Auditing tab.

   ▶ To set up auditing for a new group or user, click Add and specify the name of the user you want, and click the OK button to open the Auditing Entry box.

   ▶ To view or change auditing for an existing group or user, click the name and then the View/Edit button.

   ▶ To remove auditing for an existing group or user, click the name and then the Remove button.

Because the security log is limited in size, select only those objects that you need to audit and consider the amount of disk space that the security log will need. The maximum size of the security log is defined in Event Viewer by right-clicking Security Log and selecting the Properties option.

Event Viewer

The Event Viewer utility is used to view and manage logs of the system, program, and security events on a computer. Event Viewer gathers information about hardware and software problems and monitors Windows security events. Event Viewer can be executed by clicking on the Start button, clicking on Programs, clicking on Administrative Tools, and then clicking on Event Viewer, or by adding it to the MMC. You can also access it though the Computer Management console.

Windows Event Viewer starts with three kinds of logs:

   ▶ *Application log*—The application log contains events logged by programs. For example, a database program might record a file error in the application log. Program developers decide which events to monitor. The application log can be viewed by all users.

   ▶ *Security log*—The Security log contains valid and invalid logon attempts, as well as events related to resource use such as creating, opening, or deleting files or other objects. For example, if you have enabled logon and logon off auditing, attempts to log on to the system are recorded in the security log. By default, security logging is turned off.

▶ *System log*—The system log contains events that are logged by the Windows system components. For example, the failure of a driver or other system component to load during startup is recorded in the system log. The event types logged by system components are predetermined by Windows. The application log can be viewed by all users.

▶ *Directory service*—Appears only on domain controllers. It contains Directory service information such as Active Directory replication.

▶ *File Replication service*—Appears only on domain controllers. The File Replication service event log contains items that relate to the replication of group policies.

Event Viewer log files are also stored in the `systemroot/system32/config` folder. Event Viewer logs can be exported and archived in the following file formats:

▶ Event log files (`.evt`; the default)

▶ Comma-delimited files (`.csv`)

▶ Text files (`.txt`)

Depending on which audit options you have selected, your security logs can grow very quickly. By default, the security log in the Event Viewer can be no larger then 16MB for Windows Server 2003, 8MB for Windows XP with SP1, and 512KB for Windows XP (with no service packs).

To change the size of the log files, right-click the log in Event Viewer, and specify the maximum log file in the Properties pane. You can define the size of log files in multiples of 64KB. You can also define what happens when the maximum log size is reached. Use these options:

▶ Overwrite events as needed

▶ Overwrite events older than the specified number of days

▶ Do not overwrite events (clear log manually)

The size of the log files and how the logs are handled when the maximum log size is reached can be configured using group policies, specifically *GPO_name*\ Computer Configuration\Windows Settings\Security Settings\Event Log\.

Exam Prep Questions

1. Which two statements describe rights and permissions? (Choose two answers.)

    ○ **A.** Permissions define the type of access over an object or object attributes.

    ○ **B.** Rights define the type of access over an object or object attributes.

    ○ **C.** Permissions authorize a user to perform an action.

    ○ **D.** Rights authorize a user to perform an action.

2. How do you assign user rights to a user or group?

    ○ **A.** Use the Active Directory User and Computer Console.

    ○ **B.** Use group policies.

    ○ **C.** Use the Registry editor.

    ○ **D.** Use Windows Explorer.

3. If you need to log on directly to a Windows Server 2003 computer, you need to have what right?

    ○ **A.** Allow Logon Locally

    ○ **B.** Access This Computer from the Network

    ○ **C.** Manage System

    ○ **D.** Backup and Restore

4. When you configure the strong passwords (complexity requirements), which of the following statements are true? (Choose all that apply.)

    ○ **A.** Must contain characters from at least three of the following four classes: English uppercase, English lowercase, westernized Arabic numerals, and nonalphanumeric.

    ○ **B.** At least 6 characters.

    ○ **C.** At least 8 characters.

    ○ **D.** A maximum password age of 60 days and a minimum password age of 1 day.

    ○ **E.** Enforce password history of 8.

5. Password policies and Account lockout policies should be configured at what level?

- ○ **A.** Domain level
- ○ **B.** Site level
- ○ **C.** Organizational Unit
- ○ **D.** Any level

6. What is used to provide a single place at which all system security can be viewed, analyzed, and easily and quickly changed?

- ○ **A.** Administrative templates
- ○ **B.** Security templates
- ○ **C.** Registry files
- ○ **D.** Audit files

7. When you configure auditing, where do you see the security violations?

- ○ **A.** Log files located in the `Windows\System32\Logs` folder
- ○ **B.** Security Configuration and Analysis Tool
- ○ **C.** Event viewer
- ○ **D.** Audit event viewer

8. If you have a Windows NT application that is having problems running, which security template can you use to ease the security requirements of a Windows Server 2003 computer so that it will run?

- ○ **A.** Basic
- ○ **B.** Default
- ○ **C.** Compatible
- ○ **D.** Secure
- ○ **E.** Highly Secure

9. Where would you find the group policy option if you want to enforce that only signed drivers are loaded?

- ○ **A.** Account policies
- ○ **B.** Local Policies
- ○ **C.** System Services
- ○ **D.** Administrative Templates

10. How do you force users to log off when their logon hours expire?

- ○ **A.** Define Local Policies with group policies.
- ○ **B.** Configure the Registry.
- ○ **C.** Add an option in the boot.ini file.
- ○ **D.** When you define the hours that a user can log on, you select the Automatic logoff option.

Answers to Exam Prep Questions

1. **Answers A and D are correct.** Permissions define the types of access over an object or object attribute such as NTFS files. Rights authorize a user to perform a system-related action, such as to perform backups or restores on the system.

2. **Answer B is correct.** User rights are assigned through group policies. They are not assigned using the Active Directory User and Computer console, Registry editor, and Windows Explorer.

3. **Answer A is correct.** To log on locally to a Windows Server 2003 computer, you use group policies. The Access This Computer from the Network, Manage System, and Backup and Restore do not give you the ability to log on locally.

4. **Answers A and B are correct.** Strong passwords, defined as complex passwords, are at least six characters and have at least three of the following four: English uppercase, English lowercase, westernized numerals, and nonalphanumeric. Although it is recommended you have a maximum and minimum age and enforce password history, they are not necessary to define strong passwords.

5. **Answer A is correct.** Password policies and account lockout policies are configured only at the domain level. They cannot be configured at a site level or an organizational unit level.

6. **Answer B is correct.** Security templates can be applied to quickly update security settings. In addition, they can be used to check your security settings. Administrative templates and Registry files don't allow you to view and analyze system security settings. Audit files will show you possible security breaches but not security settings.

7. **Answer C is correct.** Security violations gathered by Windows auditing are listed in the Event viewer security logs. You cannot see the Windows security violiations using log files and security configuration and analysis tools. There is no such thing as an audit event viewer.

8. **Answer C is correct.** If you have problems because of the additional security of Windows Server 2003, you can try using the Compatible security template that will ease the security. Depending on the situation, systems by default will have the Basic or Default security templates. Secure and Highly Secure will lock down a server more then Basic or Default security templates, which could hamper older applications.

9. **Answer B is correct.** Local policies define a wide array of security settings, including enforcing signed drivers.They will not be found in Account policies, system services, or administrative templates.

10. **Answer A is correct.** To automatically configure the automatic logon when the logon hours expire, create a group policy that defines the local policy—Network security: Force Logoff When Logon Hours Expire. This cannot be done using the Registry or the `boot.ini` file. Answer D is incorrect because there is no Automatic logoff option.

Need to Know More?

For more information about using group policies, see the following articles from the Windows Server 2003 Technical Library and Windows Server 2003 Product Help in the Microsoft TechNet website (`http://technet.microsoft.com`):

▶ "Administering Group Policy with Group Policy Management Console Abstract"

▶ "Administering Group Policy with Group Policy Management Console"

12

CHAPTER TWELVE

Preparing to Administer a Server

Terms you'll need to understand:

✓ The Run as command option

✓ Computer Management console

✓ Remote server management

✓ Remote Assistance

✓ Remote Desktops snap-in

✓ Remote Desktop Connections

✓ Terminal Services Remote Administration

Techniques/concepts you'll need to master:

✓ Running programs and utilities as a different user

✓ Managing servers remotely

✓ Setting up and using Remote Assistance

✓ Configuring Terminal Services

✓ Setting up and using Remote Desktop connections

As a network administrator, you will need to access the servers to administer them. Your day-to-day tasks can include setting Active Directory, NTFS, and share permissions; installing and configuring software; or troubleshooting a problem, just to name a few. You should know the different methods and tools that are available for you to access these servers.

Taking Advantage of Server Administration Tools

To support both network security and network administration, IT support personnel should be granted sufficient network rights and permissions to accomplish their jobs, but they should not be given *carte blanche* to do anything that they want to network servers and other resources. These privileges should be sufficient but also very specifically allocated. For example, individuals in charge of data backups should have their user accounts placed in the Backup Operators group; these support technicians do not need to be members of the all-powerful Administrators group. Top-level network administrators should assign lower-level administrators to specific domain local groups that will provide them with sufficient permissions to do their jobs but nothing more. You can find the default built-in domain local security groups for an Active Directory domain in the Built-in container within the Active Directory Users and Computers (ADUC) console. The following are some of the popularly used built-in groups:

▶ *Administrators*—Have complete and unrestricted access to the domain and to servers and other resources within the domain. If they don't have the user rights by default, they can assign themselves the user rights. Of course, because this is a powerful account, membership to this group should be restricted.

▶ *Account operators*—Can manage user accounts, groups, computer accounts, and InetOrgPerson accounts. Note: Only members of the Administrators domain local group can modify the Administrators domain local group or any operator domain local group.

▶ *Backup operators*—Can back up and restore files even if they don't have permissions to the files and folders.

▶ *Print operators*—Can set up local and network printers to ensure that users can easily connect to and use printer resources.

▶ *Server operators*—Can share disk resources, log on to a server interactively, create and delete network shares, start and stop services, format the hard disk of the server, and shut down the computer. They can also back up and restore files similar to the Backup operator.

To give users access to a single server, you can assign users to the built-in local Administrators, Server operators, and Backup operators groups. In either case, you should only assign users to the most restricted group that still provides appropriate rights and permissions necessary to do their job.

> **NOTE**
>
> Members of the Domain Admins global group are automatically added to the Administrators domain local group and to the Administrators local group on each computer.

The Run As Feature

The Run as option gives administrators (and other users) the ability to run programs and system utilities under the security credentials of one user while being interactively logged on to the server as a different user. For example, an administrator named DanB can be logged on to a server or a workstation with an ordinary user account that is only a member of the Domain Users group. While logged on as the ordinary user, DanB, he can right-click any MMC snap-in tool, such as ADUC (dsa.msc), and select Run as from the pop-up menu. The Run as dialog box appears with two options to run this program—Current User (with Restricted Access) and the Following User. By selecting the second option and typing in the appropriate administrative username and password (see Figure 12.1), DanB can log in using the alternate credentials without logging out of the machine.

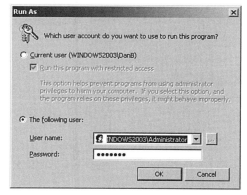

FIGURE 12.1 Running a program as a different user with the Run as option.

You can use the Run as command for all types of programs, utilities, and even Control Panel applets. For using Run as on Control Panel tools, hold down the Shift key while you right-click a Control Panel icon to display the Run as option. You might need to hold down the Shift key while you right-click to access the Run as option for other applications as well. Using Run as is a more secure way for accessing security-sensitive utilities rather than always logging on to systems as a user who is a member of the Administrators group.

You can even use the Run as command to launch an instance of the Windows Explorer under the security credentials of a different user. For example, if you are currently logged on as JoeUser, at a command prompt or at the Start, Run box, you can type `runas /noprofile /user:domain1\administrator explorer.exe` to launch an Explorer window under the security context of Domain1's Administrator account. Any folders or files that you access from *that* Explorer window are subject to the Access Control List (ACL) for the Administrator user account, not the ACL for JoeUser.

Using Run As from the Command Line

You can also use the Run as feature from the command line, both for GUI tools as well as for command-line tools. For example, you can run the Computer Management console as the administrator for the `Windows2003.local` domain by clicking Start, Run; typing `runas /user:windows2003\administrator "mmc %windir%\system32\compmgmt.msc"` in the Open box; and clicking OK. From a command prompt, you can type `runas /?` and press Enter to view the many options and syntax for this command. You can also open a command-prompt window as a different user—the administrator for a domain named `Windows2003.local`, for example—by clicking Start, Run; typing `runas /user:windows2003\administrator cmd.exe` in the Open box; and clicking OK. In addition, you can create shortcuts to administrative tools that require the administrator's password to run. For an example of how to create such a shortcut, follow these steps:

1. Right-click the Windows desktop and select New, Shortcut.

2. Type a command string such as `runas /user:windows2003\ administrator "mmc %windir%\system32\compmgmt.msc"` in the Type the Location of the Item box.

3. Click Next.

4. Type a name for the shortcut in the Type a Name for This Shortcut box, such as `Admin Computer Mgmt`.

5. Click Finish.

When you double-click the shortcut, you are prompted for the administrator password. If you do not type in the correct password for the administrator user account, the program (Computer Management, in this example) does not run.

Using Server Management Tools Remotely

Many tools are used to manage Windows servers. One commonly used tool is the Computer Management console, which is a collection of administrative tools to administer local or remote computers. To access the Computer Management console, you can open the Control Panel, double-click Administrative Tools, and double-click Computer Management. You can also right-click My Computer and select Manage.

Computer Management includes the following administrative tools:

▶ *Event Viewer*—To manage and view events that are recorded in the application, security, and system logs.

▶ *Shared Folders*—To create, view, and manage shared resources; view open files and sessions; and close files and disconnect sessions.

▶ *Local Users and Groups*—To create and manage your local user accounts and groups.

▶ *Performance Logs and Alerts*—To monitor and collect data about your computer's performance.

▶ *Device Manager*—To view the hardware devices that are installed in your computer, update device drivers, modify hardware settings, and troubleshoot device conflicts.

▶ *Removable Storage*—To track your removable storage media and to manage the libraries or data-storage systems that contain them.

▶ *Disk Defragmenter*—To analyze and defragment volumes on your hard disks.

▶ *Disk Management*—To perform disk-related tasks, such as converting disks or creating and formatting volumes. Disk Management helps you manage your hard disks and the partitions or volumes they contain.

▶ *Services*—To manage services on local and remote computers including starting, stopping, pausing, resuming, or disabling a service.

▶ *WMI Control*—To configure and manage the Windows Management Service.

▶ *Indexing Service*—To manage the Indexing service and to create and configure additional catalogs to store index information.

Computer Management, Event Viewer, and other MMC snap-ins will allow you to administer computers and servers remotely. For the Computer Management console, you can right-click the Computer Management root node and select Connect to Another Computer. From the Select Computer dialog box, click the Another Computer option and either type the name of the remote computer or click Browse to locate it. Click OK to connect to the remote computer (see Figure 12.2). You can use Computer Management (and other support tools) to remotely manage different computers as long as you are running the MMC snap-in (or other utility) under a user account that has the proper permissions to access those remote computers. Most MMC snap-ins support remote administration. For other snap-ins and tools such as Event Viewer, Services, and DNS Management (among others), you can also right-click the root node and select Connect to Another Computer to remotely manage other machines.

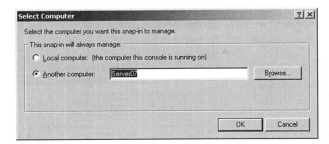

FIGURE 12.2 Connecting to a remote computer for the Computer Management console.

Adding Snap-Ins to a Custom MMC for Remote Management

You can remotely manage servers and other computers by adding snap-ins that you need into an empty MMC shell. Many MMC snap-ins give administrators the option of local focus or remote focus when adding them to a console. Once you configure all the snap-ins, you can create a custom Microsoft Saved Console (.msc) file that you can use over and over again, without having to reconfigure the console every time you use it. To create a custom MMC for remotely managing one or more computers, follow these steps:

1. Click Start, Run; type mmc; and click OK. An empty MMC appears.

2. Click File, Add/Remove Snap-in or press Ctrl+M to display the Add/Remove Snap-in dialog box.

3. Click the Add button to add snap-ins to this MMC. The Add Standalone Snap-In dialog box appears, as shown in Figure 12.3.

FIGURE 12.3 Selecting snap-ins to add to the MMC.

4. Select one of the snap-ins shown in the Available Standalone Snap-Ins list and click the Add button. If the snap-in supports remote management, a Select Computer dialog box appears, as shown in Figure 12.4 for the Disk Management snap-in.

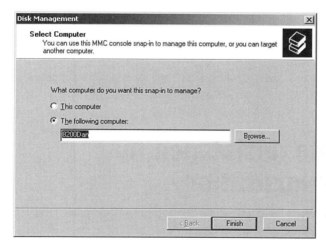

FIGURE 12.4 Selecting a remote computer to manage for the Disk Management MMC snap-in.

5. Click The Following Computer option button and type in the remote computer's name or click Browse to locate it.

6. Click Finish to add the snap-in.

7. Repeat steps 4 through 6 for each snap-in that you want to add.

8. Click Close to exit from the Add Standalone Snap-In dialog box. The snap-ins that you chose appear in the Add/Remove Snap-In dialog box, as shown in Figure 12.5.

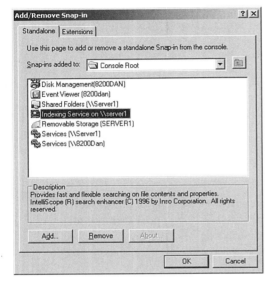

FIGURE 12.5 Viewing selected snap-ins that you loaded into the MMC for managing remote computers.

9. Click OK to close the Add/Remove Snap-In dialog box and return to the main MMC window with all the selected snap-ins loaded.

10. To save your customized console, click File, Save as; type in a filename for this MMC (*.msc) file; and click Save.

Using Remote Assistance for Remote Administration

Remote Assistance (RA) was designed primarily for help-desk personnel (or other trusted computer technicians) to assist users with general computer usage questions and to troubleshoot system problems for Windows XP Professional desktop computers. The RA feature is turned on by default on Windows XP Professional, but for security reasons, it is turned off by default on Windows Server 2003 computers.

To request remote assistance, both the RA requester and the RA provider computers must be running either Windows XP Professional or Windows Server 2003. You can make an RA request via an email message, via Windows

Messenger, or by sending an RA invitation as a file. You can use RA between two computers over an Internet connection, over a local area network (LAN) connection, or through a firewall connection to the Internet, provided that TCP port 3389 is open on the firewall at each end. This port is the same TCP port that is used for Remote Desktop connections accessing Terminal Services. If a computer is using DHCP-assigned IP addresses and the IP addresses changes between the RA request and the RA response to connect, this can also cause problems. In addition, if Network Address Translation (NAT) is used, you might need to configure the proxy server/firewall to allow RDP to function.

> **NOTE**
>
> You must be sure that TCP port 3389 is open for incoming traffic on the firewall for the requester as well as for outgoing traffic on the firewall for the provider; otherwise, RA will not work. If one location does not have a firewall for some reason, you don't need to worry about opening port 3389 for that location; all ports are open without a firewall present unless the Internet service provider (ISP) blocks certain ports.

Configuring Group Policy Settings for Remote Assistance

Windows Server 2003 Active Directory domains offer two distinct group policy object (GPO) settings for the RA feature. Both GPO settings appear in the Computer Configuration\Administrative Templates\System\Remote Assistance node. The Solicited Remote Assistance setting determines whether users can solicit help from other users via RA. When it is enabled, you must specify either Allow Helpers to Remotely Control the Computer or Allow Helpers to Only View the Computer (see Figure 12.6).

You must also specify the Maximum Ticket Time (Value), Maximum Ticket Time (Units), and the method for sending email invitations—Mailto or Simple MAPI. The Mailto option allows RA providers to reply to RA invitations via a hyperlink within the email message that connects the RA provider to the RA requester's computer. The Simple MAPI (SMAPI) option actually embeds the RA invitation file as an attachment within the email message. Double-clicking the RA invitation attachment connects the RA provider to the RA requester's computer.

The Offer Remote Assistance GPO setting determines whether another user, referred to as the "expert," is allowed to offer RA to the computer without the user requesting RA first. The expert user still cannot connect to the computer needing assistance without the user's permission, even if this GPO setting is enabled. If you enable this setting, you must select either Allow Helpers to Remotely Control the

Computer or Allow Helpers to Only View the Computer from the Permit Remote Control of This Computer drop-down list box, just as with the Solicited Remote Assistance GPO setting. You must also specify the names of the users and groups that you want to grant permission for offering RA by clicking the Helpers: Show button (see Figure 12.7).

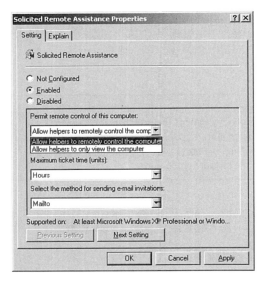

FIGURE 12.6 Enabling the Solicited Remote Assistance GPO setting and specifying its options.

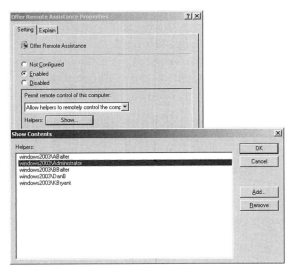

FIGURE 12.7 Enabling the Offer Remote Assistance GPO setting and specifying the authorized RA helpers.

Configuring Remote Assistance on the Client Side

In Windows Server 2003 and Windows XP Professional, if you right-click My Computer, select Properties, and click the Remote tab, you can configure the settings for RA from the client computer's perspective. As previously mentioned, RA is turned on by default for Windows XP, but it is turned off by default for Windows Server 2003. Make sure that the Turn on Remote Assistance and Allow Invitations to Be Sent from This Computer check boxes are marked if you want to use RA on the computer. If you click the Advanced button, you can configure the two option settings for RA, as shown in Figure 12.8. In the Remote Control section, you can clear the Allow This Computer to Be Controlled Remotely check box if you want to provide view-only access to RA personnel. In the Invitations section, you can change the default expiration time for RA invitations from the two drop-down list boxes. You can select from 1 to 99, and you can specify the time interval as Days, Hours, or Minutes. The default maximum time for invitations to remain open is 30 days.

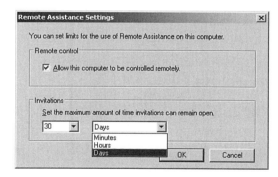

FIGURE 12.8 Specifying RA settings for an individual computer.

Requesting and Receiving RA

If you are working on a Windows XP Professional or even on a Windows Server 2003 computer, you can make a request for someone to assist you by launching the Windows Help and Support Center. From the main Help and Support Center page, find and click the Remote Assistance link. You see the Remote Assistance page where you can click the Invite Someone to Help You link, and then you can follow these steps:

1. After the RA feature loads within the Help and Support Center window, you must select how you want to contact the person whom you want to assist you—via Windows Messenger, via an email invitation, or using the advanced feature of saving the invitation as a file.

2. If you choose to save the RA invitation as a file, you must type the name that you want to appear on the invitation as the person requesting assistance in the From box.

3. Specify the Set the Invitation to Expire parameters; the default for saved invitations is one hour.

4. Click Continue.

5. Be sure to leave the Require the Recipient to Use a Password check box marked for security reasons.

6. Type a password for the person who will be assisting you and confirm it in the Type Password and the Confirm Password boxes.

7. Click the Save Invitation button.

8. When the Save as dialog box appears, choose a location on disk and accept the default filename of RAInvitation.msrcincident (unless you want to change it).

9. Click Save to save the RA invitation file.

10. In some manner (email, file transfer, copy it to a shared network location, and so on), send the invitation file to the person that you want to assist you.

11. When the assistant double-clicks the invitation file, he is prompted for the password for that invitation, as shown in Figure 12.9.

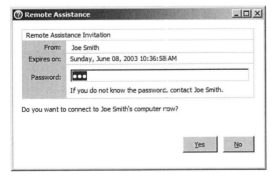

FIGURE 12.9 Initiating an RA session by responding to an RA invitation.

12. The person offering assistance must type the proper invitation password and click Yes to connect to the requester's computer.

13. On the requester's computer, a message box appears asking whether you want to grant permission to the requester to connect to your computer to view and interact with your Windows session (see Figure 12.10). Click Yes to allow the assistant to initiate the RA session.

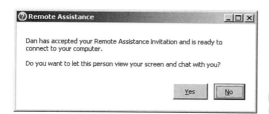

FIGURE 12.10 Accepting an assistant's offer to launch an RA session.

14. Once the requester accepts the assistant's offer for help, the RA session is initiated, as shown in Figure 12.11. Either party can disconnect from the RA session by clicking the Disconnect button.

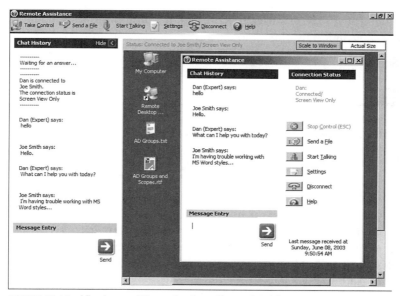

FIGURE 12.11 Viewing an RA session from the assistant's computer.

Using Terminal Services for Remote Administration

The concept of Windows Terminal Services (TS) was first introduced under the moniker Windows NT Server 4.0, Terminal Services Edition. The idea was to use screen emulation to pass mouse and keyboard input back and forth between the client and the server; it supported multiple, simultaneous remote session connections in which all the processing happened on the server computer, not on the workstations. This concept was a throwback to the days of mainframe computing, where all the processing power existed on the main ("server") computer and "dumb" terminals provided the output display and the keyboard input. You installed and configured application programs only once, on the mainframe computer.

Windows 2000 Server brought TS into the mainstream and introduced the concept of using TS for remote administration—at no extra charge! You can install TS on a Windows 2000 Server computer in Remote Administration mode. This option supports up to a maximum of two administrators logged on via TS simultaneously, and you can have one other administrator logged on to the console (working locally and interactively) at the same time. The console is typically thought of as the user that directly accesses the computer using the keyboard, mouse, and monitor. However, an administrator can also take over that session while connecting remotely. If a user is connected to the console session and an administrator logs on locally, the remote console session will close.

Windows Server 2003 works the same way for Remote Administration mode.

> **NOTE**
>
> Generally, TS on the server side is referred to as a Terminal Server. On the client side, TS is referred to as Remote Desktop Connections in Windows XP or newer. The protocol TS uses is called the Remote Desktop Protocol (RDP): Windows Server 2003 implements RDP version 5.2. Windows XP uses RDP version 5.1 and Windows 2000 uses RDP version 5.0.

Windows Server 2003 takes TS to new heights by installing TS in Remote Desktop for Administration mode by default. As an option, Terminal Server is also available on every server to support multiple user connections using Application Server mode. To install this mode, go to Control Panel, Add and Remove Programs; click Add/Remove Windows Components; and mark the check box to install Terminal Server. Under Application Server mode, you need to set up a Terminal Server Licensing Server on your network within 120 days of the first client computer successfully logging on to a Terminal Server in Application Server mode. After this 120-day period, client computers are not allowed to connect to a Terminal Server without a proper Terminal Server Client Access License (TSCAL) issued to each computer that requests a TS connection. Unlike Windows 2000 Server, all Remote Desktop Connection client computers must be issued a TSCAL; there are no built-in TSCALs for connections coming from computers running Windows 2000, Windows XP, or Windows Server 2003.

Licensed users of Windows XP Professional computers are eligible for the Terminal Server 2003 Licensing Transition Plan. Microsoft customers who own licenses for Windows XP Professional on the date that Windows Server 2003 was publicly released in the United States (April 2003) can receive TSCALs for Windows Server 2003 for the number of Windows XP Professional licenses that they own. Microsoft volume licensing customers (Enterprise Agreement, Select, and Open) must enter their volume licensing agreement information into the Terminal Server licensing administration tool on the Microsoft website. Retail and original equipment manufacturer (OEM) customers must enter their Windows XP Professional product keys into the Terminal Server activation website to receive TSCALs for Windows Server 2003.

> **NOTE**
>
> For Windows Server 2003 computers installed in the default configuration for TS Remote Desktop for Administration mode, no license server and no TSCALs are required.

Configuring TS on the Server

As previously mentioned, TS is installed automatically in Windows Server 2003. However, you must enable Remote Desktop connections to allow any RDP connections to the server. To turn on Remote Desktop Connections for a server, right-click My Computer, select Properties, and click the Remote tab. Mark the Allow Users to Connect Remotely to This Computer check box. You can click the Select Remote Users button to add or remove users who have permission to access the server using TS, as shown in Figure 12.12. Adding or removing users and groups with this dialog box is the same as adding or removing users and groups through the properties sheet for the Remote Desktop Users group itself, as shown in Figure 12.13. By default, the local and domain Administrator user accounts retain permission to log on using TS without being members of either the local or the domain Remote Desktop Users groups.

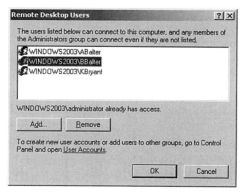

FIGURE 12.12 Enabling Remote Desktop connections and selecting Remote Desktop users.

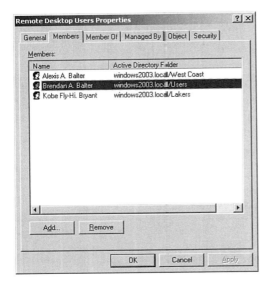

FIGURE 12.13 Viewing members of the Remote Desktop Users group.

TIP

If users will be connecting from Internet connections (without a VPN) to one or more Terminal Servers that are protected by a firewall, you must open TCP port 3389, the default port for TS traffic, on the firewall. You can use a different port for TS traffic to pass through the firewall, if desired. If you change the port on the firewall to TCP port 3393, for example, users need to specify the server name or IP address for the Terminal Server and append it with a colon (:) plus the nondefault port number in the Computer box for the RDC client—as in server1:3393 or 209.144.100.50:3393—instead of simply typing server1 or 209.144.100.50 when using the default port. Connecting over a VPN connection does not involve going through the TCP port number on a firewall; the port on the firewall is bypassed using the VPN.

Configuring RDP Settings

You can configure several parameters of the RDP using the TS Configuration utility. Click Start, (All) Programs, Administrative Tools, Terminal Services Configuration to launch this program. If you click the Server Settings node, you can view the settings that are listed and you can modify all but two of them from this window—Licensing and Permission Compatibility (see Figure 12.14). If you click the Connections node, you see the RDP-Tcp Connection listed as type Microsoft RDP 5.2 in the details pane. If you double-click this connection name, you display the properties sheet for the Remote Desktop protocol on the server. From the General tab, you can specify the Encryption Level setting. The default encryption level is Client Compatible, where all data sent between client and server is encrypted. The High level and the FIPS Compliant level increase the encryption; however, the Low level only encrypts data going from the client computer to the server. The other tabs on the RDP-Tcp Properties window are as follows:

▶ *Logon Settings*—This tab lets you set specific logon information (username, domain, and password) for all users connecting to the server using RDP. You can also specify that the server must always prompt Terminal Server users for a password. The defaults: Use client-provided logon information and do not always prompt for a password.

▶ *Sessions*—This tab allows you to override user settings for session limits and client reconnections.

▶ *Environment*—This tab lets you override user settings for a startup application program at logon time.

▶ *Remote Control*—This tab allows you to override user settings for remote-control options.

▶ *Client Settings*—This tab lets you override user settings for device redirection and maximum color depth.

▶ *Network Adapter*—This tab allows you to specify one individual network adapter or all network adapters for use with remote desktop connections. You can also limit the number of RDP connections from this dialog box.

▶ *Permissions*—This tab lets you set access permissions for users and groups for connecting via RDP. By clicking the Advanced button, selecting a user or group, and clicking Edit, you can view and modify advanced permissions for the RDP, as shown in Figure 12.15.

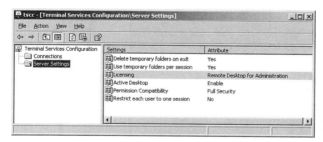

FIGURE 12.14 Viewing terminal settings.

Managing Terminal Server Sessions

If you click Start, (All) Programs, Administrative Tools, Terminal Services Manager, you can run the RDP session monitoring tool. From the Terminal Services Manager, you can view the users, sessions, and processes currently connected and running on each Terminal Server. As you can see in Figure 12.16, by right-clicking a user from the Users tab, you can connect to the current session, disconnect the user from the current session, send the user a message, remotely control the user's session, reset the session, view the current status of the session, and even log off the user from the current session. From the Sessions tab, you can view all the RDP sessions in progress. From the Processes tab, you can view all the processes that are currently active. If you right-click a process, you can select the End Process option to end that particular application or service.

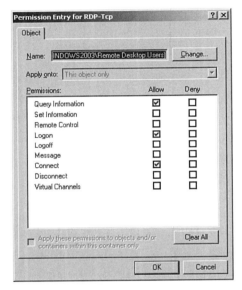

FIGURE 12.15 Viewing advanced permissions for the Remote Desktop Users group.

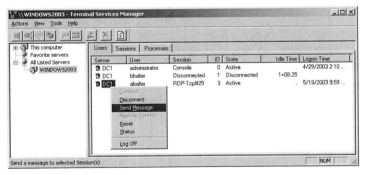

FIGURE 12.16 Monitoring user activity with the Terminal Services Manager tool.

Managing Group Policy Settings for Terminal Services

You can work with the many GPO settings for TS by opening the Group Policy Object Editor and navigating to the Computer Configuration\Administrative

Templates\Windows Components\Terminal Services node. If you are running Windows Server 2003, Enterprise Edition, or Datacenter Edition, you can make available a session directory for Remote Desktop users. By enabling the Join Session Directory GPO setting, you can specify that TS should use a session directory for tracking user sessions, which allows a group of terminal servers to locate and connect users back to disconnected remote desktop sessions. To enable this setting, you must also enable the Session Directory Server setting and the Session Directory Cluster Name setting, as shown in Figure 12.17. In addition, the Terminal Services Session Directory service must be running on the Terminal Server computers running the Enterprise or Datacenter editions of Windows Server 2003.

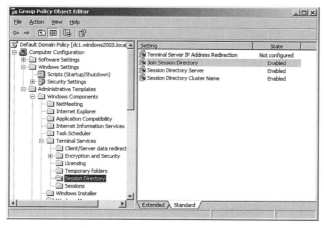

FIGURE 12.17 Specifying GPO settings for a TS session directory under Windows Server 2003, Enterprise Edition, or Datacenter Edition.

Configuring Remote Desktop Connections on the Client

Windows Server 2003 and Windows XP ship with the Remote Desktop Connection (RDC) client software, and these two operating systems install the RDC software by default. The RDC client is a big improvement over its previous cousin, the Terminal Services Client that shipped with Windows 2000 Server. The Terminal Services Client program had to be installed separately on each computer that needed to connect using TS and its feature set was somewhat limited. The RDC client supports a much richer feature set, including an enhanced color scheme for its display, support for the redirection of system sounds, and support for local printers and local disk drives for the remote client session. In addition, it enables you to use Windows keyboard combinations such as Alt+Tab within an RDC session, and you can easily save settings for each remote desktop connection for later use.

> **NOTE**
>
> You can download a self-extracting installation file for the RDC client from Microsoft's website to install on previous Windows operating systems, such as Windows 95, Windows 98, Windows Me, Windows NT 4.0, and Windows 2000. The URL for the RDC client software is `http://www.microsoft.com/windowsxp/pro/downloads/rdclientdl.asp`. Microsoft also offers a Macintosh RDC client that runs on the Mac OS 10.1 or higher; you can find it at `http://www.microsoft.com/mac/DOWNLOAD/MISC/RDC.asp`.

On Windows Server 2003 and Windows XP computers, you can find the RDC client by clicking Start, (All) Programs, Accessories, Communications, Remote Desktop Connection. When you launch the RDC client, it displays as a small window, ready to connect to a Terminal Server as soon as you type a server name or IP address in the Computer box and click Connect. If you click the Options button, you can view the tabbed dialog box showing you the wide array of settings that you can specify for each RDC session:

▶ *General*—The General tab lets you specify the computer name to connect to, and optionally, you can type in a username, password, and domain name and you can mark the Save My Password check box to have the RDC client retain this information for subsequent connections. By default, Windows Server 2003 user logon information is allowed to pass through to the Terminal Server without your having to reenter user logon credentials. Current settings are saved by default; the filename is `default.rdp` located in the My Documents folder for each user and you can open this file in any text editor, such as Notepad.

▶ *Display*—The Display tab lets you configure the resolution for the remote desktop display. It also lets you specify the number of colors to display and whether to display the connection bar when the session is in full-screen mode. The connection bar lets you easily minimize and restore the RDC window as well as disconnect the session by clicking the close (X) icon.

▶ *Local Resources*—The Local Resources tab lets you redirect sound, Windows keyboard combinations, local disk drives, local printers, and even local serial ports to the RDC session (see Figure 12.18).

▶ *Programs*—The Programs tab lets you specify an application to run when you connect to the Terminal Server. When you exit from the application program, the RDC session ends. This option works well when a user needs to access one specific program on the Terminal Server and then wants to be returned to the local computer when she exits that program.

▶ *Experience*—The Experience tab lets you customize the visual elements of the RDC session to the speed of the connection that you will be using for the RDC session (see Figure 12.19). You can select from modem speeds, broadband speeds, and LAN speed (10Mbps or higher), or you can mix and match the settings yourself (Custom).

FIGURE 12.18 Setting Local Resources redirection for the RDC client.

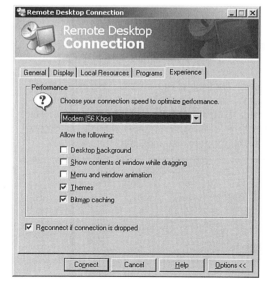

FIGURE 12.19 Specifying the user's visual experience for the RDC client based on connection speed.

TIP

Previously, pass-through of W ndows 2000 user login information to the Terminal Server was not allowed by default; us3rs were required to reenter their logon credentials at the Terminal Server logon dialog box. To change this setting, an administrator cleared the Always Prompt for Password check box on the Logon Settings tab for the RDP-Tcp properties sheet in the Terminal Services Configuration tool (see Figure 12.20).

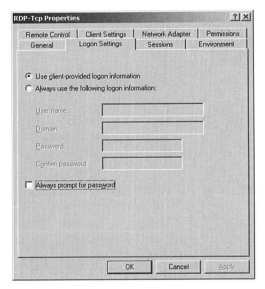

FIGURE 12.20 The Always Prompt for Password check box is cleared (disabled) by default under Windows Server 2003 for RDC logons.

NOTE

Disconnected sessions are *still active!* If you click the Close button on an RDC session window, a message box lets you know that programs continue to run while the session is disconnected (see Figure 12.21). Be sure to log out of a session if you are finished working, and you do not need to have the session continue to run while you are away. After two disconnected sessions, those administrators must reconnect to those sessions and then log off to make RDC sessions available to other administrators. Administrators can also log off users' sessions using Terminal Services Manager. Remember, the maximum number of RDC sessions for Remote Desktop for Administration is two.

FIGURE 12.21 The message box for disconnecting from an RDC session.

TIP

For Windows Server 2003 Terminal Servers, you can actually connect to a Terminal Server's console, as if you were physically there at the Terminal Server computer and logging on. Connecting to a console session allows you to get access to programs that are running within the console session, and it also lets you run applications that might not run within a normal Remote Desktop session. Simply create a shortcut to the RDC client program (`mstsc.exe`) and append the option `/console` to the target command line. For example, you can use this command line as your shortcut's target: `%systemroot%\system32\mstsc.exe /console`. To view all the other command-line options for the RDC client, click Start, Run; type `mstsc /?`; and click OK.

Using the Remote Desktops Snap-In

The Remote Desktops snap-in allows you to view multiple RDC sessions that can all be running simultaneously within one MMC window. This tool is great for centralizing remote administration using one utility for accessing multiple servers at the same time. To use the Remote Desktops snap-in and create a new connection, follow these steps:

1. Click Start, (All) Programs, Administrative Tools, Remote Desktops to launch the snap-in.

2. In the left pane, right-click the Remote Desktops node and select Add New Connection.

3. From the Add New Connection dialog box, type a server's name or IP address in the Server Name or IP Address box (see Figure 12.22). You can also click the Browse button to locate a server.

4. Type a name for this remote connection in the Connection Name box.

5. Clear the Connect to Console check box unless you want to remotely connect to a console session. Only one console session is permitted at a time: If an Administrator is currently logged on to the console, that person will be logged off when you successfully log on.

6. Type in logon information, if desired.

7. Click OK to create this new Remote Desktop connection.

TIP

By default, when you connect to an RDC session from the Remote Desktops snap-in, you are connected to the *console* session. You must clear the Connect to Console check box in the properties sheet for each Remote Desktops connection to connect to nonconsole RDC sessions.

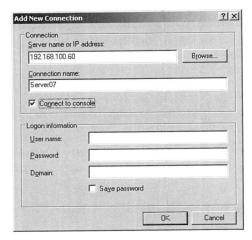

FIGURE 12.22 Adding a new connection to the Remote Desktops MMC snap-in.

To delete a connection, simply right-click the connection name and select Delete. To work with a connection's configuration settings, right-click the connection name and select Properties. Several options are only available after you create a connection—screen display settings, the option to run a program upon connection, and the option to redirect local disk drives to the remote session. Each connection's properties sheet displays three tabs—General, Screen Options, and Other. The General tab displays the same settings that you see when you create a new connection. The Screen Options tab offers you three different choices for configuring the remote display: Expand to Fill MMC Result Pane, Choose Desktop Size, or Enter Custom Desktop Size (see Figure 12.23). The Other tab lets you specify a startup program for the connection, and you can also mark the Redirect Local Drives When Logged on to the Remote Computer check box to make your local disk drives available within the RDC session (see Figure 12.24).

NOTE

If you install the Remote Desktop Web Connection Windows component, users and administrators can connect to Remote Desktop sessions using their web browsers. From the Add or Remove Programs applet in Control Panel, click Add/Remove Windows Components, select Application Server, and click Details. From the Application Server Components dialog box, select Internet Information Services, click Details, select the World Wide Web Service and click Details, and then mark the Remote Desktop Web Connection check box. Click OK for each of the preceding dialog boxes and click Next to install this component. After you install this feature on a server, users can access this server remotely by opening Internet Explorer and typing `http://server_name/tsweb` in the Address box to display the Remote Desktop Web Connection page, as shown in Figure 12.25.

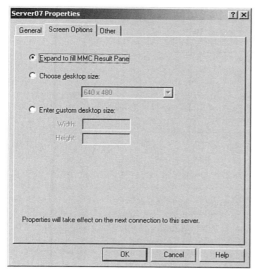

FIGURE 12.23 Setting screen options for a Remote Desktops connection.

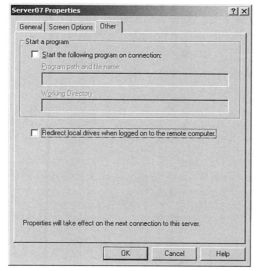

FIGURE 12.24 Specifying a startup program and local drives redirection.

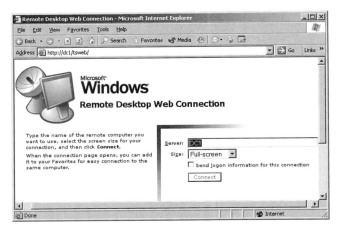

FIGURE 12.25   Accessing a server remotely using the Remote Desktop Web Connection.

Exam Prep Questions

1. You are logged on to a Windows Server 2003 member server as AlexisB and the user account you are logged on as is a member of the Domain Users group. The server is configured using default settings. How can you temporarily stop the fax service on the server without logging out and logging back on using the Administrator user account?

   ○ **A.** Click Start, Run; type services.msc; and click OK. Then, right-click the fax service and select stop.

   ○ **B.** Open a command prompt and type `net stop fax /user: windows2003.local\administrator`.

   ○ **C.** Open a command prompt, type `runas /user:windows2003.local\administrator "net stop fax"`, and then type in the proper password when prompted.

   ○ **D.** Right-click My Computer and select Manage. Expand the Services and Applications node, right-click the Fax node, and select Stop.

2. Which of the following Windows operating systems support the RA feature? (Choose two.)

   ○ **A.** Windows XP Professional

   ○ **B.** Windows Server 2003

   ○ **C.** Windows Me

   ○ **D.** Windows 2000 Professional

   ○ **E.** Windows 2000 Server

3. Which of the following Windows operating systems support TS as a server? (Choose three.)

   ○ **A.** Windows XP Professional

   ○ **B.** Windows Server 2003

   ○ **C.** Windows NT Server 4.0 Standard Edition

   ○ **D.** Windows 2000 Professional

   ○ **E.** Windows 2000 Server

   ○ **F.** Windows Me

4. Which tool do you need to use to specify settings, such as the encryption level between client and server computers, for TS on a Windows Server 2003 computer?

   ○ **A.** Terminal Services Manager

   ○ **B.** Terminal Services Configuration

   ○ **C.** Terminal Server Licensing

   ○ **D.** The Remote Desktops snap-in

5. You are the network administrator for a company that has offices in three different geographic locations—New York, New York; Dallas, Texas; and San Francisco, California. You are in Dallas, and you're trying to remotely administer a Windows Server 2003 computer named server07 in San Francisco. The San Francisco office has an Exchange Server computer installed that handles company email for the entire West Coast region. You have visited the San Francisco office before, and you've been able to access the server using an RDC within the office. From Dallas, you can send and receive SMTP and POP3 email over the Internet using the San Francisco Exchange Server. However, when you attempt to connect to server07 using an RDC and the IP address 207.107.17.77, you receive a message box that states: "The client could not connect to the remote computer. Remote connections might not be enabled for the computer or it might be too busy to accept new connections. It is also possible that network problems are preventing your connection." What is the most likely cause of this problem?

   ○ **A.** Remote Desktop connections are not enabled on server07. Mark the Allow Users to Connect to This Computer Remotely check box on the Remote tab of the System Properties window.

   ○ **B.** The Remote Desktop for Administration feature is not yet installed on server07.

   ○ **C.** The RA feature is not enabled on server07. Mark the Turn on Remote Assistance and Allow Invitations to Be Sent from This Computer check box on the Remote tab of the System Properties window.

   ○ **D.** TCP port 3389 is closed on the company's Internet firewall.

6. How can you remotely view and interact with a user's Windows desktop who is working within a Remote Desktop Connection session without using RA?

   ○ **A.** Use Terminal Services Manager to "shadow" the user's console session by right-clicking the user's name and selecting Remote Control.

   ○ **B.** Use Terminal Services Manager to shadow the user's RDC session by right-clicking the user's name and selecting Remote Control.

   ○ **C.** Use Terminal Services Configuration to shadow the user's console session by right-clicking the user's name and selecting Remote Control.

   ○ **D.** Use the Remote Desktops snap-in to shadow the user's session by making sure that the Connect to Console check box is marked in the connection's properties sheet.

7. On which of the following operating systems can you install an edition of the Microsoft RDC client software? (Choose two.)

    ○ **A.** Mac OS X 10.1 or higher

    ○ **B.** Windows NT Workstation 4.0

    ○ **C.** Windows NT Server 3.51

    ○ **D.** Windows for Workgroups 3.11

    ○ **E.** MS-DOS 6.22

8. You manage a server named Server1. Since Server1 has a public website, it has IIS installed on it. You need to be able to view the system and application logs using a web browser and the remote administration must be encrypted. What should you do?

    ○ **A.** Enable Remote Desktop.

    ○ **B.** Install the Remote Administration (HTML) Windows component.

    ○ **C.** Install the Remote Desktop Web Connection Windows component.

    ○ **D.** Enable Telnet service to automatic and start the Telnet service.

9. You are the network administrator. You have a new server running Windows Server 2003 with the default settings that has been added to your domain. You are a member of the local administrators group on the server. You need to remotely manage the server. You have no money to purchase additional software. How should you reconfigure the server?

    ○ **A.** In the system Properties dialog box, enable Remote Assistance.

    ○ **B.** In the System Properties dialog box, enable Remote Desktop.

    ○ **C.** Add our user account to the Remote Desktop Users local group.

    ○ **D.** Install Terminal Services by using Add or Remove Programs.

10. You have a Windows XP Professional computer that you use to access your web servers using Remote Desktop. You frequently need to update the contents on the web folders. Therefore, you need to copy web documents to the web folders. What should you do?

    ○ **A.** Install the Terminal Server on all your web servers. Modify the registry to allow drives.

    ○ **B.** Install the terminal server and create a new Microsoft RDP connection.

    ○ **C.** On the client computer, select the Disk Drives check box in the properties of Remote Desktop Connection.

    ○ **D.** On each client computer, select the Allow users to connect remotely to this computer check box in the System Properties dialog box.

    ○ **E.** Make sure that the user has administrative permissions on the server.

Answers to Exam Prep Questions

1. **Answer C is correct.** Only the Run as command allows you to run a system utility or a program as a different user other than the user you are currently logged on as. Answer A is incorrect because you must be at least a member of the Server Operators group to stop and start system services. Answer B is incorrect because the `net stop` and `net start` commands do not support the `/user:` option. Answer D is incorrect because, as just mentioned, you must be a member of the Server Operators or the Administrators group to stop and start system services.

2. **Answers A and B are correct.** The RA feature is only supported on Windows XP and Windows Server 2003 computers. Answers C, D, and E are incorrect because RA is not supported on these operating systems.

3. **Answers A, B, and E are correct.** Windows XP Professional supports one Remote Desktop console session, whereas Windows Server 2003 and Windows 2000 Server both support up to two simultaneous Remote Desktop connections as a server in Remote Administration mode. Answers C, D, and F are incorrect because TS as a server is not supported on these operating systems.

4. **Answer B is correct.** Terminal Services Configuration allows you to select the Connections node and double-click the RDP-Tcp connection object to specify Terminal Server properties such as the encryption level. Answer A is incorrect because Terminal Services Manager lets you administer active TS sessions. Answer C is incorrect because Terminal Server Licensing lets you work with TS licenses when the server is set up in Application Server mode. Answer D is incorrect because the Remote Desktops snap-in connects you to other Terminal Servers; it does not configure TS settings.

5. **Answer D is correct.** Because you have successfully logged on to server07 remotely within the San Francisco office, this attempt would indicate that the problem is from outside the LAN and that the firewall port 3389 is not open to allow RDP-TCP traffic. Answer A is incorrect because RDCs apparently work within the LAN. Answer B is incorrect because the Remote Desktop for Administration feature is installed by default under Windows Server 2003. Answer C is incorrect because RDCs do not depend upon the RA feature being enabled or disabled.

6. **Answer B is correct.** Answer A is incorrect because although you can use Terminal Services Manager to shadow users, you can only use Remote Control to connect to existing RDP sessions, not a console session in which the user is logged on interactively. Answer C is incorrect because you cannot use Terminal Services Configuration to shadow a user's session. Answer D is incorrect because you cannot use the Remote Desktops snap-in to shadow a user's session, especially if you mark the Connect to Console check box.

7. **Answers A and B are correct.** Answer C is incorrect because Microsoft does not publish a version of the RDC client for Windows NT Server 3.51. Answer D is incorrect because Microsoft does not publish a version of the RDC client for the 16-bit Windows for Workgroups operating system. Answer E is incorrect because Microsoft does not publish a version of the RDC client for the legacy MS-DOS operating system.

8. **Answer C is correct.** The Remote Desktop Web Connection ActiveX control allows you to access your computer through Remote Desktop via the Internet using Internet Explorer. Of course, you must have IIS to host this web feature. To add this component, you add this package from Add/Remove in the Control Panel.

9. **Answer B is correct.** Because it has been added to the domain, you need to enable Remote Desktop. Of course, you must have the appropriate permissions. By default, members of the Administrator group can connect remotely to the server. Other members must be added to the Remote Desktop Users group.

10. **Answer C is correct.** When this option is enabled, you can open My Computer on the remote server and view the disk drives from the client computer listed with the disk drives from the server.

Need to Know More?

1. Holme, Dan, and Hank Carbeck. *MCSA/MCSE Self-Paced Training Kit (Exam 70-290): Managing and Maintaining a Microsoft Windows Server 2003 Environment*. Redmond, Washington: Microsoft Press, 2003.

2. Morimoto, Rand, et. al. *Microsoft Windows Server 2003 Unleashed*. Indianapolis, Indiana: Sams Publishing, 2003.

3. Search the Microsoft Product Support Services Knowledge Base on the Internet: `http://support.microsoft.com`. You can also search Microsoft TechNet on the Internet: `http://www.microsoft.com/technet`. Find technical information using keywords from this chapter, such as Run as, administration tools, MMC, Remote Assistance, Terminal Services and Remote Desktop.

CHAPTER THIRTEEN

Preparing to Monitor Server Performance

Terms you'll need to understand:

✓ Event Viewer

✓ Task Manager

✓ System Monitor

✓ Performance logs and alerts

✓ Performance objects

✓ Performance counters

✓ Performance object instances

Techniques you'll need to master:

✓ Monitoring events with the Event Viewer

✓ Monitoring and managing applications, processes, and current system vital signs with Task Manager

✓ Using the Performance snap-in

✓ Viewing real-time server performance data with the System Monitor tool

Server performance can degrade over time as more users, more workstations, and more demands are placed on server resources. Windows Server 2003 offers administrators several built-in tools for monitoring, optimizing, and troubleshooting a server's performance. The Task Manager tool can tell us how the server's memory, network, and processor utilization are doing. The Event Viewer snap-in can show us both recent and past events that might be impacting the server's robustness. The System Monitor tool can diagram several vital aspects (or counters) of computer health in real time, as well as create a historical log of these various system counters to establish a baseline of performance over a period of time.

Understanding and Monitoring System Events

Many different processes are constantly running on computers, especially on server systems. Operating system and third-party services run in the background, application programs run in the foreground for users on Terminal Server systems, and network applications, such as Microsoft SQL Server or Exchange Server, run in the background. Don't forget about other programs that run in the foreground that administrators execute when performing routine management chores, such as the Active Directory Users and Computers console, Terminal Services Manager, and other utilities.

All the processes that run on a server communicate with the operating system, which in turn communicates with other subsystems and the computer's hardware devices. The messages that are sent back and forth between application programs and the operating system can generate different types of events. Windows Server 2003 records these events in log files. You can view the events stored in these log files by using the Event Viewer snap-in, `eventvwr.msc`. All the processes that run on a server are executing programming code that must be transferred into and out of the computer's memory. The programming code is executed by the computer's central processing unit (CPU), often called the "processor," and the executing code resides within files that are stored on disk subsystems. The data that is manipulated by these processes is also stored on disk subsystems. The System Monitor node of the Performance snap-in can track processor utilization, memory utilization, and disk utilization, among several other items.

Working with the Event Viewer

You can launch the Event Viewer snap-in tool by clicking Start, All Programs, Administrative Tools, Event Viewer, or simply click Start, Run; type `eventvwr.msc`; and click OK. Events are recorded into log files by the Event

Log service, which is configured to run at system startup by default. All Event Log files are stored in the `%systemroot%\system32\config` folder by default. Event Log files are identified with the `.evt` filename extension. These log files are not text files; you cannot view them using a simple text editor such as Notepad. You can easily save the `.evt` files in various text-readable formats, which are covered later in this chapter. On Windows Server 2003 standalone computers and domain member servers, there are just three different event logs:

▶ *Application*—This log records events that are generated by application programs and network application services such as Microsoft SQL Server and Exchange Server. The name of this log file stored on disk is `AppEvent.Evt`.

▶ *Security*—This log records success and failure notifications for audited events. Administrators can configure various auditing settings through local or group policies; the results of those audited events get recorded in the security log. Only users who have been granted the user right called Manage Auditing and the Security Log may access the security log; members of the Administrators group retain this right by default. The name of this log file stored on disk is `SecEvent.Evt`.

▶ *System*—This log records events generated by the operating system and its subsystems, such as its device drivers and services. The name of this log file stored on disk is `SysEvent.Evt`.

For Windows Server 2003 computers that have been set up as domain controllers (DCs), the Active Directory Installation Wizard (`DCPROMO.exe`) adds three other event logs, as shown in Figure 13.1. These additional logs monitor vital parts of Active Directory, such as the directory service itself, the File Replication Service, and the DNS (Domain Name System) server (if the DNS Server service is installed on the DC). The three additional event logs for DCs are the following:

▶ *Directory Service*—This log records events that are generated by the Active Directory service itself. The name of this log file stored on disk is `NTDS.Evt`.

▶ *DNS Server*—This log records DNS queries, DNS replies, and assorted other DNS-related activities. The name of this log file stored on disk is `DnsEvent.Evt`.

▶ *File Replication Service*—This log records activities related to the File Replication Service, including messages about replication problems between DCs. The name of this log file stored on disk is `NtFrs.Evt`.

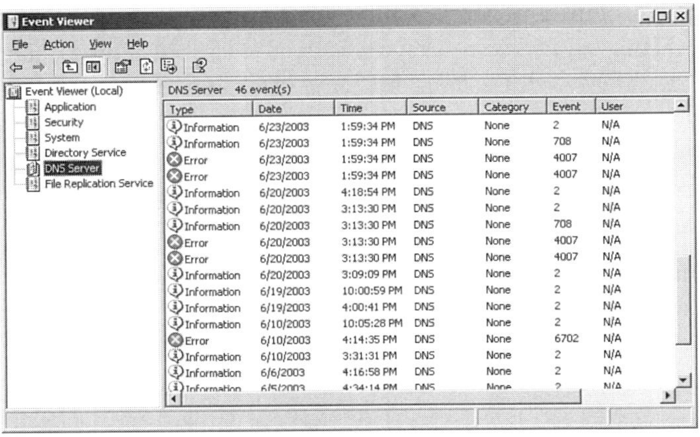

FIGURE 13.1 Looking at system events in the Event Viewer for a domain controller.

Viewing Event Logs

After you launch the Event Viewer, you can select the log you want to look at in the left pane; the events then appear in the right (details) pane, as you can see in Figure 13.1. When you double-click an event, its properties window appears, as shown in Figure 13.2. An event's properties window displays the details of the event, including the date, time, computer name, event ID, and a description of the event itself. The Event Viewer displays five types of events:

▶ *Error*—These events are recorded whenever significant problems occur, such as the loss of data or the loss of functionality. Unexpected system shutdowns and the failure of a service to start automatically at boot time are examples of events that are logged as errors.

▶ *Warning*—These events are recorded to indicate possible future problems. Low disk space for a drive volume is an example of an event that might get logged as a warning.

▶ *Information*—These events are recorded often. They indicate the successful operation of a program, a device driver, or a service. For example, Event ID 6005 indicates that "The Event Service was started"; this event usually occurs when the computer is started or restarted.

▶ *Failure Audit*—These events are recorded each time that any audited security event fails. For example, if a user attempts to log on to the computer without the proper username or password, a failure audit event is logged if the policy setting for Audit Account Logon Events is set to Success, Failure or if it's set only to Failure. You can configure Audit Policy settings at the local or group policy levels.

▶ *Success Audit*—These events are recorded each time that any audited security event succeeds. For example, if a user successfully logs on to the computer, a success audit event is logged if the policy setting for Audit Account Logon Events is set to Success, Failure or if it's set only to Success. You can configure Audit Policy settings at the local or group policy levels.

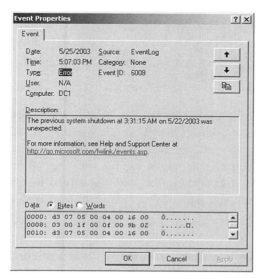

FIGURE 13.2 Viewing the Event Properties dialog.

Audit policy settings are available at the local, site, domain, DC, and organizational unit (OU) policy levels. You can use the Local Security Settings snap-in, the Default Domain Security Settings snap-in, the Default Domain Controller Security Settings snap-in, or the Group Policy Object Editor snap-in for a site or an OU to affect audit policy settings. From one of the snap-ins just mentioned, expand the Security Settings node, expand the Local Policies subnode, and select the Audit Policy subnode. Double-click the policy setting listed in the details pane to configure it, as shown in Figure 13.3.

Archiving Event Logs, Setting Options, and Filtering Events

Event logs fill up over time. By default, the maximum log size for each event log is 16,384KB. By default, when the log reaches its maximum size, it overwrites events as needed. If you want to manually clear a log, right-click the log (in the left pane of the Event Viewer) and select Clear All Events. A message box asks whether you want to save the events contained in this log before you clear them. If you click Yes, the Save As dialog box prompts you to choose a location on disk, a filename for this log, and the file type to save this log as—Event Log (.evt), Text (tab delimited, *.txt), or CSV (comma delimited, *.csv).

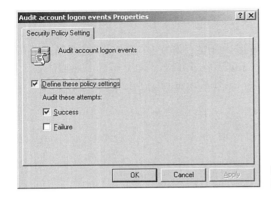

FIGURE 13.3 Configuring Audit Policy settings.

You can open logs saved in the .evt file format within the Event Viewer. You can right-click a log in the Event Viewer, select Open Log File, and then specify the location and name of the file to open it. You can also right-click the Event Viewer root node and select Open Log File to open a log file without closing any of the existing logs. You can open logs saved in the .txt file format in any text editor or word processing program. You can open logs saved in the .csv file format in applications such as Microsoft Excel or Notepad. However, the Event Viewer cannot itself open logs saved as .txt or .csv files.

If you right-click one of the Event logs in the left pane of the Event Viewer and select Properties, from the General tab, you can view and configure option settings for that specific Event Log, as shown in Figure 13.4. You can change the maximum log size, configure log overwrite settings, specify whether you're using a low-speed connection, clear the log, and restore all the default settings for the log from its properties sheet. The default setting for event logs is to overwrite events as necessary after reaching the maximum log size. Also from the log's properties sheet, you can click the Filter tab to filter and sort all the different events contained in the log (see Figure 13.5).

EXAM ALERT

If you right-click a log, you can take advantage of a new feature of Windows Server 2003 called *new log view*. When you create a new log view, you can specify how the Event Viewer presents the log instead of always modifying the default display settings for the log. You can give this new log view a custom name, and you can manage it just like any other log. If you create a custom MMC snap-in, your customized settings for each new log view are maintained while the settings for the original log on which the new log view is based are left alone.

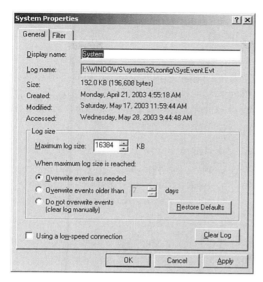

FIGURE 13.4 Configuring Event Log option settings for the System log.

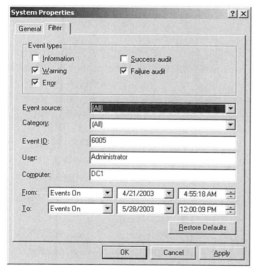

FIGURE 13.5 Setting sorting and filtering options for the System log.

Working with the System Monitor

The System Monitor tool is available as a node within the Performance snap-in, perfmon.msc. The System Monitor can display performance data about the local computer, or it can display performance data on one or more remote computers in real time. The System Monitor tool can also log a history of performance results over time for local or remote computers. To monitor system performance, you must specify performance *objects*, *counters*, and *instances* of those objects so that the System Monitor knows which areas of system performance to track and display. These performance specifiers are defined as follows:

▶ *Performance Objects*—These items are logical collections of performance metrics associated with a computer resource (CPU, disk, memory) or service that you can monitor. Processor, Memory, PhysicalDisk, and Paging File are all examples of performance objects.

▶ *Performance Object Instances*—These terms provide a method of identifying multiple performance objects of the same type. If a computer has more than one processor installed, its processor performance object displays multiple distinct instances of this object to monitor each individual processor separately.

▶ *Performance Counters*—These data items direct the System Monitor about which areas of performance to track and display. Each performance object has several performance counters associated with it. Pages/sec, Available Bytes, and %Committed Bytes in Use are all examples of counters for the Memory performance object.

In Windows Server 2003, the System Monitor tool is preconfigured with three sets of performance objects, counters, and instances (object:counter:instance) by default each time that you launch the Performance snap-in, as shown in Figure 13.6:

▶ *Memory:Pages/sec*—This performance metric is the rate at which pages are read from or written to disk to resolve hard page faults. Hard page faults occur when a process requests a page from memory, but the system cannot find it and it must be retrieved from disk. This metric is a primary indicator of the kinds of faults that cause systemwide slowdowns. *This value should remain consistently between 0 and 20 but not consistently higher than 20.*

▶ *PhysicalDisk:Avg. Disk Queue Length:_Total*—This performance metric is the average number of both read and write requests that were queued (waiting) for the selected disk during the sample interval. *This value should remain consistently between 0 and 2 but not consistently higher than 2.*

▶ *Processor:% Processor Time:_Total*—This performance metric is the percentage of elapsed time that the processor spends to execute a non-idle thread. It is calculated by measuring the duration that the idle thread is active in the sample interval and subtracting that time from interval duration. (Each processor has an idle thread that consumes cycles when no other threads are ready to run.) This metric is the primary indicator of processor activity and displays the average percentage of busy time observed during the sample interval. It is calculated by monitoring the time that the service is inactive and subtracting that value from 100%. *This value should remain consistently below the 85% mark.*

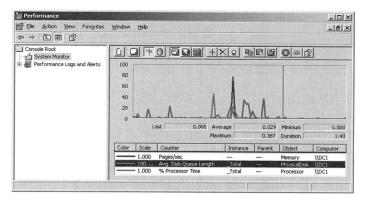

FIGURE 13.6 Watching the System Monitor in graph view with the default performance objects, counters, and instances.

NOTE

The `diskperf.exe` `-y` command is no longer required under Windows Server 2003 to enable either LogicalDisk or PhysicalDisk objects and counters. All disk objects and counters are automatically enabled on demand for Windows Server 2003 and Windows XP computers.

Monitoring System Performance

You can monitor system performance in one of two ways—real-time monitoring and logged monitoring. Real-time monitoring measures the current performance of the server's processors, memory, physical disks, and network utilization, among other metrics. You can find out what type of usage load a server is currently experiencing by monitoring subsystems in real time. You use logged monitoring to analyze server performance over an extended period of time. By recording historical performance data into log files during "normal" usage periods, you can establish a baseline of performance data that you can use to compare against future performance data to help diagnose and alleviate performance bottlenecks that might occur.

Using System Monitoring in Real Time with Task Manager

You can use either the Task Manager tool or the System Monitor tool to measure system performance in real time. You can access the Task Manager in any one of three ways:

▶ Right-click the taskbar and select Task Manager.

▶ Press Ctrl+Shift+Esc on the keyboard.

▶ Press Ctrl+Alt+Del on the keyboard and select Task Manager.

The Task Manager utility under Windows Server 2003 displays five tabs—Applications, Processes, Performance, Networking, and Users, as shown in Figure 13.7. The Applications tab shows the application programs that are currently running in the foreground; background services do not appear on this page. The Processes tab displays the processes currently running on the computer; to view all processes from all users logged on to the computer, mark the Show Processes from All Users check box. The Performance tab shows current usage of the CPUs, the CPU Usage History charts, current Page File usage, Page File Usage History chart, and current memory usage statistics. The Networking tab is new for Windows Server 2003; it charts the current network adapters' network traffic utilization (see Figure 13.8). The Users tab lists the users who are currently logged onto the console or logged on via Remote Desktop connections (see Figure 13.9).

Task Manager offers you a quick glimpse at the following items:

▶ Applications currently in use

▶ Processes currently running

▶ Current processor usage

▶ Current paging file usage

▶ Overall current memory usage

▶ Current network utilization

▶ Currently logged on users

For any other vital statistics on a system, or for more detailed and in-depth inquiries, you should use the System Monitor and the Performance Logs and Alerts tools.

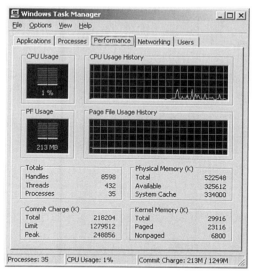

FIGURE 13.7 Monitoring system performance in real time with Task Manager.

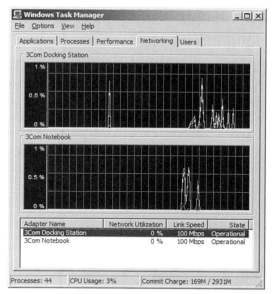

FIGURE 13.8 Monitoring a system's network utilization in real time with Task Manager.

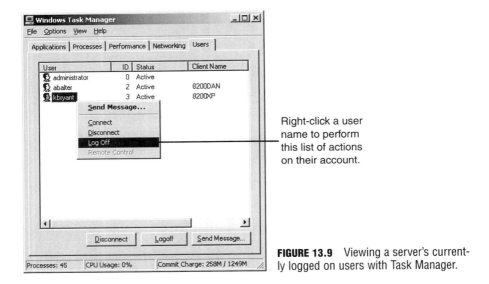

Right-click a user name to perform this list of actions on their account.

FIGURE 13.9 Viewing a server's currently logged on users with Task Manager.

Using Real-Time Monitoring with System Monitor

You can configure the System Monitor tool to display its results in any of three different views—graph, histogram, or report. The graph view is the default, and it supports the most optional settings. The histogram view is a bar-chart configuration, as shown in Figure 13.10. The report view is simply a straightforward list of the performance objects, counters, and their associated instances in a report-like format (see Figure 13.11). Using the System Monitor, you can monitor the local computer or several remote computers over a network connection.

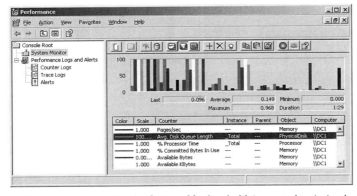

FIGURE 13.10 Watching the System Monitor in histogram view to track several performance objects and counters.

The default configuration is to monitor the local computer in real time. You can change the default settings to monitor one or more remote computers in real time. You can also choose to record the system performance of the local or remote computers to a log file using the Performance Logs and Alerts node of the Performance snap-in. You can play back and view the results of those log files using the System Monitor tool.

TIP

> To obtain the most accurate results when checking a computer's performance with System Monitor, you should monitor a computer remotely. System Monitor itself requires a certain amount of overhead to run. Therefore, when you run System Monitor on the same machine you are measuring, the performance data can be negatively affected and the results might be somewhat skewed.

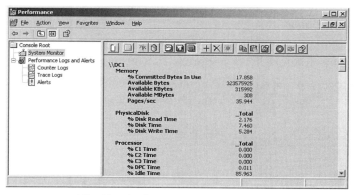

FIGURE 13.11 Watching the System Monitor in report view to track several performance objects and counters.

Adding and Removing Objects, Counters, and Instances

System Monitor offers you a variety of ways to add objects, counters, and instances to its list of monitored items; collectively, these items as referred to simply as *counters*. To add counters, you can click the plus sign (+) on the icon bar, you can press Ctrl+I on the keyboard, or you can right-click the right (details) pane in any view and select Add Counters. To both add and remove counters, you can right-click the details pane in any view, select Properties, and click the Data tab. To add counters to System Monitor, follow these steps:

1. Open the Performance snap-in and click the System Monitor node.

2. Click the plus sign (+) on the icon bar, press Ctrl+I on the keyboard, right-click the details pane and select Add Counters, or right-click the details pane and select Properties and use the Data tab.

3. From the Add Counters dialog box, select either the Use Local Computer Counters option or the Select Counters From Computer option; type in a computer name or select a remote computer.

4. Select the performance object that you want to monitor from the drop-down list box.

5. Click the All Counters option button or the Select Counters from List option button.

6. Select the counter that you want to monitor from the list of counters. Click the Explain button to view a definition of the specific counter that you have selected (see Figure 13.12).

7. Click the All Instances option button or the Select Instances from List option button.

8. Choose the instance of the object that you want to monitor. The _Total option monitors the sum of all the instances for that selected object:counter combination.

9. Click the Add button to add the selected object:counter:instance combination to System Monitor's list of performance items to monitor.

10. Repeat this process for each object:counter:instance combination that you want to add. Click Close when you are done adding counters.

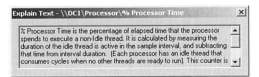

FIGURE 13.12 Adding performance counters to System Monitor with the Add Counters dialog box.

To remove counters from System Monitor, you can select the counter that you want to remove at the bottom of the details pane and press the Del key on the keyboard. You can also remove counters another way by following these steps:

1. Right-click the details pane and select Properties.

2. Select the Data tab.

3. Select the counter (or several counters) that you want to delete from the Counters list box.

4. Press the Remove button.

Using Logged Monitoring with Performance Logs and Alerts

The Performance Logs and Alerts tool in Windows Server 2003 is the other half of the Performance snap-in. Performance Logs and Alerts supports *logged monitoring* to log files larger than 1GB, up to the maximum supported file size for the file system on which the logs are stored. In addition, you can append performance data onto existing log files. Two new groups (installed by default) allow users to gather performance data for a computer *without* requiring that those users become members of the Administrators group:

▶ *Performance Log Users*—This is a local group on standalone and domain member servers and a domain local group on domain controllers. Members of this group have permission to *manage and schedule logged* performance counters, logs, and alerts on the local server or on servers within the domain, both interactively (locally) and remotely.

▶ *Performance Monitor Users*—This is a local group on standalone and domain member servers and a domain local group on domain controllers. Members of this group have permission to *monitor* performance counters, logs, and alerts on the local server or on servers within the domain, both interactively (locally) and remotely. Members of this group do not need to be members of the Administrators group or the Performance Log Users group to monitor performance.

The Performance Logs and Alerts tool offers administrators three major benefits:

▶ The ability to record system performance data at specified intervals over time using *counter logs*

▶ A method to record detailed system events after specific events occur using *trace logs*

▶ A configuration setting for being notified by the system when specific counters exceed certain preset thresholds using *alerts*

EXAM ALERT

Counter logs enable you to collect data about a server's performance over time to establish a *baseline* of normal performance for a given computer system. You should collect baseline data during periods of regular activity, not during temporary periods of high or low server usage. Baselines can only be an effective barometer of average server performance under "normal" loads; recording performance data during peak usage times does not create an accurate baseline reading, nor does recording performance at times when the system is not being used. In some cases, it might be interesting to record the system without users on it to know the minimum level of activity the system generates on its own for replication traffic and so on. This no-user baseline gives the administrators another piece of information to use when considering system upgrades. You should create and use system performance baselines for future comparison purposes when you suspect that server performance has degraded over time or when you evaluate new purchases. By comparing baseline readings with current performance results, you can quickly determine whether there is truly a performance bottleneck or whether you might need additional hardware. Remember, if you change the server's hardware configuration, you need to reestablish a baseline for that system.

Configuring Counter Logs

Counter logs enable you to collect performance data on systems over periods of time to create performance baselines, chart and analyze performance trends, and diagnose performance bottlenecks. Once you configure one or more counter logs, you can schedule these logs to record data automatically at predetermined times. You can also start and stop counter logs manually if you want. You can choose from five different types of counter log storage formats—comma delimited (.csv) text files; tab delimited (.tsv) files; binary files (.blg); binary circular files (.blg) that overwrite themselves when they reach a maximum size; and SQL database files, which require a connection to a Microsoft SQL Server computer and access to an accompanying SQL database table. To set up a new counter log, follow these steps:

1. Launch the Performance console.

2. Expand the Performance Logs and Alerts node and select the Counter Logs subnode.

3. Right-click the Counter Logs subnode and select New Log Settings.

4. Type a name for this log in the Name box and click OK.

5. From the General tab of the properties dialog box that appears (see Figure 13.13), you can perform the following tasks:

   ▶ Click the Add Objects button to add objects with *all* their associated counters to the log.

   ▶ Click the Add Counters button to add individual counters and instances to the log.

   ▶ Select one or more objects or counters from the Counters list and click the Remove button to delete them.

6. To change the sample interval, type a number or increment or decrement the interval using the up or down arrows on the Interval spinner box.

7. To change the sample interval time units, click the Units drop-down list box and select from Seconds, Minutes, Hours, or Days.

8. If you want to have the counter log record data under a specific user account's security context, type the user account name in the Run as box and then click the Set Password button to specify the proper password.

9. Click the Log Files tab to specify log-file options, as shown in Figure 13.14.

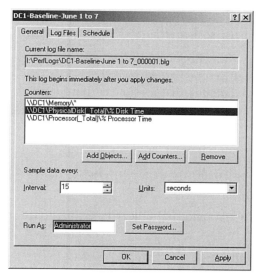

FIGURE 13.13 Adding objects and counters to a new counter log in Performance Logs and Alerts.

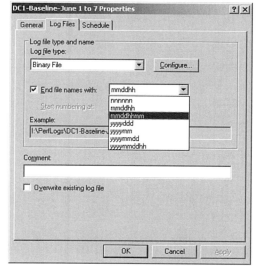

FIGURE 13.14 Specifying log-file formats for a new counter log.

10. Click the Log File Type drop-down list box to select the type of log storage format that you want for this log—binary file (default), text file (comma delimited), text file (tab delimited), binary circular file, or SQL database.

11. Click the Configure button to change the location of the log file, change the log filename, or establish a maximum log file size. If the Maximum Limit (default) option is selected, the logging will continue for this counter log until the log file uses all the available space on the disk where the log is located. Click OK for the Configure Log Files dialog box when finished.

12. Clear the End File Names with check box if you do not want the log file's name appended with a numeric sequence number or a date format.

13. If you leave the End File Names with check box marked, you can select from the nnnnnn setting or one or several date formats from the associated drop-down list box, such as mmddhh that uses the current month, day, and hour or mmddhhmm that uses the current month, day, hour, and minute.

14. Optionally, you can type a description in the Comment box.

15. Mark the Overwrite Existing Log File if you want to overwrite an existing file that has the same name.

16. Click the Schedule tab to specify start and stop times for logging to this counter log, as showr. in Figure 13.15.

17. Click OK to create the new counter log.

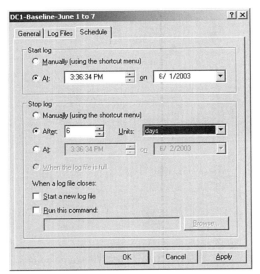

FIGURE 13.15 Scheduling start and stop times for a counter log.

To manually start a counter log to record performance data, right-click the counter log name in the details pane of Performance Logs and Alerts and select Start. The icon for the counter log turns to green, indicating that logging is occurring. To manually stop a counter log from logging data, right-click the counter log name and select Stop. To modify a counter log's settings, right-click the log and select Properties.

TIP

You can create a counter log from an existing set of counters set up in the System Monitor tool by right-clicking anywhere in the details pane of System Monitor and selecting Save As. When the Save As dialog box appears, select a location on disk to save these settings, specify the Save as Type as a Web page (`*.htm`, `*.html`) file, and click Save to save the settings file. Next, go to the Performance Logs and Alerts node, right-click the Counter Logs subnode, and select New Log Settings. Locate the settings file that you saved and click the Open button. Click OK for the message box that appears. Type a name for this new counter log in the Name box for the New Log Settings dialog box that pops up. Make any changes that you want to the new counter log's properties window that appears and click OK when you are done.

To view the results of logging to a counter log, go to System Monitor and click the View Log Data icon from the icon bar or press Ctrl+L on the keyboard. Be sure that the Source tab is selected. Click the Log Files option button, if you are not using the SQL Database logging format. Next, click the Add button, locate the log file using the Select Log File dialog box, and click Open to select the file. If you are using the SQL database logging format, click the Database option button and select the SQL System DSN and Log Set from their respective drop-down list boxes. Click the Time Range button to adjust the period of time view for displaying the log file's results; use the slider bar to shorten or lengthen the time window. Lengthening the time window gives you more of an overall view of a performance trend; shortening the time window lets you zoom in to analyze the details of system performance for a specific period of time. Click OK for the System Monitor Properties dialog box, as shown in Figure 13.16.

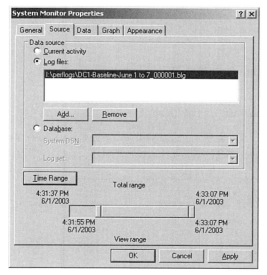

FIGURE 13.16 Setting the data source for a counter log to display its results in System Monitor.

> **NOTE**
>
> You can also create counter logs from the command line under Windows Server 2003 using the `logman.exe` tool. If you type `logman /?` at a command prompt, you can get help on the many "verbs," parameters, and options available with this tool. For example, the command line `logman create counter perf_log -c "\Processor(_Total)\% Processor Time"` creates a new counter log named `perf log` that uses the binary file format and uses the Processor object, the % Processor Time counter, and the _Total instance.

Configuring Alerts

Alerts send notifications whenever the predefined counter setting exceeds or falls beneath the specified alert threshold. When an alert is triggered based on its settings, it can perform several actions—create an entry in the application event log, send a network message to someone, initiate logging for a specific performance log, and run an application program. To create a new alert, follow these steps:

1. Launch the Performance console.

2. Expand the Performance Logs and Alerts node and select the Alerts subnode.

3. Right-click the Alerts subnode and select New Alert Settings.

4. Type a name for this Alert in the Name box and click OK.

5. From the General tab of the properties dialog box that appears (see Figure 13.17), click the Add button to add one or more counters to this alert.

6. Select either Over or Under from the Alert When the Value Is drop-down list box.

7. Type the threshold value in the Limit box.

8. You can change the sample data interval and you can configure the alert to run under a specific user account, if you desire.

9. Click the Action tab to specify the actions that you want the alert to perform when the alert is triggered, as shown in Figure 13.18.

10. Click the Schedule tab to schedule when the alert should be operating.

11. Click OK to save the settings for the new alert.

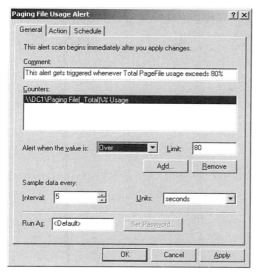

FIGURE 13.17 Configuring threshold settings for an alert.

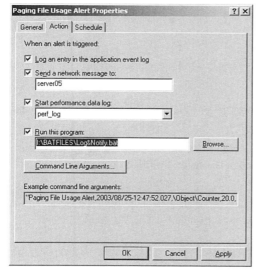

FIGURE 13.18 Configuring actions to be performed when an alert is triggered.

To manually start an alert, right-click the alert name in the details pane of Performance Logs and Alerts and select Start. The icon for the alert turns to green, indicating that the alert is operating. To manually stop an alert from scanning the system, right-click the alert name and select Stop. To modify an alert's settings, right-click the alert and select Properties.

Exam Prep Questions

1. Which of the following tools can you use to view real-time system performance data? (Choose two.)

   ○ **A.** Performance Logs and Alerts

   ○ **B.** Task Manager

   ○ **C.** Event Viewer

   ○ **D.** System Monitor

   ○ **E.** Services.msc

   ○ **F.** Logman.exe

2. Which of the following event items is not one of the five default Event Viewer event types?

   ○ **A.** Information

   ○ **B.** Error

   ○ **C.** Caution

   ○ **D.** Failure Audit

   ○ **E.** Success Audit

3. Which of the following statements about performance metrics and the System Monitor tool is correct? (Choose the best answer.)

   ○ **A.** Performance Objects are logical collections of performance measurement units associated with a computer resource (CPU, disk, memory) or service that you can monitor.

   ○ **B.** Performance Counters are logical collections of performance measurement units associated with a computer resource (CPU, disk, memory) or service that you can monitor.

   ○ **C.** Performance Object Instances are data items that instruct System Monitor to track display specific areas of performance for a computer. Each performance object has several performance counters associated with it.

   · ○ **D.** The System Monitor tool is available as an MMC snap-in named sysmon.msc.

4. Into which of the following file formats can you save event logs and which is the file format's associated application program? (Choose three.)

    ○ **A.** `.doc`—opens the log using `notepad.exe`.

    ○ **B.** `.txt`—opens the log using `notepad.exe`.

    ○ **C.** `.evt`—opens the log using Event Viewer.

    ○ **D.** `.csv`—opens the log using Microsoft Excel.

    ○ **E.** `.log`—opens the log using `notepad.exe`.

    ○ **F.** `.xls`—opens the log using Microsoft Excel.

5. As a senior network administrator for the XLM Corporation, you promote a Windows Server 2003 computer to domain controller (DC) status. This new DC is located at the company's main headquarters, where three other DCs are already sharing the user authentication role and functioning properly. Which of the following Event Logs would you expect to see when you open the Event Viewer for the first time after you have successfully promoted the server to a DC? (Choose three.)

    ○ **A.** Directory Service

    ○ **B.** Security

    ○ **C.** Local

    ○ **D.** Application

    ○ **E.** DNS Server

    ○ **F.** Internet Explorer

6. Which of the following features does the Performance Logs and Alerts tool provide to network administrators? (Choose three.)

    ○ **A.** The ability to capture and view system performance in real time

    ○ **B.** The ability to configure notifications to be sent based on predetermined system threshold settings

    ○ **C.** The ability to filter and sort system events

    ○ **D.** The ability to log details about various system events after certain other events take place

    ○ **E.** The ability to view which processes are currently running on the system

    ○ **F.** The ability to record system performance measurements during specific periods

7. To be granted permission to manage and schedule logged performance counters, logs, and alerts, you must be a member of at least one of which of the following groups? (Choose two.)

   ○ **A.** Server Operators

   ○ **B.** Account Operators

   ○ **C.** Performance Monitor Users

   ○ **D.** Performance Log Users

   ○ **E.** Administrators

8. Which of the following types of storage formats are supported by Counter Logs? (Choose three.)

   ○ **A.** `.txt` files

   ○ **B.** `.tsv` files

   ○ **C.** `.csv` files

   ○ **D.** `.blg` files

   ○ **E.** `.glb` files

   ○ **F.** `.lbg` files

9. Which of the following utilities allow you to actually gather data to store within Counter Logs in Windows Server 2003? (Choose three.)

   ○ **A.** System Monitor

   ○ **B.** Performance Monitor

   ○ **C.** Event Viewer

   ○ **D.** Logman

   ○ **E.** Elogger

   ○ **F.** Performance Logs and Alerts

10. Which of the following print spooler events and notifications are logged or enabled by default? (Choose three.)

   ○ **A.** Error events

   ○ **B.** Warning events

   ○ **C.** Notify when remote documents are printed

   ○ **D.** Show informational notifications for local printers

   ○ **E.** Beep on errors of remote documents

   ○ **F.** Information events

Answers to Exam Prep Questions

1. **Answers B and D are correct.** You can monitor a computer system in real time under Windows Server 2003 using either the Task Manager tool or the System Monitor utility. Answer A is incorrect because Performance Logs and Alerts is not designed to display performance data in real time; its results are logged. Answer C is incorrect because the Event Viewer displays system event messages, not real-time performance data. Answers E and F are incorrect because neither the Services console (`Services.msc`) nor the Licensing applet offer real-time system performance monitoring.

2. **Answer C is correct.** Caution is not one of the default event types for the Event Viewer; Warning events are one of the five default event types. Answer A is incorrect because Information is a default event type. Answer B is incorrect because Error is a default event type. Answer D is incorrect because Failure Audit is a default event type. Answer E is incorrect because Success Audit is also a default event type.

3. **Answer A is correct.** Performance Objects are logical collections of performance measurement units that are associated with a computer resource, such as a processor, a physical disk, or memory. Answer B is incorrect because Performance Counters direct System Monitor about which areas of performance to track and display. Each performance object has several performance counters associated with it. Pages/sec, Available Bytes, and %Committed Bytes in Use are all examples of counters for the Memory performance object.

   Answer C is incorrect because Performance Object Instances identify multiple Performance Objects of the same type. Answer D is incorrect because the System Monitor tool is a *node* within the `perfmon.msc` MMC snap-in—it is not a standalone MMC snap-in.

4. **Answers B, C, and D are correct.** The Event Viewer supports saving Event Logs as `.txt`, `.csv`, and `.evt` files. The `.txt` files are tab delimited; the `.csv` files are comma delimited; and the `.evt` files can only be opened by the Event Viewer. Answer A is incorrect because the Event Viewer does not support saving Event Logs as `.doc` files. Answer E is incorrect because the Event Viewer does not support saving Event Logs as `.log` files. Answer F is incorrect because the Event Viewer does not support saving Event Logs as `.xls` files.

5. **Answers A, B, and D are correct.** The Directory Service log, the Security log, and the Application log are all default event logs for a domain controller. The System log and the File Replication Service log are also default logs, but they are not listed as possible answers for this question. Answer C is incorrect because there is no such event log as a "Local" log. Answer E is incorrect because the DNS Server log is not a default event log for a DC unless the DNS Server service is also installed on that DC. The question does not indicate that the DNS Server service was installed, and you can safely assume that the DNS service is set up and working well already on the network because three other DCs are already configured and working properly. Answer F is incorrect because there is no event log for Internet Explorer.

6. **Answers B, D, and F are correct.** You can configure notifications to be sent based on predetermined threshold settings using *Alerts*. You can log details about various system events after certain other events occur by using *Trace* logs. You can record system performance measurements during specific periods using *Counter* logs. Answer A is incorrect because the ability to capture and view system performance in real time describes some of the benefits of using the System Monitor tool. Answer C is incorrect because you can filter and sort system events using the Event Viewer, not Performance Logs and Alerts. Answer E is incorrect because the Task Manager lets you view which processes are currently running on the system.

7. **Answers D and E are correct.** Users who are members of either the Performance Log Users group or the Administrators group have permission to manage and schedule logged performance counters, logs, and alerts. Answer A is incorrect because members of the Server Operators group do not have permission to manage and schedule logged performance counters, logs, and alerts. Answer B is incorrect because members of the Account Operators group do not have permission to manage and schedule logged performance counters, logs, and alerts. Answer C is incorrect because although members of the Performance Monitor Users group do have permission to *monitor* performance metrics, they do not have permission to manage *and schedule* logged performance counters, logs, and alerts.

8. **Answers B, C, and D are correct.** Counter Logs support four types of storage formats—comma delimited (`.csv`) text files; tab delimited (`.tsv`) files; binary files (`.blg`); and SQL database files, which require a connection to a Microsoft SQL Server computer. Answer A is incorrect because Counter Logs do not support `.txt` files. Answer E is incorrect because Counter Logs do not support `.glb` files. Answer F is incorrect because Counter Logs do not support `.lbg` files.

9. **Answers B, D, and F are correct.** The Performance Monitor MMC snap-in hosts the Performance Logs and Alerts node where Counter Logs can be created; the `Logman.exe` command line utility allows you to generate Counter Logs via the command line; the Performance Logs and Alerts node is located within the Performance Monitor snap-in, as previously stated. Answer A is incorrect because you cannot generate Counter Logs from the System Monitor interface; however, you can view the results of a Counter Log from the System Monitor node. Answer C is incorrect because you cannot create Counter Logs from the Event Viewer. Answer E is incorrect because no utility named "Elogger" ships with Windows Server 2003, whether it's the RTM version, the SP1 version, or the R2 Edition.

10. **Answers A, B, and F are correct.** Error events, warning events, and information events are recorded in the Event Viewer System log by default. Answer C is incorrect because the Notify When Remote Documents Are Printed check box is not marked (enabled) by default. Answer D is incorrect because the Show Informational Notifications for Local Printers check box is not marked (enabled) by default. Answer E is incorrect because the Beep on Errors of Remote Documents check box is not marked (enabled) by default.

Need to Know More?

1. Holme, Dan, and Orin Thomas. *MCSA/MCSE Self-Paced Training Kit (Exam 70-290): Managing and Maintaining a Microsoft Windows Server 2003 Environment*. Redmond, Washington: Microsoft Press, 2003.

2. Morimoto, Rand, et. al. *Microsoft Windows Server 2003 Insider Solutions*. Indianapolis, Indiana: Sams Publishing, 2003.

3. Microsoft Corporation. *Microsoft Windows Server 2003 Resource Kit*. Redmond, Washington: Microsoft Press, 2003.

4. Morimoto, Rand, et al. *Microsoft Windows Server 2003 Unleashed (R2 Edition)*. Indianapolis, Indiana: Sams Publishing, 2006.

5. Search the Microsoft Product Support Services Knowledge Base on the Internet: `http://support.microsoft.com`. You can also search Microsoft TechNet on the Internet: `http://www.microsoft.com/technet`. Find technical information using keywords from this chapter, such as system monitor, Performance Logs and Alerts, Performance Objects, Performance Object Instances, Performance Counters, Task Manager, and Event Viewer.

CHAPTER FOURTEEN

Monitoring Server Performance

Terms you'll need to understand:

✓ Server memory utilization

✓ Server processor utilization

✓ Server disk utilization

✓ Network bandwidth utilization

✓ Performance bottlenecks

✓ Print queues

Techniques you'll need to master:

✓ Monitoring server memory usage

✓ Monitoring server processor usage

✓ Monitoring server disk usage

✓ Monitoring server network usage

✓ Identifying and remedying performance bottlenecks

✓ Monitoring and optimizing server performance

✓ Managing and troubleshooting network printing

Monitoring server performance, resolving performance bottlenecks, and always striving to optimize system settings should be the goal of every network administrator. In this chapter, we go into detail to show you some of the key performance indicators that you should monitor, and we make recommendations for how to successfully resolve the performance bottlenecks that these measurements are designed to uncover. You'll learn how to use the native Windows Server 2003 performance troubleshooting tools such as System Monitor and Performance Logs and Alerts. More importantly, you'll learn how to identify several common performance bottlenecks and you'll gain insight into how to resolve those bottlenecks.

Monitoring File and Print Services

At a minimum, you should always monitor the four major performance areas that can have a significant impact on file and print server performance—processor utilization, memory utilization, disk utilization, and network utilization. These four major performance areas and the reasons for their impact on server performance are as follows:

▶ *Processor*—This is a key element in server performance. This element is measured in terms of percentages with 100% being full processor utilization. It is not good for a server to be fully utilized for prolonged periods.

The CPU Usage graph in Task Manager and the % Processor Time counter in the Performance snap-in measure processor utilization. Sustained usage of 85% or more can indicate a processor bottleneck.

▶ *Memory*—This resource is also a key element in server performance. A lack of sufficient physical memory in a server requires that it use more virtual memory. Virtual memory uses disk storage via the paging file to swap data and programs in and out of memory. Because disk is *much* slower than RAM, insufficient RAM can cause a significant system slowdown.

Memory bottlenecks occur when low memory conditions cause increased use of the paging file, and page faults occur when the system is unable to locate either data or programs in memory. Services and programs can become less responsive under these conditions.

Memory leaks occur when programs allocate memory for their own use, but they never release that allocated memory back to the system's memory pool. Over time, memory leaks can lock up a server and make it stop functioning; rebooting the server temporarily fixes the problem. A server that is running low on memory can appear to have a disk problem due to excessive swapping of application code and data from physical memory to virtual memory (the paging file). This excessive swapping is known as *thrashing*.

▶ *Disk*—Disks can be a source of performance bottlenecking on a system if all three of the following conditions exist: the sustained disk activity greatly exceeds your established baseline, the persistent disk queues exceed two per disk, *and* there is not a high amount of paging occurring on the system. Disk fragmentation can slow down disk performance; you should have all the disks on a server regularly defragmented. If the % Disk Time performance counter averages greater than 50% on a regular basis, you might have a disk bottleneck. Replacing the disk subsystem with faster drives or replacing a software RAID configuration with a hardware RAID configuration can improve disk performance.

▶ *Network*—Network throughput can have a major impact on users as they request data from network servers. Network bandwidth includes how fast bytes are sent to and from a server and how fast data packages (packets, frames, segments, and datagrams) are transferred by a server. Network bottlenecks are often caused by too many requests for data on a particular server; too much data traffic on the network segment; or a physical network problem with a hub, switch, router, or other network device. The Network Utilization graph in Task Manager can assist you with troubleshooting a possible network bottleneck. This statistic should generally average below 30% utilization.

Monitoring General Server Workload with Task Manager

You can get a quick glimpse into the server's general health and well-being by using Task Manager. Press Ctrl+Alt+Del on the keyboard and select Task Manager from the Windows Security dialog box, or right-click a blank area on the taskbar and select Task Manager to display this tool. Click the Performance tab to view current CPU Usage; CPU Usage History; current PF (Page File) Usage; Page File Usage History; total Handles, Threads, and Processes; Physical Memory; Kernel Memory; and Commit Charge statistics (listed in kilobytes). Click the Networking tab to view current network utilization percentages for each installed network adapter.

Monitoring Disk Quotas with the Event Viewer

If you enable disk quotas for one or more drive volumes, you can monitor users who exceed their disk quota entry warning level and their disk quota limit threshold in Event Viewer. You must be sure to mark the Log Events When a

User Exceeds Their Warning Level check box and the Log Events When a User Exceeds Their Quota Limit check box for these occurrences to be recorded in the System Event Log as a Category Disk, Event ID 36 logged entry. If you filter the log, it's easy to spot various kinds of warnings and errors such as this one. Figure 14.1 shows the Event Properties window for a user who hits his or her disk quota limit.

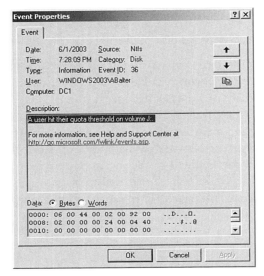

FIGURE 14.1 Monitoring disk quota thresholds for users with the Event Viewer.

Troubleshooting Server Bottlenecks with System Monitor

You can usually discover performance bottlenecks on a server whenever one or more of the system's major elements, or subsystems, shows a decline in performance as compared to its historical baseline performance statistics. This discovery is why establishing and maintaining baseline performance data for each of the major server subsystems is so important! By default, performance for each counter is displayed in graph view in System Monitor. Each counter/instance combination is assigned a different color on the graph. As you select a counter/instance in the lower half of the window, its statistics also appear just below the graph. The following metrics appear below the graph:

- ▶ *Last*—This metric shows the result for the current counter/instance as of the last recorded interval.

- ▶ *Average*—This metric shows the average result for the current counter/instance during the monitoring period.

▶ *Maximum*—This metric shows the maximum result for the current counter/instance during the monitoring period.

▶ *Minimum*—This metric shows the minimum result for the current counter/instance during the monitoring period.

▶ *Duration*—This metric shows the length of the current monitoring period.

By keeping baseline data on each server's processor (CPU), memory, disk, and network utilization, you can easily compare those baseline figures against current performance results. Use the Performance Logs and Alerts tool to log system baseline performance, and then you can compare the baseline to current system performance by loading the logged data into System Monitor and displaying a second instance of the Performance snap-in to show current performance results. Figure 14.2 shows two instances of System Monitor: The top window shows current performance, and the bottom window shows logged baseline data.

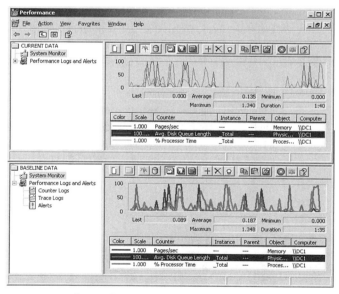

FIGURE 14.2 Comparing current system performance data (top) against logged baseline performance data (bottom).

Diagnosing and Resolving Performance Bottlenecks

In addition to monitoring and comparing current system performance metrics against baseline data, you can also keep tabs on several key areas of performance that might indicate the presence of performance problems. Tables 14.1, 14.2,

14.3, and 14.4 outline performance counters to monitor when checking for possible system bottlenecks. Each table lists general guidelines for performance counters that you should monitor, the threshold levels to check, and what remedial action that you can take to resolve the performance problem. Table 14.1 deals with processor bottlenecks, Table 14.2 deals with memory bottlenecks, Table 14.3 talks about disk bottlenecks, and Table 14.4 discusses network bottlenecks.

TABLE 14.1   Troubleshooting Processor Usage Bottlenecks

Performance Object:Counter	Unacceptable Threshold Level	Remedy
Processor:% User Time		
Processor:% Processor Time		
Processor:% Privileged Time	Sustained usage higher than 85%.	Upgrade existing CPU to a faster CPU or install additional CPUs.
System:Processor Queue Length		
Server Work Queues:Queue Length	Sustained usage higher than 2.	Upgrade existing CPU to a faster CPU or install additional CPUs.
Processor:Interrupts/sec	Varies by processor; however, substantially higher values than the baseline can indicate a hardware problem with another device in the server, such as a faulty network adapter or a failing disk controller.	Locate and replace the hardware device that is generating the high number of interrupts.

TABLE 14.2   Troubleshooting Memory Usage Bottlenecks

Performance Object:Counter	Unacceptable Threshold Level	Remedy
Memory:Page Faults/sec	Consistent page fault rates higher than 5.	Identify the processes using disproportional amounts of RAM and install more memory.
Memory:Committed Bytes	Sustained value higher than 75% of total physical RAM installed.	Identify the processes using disproportional

Table 14.2 *Continued*

Performance Object:Counter	Unacceptable Threshold Level	Remedy
		amounts of RAM and install more memory.
Memory:Available Bytes	Consistent value lower than 5% of total physical RAM installed.	Identify the processes using disproportional amounts of RAM and install more memory.
Memory:Pages/sec	Consistently higher than 20.	Identify the processes causing excessive paging and install more memory.
Memory:Nonpaged Bytes	Steady increases (compared to baseline) over time without an increased server load can indicate a memory leak.	Identify one or more programs that might have a memory leak, stop running the programs, or get updated versions.

TABLE 14.3 Troubleshooting Disk Usage Bottlenecks

Performance Object:Counter	Unacceptable Threshold Level	Remedy
PhysicalDisk:% Disk Time		
LogicalDisk:% Disk Time	Consistently higher than 50%.	First verify that excessive paging is not the cause of this problem; if not the result of excessive paging, replace the disk with a faster model.
PhysicalDisk:Current Disk Queue Length		
LogicalDisk:Current Disk Queue Length	Consistently higher than 2.	Replace the disk with a faster model.

(continues)

Table 14.3 *Continued*

Performance Object:Counter	Unacceptable Threshold Level	Remedy
PhysicalDisk:Avg. Disk Bytes/Transfer		
LogicalDisk:Avg. Disk Bytes/Transfer	Consistently lower than the server's baseline.	Replace the disk with a faster model.
PhysicalDisk:Disk Bytes/sec		
LogicalDisk:Disk Bytes/sec	Consistently lower than the server's baseline.	Replace the disk with a faster model.

TABLE 14.4 **Troubleshooting Network Usage Bottlenecks**

Performance Object:Counter	Unacceptable Threshold Level	Remedy
Server:Bytes Total/sec		
Network Interface:Bytes Total/sec	Sustained usage levels higher than the baseline averages for the server.	Replace the installed network adapters with faster models; install another network adapter; upgrade the physical network cabling, hubs, and switches.
Server:Bytes Received/sec	Sustained usage levels higher than 50% of the network adapter's bandwidth rating.	Replace the installed network adapters with faster models; upgrade the physical network cabling, hubs, and switches.
Network Interface:Bytes Sent/sec	Sustained usage levels lower than the baseline averages for the server.	Replace the installed network adapters with faster models; upgrade the physical network cabling, hubs, and switches.

Monitoring and Optimizing Application Server Performance

As discussed throughout this chapter, monitoring system performance is an important task for an administrator to perform on a regular basis. You can use System Monitor to display real-time data and to display the results of log files you created with the Performance Logs and Alerts tool. There are four major areas of server performance to monitor that will help identify and resolve performance slowdowns—processor, memory, disk, and network utilization. In this section, we show you how to set up the appropriate performance counters to make sure that a server is running smoothly.

Monitoring Processor Usage

One or more CPUs are the heart of any computer system. Processors on application servers tend to experience more activity than processors on file and printer servers; generally, more numbers are being crunched on an application server. You can monitor processor performance in any of the following ways:

- ► Run Task Manager and view real-time performance data from the Performance tab.

- ► Open the Performance snap-in and select System Monitor to view real-time data. Add performance counters for

  - ► Processor:% Processor Time

  - ► System:Processor Queue Length

  - ► Server Work Queues:Queue Length

  - ► Processor:Interrupts/sec

- ► Open the Performance snap-in and select Performance Logs and Alerts to collect logged data or establish baseline averages for the server. Add performance counters for

  - ► Processor:% Processor Time

  - ► System:Processor Queue Length

  - ► Server Work Queues:Queue Length

  - ► Processor:Interrupts/sec

- ► Monitor these counters and watch for the threshold levels listed in Table 14.1 in the previous section "Diagnosing and Resolving Performance Bottlenecks."

Monitoring Memory Usage

Lack of adequate RAM is a common cause for poor server performance. Symptoms related to inadequate memory include excessive paging or a high rate of hard page faults. You can monitor memory performance in any of the following ways:

▸ Run Task Manager and view real-time performance data from the Performance tab.

▸ Open the Performance snap-in and select System Monitor to view real-time data. Add performance counters for

   ▸ Memory:Nonpaged Bytes

   ▸ Memory:Pages/sec

   ▸ Memory:Available Bytes

   ▸ Memory:Committed Bytes

   ▸ Memory:Page Faults/sec

▸ Open the Performance snap-in and select Performance Logs and Alerts to collect logged data or establish baseline averages for the server. Add performance counters for

   ▸ Memory:Nonpaged Bytes

   ▸ Memory:Pages/sec

   ▸ Memory:Available Bytes

   ▸ Memory:Committed Bytes

   ▸ Memory:Page Faults/sec

▸ Monitor these counters and watch for the threshold levels listed in Table 14.2 in the previous section.

Monitoring Disk Usage

Disk storage can be a significant source of performance bottlenecking on a server because of the fact that the disks are mechanical. Therefore, disk response times are generally much slower than the access times for nonmechanical components such as the processor, memory, or even network I/O. You can monitor PhysicalDisk counters, LogicalDisk counters, or both. PhysicalDisk counters measure individual hard disk drives. LogicalDisk counters measure logical partitions or volumes stored on physical disks. LogicalDisk counters help you isolate the source of bottlenecks to a particular logical drive volume so that you can more easily identify where disk access requests are coming from. You can monitor disk performance in the following ways:

▸ Open the Performance snap-in and select System Monitor to view real-time data. Add performance counters for

   ▸ PhysicalDisk:% Disk Time or LogicalDisk:% Disk Time

- ► PhysicalDisk:Current Disk Queue Length or LogicalDisk:Current Disk Queue Length

- ► PhysicalDisk:Avg. Disk Bytes/Transfer or LogicalDisk:Avg. Disk Bytes/Transfer

- ► PhysicalDisk:Disk Bytes/sec or LogicalDisk:Disk Bytes/sec

► Open the Performance snap-in and select Performance Logs and Alerts to collect logged data or establish baseline averages for the server. Add performance counters for

- ► PhysicalDisk:% Disk Time or LogicalDisk:% Disk Time

- ► PhysicalDisk:Current Disk Queue Length or LogicalDisk:Current Disk Queue Length

- ► PhysicalDisk:Avg. Disk Bytes/Transfer or LogicalDisk:Avg. Disk Bytes/Transfer

- ► PhysicalDisk:Disk Bytes/sec or LogicalDisk:Disk Bytes/sec

► Monitor these counters and watch for the threshold levels listed in Table 14.3, in the previous section.

Monitoring Network Usage

Network usage bottlenecks can be difficult to troubleshoot because many factors can influence network bandwidth availability and because the larger networks become, the more complex they become. If you determine that network throughput is the source of your server's bottleneck, you can take some constructive measures such as the following:

- ► Add servers to distribute network traffic.

- ► Segment the network into smaller subnets and connect each subnet to a separate network card on the server.

- ► Remove network bindings from unneeded network cards.

- ► Install the latest networking equipment such as 100Mb or 1,000Mb (Gigabit) switches, hubs, routers, and cabling.

You can monitor network performance in the following ways:

- ► Run Task Manager and view real-time performance data from the Networking tab. *In general, sustained network utilization should be lower than 30%.*

▶ Open the Performance snap-in and select System Monitor to view real-time data. Add performance counters for

  ▶ Server:Bytes Total/sec

  ▶ Network Interface:Bytes Total/sec

  ▶ Server:Bytes Received/sec

  ▶ Network Interface:Bytes Sent/sec

▶ Open the Performance snap-in and select Performance Logs and Alerts to collect logged data or establish baseline averages for the server. Add performance counters for

  ▶ Server:Bytes Total/sec

  ▶ Network Interface:Bytes Total/sec

  ▶ Server:Bytes Received/sec

  ▶ Network Interface:Bytes Sent/sec

▶ Monitor these counters and watch for the threshold levels listed in Table 14.4 in the previous section.

Exam Prep Questions

1. Maintaining a historical record of server performance for later comparative analysis is commonly referred to as which of the following terms: (Choose the best answer.)

   ○ **A.** Performance tracking

   ○ **B.** Bottlenecking

   ○ **C.** Baselining

   ○ **D.** Threshold monitoring

   ○ **E.** Performance standardizing

   ○ **F.** Foundation monitoring

2. Which of the following event items is not one of the five default Event Viewer event types?

   ○ **A.** Information

   ○ **B.** Error

   ○ **C.** Caution

   ○ **D.** Failure Audit

   ○ **E.** Success Audit

3. Which of the following items serve as performance metrics for specifying different computer resources to monitor? (Choose three.)

   ○ **A.** Objects

   ○ **B.** Counters

   ○ **C.** Cycles

   ○ **D.** Initiators

   ○ **E.** _Totals

   ○ **F.** Instances

4. Using the Performance Logs and Alerts tool, Jane, the network administrator, adds performance counters such as Memory:Pages/sec, PhysicalDisk:Avg. Disk Queue Length:_Total, and Processor:% Processor Time:_Total to a new counter log. She schedules this new counter log to start on Monday morning at 8:00 a.m., and she schedules the log to stop on Wednesday evening at 10:00 p.m. The company that Jane works for has a very seasonal business; computer usage is extremely high during this time of year due to increased marketing, sales, and accounting activities. Collecting this type of performance data can be referred to as

○ **A.** Establishing a baseline

○ **B.** Viewing real-time data

○ **C.** Logged performance monitoring

○ **D.** Collecting histogram data

5. As a network administrator for ABC Company, Inc., you notice from the performance logs you keep on Server03 that the Memory:Page Faults/sec performance object:counter continues to show a consistent page fault rate of 7. This rate is more than the baseline figure of 5 for this server. Should you take some course of action to remedy this situation, or does this performance metric fall within a normal range? (Choose the best answer.)

○ **A.** Do nothing; this measurement is not indicative of a performance bottleneck.

○ **B.** Install more RAM into Server03.

○ **C.** Install more disk space for Server03.

○ **D.** Increase the size of the paging file on Server03 and store the paging file on the fastest disk with the most free space.

○ **E.** Replace the existing disks with faster disks into Server03.

○ **F.** Stop playing "Doom" on Server03 during production hours.

6. As a network administrator for XYZ Company, Inc., you notice from the performance logs you keep on Server04 that the Server:Bytes Received/sec performance object:counter continues to show a sustained usage rate of between 35% to 40% of the network bandwidth rating for the network adapter that is installed in the server. Should you take some course of action to remedy this situation, or does this performance metric fall within a normal range? (Choose the best answer.)

○ **A.** Do nothing; this measurement is not indicative of a performance bottleneck.

○ **B.** Install more RAM into Server04.

○ **C.** Install more disk space for Server04.

○ **D.** Install a second network adapter into Server04.

○ **E.** Replace the existing network adapter on Server04 with a newer and faster network adapter.

7. As a network administrator for Widgets R Us, LLC, you notice from the performance logs you keep on Server05 that the Server Work Queues:Queue Length performance object:counter continues to show a sustained usage rate of 3. Should you take some course of action to remedy this situation, or does this performance metric fall within a normal range? (Choose the best answer.)

○ **A.** Do nothing; this measurement is not indicative of a performance bottleneck.

○ **B.** Install more RAM into Server05.

○ **C.** Increase the size of the paging file on Server05.

○ **D.** Install an additional processor into Server05.

○ **E.** Replace the existing network adapter on Server04 with a newer and faster network adapter.

8. As a network administrator for Exam Cram IT Services Corporation, you notice from the performance logs you keep on Server07 that the Physical Disk:Current Disk Queue Length performance object:counter continues to show a consistent usage level of 2. Should you take some course of action to remedy this situation, or does this performance metric fall within a normal range? (Choose the best answer.)

○ **A.** Do nothing; this measurement is not indicative of a performance bottleneck.

○ **B.** Install more RAM into Server07.

○ **C.** Increase the size of the paging file on Server07.

○ **D.** Install an additional processor into Server07.

○ **E.** Replace the existing disk(s) on Server07 with a newer and faster network adapter.

Answers to Exam Prep Questions

1. **Answer C is correct.** Baselining is an important part of performance monitoring and optimization. Baselining requires that you create a historical log of key performance counters for each server over a period of time—these measurements can later be compared to current server performance to find possible bottlenecks. Answer A is incorrect because performance baselining has a more specific purpose than general performance tracking. Answer B is incorrect because bottlenecking means that some aspect of server performance is slowed; it does not mean baselining. Answer D is incorrect because a term such as "threshold monitoring" is not synonymous with the term baselining. Answer E is incorrect because a term such as "performance standardizing" is not synonymous with the term baselining. Answer F is incorrect because a term such as "foundation monitoring" is not synonymous with the term baselining.

2. **Answer C is correct.** Caution is not one of the default event types for the Event Viewer; Warning events are one of the five default event types. Answer A is incorrect because Information is a default event type. Answer B is incorrect because Error is a default event type. Answer D is incorrect because Failure Audit is a default event type. Answer E is incorrect because Success Audit is also a default event type.

3. **Answers A, B, and F are correct.** You use objects, counters, and instances of objects to measure system performance using System Monitor and Performance Logs and Alerts. Answer C is incorrect because cycles are not performance metrics. Answer D is incorrect because initiators are not performance metrics. Answer E is incorrect because _Totals are not performance metrics.

4. **Answer C is correct.** The Performance Logs and Alerts tool collects performance data over time and records that data into log files. Answer A is incorrect because although you should use the Performance Logs and Alerts tool to create performance baseline data, you should not attempt to collect performance data as a baseline during peak usage times. Answer B is incorrect because you can only view real-time data using System Monitor or the Task Manager. Answer D is incorrect because both real-time data and logged performance data can be viewed as a histogram using the System Monitor tool; a histogram is a view, not a type of data.

5. **Answer B is correct.** If the performance object:counter Memory:Page Faults/sec is consistently higher than 5, this represents an unacceptable threshold level for server memory performance. In addition, since the baseline figure for this server is 5, this performance statistic indicates that the server is now consistently under a heavier load than it has been in the past. You should identify the process(es) responsible and install more RAM if the process(es) must continue to run on the server. Answer A is incorrect because this measurement does indicate that a performance bottleneck exists for the memory on Server03. Answer C is incorrect because installing more disk space for Server03 will not fix this performance bottleneck for the memory object. Answer D is incorrect because increasing the size of the paging file for Server03 will not fix this performance bottleneck for the memory object. Answer E is incorrect because replacing the disks on Server03 with faster disks will not fix this performance bottleneck for the memory object. Answer F is incorrect, of course, because no one should ever play games or use any production server for any unauthorized or nonessential use at any time.

6. **Answer A is correct.** If the performance object:counter Server:Bytes Received/sec shows sustained usage levels of more than 50%, this represents an unacceptable threshold level for server network adapter performance. However, since the logged performance levels indicate a sustained usage rate of less than 50%, you do not need to take any action. Answer B is incorrect because no action needs to be taken and installing additional RAM would not affect network adapter performance anyway. Answer C is incorrect because no action needs to be taken and installing additional disk space would not affect network adapter performance anyway. Answer D is incorrect because no action needs to be taken and installing a second network adapter is not necessary. Answer E is incorrect because no action is necessary and replacing the existing network adapter with a newer and faster model is not necessary based on the available information.

7. **Answer D is correct.** If the performance object:counter Server Work Queues:Queue Length shows a sustained usage level of more than 2, this represents an unacceptable threshold level for server CPU performance. Installing a second processor will help to balance and reduce the processing load on Server05. Answer A is incorrect because the

historical logged performance results indicate that there is a bottleneck and remedial action should be taken. Answer B is incorrect because installing additional RAM would not improve the server's processing performance. Answer C is incorrect because increasing the size of the paging file would not improve the server's processing power. Answer E is incorrect because replacing the existing network adapter with a newer and faster model would not resolve the issue with the overloaded processor performance.

8. **Answer A is correct.** If the performance object:counter Physical Disk:Current Disk Queue Length consistently shows a usage level of 2 or lower, this does *not* represent an unacceptable threshold level for server disk performance. A consistent usage higher than 2 would indicate a disk performance bottleneck. Answer B is incorrect because installing additional RAM would not improve the server's disk performance for this specific bottleneck. Answer C is incorrect because increasing the size of the paging file would not improve the server's disk performance for this specific bottleneck. Answer E is incorrect because replacing the existing network adapter with a newer and faster model would not resolve the issue with the server's slow disk performance.

Need to Know More?

1. Scales, Lee, and John Michell. *MCSA/MCSE 70-290 Training Guide: Managing and Maintaining a Windows Server 2003 Environment.* Indianapolis, Indiana: Que Publishing, 2003.

2. Jones, Don. *Windows Server 2003 Weekend Crash Course.* New York, New York: Wiley Publishing, Inc., 2003.

3. Snedaker, Susan. *The Best Damn Windows Server 2003 Book Period.* Rockland, Massachusetts: Syngress Publishing, Inc., 2004.

4. Williams, Robert, and Mark Walla. *The Ultimate Windows Server 2003 System Administrator's Guide.* Boston, Massachusetts: Addison Wesley Professional, 2003.

5. Search the Microsoft Product Support Services Knowledge Base on the Internet: http://support.microsoft.com. You can also search Microsoft TechNet on the Internet: http://www.microsoft.com/technet. Find technical information using keywords from this chapter, such as memory utilization, processor utilization, disk utilization, network bandwidth utilitization, performance monitoring, baselines, and performance bottlenecks.

CHAPTER FIFTEEN

Maintaining Device Drivers and Hardware

Terms you'll need to understand:

✓ Device Manager

✓ Driver signing

✓ Driver roll back

✓ Hardware profiles

✓ Add Hardware Wizard

✓ Windows Firewall

✓ Wi-Fi Protected Access (WPA)

✓ Wireless Provisioning Services (WPS)

✓ Network adapter or network interface card (NIC)

Techniques you'll need to master:

✓ Installing, configuring, and troubleshooting hardware devices and drivers

✓ Updating drivers and system files

✓ Configuring and using hardware profiles

✓ Rolling back drivers to a previous version

✓ Managing and troubleshooting driver signing

✓ Configuring Windows Firewall settings

The term "computer hardware" includes any physical device that is connected to or installed in a computer. It includes equipment connected to the computer at the time that it is manufactured as well as equipment that you add later. Modems, disk drives, CD-ROM drives, printers, network cards, keyboards, display adapter cards, and USB cameras are all examples of devices. Each device attached to a system must also have a corresponding software driver, which enables the device to interface (communicate) with the computer's operating system. Administering and troubleshooting hardware devices and their associated drivers is vital to maintaining server uptime. Administering, diagnosing, and resolving hardware-related issues is the focus of this chapter.

Managing Hardware Devices and Drivers

Windows Server 2003 offers full support for Plug and Play (PnP) devices and offers limited support for non–Plug and Play devices. Be sure to always consult the latest Windows Server 2003 Hardware Compatibility List (HCL) before installing a new device to verify that the device is supported. You can access the online version of the HCL at `http://www.microsoft.com/hwdq/hcl/search.asp`. Of course, even if it's on the HCL, it's not a bad idea to test a device yourself to be sure that it will work with Windows Server 2003 and the existing hardware that you will be connecting it to.

For a device to work properly with Windows Server 2003, you must install software (a device driver) on the computer. Each hardware device has its own unique device driver, which the device manufacturer typically supplies. However, many Microsoft-tested and certified device drivers are included on the Windows Server 2003 CD-ROM, and these drivers often work even better with Windows Server 2003 than other drivers that might not be certified. Expect Microsoft to recommend using those drivers that have been tested and certified for a given device rather than any other drivers that might be offered from a manufacturer because Microsoft knows that the tested and certified drivers offer much more compatibility than untested drivers.

Because Windows Server 2003 manages your computer's resources and configuration based on PnP standards, you can install most PnP hardware devices without restarting your computer. Windows Server 2003 automatically identifies (enumerates) the new hardware and installs the drivers it needs. Windows Server 2003 fully supports computers with Basic Input/Output System (BIOS) versions that are compliant with the Advanced Configuration and Power Interface (ACPI) specification. Windows Server 2003 also supports computers with certain BIOS versions that are compliant with the older Advanced Power Management (APM) specification. Just remember that ACPI-compliant computers and hardware devices usually make your Windows Server 2003 hardware setup experiences more enjoyable.

Installing, Configuring, and Managing Devices

You might need to configure devices on Windows Server 2003 machines using the Add Hardware Wizard in the Control Panel or by clicking the Add Hardware Wizard button from the Hardware tab on the System Properties window. Keep in mind that in most cases, you need to be logged on to the local computer as a member of the Administrators group to add, configure, and remove devices. Many devices completely configure themselves without any administrator intervention at all; other devices require some administrative effort.

Installing PnP Devices and Non-PnP Devices

Connect the device to the appropriate port or slot on your computer according to the device manufacturer's instructions. You might need to start or restart your computer, but this step happens much less often than it did with previous versions of Windows. Plan for necessary downtime on production servers. If you are prompted to restart your server, do so only when it is appropriate for the users' environment.

Server reboots should be performed during nonproduction hours, if at all possible. Restarting a server during peak hours requires that all users exit all application programs that are accessing data stored on the server. Users then must wait for the server to come back online before they can resume their work. If, for some unknown reason, the server fails to restart properly, users lose valuable productivity time until the server's problem can be diagnosed and repaired.

For PnP devices, Windows Server 2003 should detect the device and then immediately start the Found New Hardware Wizard. If a new device does not immediately install, you might need to use a special setup driver disk, CD-ROM, or DVD from the manufacturer that ships with the device. (Typically, you can also download updated drivers from the device manufacturer's website.) If you are still unable to install the device, or if you are installing a non-PnP device, perform the following manual installation steps:

1. Click the Add Hardware icon in the Control Panel.

2. Click Next and then click Yes, I Have Already Connected the Hardware. Click Next again.

3. Scroll down the Installed Hardware list to the very bottom, select Add a New Hardware Device, and click Next.

4. Select one of the following options:

   ▶ *Search for and Install the Hardware Automatically (Recommended)*— Perform this step if you want Windows Server 2003 to try to detect the new device that you want to install.

   ▶ *Install the Hardware That I Manually Select from a List (Advanced)*— Perform this step if you know the type and model of the device you are installing and you want to select it from a list of devices.

5. Click Next, and then follow the instructions on your screen.

6. You might be prompted to restart your computer, depending on the type of device you just installed.

Troubleshooting Installed Devices with the Add Hardware Wizard

Sometimes, the Windows Server 2003 PnP enumeration does not automatically recognize an installed device. If this happens, or if the device fails to function, you should troubleshoot the device by performing the following steps:

1. Click the Add Hardware icon in the Control Panel.

2. Click Next and then click Yes, I Have Already Connected the Hardware. Click Next again.

3. Select the installed hardware device that you are having trouble with and click Next, as shown in Figure 15.1. Keep in mind that if a hardware device has completely failed, it might not appear in the list of installed devices.

4. Follow the subsequent instructions on your screen. Click Finish to launch the Hardware Update Wizard or to go through a hardware troubleshooter from the Windows Server 2003 Help and Support Center, depending on the device in question, to try to resolve the problem. Otherwise, click Cancel to exit the Add Hardware Wizard.

Troubleshooting Hardware with Device Manager

The Windows Server 2003 Device Manager is quite similar to the Device Manager in Windows XP and Windows 2000. The Device Manager window displays all the hardware devices connected to the computer. You can view the devices by type or by connection, or you can view the resources that the devices use or how the resources are connected to each device by selecting the appropriate option from the View menu (see Figure 15.2). Device Manager gives administrators the power to update device drivers, enable or disable devices, uninstall devices, scan for hardware changes, roll back drivers, and even work with resource settings for devices, all in one centralized interface.

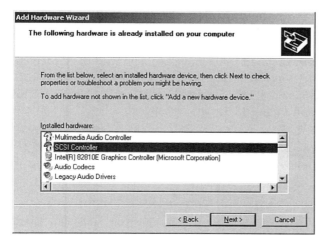

FIGURE 15.1 Troubleshooting hardware devices with the Add Hardware Wizard.

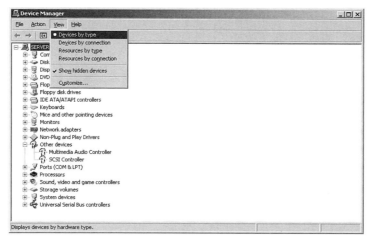

FIGURE 15.2 The display options from the View menu in Device Manager.

To run Device Manager, follow these steps:

1. Right-click My Computer from the Windows desktop or from the Start menu and select Properties. Alternatively, you can double-click the System icon from the Control Panel.

2. From the System properties window, click the Hardware tab and then click the Device Manager button.

When you view devices by type, Device Manager categorizes devices into logical groups such as computer, disk drives, display adapter, and so on. To work with an individual device, click the plus sign to expand the appropriate category and then right-click the device itself and select Properties to display its properties sheet. Devices that are not set up or functioning properly have their categories automatically expanded, and each problem device is shown with a yellow question mark or an exclamation point to denote a problem with the device. To enable or disable a device from its properties sheet, click the Device Usage drop-down list box and select either Use This Device (Enable) or Do Not Use This Device (Disable), as shown in Figure 15.3.

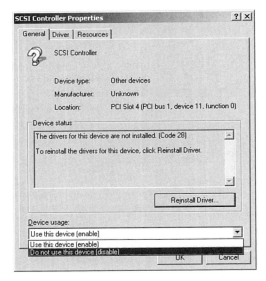

FIGURE 15.3 The properties sheet for a device from Device Manager.

To install or reinstall a driver for a device, perform the following steps:

1. Open Device Manager and expand the device category that you want to work with.

2. Right-click the device for which you want to install or reinstall drivers.

3. Click the Reinstall Driver button from the General tab and follow the onscreen instructions. You might need the CD-ROM or disk containing the device drivers from the manufacturer.

Managing Device Drivers and System Updates

Keeping drivers and system files updated ensures that your operating system performs at its peak level. Because Microsoft has thoroughly tested Microsoft digitally signed drivers for compatibility with Windows Server 2003, it recommends using these signed drivers whenever possible as they are sometimes more stable than unsigned drivers. The `driver.cab` cabinet file is stored in the `\i386` folder on the Windows Server 2003 CD-ROM, and this file contains all the drivers that Windows Server 2003 works with at the time that the operating system is released to manufacturing. This cabinet file is copied to the `%systemroot%\Driver Cache\i386` folder when Windows Server 2003 is installed. Whenever a driver is updated, Windows Server 2003 looks in the `driver.cab` file first. The location of `driver.cab` is stored in a Registry key, and you can change it if you use the Registry Editor (`regedit.exe`) and navigate to `HKLM\Software\Microsoft\Windows\CurrentVersion\Setup\DriverCachePath`.

Manually Updating Device Drivers

Automatic updates might be convenient for desktop computers, but when it comes to servers, it's a good idea to be more vigilant and protective. One bad driver can severely cripple or completely disable an important server. Be sure to test all updated drivers and other critical system files on test machines in a nonproduction environment before you deploy them. To update drivers on individual components, such as network cards or SCSI disk controllers, perform the following steps:

1. Open Device Manager and expand the device category where the device that you want to update is located.

2. Perform one of these two steps:

   ▶ Right-click the device that you want to update, select Update Driver from the right-click menu, and follow the onscreen instructions.

   ▶ Right-click the device that you want to update and select Properties from the right-click menu. Click the Driver tab, click the Update Driver button, and follow the onscreen instructions.

TIP

You can use the Driver Verifier utility to troubleshoot and isolate driver problems. It is not enabled by default. To use it, you must enable it by running the Driver Verifier Manager part of `verifier.exe` by executing it from the GUI first or by changing a Registry setting and then restarting the computer. When you run the Driver Verifier tool (`verifier.exe`) from the command line, it offers several options for troubleshooting drivers. For example, if you run the command `verifier /all`, it verifies all the drivers installed on the system. See the Microsoft Knowledge Base article 244617 for more information.

Using Driver Roll Back

Driver roll back was first introduced as a new feature in Windows XP and was also included in Windows Server 2003. If you encounter problems with a hardware device after you install an updated driver for it, you can easily revert back to the previously installed software driver for that device by using the Roll Back Driver option within Device Manager. Follow these steps to roll back a driver for a specific device:

1. Open Device Manager and expand the device category where the device driver that you want to roll back is located.

2. Right-click the device and select Properties.

3. Click the Driver tab.

4. Click the Roll Back Driver button.

Managing and Troubleshooting Device Conflicts

You can configure, diagnose, and modify settings for hardware devices using the Device Manager. Each resource—for example, a memory address range, interrupt request (IRQ), input/output (I/O) port, Direct Memory Access (DMA) channel, and so on—assigned to each device must be unique or the device won't function properly. For PnP devices, Windows Server 2003 attempts to ensure automatically that these resources are configured properly. If a device has a resource conflict or is not working properly, you see a yellow circle with an exclamation point inside it next to the device's name. If a device has been improperly installed or if it's been disabled, you see a red X next to the device name in Device Manager.

TIP

If you're having trouble with a particular device, sometimes it's helpful to simply uninstall the device's driver, reboot the computer, and then attempt to reinstall the driver.

Because PnP devices automatically invoke the installation procedure from Windows Server 2003, it's often better to disable a particular device rather than uninstall its driver if you do not want the operating system to attempt to install it each time the server restarts.

Occasionally, two devices require the same resources, but keep in mind that this does not always result in a device conflict—especially if the devices are PnP compliant. If a conflict arises, you can manually change the resource settings to be sure that each setting is unique. Sometimes, two or more devices can share resources, such as interrupts on Peripheral Connection Interface (PCI) devices, depending on the drivers and the computer. For example, you might see Windows Server 2003 share IRQ 9 or 10 among multiple PCI devices, such as USB host controllers, SCSI adapters, and audio controllers. In many instances, you cannot change resource settings for PnP devices because no other settings are available.

When you install a non-PnP device, the resource settings for the device are not automatically configured. Depending on the type of device you are installing, you might have to manually configure these settings. The appropriate range of settings should appear in the user's manual that ships with your device. To change resource settings for a device, follow these steps:

1. Open Device Manager and expand the device category where the device is located.

2. Right-click the device for which you want to adjust its resource settings and select Properties.

3. Click the Resources tab and clear the Use Automatic Settings check box (if available). If the Use Automatic Settings check box is dim (unavailable), you cannot change the resource settings for this device.

4. Choose one of the following courses of action:

   ▶ Click the Settings Based on drop-down list box to select from the predefined list of settings.

   ▶ Click a Resource Type item shown in the Resource Settings list box and then click the Change Setting button to individually modify the resource's setting. Change the setting and click OK. Repeat this action for each resource setting that you want to change.

5. Click OK for the device's properties sheet to return to the Device Manager window.

EXAM ALERT

Generally, you should not change resource settings manually because when you do so, the settings become fixed and Windows Server 2003 then has less flexibility when allocating resources to other devices. If too many resources become fixed, Windows Server 2003 might not be able to install new PnP devices. In addition, if you manually change resource settings to incompatible values, the device might no longer function or it might function improperly.

Uninstalling and Reinstalling Device Drivers

If you need to uninstall a driver for a particular device, simply open Device Manager and locate the device that you want to uninstall. Right-click the device name and select Uninstall. Click OK in the Confirm Device Removal dialog box. The driver for an installed device does not get deleted from the system. When the computer restarts, Windows Server 2003 attempts to reinstall the PnP device unless you designate the device as disabled from its properties sheet in Device Manager. If you need to reinstall a driver for a non-PnP device, perform the following steps:

1. Right-click My Computer and select Properties.

2. Click the Hardware tab and click the Add Hardware Wizard button to launch the wizard and then click Next.

3. Click Yes, I Have Already Connected the Hardware and then click Next.

4. Select the device that you want to reinstall from the Installed Hardware list box and click Next.

5. Follow the instructions that the wizard displays to finish the reinstallation process.

Managing and Troubleshooting Driver Signing

Microsoft touts digital signatures for device drivers as a method for improving the overall quality of software drivers. Better quality device drivers, in turn, help reduce support costs for vendors and help lower the total cost of ownership (TCO) for customers. Windows Server 2003 uses the same type of driver-signing process as Windows XP and Windows 2000 to make sure that drivers have been certified to work correctly with the Windows Driver Model (WDM) in Windows Server 2003. Depending on the Driver Signing Options configured for each specific Windows Server 2003 computer, you might be allowed to install nondigitally signed drivers without any warning, you might be warned but still permitted to proceed with installing nondigitally signed drivers (see Figure 15.4), or you might be completely prevented from installing drivers that do not have digital signatures.

If your server is experiencing a device-driver problem, it might be because you are using a driver that was not correctly (or specifically) written for Windows Server 2003. To identify such drivers, you can use the Signature Verification tool. This utility, `sigverif.exe`, helps you quickly identify unsigned drivers. Feel free to take advantage of this tool whether a device is not currently working or if you simply want to make sure that all drivers in use are properly signed. To use this digital-signature verification tool, perform the following steps:

1. Click Start, Run; type `sigverif.exe`; and click OK to launch the program.

2. Click the Advanced button.

3. Select the option Look for Other Files That Are Not Digitally Signed.

4. Mark the Include Subfolders check box.

5. Click the Logging tab to make any changes for the log file and then click OK. Note the log file name: `sigverif.txt`.

6. Click Start to run the signature-verification process.

7. After the process finishes, the Signature Verification Results windows will appear. Review the list of unsigned drivers and click Close to exit. You can review the results again later by double-clicking the `sigverif.txt` log file located by default in the `%systemroot%` folder (for example, `C:\Windows`).

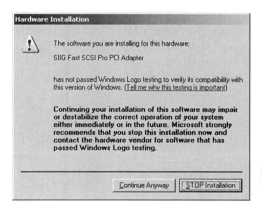

FIGURE 15.4 A Hardware Installation warning message box about installing an unsigned device driver.

Setting Driver Signing Options via System Properties

Windows Server 2003 offers administrators some control over whether users can install signed drivers, unsigned drivers, or both for a chosen device. Signed drivers are software device drivers that have been tested by Microsoft for compatibility with Windows Server 2003 (or other versions of Windows). Microsoft issues a catalog (`*.cat`) file that contains a digital signature for each device driver that successfully passes its compatibility test. Manufacturers then distribute the associated catalog file as part of each device driver's set of installation files. Unsigned drivers are drivers that either have not been tested or drivers that are actually not compatible with specific versions of Windows: These drivers do not include catalog files as part of their set of installation files.

To change the system's driver-signing options, right-click My Computer, select Properties, click the Hardware tab, and click the Driver Signing button. Select one of the following actions for the operating system to take (as shown in Figure 15.5) when you attempt to install an unsigned device driver:

▶ *Ignore*—This option bypasses driver-signing checks, allowing the user to proceed with the driver installation even if a driver is not signed.

▶ *Warn*—This option issues a dialog box warning if an unsigned driver is encountered during a device driver installation. It gives the user the option of continuing with the installation or terminating the device driver's setup. This setting is the default.

▶ *Block*—This option is the most restrictive of the three settings. To prevent the installation of any unsigned device drivers, you should select this option.

When you are logged on to the server as the administrator or a member of the Administrators group, the Administrator Option for driver signing is also available. If you mark the Make This Action the System Default check box, the driver-signing setting that you have chosen will become the default setting for all other users who log on to this server.

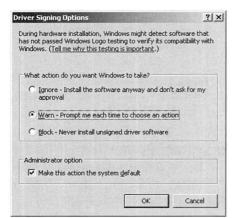

FIGURE 15.5 The Driver Signing Options dialog box for unsigned device driver installation behavior.

NOTE

Nonadministrator users can make the driver-signing policy for a given system more stringent than the current default setting; however, they cannot make the driver-signing policy more liberal.

Setting Driver Signing Options via Policy Settings

Instead of modifying the driver-signing options from the GUI, you can manipulate Windows Server 2003 driver-signing options using either a Local Policy setting or a Group Policy setting. Both the Local Policy setting and the Group Policy Object (GPO) setting appear in the Local Policies, Security Options container named Devices: Unsigned Driver Installation Behavior. The three options for the unsigned driver behavior policy are the same as the options in the System Properties window shown earlier in Figure 15.5; they are just worded differently, as shown in Figures 15.6 and 15.7. To configure driver-signing options using Local Policy for a standalone server or a member server, follow these steps:

1. Click Start, Programs, Administrative Tools, Local Security Policy.

2. Expand the Local Policies node and select the Security Options subnode.

3. Double-click the Devices: Unsigned Driver Installation Behavior policy, select one of the following options, and click OK:

   ▶ *Silently Succeed*—Selecting this setting ignores whether a driver is signed or not, allowing the user to proceed with the driver installation.

   ▶ *Warn but Allow Installation*—Selecting this setting issues a dialog box warning if an unsigned driver is encountered during a device installation. It gives the user the option of continuing with the installation or terminating the device's setup.

   ▶ *Do Not Allow Installation*—This option is the most restrictive of the three settings. To prevent the installation of any unsigned device drivers, you should select this option.

4. Exit from the Local Security Settings console.

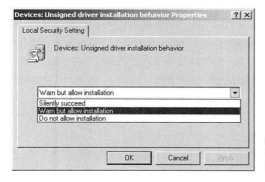

FIGURE 15.6 The Local Policy setting for Devices: Unsigned Driver Installation Behavior.

Of course, because GPOs are applied via the LDSO (local, domain, site, organizational unit) methodology, Local Policy settings can be overridden by Group

Policy settings within an Active Directory environment. Configuring the Group Policy for Devices: Unsigned Driver Installation Behavior is quite similar to working with the Local Policy setting; however, you must use the Group Policy Object Editor Microsoft Management Console (MMC) snap-in instead of the Local Security Settings MMC snap-in. To configure driver-signing options using Group Policy, follow these steps:

1. Log on to an Active Directory domain controller as the administrator or as a member of the Administrators group.

2. Click Start, Programs, Administrative Tools, Domain Security Policy to affect all member computers within the domain, or click Start, Programs, Administrative Tools, Domain Controller Security Policy to affect only domain controllers within the domain.

3. For either the Default Domain Security Settings console or the Default Domain Controller Security Settings console, expand the Local Policies node and select the Security Options subnode.

4. Double-click the Devices: Unsigned Driver Installation Behavior policy, select one of the following options, and click OK:

    ▶ *Silently Succeed*—Selecting this setting ignores whether a driver is signed or not, allowing the user to proceed with the driver installation.

    ▶ *Warn but Allow Installation*—Selecting this setting issues a dialog box warning if an unsigned driver is encountered during a device installation. It gives the user the option of continuing with the installation or terminating the device's setup.

    ▶ *Do Not Allow Installation*—This option is the most restrictive of the three settings. To prevent the installation of any unsigned device drivers, you should select this option.

5. Exit from the security settings console.

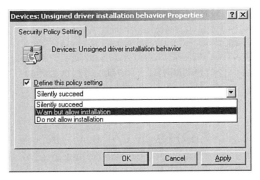

FIGURE 15.7 The Group Policy Object setting for Devices: Unsigned Driver Installation Behavior under Active Directory.

Working with Network Interface Cards (NICs)

Most, if not all, NICs on the market today are PnP PCI devices that Windows Server 2003 installs automatically. (Increasingly, Ethernet connector support is built into the motherboard.) If necessary, you can attempt to install non-PnP network adapters, or PnP NICs that don't get detected automatically, by using the Add New Hardware applet in the Control Panel. You can access the Network Connections applet from the Control Panel or by clicking Start, Settings, Network Connections if you use the classic Start menu. The following options are available from the Advanced menu of the Network Connections window:

▶ *Operator-Assisted Dialing*—You can enable or disable this feature for dial-up connections.

▶ *Remote Access Preferences*—You configure location information for dial-up connections with this option for settings such as country/region, area code/city code, carrier code, outside line access code, and tone or pulse dialing. You also can configure Autodial, Callback, and Diagnostics settings from this option.

▶ *Network Identification*—This option displays the Computer Name tab from the System Properties window where you can change the server's NetBIOS name and join the server to a domain or a workgroup.

▶ *Bridge Connections*—You can join together multiple network connections to form a network bridge by first selecting the connections in the Network Connections window and then clicking this option.

▶ *Advance Settings*—You can make changes to the binding order of protocols, bind and unbind protocols to network adapters, and modify the network provider order by selecting this option.

▶ *Optional Networking Components*—You can install or remove Windows Server 2003 additional networking components such as Management and Monitoring Tools, Networking Services, and Other Network File and Print Services (such as support for Macintosh and UNIX computers) by selecting this option.

Configuring Networking Connections and Protocols

Each network adapter has its own separate icon in the Network Connections folder. Right-click a network adapter icon (network connection) to access its properties. In the properties dialog box, you can install protocols, change addresses, or perform any other configuration changes for the connection. The properties window for each network connection has three tabs: General,

Authentication, and Advanced. The General tab displays the network adapter (NIC) for the connection along with the networking components for the connection. (Client for Microsoft Networks, File and Printer Sharing for Microsoft Networks, and Internet Protocol are the defaults.) You can also install, configure, and uninstall networking components from the General tab.

The Authentication tab is where you can enable or disable IEEE 802.1x authentication, which is enabled by default. You can select the Extensible Authentication Protocol (EAP) to be used on the system from the EAP Type drop-down list box: MD5-Challenge, Protected EAP (PEAP), or Smart Card or Other Certificate (default).

New to **SP1**   New to **R2**   Under Windows Server 2003 SP1 and under the R2 Edition, the Advanced tab of a network connection's properties window is where you can turn on, turn off, and configure the Windows Firewall (formerly known as the Internet Connection Firewall [ICF] feature under the RTM edition). If you have two or more network adapters installed in the computer, you'll also see the Internet Connection Sharing (ICS) option displayed.

Click the Settings button to configure the properties for Windows Firewall, as shown in Figure 15.8. You can also access the Windows Firewall settings by double-clicking the Windows Firewall icon in the Control Panel. The General tab is where you turn the Windows Firewall on or off. When the Windows Firewall is enabled, you can mark the Don't Allow Exceptions check box to ensure that the software firewall blocks all incoming access to your computer. Outgoing connections are not monitored or blocked by Windows Firewall.

> **TIP**
>
> Under SP1 and R2, you can configure Internet Connection Sharing (ICS) on a domain controller by enabling the Routing and Remote Access (RRAS) feature and turning on Network Address Translation (NAT) within the RRAS MMC snap-in. The ICS option is no longer available on a domain controller computer from the Advanced tab of a network connection's properties sheet under SP1 and R2.

The Exceptions tab allows you to selectively block and unblock specific programs and services, as shown in Figure 15.9. You can add programs and ports to the Programs and Services list by clicking the Add Program or Add Port buttons, respectively. You can edit one of the listed programs, services, or ports by selecting the item and then clicking the Edit button. By default, the Windows Firewall notifies the user when it blocks a program. You can disable this behavior by clearing the check box titled Display a Notification When Windows Firewall Blocks a

Program. Any time that you add or edit a program or a port to be unblocked, you also have the option of specifying the set (or scope) of computers or devices for which the program or port is unblocked. To set the scope, click the Change scope button when you are adding or editing a program, service, or port for the list of exceptions.

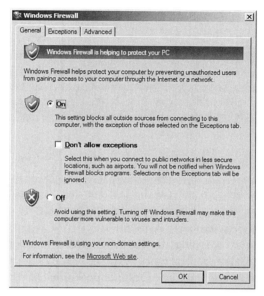

FIGURE 15.8 The General tab of the Windows Firewall properties window under SP1 and R2.

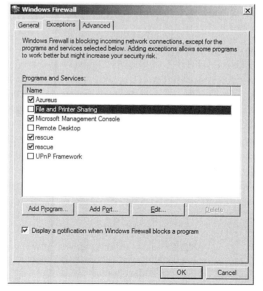

FIGURE 15.9 The Windows Firewall Exceptions tab for choosing which programs and services should be blocked from incoming Internet and network connections.

The Advanced tab allows you to choose which network connections will use the Windows Firewall. *By default, all network connections use the Windows Firewall.* To turn off the Windows Firewall for specific network connections, simply clear the check box next to the appropriate connection (see Figure 15.10). Instead of disabling the Windows Firewall entirely for specific network connections, you can selectively disable the Windows Firewall from blocking individual services for each network connection.

EXAM ALERT

When you apply SP1 to an *existing* Windows Server 2003 computer—or if you upgrade an existing server to the R2 Edition—the Windows Firewall is turned *off* by default. When you perform a *clean install* of Windows Server 2003 SP1 or R2 (not an update or upgrade), the Windows Firewall is turned *on* by default.

From the Advanced tab, select the network connection and then click the Settings button to view the Advanced Settings dialog box. On the Services tab, you can exclude individual services from being blocked, such as the File Transfer Protocol (FTP). On the ICMP tab, you can specify which types of Internet Control Message Protocol (ICMP) requests the computer will respond to. ICMP is generally used for troubleshooting purposes by using the **P**acket **I**nter**N**et **G**roper (PING) command. You can allow or disallow several types of ICMP requests, such as Allow Incoming Echo Request and Allow Outgoing Destination Unreachable.

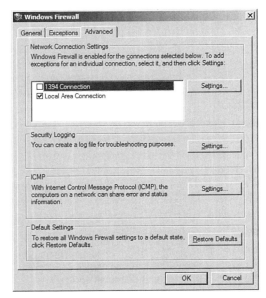

FIGURE 15.10 The Windows Firewall Advanced tab lets you exclude specific network connections.

The Advanced tab of the Windows Firewall dialog box also gives you the ability to turn on security logging. In the Security Logging section, click the Settings dialog box. You can accept the default log filename and location, or you can change these options to suit your needs. *The default security log filename is **pfirewall.log**, and it's located in %windir% folder. The log file's default size limit is 4096KB.*

TIP

If you find that you need to restore all the default settings for the Windows Firewall, you're in luck. From the Windows Firewall Advanced tab, just click the Restore Defaults button!

TCP/IP is the default protocol installed by Windows Server 2003, and it cannot be uninstalled. The properties window for Internet Protocol (TCP/IP) now sports a new tab that was not present under Windows 2000 Server—Alternate Configuration. By using the Alternate Configuration tab, you can set up alternate IP settings that will be used if no Dynamic Host Configuration Protocol (DHCP) server is available. By clicking the Advanced button from the Internet Protocol (TCP/IP) Properties window, you can add default gateway IP addresses and metrics, configure DNS settings, configure WINS settings, and set up TCP/IP filtering, among other things.

Wireless Networking Support

Windows Server 2003 and Windows XP both include support for the IEEE standard 802.11 for wireless networks. The Wireless Configuration service is installed and enabled at startup by default. This service is responsible for handling the automatic configuration of wireless network adapters. Wireless network support under Windows Server 2003 includes a new roaming feature that enables the operating system to detect a move to a new wireless access point and forces re-authentication to verify appropriate network access at a new location. By default, wireless network support under Windows Server 2003 uses the zero client configuration feature to automatically configure and use IEEE 802.1x authentication on the wireless network. (It includes the different "flavors" of wireless networking—802.11a, 802.11b, 802.11g, and so on.)

New to **SP1** | New to **R2** You can configure wireless networking settings by opening the Network Connections applet from the Control Panel, right-clicking the wireless connection you want to modify, and selecting Properties. From the wireless connection's Properties dialog box, you can enable or disable the automatic wireless configuration, set up or disable IEEE 802.1x authentication, and specify a connection to a wireless network with or without a Wired Equivalent Privacy (WEP) or a Wi-Fi Protected Access (WPA) Network Key, as shown in Figure 15.11. Prior to SP1 and R2, Windows Server 2003 did not support WPA encryption.

FIGURE 15.11 The Wireless Network Properties window.

Wireless Provisioning Services (WPS)

WPS facilitates the use of wireless hotspots while enhancing wireless security. WPS with Windows Server 2003 Service Pack 1 (and with R2), along with Microsoft Internet Authentication Service (IAS), allows users' computers to more easily detect, connect, and move between wireless hotspots with stronger security. An IAS server is also known as a Radius server.

WPS uses and extends the wireless services already built into Windows XP and Windows Server 2003. WPS takes advantage of Windows' Wireless Zero Configuration (WZC) feature in conjunction with Windows' wireless security features, such as Protected Extensible Authentication Protocol (PEAP) and WPA. Windows Server 2003 IAS under SP1 and R2 now supports guest authentication of client computers during the wireless network provisioning stage.

WPS adds support for Wireless Internet Service Providers (WISPs) and other organizations to send provisioning and configuration information to a mobile computer that is requesting to connect to the wireless network. WPS provides a standardized method for WISPs to offer wireless services at multiple locations and allows the WISPs to use multiple network names, commonly referred to as service set identifiers (SSIDs). Wireless users can register with a WISP at any location and they can be pre-provisioned for authentication and re-authentication.

When a wireless user downloads the provisioning configuration data, the user can automatically connect to the wireless network. For each future visit, the user can be authenticated on the same WISP's network even when the user visits different hotspot locations. The WZC service automatically selects the appropriate network for the WISP according to the provisioning information supplied by client computer. In addition, WSP provides automatic and seamless roaming between different wireless providers.

WPS automatically keeps the wireless client computers updated with the correct provisioning information. This automatic updating enables each WISP to modify network settings, add new locations, and make other network configuration changes without disrupting the wireless service and without requiring users to reconfigure the wireless network settings on their computers. Under WPS, the following four phases get set into motion each time that a user connects a computer to a WISP and establishes a wireless account for the first time:

1. The client computer detects the WISP's network at a Wi-Fi hotspot location.

2. The user is authenticated using a guest account, and the client computer is connected to the wireless network.

3. The client computer gets provisioned, and the user establishes an account with the WISP.

4. The user is authenticated on the wireless network using the new user account credentials.

Multiprocessor Support and Hardware Abstraction Layer

Windows Server 2003 supports up to two processors (CPUs) for the Web edition, and it supports more than two processors on the Standard, Enterprise, and Datacenter editions. When more than one processor is present in the computer at the time that the operating system is installed, Windows Server 2003 installs either the ACPI Multiprocessor Hardware Abstraction Layer (HAL) or the MPS Multiprocessor HAL. These HALs enable the operating system to support symmetric multiprocessing (SMP), which spreads different processing tasks among the installed CPUs. However, if Windows Server 2003 is installed with just one CPU present (a uniprocessor system) and you later want to add one or more additional processors (to create a multiprocessor system), you must use the Hardware Update Wizard to install a new HAL, which enables support for multiple processors. To install support for multiple CPUs, perform the following steps:

1. Right-click My Computer and then select Properties.

2. Click the Hardware tab and then click the Device Manager button.

3. Expand the Computer node and note the type of support you currently have.

4. Right-click the icon for the current type of PC that is installed and select Update Driver to launch the Hardware Update Wizard.

5. Select the option Install from a List or Specific Location (Advanced) and click Next.

6. Click the option Don't Search. I Will Choose the Driver to Install and click Next.

7. Select the appropriate type of computer from the Model list box, or click the Have Disk button if you have a disk or CD from the manufacturer, and then click Next.

8. Click Finish to exit from the wizard. You must restart the computer for the change to take effect.

> **CAUTION**
>
> Changing a server's HAL is never a trivial matter. You should take great care whenever attempting to install a HAL. If you upgrade the BIOS from supporting APM to ACPI, you need to reinstall Windows Server 2003 so that the operating system will properly support that type of upgrade.

Windows Server 2003 only supports a few very specific HAL updates because the installation of an incorrect HAL can render the operating system unusable. For a server with the MPS Multiprocessor HAL installed, you can update the system to either of the following two HAL options:

▶ Standard PC HAL

▶ MPS Multiprocessor HAL (this is a reinstallation option)

For a server with the ACPI Multiprocessor HAL installed, you can update the system to any one of the following three HAL options:

▶ MPS Multiprocessor HAL

▶ ACPI PC HAL

▶ ACPI Multiprocessor HAL (this is a reinstallation option)

NOTE

You cannot switch to the MPS Uniprocessor HAL or the ACPI Uniprocessor HAL if the computer already has a Multiprocessor HAL installed. To install a Uniprocessor HAL for Multiprocessor HAL systems, you must reinstall Windows Server 2003.

Managing Hardware Profiles

A *hardware profile* stores configuration settings for a collection of devices and services. Windows Server 2003 can store different hardware profiles so that you can meet different needs for various device and service settings depending on the circumstances. One example is a server that might have one or more external hard drives or tape backup drives connected, and perhaps those devices interfere with the server when it's in production; you can disable those devices during production hours. You select hardware profiles when the server boots. Hardware profiles can store alternate network settings and various hardware configuration options that you can select each time the system restarts.

You can enable and disable devices for a specific hardware profile through their properties dialog boxes in Device Manager. You manage enabling and disabling of services in each hardware profile by using the Services MMC snap-in, as shown in Figure 15.12. You create and manage hardware profiles using the System applet in the Control Panel, or by right-clicking My Computer and choosing Properties. Once inside the System applet, click the Hardware tab and click the Hardware Profiles button to open the Hardware Profiles dialog box, shown in Figure 15.13. At installation, Windows Server 2003 creates a single hardware profile called Profile 1 (Current), which you can rename later. You are only prompted to select a hardware profile at system startup when two or more hardware profiles are stored on your machine. You can create and store as many hardware profiles on your machine as you like. You select the desired hardware profile at Windows Server 2003 startup to specify which device and service configuration settings you need for the current session.

To configure a hardware profile, copy the default profile and rename it appropriately. Restart the computer and select the profile you want to configure, if you are configuring hardware devices. From Device Manager, in the properties dialog box for any device, you can specify whether that device is enabled or disabled for the current profile. To configure services, you can specify for which hardware profile a particular service is enabled or disabled; the computer does not need to be restarted with a specific hardware profile when you configure services.

Chapter 15: Maintaining Device Drivers and Hardware

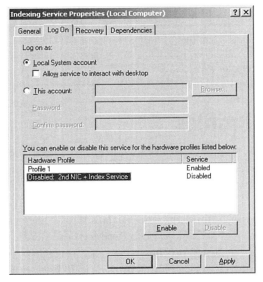

FIGURE 15.12 Disabling the indexing service for a specific hardware profile.

FIGURE 15.13 Working with the Hardware Profiles dialog box.

If Windows Server 2003 detects that your computer is a portable (laptop or notebook), it tries to determine whether your system is docked or undocked; it then selects the appropriate hardware profile for the current conditions. When more than one hardware profile is present, Windows Server 2003 displays the Hardware Profile/Configuration Recovery menu each time the computer restarts, as shown in Figure 15.14.

> **TIP**
>
> Don't confuse *hardware* profiles with *user* profiles: The two are not related! Hardware profiles deal with devices and services settings for the entire computer; user profiles deal with user configuration settings for individual users.

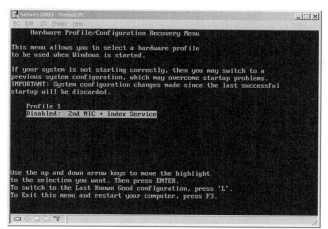

FIGURE 15.14 The Hardware Profile/ Configuration Recovery menu.

Managing Card Services

Card services play an important role in Windows Server 2003 for security purposes because of the compact size and tamper-resistant qualities of today's high-tech card-like devices. Support for card services includes PC Cards as peripheral devices and smart card technology for logon authentication. The operating system supports both the PC Card (formerly known as PCMCIA) standard as well as the CardBus (PC Card 32) standard. The many benefits of these devices include their convenient size, low power requirements, and support for the PnP standard. The CardBus specification is a combination of the PC Card 16 standard and the Peripheral Component Interconnect (PCI) standard. This combination provides 32-bit performance and the PCI bus in a compact, portable package. You can find several types of PC Cards that are often used in mobile computers: network adapter cards, hard drive cards, modem cards, wireless network cards, and so on.

Support for smart card technology is fully integrated into Windows Server 2003. Smart cards play an important role in Windows Server 2003's Public Key Infrastructure (PKI) security architecture for logon authentication and other security-related services. Smart cards are credit card–size devices that have integrated circuits built into them. These electronic cards securely store both public and private encryption keys and also perform cryptographic functions such as digital-signature and key-exchange operations.

Windows Server 2003 and Windows XP support only PnP-compliant smart card reader devices. Smart card readers connect to standard PC interfaces such as serial (RS-232) ports, PS/2 ports, USB ports, and PC Card slots. To install a smart card reader, use the Add Hardware applet in the Control Panel. Smart card configurations typically use the Extensible Authentication Protocol-Transport Level Security (EAP-TLS) authentication protocol. When you use a smart card to log on to a Windows Server 2003 computer, or to log on to a Windows XP Professional computer, at least one Cryptographic Service Provider (CSP) service must be installed and running on the system. CSPs enable other application programs to have access to the cryptographic services of a smart card, such as digital signature, key generation, and key exchange.

Before a user can log on to a system with a smart card, the user must be enrolled for a smart card certificate by an administrator who has the proper security privileges to enroll other users. This enrollment process creates a certificate and a public encryption key for the user. The user also needs to create or to be assigned a personal identification number (PIN) code, which he or she must use in conjunction with the smart card when logging on to a smart card–enabled computer.

Exam Prep Questions

1. Aaron is a network administrator for his company. One of the company's servers has just been upgraded to Windows Server 2003 from Windows 2000 Server. Unfortunately, one of the internal SCSI adapters cannot be installed because the operating system cannot find a suitable driver for it. Each time the system restarts, the PnP feature attempts to install the SCSI adapter without any success. Which is the easiest and fastest way to avoid having Windows Server 2003 try to install the device until the manufacturer publishes a driver that is compatible with Windows Server 2003?

   ○ **A.** Uninstall the SCSI adapter in Device Manager.

   ○ **B.** Physically remove the SCSI adapter from the server.

   ○ **C.** In Device Manager, right-click the SCSI adapter and select Disable.

   ○ **D.** Create a new hardware profile, restart the server using the new hardware profile, and disable the SCSI adapter for the new hardware profile.

2. Which of the following unsigned driver options are available under Windows Server 2003 from the graphical user interface? (Choose three.)

   ○ **A.** Install for administrators only

   ○ **B.** Ignore

   ○ **C.** Prompt

   ○ **D.** Block

   ○ **E.** Warn

   ○ **F.** PnP drivers only

3. You are the network administrator for your ABC Company. You want to enable the logging feature for the Windows Firewall under Windows Server 2003 Standard Edition SP1 on two of ABC Company's servers. What is the default name and location of the Windows Firewall security log?

   ○ **A.** Wfirewall.txt located in %windir%

   ○ **B.** Pfirewall.log located in %windir%

   ○ **C.** Wfirewall.txt located in %windir%\System32

   ○ **D.** Wfirewall.log located in %windir%\Pfirewall

   ○ **E.** Pfirewall.log located in %windir%\Wfirewall

   ○ **F.** Winfwlog.txt located in %windir%

4. Brendan is a network administrator who is responsible for deploying 1,000 new Windows XP Professional desktop computers within an Active Directory domain in a Windows Server 2003 network environment. What is the easiest, most dynamic, and most effective way for him to ensure that all the new desktop computers do not allow any unsigned device drivers to be installed?

   ○ **A.** Set the Unsigned Driver Options to Block in the System Properties window for a model computer. Then, image that model machine using the Sysprep tool and a third-party disk cloning software utility, such as Ghost, and copy the image to each of the 1,000 new workstations.

   ○ **B.** Use a GPO for the Default Domain Policy, or create a GPO for an OU where all the workstations will be placed. In the GPO, go to the Computer Policy, Security Settings, Local Policies, Security Options node. Set the Devices: Unsigned Driver Installation Behavior policy to Do Not Allow Installation. Mark the No Override check box for the GPO.

   ○ **C.** Keep the default installation setting for Unsigned Driver Options under Windows XP Professional because it is Block—Never Install Unsigned Driver Software.

   ○ **D.** As a local computer policy, set the Devices: Unsigned Driver Installation Behavior policy to Do Not Allow Installation for a model computer. Then, image that model machine using the Sysprep tool and a third-party disk cloning software utility, such as Ghost, and copy the image to each of the 1,000 new workstations.

5. As a consultant, you have several clients running Windows Server 2003 SP1 and Windows Server 2003 R2 on their corporate LANs. One of your clients calls, requesting that you connect his notebook computer to his corporate server using a Remote Desktop Connection. Your client has a high-speed Internet connection at his remote location, and he has Windows Firewall (WF) enabled on the server. You advise your client to attempt to connect to office network via a VPN (Virtual Private Network) connection. The client calls you back and tells you that he is having problems connecting to the server at his office over the VPN. In troubleshooting this issue, what is the most logical thing you should do first?

   ○ **A.** Disable Windows Firewall on the VPN connection on the server

   ○ **B.** Ensure that Windows Firewall on the VPN connection is enabled on the server

   ○ **C.** Check the Dial Another Connection First box on the General tab of the VPN Properties dialog box on the notebook computer

   ○ **D.** Disable your client's high speed Internet connection and advise your client to dial into the network at his office

6. You want to host a company website from your office on a Windows Server 2003 R2 Web Edition computer. You want to enable some of your employees to access the website and add content via FTP. You create the site, register its name, and enable Windows Firewall. Later, you receive reports that your employees and associates have no problems accessing the website; however, no one can upload any files to the web server via FTP. What can you do to resolve the issue?

- ○ **A.** Go to the Advanced tab of the Window Firewall properties dialog box. In the Network Connection Settings section, select the VPN connection and click the Settings button. Ensure that the FTP check box on the Services tab of the Advanced Settings dialog box is checked.

- ○ **B.** Go to the Advanced tab of the Window Firewall properties dialog box. In the Network Connection Settings section, select the VPN connection and click the Settings button. Ensure that the FTP box on the Services tab of the Advanced Settings dialog box is unchecked.

- ○ **C.** Go to the Advanced tab of the Window Firewall properties dialog box. In the Network Connection Settings section, select the HTTP connection and click the Settings button. Ensure that the HTTP check box on the Services tab of the Advanced Settings dialog box is checked.

- ○ **D.** Go to the Advanced tab of the Window Firewall properties dialog box. In the Network Connection Settings section, select the HTTP connection and click the Settings button. Ensure that the HTTP check box on the Services tab of the Advanced Settings dialog box is unchecked.

7. Under Windows Server 2003, where can you change the network binding order of protocols in addition to unbinding protocols to network adapters?

- ○ **A.** From the Network Connections window, click the Advanced menu and then select Advanced Settings.

- ○ **B.** From the Network Connections window, click the Advanced menu and then select Optional Networking Components.

- ○ **C.** In Device Manager, right-click Network Adapters and then click Properties.

- ○ **D.** In Device Manager, right-click a network adapter name, select Properties, and click the Advanced tab.

8. How can you set up a new hardware profile for disabling a network interface card on a Windows Server 2003 computer? (Choose two.)

- ○ **A.** Copy an existing profile from the Hardware Profiles dialog box and name it **NIC Disabled** by clicking the Hardware Profiles button on the System Properties window.

- ○ **B.** Create a new hardware profile by copying the `LocalService` folder in the `%systemdrive%\Documents and Settings` folder and name it **NIC Disabled**.

- ○ **C.** In Device Manager, right-click the device and select Properties. Click the Log on tab, select the Hardware Profile NIC Disabled, and click Disable.

- ○ **D.** Restart the system under the new profile named NIC Disabled. Open Device Manager, right-click the network interface card that you want to disable, and select Disable.

- ○ **E.** Create a new user account named **NIC Disabled** and log on using that user account each time that you want the computer to start up with the NIC disabled.

9. Which of the following operating system services and features does Wireless Provisioning Services (WPS) utilize under Windows Server 2003 SP1 and R2? (Choose four.)

- ○ **A.** WEP
- ○ **B.** WPA
- ○ **C.** WZC
- ○ **D.** IIS
- ○ **E.** IAS
- ○ **F.** PEAP
- ○ **G.** WISP
- ○ **H.** ISA

10. If you add a second processor to a Windows Server 2003, Standard Edition computer after the operating system has already been installed, what procedure must you follow for Windows Server 2003 to take advantage of that second processor?

- ○ **A.** Reinstall the operating system.
- ○ **B.** The Standard Edition does not support more than one processor.
- ○ **C.** Upgrade the HAL driver from Uniprocessor to Multiprocessor in Device Manager.
- ○ **D.** Upgrade the HAL driver from Uniprocessor to DualProcessor in Device Manager.

Answers to Exam Prep Questions

1. **Answer C is correct.** It offers the easiest and fastest way to stop Windows Server 2003 from repeatedly attempting to install a driver for the SCSI device. Answer A is incorrect because it would only result in having the operating system redetect the device each time it restarts, and then it would continue to try to install the device. Answer B is incorrect because you would have to take the server out of production to power it down and physically remove the SCSI adapter. Answer D is incorrect because it is easier to simply disable the device until a suitable driver becomes available instead of creating a new hardware profile and having to restart the computer under that profile to disable the SCSI adapter.

2. **Answers B, D, and E are correct.** Answers A, C, and F are incorrect because Windows Server 2003 offers only three options for unsigned driver installation behavior from the System Properties window—Ignore, Warn, or Block.

3. **Answer B is correct.** The default filename for the Windows Firewall log file is Pfirewall.log, and its default location is the %windir% folder, which is usually the C:\Windows folder. Answer A is incorrect because the default log filename is not Wfirewall.txt. Answer C is incorrect because the default log filename is not Wfirewall.txt. Answer D is incorrect because the default log file name is not Wfirewall.log. Answer E is incorrect because even though the default log filename is Pfirewall.log, it is not located in the %windir%\Wfirewall folder by default. Answer F is incorrect because the default log filename is not Winfwlog.txt.

4. **Answer B is correct.** Using a GPO setting for the domain or for the OU in which the workstations are placed is the fastest and easiest way to implement an unsigned driver signing policy. A GPO setting is also the most flexible because you can change it at any time, and the change will be propagated to all the workstations simultaneously. Answer A is incorrect because setting a local configuration and imaging it out is only a static solution and the local configuration can be overridden by a GPO setting. Answer C is incorrect because the default setting for Unsigned Driver Options is not Block, it is Warn—Prompt Me Each Time to Choose an Action. Answer D is incorrect because disk cloning solutions create static configurations rather than configurations that you can easily change later on a mass scale, such as GPO settings.

5. **Answer A is correct.** Because it will interfere with the operation of file sharing and other VPN functions, you should not enable WF on VPN connections. Answer B is incorrect because, by default, the option is already enabled. Answer C is incorrect because you would have the same problems with WF. Although it seems that answer D would work, nothing in the scenario suggests that it is possible to dial in to the network.

6. **Answer A is correct.** Any service associated with a specific network connection that you want to provide for remote clients must be enabled on the Services tab of the Advanced Settings page for the WF properties dialog box. Answer B is incorrect because the FTP service option must be checked (selected), not cleared (unchecked). Answer C is incorrect because the scenario clearly indicates that users are able to connect to the website, so the HTTP option must have already been allowed (checked). Answer D is incorrect because that would cause users to not be able to connect to the website, which is counterproductive.

7. **Answer A is correct.** You can change network protocol binding order, and you can bind and unbind protocols to network adapters from the Advance Settings dialog from the Advanced menu in the Network Connections window. Answer B is incorrect because the protocol binding options do not appear under the Optional Networking Components. Answers C and D are incorrect because you cannot change protocol bindings from Device Manager.

8. **Answers A and D are correct.** You create hardware profiles by either renaming an existing profile or copying an existing profile from the Hardware Profiles dialog box. You must first create a hardware profile and then start the server under that profile to enable or disable devices for that profile. Answer B is incorrect because you cannot create hardware profiles from the `%systemdrive%\Documents and Settings` folder. Answer C is incorrect because devices do not have a Log On tab for their properties windows; you configure services for hardware profiles in this manner. Answer E is incorrect because you cannot implement a hardware profile by creating any type of user account, nor by logging on to the computer under a particular user account.

9. **Answers B, C, E, and F are correct.** WPS under Windows Server 2003 SP1 and R2 uses Wi-Fi Protected Access (WPA), Wireless Zero Configuration (WZC), Internet Authentication Service (IAS), and Protected Extensible Authentication Protocol (PEAP) to provide its wireless provisioning services. Answer A is incorrect because WPS does not rely on Wired Equivalent Privacy (WEP) for its wireless security services. Answer D is incorrect because WPS does not rely on Internet Information Services (IIS) for its provisioning services. Answer G is incorrect because WISP stands for Wireless Internet Service Provider, which is not an operating system service or feature. Answer H is incorrect because WPS does not rely on Microsoft's Internet Security and Acceleration (ISA) server for its provisioning services.

10. **Answer C is correct.** All editions of Windows Server 2003 support at least up to two processors: You use Device Manager to right-click the computer type (HAL) and select Update Driver from the right-click menu to launch the Hardware Update Wizard. Answer A is incorrect because you do not need to reinstall the operating system to add support for a second processor. Answer B is incorrect because all editions support at least two processors. Answer D is incorrect because Windows Server 2003 allows you to switch from a Uniprocessor HAL to a Multiprocessor HAL, but you cannot switch from a Multiprocessor HAL to a Uniprocessor HAL.

Need to Know More?

1. Jones, Don. *Windows Server 2003 Weekend Crash Course*. New York, New York: Wiley Publishing, Inc., 2003.

2. Scales, Lee, and John Michell. *MCSA/MCSE 70-290 Training Guide: Managing and Maintaining a Windows Server 2003 Environment.* Indianapolis, Indiana: Que Publishing, 2003.

3. Williams, Robert, and Mark Walla. *The Ultimate Windows Server 2003 System Administrator's Guide*. Boston, Massachusetts: Addison Wesley Professional, 2003.

4. Snedaker, Susan. *The Best Damn Windows Server 2003 Book Period.* Rockland, Massachusetts: Syngress Publishing, Inc., 2004.

5. Search the Microsoft Product Support Services Knowledge Base on the Internet: `http://support.microsoft.com`. Find technical information using keywords from this chapter such as driver signing, Plug and Play, Device Manager, driver roll back, Windows Firewall, wireless provisioning services, and hardware profiles.

CHAPTER SIXTEEN

Managing Disks

Terms you'll need to understand:

✓ Intel Itanium-based servers

✓ Master Boot Record (MBR) disk partitioning

✓ Globally Unique Identifier (GUID) partition table (GPT) disks

✓ Basic versus dynamic disks

✓ Partitions and volumes

✓ Simple, spanned, and striped volumes

✓ Mirrored and RAID-5 volumes

✓ Diskpart.exe utility

Techniques you'll need to master:

✓ Administering 32-bit MBR disks

✓ Administering 64-bit GPT disks

✓ Using the Disk Management console

✓ Using the Disk Defragmenter

✓ Configuring and troubleshooting RAID-5 volumes

✓ Configuring and troubleshooting mirrored volumes

✓ Using diskpart.exe to manage disk drives and volumes from the command line

Managing a server's physical disk drives is vital for meeting the needs of network users, while at the same time safeguarding their data. If you are familiar with managing hard disks and volumes under Windows 2000 Server, you should feel quite at home working with disk storage administration in Windows Server 2003. You can manage the hard disks under Windows Server 2003 using the Disk Management console in both the Server and Professional editions of Windows 2000. For administrators who are more accustomed to working with Windows NT 4.0 Server, Windows Server 2003 introduces you to some new concepts that appeared in Windows 2000, such as basic and dynamic disk storage. Even so, the Disk Management Microsoft Management Console (MMC) snap-in does share a resemblance to the old Disk Administrator utility of Windows NT 4.0. This chapter focuses on managing hard disks in a Windows Server 2003 environment.

Disk Partitioning

Windows Server 2003 supports two types of disk partitioning styles: Master Boot Record (MBR) and GUID partition table (GPT). MBR disks have been used as standard equipment on IBM-compatible personal computers since the days of MS-DOS. MBR disks support volume sizes up to 2 terabytes (TB) and allow up to four primary partitions per disk. Alternatively, MBR disks support three primary partitions, one extended partition, and an unlimited number of logical drive letters.

GPT disks are supported on computers equipped with Intel Itanium-based processors and also on some non-Itanium–based computers, depending on the Microsoft operating system installed (see the following Exam Alert). Itanium-based computers use the Extensible Firmware Interface (EFI) instead of using a basic input/output system (BIOS) as the interface between the computer's hardware devices, its firmware, and the operating system.

> **EXAM ALERT**
>
> GPT disks are supported by Windows XP Professional x64 Edition, Windows XP Professional x64 (Itanium) Edition, all (32-bit–based) releases of Windows Server 2003 Service Pack 1 or later, all releases of Windows Server 2003 x64 Edition, and the Windows Server 2003 Editions for Intel Itanium-based (IA64) systems. However, only Itanium-based computers support booting from a GPT disk. The other Microsoft operating systems just mentioned that support GPT disks only support this disk partitioning style for reading and writing data on GPT disks.

GPT disks support volume sizes up to 18 exabytes (EB) and can store up to 128 partitions on each disk! Eighteen exabytes are roughly equivalent to 18 billion gigabytes—try using up that much storage! Critical system files are stored on GPT partitions, and GPT disks store a duplicate set of partition tables to ensure that partitioning information is retained. The Disk Management MMC snap-in identifies disks as either MBR or GPT. You can use GPT disks in the same way as you use MBR disks; however, you must be aware of the following character- istics and restrictions:

▶ On Intel Itanium-based computers, the Windows operating system loader files and the boot partition must be stored on a GPT disk. Any additional disks can be partitioned as MBR or GPT.

▶ You can convert a GPT disk to an MBR disk, and you can convert an MBR disk to a GPT provided that the disk has no data on it.

▶ Microsoft does not support mirroring the EFI System Partition (ESP) because ESPs only support manual replication and synchronization of these volumes. Because the ESP stores the files necessary for booting an Intel Itanium-based (IA64) computer using a GPT disk, this partition is critical to the successful operation of an Intel Itanium-based computer.

▶ Microsoft does not support GPT disks on removable media, such as Universal Serial Bus (USB) or IEEE 1394 (FireWire) disks. Cluster disks that use shared SCSI connections or Fibre channel connections used by Microsoft Cluster Services (MCS) are not supported for GPT disks.

▶ If you install one or more GPT disks into a computer that runs a 32-bit version of Windows XP or Windows Server 2003, the 32-bit Disk Management console displays each GPT disk as a basic MBR disk that contains just a single partition and the data on the partition is inaccessible.

▶ Both GPT disks and MBR disks can be part of a dynamic disk group. GPT disks and MBR disks can also coexist within the same computer.

▶ You can create dynamic volumes consisting of spanned, striped, mirrored, and RAID-5 volumes using any combination of GPT and MBR disks. Because of MBR disk cylinder alignment limitations, you can run into problems when you attempt to mirror a GPT-based disk volume to an MBR-based disk. To avoid this issue, mirror the MBR disk volume to the GPT disk, instead of trying to mirror a GPT disk volume to an MBR disk.

▶ You can create partitions on basic GPT disks with the EFI firmware tool, `diskpart.efi`, with 64-bit version of the `diskpart.exe` command-line tool, or from within the 64-bit edition of the Disk Management console.

Disk Storage Management

All 32-bit and 64-bit editions of Windows Server 2003 support two types of hard disk storage: basic and dynamic. Microsoft introduced these two concepts with Windows 2000 Server. All disks begin as basic disks until a server administrator converts them to dynamic status, one physical disk at a time. The biggest advantage that dynamic disks offer when compared to basic disks is that you can create software-based fault-tolerant volumes via the operating system from the volumes stored on dynamic disks; you cannot create fault-tolerant disk sets (volumes) from partitions stored on basic disks. Fault-tolerant volumes under Windows Server 2003 are mirrored volumes and Redundant Array of Independent Disks level 5 (RAID-5) volumes only. Of course, you can always implement a hardware RAID solution using a RAID controller and the disks can retain their basic status, or they can be converted to dynamic status under Windows Server 2003.

Basic Disks

A basic disk under Windows Server 2003 is essentially the same as the disk configuration under earlier versions of Windows: It is a physical disk with primary and extended partitions. Prior to Windows 2000, Microsoft did not call disks *basic* because that was the only type of disk available. There were no dynamic disks. You can create up to three primary partitions and one extended partition on a basic disk or up to four primary partitions. You can create a single extended partition with logical drives on a basic disk. You can also extend a basic partition, but only by using the `diskpart.exe` command-line tool, which is covered in a note in the section "Partitions and Logical Drives on Basic Disks" later in the chapter. Extending a disk increases the size of one of the basic disk's partitions by using some or all of any existing contiguous unallocated space on the basic disk. In other words, you gain more disk storage while maintaining the same drive letter for the basic partition.

Basic disks store their configuration information in the Partition Table, which is stored on the first sector of each hard disk. The configuration of a basic disk consists of the partition information on the disk. Fault-tolerant disk sets inherited from Windows NT 4 Server are based on these simple partitions, but they extend the configuration with some extra partition relationship information, which is stored on the first track of the disk. Windows NT Server 4.0 fault-tolerant disk sets use basic disks.

Under Windows NT Server 4.0, basic disks can contain spanned volumes (called *volume sets* in Windows NT 4.0), mirrored volumes (called *mirror sets* in

Windows NT 4.0), striped volumes (called *stripe sets* in Windows NT 4.0), and RAID-5 volumes (called *stripe sets with parity* in Windows NT 4.0) that were created using Windows NT 4.0 or earlier. The section "Basic Partitions" later in this chapter covers these kinds of hard disk configurations. Under Windows Server 2003, Windows XP, and Windows 2000, basic disks cannot contain any of the just mentioned disk configurations; such disk configurations are reserved for dynamic disks. For Windows 2000 and later operating systems, basic disks can store only "partitions"; dynamic disks can store only "volumes."

EXAM ALERT

Mirrored and RAID-5 volumes are fault-tolerant volumes that are only available under the Windows 2000 Server or the Windows Server 2003 family of server operating systems. You cannot create these types of volumes on basic or dynamic disks using a desktop operating system such as Windows XP Professional or Windows 2000 Professional. Fault-tolerant volumes are designed to withstand a single disk failure within a set of disks and to continue functioning until the failed disk is replaced. A mirror set (called a *mirrored volume* in Windows Server 2003) duplicates data to a second physical disk; a stripe set with parity (called a *RAID-5 volume* in Windows Server 2003) writes data across several disks (between 3 and 32 physical disks) and stores parity information across all the drives to be able to retrieve data in the event of a single failed disk. RAID-5 volumes cannot recover data if more than one drive in the set fails at the same time.

Dynamic Disks

A Windows Server 2003 dynamic disk is a physical disk configuration that does not use partitions or logical drives, and the Master Boot Record (MBR) is not used. Instead, the basic partition table is modified and any partition table entries from the MBR are added as part of the Logical Disk Manager (LDR) database that stores dynamic disk information at the end of each dynamic disk. Dynamic disks can be divided into as many as 2,000 separate volumes, but you should limit the number of volumes to 32 for each dynamic disk to avoid slow boot time performance.

Dynamic disks do not have the same limitations of basic disks. For example, you can extend a dynamic disk "on-the-fly" without requiring a reboot. Dynamic disks are associated with disk groups, which are disks that are managed as a collection. This managed collection of disks helps organize dynamic disks. All dynamic disks in a computer are members of the same disk group. Each disk in a disk group stores replicas of the same configuration data. This configuration data is stored in the 1MB LDR region at the end of each dynamic disk.

Dynamic disks support five types of volumes: simple, spanned, mirrored, striped, and RAID-5. (The section "Dynamic Volumes" later in this chapter covers these volumes in detail.) You can extend a volume on a dynamic disk. Dynamic disks can contain a virtually unlimited number of volumes, so you are not restricted to four volumes per disk as you are with basic disks. Regardless of the type of file system, only computers running Windows XP Professional, Windows 2000 Professional or Server, or Windows Server 2003 can directly access dynamic volumes on hard drives that are physically connected to the computer. However, computers running other operating systems can access dynamic volumes remotely when they connect to shared folders over the network.

Managing Basic Disks and Dynamic Disks

When you install Windows Server 2003, the system automatically configures the existing hard disks as basic NTFS disks, unless they have been configured as dynamic from a previous installation. Windows Server 2003 does not support dynamic disks on mobile PCs (laptops or notebooks). If you're using an older desktop machine that is not Advanced Configuration and Power Interface (ACPI) compliant, the Convert to Dynamic Disk option (covered in the section "Converting Basic Disks to Dynamic Disks" later in this chapter) is not available. Dynamic disks have some additional limitations. You can install Windows Server 2003 on a dynamic volume that you converted from a basic disk, but you cannot extend either the system or the boot volume on a dynamic disk. Any troubleshooting tools that cannot read the dynamic disk management database work only on basic disks.

EXAM ALERT

Dynamic disks are only supported on computers that use the Small Computer System Interface (SCSI), Fibre Channel, Serial Storage Architecture (SSA), Integrated Drive Electronics (IDE), Enhanced IDE (EIDE), or Ultra Direct Memory Access (DMA) interfaces. Portable computers, removable disks, and disks connected via Universal Serial Bus (USB) or FireWire (IEEE 1394) interfaces are not supported for dynamic storage. Dynamic disks are also not supported on hard drives with a sector size of less than 512 bytes. Cluster disks—groups of several disks that serve to function as a single disk such as storage area networks (SANs)—are not supported either.

Basic and dynamic disks are nothing more than Windows Server 2003's way of looking at a hard disk configuration. If you're migrating to Windows Server 2003 from Windows NT 4, the dynamic disk concept might seem odd in the beginning, but once you understand the differences, working with dynamic disks is not complicated. You can format partitions with the FAT16, FAT32, or

New Technology File System (NTFS) on a basic or a dynamic disk. However, you can only format a dynamic volume as NTFS from the Disk Management console because NTFS is the most stable, secure, and feature-rich file system for Windows Server 2003. You must use Windows Server 2003 Explorer to format a dynamic volume as FAT or FAT32. Table 16.1 compares the terms used with basic and dynamic disks.

TABLE 16.1   Terms Used with Basic and Dynamic Disks

Basic Disks	Dynamic Disks
Active partition	Active volume
Extended partition	(Not applicable)
Logical drive	Simple volume
Mirror set	Mirrored volume (servers only)
Primary partition	Simple volume
Stripe set	Striped volume
Stripe set with parity	RAID-5 volume (servers only)
System and boot partitions	System and boot volumes
Volume set	Spanned volume

EXAM ALERT

Windows Server does not support formatting partitions or volumes larger than 32GB as FAT32. Partitions or volumes larger than 32GB that have been upgraded from previous operating systems can be mounted and used under Windows Server 2003. Partitions or volumes larger than 32GB that have been created by third-party utilities can also be mounted and used under Windows Server 2003.

When you install a fresh copy of Windows Server 2003 or when you perform an upgrade installation from Windows NT 4.0 Server with SP5, the computer system defaults to basic disk storage. One or more of the disk drives could already be configured as dynamic if you upgraded from Windows 2000 Server (or if you import a "foreign disk" from a Windows 2000 Server or from another Windows Server 2003 computer). A disk is considered "foreign" when you move it from one computer to another computer, until you select the import option for it in the Disk Management console. Dynamic disks are proprietary to Windows Server 2003, Windows 2000, and Windows XP Professional. On desktop operating systems, such as Windows 2000 Professional and Windows XP Professional, dynamic disks provide support for advanced disk configurations, such as disk striping and disk spanning. On Windows Server 2003 and Windows 2000 Server computers, dynamic disks provide support for fault-tolerant configurations, such as disk mirroring and disk striping with parity (also known as RAID-5).

Converting Basic Disks to Dynamic Disks

From the graphical user interface (GUI), you use the Windows Server 2003 Disk Management console (an MMC snap-in) to upgrade a basic disk to a dynamic disk. To access Disk Management, click Start, Administrative Tools, Computer Management or right-click the My Computer icon on the Start menu and click Manage. If you are using the Classic Start menu, click Start, Administrative Tools, Computer Management or simply right-click the My Computer icon on the desktop and select Manage. You'll find Disk Management by expanding the Storage folder. You must be a member of the local Administrators group or the backup operators group, or else the proper authority must be delegated to you if you are working within an Active Directory environment to make any changes to the computer's disk-management configuration.

For the conversion to succeed, any disks to be converted must contain at least 1MB of unallocated space. Disk Management automatically reserves this space when creating partitions or volumes on a disk, but disks with partitions or volumes created by other operating systems might not have this space available. (This space can exist even if it is not visible in Disk Management.) Windows Server 2003 requires this minimal amount of disk space to store the dynamic database, which the operating system that created it maintains. Before you convert any disks, close any programs that are running on those disks. After you convert a disk to dynamic, remember that you can have only one operating system that is bootable on each dynamic disk!

> **NOTE**
>
> Many third-party disk partitioning utilities do not automatically leave the necessary 1MB of space at the end of a disk for converting a basic disk to dynamic. If you use tools such as Partition Magic, you need to manually allocate the required 1MB of disk space with these tools.

To convert a basic disk to a dynamic disk from the Disk Management console, perform the following steps:

1. Open the Disk Management console.

2. Right-click the basic disk that you want to convert to a dynamic disk, and then click Convert to Dynamic Disk (see Figure 16.1).

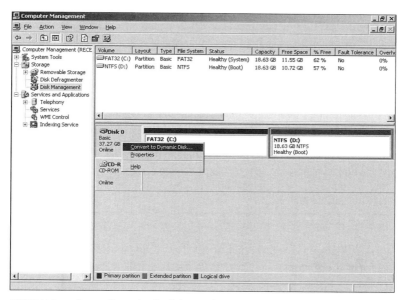

FIGURE 16.1 Converting a basic disk to a dynamic disk with Disk Management.

When you upgrade an empty basic disk to a dynamic disk, you do not need to reboot. However, if you convert a basic disk that already has partitions on it, or if the basic disk contains the system or boot partitions, you must restart your computer for the change to take effect. The good news is that you do not need to select a special command such as Commit Changes Now (as with Windows NT 4.0) before restarting your computer or closing the Disk Management tool.

NOTE

If you use a basic disk for storing volume shadow copies of files using the Volume Shadow Copy Service (VSS), you must take special measures to avoid losing shadow-copy data if you convert the disk to a dynamic disk. For a nonboot volume that stores shadow-copy data for a different volume, you first need to dismount the volume where the original files are stored. After you take that volume offline, you should convert the basic disk containing the shadow-copy volume to a dynamic disk. Immediately following the conversion, you must bring the volume that holds the original files back online within 20 minutes or you will lose the existing shadow-copy data for that volume. If the shadow-copy volume is also the boot volume, you can convert the disk to dynamic without having to take the original volume offline to avoid losing shadow-copy data.

TIP

You can mount and dismount volumes from the command line with the `mountvol.exe` command. On basic disks, if you type `mountvol x: /p`, where *x:* represents the volume's drive letter, you can dismount a volume and take it offline. Unfortunately, the `/p` parameter is not supported on dynamic disks. The command `mountvol x: /l` displays the specified drive letter's volume ID. By using the syntax `mountvol x: volume_ID`, you can assign a drive letter to the volume and remount it to bring it back online. For example, the command `mountvol S: \\?\Volume{55e769f0-40d5-11d4-b223-806d6172696f}\` would assign drive letter S: to the volume ID specified. You can also use Disk Management to mount and dismount volumes from the GUI. You can mount and dismount volumes by right-clicking a volume and selecting Change Drive Letter and Paths. By removing the drive letter and any other paths (mount points) for the volume, you take the volume offline.

To convert a basic disk to a dynamic disk from the Windows Server 2003 command line, perform these steps:

1. Open a command prompt window, type **diskpart**, and press Enter.

2. Type `commands` or `help` to view a list of available commands.

3. Type `select disk 0` to select the first hard disk (`select disk 1` to select the second hard disk, and so on) and press Enter.

4. Type `convert dynamic` and press Enter (see Figure 16.2).

5. Type **exit** to quit the `diskpart.exe` tool and then restart the computer to have the new configuration take effect.

FIGURE 16.2 Using the `diskpart.exe` command-line tool to convert a basic disk to a dynamic disk.

NOTE

In addition to the `diskpart` command, Windows Server 2003 administrators can take advantage of another command-line tool for managing FAT, FAT32, and NTFS file systems—`fsutil.exe`. With `fsutil`, Windows Server 2003 administrators can perform tasks such as managing disk quotas, managing mount points, and several other advanced disk-related tasks. Type **fsutil** at a command prompt to view a list of supported commands.

When you convert a basic disk to a dynamic disk, any existing partitions on the basic disk become simple volumes on the dynamic disk. Any existing mirror sets, stripe sets, stripe sets with parity, or volume sets become mirrored volumes, striped volumes, dynamic RAID-5 volumes, or spanned volumes, respectively. Once you convert a basic disk to a dynamic disk, you cannot change the volumes back to partitions. Instead, you must first delete all dynamic volumes on the disk, right-click the disk in Disk Management, and then select the Convert to Basic Disk option.

EXAM ALERT

Converting to a dynamic disk is a one-way process. Yes, you can convert a dynamic disk back to a basic disk, but you'll lose all your data. Obviously, this loss is a major consideration! If you find yourself needing to do it, first back up your data and then you can delete all the volumes on the disk, convert the disk to basic, and restore your data.

Because the conversion process from basic to dynamic is per physical disk, a disk has all dynamic volumes or all basic partitions; you won't see both on the same physical disk. Remember, you do not need to restart your computer when you upgrade from an empty basic to a dynamic disk from the Disk Management console. However, you do have to restart your computer if you use the `diskpart.exe` command-line tool for the conversion; if you convert a disk containing the system volume, boot volume, or a volume with an active paging file; or if the disk contains any existing volumes or partitions.

EXAM ALERT

When you upgrade or convert a basic disk to a dynamic disk, at least 1MB of free space must be available for the dynamic disk database. Under normal circumstances, this requirement should not be a problem.

Converting Dynamic Disks Back to Basic Disks

You must remove all volumes (and therefore all data) from a dynamic disk before you can change it back to a basic disk. After you convert a dynamic disk back to a basic disk, you can only create partitions and logical drives on that disk. After being converted from a basic disk, a dynamic disk can no longer contain partitions or logical drives, nor can any operating systems other than Windows Server 2003, Windows 2000, or Windows XP Professional access it. To revert a dynamic disk to a basic disk, perform the following steps:

1. Back up the data on the dynamic disk.

2. Open Disk Management.

3. Delete all the volumes on the disk.

4. Right-click the dynamic disk that you want to change back to a basic disk and then click Convert to Basic Disk.

5. Restore the data to the newly converted basic disk.

Moving Disks to Another Computer

To move disks to another computer, perform the following steps:

1. Before you disconnect the disks, use Disk Management on the source computer and make sure that the status of all volumes on each of the disks is healthy. For any volumes that are not healthy, repair the volumes before you move the disks.

2. If the disks are dynamic, right-click each disk and select Remove Disk.

3. Power off the computer, remove the physical disks, and then install the physical disks on the target computer.

4. When you restart the target computer, the Found New Hardware dialog box should appear. If not, click Start, Control Panel, Add Hardware to launch the Add Hardware Wizard. Use the wizard to properly install the disks on the computer.

5. Open Disk Management on the target computer.

6. Click Action, Rescan Disks from the menu bar.

7. For any disks that are labeled Foreign, right-click on them, click Import Foreign Disks, and then follow the instructions provided by the Disk Management console.

> **EXAM ALERT**
>
> You can move dynamic disks only to Windows Server 2003, Windows 2000, or Windows XP Professional computers.

Reactivating a Missing or Offline Disk

A dynamic disk can become "missing" or "offline" when it is somehow damaged, it suddenly loses power, or it has its data cable disconnected while still powered on. Unfortunately, you can reactivate only dynamic disks—not basic disks.

To reactivate a missing or offline dynamic disk, perform the following steps:

1. Launch the Disk Management console.

2. Right-click the disk marked Missing or Offline and then select the Reactivate Disk option.

3. After the disk is reactivated, the disk should be labeled as "online."

4. Exit from the Disk Management MMC.

Basic Partitions

Basic disks include partitions and logical drives, as well as special partition sets created using Windows NT 4.0 or earlier operating systems. Before Windows 2000, basic disks contained all partition types: primary partitions, extended partitions with logical drives, volume sets, stripe sets, mirror sets, and stripe sets with parity (also known as RAID-5 sets). For Windows Server 2003, Windows 2000, and Windows XP Professional, these volumes can be created only on dynamic disks and they have been renamed to simple volumes, spanned volumes, striped volumes, mirrored volumes, and RAID-5 volumes. Under Windows Server 2003, you can create basic partitions on basic disks only. In addition, you can create fault-tolerant volumes (mirrored volumes and RAID-5 volumes) only on dynamic disks under a Windows 2000 or a Windows Server 2003 operating system. See the upcoming section "Dynamic Volumes" to find out how to migrate data from striped sets or volume sets that are stored on a basic disk under Windows NT 4.0 Workstation or Windows 2000 Professional.

> **NOTE**
>
> Only Microsoft server operating systems support fault-tolerant features such as mirrored volumes and RAID-5 volumes. Windows Server 2003 and Windows 2000 Server operating systems require fault-tolerant volumes to be stored on dynamic disks. Desktop (client-side) operating systems, such as Windows XP Professional and Windows 2000 Professional, do not support any type of fault-tolerant volumes, even though they do support dynamic disks.

Partitions and Logical Drives on Basic Disks

You can create primary partitions, extended partitions, and logical drives only on basic disks. You should create basic disks rather than dynamic disks if your computer also runs a down-level Microsoft operating system, such as Windows NT 4.0 Server. You must be a member of the local Administrators group or the backup operators group, or else the proper authority must be delegated to you (if you are working within an Active Directory environment) to create, modify, or delete basic volumes.

Partitions and logical drives can reside only on basic disks. You can create up to four primary partitions on a basic disk or up to three primary partitions and one extended partition. You can use the free space in an extended partition to create multiple logical drives.

> **NOTE**
>
> You can extend a basic partition, but it must be formatted as NTFS, it must be adjacent to contiguous unallocated space on the same physical disk, and it can be extended only onto unallocated space that resides on the same physical disk. With these requirements met, you can perform only the extension using the `diskpart.exe` command-line utility.

> **TIP**
>
> On a local computer set up in a dual-boot configuration, you should create basic partitions on basic disks. In this way, the computer can run earlier versions of Microsoft operating systems (prior to Windows 2000), and those earlier versions will be able to access those basic partitions (drive letters). For example, if a computer dual boots between Windows Server 2003 and Windows NT 4.0 Server, the Windows NT 4.0 Server operating system would not be able to access any data stored on a dynamic disk on the same computer.

Creating or Deleting a Partition or Logical Drive

To create or delete a partition or logical drive, you can use the `diskpart.exe` command-line tool or the GUI and perform the following steps:

1. Open the Disk Management console.

2. Perform one of the following options:

   ▶ Right-click an unallocated region of a basic disk and click New Partition.

   ▶ Right-click an area of free space within an extended partition and click New Logical Drive.

   ▶ Right-click a partition or logical drive and select Delete Partition to remove that partition or logical drive. Click Yes to confirm the deletion.

3. When you choose to create a new partition or logical drive, the New Partition Wizard appears. Click Next to continue.

4. Click Primary Partition, Extended Partition, or Logical Drive and answer the prompts regarding disk space allocation and so on as requested by the wizard to finish the process.

You must first create an extended partition before you can create a new logical drive, if no extended partition exists already. If you choose to delete a partition, all data on the deleted partition or logical drive is lost. You cannot recover deleted partitions or logical drives. You cannot delete the system partition, boot partition, or any partition that contains an active paging file. The operating system uses one or more paging files on disk as virtual memory that can be swapped into and out of the computer's physical random access memory (RAM) as the system's load and volume of data dictate.

EXAM ALERT

Windows Server 2003 requires that you delete all logical drives and any other partitions that have not been assigned a drive letter within an extended partition before you delete the extended partition itself.

Dynamic Volumes

What were called sets (such as mirror sets and stripe sets) under previous operating systems are now called volumes (such as mirrored volumes and striped volumes) in Windows Server 2003, Windows 2000, and Windows XP. Dynamic volumes are the only type of volume that you can create on dynamic disks. With dynamic disks, you are no longer limited to four volumes per disk (as you are with basic disks). You can install Windows Server 2003 onto a dynamic volume; however, these volumes must contain the partition table (which means that these volumes must have been converted from basic to dynamic under Windows Server 2003, Windows XP Professional, or Windows 2000). You cannot install Windows Server 2003 onto dynamic volumes that you created directly from unallocated space. Only computers running Windows XP Professional, the Windows 2000 family of operating systems, or the Windows Server 2003 family of products can access dynamic volumes. The five types of dynamic volumes are simple, spanned, mirrored, striped, and RAID-5. Windows Server 2003 supports all five dynamic volume types. Windows XP Professional and Windows 2000 Professional support only simple, spanned, and striped dynamic volumes. You must be a member of the local Administrators group or the backup operators group, or you must have the proper permissions delegated to you (if you are working within an Active Directory environment) to create, modify, or delete dynamic volumes.

EXAM ALERT

When you create dynamic volumes on dynamic disks using the Disk Management console, you only have the option of formatting new dynamic volumes with the NTFS file system. However, you can use the `format.exe` command at a command prompt window to format a dynamic volume using the FAT or FAT32 file system. For example, you can create a new dynamic volume using Disk Management; do not format the drive, and be sure to assign a drive letter to it. Then, at a command prompt, type `format x: /fs:fat32`, where `x:` represents the drive letter and `fat32` represents the file system that you want to format on the volume. You can alternatively specify `fat` or `ntfs` as the file system when you use the `format` command.

Simple Volumes

A simple volume consists of disk space on a single physical disk. It can consist of a single area on a disk or multiple areas on the same disk that are linked together. To create a simple volume, perform the following steps:

1. Open Disk Management.

2. Right-click the unallocated space on the dynamic disk where you want to create the simple volume and then click New Volume.

3. Using the New Volume Wizard, click Next, click Simple, and then follow the instructions and answer the questions asked by the wizard.

Here are some guidelines about simple volumes:

▶ You can create simple volumes on dynamic disks only.

▶ Simple volumes are not fault tolerant.

▶ Simple volumes cannot contain partitions or logical drives.

▶ Neither MS-DOS nor Windows operating systems other than Windows Server 2003, Windows XP Professional, and Windows 2000 can access simple volumes.

Spanned Volumes

A spanned volume consists of disk space from more than one physical disk. You can add more space to a spanned volume by extending it at any time. To create a spanned volume, perform the following steps:

1. Open Disk Management.

2. Right-click the unallocated space on one of the dynamic disks where you want to create the spanned volume and then click New Volume.

3. Using the New Volume Wizard, click Next, click Spanned, and then follow the instructions and answer the questions asked by the wizard.

Here are some guidelines about spanned volumes:

▶ You can create spanned volumes on dynamic disks only.

▶ You need at least two dynamic disks to create a spanned volume.

▶ You can extend a spanned volume onto a maximum of 32 dynamic disks.

▶ Spanned volumes cannot be mirrored or striped.

▶ Spanned volumes are not fault tolerant.

Extending Simple or Spanned Volumes

Simple volumes are the most basic volumes on dynamic disks. If you extend a simple volume to another dynamic disk, it automatically becomes a spanned volume. You can extend a simple volume to make it a spanned volume, and you can also further extend a spanned volume to add disk storage capacity to the volume. To extend a simple or a spanned volume, perform the following steps:

1. Open Disk Management.

2. Right-click the simple or spanned volume you want to extend, click Extend Volume, and then follow the instructions and answer the questions asked by the Extend Volume Wizard.

You should be aware of the many rules about extending a simple or a spanned volume:

▶ You can extend a volume only if it contains no file system or if it is formatted using NTFS. You cannot extend volumes formatted using FAT or FAT32.

▶ After a volume is extended onto multiple disks (spanned), you cannot mirror the volume, nor can you make it into a striped volume or a RAID-5 volume.

▶ You cannot extend boot volumes, system volumes, striped volumes, mirrored volumes, and RAID-5 volumes.

▶ After a spanned volume is extended, no portion of it can be deleted without the entire spanned volume being deleted.

▶ You can extend a simple or a spanned volume only if the volume was created as a dynamic volume under Windows Server 2003. You cannot extend a simple or spanned volume that was originally converted from basic to dynamic under Windows 2000 or Windows XP Professional.

▶ You can extend simple and spanned volumes on dynamic disks onto a maximum of 32 dynamic disks.

▶ Spanned volumes write data only to subsequent disks as each disk volume fills up. Therefore, a spanned volume writes data to physical disk 0 until it fills up, then it writes to physical disk 1 until its available space is full, then it writes to physical disk 2, and so on. However, if just one disk fails as part of the spanned volume—*all the data contained on that spanned volume is lost.*

Which One Is the Boot Partition or Volume?

The boot partition is a partition on a basic disk that contains the Windows Server 2003 operating system files; the default location is C:\Windows. The boot volume is the same as the boot partition, but the term *volume* is used when it is located on a dynamic disk.

The system partition is a partition on a basic disk that stores the files necessary for the operating system to load when the computer is starting up, such as the ntldr file, ntdetect.com, and boot.ini. The system volume is the same as the system partition, but the term *volume* is used when it is located on a dynamic disk. The system partition or volume is often the same as the boot partition or volume, but of course, this setup is not required and many times the operating system files are stored in an entirely different partition or volume. Just remember:

▶ *Boot*—The drive letter where the \Windows (%windir%) folder is located

▶ *System*—The drive letter where the computer's boot-up files are located, usually the C: drive

Seems backward, doesn't it?

Striped Volumes

A striped volume stores data in stripes on two or more physical disks. Data in a striped volume is allocated alternately and evenly (in stripes) to the disks contained within the striped volume. Striped volumes can substantially improve the speed of access to the data on disk. Striped volumes are often referred to as

RAID-0; this configuration tends to enhance performance, but it is not fault tolerant. To create a striped volume, perform the following steps:

1. Open Disk Management.

2. Right-click unallocated space on one of the dynamic disks where you want to create the striped volume and select New Volume from the menu that appears.

3. Using the New Volume Wizard, click Next, select the Striped option, and follow the instructions and answer the questions asked by the wizard.

Here are some guidelines about striped volumes:

▶ You need at least two physical dynamic disks to create a striped volume.

▶ You can create a striped volume onto a maximum of 32 disks.

▶ Striped volumes are not fault tolerant.

▶ For increased volume capacity, select disks that contain similar amounts of available disk space. A striped volume's capacity is limited to the space available on the disk with the smallest amount of available space.

▶ Whenever possible, use disks that are the same model and from the same manufacturer.

▶ Striped volumes cannot be extended or mirrored. If you need to make a striped volume larger by adding another disk, you first have to delete the volume and then re-create it.

Mirrored Volumes and RAID-5 Volumes

You can create mirrored volumes and RAID-5 volumes only on dynamic disks running on Windows Server 2003 or Windows 2000 Server computers. Both mirrored volumes and RAID-5 volumes are considered fault tolerant because these configurations can handle a single disk failure and still function normally. Mirrored volumes and RAID-5 volumes both require that an equal amount of disk space be available on each disk that will be a part of these volumes. A mirrored volume must use two physical disks—no more and no fewer than two physical hard disk drives. A RAID-5 volume must use at least three physical hard disks up to a maximum of 32 physical disks.

Many network administrators and consultants agree that hardware-based fault-tolerant solutions are more robust and reliable than software-based fault-tolerant configurations. By installing one or more RAID controller adapter cards into a server, you can set up several different types of hardware fault tolerance, such as mirroring, RAID-5, RAID 10 (mirrored volumes that are part of a striped array set), and RAID 0+1 (striped volumes that are part of a mirrored set). When you use hardware RAID, you can retain basic disks or you can convert disks to dynamic; hardware RAID is hidden to Windows Server 2003. Of course, it's less expensive to implement a software solution, such as setting up mirrored volumes or RAID-5 volumes using the Disk Management console in Windows Server 2003, but often the performance, reliability, and flexibility of hardware-based RAID far outweighs its extra cost.

Working with Mirrored Volumes

A mirrored volume uses volumes stored on two separate physical disks to "mirror" (write) the data onto both disks simultaneously and redundantly. This configuration is also referred to as RAID-1. If one of the disks in the mirrored configuration fails, Windows Server 2003 writes an event into the system log of the Event Viewer. The system functions normally (unless the second disk fails) until the failed disk is replaced and then the volume can be mirrored again. Mirrored volumes cost you 50% of your available storage space because of the built-in redundancy. If you mirror two 70GB disks, you are left with just 70GB of space rather than 140GB.

You can make mirrored volumes more robust by installing a separate hard disk controller for each disk; technically, this is known as disk duplexing. Disk duplexing is better than disk mirroring because you alleviate the single point of failure by having one controller for each disk. Under Windows Server 2003, disk duplexing is still referred to as disk mirroring. You can create mirrored volumes only by using dynamic disks. To create a new empty mirrored volume from unallocated space, perform the following steps:

1. Open Disk Management.

2. Right-click an area of unallocated space on a dynamic disk and select New Volume.

3. Click Next for the New Volume Wizard welcome window.

4. Click Mirrored as the volume type option and click Next.

5. Select one of the available dynamic disks and click Add (see Figure 16.3).

6. Enter the amount of storage space to be used (in MB) for this mirrored volume, up to the maximum available space on the first disk that you selected, and then click Next.

7. Assign the new volume a drive letter, mount the volume in an empty NTFS folder, or choose not to assign the volume a drive letter or path and click Next.

8. Choose whether to format the new mirrored volume. If you choose to format the new volume, specify the following settings:

   ▸ File system (NTFS is the only option for dynamic volumes under the Disk Management console).

   ▸ Allocation unit size.

   ▸ Volume label.

   ▸ Mark the check box to Perform a Quick Format (if desired).

   ▸ Mark the check box to Enable File and Folder Compression (if desired).

9. Click Next to continue.

10. Click Finish to complete the New Volume Wizard.

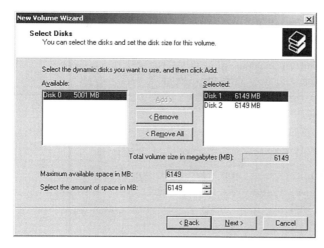

FIGURE 16.3 Using the Select Disks dialog box to create a mirrored volume with the New Volume Wizard.

To create a mirrored volume from a boot or system volume, or to create a mirrored volume from an existing volume that already contains data, perform the following steps:

1. Open Disk Management.

2. Right-click an existing dynamic volume and select Add Mirror.

3. Select one of the available dynamic disks on which to create the redundant volume and click Add Mirror (see Figure 16.4).

FIGURE 16.4 Using the Add Mirror dialog box to create a mirrored volume from an existing dynamic volume.

TIP

When you add a mirrored volume to the boot volume, Windows Server 2003 automatical-ly adds an entry to the computer's `boot.ini` file (located on the system volume or par-tition) as an additional startup option that displays each time the server reboots. Unless your primary mirror disk is the system volume, this option allows you to boot to the sec-ondary disk in the mirror without using a boot disk if the primary disk in the mirror fails. The additional startup option displays like this: `Boot Mirror X: - secondary plex`, where `X:` represents the secondary mirror drive letter.

You should be aware of some important issues and guidelines before you attempt to mirror system or boot volumes:

▶ When you mirror volumes stored on ATA disks, you must change the jumper switch on the nonfailed drive to the master position (upon restart) if the master disk on the primary IDE channel fails, until you replace the failed disk.

▶ Microsoft does not recommend mirroring the system volume using one ATA disk and one SCSI disk because the system can encounter startup problems if one of the drives fails.

▶ If you plan to use separate SCSI controllers for each SCSI disk that you will mirror, you should use identical controllers from the same manufac-turer.

▶ For a mirrored system volume, be sure to run a test to simulate a disk failure and attempt to start the system from the remaining mirrored vol-ume. Perform this test regularly as part of your backup routine *before* a real failure occurs.

EXAM ALERT

If you mirror the system volume of a Windows Server 2003 computer, be sure to create a system boot disk in case the computer does not boot normally after one disk fails as part of the mirrored volume. You can make a system boot disk by formatting a blank disk under Windows Server 2003 and copying the following Windows Server 2003 startup files onto the disk: `ntldr`, `ntdetect.com`, `boot.ini`, and `ntbootdd.sys`, if it exists. Edit the `boot.ini` file so that the ARC path points to the correct `partition()` number for the nonfailed boot volume hard disk. See Microsoft Knowledge Base article #325879 for more information.

You can stop mirroring a volume by either breaking or removing the mirror. When you break a mirrored volume, each volume that makes up the mirror becomes an independent simple volume, and they are no longer fault tolerant. When you remove a mirrored volume, the removed mirrored volume becomes unallocated space on its disk, whereas the remaining mirrored volume becomes a simple volume that is no longer fault tolerant. All data that was stored on the removed mirrored volume is erased. To break a mirrored volume, perform the following steps:

1. Open Disk Management.

2. Right-click one of the mirrored volumes that you want to break and select Break Mirrored Volume (see Figure 16.5).

3. Click Yes in the Break Mirrored Volume message box (see Figure 16.6).

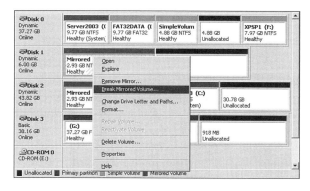

FIGURE 16.5 The right-click menu options for breaking a mirrored volume in the Disk Management console.

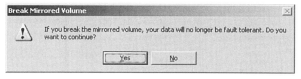

FIGURE 16.6 The Break Mirrored Volume message box.

If you want to completely destroy one of the mirrored volumes and leave just one of the volumes intact, you need to perform a removal procedure instead of simply breaking the mirrored volumes. To remove a mirrored volume, perform the following:

1. Open Disk Management.

2. Right-click a mirrored volume and then select Remove Mirror.

3. At the Remove Mirror dialog box, select the disk from which you want to completely erase the mirrored volume and turn the volume into unallocated space. The remaining volume will stay with all of its data intact as a simple volume (see Figure 16.7).

4. Click the Remove Mirror button.

5. Click Yes to confirm the removal action at the Disk Management message box that appears.

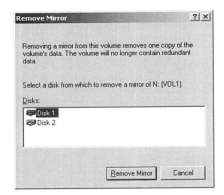

FIGURE 16.7   The Remove Mirror dialog box.

Working with RAID-5 Volumes

Windows Server 2003 supports disk striping with parity (RAID-5) volumes with the Disk Management console and through the `diskpart.exe` command-line utility. You need a minimum of three physical disks to create a RAID-5 volume. You are limited to a maximum of 32 physical disks in creating a RAID-5 volume under Windows Server 2003. In creating a fault-tolerant volume using a RAID-5 configuration, you effectively lose an amount of storage equivalent to the capacity of one of the disks due to parity information that gets stored across all the disks (disk striping with parity). For example, if you use three 70GB disks, your RAID-5 volume will be able to store up to approximately 140GB of data. The remaining 70GB is used for storing the important parity data across all three disks in case of a failure—a 33% loss of available storage capacity. However, as you add disks to a RAID-5 volume, the percentage of lost storage space diminishes. For example, if you use five 70GB disks, you would again lose 70GB of available storage capacity, but that accounts only for a 20% overall loss in capacity (70GB divided by 350GB total available disk space equals .20, or 20%). In the event that one disk within the RAID-5 volume fails, the remaining disks can re-create the data stored on the failed disk as soon as a new disk is installed to replace the failed disk. To create a RAID-5 volume using Disk Management, perform the following steps:

1. Open Disk Management. Be sure that the computer has three or more dynamic disks—each with unallocated space.

2. Right-click an area of unallocated space on one of the dynamic disks that you want to use for the RAID-5 volume and select New Volume.

3. Click Next for the Welcome to the New Volume Wizard window.

4. Select the RAID-5 option button and click Next.

5. Select each available disk that you want to use as part of the RAID-5 volume from within the Available list box and click Add for each one (see Figure 16.8). You must select at least three disks and no more than 32 disks.

6. Select any disks that you do not want to use as part of the RAID-5 volume within the Selected list box and click Remove to remove any disks that you do not want to include as a part of the RAID-5 volume.

7. Enter the storage capacity that you want for the RAID-5 volume in the Select the Amount of Space in MB spin box and click Next to continue.

8. Choose to assign the volume a drive letter, mount the volume in an empty NTFS folder, or choose to not assign a drive letter or path to the new RAID-5 volume and click Next.

9. Choose whether to format the new RAID-5 volume. If you choose to format the new volume, specify the following settings:

   ▶ File system (NTFS is the only option for dynamic volumes under the Disk Management console).

   ▶ Allocation unit size.

   ▶ Volume label.

   ▶ Mark the check box to Perform a Quick Format (if desired).

   ▶ Mark the check box to Enable File and Folder Compression (if desired).

10. Click Next to continue.

11. Click Finish to complete the New Volume Wizard.

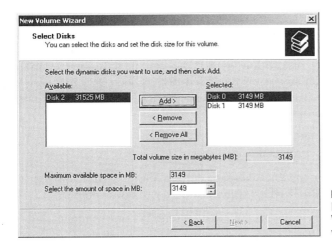

FIGURE 16.8 The Select Disks dialog box of the New Volume Wizard for a RAID-5 volume.

NOTE

Mirrored and RAID-5 volumes are available only on computers that are running Windows Server 2003 or Windows 2000 Server. Windows XP Professional and Windows 2000 Professional computers can use basic and dynamic disks, but they cannot host software-based fault-tolerant disk configurations such as mirrored volumes and striped sets with parity (RAID-5) volumes. You can, however, use a computer running Windows XP Professional (or Windows 2000 Professional) to create mirrored and RAID-5 volumes on a remote computer running the Windows Server 2003 or the Windows 2000 Server network operating system. The Disk Management MMC snap-in can administer both local and remote disk storage.

If one disk within a RAID-5 volume is intermittently failing, you can attempt to reactivate it by right-clicking the disk and selecting Reactivate Disk. If one disk within a RAID-5 volume appears to be permanently failed, you can replace that failed disk with another dynamic disk attached to the computer or you can install a new disk. To regenerate the RAID-5 volume, right-click the RAID-5 volume on the failed disk and select Repair Volume. The replacement disk must contain at least as much unallocated space as that used by the failed disk for the RAID-5 volume.

Troubleshooting Issues on Basic and Dynamic Disks

You should use basic disks and dynamic disks appropriately. In certain instances, you cannot use basic disks and partitions; in other situations, you cannot use dynamic disks and volumes. Understanding when and where you can use these two kinds of storage is key to implementing robust server storage policies and procedures. Knowing how to structure basic and dynamic storage allows you to plan properly for upgrading existing servers and for installing new ones.

Installing Windows Server 2003 on a Dynamic Disk

If you create a dynamic volume from unallocated space on a dynamic disk under Windows 2000, Windows XP, or Windows Server 2003, you cannot install a copy of Windows Server 2003 on that volume. This setup limitation occurs because the Windows Server 2003 setup program recognizes only dynamic volumes that contain partition tables. Partition tables appear in basic volumes and in dynamic volumes only when they have been converted from basic to dynamic. If you create a new dynamic volume on a dynamic disk, that new dynamic volume does not contain a partition table.

Extending a Volume on a Dynamic Disk

If you convert a basic volume to a dynamic volume (by converting the basic disk to a dynamic disk), you can install Windows Server 2003 on that volume, but you cannot extend the volume. The limitation on extending volumes occurs because the boot volume, which contains the Windows Server 2003 system files, cannot be part of a spanned volume. If you extend a simple volume that contains a partition table (that is, a volume that was converted from basic to dynamic), Windows Server 2003 Setup recognizes the spanned volume but cannot install to it, because the boot volume cannot be part of a spanned volume.

You can extend volumes that you create after you convert a basic disk to a dynamic disk. You can extend volumes and make changes to the disk configuration without rebooting your computer (in most cases). If you want to take advantage of these features in Windows Server 2003, you must convert a disk from basic to dynamic status. Use dynamic disks if your computer runs only Windows Server 2003 and you want to create more than four volumes per disk or if you want to extend, stripe, or span volumes onto one or more dynamic disks.

Upgrading from Windows NT Server 4.0 with Basic Disks

If you need to upgrade a computer running Windows NT Server 4.0 that has hard drives configured as volume sets, striped sets, mirror sets, or striped sets with parity, you must first back up all the data stored on each particular set.

Windows Server 2003 does not support volume sets, stripe sets, mirror sets, or stripe sets with parity on basic disks. These four types of special storage sets are supported only by dynamic disks under Windows Server 2003.

To migrate data on volume sets, stripe sets, mirror sets, or stripe sets with parity from Windows NT Server 4.0 to Windows Server 2003, perform the following steps:

1. Under Windows NT Server 4.0, back up the data.

2. Delete the special storage sets.

3. Upgrade the operating system to Windows Server 2003.

4. Convert the appropriate hard disks from basic to dynamic disks.

5. Create the appropriate dynamic volumes.

6. Restore the backed-up data.

TIP

If you upgrade a computer to Windows Server 2003 from Windows NT Server 4.0 without backing up the data stored on mirror sets or stripe sets with parity on basic disks, the operating system will not mount those volumes. However, if you install the Windows Server 2003 support tools on the installation CD-ROM in the \support\tools folder, you can utilize the ftonline.exe command-line tool. Ftonline will mount fault-tolerant volume sets stored on basic disks. Ftonline is designed to be a temporary measure, and it allows you to access the data stored on fault-tolerant volumes in read-only mode so that you can copy the data onto dynamic fault-tolerant volumes.

Diagnosing Hard Disk Problems

Physical disk problems do occur because disks are mechanical devices. Both the Add Hardware Wizard and Device Manager can assist you in troubleshooting physical disk problems and disk device driver problems. To diagnose disk or disk device driver problems, perform the following steps:

1. Right-click My Computer from the Start menu or from the Windows desktop and click Properties.

2. For the System Properties dialog box, click the Hardware tab and then click the Add Hardware Wizard button.

3. Click Next for the welcome window and then the wizard will search for new hardware devices that you have connected to the computer.

4. Click Yes, I Have Already Connected the Hardware and then click Next.

5. Select the hardware device that you want to diagnose and fix from the Installed Hardware list box and click Next.

6. The wizard will inform you of the device's current status. Click Finish to launch the Help and Support Center's troubleshooter window to assist you with diagnosing the problem, or click Cancel to exit the wizard.

Another way to troubleshoot hardware problems is with Device Manager. Right-click My Computer from the Start menu or from the Windows desktop and select Properties. From the System Properties dialog box, click the Hardware tab and then click the Device Manager button. Expand the hardware category that you need to troubleshoot. Right-click the device that you want to inquire about and select Properties to display the device's properties sheet, as shown in Figure 16.9. All the pertinent information about the device is available from this window, including its device status as determined by the operating system. Hard disks display four tabs on their properties sheets: General, Policies, Volumes, and Driver. The General tab shows device status and other basic information. The Policies tab displays options for enabling and disabling write caching (for ATA and SCSI disks only) and for optimizing for either quick removal or performance (for USB and FireWire disks only), as shown in Figure 16.10.

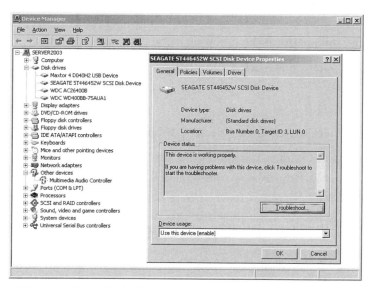

FIGURE 16.9 Using Device Manger to troubleshoot hardware problems.

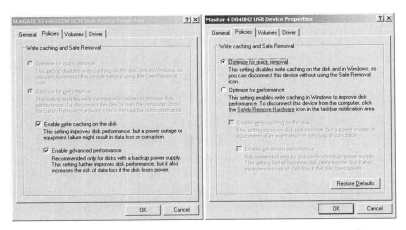

FIGURE 16.10   Using disk device policies for specifying different options for removable and nonremovable drives.

Detecting and Repairing Disk Errors

In Windows Server 2003, you can use the Error-Checking tool to check for file system errors and bad sectors on the computer's hard disks. It's a good idea to periodically run this utility as a proactive step in monitoring a server's hard disks and for repairing any minor issues before they turn into big problems. To run the Error-Checking tool, perform the following steps:

1. Open My Computer, right-click the local disk that you want to check, and select Properties.

2. Click the Tools tab.

3. Under Error-Checking, click the Check Now button.

4. Under Check Disk Options, mark both the Automatically Fix File System Errors check box and the Scan for and Attempt Recovery of Bad Sectors check box.

5. Click the Start button to begin the error-checking process. After the process finishes, a message box will notify you of any errors.

All files must be closed for the Error-Checking utility to run. The volume (drive letter) is not available to run any other tasks while this process is running. If the volume is currently in use, a message asks whether you want to reschedule the disk checking for the next time you restart the system. The next time you restart the computer, the Error-Checking tool runs. If your volume is formatted as NTFS, Windows Server 2003 automatically logs all file transactions, replaces bad clusters, and stores copies of key information for all files on the NTFS volume.

Removable Storage Support

Windows Server 2003 provides removable storage services for applications and network administrators that enhance the sharing and management of removable media hardware such as backup tape drives, optical discs, and automated (robotic) media pool libraries. Removable storage and media support in Windows Server 2003 precludes the need for third-party software developers to write custom application programs to support each different type of removable media device. In addition, removable storage services allow organizations to leverage their investment in expensive removable storage equipment by having multiple removable storage applications share these devices.

Windows Server 2003 Removable Storage implements a set of Application Programming Interfaces (APIs) that enable third-party software solutions to catalog all removable media, such as DVDs, tapes, and optical discs. Both offline (shelved) and online (housed in a library) media can be cataloged. Removable Storage organizes media using media pools. These media pools control access to the removable media, categorize the media according to each type of use, and permit applications to share the media. Removable Storage tracks the application programs that share the removable media. Removable Storage is logically structured into five basic components: media units, media libraries, media pools, work queue items, and operator requests. You manage Removable Storage from the MMC snap-in named, strangely enough, Removable Storage. The Removable Storage snap-in is also available as part of the default Computer Management console.

The Disk Defragmenter Tool

The Disk Defragmenter utility rearranges files, programs, and unused space on your server's hard disks, allowing programs to run faster and data files to open more quickly. Putting the pieces of files and programs in a more contiguous arrangement on disk reduces the time the operating system needs to access requested items. To run Disk Defragmenter, perform the following steps:

1. Click Start, All Programs, Accessories, System Tools and click Disk Defragmenter. Alternatively, you can right-click a drive letter in My Computer, select Properties, click the Tools tab, and click Defragment Now. You can also run the Disk Defragmenter from the Computer Management console.

2. Select which disks you want to defragment and any additional options you want to set.

3. Click the Analyze button to determine whether the disks could benefit from a defragmenting procedure. The Disk Defragmenter will display a message box informing you of its findings, as shown in Figure 16.11.

4. Click View Report to see the details for the level of fragmentation on the disk, as shown in Figure 16.12.

5. Click the Defragment button to start the defragmentation process on the disk that you have selected.

6. After the defragmentation procedure is complete, a message box pops up to alert you. Click View Report to read the details about the improved level of fragmentation on the disk, or click Close to return to the Disk Defragmenter console and you can then exit the program or you can select another disk to analyze or defragment.

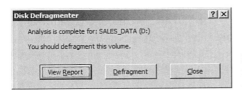

FIGURE 16.11 The Disk Defragmenter's message box after performing an analysis of a disk.

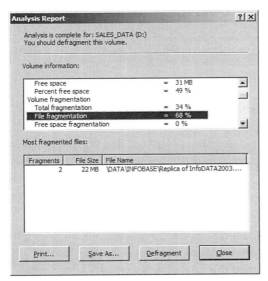

FIGURE 16.12 The Disk Defragmenter's Analysis Report dialog box.

> **TIP**
>
> Windows Server 2003 ships with a command-line version of the disk defragmenter—
> `defrag.exe`. You can run this program within a batch file or inside of a Windows script,
> which in turn can be scheduled to run automatically using the Scheduled Tasks folder.

> **TIP**
>
> On NTFS volumes, Windows Server 2003 reserves a portion of the free space for a sys-
> tem file called the Master File Table (MFT). The MFT is where Windows stores all the
> information it needs to retrieve files from the volume. Windows stores part of the MFT at
> the beginning of the volume, and Windows reserves the MFT for exclusive use, so the
> Disk Defragmenter cannot and does not move files to the beginning of volumes.

The `chkdsk` and `chkntfs` Command-Line Tools

The `chkdsk.exe` command-line utility runs diagnostic tests on the file system for a drive letter and generates a report. It also corrects file-system errors when you use the `/f` option. If the computer is powered down suddenly due to a loss of power, Windows Server 2003 marks each drive volume as "dirty" by setting the dirty bit on each drive volume. When the system restarts, `chkdsk.exe` automatically runs for each drive volume marked as dirty. For system and boot partitions and volumes, you can specify for `chkdsk.exe` to run during the next restart by typing the command `chkntfs /c` at a command prompt. Extensive help information is available for both `chkdsk.exe` and `chkntfs.exe` utilities by simply typing `chkdsk /?` or `chkntfs /?` at any command-prompt window.

Exam Prep Questions

1. Which of the following hard disk configurations is the boot volume under Windows Server 2003? (Choose two.)

   ○ **A.** The C: drive (a dynamic disk) that contains the boot files such as `ntldr`, `ntdetect.com`, and `boot.ini`, whereas the `\Windows` folder is located on a different drive letter

   ○ **B.** The E: drive (a basic disk), where the `\Windows` folder is located

   ○ **C.** The F: drive (a dynamic disk), where the `\Windows` folder is located

   ○ **D.** The C: drive (a dynamic disk), where the boot files such as `ntldr`, `ntdetect.com`, and `boot.ini` are stored and where the `\Windows` folder is also located

   ○ **E.** The G: drive, where the Windows Server 2003 CD-ROM is located

2. Which of the following types of hard disks can you convert from basic disks to dynamic disks under Windows Server 2003? (Choose four.)

   ○ **A.** EIDE (ATA) hard disks

   ○ **B.** SCSI hard disks

   ○ **C.** USB hard disks

   ○ **D.** IEEE 1394 (FireWire) hard disks

   ○ **E.** Fibre Channel disks

   ○ **F.** Ultra DMA disks

   ○ **G.** Solid-state keychain (flash) disks

3. Which of the following types of fault-tolerant (RAID) configurations (without using a RAID controller or third-party software) can you set up using either Disk Management or the `diskpart.exe` command-line tool under Windows Server 2003? (Choose three.)

   ○ **A.** RAID 0

   ○ **B.** RAID 2

   ○ **C.** RAID 5

   ○ **D.** RAID 1

   ○ **E.** RAID 0+1

   ○ **F.** RAID 10

4. How can an administrator create and format a new 33GB dynamic volume as FAT32 under Windows Server 2003?

   ○ **A.** Use the Disk Management console and the New Volume Wizard to create a new 33GB volume on an existing dynamic disk, and have the wizard format it as FAT32.

   ○ **B.** Use the Disk Management console and the New Volume Wizard to create a new 33GB volume on an existing dynamic disk. Use the `format.exe` tool at a command prompt to format the volume as FAT32.

   ○ **C.** At a command prompt, use the `diskpart.exe` tool to create a new 33GB volume on a dynamic disk and use the `format.exe` tool to format the volume as FAT32.

   ○ **D.** Use the Disk Management console and the New Partition Wizard to create a new 33GB partition on an existing basic disk. Use the `format.exe` tool at a command prompt to format the volume as FAT32.

   ○ **E.** You cannot format a 33GB volume or partition as FAT32 under Windows Server 2003 using Disk Management or the `format.exe` command-line tool.

5. On which of the following hard-disk configurations can you install a fresh copy of Windows Server 2003? (Choose two.)

   ○ **A.** On a basic partition

   ○ **B.** On a dynamic volume that was created from unallocated space

   ○ **C.** On a dynamic volume that was upgraded from a basic volume

   ○ **D.** On a basic volume that is part of a removable disk

   ○ **E.** On a dynamic disk that already has Windows XP Professional installed on it

6. How many primary partitions without an extended partition can reside on a basic MBR disk under Windows Server 2003?

   ○ **A.** 3

   ○ **B.** 4

   ○ **C.** 1

   ○ **D.** 128

7. Which of the following statements are true about basic disks under Windows Server 2003? (Choose two.)

   ○ **A.** Basic disks are not supported under Windows Server 2003.

   ○ **B.** Basic disks that were configured as one disk striping with parity set under Windows NT Server 4.0 are mounted automatically after the server is upgraded to Windows Server 2003.

    ◯ **C.** Basic disks can only be formatted as FAT or FAT32.

    ◯ **D.** You cannot convert dynamic disks back to basic disks without deleting all data and volumes on the disks first.

    ◯ **E.** IEEE 1394 disks can only be basic disks.

8. How can you extend a basic volume under Windows Server 2003? (Choose three.)

    ◯ **A.** You must extend the basic volume onto unallocated space on the same physical disk.

    ◯ **B.** The basic volume must be formatted as FAT or FAT32.

    ◯ **C.** You cannot extend a basic volume; you can only extend a simple volume that resides on a dynamic disk. The simple volume becomes a spanned volume.

    ◯ **D.** The basic volume must be formatted as NTFS.

    ◯ **E.** The basic volume must be located physically adjacent to the unallocated space onto which you will extend the volume.

    ◯ **F.** You can only use the Disk Management console to extend the basic volume.

9. How can you schedule regular disk-defragmentation procedures under Windows Server 2003?

    ◯ **A.** Install a third-party product.

    ◯ **B.** Use the Disk Defragmenter console.

    ◯ **C.** Use the `defrag.exe` command-line tool.

    ◯ **D.** You cannot schedule disk defragmentation.

10. Which of the following hardware-storage configurations is considered a best practice if you are going to set up RAID 1 fault tolerance using only software settings that are available natively under Windows Server 2003?

    ◯ **A.** Install one RAID controller.

    ◯ **B.** Install one fibre channel controller.

    ◯ **C.** Install two SCSI controllers—one for each physical disk.

    ◯ **D.** Install three SCSI controllers—one for each physical disk.

Answers to Exam Prep Questions

1. **Answers C and D are correct.** The boot volume is a dynamic disk that contains the Windows files (the `\Windows` folder by default). The system volume is a dynamic disk that stores the boot files such as `ntldr`, `ntdetect.com`, and `boot.ini`. The system volume and the boot volume can be one and the same. Answer A is incorrect

because the `\Windows` folder is located on a different drive letter; this answer would be the system volume, not the boot volume. Answer B is incorrect because the boot volume is stored on a dynamic disk; the boot partition is stored on a basic disk. Answer E is incorrect because a CD-ROM drive is never considered a boot or system volume or partition.

2. **Answers A, B, E, F, and G are correct.** These types of hard disks are compatible with Windows Server 2003 dynamic disks. Answers C and D are incorrect because Windows Server 2003 dynamic disks are not supported on USB Version 1.1 or 2.0 hard disks nor are dynamic disks supported on IEEE 1394 disks.

3. **Answers A, C, and D are correct.** Windows Server 2003 supports disk striping (RAID 0), disk striping with parity (RAID 5), and disk mirroring (RAID 1). Answer B is incorrect because Windows Server 2003 does not natively support hammering code error-correcting code (ECC) disk configurations (RAID 2). Answer E is incorrect because Windows Server 2003 does not natively support striped volumes that are part of a mirrored set (RAID 0+1). Answer F is incorrect because Windows Server 2003 does not natively support mirrored volumes that are part of a striped array set (RAID 10).

4. **Answer E is correct.** Windows Server does not support formatting partitions or volumes larger than 32GB as FAT32. Answers A, B, C, and D are all incorrect because Windows Server 2003 only supports formatting partitions or volumes larger than 32GB as NTFS. Partitions or volumes larger than 32GB that have been upgraded from previous operating systems can be mounted and used under Windows Server 2003. Partitions or volumes larger than 32GB that have been created by third-party utilities can also be mounted and used under Windows Server 2003.

5. **Answers A and C are correct.** You can install a fresh copy of Windows Server 2003 onto a basic partition and onto a dynamic volume if the volume was originally a basic partition that was upgraded to dynamic because Windows Server 2003 can only be installed on a disk that contains a partition table. Answer B is incorrect because a dynamic volume that is created from unallocated space does not contain a partition table. Answer D is incorrect because Windows Server 2003 Setup does not support installation onto removable media such as USB disks or IEEE 1394 (FireWire) disks. Answer E is incorrect because you can install only one operating system per dynamic disk.

6. **Answer B is correct.** You can create up to four primary partitions on a basic disk without an extended partition. Answer A is incorrect because you are limited to three primary partitions only if there is an extended partition on the disk. Answer C is incorrect because you can have more than one primary partition on a basic disk. Answer D is incorrect because you are limited to a maximum of four primary partitions on a basic MBR disk; a basic GPT disk can host up to 128 partitions.

7. **Answers D and E are correct.** To convert dynamic disks back to basic disks, you must remove all volumes on the disk, which means that all data must be removed as well. IEEE 1394 (or FireWire) disks cannot be converted to dynamic; therefore, they can only be basic disks. Answer A is incorrect because basic disks are supported under Windows Server 2003. Answer B is incorrect because basic disk sets that were created under previous versions of Microsoft server products are not mounted by the operating system; you must use the `ftonline.exe` tool on the setup CD-ROM. Answer C is incorrect because basic disks (and dynamic disks) can be formatted as FAT, FAT32, or NTFS.

8. **Answers A, D, and E are correct.** You can extend a basic volume formatted as NTFS onto adjacent, unallocated space on the same physical disk. Answer B is incorrect because the basic volume must be formatted as NTFS, not FAT or FAT32. Answer C is incorrect because you can extend a basic volume if certain requirements are met. Answer F is incorrect because you can only use the `diskpart.exe` command-line tool to extend a basic volume.

9. **Answer C is correct.** You can put the `defrag.exe` command into a batch file or script and then you can schedule that batch file or script using the Scheduled Tasks folder. Answer A is incorrect because you do not need to purchase and install a third-party product to schedule disk defragmentation. Answer B is incorrect because you cannot natively schedule disk-defragmentation events using the Disk Defragmenter console. Answer D is incorrect because you can schedule disk defragmentation under Windows Server 2003.

10. **Answer C is correct.** RAID 1 is referred to as disk mirroring, which uses only two physical disks. A best practice is to connect each disk to a separate controller to eliminate a single point of failure—which is known as disk duplexing. Answer A is incorrect because a RAID controller is used for configuring hardware-based RAID, not software-based RAID. Answer B is incorrect because installing just one controller for two physical disks creates a single point of failure; it does not matter which type of controller is used: EIDE, SCSI, or Fibre Channel. Answer D is incorrect because RAID 1 (disk mirroring) can only use two physical disks. Installing three controllers for three separate disks might bode well for using RAID-5 under Windows Server 2003, but you cannot use three disks for disk mirroring.

Need to Know More?

1. Boswell, William. *Inside Microsoft Windows Server 2003.* Boston, Massachusetts: Addison Wesley Professional, 2003.

2. Holme, Dan, and Orin Thomas. *MCSA/MCSE Self-Paced Training Kit (Exam 70-290): Managing and Maintaining a Microsoft Windows Server 2003 Environment.* Redmond, Washington: Microsoft Press, 2003.

3. Stanek, William R. *Microsoft Windows Server 2003 Inside Out.* Redmond, Washington: Microsoft Press, 2004.

4. Williams, Robert, and Mark Walla. *The Ultimate Windows Server 2003 System Administrator's Guide.* Boston, Massachusetts: Addison Wesley Professional, 2003.

5. Search the Microsoft Product Support Services Knowledge Base on the Internet: `http://support.microsoft.com`. You can also search through Microsoft TechNet on the Internet: `http://www.microsoft.com/technet`. Find technical information using keywords from this chapter, such as MBR disks, GPT disks, Intel Itanium processors, basic disks, dynamic disks, RAID-5, mirrored volumes, spanned volumes, diskpart.exe, boot volume, and system volume.

CHAPTER SEVENTEEN

Managing Data Storage

Terms you'll need to understand:

✓ CD-recordable and DVD-recordable media

✓ USB storage devices

✓ NTFS data compression

✓ Compressed (zipped) folders

✓ Encrypting File System (EFS)

✓ EFS Recovery Agents

✓ NTFS Disk quotas

✓ Shadow Copies of Shared Folders

✓ Previous versions of files and folders

Techniques you'll need to master:

✓ Managing USB storage devices

✓ Working with data compression

✓ Managing data encryption

✓ Setting up EFS Recovery Agents

✓ Establishing NTFS disk quotas

✓ Configuring Shadow Copies of Shared Folders

✓ Accessing previous versions of files and folders

As disk storage technology continues to improve and as the demand for data storage continues to increase, the role of managing data storage becomes even more critical and more complex. Mobile storage devices, such as USB 2.0 memory drives and DVD-recordable media, have become commonplace. Today's increasingly large data storage capacities for all devices, large and small, would have amazed IT managers just a few years ago.

While the advances in data storage technology allow for incredible convenience and provide the opportunity for disk-based backups and continuous data protection, these advances also pave the way for more potential threats. Portable storage devices put data theft within any employee's reach. Volumes of private data require regular backups and important safeguards. This chapter deals with the tools that Windows Server 2003 SP1 and R2 offer you for managing and protecting your organization's most-prized asset—information.

Managing Portable Media and Devices

Never before in the history of information technology have we seen such proliferation of low-cost, ultra-small footprint storage devices. Not only must we concern ourselves with CD- and DVD-recordable media, but with nonvolatile memory USB 2.0 devices (flash drives, thumb drives, jump drives, and so on) and extremely small USB 2.0 hard disk drives as well. At the time this book is being written, you can buy flash drives with capacities of 6GB or more and you can purchase very small portable hard drives with capacities of 120GB or more. As has been the case since the advent of digital storage, these capacities will continue to increase over time. Network administrators must know how to work with these devices and how to limit their ability to copy (steal) data from the network and from workstations.

Supporting CD-recordable and DVD-recordable Media

Windows Server 2003 supports a variety of read-only memory (CD-ROM and DVD-ROM), recordable (CD-R, DVD-R, DVD+R), rewritable (CD-RW, DVD-RW, DVD+RW), and DVD random access memory (DVD-RAM) drives and discs. Check with the most recent HCL or your hardware vendor to see whether your CD or DVD device works with Windows Server 2003.

If the CD or DVD device is PnP compliant, you can rely on Windows Server 2003 to detect the device and install the appropriate drivers as well as allocate system resources for the device. If you are using a CD or DVD drive that is not PnP compliant, use the Add Hardware applet in the Control Panel to install the drivers and assign resources for the device.

The Windows Server 2003 Compact Disc File System (CDFS) reads CDs that are formatted according to the ISO 9660 standard. Windows Server 2003 also supports the Joliet standard, which is an extension to the ISO 9660 standard that supports Unicode characters and a folder hierarchy extending deeper than eight levels of subfolders. Windows Server 2003 also offers integrated support for writing data directly onto CD-R and CD-RW media without requiring any third-party CD-burning software.

A DVD drive needs either a hardware or software decoder to play DVD-based movies on your Windows Server 2003 computer. Fortunately, the current version of Windows Media Player, which ships with all Windows versions, has a built-in DVD decoder component. The computer also requires a Windows Server 2003–compatible sound card and video display card with their respective drivers to play multimedia DVD titles. Your DVD decoder must be Windows Server 2003 compliant to play movies under Windows Server 2003 if you upgrade from a previous Windows Server version. You do not need a decoder for reading data DVDs. Windows Server 2003 supports the Universal Disk Format (UDF) file system on DVDs (and CDs) for read-only access to data. However, in general, servers should not be used for playing any types of movies or video clips to entertain the IT staff.

Writing Files and Folders to CD-R and CD-RW Media

Under Windows Server 2003, the ability to write to CD-R and CD-RW media is disabled by default. You must first enable the IMAPI CD-Burning COM Service before you can burn any CDs. To turn on this service, click Start, Run; type `services.msc`; and click OK. Double-click the IMAPI CD-Burning COM Service and change the startup type to Automatic. Click Start to run the service without having to reboot the server. If you set the startup type to Automatic, the computer will be ready to create CDs every time that it restarts. To write to CD-R and CD-RW media under Windows Server 2003 without third-party software, follow these steps:

1. Right-click individual files (and folders), or right-click selected groups of files (and folders) and select Send to CD-R (or CD-RW) Drive. Repeat this step for all files and folders that you want to write to the CD. You can also copy and paste or drag and drop files and folders onto the CD-R/ CD-RW drive letter in My Computer.

2. Open the CD-R/CD-RW drive in My Computer or the Windows Explorer to review all of the files and folders that have been placed there for creating the CD.

3. Click Write These Files to CD from the left task pane, or click the File menu and select Write These Files to CD.

4. In the CD Writing Wizard dialog that appears, type in a name for this new CD. Be sure that a blank CD-R or CD-RW disc is in the drive and click Next. The data will be written to the CD.

5. Click Finish when the wizard finishes writing the data to the CD.

When you are selecting files and folders for CD burning by either copying them into the CD-R/CD-RW drive or by using the Send to right-click menu option, they are temporarily stored in a CD burning staging area. This staging area is a hidden folder located, by default, in `%systemdrive%\Documents and Settings\`*username*`\Local Settings\Application Data\Microsoft\CD Burning`. The environment variable `%systemdrive%` represents the drive letter where the operating system is installed—for example, C: if Windows Server 2003 is installed in `C:\Windows`. Windows Server 2003 does not natively support writing data to DVD-R, DVD-RW, DVD+R, or DVD+RW media. However, some third-party utilities do support writing to DVD-based media from Windows Server 2003. Of course, Windows Server 2003 can read DVD-based media. Windows Server 2003 does support DVD-RAM drives and discs and uses the FAT32 file system for read and write operations on DVD-RAM media.

Configuring CD-R/CD-RW Device Settings

You can configure settings for desktop CD recording by right-clicking the CD-R/CD-RW drive letter in My Computer and selecting Properties. From its properties sheet, you can click the Recording tab to modify the drive's CD-burning characteristics as shown in Figure 17.1. From the Recording tab, you can enable or disable CD recording on the drive, and you change the drive letter where temporary files are stored before CDs are burned (the staging area). You can also select the writing speed for CD burning and you can specify whether the CD media should be ejected after each CD has been burned.

Installing, Configuring, and Troubleshooting USB Devices

Windows Server 2003 offers built-in support for many USB devices. Because all USB devices fully support PnP, USB peripherals are easily connected to (and disconnected from) Windows Server 2003 computers that have USB ports by using standard USB cables and connectors. Windows Server 2003 and Windows XP Professional with Service Pack 1 (SP1) provide support for the USB 2.0 specification and are fully backward compatible with the USB 1.1 standard. In theory, USB devices can be safely connected and disconnected while the computer is running. Windows Server 2003 detects USB devices when they are plugged into the computer and attempts to install the proper device driver for each detected USB device. If Windows Server 2003 cannot locate an appropriate device driver, it prompts you to insert a driver disk or CD-ROM from the manufacturer of the device.

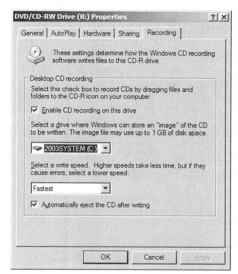

FIGURE 17.1 The Recording tab of the properties sheet for a CD-R/CD-RW drive.

Working with USB Controllers and Hubs

To support USB, a computer needs either a USB host controller built into the motherboard or a USB controller adapter card installed. The USB host controller directs all USB traffic and also serves as a hub to which USB devices connect. You can connect additional (external) USB hubs to connect multiple USB devices to the host controller, which is also known as the root hub. Hubs are either self-powered or bus-powered. Some devices, such as mice and keyboards, can function fine when plugged into bus-powered USB hubs. Other devices, such as external hard drives, printers, and scanners, might require more power than bus-powered hubs can provide. You should connect these kinds of USB devices to self-powered hubs, although some provide their own standard power cords. USB supports up to a maximum of 127 devices connected to one USB host controller (root hub) with no more than seven tiers (seven layers of USB hubs daisy-chained together). You can use no more than five external hubs in one physical chain of hubs. Each device can be no more than five meters away from the port of the hub that it is connected to.

> **NOTE**
>
> USB devices that install and function properly under Windows 98, Windows Me, Windows 2000, or Windows XP are not guaranteed to work under Windows Server 2003. Be sure to check for upgraded drivers before you upgrade a computer to Windows Server 2003. Verify that USB peripherals are on the Windows Server 2003 HCL, or check with the USB device vendor regarding compatibility with Windows Server 2003.

Viewing Power Allocations for USB Hubs

The USB root hub is allocated a certain amount of power that any bus-powered USB hubs and USB devices connected to it must share. As you add USB devices, less power is available to each connected device. To view power allocations for USB hubs, perform the following steps:

1. Open Device Manager.

2. Expand the entry for Universal Serial Bus Controllers.

3. Right-click USB Root Hub and then click Properties.

4. Click the Power tab to view the power consumed by each device in the Attached Devices list.

> **TIP**
>
> As mentioned previously, hubs for USB devices are either self-powered or bus-powered. Self-powered hubs (hubs plugged into an electrical outlet) provide maximum power to the device, whereas bus-powered hubs (hubs plugged only into another USB port) provide minimum power. You should plug devices that require a lot of power, such as cameras and hard drives, into self-powered hubs.

> **NOTE**
>
> In Device Manager, the Universal Serial Bus Controllers node appears only if you have a USB port installed on the computer. The Power tab appears only for USB hubs.

Troubleshooting USB Devices

Sometimes, when you install a USB device on a computer, the computer might start functioning poorly or the system might even freeze entirely. If the system remains unresponsive (frozen) for two or more minutes, it's probably locked up and won't recover on its own. In such an event, the first step to take is to power off the computer, wait about 60 seconds, and then power it back on. You might even need to completely disconnect the power cord for some newer devices that are power-management aware. If that doesn't help, try one or more of the following steps:

▶ Follow the manufacturer's installation instructions, which might require that you run a setup program before connecting the USB device to the computer.

▶ Connect the device to a different computer to verify that it is not defective.

▶ Plug the device directly into a USB root hub on the back of the computer instead of plugging it into a USB hub that is daisy-chained off the root hub.

▶ Look at the Windows Server 2003 event log for USB-related error messages.

▶ Check Device Manager to verify that all USB devices on the Universal Serial Bus Controllers tree are operating correctly.

▶ Check whether one or more USB devices are drawing more power (more than 500 milliamps) than the bus or hub can provide. Use a separate power adapter for high power consumption devices (if available) or use a self-powered USB hub for such devices.

▶ Replace the USB cables.

▶ Make sure that no more than five hubs are connected in one continuous chain.

Managing Data Compression, Data Encryption, and Storage Quotas

Windows Server 2003 (and Windows XP) supports two types of data compression: NTFS compression and Compressed (Zipped) Folders. Files and folders compressed using the Compressed (Zipped) Folders feature remain compressed under all three supported file systems: NTFS, FAT, and FAT32. Compressing any system folders, such as the \Windows folder or the \Program Files folder, is not recommended and should be avoided. Compressed (Zipped) Folders are identified by a zipper symbol that is part of the folder's icon.

Windows Server 2003 also supports data encryption through the Encrypting File System (EFS). EFS supports only NTFS-formatted partitions and volumes. EFS provides protection for personal and confidential documents and other files by only allowing the user who originally encrypted a file to access that file.

Other users may be granted shared permission to access an encrypted file by the original user who encrypted it. The only other users who have access to an encrypted file are users who are designated as Data Recovery Agents (DRAs) by an administrator.

Compressed (Zipped) Folders

To create a Compressed (Zipped) Folder, right-click a folder, point to Send To, and click Compressed (Zipped) Folder. This action actually creates a Zip file that Windows Server 2003 recognizes as a Compressed (Zipped) Folder that contains the folder you selected to be compressed along with all of that folder's contents. You can also use any popular third-party utility, such as WinZip or PKZip, to read, write, add to, or remove files from any Compressed (Zipped) Folder. Unless you install such a third-party zip utility, Windows Server 2003 displays standard zip *files* as Compressed (Zipped) *Folders*.

NTFS Data Compression

The NTFS file system under Windows Server 2003 enables you to compress individual files and folders so that they occupy less space on an NTFS drive partition or volume. Any Windows- or MS-DOS–based program can read from and write to NTFS compressed files without having to decompress them first. The compressed files decompress when opened and recompress when closed. The Windows Server 2003 NTFS file system handles this entire process transparently to the user. Setting the compression state (compressed or uncompressed) on a file or folder is as simple as setting a file or folder attribute.

NTFS Compressed folders and files have their folder and filenames displayed in the color blue when you view them in My Computer and in the Windows Explorer. You can turn off this default color distinction in My Computer or Windows Explorer by clicking Tools, Folder Options, View and marking the box next to Show Encrypted or Compressed NTFS Files in Color. To compress or uncompress a file or folder, follow these steps:

1. Open Windows Explorer or My Computer.

2. Right-click the file or folder that you'd like to compress or uncompress and select Properties.

3. On the General tab, click the Advanced button.

4. From the Advanced Attributes dialog box, mark (or clear) the Compress Contents to Save Disk Space check box to compress (or uncompress) the file or folder that you selected (see Figure 17.2).

5. Click OK for the Advanced Attributes dialog box and then click OK for the properties window.

FIGURE 17.2 Configuring NTFS file and folder compression from the Advanced Attributes dialog box.

Instead of compressing individual files or folders, you can choose to compress an entire NTFS drive volume. To compress an entire NTFS volume, right-click an NTFS drive volume in My Computer or Windows Explorer, select Properties, and mark the check box labeled Compress Drive to Save Disk Space. Click OK to close the drive volume's Properties window. For command-line junkies, you can use the compact.exe tool to compress and uncompress folders and files. If a lot of files are compressed on a server and many users access those files, the compression and decompression operations can degrade server performance.

Compressed files that are moved to FAT or FAT32 drive volumes become uncompressed. Compressed files that are moved or copied to uncompressed folders stored on NTFS drive volumes become uncompressed. Compressed files that are moved or copied to compressed folders stored on NTFS drive volumes remain compressed. Finally, uncompressed files that are moved or copied to compressed folders become compressed.

NTFS Data Encryption

The NTFS file system for Windows Server 2003 also supports data encryption. Just as with NTFS data compression, you set data encryption as an advanced attribute for a file or folder. NTFS data encryption is known as the Encrypting File System (EFS). EFS is an enhanced security feature that Microsoft provides as a secure method for keeping confidential documents private. Microsoft designed EFS to ensure the confidentiality of sensitive data. EFS employs public key/private key cryptography. EFS works only with the NTFS 5 file system under Windows Server 2003, Windows XP, and Windows 2000. EFS encryption and decryption is transparent to users.

EXAM ALERT

You can either compress or encrypt files and folders, but you can't use both compression and encryption on the same file or folder.

Folders that are encrypted using EFS set the encryption attribute on files that are moved or copied into them; those files automatically become encrypted once they reside in that folder. Files that are encrypted using EFS remain encrypted even if you move or rename them. Encrypted files that you back up or copy also retain their encryption attributes as long as they reside on NTFS-formatted drive volumes. EFS leaves no file data remnants behind after it modifies an encrypted file, nor does it leave any traces of decrypted data from encrypted files in temporary files or in the Windows Server 2003 paging file.

You can encrypt and decrypt files and folders from the graphical user interface (GUI) using Windows Explorer or My Computer, as well as from the command line by using the `cipher.exe` tool. Encrypted folders and files have their folder and filenames displayed in the color green in My Computer and Windows Explorer. You can turn off this default color distinction by clicking Tools, Folder Options, View in My Computer or Windows Explorer. To encrypt a file or folder from the GUI, follow these steps:

1. Open Windows Explorer or My Computer.

2. Right-click the file or folder that you'd like to encrypt or unencrypt and select Properties.

3. On the General tab, click the Advanced button.

4. From the Advanced Attributes dialog box, mark (or clear) the Encrypt Contents to Secure Data check box to encrypt (or unencrypt) the file or folder that you selected. Click OK to close the Advance Attributes dialog box and then click OK for the properties sheet to apply this setting. (When you encrypt a folder, you are prompted to select between applying this setting to the folder only and applying it to the folder, subfolders, and files.)

5. To share access to an encrypted file, click the Details button from the Advanced Attributes dialog box. *You cannot share access to encrypted folders.*

6. From the Encryption Details dialog box, click the Add button to add more users' EFS certificates to the encrypted file to share access with those users, as shown in Figure 17.3.

7. From the Select User dialog box, click the user whose EFS certificate you want to add for shared access to the encrypted file and click OK. You see only certificates for users who have encrypted a folder or file previously.

8. Click OK for the Encryption Details dialog box.

9. Finally, click OK for the Advanced Attributes dialog box, and then click OK for the properties window.

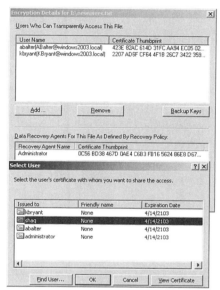

FIGURE 17.3 Adding users for shared access to an EFS-encrypted file.

After a file has the encryption attribute, only the user who originally encrypted the file, a user who has been granted shared access to the encrypted file, or a designated Data Recovery Agent (DRA) who was the DRA at the time the file was encrypted may access it. DRAs do not need to be granted shared access to encrypted files; they have access by default. Any other users who attempt to access an encrypted file are unable to view the contents of the encrypted file—the application program will open, but the contents of the encrypted file are not displayed. Some applications display an Access Is Denied message when an unauthorized user opens an encrypted file.

EXAM ALERT

DRAs are users who are designated as recovery agents for encrypted files. Only DRAs have the ability to decrypt any encrypted file regardless of which user encrypted it.

You must keep in mind, however, that any user with the necessary NTFS access permissions can still move encrypted files within the same drive volume or even delete them entirely; therefore, the enforcement of proper NTFS permissions remains extremely important for encrypted files. However, any user who did not encrypt a specific file, who does not have shared access to the encrypted file, and who is not a DRA will receive an Access Is Denied error message if they attempt to copy the encrypted file to any drive letter that is not formatted as NTFS. They will also receive an Access Is Denied error message if they attempt to move the encrypted file to a different NTFS drive letter.

The user who encrypted a file, any user with shared access to an encrypted file, and the DRA can all freely move and copy an encrypted file to any location, including FAT or FAT32 drive letters. These users will receive a warning message if they attempt to move or copy an encrypted file to a FAT or FAT32 drive letter informing them that the encrypted file will lose its encryption if the file is moved or copied to a FAT or FAT32 drive letter. The default DRAs are as follows:

▶ The local administrator user account on Windows 2000 nondomain member (standalone) computers. Standalone Windows XP and standalone *Windows Server 2003 computers have no DRAs by default.*

▶ The domain administrator user account on Windows Server 2003 or Windows 2000 Server domain controllers and for Windows Server 2003, Windows XP, and Windows 2000 domain member computers.

NTFS Disk Quotas

NTFS disk quotas track and control disk usage on a per-user, per-drive letter (partition or volume) basis. You can apply disk quotas only to NTFS-formatted drive letters under Windows Server 2003, Windows XP Professional, and Windows 2000. Quotas are tracked for each drive letter, even if the drive letters reside on the same physical disk. The per-user feature of quotas enables you to track every user's disk space usage regardless of which folder the user stores files in. To enable disk quotas, open Windows Explorer or My Computer, right-click a drive letter and select properties, click the Quota tab, and configure the options as shown in Figure 17.4.

EXAM ALERT

NTFS Disk quotas do not use compression to measure disk-space usage, so users cannot obtain or use more space simply by compressing their own data.

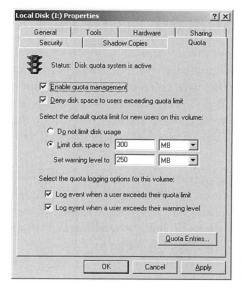

FIGURE 17.4 Configuring the NTFS disk quota system.

After you turn on the disk quota system, you can establish individual disk-quota limits for each user by clicking the Quota Entries button at the bottom of the Quota tab. By default, only members of the Administrators group can view and change quota entries and settings. In addition, all members of the Administrators group inherit unlimited disk quotas by default. NTFS disk quotas are based on file ownership; operating system accounts are not immune to disk quotas. System accounts such as the local system are also susceptible to running out of disk space because of disk quotas having been set. From the Quota Entries window (see Figure 17.5), you can change an existing quota entry for a user by double-clicking the quota entry. To set up a new quota entry for a user, click the Quota menu and select the New Quota Entry option. When a user no longer stores data on a volume, you should delete the user's disk-quota entries. The catch is that you can only delete the user's quota entries after you remove all the files that the user owns or after another user takes ownership of the files.

Quota Entries for Local Disk (I:)

Quota Edit View Help

Status	Name	Logon Name	Amount Used	Quota Limit	Warning Level	Percent Used
OK	Kobe Fly-Hi. Bryant	KBryant@windows2003.local	0 bytes	200 MB	150 MB	0
OK		ESWANSON@WINDOWS2003.LOCAL	0 bytes	200 MB	150 MB	0
OK	Brendan A. Balter	BBalter@windows2003.local	0 bytes	200 MB	150 MB	0
OK	Alexis A. Balter	ABalter@windows2003.local	0 bytes	200 MB	150 MB	0
OK		BUILTIN\Administrators	2.93 GB	No Limit	No Limit	N/A
OK		NT AUTHORITY\NETWORK SERVICE	244 KB	300 MB	250 MB	0
OK		NT AUTHORITY\LOCAL SERVICE	219 KB	300 MB	250 MB	0

7 total item(s), 1 selected.

FIGURE 17.5 Configuring NTFS disk quota entries for users.

Shadow Copies of Shared Folders

Windows Server 2003 introduces a new feature called shadow copies of shared folders. Shadow copies, when configured, automatically create backup copies of the data stored in shared folders on specific drive volumes at scheduled times. The drive volumes must be formatted as NTFS. Shadow copies are set up per individual drive volume, and the copies are created at scheduled times by the new Volume Shadow Copy service (VSS) in conjunction with the Task Scheduler service.

By default, shadow copies are stored on the same drive letter as where the shared folders are located. Shadow copies allow users to retrieve previous versions of files and folders on their own, without requiring IT personnel to restore files or folders from backup media. This feature reduces IT staffing overhead and allows users to almost instantly restore deleted or damaged data files by themselves.

Setting Up Shadow Copies

Best practice dictates that you should place the shadow copies on a separate physical disk, if possible, as an extra fault-tolerant measure. At least 100MB of free space must be available on a drive volume or partition where shadow copies are to be stored. Obviously, you might need more disk space depending on the size of the data in the shared folders that are being shadowed. To set up shadow copies for a drive letter, follow these steps on a Windows Server 2003 computer:

1. From My Computer or Windows Explorer, right-click an NTFS drive volume, select Properties, and click the Shadow Copies tab. Alternatively, from the Computer Management console, right-click the Shared Folders node and select All Tasks, Configure Shadow Copies.

2. From the Shadow Copies tab, select the drive volume that you want to shadow and then click the Settings button.

3. From the Settings dialog box, click the Located on This Volume drop-down list box to select the drive letter where the shadow copies for this drive volume will be stored (see Figure 17.6). You can select the same volume or a different NTFS drive volume.

4. Select a maximum size by clicking either the No Limit option, or click the Use Limit option and type the storage restriction in the spinner box.

5. Click the Schedule button to specify how often you want to create shadow copies for this drive volume.

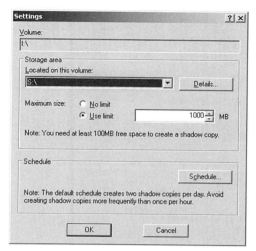

FIGURE 17.6 Configuring drive volume storage options from the Settings dialog box for shadow copies of shared folders.

6. From the Schedule tab, you have two daily scheduled shadow copies set up by default: 7:00 a.m. and 12:00 Noon, Monday through Friday of each week (see Figure 17.7).

   ▶ To accept the defaults, make no changes.

   ▶ To set up an additional scheduled shadow copy, click the New button.

   ▶ To remove an existing scheduled shadow copy, select the schedule from the drop-down list box and click the Delete button.

   ▶ To modify an existing scheduled shadow copy, select the schedule from the drop-down list box and make the appropriate changes to the Scheduled Task drop-down list box, the Start Time spinner box, and the Schedule Task section.

7. Click OK to save your settings for the shadow copies scheduling.

8. Click OK to save your settings for the Settings dialog box and return to the Shadow Copies tab. Shadow copies for the drive volume are now enabled, as shown in Figure 17.8.

   ▶ You can manually create additional shadow copies by clicking the Create Now button.

   ▶ You can delete previous shadow copies by selecting one of the date and time stamps in the Shadow Copies of Selected Volume list box and clicking the Delete Now button.

   ▶ To disable shadow copies for a volume, select the volume and click the Disable button.

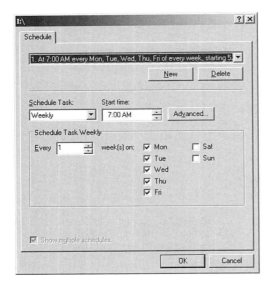

FIGURE 17.7 Scheduling shadow copies of shared folders.

9. Click OK to close the properties window for the Shadow Copies tab.

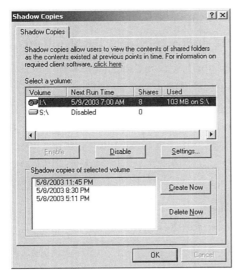

FIGURE 17.8 Setting up and managing Shadow Copies of Shared folders.

EXAM ALERT

Windows Server 2003 stores up to a maximum of 64 shadow copy snapshots per shadow-copy–enabled partition or volume. Keep this in mind when setting up a daily schedule for shadow copies to be created. After 64 shadow copy snapshots are created, each subsequent snapshot overwrites the oldest snapshot.

Accessing Previous Versions of Files from Shadow Copies

For users to be able to access shadow copies of shared folders from their workstations, administrators must install client software on those computers. You find this software on a Windows Server 2003 computer in the `%systemroot%\system32\clients\twclient` folder. For the x86 platform (Intel-compatible 32-bit CPUs), double-click the `twcli32.msi` file to install the Previous Versions Client program.

After you install the Previous Versions software, when a user selects a data file that has one or more shadow copies available, the View Previous Versions option will appear in the File and Folder task pane in Windows Explorer and My Computer. A Previous Versions tab is also available when a user views the properties sheet for a data file that has one or more shadow copies, as shown in Figure 17.9. The Previous Versions tab gives you the option to View, Copy, or Restore a previous version of a file or folder. You can use the Copy option to store a copy of a previous version to a different drive letter or folder than its original location. You can copy a previous version to a FAT, FAT32, or NTFS drive letter.

EXAM ALERT

To access previous versions of files using the Shadow Copies of Shared Folders feature, you must navigate to the folder where the file(s) you want to restore is (are) stored using a Uniform Naming Convention (UNC) path or via a mapped network drive letter! If you are accessing the file(s) over the network, this is not a problem, of course. But if you are working with the file(s) locally on a Windows Server 2003 computer, you must navigate to the files through a UNC path. The Previous Versions link does not appear, and the Previous Versions tab does not exist on a file's properties sheet when you view the file from a local drive letter window.

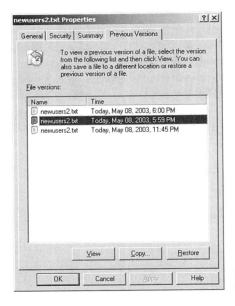

FIGURE 17.9 Viewing available previous versions of a file from its properties sheet.

NOTE

You can only install the Previous Versions Client software on Windows XP or later operating systems. You must install the Previous Versions Client to retrieve shadow-copy versions of files. Computers running Windows 2000 SP3 and Windows 98 are also supported for retrieving previous versions of folders and files from a shared network folder stored on a Windows Server 2003 computer where shadow copies have been set up. You must download and install the Shadow Copy Client software at `http://www.microsoft.com/windowsserver2003/downloads/shadowcopyclient.mspx`.

Windows 2000 SP3 computers and Windows 98 computers must have the Shadow Copy Client software installed on the Windows Server 2003 computer where the shadow copies are stored as well as having this software installed on the workstations.

Exam Prep Questions

1. Which of the following characteristics of shadow copies are true? (Choose the best three answers.)

   ○ **A.** Previous versions of files stored as shadow copies are available under Windows 2000 Professional as long as you install the Previous Versions Client software.

   ○ **B.** You must store shadow copies on NTFS drive volumes.

   ○ **C.** You can only make shadow copies from files stored on NTFS drive volumes.

   ○ **D.** Shadow copies are enabled by default on the %systemdrive% volume.

   ○ **E.** You must store shadow copies on an NTFS drive volume other than the drive volume being shadowed.

   ○ **F.** You can schedule shadow copies to occur automatically, and you can create them manually.

2. How can you set disk quotas on an NTFS drive letter for the Remote Desktop Users group and for the Administrators group? (Choose the best answer.)

   ○ **A.** Right-click the drive letter in My Computer, select Properties, click the Quota tab, and mark the check boxes for Enable Quota Management and Deny Disk Space to Users Exceeding Quota Limit. Click Apply and click the Quota Entries button. Configure quota entries for the Remote Desktop Users group and for the Administrators group.

   ○ **B.** Right-click the drive letter in My Computer, select Properties, click the Quota tab, and mark the check boxes for Enable Quota Management and Deny Disk Space to Users Exceeding Quota Limit. Click Apply and click the Quota Entries button. Configure quota entries for the Remote Desktop Users group.

   ○ **C.** Right-click the drive letter in My Computer, select Properties, click the Quota tab, and mark the check boxes for Enable Quota Management and Deny Disk Space to Users Exceeding Quota Limit. Click Apply and click the Quota Entries button. Configure quota entries for each member of the Remote Desktop Users group.

   ○ **D.** Create a new local group named Super Users and make all the members of the Power Users group and the Administrators group members of this new group. Right-click the drive letter in My Computer, select Properties, click the Quota tab, and mark the check boxes for Enable Quota Management and Deny Disk Space to Users Exceeding Quota Limit. Click Apply and click the Quota Entries button. Configure quota entries for the Super Users group.

3. Brandy wants to move an NTFS-compressed file from NTFS drive D: to an uncompressed folder on NTFS drive F:. What will happen to the file when she performs this
   operation? (Choose the best answer.)

   ○ **A.** The compressed file will become uncompressed when it is moved to drive F:.

   ○ **B.** The compressed file will remain compressed when it is moved to drive F:.

   ○ **C.** Windows Server 2003 will prompt the user whether the file should remain
   compressed or should be uncompressed after it is moved.

   ○ **D.** Brandy will receive an error message when she attempts to move the file to
   an uncompressed folder.

4. Nicole encrypts an NTFS folder named SECRET DOCS on the hard drive of a Windows
   Server 2003 computer. Nicole is the only user with access to all the encrypted files in
   the SECRET DOCS folder (except for the DRA). Nicole shares the computer with her
   associate, Aaron. Aaron is not the DRA. Later, Aaron logs on to the same computer and
   attempts to copy one of the files stored inside of the SECRET DOCS folder, named
   Salaries.xls, to a floppy disk in drive A. After that, Aaron tries to move the same
   file to an unencrypted folder on the same NTFS drive volume named PUBLIC DOCS.
   What are the results of Aaron's file operations? (Choose the best answer.)

   ○ **A.** Aaron will receive an error message for trying to copy the encrypted file to
   a floppy disk, but he will be able to move the encrypted file to the PUBLIC
   DOCS unencrypted NTFS folder, where the file will remain encrypted.

   ○ **B.** Aaron will receive an error message for trying to copy the encrypted file to
   a floppy disk, and he will also receive an error message for attempting to
   move the encrypted file to the PUBLIC DOCS unencrypted NTFS folder.

   ○ **C.** Aaron will receive an error message for trying to copy the encrypted file to a
   floppy disk, but he will successfully move the encrypted file to the PUBLIC
   DOCS unencrypted NTFS folder, where it will lose its encryption attribute.

   ○ **D.** Aaron will successfully copy the encrypted file to a floppy disk, where it will
   remain encrypted, and he will successfully move the encrypted file to the
   PUBLIC DOCS unencrypted NTFS folder.

5. As a network administrator for her company, Alexis wants to create scripts that will
   automate the process of encrypting and decrypting files using the Encrypting File
   System (EFS). She may create .bat files for the scripts or she may use program
   scripts for use with the Windows Script Host (WSH). Which of the following commands
   can she use in a script file to encrypt and decrypt files? (Choose the best answer.)

   ○ **A.** attrib.exe

   ○ **B.** cisvc.exe

   ○ **C.** cipher.exe

   ○ **D.** convert.exe

   ○ **E.** change.exe

   ○ **F.** compact.exe

6. As a network administrator for his company, Brendan needs to set up Shadow Copies of Shared Folders on the D: drive of a newly installed Windows Server 2003 file server for the Sales division. Corporate management requires that the server must store at least two weeks worth of previous versions of files. The managers of the Sales division want to maximize the number of shadow copies available on a daily basis. Given these constraints, how many times a day should Brendan schedule Shadow Copies to be created, assuming a five-day work week? (Choose the best answer.)

- ○ **A.** Eight times per day
- ○ **B.** Six times per day
- ○ **C.** Four times per day
- ○ **D.** Seven times per day
- ○ **E.** Five times per day
- ○ **F.** Eight days a week

7. Which of the following features are only supported by the NTFS file system? (Choose the best three answers.)

- ○ **A.** Shadow Copies of Shared Folders
- ○ **B.** Compressed (Zipped) Folders
- ○ **C.** Encrypting File System (EFS)
- ○ **D.** Disk quotas
- ○ **E.** Drive letter onto which you copy the previous version of a file
- ○ **F.** USB Storage Devices

8. Alison is an employee for XYZ Corporation in the Marketing department. Alison has been working on a very important Microsoft Excel worksheet that needs to be kept confidential. She encrypts the worksheet using EFS and she stores it in T:\data\alison. Her co-worker, Dan, notices the worksheet and tries to open the file to read it.

Dan and Alison are both members of the same security groups, so both users have the same NTFS access permissions to the Excel file. Neither Alison nor Dan has administrator-level permissions. When Dan tries to open the file, Excel opens but the contents of the worksheet do not display because the file has been encrypted by Alison. Because Dan cannot read the file, he attempts to move the file to a folder named "Dan's Stuff" on the T: drive. The "Dan's Stuff" folder is not encrypted under EFS. What happens when Dan tries to move this file? (Choose the best answer.)

- ○ **A.** The file is moved and remains encrypted.
- ○ **B.** Dan receives an Access Is Denied error message.
- ○ **C.** The file is moved and becomes unencrypted.
- ○ **D.** The file is copied to T:\Dan's Stuff and remains encrypted.

9. Windows Server 2003 natively supports read and write operations for which of the following types of media? (Choose the three best answers.)

   ○ **A.** DVD-RW

   ○ **B.** CD-R

   ○ **C.** DVD+RW

   ○ **D.** CD-RW

   ○ **E.** DVD-RAM

   ○ **F.** DVD+R

Answers to Exam Prep Questions

1. **Answers B, C, and F are correct.** You must store shadow copies on NTFS drive volumes, you can only make shadow copies from files stored on NTFS drive volumes, and you can schedule shadow copies to run automatically and create them manually. Answer A is incorrect because previous versions of files stored as shadow copies can only be retrieved under Windows XP and Windows Server 2003 with the Previous Versions Client software installed. Answer D is incorrect because shadow copies are not enabled by default for any drive volume. Answer E is incorrect because you can store shadow copies on any available NTFS drive volume, including the drive volume being shadowed.

2. **Answer C is correct.** Windows Server 2003 supports disk quotas on NTFS drive volumes only for individual users, not for groups. Therefore, you would have to create a quota entry for *each member* of the Remote Desktop Users group—you cannot assign a quota limit to a group. All members of the Administrators group inherit a no-limit disk quota by default, so you cannot set quotas on members of this group. Answer A is incorrect for the reasons just cited. Answer B is incorrect because you cannot set quotas on groups. Answer D is incorrect for the same reason.

3. **Answer A is correct.** When you move a compressed file from one NTFS volume to a different NTFS volume, the file inherits the compression attribute from the target location. Answer B is incorrect because an NTFS compressed folder or file retains its compression attribute only when it is moved to another folder on the same NTFS volume. Answer C is incorrect because Windows Server 2003 never prompts the user as to whether a folder or file should remain compressed or uncompressed. Answer D is incorrect because Windows Server 2003 does not generate error messages for moving compressed files to an uncompressed folder.

4. **Answer A is correct.** Only the user who originally encrypted the file (or any users given shared access to the encrypted file) may copy the file to a non-NTFS drive volume or to any type of removable media. In addition, only the user who originally encrypted the file (or any users given shared access to the encrypted file) may copy the file or move it to a folder located on a different NTFS volume. A user without shared access to an encrypted file is permitted to move the file only to another folder

located on the same NTFS volume, where the file remains encrypted. Answer B is incorrect because, although Aaron will receive an error message when he attempts to copy the file to a floppy disk, he will not receive an error message when he attempts to move the encrypted file to an unencrypted NTFS folder located on the same NTFS volume. Answer C is incorrect because, although Aaron will receive an error message when he attempts to copy the file to a floppy disk, he will be allowed to move the encrypted file to an unencrypted NTFS folder located on the same NTFS volume, but the file will not lose its encryption attribute. Answer D is incorrect because Aaron will receive an error message when he attempts to copy the encrypted file to a floppy disk.

5. **Answer C is correct.** The `cipher.exe` command allows you to encrypt and decrypt files from the command line for EFS. Answer A is incorrect because the `attrib.exe` command does not provide encryption or decryption features. Answer B is incorrect because `cisvc.exe` is used for the Content Index Service, not for EFS. Answer D is incorrect because the `convert.exe` command is used for converting a FAT or FAT32 partition or volume into an NTFS partition or volume. Answer E is incorrect because the `change.exe` command is used for terminal services only. Answer F is incorrect because the `compact.exe` tool is a command-line utility used to compress and uncompress files and folders stored on NTFS drive letters.

6. **Answer B is correct.** Because the maximum number of shadow copy snapshots that can be stored by a Windows Server 2003 computer is 64, six times a day is the best answer. Six shadow copies multiplied by 10 work days (5 days per week multiplied by 2 weeks) equals 60 shadow copies—just beneath the maximum threshold of 64. Answer A is incorrect because if Brendan were to schedule eight shadow copies per day, 8 multiplied by 10 work days equals 80 shadow copies. Since the maximum number of stored shadow copies is 64, the oldest shadow copies would be overwritten during each previous two-week period and this would not provide for a full two week's worth of previous versions of data files. Answer C is incorrect because although 4 multiplied by 10 work days is less than the maximum of 64 shadow copies stored within a two week period, this schedule does not maximize the number of shadow copies that can be stored on a daily basis. Answer D is incorrect because if Brendan were to schedule seven shadow copies per day, 7 multiplied by 10 work days equals 70 shadow copies. Since the maximum number of stored shadow copies is 64, the oldest shadow copies would be overwritten during each previous two-week period and this would not provide for a full two week's worth of previous versions of data files. Answer E is incorrect because although 5 multiplied by 10 work days is less than the maximum of 64 shadow copies stored within a two-week period, this schedule does not maximize the number of shadow copies that can be stored on a daily basis. Answer F is incorrect because it is the title of a song by the Beatles—this is a joke answer.

7. **Answers A, C, and D are correct.** Shadow Copies of Shared Folders can only be created on NTFS drive letters; you can only use EFS on NTFS-formatted drive letters; and disk quotas are only available on NTFS partitions and volumes. Answer B is incorrect because Compressed (Zipped) Folders are supported under the FAT, FAT32, and NTFS file systems. Answer E is incorrect because you can copy the previous version of a file or folder onto a drive letter formatted as FAT, FAT32, or NTFS. Answer F is incorrect because USB storage devices can be formatted as FAT, FAT32, or NTFS.

8. **Answer A is correct.** Users who have the proper NTFS security permissions can move an EFS-encrypted file from one folder to another as long as the folder resides on the same NTFS partition or volume. Answer B is incorrect for the same reason as Answer A—Dan would have received an Access Is Denied error message if he had tried to copy the file. Answer C is incorrect because even though the file may be moved, it cannot be unencrypted when a user who does not have shared access to the encrypted file simply moves it to another location. Answer D is incorrect because the question stipulates that the file was moved, not copied and an attempt to copy the file would result in an Access Is Denied error message.

9. **Answers B, D, and E are correct.** Windows Server 2003 *natively* supports read and write operations for CD-R, CD-RW, and DVD-RAM media. Answer A is incorrect because Windows Server 2003 supports read access for DVD-RW media without requiring third-party software; however, it does not support writing to DVD-RW media without third-party software. Answer C is incorrect because Windows Server 2003 supports read access for DVD+RW media without requiring third-party software; however, it does not support writing to DVD+RW media without third-party software. Answer F is incorrect because Windows Server 2003 supports read access for DVD+R media without requiring third-party software; however, it does not support writing to DVD+R media without third-party software.

Need to Know More?

1. Jones, Don. *Windows Server 2003 Weekend Crash Course*. New York, New York: Wiley Publishing, Inc., 2003.

2. Snedaker, Susan. *The Best Damn Windows Server 2003 Book Period*. Rockland, Massachusetts: Syngress Publishing, Inc., 2004.

3. Stanek, William R. *Microsoft Windows Server 2003 Inside Out*. Redmond, Washington: Microsoft Press, 2004.

4. Williams, Robert, and Mark Walla. *The Ultimate Windows Server 2003 System Administrator's Guide*. Boston, Massachusetts: Addison Wesley Professional, 2003.

5. Search the Microsoft Product Support Services Knowledge Base on the Internet: http://support.microsoft.com. You can also search through Microsoft TechNet on the Internet: http://www.microsoft.com/technet. Find technical information using keywords from this chapter, such as USB storage devices, encrypting file system (EFS), NTFS compression, compressed (zipped) folders, NTFS disk quotas, data recovery agents (DRAs), shadow copies of shared folders, and previous versions client.

CHAPTER EIGHTEEN

Managing Disaster Recovery and Data Backup Procedures

Terms you'll need to understand:

✓ Safe Mode

✓ Recovery Console

✓ Automated System Recovery (ASR)

✓ Last Known Good Configuration

✓ In-band management

✓ Out-of-band management

✓ Special Administration Console (SAC)

✓ NTBackup.exe

✓ Copy backups

✓ Daily backups

✓ Normal backups

✓ Incremental backups

✓ Differential backups

✓ System State backups

✓ NTDSUTIL.exe

✓ Primary restores

✓ Authoritative restores

✓ Directory Services Restore Mode

Techniques you'll need to master:

✓ Creating a startup disk

✓ Troubleshooting Windows Server 2003 startup problems

✓ Using Safe Mode to troubleshoot server problems

✓ Installing and using the Recovery Console

✓ Creating an Automated System Recovery (ASR) Backup

✓ Using the Special Administration Console (SAC) in Emergency Management Services (EMS)

✓ Performing different types of backups

✓ Performing a restore operation

✓ Backing up and restoring the System State

✓ Scheduling automatic backups

✓ Performing primary restores

✓ Performing authoritative restores

✓ Using Directory Services Restore Mode

A comprehensive, fully tested disaster recovery plan should be an integral part of any IT department's policies and procedures. Windows Server 2003 has a number of features to get the server up and running in the event of operating system (OS) file corruption or data loss. Emergency Management Services (EMS) allows you to perform out-of-band remote server management when you cannot access a server using a standard network connection.

The process of backing up valuable data files and folders simply involves copying that data to one or more different locations where you can retrieve it later, if you need it. You might need to restore data from backup because of a hardware failure or because someone accidentally or intentionally ruins or deletes some data. Reliable, up-to-date backups of user and system data are the cornerstone of any sound data protection and preservation policy. Numerous third-party data backup products on the market offer all sorts of fancy features, but the Windows Backup Utility does a fine job of safeguarding and restoring server data, as long as you use it properly. In this chapter, you'll learn how to prepare for disaster scenarios so that your network can recover quickly should such a situation occur.

Preparing for Disaster Recovery Situations

Reliable and up-to-date server backups are a critical part of any sound network maintenance and disaster recovery plan. A backup plan can only be judged "sound" in the context of the data-recovery requirements. For example, questions such as "What do you need to restore in the event of a catastrophe?" are appropriate to determine what kinds of precautions are necessary.

Even so, some measures are required and considered best practice in all environments. It is not considered optional to run daily backups on all servers. If the tape drive does not have the capacity to perform a daily full backup, consider weekly full backups and daily differential backups instead. Differential backups do not reset the archive bit, so it only takes two backup sets to perform a complete restore—one set with the full backup and one set with the latest differential backup. Shadow copies of shared folders can prevent the need to ever restore data files from a tape backup. In addition, creating a Windows Server 2003 start-up disk, installing the Recovery Console, and configuring Emergency Management Services (EMS) before you have server startup problems can get you out of trouble if your server refuses to start.

Booting Windows Server 2003 with a Startup Disk

In some cases, Windows Server 2003 computers might not start properly. Windows Server 2003 computers might fail to start when the boot record, or files required to start Windows Server 2003, somehow become corrupted or get deleted. Complete the following steps to create a startup disk for a Windows Server 2003 computer:

1. Format a blank floppy disk in a machine running the Windows Server 2003 operating system. In My Computer, right-click the floppy drive icon, select Format, mark the Quick Format check box, and click OK.

2. Copy the following files to the floppy disk: boot.ini, ntdetect.com, ntldr, plus bootsect.dos (if the machine is in a dual-boot configuration) and ntbootdd.sys, if these files exist on the computer that you want to use this startup disk on.

3. Make sure to test the startup disk by placing the disk in the floppy drive, restarting the server, and verifying that the server starts properly.

4. Label the disk as the Windows Server 2003 startup disk with the server name and date it was created. Make sure to update this disk if you change the disk configuration on the server.

If you did not create a startup disk ahead of time, you can copy the startup files from an existing Windows Server 2003 computer. You might need to make some adjustments to the boot.ini file if the server you are trying to repair starts from a different partition. The boot.ini file resides on the system drive on every Windows Server 2003 computer. This file contains the Advanced RISC Computing (ARC) path specifications that define where the operating-system partition (or volume) is physically located on the computer's hard drives. The boot.ini file handles single-boot, dual-boot, and multiboot configurations. This file also determines which operating system is the default, when more than one operating system is installed, and the amount of time before the default operating system loads. Refer to Microsoft Knowledgebase article 317526, which you can find at http://support.microsoft.com/default.aspx?scid=kb;en-us;317526, for more information on editing boot.ini files.

Using Safe Mode to Recover a Server

If the server does not start after you install a device driver, new software, or a new service, you can use Safe Mode to start the server with a minimal amount of services and drivers. Once the server is running in Safe Mode, you can disable or remove the offending driver, software program, or service. Table 18.1 lists the available Safe Mode options for Windows Server 2003.

TABLE 18.1 Safe Mode Startup Options for Windows Server 2003

Safe Mode Options	When to Use
Safe Mode	Remove offending program, driver, or service that prevents Windows Server 2003 from starting.
Safe Mode with Networking Support	Use to verify that network components are working properly.
Safe Mode with Command Prompt	Use to run command-line utilities only. After logon, only a command prompt appears. Try running this option if Safe Mode does not work.

Accessing Safe Mode

The Safe Mode options are installed by default on all Windows Server 2003 editions. If the server does not start after you install a service pack, install new hardware, or make some other change to the server, uninstall the service pack or hardware in Safe Mode. If the server starts up after you remove the offending files, you can be confident that the item you removed was the source of the problem. To access Safe Mode, complete the following steps:

1. Restart the server.

2. Before the Windows Server 2003 splash screen appears, press the F8 key.

3. Use the arrow keys to select one of the listed Safe Mode options and press Enter.

4. Log on to the server as the administrator; a message box will inform you that you have logged on using Safe mode, as shown in Figure 18.1.

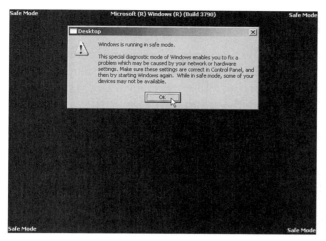

FIGURE 18.1 Logging on to Windows Server 2003 under Safe Mode.

Using Last Known Good Configuration

If you have difficulty starting the server, you can use the Last Known Good Configuration to restore the settings of the server, which the server saved automatically at the last successful logon. Using the Last Known Good Configuration restores information for the Registry subkey `HKEY_LOCAL_MACHINE\SYSTEM\CurrentControlSet`. Any updated drivers are restored to the previous version if you use the Last Known Good Configuration. Complete the following steps to start Windows Server 2003 with the Last Known Good Configuration:

1. Restart the Server.

2. Before the Windows Server 2003 splash screen appears, press the F8 key.

3. Select the Last Known Good Configuration and press Enter.

4. Use the arrow keys to select an operating system and press Enter, if the computer has multiple instances of an operating system installed.

TIP

Although Microsoft recommends trying the Last Known Good Configuration before using Safe Mode, use Safe Mode first. Often the Last Known Good Configuration returns the server to a much earlier state than anticipated. Because Safe Mode does not update the Last Known Configuration registry key, you still have this option available if Safe Mode does not resolve the problem.

Whenever you make a major change to a server, restart the server to verify that it starts properly. If it does not start, you can quickly reverse the changes using Safe Mode. If you do not verify that the server restarts, it will be more difficult to determine the cause of a startup problem at a (potentially much) later date when a server restart is mandatory.

Working with the Recovery Console

If a startup disk, Safe Mode, and the Last Known Good Configuration all fail to start the server, use the Recovery Console. The Recovery Console in Windows Server 2003 provides a command-prompt–only environment that you can use for the following:

▶ Enabling or disabling services that prevent Windows Server 2003 from properly starting.

▶ Reading, writing, and copying files on a local drive. The Recovery Console enforces NTFS permissions.

▶ Formatting hard disks.

▶ Repairing a boot sector.

To use the Recovery Console, you must log on to the server using the local administrator account. You can either preinstall the Recovery Console, or you can run it directly from the Windows Server 2003 CD-ROM. To install the Recovery Console, complete the following steps:

1. Insert the Windows Server 2003 CD into the computer's CD-ROM drive.

2. Click Start, Run; type `cmd` in the Open box; and click OK.

3. At the command prompt, type the letter of the CD-ROM drive and a colon (:), and press Enter. (For example, type `R:` and press Enter.)

4. Type `cd\i386` and press Enter.

5. Type `winnt32 /cmdcons` and press Enter. Windows Server 2003 might check for any updates to the software before installing the Recovery Console.

6. After the installation is finished, click Yes, and then click OK.

To run the Recovery Console, restart Windows Server 2003 and select the Microsoft Windows Recovery Console from the Please Select the Operating System to Start screen.

Starting the Recovery Console from the Windows Server 2003 CD

As an alternative, you can start the Recovery Console by booting the server from the Windows Server 2003 CD-ROM. This step is useful if the Recovery Console was not previously installed or if the server does recognize the boot hard drive.

Complete the following steps to start the Recovery Console from the Windows Server 2003 CD-ROM:

1. Insert the Windows Server 2003 CD-ROM into the CD drive.

2. If necessary, press a key to boot from the CD.

3. Press R to select the Repair/Recover option.

Logging On to the Recovery Console

Once the Recovery Console screen boots, you must specify which Windows Server installation that you want to log on to. On a multiboot server, you can log on to any of the available Microsoft operating systems that are compatible with the Recovery Console, such as Windows 2000, Windows XP, and Windows Server 2003. Complete the following steps to log on to the Recovery Console:

1. Type the number of the Windows installation you want (usually 1) and press Enter.

2. Type the password for the local administrator account and press Enter (see Figure 18.2).

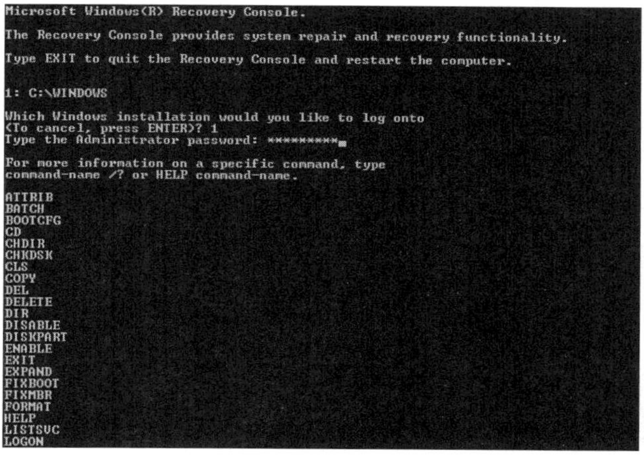

FIGURE 18.2 The Recovery Console screen showing available commands.

Recovery Console Commands

Once you successfully log on to the Recovery Console, you can type help and press Enter at the command prompt to display a list of Recovery Console commands. Recovery Console commands include valuable tools such as bootcfg to repair a system's boot configuration, disable and enable to disable or enable a system's services and device drivers, fixboot to write a new boot sector onto the system partition (x86-based computers only), and fixmbr to repair the master boot record (x86-based computers only).

EXAM ALERT

Prior to R2, the Recovery Console was not available as a startup option for the x64 Edition of Windows Server 2003. Under R2, you can now install the Recovery Console as a startup option on the x64 Edition; you also can access the Recovery Console by booting from the Windows Server 2003 x64 Edition CD or DVD media.

The Automated System Recovery Feature

Automated System Recovery (ASR) is a new feature in Windows XP and Windows Server 2003. ASR is integrated within the Windows Backup Utility (NTBackup.exe), and you can use it to recover a system that does not start. You can think of it as a system restore CD that commonly ships with many new OEM computers from vendors such as Dell, HP, and IBM. The ASR has two parts—backup and recovery. Restoring an ASR backup brings the server back to the state at the point in time when the ASR set was originally created. Whenever you perform an operation that is potentially damaging to the operating system (installing service packs, driver upgrades, hardware upgrades, and so on), consider creating an ASR backup set. If anything goes wrong, you can quickly restore the server back to its original configuration without much trouble.

NOTE

Note that *ASR only saves the Windows Server 2003 operating-system configuration!* It saves the system state, system services, and the operating-system components, but it *does not back up any user data files.* Any data files that are stored on the operating-system drive volume (%systemdrive%) are destroyed during an ASR restore. ASR creates a boot floppy, which contains backup information and disk configuration settings. ASR gives administrators the ability to quickly reinstall Windows Server 2003, if necessary, with all the required drivers already in place. You can then perform a restore operation from a full system backup, if needed.

Creating an ASR Backup Set

You must use the Windows Server 2003 Backup Utility to create ASR backup sets. You cannot perform an ASR restore unless you have first created an ASR backup set. It's a good idea to periodically create updated ASR backup sets to ensure that the ASR backup is as current as possible should you ever need to use it. Complete the following steps to create an ASR backup setup:

1. Click Start, (All) Programs, Accessories, System Tools, Backup.

2. Click the Advanced Mode link on the Welcome window.

3. Click the Automated System Recovery button on the Backup Utility Advanced Mode page to start the ASR Wizard.

4. Click Next for the Welcome to the Automated System Recovery Preparation Wizard window.

5. Select the Backup Media Type in the drop-down list box and then select the backup media or type the backup file name in the dialog box on the Backup Destination page (Figure 18.3).

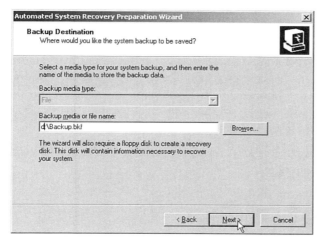

FIGURE 18.3 Selecting the backup destination using the ASR Wizard.

6. Click Next. If you are backing up to file, be sure not to store the backup file on the same drive as the operating system (usually the C:\ drive).

7. Click Finish to complete the media backup portion of the ASR backup procedure. After the ASR media backup finishes, you are prompted to create a boot disk to complete the ASR backup (see Figure 18.4). Make sure to label the disk with the backup filename, creation date, and time.

FIGURE 18.4 Creating the boot floppy for ASR.

NOTE

The ASR backup procedure actually generates a shadow copy to create a snapshot of the necessary operating-system information. During the restore process, ASR formats the operating-system drive volume and then copies the original default operating system files onto it. You must have your ASR backup files stored somewhere other than the system partition. *If you save the ASR backup file on the* `%systemdrive%` *volume (usually the* `C:\` *drive) and later perform an ASR restore, it will fail because ASR will format the* `%systemdrive%` *volume and destroy your ASR backup file.*

Restoring a Server Using ASR

Use the ASR to restore the entire operating system on a server that does not start. *When you restore a backup set using ASR, the system will format and destroy any data contained on the operating-system drive, referenced by the system environment variable* `%systemdrive%`*!* (This drive volume is usually drive `C:\`.) Any other drive volumes on the server that do not contain operating-system files are not formatted. ASR only restores the operating system and related files. If you have any other data on the operating system drive, you will lose this data and will have to restore the data from another backup method. To use an ASR restore set, you must have the following:

▶ An ASR backup set created as a file on a hard disk (other than the system volume) or on a backup tape.

▶ Floppy disk created by the ASR.

▶ Windows Server 2003 CD or DVD media.

▶ Optional, but highly recommended: a recent backup of all nonoperating–system data files that are stored on the operating system drive (usually `C:`).

TIP

If you have a tape drive or other mass-storage device where the ASR backup set was created, and, if its device driver is not included on the Windows Server 2003 CD-ROM, make sure to have this driver available on a floppy disk or some other accessible location. Without the driver, your ASR restore process will fail because Windows will not be able to read the data on the device.

Assuming that you have all the necessary components for an ASR restore, you can begin the restore process. To restore an ASR backup set, complete the following steps:

1. Insert the Windows Server 2003 CD-ROM into the CD-ROM drive.

2. Restart the server. If prompted, press a key to boot from the CD.

3. If you have a third-party SCSI or RAID driver, press the F6 key, when prompted.

4. Press the F2 key to run the ASR restore, when prompted.

5. Insert the ASR disk into the disk drive and press any key on the keyboard. The ASR restore loads the necessary files to restore your operating system.

6. If you installed a third-party SCSI or RAID driver, press the F6 key again, when prompted, after the system restarts.

7. When the server reboots, remove the ASR disk, but leave the Windows Server 2003 CD in the drive (see Figure 18.5). When the server reboots, make sure the server does not start from the CD.

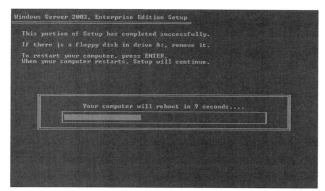

FIGURE 18.5 Restarting the computer after the character-based phase of an ASR restore.

8. If you installed a third-party SCSI or RAID driver, after the system restarts, press the F6 key when prompted.

9. When prompted, select the backup file that you want to restore from the Data Recovery Source window. The ASR Wizard then displays a summary window listing the ASR restore settings (see Figure 18.6).

10. Click Finish to begin the ASR restore using the Windows Backup Utility media. After this restore procedure is complete, the system will restart.

EXAM ALERT

The ASR floppy disk that gets created contains three files—`asr.sif`, `asrpnp.sif`, and `setup.log`. If you misplace the ASR floppy disk, you can use the Windows Server 2003 Backup Utility on a different Windows Server 2003 computer to restore the `asr.sif` and `asrpnp.sif` files from the ASR media backup set onto a blank floppy disk. You can then use that floppy disk as the ASR floppy disk during the ASR restore operation.

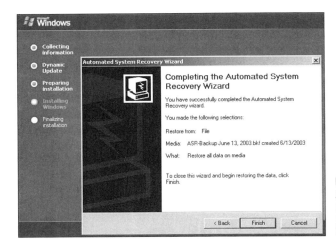

FIGURE 18.6 Viewing the ASR Wizard summary window before launching the media restore using the Windows Backup Utility.

Emergency Management Services

Emergency Management Services (EMS) is a new feature in Windows Server 2003. EMS allows an administrator to perform remote management and system recovery tasks when the server is not available. It includes support for headless servers and out-of-band management. Headless servers are servers that do not have a local keyboard, mouse, and video monitor directly connected to the server. Out-of-band management support allows an administrator to remotely access a server though a connection other than the normal network (Ethernet) connection or system console. Typically, you perform out-of-band management via a modem or serial port.

Out-of-Band Management

Out-of-band management is useful when the server is not accessible via the regular network port or the system console. The primary goal of out-of-band management is to restore the state of the server to a point where you can use in-band management. The functionality of EMS is partially dependent upon the hardware or firmware support of the server where EMS is installed. The server must support Serial Port Console Redirection (SPCR) for EMS to work. Check with your server vendor to verify the extent of SPCR support. SPCR redirects video output to and accepts keyboard input from a serial port. The server is remotely accessed via terminal emulation (VT100, VT100+, and VT-UTF8 terminal emulation modes are supported) through two consoles: Special Administration Console (SAC) and !Special Administration Console (!SAC).

EMS with New Installations of Windows Server 2003

If your server supports SPCR, EMS is enabled by default during the installation of Windows Server 2003. EMS configures itself by reading the settings in the SPCR table. At the end of the text mode setup, you are prompted to allow setup to automatically configure your system with no user intervention (using unattend.txt and winnt.sif files) or to enter the GUI mode setup. For more information on unattend.txt, winnt.sif, and Remote Installation Services (RIS), refer to http://support.microsoft.com/default.aspx?scid=kb;en-us;308662.

The unattend.txt and winnt.sif files are necessary to perform a remote installation of Windows Server 2003. You can change two EMS parameters in these files to modify the behavior of EMS. These parameters appear in Table 18.2.

TABLE 18.2   EMS Parameters in unattend.txt and winnt.sif Files

[Data] Parameter	Possible Values
EMSPort={com1¦com2¦useBiosSettings}	Com*x* (where *x* specifies serial port 1 or 2). This option is valid for x86-based systems only. UseBiosSettings instructs the operating system to detect firmware that supports EMS and uses SPCR settings. If an SPCR table is not present, EMS is not enabled, which is the default setting for Advanced Configuration and Power Interface (ACPI) systems.
EMSBaudRate=*value*	9600 baud is the default, with other values of 19200, 57600, and 115200 possible, depending on the capabilities of the serial port. You must use this parameter with EMSPort=, or the parameter is ignored.

EMS with Existing Installations of Windows Server 2003

On x86-based systems, you can also enable, configure, or disable EMS on an existing Windows Server 2003 computer using the BOOTCFG command. The bootcfg.exe command allows you to add or change the EMS headless redirection settings for EMS. Table 18.3 displays the list of available commands that appear when you type the command `bootcfg /ems /?`.

TABLE 18.3   Available EMS Command-Line Options for `bootcfg.exe`

Parameter List	Value	Description
/EMS	*value*	ON, OFF, EDIT Note: EDIT changes the current settings; you cannot use /ID with EDIT.
/S	*system*	Specifies the remote system to connect to.
/U	[*domain*\]*user*	Specifies the user context under which the command should execute.
/P	[*password*]	Specifies the password for the given user context. Prompts for input if omitted.
/PORT	*port*	Specifies the COM port for redirection. Valid ports are COM1, COM2, COM3, COM4, and BIOSSET (EMS uses BIOS settings).
/BAUD	*baudrate*	Specifies the baud rate for redirection. Valid baud rates are 9600, 19200, 57600, and 115200.
/ID	Booted	Specifies the boot entry ID to add the EMS option. This parameter is required when the EMS value is ON or OFF.

The /ID switch is required for the /EMS ON or /EMS OFF options. The following examples show how you can use `bootcfg.exe` with the /EMS ON or /EMS OFF command-line options for enabling or disabling EMS and specifying the boot entry identifier:

▶ BOOTCFG /EMS ON /PORT COM1 /BAUD 19200 /ID 1

▶ BOOTCFG /EMS ON /PORT BIOSSET /ID 3

▶ BOOTCFG /EMS OFF /S *system* /ID 2

▶ BOOTCFG /EMS EDIT /PORT com2 /BAUD 115200

▶ BOOTCFG /EMS OFF /S *system* /U *domain\user* /P *password* /ID 2

Special Administration Console

The Special Administration Console (SAC) is a set of command-line utilities that allows you to perform out-of-band management for a Windows Server 2003 computer. The SAC is the primary interface for EMS. Table 18.4 lists some of the available SAC commands.

TABLE 18.4 SAC Commands

Command	Description
ch	Lists all channels.
Cmd	Creates Windows command-prompt channels. To use a command-prompt channel, you must provide valid logon credentials. You must log on to each command-prompt instance.
Crashdump	Manually generates a Stop error message and forces a memory dump file to be created.
restart	Restarts the computer.
S	If no parameters are passed, this command displays the current date using the 24-hour clock format. You can set the system time by providing the date and, optionally, the time in this format: *mm/dd/yyyy hh:mm*.
shutdown	Shuts down the computer. Do not use this command unless you can be physically present at the computer when you are ready to restart it.
T	Lists the processes and threads that are currently running.
? or help	Lists the available commands.

!Special Administration Console

The !Special Administration Console (!SAC) is separate from both the SAC and Windows Server 2003 command-line utilities. You should use it when the SAC is unavailable. !SAC contains a subset of the SAC command-line options. Some of the available !SAC commands appear in Table 18.5.

TABLE 18.5 !SAC Commands

Command	Description
restart	Restarts the server immediately.
D	Displays all log entries (screen pauses at each page of information).
Id	Displays computer identification.
Q	Quits !SAC and resumes normal out-of-band port operation.
? or Help	Lists available commands.

Summary of Disaster Recovery Options

Windows Server 2003 offers you several options for restoring data files and troubleshooting server startup problems. You should create an ASR backup set after you complete the installation and configuration of every Windows Server 2003 computer. You should also create a new, updated ASR backup set prior to making any major OS, hardware, service pack, or device driver changes to the system. Be sure not to save the ASR backup file on the same drive as the operating system, if you don't save the ASR backup to tape or some other media besides a local disk. To fully leverage ASR, only store operating-system files on the system drive volume (%systemdrive%).

Administrators and users can restore data using the shadow copies of shared folders feature along with the Previous Versions Client software that you can install only on Windows XP and Windows Server 2003 computers. If a file is corrupted, damaged, or accidentally deleted, you can use shadow copies to restore the file. You must properly configure shadow copies on a Windows Server 2003 computer and install the Previous Version Client on a workstation to access the shadow copy versions of files. The following list details the different disaster recovery techniques that you can choose when a Windows Server 2003 computer does not restart.

- *Boot the server using a startup disk*—You should create a startup boot disk after Windows Server 2003 is finalized and prior to any startup problems. In general, the startup disk only works if boot.ini, ntdetect.com, ntldr, or the MBR is damaged on the server, but the hard disk that contains the Windows Server 2003 operating system files must be available.

- *Boot the server using Safe Mode*—Use this option when you suspect that the server is not booting because of a recently installed program, service pack, or driver.

- *Boot the server using Safe Mode with Networking Support*—Use this option to verify that networking components are working properly.

- *Boot the server using Safe Mode with Command Prompt*—This option gives you a command-prompt–only environment. Use this option if the other Safe Mode options fail to start the server.

- *Boot the server using the Last Known Good Configuration*—Use this option after trying all of the Safe Mode options. Booting with this option might return the server to an earlier state than anticipated, so be careful.

- *Boot the Recovery Console*—Use this option after trying the Last Known Good Configuration. The Recovery Console is especially useful for copying files to a local drive. You can also use it to access NTFS volumes and partitions from previous Windows Server versions, such as Windows NT and Windows 2000.

- *Use the EMS SAC and !SAC utilities*—Use these options to restore the server to a point where you can use in-band management. Use these features if the server does not start or if you do not have local or network access to the server. Make sure that EMS is properly configured and that your hardware supports console redirection *before* you use these techniques.

▶ *Perform an ASR restore*—Use this option as a last resort. An ASR restore destroys all files on the operating-system drive volume (`%systemdrive%`). It only restores operating-system files, not data files. Make sure that you have an ASR backup set, the Windows Server 2003 CD-ROM or DVD-ROM media, and the ASR-created disk *prior* to attempting an ASR restore.

Managing Backup and Restore Procedures

How frequently you need to back up your organization's data depends on how often it gets updated and how important that data is to the organization. Which data should get backed up is an easier question: If you or someone in the company needs the information that certain data files contain, or if you need it for archival or legal purposes, it needs to get backed up. For these reasons, most organizations employ consistent, regularly scheduled backup operations for all computers that store valuable data.

The Shadow Copies of Shared Folders feature is a nice way to complement regular backup procedures, but shadow copies should *never* be a replacement for a regularly scheduled backup routine. Shadow Copies of Shared Folders is covered in Chapter 17, "Managing Data Storage."

TIP

It's always a good idea to set up a rotating system for server data backups. Your organization might want or need data backups to be maintained over a period of several weeks or more. At a minimum, keep at least one week's worth of backups before overwriting previous backup sets. Keeping at least two weeks' worth of previous backup sets is an even better idea. In addition, you might want to archive data by taking a backup set out of the normal rotation and keeping it in a safe location, off the premises. You might decide to keep one backup set per month as an archive so that you can retrieve older data after several months, if necessary. Keeping recent backups offsite as part of your normal backup rotation is a very important thing to do. Catastrophes such as fire, theft, acts of nature, or acts of violence can completely destroy an entire data center; offsite backups provide invaluable insurance against such unexpected events.

Backing Up Data Files

The Windows Server 2003 Backup Utility offers several different types of backups that you can use for backing up data files. The various types of backups determine which files get backed up and whether each backed-up file's archive bit gets cleared (turned off) or left alone. Each and every file stored on Windows– and MS-DOS–based computers retains at least four attributes that you can manipulate: R (Read-Only), S (System), H (Hidden), and A (Archive). The archive attribute (or bit) specifies whether the file has been modified since that last backup or since the last time the archive bit was cleared. Both normal backups and incremental backups clear (turns off) the archive bit for each file that gets backed up. As soon as a file that was previously backed up (archive bit off) gets modified, its archive bit gets set (turned on) to indicate that the file needs to be backed up again because its data has changed. The Windows Backup Utility offers five backup types to choose from when you perform a data backup:

- *Normal*—All files that are selected for backup are backed up, and each backed-up file's archive bit is cleared.

- *Copy*—This setting backs up all selected files, but each backed-up file's archive bit is not changed; files that have their archive bits set remain that way. In this way, a copy backup that is performed will not interfere with your regular backup procedures, but it allows you to back up your files onto a tape (or other media), which will not be included with your normal backup sets. This procedure is often used to produce month-end or year-end data archives.

- *Differential*—This setting only backs up files that have their archive bits set (turned on) to indicate that they have been modified since the last normal or incremental backup. Each backed-up file's archive bit is not changed; in this way, you can perform other types of backups on these files at a later time, such as a Daily backup or a Copy backup. Daily backups and Copy backups do not change the archive bit on the backed-up files. Therefore, you can continue to run Differential backups after Daily or Copy backups are run without concern that the Differential backups will not accurately capture the data that has been modified since the last Normal or Incremental backups were completed.

- *Incremental*—This setting only backs up files that have their archive bits set (turned on) to indicate that they have been modified since the last normal or incremental backup. However, each backed-up file's archive bit is cleared (turned off) to indicate that it has been backed up.

▶ *Daily*—This setting only backs up files that have been modified or created on the same day as the backup is run (today). Each backed-up file's archive bit is not changed. Daily backups can be convenient when you are performing normal backups each night, but you want to have some added insurance by creating a backup set that contains all the data that was modified during the current day. Before you do something to the server such as add memory or install one or more additional hard drives, you can run a daily backup fairly quickly as compared to a normal backup. If all goes well, you can discard the daily backup; if things don't go so well, you have the daily backup to restore from in addition to your regularly scheduled backups.

NOTE

Be sure that no NT File System (NTFS) disk quotas are in effect for the users responsible for backing up data on the server's drive volumes. NTFS disk quotas can prohibit backup operations by restricting a user's access to a drive volume. Chapter 17 discusses NTFS disk quotas.

To back up server data, you must be logged on to the computer as a member of the Backup Operators group, a member of the Server Operators group (in a domain environment), or a member of the Administrators group. From the Backup Utility, you can back up files and folders that are stored on the local computer, or you can back up files and folders that are stored on remote computers over the network, assuming that the user account you are logged on with has the proper permissions for backing up the remote computer. To perform a data backup, follow these steps:

1. Click Start, (All) Programs, Accessories, System Tools, Backup, or click Start, Run; type `NTBackup.exe`; and click OK.

2. At the Welcome to the Backup or Restore Wizard window, click the Advanced Mode link to switch to Advanced Mode. (The default is Wizard Mode.)

3. From the Welcome tab (in Advanced Mode), click the Backup tab instead of using the Backup Wizard (Advanced) for even more control over the backup process.

4. From the Backup tab, expand the drive volumes to select the folders and files that you want to back up (see Figure 18.7). Marking a check box for a parent container automatically selects all child objects within the container. You can select local drives, mapped network drives, and network shared folders on remote computers without local drive letter mappings.

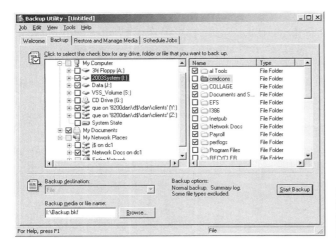

FIGURE 18.7 Selecting files to be backed up with the Windows Server 2003 Backup Utility.

5. From the drop-down list box, select the Backup Destination—such as tape or file. Backup files get the filename extension .bkf, as in backup.bkf. Be sure not to back up to a file stored on the same server as the server that you are backing up, or else copy the backup file to different media or to a network location immediately after the backup finishes.

6. If backing up to a file, type the full path and filename, or click Browse to navigate to a location for the backup file.

7. Click Start Backup to enter descriptions and choose various options for the Backup Job Information dialog box, as shown in Figure 18.8.

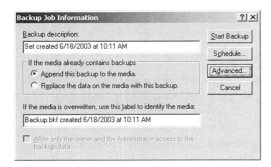

FIGURE 18.8 Adding descriptions and choosing options at the Backup Job Information dialog box.

8. Type a description in the Backup Description box or accept the default text.

9. Select either the Append This Backup to the Media option or the Replace the Data on the Media with This Backup option, if the media already has stored backups on it.

10. Type a label description in the If the Media Is Overwritten, Use This Label to Identify the Media box, or accept the default text.

11. For tape backups, you can mark the Allow Only the Owner and the Administrator Access to the Backup Data check box, if you want.

12. Click the Advanced button to configure Advanced Backup Options, as shown in Figure 18.9.

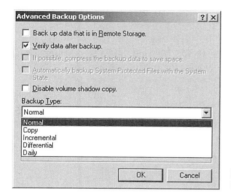

FIGURE 18.9 Configuring Advanced Backup Options.

13. Mark the check box labeled Back Up Data That Is in Remote Storage, if desired.

14. Mark the check box labeled Verify Data After Backup, if desired. As a best practice, you should always verify backup jobs; the default setting has Verify turned off.

15. For tape backups, you can mark the check box labeled If Possible, Compress the Backup Data to Save Space.

16. For System State backups, you can mark the Automatically Backup System Protected Files with the System State.

17. You can mark the Disable Volume Shadow Copy check box, but this move is not recommended. (See the note following these steps.)

18. Select the type of backup to perform from the Backup Type drop-down list box.

19. Click OK to save your Advanced Backup Options and return to the Backup Job Information dialog box.

20. Click the Start Backup button to begin the backup operation for this backup job. The Backup Progress window appears.

21. The Backup Utility notifies you when the backup operation is finished (see Figure 18.10).

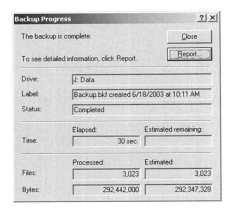

FIGURE 18.10 Viewing the Backup Progress window after the backup job finishes.

22. You can click the Report button to view and print the Backup Report log file for the completed backup job (see Figure 18.11).

FIGURE 18.11 Viewing the Backup Status report log after the backup job finishes. Note that the backup has been verified.

23. Close the report log (Notepad) window when you are finished viewing the report, and then click the Close button to finish the backup job.

NOTE

By default, Windows XP Professional and Windows Server 2003 computers first create a shadow copy of the files that you select for backup. The files are then copied (or backed up) from the shadow copy "snapshot," rather than copied directly from the files themselves. This procedure allows files that are open or locked to be backed up instead of being skipped because they cannot be backed up while they are in use.

Backing Up the System State

A computer's System State data contains most of the operating system's vital configuration settings, important databases, and critical files for Windows 2000, Windows XP, or Windows Server 2003. These vital software components include the Windows Registry, the COM+ Class Registration database, boot files and system files such as `ntldr` and `ntdetect.com`, the Certificate Services database (if the computer runs Certificate Services), the Active Directory database and the `SYSVOL` folder contents (if the computer is a DC), operating-system files that are protected by Windows File Protection, the Internet Information Services (IIS) metabase (if IIS is installed), and cluster service information (if the computer is part of a cluster).

As a separate operation from your full system backup procedures, you should also back up each server's System State data on a frequent and regular basis because this information is critical to the successful operation of a Windows Server 2003 computer. To back up a computer's System State, simply follow the steps outlined in the previous section, "Backing Up Data Files," and mark the System State check box as the item that you want to back up in the Windows Server 2003 Backup Utility (see Figure 18.12). You can back up the System State to tape or to a file, just like any other data backup. If you back up the System State to a file, you can copy the backup file to some other media, such as a CD-R/CD-RW or writable DVD.

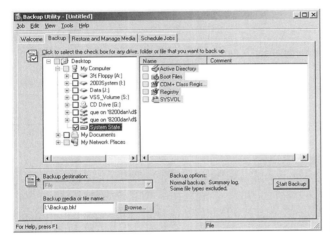

FIGURE 18.12 Selecting the System State check box to back up System State data.

Using the Windows Backup Utility from the Command Line

You can use the same executable program for the graphical Backup Utility program from the command line. You can use the NTBackup.exe program at a command prompt to run backup operations only; you cannot perform restores from the command line. You can also use NTBackup.exe in batch files to create an entirely customized backup routine that you can schedule to run at various times using the Task Scheduler and the Scheduled Tasks folder. If you type NTBackup.exe without any parameters after it, the graphical Backup Utility program runs. To see the entire list of available command-line options that you can use with NTBackup.exe, type **NTBackup.exe /?** at a command prompt.

If you use the NTBackup.exe program at a command prompt, it only backs up entire folders. Instead, you can use wildcard characters (such as ? and *) to select groups of files to back up, such as using *.doc to indicate that all files with the .doc extension should be backed up. An example of using NTBackup.exe to back up the

E: drive on the local computer, assigning the backup job name "Sample Backup of E" and using a file backup to the file named "SampleBackup.bkf" on drive N:, is `NTbackup backup E: /j"Sample Backup of E" /f"N:\SampleBackup.bkf"`.

Setting Backup Utility Defaults

You can set global default options for all backup and restore jobs using the graphical Backup Utility interface. These customizable default settings include whether to perform verifications of backup jobs; whether to replace files that already exist on the computer during a restore operation; which backup type should be the default; the level of logging that you want for backup jobs; and which files, if any, that you want excluded from all backup jobs. To configure default settings for backup and restore operations, follow these steps:

1. Run the Backup Utility in graphical Advanced Mode.

2. Click Tools, Options from the menu bar.

3. From the General tab, mark or clear the check box for each option that you want to turn on or off as a global program default. The options on this tab include Verify Data After the Backup Completes and Back Up the Contents of Mounted Drives (see Figure 18.13).

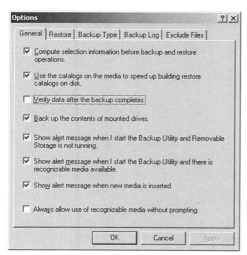

FIGURE 18.13 Specifying global default backup options from the General tab.

4. Click the Restore tab to specify which action that the Backup Utility should take when restoring a file that already exists in the same folder where the file is supposed to be restored:

> ▸ Do Not Replace the File on My Computer (Recommended).

> ▸ Replace the File on Disk Only if the File on Disk Is Older.

> ▸ Always Replace the File on My Computer.

5. Click the Backup Type tab to indicate the default backup type for backup jobs to use—normal, copy, differential, incremental, or daily.

6. Click the Backup Log tab to specify the level of logging that you want enabled by default:

> ▸ *Detailed*—Logs All Information, Including the Names of All the Files and Folders

> ▸ *Summary*—Logs Only Key Operations, Such as Loading a Tape, Starting the Backup, or Failing to Open a File

> ▸ *None*—Do Not Log

7. Click the Exclude Files tab to specify any files that you do not want backed up by default. (You can use wildcards to specify groups of files by filename extension.) Several files are already listed by default (see Figure 18.14). You can specify files to exclude from backup jobs for all users, and you can specify files to exclude from backup jobs only for members of the Administrators group. Excluded files for Administrator users are only excluded when someone logs on to the computer as a member of the Administrators group to perform a backup.

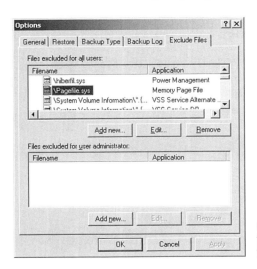

FIGURE 18.14 Specifying files to exclude from backups by default for all users and for members of the Administrators group.

8. Click OK to save your global default settings.

Scheduling Backup Jobs

You can easily schedule backup jobs to run automatically at predetermined times using the graphical Backup Utility as well as by specifying the proper parameters for the `NTBackup.exe` program on the command line. For the Backup Utility, you can schedule a backup job to run when you create the backup job, or you can click the Add Job button in the bottom-right corner of the Schedule Jobs tab to launch the Backup Wizard to set up a new scheduled backup job (see Figure 18.15).

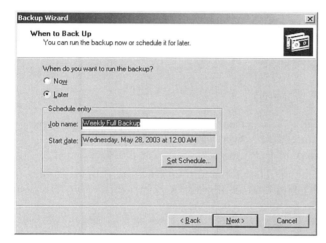

FIGURE 18.15   Running the Backup Wizard by clicking the Add Job button on the Schedule Jobs tab.

To schedule a new backup job that you set up from the Backup tab, take these steps:

1. Follow the steps listed in the section titled, "Backing Up Data Files," and click the Schedule button when you get to the Backup Job Information dialog box, after you configure any advanced backup options for the job.

2. Click Yes when you are prompted to save the backup selections. The backup job's settings are saved to a file with the `.bks` extension.

3. At the Set Account Information dialog box, type the user account name or accept the logged-on user account name (default), type the user account's password, and confirm the password.

4. Click OK.

5. At the Scheduled Job Options dialog box, type a name for this backup job in the Job Name box.

6. Click the Backup Details tab to view a summary of the name for this backup job, the backup device or file that is to be used, and a description of the options configured for this backup job (see Figure 18.16).

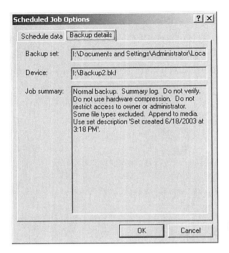

FIGURE 18.16   The Backup Details tab on the Scheduled Job Options dialog box.

7. Click back on the Schedule Data tab and then click the Properties button to schedule the backup job (see Figure 18.17).

FIGURE 18.17   The Schedule Job dialog box for scheduling backup jobs to run automatically.

8. Click OK to save the schedule settings. The scheduled backup job appears on the calendar for the Scheduled Jobs tab for each time that it is scheduled to run.

Managing Backup Storage Media

The Removable Storage Manager (RSM) in Windows Server 2003 is responsible for managing storage media that you can use for backup and restore operations. The RSM provides removable storage services for applications and network administrators that enhance the sharing and management of removable media hardware such as backup tape devices, optical disc drives, and automated (robotic) media-pool libraries. Removable storage and media support in Windows Server 2003 precludes the need for third-party software developers to write custom application programs to support each different type of removable media device. In addition, removable storage services allow organizations to leverage their investment in expensive removable-storage equipment by having multiple removable-storage applications share these devices.

> **NOTE**
>
> You cannot back up data files directly to optical media using the Windows Server 2003 Backup Utility. However, you can back up data to a file, instead of backing up to tape, and you can copy the backup file to recordable media of this type. During a restore operation, the Backup Utility does support reading a backup file from these recordable media types, so you can restore from recordable and rewritable CDs and DVDs without a problem.

The Windows Server 2003 Removable Storage service implements a set of APIs that enable third-party software solutions to catalog all removable media, such as CDs, DVDs, tapes, and optical discs. You can catalog both offline (shelved) as well as online (housed in a library) media. The Removable Storage service organizes media using *media pools*. These media pools control access to the removable media, categorize the media according to each type, and permit the media to be shared by applications. The Removable Storage service tracks the application programs that share the removable media. The Removable Storage feature is logically structured into five basic components: media units, media libraries, media pools, work queue items, and operator requests (see Figure 18.18). You can manage removable storage from the Computer Management console or from the Microsoft Management Console (MMC) snap-in named Removable Storage.

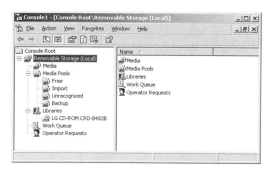

FIGURE 18.18 Managing backup storage media with the Removable Storage snap-in.

Configuring Security for Backup Operations

By default, all user accounts retain the appropriate rights and permissions to back up their own folders and files, but ordinary users cannot back up folders and files that are owned by other users. Only members of the Backup Operators group, the Server Operators group, and the Administrators group have the ability to back up and restore all files stored on a server regardless of which users own those folders and files. Members of these three groups retain both the Back Up Files and Directories user right and the Restore Files and Directories user right on standalone servers, member servers, and domain controllers.

Local or group policy settings are responsible for controlling user rights assignments. For standalone and member server Windows Server 2003 computers, the Backup Operators group and the Administrators group are assigned these backup and restore rights by default in the Local Security Settings MMC snap-in. For DCs, the Backup Operators group, the Server Operators group, and the Administrators group are assigned these backup and restore rights in the Default Domain Controller Security Settings MMC snap-in (see Figures 18.19 and 18.20). The location for these two policy settings is `Computer Configuration\Windows Settings\Security Settings\Local Policies\User Rights Assignment`.

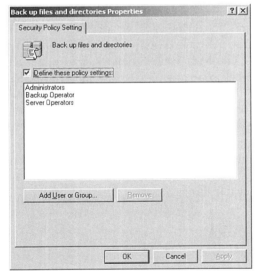

FIGURE 18.19 Viewing the default members of the Back Up Files and Directories security policy setting for a DC.

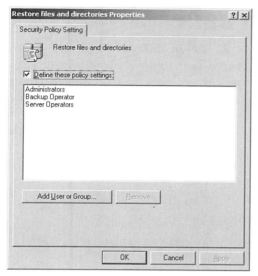

FIGURE 18.20 Viewing the default members of the Restore Files and Directories security policy setting for a DC.

For increased security, you might consider removing the Backup Operators group (in domain and standalone environments) and the Server Operators group (in domain environments) from both the Back Up Files and Directories user rights assignment policy and from the Restore Files and Directories user rights assignment policy. In their place, you can create two different groups, such as "Backup Admins" and "Restore Admins." You can then add the appropriate user accounts to these custom groups, and you can add the Backup Admins group to the Back Up Files and Directories policy setting, while adding only the Restore Admins group to the Restore Files and Directories policy setting. In this way, you are separating the backup and restore user rights into two distinct groups, which enables you to allow only certain users to back up data and only certain other users to restore that data.

EXAM ALERT

For even more protection, users can mark the Allow Only the Owner and the Administrator Access to the Backup Data check box from the Backup Job Information dialog box. However, this additional security measure is only available if you select the Replace the Data on the Media with This Backup option instead of the Append This Backup to the Media option. When you enable this security option, only a member of the Administrators group or the user who created the backup set can restore the files and folders contained within the backup set.

Restoring Backup Data

Restoring data from a backup set using the Backup Utility is a fairly straightforward process. You cannot restore backup data from a command prompt using the NTBackup.exe command-line program; you must use the Backup Utility GUI. By default, you must be a member of the Backup Operators group, the Server Operators group (in a domain environment), or the Administrators group to perform a restore operation. To restore backup data, follow these steps:

1. Run the Backup Utility program.

2. Click the Advanced Mode link, if the program is not already in Advanced Mode.

3. Click the Restore and Manage Media tab.

4. Expand the media item that you want to restore from and then expand the backup set that you want to restore from.

5. Mark the check box for each drive letter, folder, or individual file that you want to restore. Marking a parent drive letter or folder selects all the child folders and files contained within it. Clear each item that you do not want to restore (see Figure 18.21).

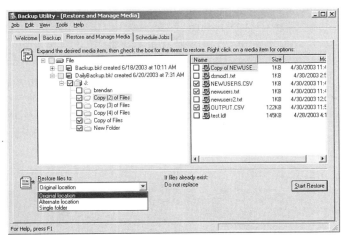

FIGURE 18.21   Selecting folders and files to restore using the Windows Backup Utility.

6. From the Restore Files to drop-down list box, select where you want the restored files to be copied to—Original Location, Alternate Location, or Single Folder. If you select Alternate Location or Single Folder, type in the path (drive letter and folder name) or click the Browse button to select the restore path for the Alternate Location box.

7. Click the Start Restore button to begin the restore operation.

8. When the Confirm Restore message box appears, click the Advanced button to specify advanced restore options.

9. From the Advanced Restore Options dialog box (see Figure 18.22), make sure that the Restore Security check box is marked, which is the default. This option restores all NTFS security settings for the restored files and folders, if you are restoring onto an NTFS drive volume. Other options include restoring junction points and preserving existing mount points.

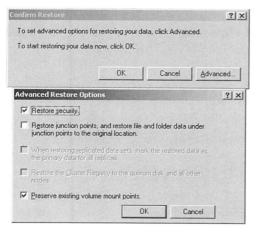

FIGURE 18.22 Setting advanced restore options.

10. Click OK to save the advanced restore options settings, and then click OK to begin restoring the data.

11. The Restore Progress window keeps you updated on the progress of the restore job, and it notifies you when the restore is finished. Click the Report button to view the Restore Report log.

12. Click the Close button to finish the restore operation.

NOTE

You can back up data files from FAT, FAT32, and NTFS drive volumes with the Windows Server 2003 Backup Utility. However, when you restore the data files, you should restore them onto the same file system as they were stored on originally. This concept is especially critical if you attempt to restore files that were backed up from an NTFS drive volume onto a FAT or FAT32 drive volume: NTFS security permissions, NTFS disk quotas, NTFS data compression attributes, and Encrypting File System (EFS) data encryption attributes all become lost for the restored data files when they are restored onto a FAT or FAT32 drive volume.

Restoring System State Data

You can easily restore a backup of a computer's System State data using the Windows Server 2003 Backup Utility in much the same way as you perform a restore operation for user data. However, a System State restore operation for a DC is more complex than a System State restore operation for a member server or a standalone server. Performing a restore operation for a DC is covered in the following section, "Restoring the System State for DCs." To restore a computer's System State, follow these steps:

1. Run the Backup Utility program.

2. Click the Advanced Mode link, if the program is not already in Advanced Mode.

3. Click the Restore and Manage Media tab.

4. Expand the media item that you want to restore from and then expand the backup set that you want to restore from.

5. Mark the check box for the System State item (see Figure 18.23).

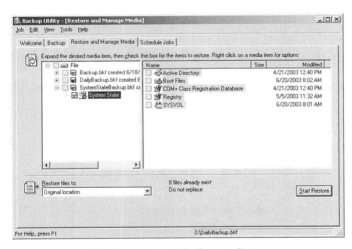

FIGURE 18.23 Selecting to restore the System State.

6. From the Restore Files to drop-down list box, select the Original Location option.

7. Click the Start Restore button to begin the restore operation.

8. Click OK for the Warning message box that appears, informing you that "Restoring the System State will always overwrite current System State unless restoring to an alternate location."

9. Next, the Confirm Restore message box appears. Click OK to begin the restore operation, or click Advanced to specify Advanced Restore Options and then begin the restore.

10. The Restore Progress window keeps you updated on the progress of the restore job and it will notify you when the restore is finished. Click the Report button to view the Restore Report log.

11. Click the Close button to finish the System State restore process.

12. For a System State restore, you might be prompted to restart the computer. Click Yes to restart the computer immediately, or click No and you can restart it later.

Restoring the System State for DCs

Windows Server 2003 computers that act as DCs store Active Directory data within the SYSVOL folder and within the Active Directory database (ntds.dit) file. The objects contained within the SYSVOL folder and the Active Directory database are always open and being accessed by the directory service. The shadow copy service cannot help with this condition for Active Directory files because the data is always in a state of flux due to replication of the data between DCs. Therefore, you must reboot a DC and select Directory Services Restore Mode from the Windows Advanced Options startup menu (see Figure 18.24) to perform a restore of its System State and the DC's Active Directory database. You still use the Windows Server 2003 Backup Utility to perform the System State restore, but the restore operation must occur while the computer is in Directory Services Restore Mode.

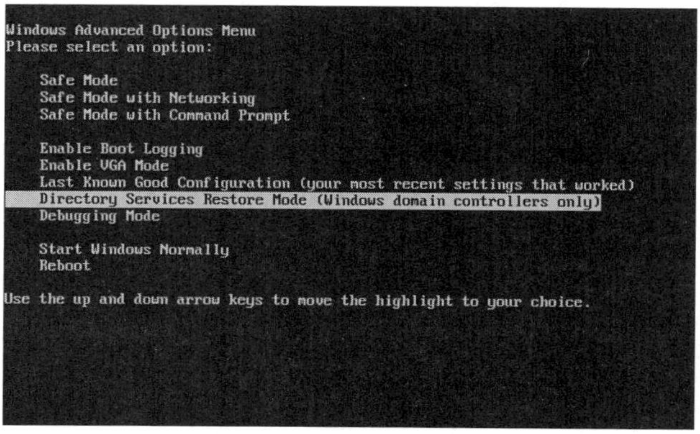

FIGURE 18.24 Restarting a DC in Directory Services Restore Mode to restore the System State.

Because Active Directory uses multimaster replication to synchronize all the DC databases throughout an Active Directory domain, performing a normal restore is not sufficient when objects such as user accounts, groups, or organizational units get accidentally deleted or incorrectly modified. All objects in Active Directory are assigned Update Sequence Numbers (USNs) that determine which objects are the most up-to-date when replication occurs between DCs. After you perform a normal, or nonauthoritative, restore, the restored objects retain their previous USNs; objects that had been deleted with older USNs will become deleted again when the DC is restarted in normal mode and replication takes place.

> **NOTE**
>
> If a DC goes down completely and you have to rebuild it from scratch, you can perform a normal restore. After the DC comes back online, Active Directory replication synchronizes the DC with the most recent updates from the other DCs in the domain. For such a scenario, an authoritative restore is not necessary. Authoritative restores should always be done with great caution and only in coordination with the responsible administrative personnel who manage the other DCs within the same domain.

To ensure that the restored Active Directory objects do not get deleted again via replication, you must use the `ntdsutil.exe` command-line tool to mark the restored Active Directory objects as authoritative while the computer is still in Directory Services Restore Mode. An authoritative restore marks and updates the USNs for each object that is marked as authoritatively restored; Active Directory objects with newer USNs appear newer than objects on other DCs that have older USNs. Objects with older USNs are discarded, and the objects with newer USNs are replicated throughout the domain or forest.

To run `ntdsutil.exe`, open a command prompt, type **ntdsutil**, and press Enter. At any NTDSUTIL: prompt, you can type **help** to view a list of available commands. In the following step-by-step example, the entire Active Directory database is marked as authoritative to demonstrate how to perform an authoritative restore. In the real world, you would be more likely to mark an object or a subtree as authoritative, not the entire database. To restore the System State and Active Directory database on a Windows Server 2003 DC, follow these steps:

1. Restart the computer, press the F8 key during the startup process, select Directory Services Restore Mode from the Windows Advanced Options startup menu, and then press Enter.

2. Log on to the DC as the administrator under Safe Mode (Directory Services Restore Mode). You must log on with the administrator password that was created for Directory Services Restore Mode at the time that the computer was promoted to a DC using the Active Directory Installation Wizard (`dcpromo.exe`).

3. Perform the System State restore operation using the Backup Utility, as outlined in the previous section, "Restoring System State Data."

4. After the System State restore operation is successful and finished, open a command prompt.

5. At a command prompt, type **ntdsutil** and press Enter.

6. At the NTDSUTIL: prompt, type **authoritative restore** and press Enter.

7. At the Authoritative Restore: prompt, you can type **help** to view a list of available commands for marking Active Directory objects as "authoritative."

8. To mark the *entire restored Active Directory database as authoritative*, type **restore database** at the Authoritative Restore: prompt and press Enter (see Figure 18.25).

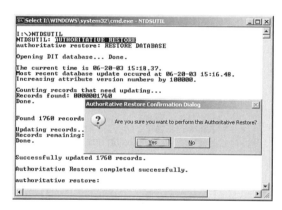

FIGURE 18.25   Using the ntdsutil.exe tool to mark a restored Active Directory database as authoritative.

9. Click Yes when the confirmation dialog box appears. Be extremely cautious and make sure that you understand all the ramifications of this action before you attempt to mark the entire Active Directory database as authoritative. Changes made to Active Directory objects on other DCs might be lost when you mark one DC's database as authoritative and replication takes place.

10. You are notified when the authoritative restore is complete by the ntdsutil program.

11. Type **quit** for the authoritative restore prompt.

12. Type **quit** at the NTDSUTIL: prompt to exit the utility and return to the Windows Server 2003 command prompt.

13. Restart the computer under Windows Server 2003 normally.

If you have only one DC in the domain or if you need to rebuild an entire domain from backup when all DCs have been lost, you should perform a primary restore. A primary restore lets you restore the domain's first replica set as well as letting you restore Active Directory and the SYSVOL folder on a stand-alone DC or on the first DC within a forest.

To perform a primary restore of Active Directory from a System State backup, you still must boot the computer into Directory Services Restore Mode; however, you do not need to use the NTDSUTIL program. After you select the System State item for the restore in the Windows Backup Utility, click Start Restore, click OK for the Warning dialog box, and then click the Advanced button to specify advanced restore options. You must mark the When Restoring Replicated Data Sets, Mark the Restored Data as the Primary Data for All Replicas check box to specify that the restore operation is a primary restore (see Figure 18.26). After selecting this option, start the restore job; you can boot Windows normally after the restore job finishes.

FIGURE 18.26 Using the Advanced Restore Options dialog box to designate the restored Active Directory database as primary.

Exam Prep Questions

1. Which type of backup can you perform using the Windows Server 2003 Backup Utility if you only want to back up files that have their archive bits set and you want the backup job to clear each file's archive bit after each file has been backed up?

   ○ **A.** Incremental

   ○ **B.** Differential

   ○ **C.** Normal

   ○ **D.** Copy

2. When will booting a Windows Server computer from a startup disk not work?

   ○ **A.** When the `boot.ini` file is corrupted

   ○ **B.** When the boot hard drive that stores the operating-system files has a hardware failure

   ○ **C.** When the `ntdetect.com` file is corrupted

   ○ **D.** When the `ntldr` file is corrupted

   ○ **E.** When the CD-ROM drive is not working

3. What strategies can you use to troubleshoot a server that does not start properly? (Choose four.)

   ○ **A.** Use a Windows Server 2003 startup disk to try to boot the server.

   ○ **B.** Use Safe Mode to try to start the server.

   ○ **C.** Perform an Automated System Recovery (ASR) backup.

   ○ **D.** Implement shadow copies on the server.

   ○ **E.** Use the Last Known Good Configuration to try to start the server.

   ○ **F.** Run the Recovery Console on the server and run the `DISABLE` command to prevent a service from loading upon startup.

   ○ **G.** Install the Previous Versions software on the server.

4. Alexis is a member of the Backup Operators group on a Windows Server 2003 computer. The server's data drive volume contains more than 25GB of data files that need to be backed up. Alexis's user account is currently subject to a 500MB NTFS disk-quota entry and disk quotas are enabled on the drive volume. What must the network administrator do to allow Alexis to back up the entire data volume without unnecessarily compromising security?

   ○ **A.** Make Alexis a member of the Administrators group.

   ○ **B.** Make Alexis a member of the Server Operators group.

   ○ **C.** Grant Alexis the Backup Files and Directories user right on the server.

   ○ **D.** Assign Alexis an unlimited disk-quota entry for the data volume.

5. Which of the following is not true about the Recovery Console? (Choose two.)

   ○ **A.** The Recovery Console can be preinstalled and run directly from the hard drive.

   ○ **B.** You can run the Recovery Console from the Windows Server 2003 CD-ROM.

   ○ **C.** The Recovery Console does not enforce NTFS permissions.

   ○ **D.** The Recovery Console can repair a boot sector on the hard drive with the FIXBOOT command.

   ○ **E.** The Recovery Console command LISTSVC lists all available services and drivers running on the computer.

   ○ **F.** You must install the Recovery Console to perform an ASR restore.

6. Which of the following will prevent a successful ASR restore? (Choose three.)

   ○ **A.** Storing the ASR Backup file on the same drive as the operating system

   ○ **B.** Losing the ASR floppy disk

   ○ **C.** A boot-sector virus on the operating system drive

   ○ **D.** A failed CD-ROM drive

   ○ **E.** A missing or damaged ntdetect.com file on the operating-system drive volume

   ○ **F.** A missing ntldr file on the operating-system drive

7. In which of the following ways can you perform a restore operation using the Windows Server 2003 Backup Utility? (Choose three.)

○ **A.** From backup tape

○ **B.** From DVD recordable or rewritable media

○ **C.** From an external USB hard drive

○ **D.** By using the NTBackup.exe tool from a command prompt

○ **E.** By restoring a remote computer's System State over the network

○ **F.** By selecting Advanced Restore Options to mark the restored data as authoritative for Active Directory

8. Which communication channels can you use to perform out-of-band management on a headless server under EMS? (Choose two.)

○ **A.** Primary network connection

○ **B.** Serial port

○ **C.** Modem

○ **D.** USB port

○ **E.** Parallel port (lpt)

○ **F.** SCSI port

9. Which is the best way to restrict a tape backup set from being restored by just any member of the Backup Operators group?

○ **A.** Apply appropriate NTFS security permissions on the backup set.

○ **B.** Remove all users from the Backup Operators group.

○ **C.** Revoke the Restore Files and Directories user right from the Backup Operators group.

○ **D.** Mark the Allow Only the Owner and the Administrator Access to the Backup Data check box for the Backup Job Information dialog box when you run a backup job.

10. Which Safe Mode option should you use when the other Safe Mode options fail?

○ **A.** Safe Mode

○ **B.** Safe Mode with Command Prompt

○ **C.** Safe Mode with Networking Support

○ **D.** Safe Mode with EMS Support

○ **E.** Safe Mode with SAC Support

Answers to Exam Prep Questions

1. **Answer A is correct.** Incremental backups only back up files that have their archive bit set and each backed up file has its archive bit cleared. Answer B is incorrect because differential backups do not clear each file's archive bit. Answer C is incorrect because normal backups back up all files, not just files that have their archive bits set. Answer D is incorrect because a copy backup backs up all files and does not clear each backed-up file's archive bit.

2. **Answer B is correct.** To use a Windows Server 2003 startup disk, the hard drive that stores the operating-system files must be functioning. Answer A is incorrect because a startup disk can normally boot the server when the boot.ini file is corrupted. Answer C is incorrect because a startup disk can normally boot the server when the ntdetect.com file is corrupted. Answer D is incorrect because a startup disk can normally boot the server when the ntldr file is corrupted. Answer E is incorrect because a startup disk does not use the CD-ROM during the boot process.

3. **Answers A, B, E, and F are correct.** A Windows Server 2003 Startup disk can start a server that has a damaged boot.ini, ntdetect.com, or ntldr file or damaged master boot record. All Safe Modes are useful to troubleshoot server startup problems. Using the Last Known Good Configuration can start a server when the last successful logon is a good configuration. Using the Recovery Console to disable one or more services that might be preventing Windows Server 2003 from starting is a valid method for troubleshooting server startup problems. Answer D is incorrect because shadow copies allow users to restore files when the server is up and running. Answer G is incorrect because the Previous Versions software only serves to restore data files from shared folders stored on drive volumes where shadows copies are enabled.

4. **Answer D is correct.** Assigning an unlimited disk-quota entry for Alexis allows her to back up all the data files on the volume. Answer A is incorrect because even though members of the Administrators group have unlimited disk quotas by default, the network administrator would be granting much more authority to Alexis than she needs to do her job. Answer B is incorrect because making Alexis a member of the Server Operators group would not solve her disk-quota restriction. Answer C is incorrect because Alexis already has this user right by being a member of the Backup Operators group.

5. **Answers C and F are correct.** The Recovery Console does enforce NTFS permissions, and you can perform an ASR restore without first installing the Recovery Console. Answer A is incorrect because it is true that the Recovery Console can be preinstalled and run directly from the hard drive. Answer B is incorrect because it is true that you can run the Recovery Console from the Windows Server 2003 CD-ROM. Answer D is incorrect because it is true that the Recovery Console can repair a boot sector on the hard drive with the FIXBOOT command. Answer E is incorrect because it is true that the Recovery Console command LISTSVC lists all available services and drivers running on the computer.

6. **Answers A, B, and D are correct.** If you store the ASR backup file on the operating-system drive, you will be unable to complete the ASR process because an ASR restore formats the operating-system drive as part of the ASR restore process. If you do not have the ASR floppy, or an ASR floppy disk that you created by restoring the files from backup media, you cannot start the ASR restore process. The ASR restore procedure copies files from the Windows Server 2003 CD-ROM to complete the restore process, so you must have the CD available. Answer C is incorrect because an ASR restore formats the operating-system drive; therefore, it does not matter what is currently contained on the drive before the ASR restore starts. Answer E is incorrect because a missing or damaged `ntdetect.com` file does not affect an ASR restore. Answer F is incorrect because a missing `ntldr` file does not affect an ASR restore.

7. **Answers A, B, and C are correct.** You can restore from backup tape, from DVD recordable or rewritable media, and from any type of external hard drive. Answer D is incorrect because you cannot use the `NTBackup.exe` command-line tool to perform a restore. Answer E is incorrect because you cannot restore a computer's System State remotely. Answer F is incorrect because you cannot mark restored System State data as authoritative from the Backup Utility; you must use `NTDSUTIL` for that purpose. You can, however, use the Backup Utility to mark restored System State data as primary for Active Directory objects.

8. **Answers B and C are correct.** Both serial ports and modems are supported in Windows Server 2003 for remote out-of-band management. Answer A is incorrect because managing a server with a primary network connection is considered in-band management. Answers C and D are incorrect because USB ports and parallel ports (lpt) are not supported for out-of-band management. Answer F is incorrect because SCSI ports are not supported for out-of-band management.

9. **Answer D is correct.** Answer A is incorrect because you cannot apply NTFS permissions on a tape backup set. Answer B is incorrect because removing all users from the Backup Operators group allows only administrators to create backups. Answer C is incorrect because revoking the Restore Files and Directories user right from the Backup Operators group means that only administrators can perform restores for any backup sets.

10. **Answer B is correct.** The Safe Mode with Command Prompt option only starts the command-line utilities. Answers A and C are incorrect because these two Safe Mode options require more resources to start than the Safe Mode with Command Prompt option. Answers E and E are incorrect because there is no Safe Mode option with EMS or SAC support.

Need to Know More?

1. Boswell, William. *Inside Windows Server 2003*. Boston, Massachusetts: Addison-Wesley, 2003.

2. Honeycutt, Jerry. *Introducing Microsoft Windows Server 2003*. Redmond, Washington: Microsoft Press, 2003.

3. Jones, Don, and Mark Rouse. *Microsoft Windows Server 2003 Delta Guide*. Indianapolis, Indiana: Sams Publishing, 2003.

4. Search the Microsoft Product Support Services Knowledge Base on the Internet: http://support.microsoft.com. You can also search Microsoft TechNet on the Internet: http://technet.microsoft.com. Find technical information using keywords from this chapter, such as Safe Mode, Automated System Recovery, Emergency Management Services, Recovery Console, and Last Known Good Configuration, Backup Utility, NTBackup, backup types, System State, authoritative restore, NTDSUTIL, and Directory Services Restore Mode

CHAPTER NINETEEN

Software Maintenance Using Windows Server Update Services

Terms you'll need to understand:

✓ Windows Server Update Service (WSUS)

✓ Security updates

✓ Service packs

Techniques/concepts you'll need to master:

✓ Describe the benefits of WSUS.

✓ Install and configure WSUS.

✓ Configure users to get updates from a WSUS server.

It is important that you keep your systems up-to-date with updates and security patches. If your system is not kept up-to-date, it may not run as reliably as it should, and it would not be as resistant against viruses and other forms of denial of service (DoS) attacks.

You could manually log in to each computer within your organization and go to the http://update.microsoft.com website to download and install the updates. Unfortunately, if you have hundreds of computers, this approach is impractical because of the labor and because hundreds of computers downloading patches also use valuable bandwidth. In addition, you often want a way to control what updates get applied since updates might cause problems with certain applications.

Another option is to configure each computer for automatic updates. To enable automatic updates, open the System Properties using the Control Panel and select the Automatic Updates tab. Select Automatic (recommended). Unfortunately, hundreds of computers downloading patches might use valuable bandwidth and you do not have a way to control which updates get applied.

Microsoft Updates

To overcome these problems, you can set up a Windows Server Update Services (WSUS) server to provide a central point for client computers and servers to acquire updates. With WSUS, you can also update Microsoft Office, Microsoft SQL, Microsoft Exchange, and other Microsoft applications.

> **NOTE**
>
> The server exam may include questions on Software Update Service (SUS). SUS has been retired and replaced by WSUS. WSUS offers more updates than just Windows, provides reporting capabilities, and gives administrators more control over the update process.

WSUS is provided free from Microsoft. The software and step-by-step guides can be found at http://www.microsoft.com/windowsserversystem/updateservices/default.mspx.

When installing WSUS, the minimum requirement for a server to handle 500 clients is

- ▶ Pentium III processor
- ▶ 1GB of RAM
- ▶ 1GB disk space on the system volume
- ▶ 30GB for security packages

You also will need a SQL server. If you do not have a dedicated SQL server, you can download and install SQL Server 2000 Desktop Engine (WMSDE).

After WSUS is installed, the WSUS server will need to be able to communicate with the Microsoft update sites so that it can download the updates.

To configure WSUS, use the WSUS administration website located at `http://servername/WSUSAdmin`, where *servername* is the DNS name of the server on which WSUS is installed. You can also open Administrative Tools and click Microsoft Windows Server Update Services. To run the WSUS console, you must be a member of the WSUS Administrators or the local Administrators security groups on the server on which WSUS is installed.

These are the five primary administrative tasks for managing WSUS:

- ► Review status information, such as computers requiring updates.

- ► Review and approve updates for distribution to clients.

- ► Generate reports on the status of updates, computers, synchronization, and WSUS settings.

- ► Manage computers and computer groups.

- ► Configure WSUS options for synchronization, automatic approval, and assigning computers to groups.

By default, only critical updates and security updates are downloaded. You can select specific products and update classifications, such as Microsoft Office, Microsoft Exchange, Microsoft SQL, and so forth. You can also limit the versions of Windows that it will update and the languages that are available to limit the size of the database and archive of the updates (see Figure 19.1).

WSUS enables you to specify which updates you want, including

- ► Microsoft Server 2003

- ► Windows XP

- ► Office XP

- ► Office 2003

It also enables you to specify the update classifications, including

- ► Critical updates
- ► Security updates
- ► Service packs
- ► Patch rollups
- ► Tools
- ► Updates
- ► Drivers

FIGURE 19.1 You access Windows Server Update Services management console using Internet Explorer.

To limit which computers get updates and which updates are sent to the specified computers, you define computer groups. This allows you to configure test computers for updates before rolling out updates to all computers. After a client computer makes contact with the WSUS server for the first time, it will be listed on the Computers page of the WSUS administration site. You must approve them to initiate deployment of updates.

EXAM ALERT

Before computers can get updates, they must be first approved to receive updates. Then the individual updates must be approved to be distributed.

After the updates have been downloaded from Microsoft or another WSUS server, you will need to approve which updates will be propagated to the client computers. When you approve updates, you can choose to install, detect only, remove, or decline. After detection, you can view how many computers do not have the update installed and need it. If the number of computers needing an update is zero, all client computers are up-to-date. The install approval option installs the update for the selected computer groups.

By default, updates are not downloaded until they are approved for installation. Using the WSUS console, you can run reports to show how many computers have been updated, a list of those computers updated, the status of computers, and synchronization results (see Figure 19.2).

FIGURE 19.2 After the updates have been synchronized on the server, you then have to specify which updates are approved.

To configure the client computers to use the WSUS server, you can configure the registry or you can use group policies. To configure WSUS with group policies, perform the following:

1. In Group Policy Object Editor, expand Computer Configuration, expand Administrative Templates, expand Windows Components, and then click Windows Update (see Figure 19.3).

2. In the Details pane (right side), double-click Specify intranet Microsoft update service location.

3. Click Enabled, and type the HTTP URL of the same WSUS server in the Set the Intranet Update Service for Detecting Updates box and in the Set the Intranet Statistics Server box. For example, type http://servername in both boxes.

4. Click OK.

5. Double-click Configure Automatic Updates.

6. Click Enabled, and specify the type of updates and type of the install (see Figure 19.4). The type of updates include

   ▶ 2-Notify for Download and Notify for Install

   ▶ 3-Auto Download and Notify for Install

   ▶ 4-Auto Download and Schedule the Install

7. Click OK.

After you establish a group policy, it might take a few minutes for the group policy to take effect. Therefore, you might want to refresh the group policy by using gpudate /force if you want more immediate results.

EXAM ALERT

To configure the client computers to use the WSUS server, you can configure the Registry or use group policies.

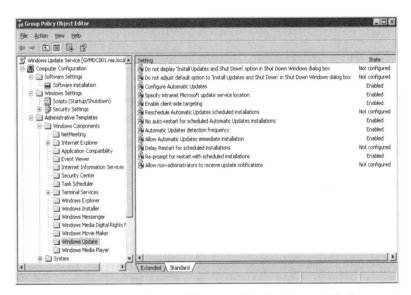

FIGURE 19.3 You can use Group policies to enable clients to use WSUS servers to receive updates.

Although WSUS does not provide built-in backup tools, you can use normal backup tools such as backup utility that comes with Microsoft Windows to backup and restore the WSUS database and update the file storage folder. It is recommended that when you backup the database (MSSQL$WSUS), you should stop the database to prevent inconsistencies.

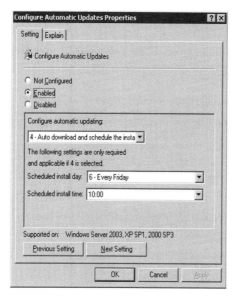

FIGURE 19.4 One setting using group policies is when and how updates will be installed.

Exam Prep Questions

1. You need to install WSUS on a server named Server1. Server1 has limited hard drive space. You must install Microsoft critical updates. What do you need to do to make sure that you do not run out of disk space?

   ○ **A.** Clear the selection of all locales not used on your network.

   ○ **B.** Select the option to maintain the updates on a Windows Update server.

   ○ **C.** Modify the default home page to `http://windowsupdate.microsoft.com`.

   ○ **D.** Modify the proxy server setting in IE to `http://Server1`.

2. What is the primary site that allows a user to quickly and easily install service packs and security patches?

   ○ **A.** `http://update.microsoft.com`

   ○ **B.** `http://download.microsoft.com`

   ○ **C.** `http://www.microsoft.com/wsus`

   ○ **D.** `http://www.Microsoft.com/security`

3. What is the Successor to Software Update Service (SUS)?

   ○ **A.** SUS 2.0

   ○ **B.** WSUS

   ○ **C.** SUS+

   ○ **D.** Enhanced SUS

4. What is the best method to make sure that all clients are receiving updates from the WSUS server?

   ○ **A.** Modify the registry on each client computer.

   ○ **B.** Modify the login script to execute the WSUS.EXE //Servername.

   ○ **C.** Enable the WSUS server by using DHCP options.

   ○ **D.** Use group policies.

5. If you do not want an update to be sent to a workstation using WSUS, what do you need to do?

   ○ **A.** Don't approve the update.

   ○ **B.** Right-click the update on the workstation's Add/Remove Programs and specify the Deny Update permission.

○ **C.** Use your firewall to block the update.

○ **D.** Send an email to Microsoft not to release the patch.

6. The WSUS administrative website can be found where?

○ **A.** `http://localhost/WSUS`

○ **B.** `http://`*servername*`/WSUS`, where *servername* is the DNS name of the server on which WSUS is installed

○ **C.** `http://`*servername*`/WSUSAdmin`, where *servername* is the DNS name of the server on which WSUS is installed

○ **D.** `http://update.microsoft.com`

Answers to Exam Prep Questions

1. **Answer A is correct.** To minimize the size of disk space, you can specify the locale, which version of software, and which type of updates will be updated. To minimize the size of disk space used, only download what is needed. The option in answer B does not exist, and option C would not automatically download and install updates. Answer D has nothing to do with automatic updates.

2. **Answer A is correct.** The `http://update.microsoft.com` website is a site that allows users to scan their own computers and choose which updates to install and download. The website in answer A enables you to download Microsoft software, not to download and install updates. The website in answer C enables you to download WSUS and explains what WSUS is. The website in Answer D discusses security in general but does not perform updates.

3. **Answer B is correct.** SUS is no longer available from Microsoft. It has been replaced by WSUS, which offers more control and more updates. Answers A, C, and D do not exist.

4. **Answer D is correct.** The easiest way to configure users to use a WSUS server is to create a group policy. Answer A is incorrect because configuring each user's Registry individually is time-consuming. Answer B and C do not exist as commands or options.

5. **Answer A is correct.** By default, you must approve the updates before they are sent to the workstations using the WSUS administrative website. Answers B, C, and D options do not exist.

6. **Answer C is correct.** Answer A is incorrect because the localhost will work only if you are logged on to the server that has WSUS. Answer B is the address that will be used to receive updates, not to access the administrative console. Answer D is incorrect because that is the Microsoft update site, not the WSUS site.

Need to Know More?

1. For more information about WSUS, including overview and a step-by-step guide, visit the following website: `http://www.microsoft.com/windowsserversystem/updateservices/default.mspx`

2. For more information about patch management, visit the following website: `http://www.microsoft.com/technet/security/topics/patchmanagement.mspx`

Securing Windows Server 2003

Terms you'll need to understand:

✓ Security

✓ Defense-in-depth model

✓ Written security policy

✓ Hardening

✓ Stateful firewall

✓ Firewall

✓ Microsoft Baseline Security Analyzer

Techniques/concepts you'll need to master

✓ Describing the Defense-in-Depth model as it relates to securing an organization.

✓ Physically securing a system.

✓ Describing the importance of keeping your system up to date.

✓ Describing the methods to harden Windows Server 2003 machines.

✓ Listing the features of the Windows firewall.

✓ Installing and running the Microsoft Baseline Security analyzer to identify security problems.

Security is a high concern and a major responsibility for network administrators. When you, as a network administrator, examine your network environment, you need to assess the risks you currently face, determine an acceptable level of risk, and maintain risk at or below that level. Risks are reduced by increasing the security of your network environment. This chapter looks at how to secure Windows Server 2003.

Security Challenges

Need to know is a basic security concept that says information should be limited to only those individuals who require it. When planning for how you assign the rights and permissions to the network resources, follow these two main rules:

▶ Give the rights and permissions for the user to do his job.

▶ Don't give any additional rights and permissions that a user does not need.

Although you want to keep these resources secure, you want to make sure that the users can easily get what they need. For example, give users access to the necessary files, and give them only the permissions they need. If they need to read a document but don't need to make changes to it, they need to have only the read permission. When you give a person or group only the required amount of access and nothing more, this is known as the rule of *least privilege*.

As a general rule, the higher the level of security in an organization, the more costly it is to implement security measures. Unfortunately, at a higher level of security, the functionality of the network might be reduced. Sometimes, extra levels of security result in systems that are too complex for users. For example, if the authentication process in a system is too complex, some customers will not bother to use the system or will create unintended weaknesses in the system by writing passwords down, or teams will share a single user ID so that the system can remain logged in during the work day. Either of these consequences will fundamentally negate any security procedures created by administrators, so it is often wiser to institute security measures that make sense and are appropriate for the work environment in which they are used.

If you compare security threats between small and medium-sized organizations, you will notice some differences. Small and medium-sized organizations typically have the following:

▶ Fewer formal procedures and fewer resources devoted to security.

▶ Because the organization has a more limited budget, servers often have a variety of roles, which give a larger attack surface.

- Limited resources to implement security solutions.

- Lack of security expertise.

- Use of older systems that might not offer enhanced or up-to-date security.

No matter the size of the organization, you should be aware that security breaches often happen because of the following:

- Many computers do not have updated antivirus software.

- Spyware infects many computers, which often causes slow performance, unreliable computers, and further security breaches.

- Many organizations do have not have a plan to keep their system's up-to-date security patches or do not apply updates because they are afraid that it will break other applications.

- Internal or accidental threats make up a high percentage of attacks.

Defense-in-Depth Model

In addition to authentication, when building a defense, you should use a layered approach, called the defense-in-depth model, which includes securing the network infrastructure, the communication protocols, servers, applications that run on the server, and the file system. When you configure a strong layered defense, an intruder has to break through several layers to reach his or her targets.

The defense-in-depth model includes the following two base layers:

- *Policies, procedures, and awareness layer*—The layer that guides all of the other layers is the layer that includes security policies, security procedures, and security education programs for users.

- *Physical security layer*—The layer that prevents intruders from physically accessing servers and network equipment. It includes security guards, locks, and tracking devices.

On top of the base layers, you will find the core layers:

- *Perimeter layer*—Firewalls and virtual private networks that limit access in and out of the network.

- *Internal network layer*—Internal network infrastructure including Network segmentation, Internet Protocol security (IPSec), and network intrusion-detection systems (NIDS).

▶ *Host layer*—The operating system/Network operating system security components, including hardening practices, strong authentication methods, update management tools, and host-based intrusion detection systems (HIDS).

▶ *Application layer*—Application security components, including application hardening practices and antivirus and anti-spyware software.

▶ *Data layer*—Access to data files and databases, including using access control lists (ACLs), encryption, and the Encrypting File System (EFS).

While this exam focuses on the Windows Server 2003 operating system, you should remember that server security is only part of an effective overall security strategy. To truly secure your network, you have to look at all components of the network.

Microsoft Server Security

As you can imagine, much has to be done to secure a network and its servers. For Windows Server 2003, Microsoft has created several documents that will greatly help you to secure your system. Two key documents include

▶ *Threats and Countermeasures Guide*—A reference for all Windows security settings that provides countermeasures for specific threats against current versions of the Microsoft Windows operating systems. It provides a reference to many of the security settings that are available in the current versions of the Microsoft Windows operating systems.

▶ *Windows Server 2003 Security Guide*—Provides specific recommendations about how to harden computers that run Microsoft Windows Server 2003 with Service Pack 1 (SP1).

Physically Secure the System

Before you start securing the system using the Windows operating system, you need to physically secure the server. Therefore, the following is recommended:

▶ Store servers in a locked room. The servers should also be in a server rack that contains a lock.

▶ Disable floppy drives, Universal Serial Bus (USB) ports, and CD-ROM drives from booting on a server.

▶ Have a password to access the server Basic Input/Output System (BIOS).

You should also consider using turnstiles, video cameras, motion detectors, and any other devices that will monitor a facility. A turnstile will limit the pathway for a person entering a facility or limit the number of people entering a facility at one time. Video cameras can be used to spot security breaches and to make recordings that could be used in criminal and civil court. Motion detectors can be used to detect possible security breaches.

Service Packs and Security Fixes

Some of the recommendations discussed in these guides have already been mentioned throughout this book:

> ▶ It is important to update machines to the latest service pack and available security updates. This is because service packs are intended to make a system more secure and more stable while protecting against most attacks.

> ▶ It is also important to use group policies to harden the server and your client computers.

> ▶ You should also use group policies to implement a secure password policy to make sure that users change their passwords on a regular basis and that they are strong passwords.

> ▶ You should also implement account lockout policies to prevent intruders from guessing passwords.

Service packs are traditionally a convenient bundling of existing updates for a product. The Windows Server 2003 SP1 is more than that. Besides containing the latest updates for Windows Server 2003, it also adds new features and enhancements to Windows Server 2003 designed to enhance security, improve reliability, and simplify administration.

Windows Server 2003 SP1 includes improvements to functionality that originally shipped with Windows Server 2003. Such enhancements make a great product better and raise the security, reliability, and productivity of Windows Server 2003. Some of the key enhancements include

> ▶ Enhanced security that helps combat malicious code from launching attacks from areas of computer memory that should not run code.

> ▶ Internet Information Services (IIS) 6.0 metabase auditing that allows tracking which user accessed the metabase if it becomes corrupted.

> ▶ Stronger defaults and privilege reduction on services such as Remote Procedure Call (RPC) and Distributed Component Object Model (DCOM) by requiring greater authentication for calls of these services.

▶ Windows Firewall is the successor to the Internet Connection Firewall. Windows Firewall is a host (software) firewall.

▶ Security Configuration Wizard (SCW) that asks users questions about the role their servers fill, and then stops all services and blocks ports that aren't necessary to perform those roles.

Hardening Windows Server 2003

As described in the Windows Server 2003 Security Guide, you should disable services that are not required. Any service or application is a potential point of attack. Therefore, disable or remove all unneeded services and applications. If you are not using pre-Windows 2000 clients, you can also disable older authentication methods such as LAN Manager and NTLMv1 authentication and storage of LAN Manager hashes.

Other items that you should consider are

▶ Renaming the built-in Administrator account.

▶ Disabling the Guest account. If not, consider renaming the guest account.

▶ Assigning long and complex passwords or passphrases to the built-in Administrator and Guest accounts.

▶ Using scripts or third-party utilities to periodically verify local passwords on all workstations and servers in the enterprise. Note: MBSA offers some of these tools, which will be discussed later in this chapter.

▶ Using different passwords for the built-in Administrator and Guest accounts on each server.

▶ Using restricted groups to limit the membership of administrative groups.

▶ Restricting the users who can log on to the servers locally.

▶ Denying logons using Terminal Services for the Built-In Administrator, Support_388945a0, Guest accounts, and service accounts other than the system service accounts.

▶ Not configuring a service to log on by using a domain account. Instead, use a local account for each service.

▶ Using NTFS permissions to secure files and folders.

Windows Firewall

Windows Firewall is a software-based, stateful host firewall that is included with Microsoft Windows XP Service Pack 2 and Microsoft Windows Server 2003 Service Pack 1. The features of the Windows Firewall include

- ▶ A stateful firewall keeps track of traffic conversations so that it can keep track of what traffic is allowed in from the outside, preventing unsolicited traffic.

- ▶ If you enable audit logging, audit events are logged in the security events logs. By monitoring the security logs, you can quickly react to attacks on your network.

- ▶ You can configure the port to receive only network traffic from a source network address or a network subnet.

- ▶ If you discover a security issue in one or more service or applications, you can switch into a client-only mode that prevents unsolicited inbound traffic without having to reconfigure the firewall; all static ports are closed and all connections are dropped.

- ▶ Like most firewalls, you can use a Windows Firewall exceptions list that allows you to accept connections automatically even if they are unsolicited.

- ▶ Because it is a Windows component, it can be configured with Group Policies including defining program exceptions, allowing ICMP (used by the ping and tracert commands), prohibiting notifications, allowing file and printer sharing exceptions, and allowing logging.

Although the Firewall software is a great tool, it can be a hindrance in some situations. If you have a network application that is having problems with communications, those problems might be caused by the firewall on the server or the workstation. Therefore, you will have to establish some exceptions or turn off the firewall so that the network application will work.

Microsoft Baseline Security Analyzer

As part of Microsoft's Strategic Technology Protection Program, and in response to direct customer need for a streamlined method of identifying common security misconfigurations including missing security patches, blank passwords and other forms of weak passwords, and unnecessary services, Microsoft developed the Microsoft Baseline Security Analyzer (MBSA). The MBSA includes a graphical and command-line interface that can perform local or remote scans of

Windows systems. MBSA runs on Windows 2000, Windows Server 2003, and Windows XP systems Internet Information Services (IIS) 4.0, 5.0, and 6.0, SQL Server 7.0, 2000 and 2005, Internet Explorer 5.01 and later, and Office 2000 and later. MBSA creates and stores individual XML security reports for each computer scanned and displays the reports in the graphical user interface in HTML (see Figure 20.1).

To download MBSA, visit the following website: `http://www.microsoft.com/technet/security/tools/mbsahome.mspx`.

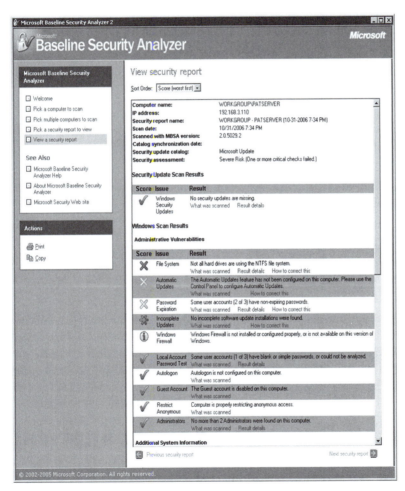

FIGURE 20.1 A Microsoft Baseline Security Analyzer report.

Exam Prep Questions

1. You are the network administrator for your company. You have Windows Server 2003 and Windows XP computers. You would like to verify the security settings to make sure that your systems are secure. What tool can you use to quickly scan your systems that you manage?

   ○ **A.** Microsoft Baseline Security Analyzer (MBSA)

   ○ **B.** Security Configuration and Analysis console

   ○ **C.** gpresult.exe

   ○ **D.** Resultant Set of Policy console in planning mode

2. Which of the following is included in Windows Server 2003 SP1?

   ○ **A.** MBSA

   ○ **B.** WSUS

   ○ **C.** Windows firewall

   ○ **D.** Administrative Tools 2.5

3. Why is it important to have the most up-to-date service packs and security patches? (Choose two answers.)

   ○ **A.** To make your machine more resistant against viruses and other forms of malware

   ○ **B.** To help keep hackers out of your system

   ○ **C.** To make your system legal

   ○ **D.** To test your machine against RPC attacks

4. Which of the following are not recommended hardening procedures?

   ○ **A.** Rename the administrator.

   ○ **B.** Use NTFS on your machine.

   ○ **C.** Restrict who has the log on local right.

   ○ **D.** Disable all service accounts.

5. Which of the following are recommended methods to physically secure your system?

   ○ **A.** Use locked doors.

   ○ **B.** Use a password for a folder.

   ○ **C.** Place passwords on your floppy disks and CD drives.

   ○ **D.** Use strong passwords.

6. Why are written security policies so important?

   ○ **A.** They give proof of who to prosecute if an intruder is detected.

   ○ **B.** They list who are the administrators of your network.

   ○ **C.** They provide a foundation that helps guide an organization in developing sound security practices.

   ○ **D.** They specify the newest viruses.

7. What model describes several security mechanisms to protect network resources? If one mechanism is compromised, several other mechanisms are used to protect the resources.

   ○ **A.** LaPadula Model

   ○ **B.** Defense-in-Depth Model

   ○ **C.** Mandatory access control model

   ○ **D.** Role-based access control model

Answers to Exam Prep Questions

1. **Answer A is correct.** Microsoft Baseline Security Analyzer (MBSA) can be used to scan your own computer or other remote computers for any kind of security problem, including password security, disk security, account security, and security patches. Answer B is incorrect because it is used to compare security settings within group policies. MBSA does more in checking security settings and weaknesses. Answers C and D are incorrect because gpresult.exe and Resultant Set of Policy are used to give you the overall effect of group policies.

2. **Answer C is correct.** Windows firewall is available in Windows Server 2003 SP1. MBSA and WSUS are available free from Microsoft. Answers A and B are incorrect because MBSA and WSUS are not included with SP1. Answer D is incorrect because Administrative Tools 2.5 does not exist.

3. **Answers A and B are correct.** Security patches are essential to keep your system secure. They will make your system more resistant against viruses and prevent intruders from

accessing your machine. Answer C is incorrect because service packs and security patches do not make a system legal. Answer D is incorrect because although it might make your system more resistant against RPC attacks, it does not test your machine.

4. **Answer D is correct.** Answer D is correct because it is recommended that you use service accounts to run certain applications that are running in the background. Renaming the administrator (answer A) and making sure that you use NTFS so that you can assign NTFS permissions (answer B) and who can log on locally (answer C) are all important steps in hardening your machine. Because you will most likely have applications or services that need access to your network, it is best to create service accounts and run those applications and services running under the service account. Therefore, you should not disable your service accounts. You should disable any unused service accounts.

5. **Answer A is correct.** Of these answers, only locked doors will physically secure your system. If a hacker can physically access a server, he can bypass most security mechanisms, including using passwords. Answers B and C are incorrect because you cannot use a password for folders or for floppy disks and CD drives.

6. **Answer C is correct.** Written security policies enable an organization to develop sound security practices. They describe the steps taken if an intrusion is detected. They also specify methods used in protecting your systems from viruses. Answer A is incorrect because written security policies do not give proof of who to prosecute if an intruder is detected. Answer B is incorrect because they should not list the administrators of your network. Answer D is incorrect because security policies do not specify the newest viruses.

7. **Answer B is correct.** The Defense-in-Depth model is used to establish several layers of security. If one layer is compromised, the attacker or intruder must break through additional layers to get to the network resources. The LaPadula, mandatory access control model, and role-based access control models are models that specify how resources are controlled. Answers A, C, and D are incorrect because they describe access models.

Need to Know More?

For more information about security with Windows Server 2003 and other Microsoft products, visit the following website: `http://www.microsoft.com/security/default.mspx`.

You should also search for and download the Threats and Countermeasures Guide and Windows Server 2003 Security Guide from Microsoft.com. These and many other useful documents can be found at `http://www.microsoft.com/technet/security/guidance/serversecurity.mspx`.

You can also refer to Ben Smith and Brian Komar, *Microsoft Security Resource Kit, Second Edition*. Redmond, WA: Microsoft Press, 2005.

21

CHAPTER TWENTY-ONE

Practice Exam 1

Now it's time to put to the test the knowledge that you've learned from reading this book! Write down your answers to the following questions on a separate sheet of paper. You will be able to take this sample test multiple times this way. After you answer all the questions, compare your answers with the correct answers in Chapter 22, "Answers to Practice Exam 1." The answer keys for both exams immediately follow each Practice Exam chapter. Good luck!

Exam Questions

1. What Windows 2003 Server utility program can you use as a non-administrator to troubleshoot hardware that does not function correctly?

   ○ **A.** Hardware Troubleshooter

   ○ **B.** Add or Remove Programs

   ○ **C.** Add New Hardware Wizard

   ○ **D.** `msconfig.exe`

2. As an administrator, you want to be sure that no unsigned drivers are installed on your computer. What steps can you take?

   ○ **A.** Choose Block and also mark the Make This Action the System Default check box in the Driver Signing Options dialog box from the System Properties window.

   ○ **B.** Choose the Ignore option and also mark the Make This Action the System Default check box in the Driver Signing Options dialog box from the System Properties window.

   ○ **C.** Choose Ignore in the Driver Signing Options dialog box from the System Properties window.

   ○ **D.** Choose Block in the Driver Signing Options dialog box from the System Properties window.

3. Morgan is trying to install a new network scanner on the company's Windows Server 2003 computer, but it is not allowing her to begin the installation. The scanner driver was not included with Windows, but it has a Designed for Windows logo, and she has the CD containing the signed driver. What is the most likely cause of the installation problem?

   ○ **A.** She is not a member of the Power Users group.

   ○ **B.** She is not a member of the Administrators group.

   ○ **C.** The scanner is not approved by Microsoft.

   ○ **D.** The software was written for Windows 3.1.

4. Gina has been given the task of bringing another Active Directory domain online in her corporate network. She does not have enough time to purchase a new server, but she does have several computers running Windows Server 2003, Web Edition, that are underutilized at the moment. She decides to use one of them as a domain controller (DC) for the new domain but cannot promote it. Why not?

     ○ **A.** The computer does not have enough RAM to become a DC.

     ○ **B.** The paging file is not on the boot drive, which is a requirement for DCs.

     ○ **C.** Only Windows Server 2003, Enterprise Edition, can be a DC.

     ○ **D.** Windows Server 2003, Web Edition, cannot be a DC.

5. Your company's server is beginning to experience slowdowns that you associate with having only a single processor. To alleviate the problems, you install a second processor in the computer. What application can you run in Windows Server 2003 to enable the second processor?

     ○ **A.** `procup.exe` in the `\support` directory of the Windows Server 2003 CD-ROM

     ○ **B.** Device Manager from the System Control Panel

     ○ **C.** Processor MMC in the Computer Management MMC

     ○ **D.** `setup.exe` from the Windows Server 2003 CD-ROM, choosing the Upgrade to Multiple Processors option

6. A Windows Server 2003 computer in your office has a special video-editing card installed in a PCI slot. This card is vital to the operation of your company. You've been having some minor problems with the card, and you installed a new set of drivers that the manufacturer just released. Unfortunately, the card is now corrupting all the data it processes. What is the best way to solve this problem?

     ○ **A.** In Device Manager, go into the properties of the device, choose the Drivers tab, and select Roll Back Driver.

     ○ **B.** Reinstall the original driver from the CD-ROM included with the device.

     ○ **C.** Download and install the latest beta driver from the manufacturer's website.

     ○ **D.** Manually delete the files associated with the new driver.

7. Mike works in a small company that has recently acquired a new server preinstalled with Windows Server 2003, Standard Edition. The server was purchased with a CD/RW drive so that all employees could copy project data files to the server and then burn archive CDs. Mike's IT department made sure that the drive was on the Hardware Compatibility List when purchasing the server. Mike is attempting to burn an archive CD, but when he right-clicks on the server's CD/RW drive, he does not see Write These Files to CD as a choice. What does he need to do to enable CD burning on Windows Server 2003?

     ○ **A.** Select CD Burning from Add/Remove Windows Components inside the Add/Remove Programs Control Panel.

○ **B.** Enable CD burning in the local security policy of the Windows Server 2003 computer.

○ **C.** Enable the IMAPI CD-Burning COM Service in the Services MMC snap-in to start automatically.

○ **D.** Update the burner's firmware to a version compatible with Windows Server 2003.

8. While updating your Windows Server 2003 computer, you decide to install a new video driver. Upon rebooting, your monitor reports "Signal out of range." You want to maintain the new driver, but you need to access the display. How can you gain access to the display again so you can change the video settings to functional settings for your environment?

○ **A.** Hold down Ctrl+Alt+Tab and press 1 to force the computer to switch to 640 × 480 resolution.

○ **B.** While booting the machine, press F8 to gain access to the advanced boot menu. Choose Enable VGA Mode to boot into 640 × 480 with 16 colors so that you can fix the video settings.

○ **C.** While booting the machine, press F8 to gain access to the advanced boot menu. Choose Safe Mode so that you can roll the driver back to the previous version.

○ **D.** Hold down V on the keyboard as the computer boots to enable VGA mode.

9. Johanna has a maintenance program that she needs to run on her Windows Server 2003 computer once per month. The application is extremely resource intensive, and Johanna would like to have as few applications and services loaded as possible when she runs the application. What feature of Windows Server 2003 will help Johanna configure her server to have very few services and devices loaded when she needs to run her application?

○ **A.** Hardware profiles

○ **B.** User profiles

○ **C.** Hardware configuration

○ **D.** Device selection

10. A catastrophic failure causes you to lose two drives in your eight-drive RAID-5 volume. Choose all the tasks related to recovering the data and regaining fault tolerance. (Choose two.)

○ **A.** Replace one drive and allow the rebuild process to begin.

○ **B.** Replace the two failed drives.

○ **C.** Move the remaining drives into a dedicated recovery server and rebuild the array.

○ **D.** Restore the information from your most recent tape.

○ **E.** In Logical Disk Management, right-click the failed volume and choose Restore from Shadow Copy.

11. Windows Server 2003 supports legacy file-system types, such as FAT and FAT32, as well as the latest NTFS file system. Which partition schemes does Windows Server 2003 support on a single IDE hard drive, if you have one extended partition on the same drive? (Choose two answers.)

○ **A.** Two primary partitions

○ **B.** Four primary partitions

○ **C.** Three simple volumes

○ **D.** One simple volume and one extended partition

○ **E.** Three primary partitions

12. You are the network administrator for your domain. On your domain, you have 15 Windows Server 2003 computers and 2,500 Windows XP Professional computers. All servers are located in the Servers OU, and all Windows XP computers are located in Client OU. When you install and configure Windows Server Update Services (WSUS) on Server1, you want to configure the client computers to obtain the updates from Server1. What should you do?

○ **A.** Create a group policy named WSUS and link it to the Client OU. Open the WSUS GPO and enable the Configure Automatic Update policy to automatically download updates.

○ **B.** Create a Group Policy object (GPO) named WSUS and link it to the Clients OU. Open the WSUS GPO and enable the Specify intranet Microsoft update service location policy to use http://Server1 as the value for the update server.

○ **C.** Create a group policy object (GPO) named WSUS and link to the domain. Open the WSUS GPO and enable the Specific intranet Microsoft update service location policy to use http://server1 as the value for the update server.

○ **D.** Create a Group Policy object (GPO) named WSUS and link it to the domain. Open the WSUS GPO and enable the Configure Automatic Update policy to automatically download updates.

13. Which of the following is not a true statement about striped volumes in Windows Server 2003?

- ○ **A.** Striped volumes provide no fault tolerance for data stored on them.
- ○ **B.** Striped volumes may be created onto a maximum of 32 disks.
- ○ **C.** Striped volumes may be extended to add more storage space.
- ○ **D.** Striped volumes provide better performance than simple volumes.

14. On a multiboot computer with Windows Server 2003, Windows XP Professional, and Windows NT 4.0 Server with SP6, what types of storage volumes are natively accessible to all of these operating systems? (Choose three.)

- ○ **A.** Primary partition formatted with FAT
- ○ **B.** Extended partition formatted with FAT32
- ○ **C.** Extended partition formatted with NTFS
- ○ **D.** Simple volume formatted with FAT32
- ○ **E.** Stripe set formatted with NTFS
- ○ **F.** RAID-5 volume formatted with NTFS
- ○ **G.** Logical drive formatted with FAT

15. What is the preferred method for running the Disk Defragmenter utility on Windows Server 2003?

- ○ **A.** Log on to the computer as a user with local administrative privileges and run Disk Defragmenter.
- ○ **B.** Log on to a different computer as a domain administrator and launch the defragmenter remotely to ensure the least performance impact.
- ○ **C.** Log on to the computer as a user without administrative privileges, right-click the Disk Defragmenter icon and choose Run as, and type in the credentials of a user account with administrative privileges.
- ○ **D.** Log on to the computer as an administrative user using Terminal Services and launch Disk Defragmenter.

16. Which of the following defines the system partition in Windows Server 2003?

- ○ **A.** A simple volume on a dynamic disk that contains the \Windows folder
- ○ **B.** A spanned volume on a basic disk that contains the boot files such as ntldr, ntdetect.com, and boot.ini
- ○ **C.** A partition on a basic disk that contains the boot files such as ntldr, ntdetect.com, and boot.ini
- ○ **D.** A partition on a dynamic disk that contains the \Windows folder

17. After moving a hard disk that contains data from an old Windows Server 2003 computer to a new one, it is listed as Foreign in Disk Management. What can you do to make the data accessible in the new server?

- ○ **A.** In Disk Management, right-click on the disk and choose Import Foreign Disks.

- ○ **B.** In Device Manager, enter the properties of the disk and choose Activate This Disk.

- ○ **C.** In Disk Management, right-click on the disk and choose Activate This Disk.

- ○ **D.** In Device Manager, enter the properties of the disk and choose Import Foreign Disks.

18. You believe that one of the drives in your mirrored volume is beginning to fail. You want to break the mirror and replace the failing drive. The mirrored volume consists of the physical disks numbered 2 and 3 in Disk Management. The drive letter assigned to the volume is H:. You want to be sure that Disk 3 retains the H: drive letter designation because it is the good disk and it will be retained. You also want to retain the data on the possibly failing disk as a failsafe option in case problems arise during the replacement process. How can you accomplish this? (Choose three.)

- ○ **A.** Right-click Disk 3 and choose Remove Mirror.

- ○ **B.** Right-click Disk 3 and choose Break Mirrored Volume.

- ○ **C.** Right-click Disk 2 and choose Break Mirrored Volume.

- ○ **D.** Right-click the remaining H: drive, choose Add Mirror, and then choose a dynamic disk with enough unallocated space.

- ○ **E.** Ensure the new mirrored volume reports a status of Healthy.

- ○ **F.** Right-click Disk 2 and choose Remove Mirror.

- ○ **G.** Right-click on the remaining H: drive and choose Add Mirror, choosing another simple volume that is the same size or larger than the volume you are mirroring.

19. Which of the following command-line tools can you use to remove a user from Active Directory?

- ○ **A.** dsquery
- ○ **B.** dsrm
- ○ **C.** dsmove
- ○ **D.** dsadd
- ○ **E.** dsget
- ○ **F.** net user

20. You are the network administrator for your Active Directory domain. All domain con-trollers run Windows Server 2003. Each domain controller has a locally attached tape drive. The backup process must be able to fulfill the following requirements:

> ▶ If the server fails, you must recover the System.

> ▶ The system configuration and all current dynamic disk configurations must be backed up.

> ▶ Other data partitions do not need to be backed up.

What should you do?

○ **A.** Use the Backup utility to back up the system files and to create an Automated System Recovery (ASR) disk.

○ **B.** Use the Backup utility to back up the contents of all mounted drives.

○ **C.** Use the Backup utility to back up only the System State data.

○ **D.** Use the Copy command to copy C:\windows and its subfolders to a shared folder on the network.

○ **E.** Use the Xcopy command to copy C:\windows and its subfolders to a shared folder on the network.

21. Which networking components must be present on the network to install Active Directory? (Choose two.)

○ **A.** Windows Internet Name Service (WINS)

○ **B.** Domain Name System (DNS)

○ **C.** Kerberos

○ **D.** Remote Procedure Call (RPC)

○ **E.** Transmission Control Protocol/Internet Protocol (TCP/IP)

○ **F.** NetBIOS

22. You plan to raise the functional level of your Active Directory forest to Windows Server 2003. What must you do to fulfill the requirements necessary to perform this upgrade? (Choose two.)

○ **A.** Upgrade all the workstations to Windows 2000 Professional or Windows XP Professional.

○ **B.** Upgrade all Windows NT 4.0 member servers to Windows Server 2003.

○ **C.** First upgrade the forest to Windows 2000 native mode.

○ **D.** Make sure that all DCs are running Windows 2003 Server.

    ○ **E.** Raise the domain functional level on all DCs to at least Windows 2003 native mode.

    ○ **F.** Raise the domain functional level of all the domains in the forest to at least Windows 2000 native mode.

23. How can you identify a prestaged computer account in Active Directory? (Choose two.)

    ○ **A.** By its fully qualified domain name (FQDN)

    ○ **B.** By its TCP/IP address

    ○ **C.** By its computer name

    ○ **D.** By its globally unique identifier (GUID)

    ○ **E.** By its security identifier (SID)

    ○ **F.** By its universally unique identifier (UUID)

24. You have reset the computer account password, but now the user can no longer log on to the domain. What must you do to fix it?

    ○ **A.** Reset the user account password.

    ○ **B.** Rejoin the computer to the domain.

    ○ **C.** Reboot the workstation.

    ○ **D.** Reset the security identifier.

25. Users on Windows 98 computers who log on to a Windows NT Server 4.0 domain need to be able to access shared folders and printers within a Windows Server 2003 Active Directory environment. What must be in place for this access to occur?

    ○ **A.** A one-way trust

    ○ **B.** The `dsclient.exe` utility installed on all Windows 98 computers

    ○ **C.** The Kerberos authentication protocol

    ○ **D.** DNS configured on the Windows 98 computers

26. For a domain set at the Windows 2000 mixed domain functional level, which type of group scope can contain accounts and global groups from any domain in the forest?

    ○ **A.** Universal groups

    ○ **B.** Domain local groups

    ○ **C.** Security groups

    ○ **D.** Global groups

27. A user complains that she is not able to access a resource that she once could. You suspect that it is a group-policy issue. What is the best way to determine whether group policy is the problem?

- ○ **A.** Check the group policy for the OU the user is in.
- ○ **B.** Use `dsquery`.
- ○ **C.** Use `dsget`.
- ○ **D.** Run the RSoP Wizard.

28. MartyB belongs to the Domain Admins group within the CORINTH.LOCAL domain. The Domain Admins group is a group that belongs to the local Administrators group on Windows XP workstations, which are also joined to the CORINTH domain. Which `runas` command (or commands) does MartyB need to run to execute the Computer Management console with domain administrative credentials? (Choose two.)

- ○ **A.** `runas /user:MARTYB "mmc %windir%\system32\compmgmt.msc"`
- ○ **B.** `runas /user:CORINTH\MARTYB "mmc %windir%\system32\compmgmt.msc"`
- ○ **C.** `runas /user:MARTYB@CORINTH.LOCAL "mmc %windir%\system32\compmgmt.msc"`
- ○ **D.** `runas /user:LOCAL\MARTYB "mmc %windir%\system32\compmgmt.msc"`
- ○ **E.** `runas /user:Administrator\MARTYB "mmc %windir%\system32\compmgmt.msc"`

29. You are a network administrator for a clothing manufacturer headquartered in Sacramento, California. The manufacturing facilities are located in Reno, Nevada, and St. Paul, Minnesota. Both manufacturing facilities are connected to the corporate office by a VPN tunnel over the Internet. You are working from the Sacramento location and you were sent an email request for Remote Assistance (RA) from the local technician in St. Paul. When you attempted to make an RA connection to a Windows 2003 server located in St. Paul, the connection fails. What are two possible reasons for the failure? (Choose two.)

- ○ **A.** The RA invitation has expired.
- ○ **B.** RA has not been enabled on the server.
- ○ **C.** TCP port 3389 is blocked on the firewall.
- ○ **D.** UDP port 3389 is blocked on the firewall.
- ○ **E.** You do not have administrative permissions on the server.

30. You are a Windows Server 2003 network administrator running Terminal Services in Application Server mode. After a period of 120 days, your Terminal Server users complain that they can no longer access the Terminal Server. Upon examination of the problem, you realize that you have additional steps to finish. Each correct step is only a portion of the solution. (Choose two.)

- ○ **A.** Upgrade each client computer to Windows XP Professional or Windows 2000 Professional with SP3.

- ○ **B.** Install the proper number of Terminal Server Client Access Licenses (TSCALs).

- ○ **C.** Reboot the Terminal Server every four months.

- ○ **D.** Install a Terminal Server License Server on your network.

- ○ **E.** Uninstall Terminal Services and restore the System State from backup. Reinstall Terminal Services and ensure that the users can connect.

31. Which port needs to be open on the firewall that will enable an external user to connect to an internal Terminal Server that is listening on the default port?

- ○ **A.** TCP port 21
- ○ **B.** TCP port 8000
- ○ **C.** TCP port 3398
- ○ **D.** TCP port 3389

32. You manage two network administrators. Each administrator has left for the day, and you receive a call that a remote Windows 2003 web server is not responding to HTTP requests. You attempt to establish a connection to this server, but you receive a message that the maximum number of connections has been reached. Through investigation, you realize that your two network administrators left their sessions running. What Terminal Services tool can you use to disconnect one of the sessions so that you can use Terminal Services to connect to the remote web server?

- ○ **A.** Terminal Services Manager
- ○ **B.** Terminal Services Configuration
- ○ **C.** Terminal Services Licensing
- ○ **D.** Managing Your Server—Terminal Services Edition

33. Which Terminal Services administration tool would you use to view users, sessions, and processes for current connections running on each Terminal Server?

- ○ **A.** Active Directory Users and Computers
- ○ **B.** Terminal Services Configuration

○ **C.** Terminal Services Manager

○ **D.** Terminal Services Licensing

34. You realize that you have just sent an RA invitation by email to the wrong technician. You want the invitation to expire immediately. What steps do you need to perform to ensure that the invitation expires before the default of one hour?

○ **A.** Open the Help and Support Center, click the View Invitation Status option, select the proper Invitation, and then click the Expire button.

○ **B.** Open the Help and Support Center, click the Invite Someone to Help You option, select the proper invitation, and then click the Expire button.

○ **C.** Open the Help and Support Center, click the Invite Someone to Help You option, select the proper invitation, and then click the Delete button.

○ **D.** Open the Control Panel, click the View Invitation Status option, select the proper invitation, and then click the Expire button.

35. Under which Registry subkey will you find the Group Policy Object (GPO) settings for the Remote Assistance feature?

○ **A.** User Configuration\Administrative Templates\System\Remote Assistance

○ **B.** Computer Configuration\Administrative Templates\System\Remote Assistance

○ **C.** Computer Configuration\Windows Settings\Security Settings\Remote Assistance

○ **D.** Computer Configuration\Security Settings\System\Remote Assistance

36. As the network administrator, to better protect your network from data loss through accidental overwrites and deletions, you come up with the following strategies for Server1:

▶ Incremental backups of the server at 8:00 p.m. nightly

▶ Full backups of the server on Sundays at 12 noon

▶ Shadow Copies of Shared Folders scheduled to run twice daily at 10:00 a.m. and 3:00 p.m. for the E: drive

On Thursday, you are working on a document that you stored in the E:\SpecialDocs folder on the server. It contains sensitive information, so instead of sharing the folder, you connect to it using a Remote Desktop Connection to work on the file. You realize that you deleted some information from the file last Monday morning that you now need. Where can you find the latest copy of the document that has the information you need?

    ○ **A.** On Monday night's incremental backup tape

    ○ **B.** In the Previous Versions tab on the properties sheet for the file, as long as you connect over the network using the UNC path `\\server1\e$\ specialdocs`

    ○ **C.** On Sunday's full backup tape

    ○ **D.** In the Previous Versions tab on the properties for the file by logging on to the server locally or via Remote Desktop Connection

37. Which three files are required if you need to boot a Windows Server 2003, Web Edition, computer from a floppy disk? (Choose three.)

    ○ **A.** `ntldr`

    ○ **B.** `io.sys`

    ○ **C.** `boot.ini`

    ○ **D.** `ntdetect.com`

    ○ **E.** `boot.sys`

    ○ **F.** `bootsect.dos`

38. Which options are presented to you when you boot the server and press the F8 key to enter the Advanced Startup Options menu? (Choose three.)

    ○ **A.** Safe Mode with Recovery Console

    ○ **B.** Safe Mode with Networking Support

    ○ **C.** Safe Mode with Command Prompt

    ○ **D.** Recovery Console

    ○ **E.** Automated System Recovery (ASR)

    ○ **F.** Last Known Good Configuration

39. While you are working with another operating system on a Windows Server 2003 computer configured for dual-booting, a system-level command overwrites the boot sector. Now, whenever you boot the computer, it boots straight into the other operating system without giving you a chance to even select Windows Server 2003. You want to restore the Windows Server 2003 boot menu for choosing which operating system to run. What steps must you take? (Choose two.)

    ○ **A.** Use the Windows Server 2003 CD-ROM to boot the computer into the Recovery Console.

    ○ **B.** After booting into Windows Server 2003, be sure the operating system selection timeout is greater than zero in the System applet in the Control Panel.

○ **C.** Execute `fixboot` from the Recovery Console prompt.

○ **D.** Boot with an MS-DOS–based startup disk and execute `fdisk /mbr` to repair the master boot record.

○ **E.** Perform an ASR to repair the boot sector.

40. Marty wants to create an ASR backup of his company's Windows Server 2003 computer. He has a variety of media that he could create the backup set on. Which media will allow him to successfully recover his server with the fewest configuration changes or questions?

○ **A.** A SCSI hard drive that stores both the system and boot volumes

○ **B.** A tape drive that requires a special driver from the manufacturer

○ **C.** A write once, read many (WORM) optical drive that requires a manufacturer-provided device driver connected to the server via a SCSI cable

○ **D.** An IDE hard drive used for data storage only

41. What must your server hardware support to use Emergency Management Services (EMS) in Windows Server 2003?

○ **A.** SPCR (Serial Port Console Redirection)

○ **B.** OOBM (Out-of-Band Management)

○ **C.** NTFS (New Technology File System)

○ **D.** IPv6 (TCP/IP version 6)

42. Which disaster-recovery tools allow you to disable a service that you believe is causing your Windows Server 2003 computer to crash on a regular basis? (Choose three.)

○ **A.** Recovery Console

○ **B.** Safe Mode with Networking Support

○ **C.** ASR

○ **D.** EMS Special Administration Console (SAC)

○ **E.** Safe Mode

○ **F.** Directory Services Restore Mode

43. Vinnie is troubleshooting a startup problem on his Windows Server 2003 computer. He is able to start the computer using Safe Mode but not Safe Mode with Networking. What assumption can Vinnie make about the problem his server is having?

○ **A.** A recently installed video driver is causing the problems.

○ **B.** A recently updated network driver is causing the problems.

○ **C.** A corrupted shared folder is causing the problems.

○ **D.** A corrupted boot sector is causing the problems.

44. You want to implement Shadow Copies of Shared Folders on all your data drive volumes to help protect your users' data from accidental deletion and overwrites. You have two Windows Server 2003, Standard Edition, computers—each configured with NTFS drive volumes; you also have one Windows Server 2003, Enterprise Edition, server configured with FAT32 volumes. Additionally, you have one Windows 2000 Advanced Server computer configured with FAT32 drive volumes, and you have one Windows Server 2003, Web Edition, computer configured with dynamic disks, running NTFS. Which computers are capable of creating shadow copies? (Choose two.)

○ **A.** The Windows Server 2003, Standard Edition, computers

○ **B.** The Windows Server 2003, Enterprise Edition, computer

○ **C.** The Windows 2000 Advanced Server computer

○ **D.** The Windows 2000 Advanced Server computer after you install the Previous Versions client

○ **E.** The Windows Server 2003, Web Edition, computer

45. Using the Windows 2003 Backup Utility, which type of backup should you perform if you only want to back up those files that have their archive bits set and you do not want to have them cleared?

○ **A.** Incremental

○ **B.** Copy

○ **C.** Normal

○ **D.** Daily

○ **E.** Differential

46. Vireya is a system administrator for a large automobile manufacturer. She administers a Windows Server 2003 Active Directory domain. Both the domain and the forest are running at the Windows Server 2003 functional level. On a Thursday at 6:00 p.m., one of the member servers that controls an assembly-line robot experienced a catastrophic hard-disk crash. The server must be restored from tape backup. Based on the following backup schedule, which backup tapes does Vireya need to use to restore the server as quickly as possible?

Backup Schedule:

Monday—Incremental backup at 12:30 a.m.

Tuesday—Incremental backup at 12:30 a.m.

Wednesday—Incremental backup at 12:30 a.m.

Thursday—Incremental backup at 12:30 a.m.

Friday—Normal backup at 12:30 a.m.

- ○ **A.** Friday, Monday, Tuesday, Wednesday, Thursday
- ○ **B.** Monday, Tuesday, Wednesday, Thursday
- ○ **C.** Friday, Thursday
- ○ **D.** Friday, Wednesday
- ○ **E.** Monday, Thursday

47. You are the administrator of a Windows Server 2003 domain. You have a Windows Server 2003 member server that contains a large number of shared folders and has the following backup schedule:

Sunday—Normal backup at 1:45 a.m.

Monday—Differential backup at 1:45 a.m.

Tuesday—Differential backup at 1:45 a.m.

Wednesday—Differential backup at 1:45 a.m.

Thursday—Differential backup at 1:45 a.m.

Friday—Differential backup at 1:45 a.m.

Saturday—Differential backup at 1:45 a.m.

Thursday afternoon, you experience a hard-disk failure. Which backup tapes do you need to quickly restore this server?

- ○ **A.** Sunday, Monday, Tuesday, Wednesday, Thursday
- ○ **B.** Thursday only
- ○ **C.** Sunday and Thursday only
- ○ **D.** Friday, Saturday, Sunday, Monday, Tuesday, Wednesday, Thursday

48. Robert is the network administrator of Clamberto Enterprises, a large financial firm in Hastings, Minnesota. One Windows Server 2003 computer that Robert is responsible for runs a vital financial transaction-processing application. For disaster recovery, he uses the Windows Server 2003 Backup Utility to back up his server early each morning. Saturday night at 11 p.m., Robert receives a call from the police department informing him that his data center has been broken into. Upon Robert's inspection, he sees that his financial server is missing. For Robert, the first order of business is to get this financial server up and running as quickly as possible. He has identical hardware so that he can re-create the missing server, and fortunately, no backup tapes are missing. Robert's routine backup schedule is as follows:

Sunday—Normal backup at 1:45 a.m.

Monday—Differential backup at 1:45 a.m.

Tuesday—Incremental backup at 1:45 a.m.

Wednesday—Differential backup at 1:45 a.m.

Thursday—Incremental backup at 1:45 a.m.

Friday—Incremental backup at 1:45 a.m.

Saturday—Differential backup at 1:45 a.m.

Which backup tapes does Robert need to restore the data as quickly as possible?

- ○ **A.** Sunday, Tuesday, Thursday, Friday, and Saturday
- ○ **B.** Sunday, Monday, Wednesday, and Saturday
- ○ **C.** Sunday and Saturday
- ○ **D.** Sunday, Monday, Wednesday, and Saturday
- ○ **E.** Sunday, Monday, Tuesday, Wednesday, Thursday, Friday, and Saturday

49. You are the network administrator for a Windows Server 2003 standalone server. You are creating a backup routine that will allow for the shortest possible time to restore from the backup. You are not worried about the amount of time it takes to back up the files and folders. Assume that this server is using a Sunday through Saturday backup schedule. Which routine guarantees the quickest restore if a failure occurs on a Friday?

- ○ **A.** A normal backup on Sunday, followed by differential backups Monday through Saturday
- ○ **B.** A normal backup on Sunday, followed by incremental backups Monday through Saturday
- ○ **C.** A daily backup on Sunday, followed by differential backups Monday through Saturday
- ○ **D.** A daily backup on Sunday, followed by incremental backups Monday through Saturday
- ○ **E.** All normal backups each day

50. Which default groups allow backing up and restoring of files and folders on a Windows 2003 Server? (Choose three.)

- ○ **A.** Administrators
- ○ **B.** Account Operators
- ○ **C.** Backup Operators
- ○ **D.** Print Operators
- ○ **E.** Users
- ○ **F.** Server Operators

51. You are executing `NTBackup.exe` from the command line on a computer named Server01. Your goal is to do a normal backup of Server01 that includes the C$ administrative share and back it up to the d$ administrative share. You want to ensure that backup verification is enabled and that access is restricted to the administrator and to you, the person performing the backup operation. What command-line entry will accomplish this goal?

- ○ **A.** `ntbackup backup \\server01\c$ /J "Command Line Backup" /F \\server01\d$\backup.bkf /R:no /M normal`
- ○ **B.** `ntbackup backup \\server01\c$ /J "Command Line Backup" /F \\server01\d$\backup.bkf`
- ○ **C.** `ntbackup backup \\server01\c$ /J "Command Line Backup" /F \\server01\d$\backup.bkf /M normal /R:yes /V:yes`
- ○ **D.** `ntbackup backup \\server01\c$ /J "Command Line Backup" /F \\server01\d$\backup.bkf /V:yes /M copy`

52. Orin is unsure which components are included in a backup of the Windows 2003 System State. He made five lists of those components he believes are backed up. Which lists are correct? (Choose two.)

- ○ **A.** COM+ class registration database, SYSVOL, Active Directory database, C$ administrative share
- ○ **B.** COM+ class registration database, SYSVOL, Active Directory database, `%systemroot%\system32` folder
- ○ **C.** Active Directory database, COM+ class registration database, SYSVOL, Certificate Services database
- ○ **D.** COM+ class registration database, SYSVOL, Active Directory database, Certificate Services database, Windows Registry, `%systemdrive%` folder

○   **E.** COM+ class registration database, SYSVOL, Active Directory database, operating-system files that are protected by Windows File Protection, Windows Registry, IIS metabase

53. For Windows Server 2003 DCs, which additional event logs are added to Event Viewer? (Choose two.)

  ○   **A.** System performance

  ○   **B.** Directory Service

  ○   **C.** File Replication Service

  ○   **D.** Security

  ○   **E.** Application

  ○   **F.** DNS server

54. Event Viewer opens saved files using only which file format?

  ○   **A.** `.doc`

  ○   **B.** `.evt`

  ○   **C.** `.csv`

  ○   **D.** `.txt`

  ○   **E.** `.pdf`

55. What metric within the default configuration of System Monitor indicates good performance for Memory:Pages/Sec on a Windows Server 2003 computer?

  ○   **A.** Between 0 and 2

  ○   **B.** Between 10 and 30

  ○   **C.** Between 0 and 20

  ○   **D.** Between 20 and 40

56. To get the most accurate results when measuring a computer's performance, which best practice should you implement?

  ○   **A.** Use Task Manager.

  ○   **B.** Use System Monitor in default mode.

  ○   **C.** Log the information.

  ○   **D.** Monitor the computer remotely.

57. Which default group allows members to manage performance counters, logs, and alerts on the local computer or, on servers within the domain, both interactively (locally) and remotely?

- ○ **A.** Performance Monitor Users group
- ○ **B.** Power Users group
- ○ **C.** Performance Log Users group
- ○ **D.** Local Administrators group

58. You use the Event Viewer primarily for viewing what type of data?

- ○ **A.** Network data
- ○ **B.** Performance data
- ○ **C.** Logged data
- ○ **D.** Real-time data

59. You want to run an application after an event exceeds your predefined threshold. Which monitoring component should you use?

- ○ **A.** Performance Monitor
- ○ **B.** Counter log
- ○ **C.** Trace log
- ○ **D.** Alert

60. As a network administrator, you are responsible for ensuring a high level of perform-ance for the network and the servers for all the users in your company. What must you do first to be able to document changes in the future that might degrade the perform-ance of your network over time?

- ○ **A.** Save the event logs in the .csv format.
- ○ **B.** Establish a baseline.
- ○ **C.** Set up performance logs at peak usage times.
- ○ **D.** Set up trace logs.

Answers to Practice Exam 1

1. A	**21.** B, E	**41.** A
2. A	**22.** D, F	**42.** A, B, E
3. B	**23.** D, F	**43.** B
4. D	**24.** B	**44.** A, E
5. B	**25.** A	**45.** E
6. A	**26.** B	**46.** A
7. C	**27.** D	**47.** C
8. B	**28.** B, C	**48.** A
9. A	**29.** A, C	**49.** E
10. B, D	**30.** B, D	**50.** A, C, F
11. A, E	**31.** D	**51.** C
12. B	**32.** A	**52.** C, E
13. C	**33.** C	**53.** B, C
14. A, C, G	**34.** A	**54.** B
15. C	**35.** B	**55.** C
16. C	**36.** B, C	**56.** D
17. A	**37.** A, C, D	**57.** C
18. B, D, E	**38.** B, C, F	**58.** C
19. B	**39.** A, C	**59.** D
20. A	**40.** D	**60.** B

Question 1

Answer A is correct because the Hardware Troubleshooter makes suggestions based on user input and is an extension of the Windows Server 2003 Help and Support Center. The Add New Hardware Wizard is limited because it will try to install drivers for a device that does not already have them. Answer B is incorrect because the Add or Remove Programs applet does not diagnose or fix hardware problems. Answer D is incorrect because the `msconfig` utility must be run by a member of the Administrators group, and it manages system-configuration settings, not hardware and device drivers.

Question 2

Answer A is correct. On the Hardware tab of the System Control Panel, you click the Driver Signing button to get into Driver Signing options. Your choices at this point are Ignore, meaning allow any driver; Warn, which is the default; and Block, which stops all nonsigned driver installation. Also, making it the system default imposes your choice on all the other users of the computer. Answer B is not correct because Ignore allows all drivers. Answer C is not correct because the location of the Driver Signing options is incorrect. Answer D is not correct because Make This Action the System Default is not chosen; the next user to log on could change the setting herself.

Question 3

Answer B is correct. Drivers that are signed by Microsoft typically install for any user without a problem, except in a few special cases. If the drivers are not already on the computer or extra configuration is necessary, for instance, you must be a member of the Administrators group to complete the installation. Answer A is not correct because the Power Users group does not give you the proper permissions for installing hardware. Answer C is not correct because the question states that it is. Answer D is not correct because the logo program and signed drivers are recent developments. If the software were truly developed for Windows 3.1, the installation would stop because software developed for Windows 3.1 will not run on Windows Server 2003.

Question 4

Answer D is correct. Microsoft does not allow Windows Server 2003, Web Edition, to act as a domain controller (DC); it can be a member server, but not a DC. Answer A is not correct because if the computer has enough RAM to run Windows Server 2003, it has enough RAM to be a DC, although busy DCs can

benefit from more RAM. Answer B is not correct because there is no requirement for the placement of the paging file. Answer C is not correct because
Standard Edition can also be a DC.

Question 5

Answer B is correct. To enable multiple processors in Windows Server 2003,
you must update the hardware abstraction layer (HAL) to use the new processors. You can change the HAL by changing the "computer driver" in the Device
Manager from uniprocessor to multiprocessor. Answer A is not correct because
such an application does not exist. Answer C is not correct because although you
can access the Device Manager from Computer Management, there is no
Processor Microsoft Management Console. Answer D is not correct because
you do not need to rerun Windows Server 2003 installation at all for the
upgrade to be successful.

Question 6

Answer A is correct. Windows Server 2003 includes the Roll Back Driver function first introduced in Windows XP. It gives you the ability to get back to a previous version of the driver simply by clicking a button. Answer B is not correct
because, although it might work, it is not the best solution. Complications could
arise from installing the old driver over the new driver that will not arise from
simply rolling back. Answer C is not correct because in a production environment, beta drivers are never the best solution and might introduce more problems than they solve. You should definitely communicate your problems with
this latest driver to the manufacturer, however, so it can work on a solution.
Answer D is not correct because of the extreme danger it poses to completely
disabling your device, if not your server. Device drivers are too intertwined with
the core operating system and Registry to attempt manual removal.

Question 7

Answer C is correct. On Windows Server 2003, the CD-burning service is disabled by default because most environments won't attempt to burn from a server. For those computers that do need this ability, simply enable the service, start
it, and use the burner. Answer A is not correct because burning is installed by
default, just not enabled; it actually is not available as a component to add or
remove. Answer B is not correct because burning is not controlled via the local
security policy. Answer D is not correct because the machine was preinstalled
with Windows Server 2003, and the drive is on the Hardware Compatibility
List, so compatibility is not an issue.

Question 8

Answer B is correct. VGA Mode is the lowest common denominator supported by virtually all computers, video cards, and monitors. By booting into VGA Mode, you can set a resolution, color depth, and refresh rate applicable to your hardware and reboot using the new settings. Answer A is not correct because the key combination does not function. Answer C is not correct because it does not allow you to maintain the new driver, which is a requirement of the question. Answer D is not correct because holding down V does not enable VGA mode.

Question 9

Answer A is correct. Hardware profiles give you the ability to choose a "set" of drivers and services to load at boot time. If your server is configured with multiple hardware profiles, and it cannot determine which profile is correct at boot time, it prompts you to choose. Johanna can create a new hardware profile, boot into it, disable all services and devices her application and the server do not rely on, reboot in the regular profile, and then just reboot into the "slim" profile once a month when she needs to run her application. Answer B is not correct because user profiles do not afford you the ability to disable services and devices at boot time. Johanna would have to manually turn off all services she did need and then restart them when her application was done. Answer C is not correct because although configuring your hardware by disabling it in Device Manager might release resources, it is a manual process that you must do each time the application needs to run. Answer D is not correct because Windows Server 2003 does not have such a feature.

Question 10

Answers B and D are correct because two drives in the RAID-5 set died. This means that the redundancy information is lost. At this point, restoring from backup is the only solution. Answer A is not correct because two drives have failed, so replacing one has no effect. Answer C is not correct because even if you have a dedicated "recovery" server, it cannot recover the redundancy information lost from losing two drives. Answer E is not correct because Windows Server 2003 does not maintain enough information elsewhere to recover from two failed drives in a RAID 5 array.

Question 11

Answers A and E are correct. The drive is a basic disk because it already has an extended partition on it. It only supports primary and extended partitions. With a maximum of four partitions—one of which can be extended—only the answers containing two or three primary partitions are correct. Answer B is not correct because you cannot have five partitions on a basic disk. Answer C is incorrect because simple volumes only appear on dynamic disks, and the question deals with a basic disk. Similarly, Answer D is incorrect because it mixes volumes and partitions, which cannot exist on the same physical disk.

Question 12

Answer B is correct because you have to create a GPO. In the GPO, you need to enable the specific intranet Microsoft update service location policy. You should only link the group policy to the Clients OU so that it will not affect the servers. Answers A and D do not specify the intranet Microsoft update service location. Answer C links the OU to the domain level. The client OU will be better because you only want it to automatically update the clients and not the servers located in the server OU.

Question 13

Answer C is the correct choice because you cannot extend a striped volume—one of the main limitations of using striped volumes. Answer A is not correct because fault tolerance is not available on a striped volume. Answer B is not correct because 32 disks are the maximum you can use in a striped volume. Answer D is not correct because the performance of a striped volume is better than a simple volume; the data is written to and read from multiple drives at the same time.

Question 14

Answers A, C, and G are correct because all three operating systems support these combinations of drive configurations and file systems. Answer B is not correct because Windows NT 4.0 Server does not support FAT32 natively. Likewise, you can rule out Answers D and F because Windows NT 4.0 Server does not support dynamic disks; therefore, it does not support dynamic volumes. Answer E is not correct because Windows Server 2003 does not *natively* support stripe sets, which would have been created on Windows NT 4.0 because of the name, "stripe set." Windows Server 2003 can *use* stripe sets but only after mounting them with an additional tool found on the Windows Server 2003 CD-ROM.

Question 15

Answer C is correct because it provides the ability to run Disk Defragmenter without compromising the security of the computer by logging on as an administrative user. Answer A is not correct because it is not recommended to use the computer while logged on with administrative credentials. Answer B is not correct because you must run Disk Defragmenter locally on a computer. Answer D is not correct because it exposes the computer to risks by using it as a user with administrative privileges as well as adding the overhead of the Terminal Services session to the computer.

Question 16

Answer C is correct because the question asks about the system *partition*. Partitions exist only on basic disks, and the system partition contains the files necessary to boot the computer. Answer A is not correct because it refers to the boot volume, which contains the operating system. Answer B is not correct for several reasons. A spanned volume and a basic disk are mutually exclusive: Spanned volumes exist only on dynamic disks. Also, the system volume—and boot volume—must be on a simple volume rather than on a spanned volume or on any other volume. Answer D is incorrect because partitions and dynamic disks are mutually exclusive, and the \Windows folder is the boot volume or partition rather than the system volume or partition.

Question 17

Answer A is correct because a dynamic disk moved from one Windows 2000, Windows XP Professional, or Windows Server 2003 computer to a different computer is listed with a status of Foreign in Disk Management. You can simply right-click the disk and import it to make it available in the new computer. Answer B is not correct because Device Manager is not the appropriate tool to use. Answer C is not correct because Activate This Disk is not a valid choice to render the foreign disk operable. Answer D is not correct—again because Device Manager is not the correct tool to use.

Question 18

Answers B, D, and E are correct because they explain the procedure for breaking and replacing a mirrored volume. You must right-click on Disk 3 and break the mirror from there for Disk 3 to retain the existing drive letter. Also, when creating a mirror, you must choose a dynamic disk with enough unallocated space, and you want to be sure that the status of the new mirrored volume is Healthy. Answer A is incorrect because it removes the volume completely from Disk 3. Answer C is not correct because it gives Disk 2 the H: drive letter. Answer F is incorrect because, although Disk 3 retains the H: drive letter, the volume is removed completely from Disk 2, which does not meet the objective of retaining the data. Answer G is not correct because to add a mirror to an existing simple volume, you must choose another dynamic disk with enough unallocated space. You cannot create a mirror from two existing simple volumes.

Question 19

Answer B is correct. You can use the `dsrm` command for removing objects in Active Directory. Answer A is incorrect because you use `dsquery` for performing search operations. Answer C is incorrect because you use the `dsmove` command to move or rename objects in Active Directory. Answer D is incorrect because you use `dsadd` for adding objects to Active Directory. Answer E is incorrect because you use `dsget` for displaying properties of objects in Active Directory. You use the `net user` command for adding users and for viewing user information.

Question 20

Answer A is correct. The ASR saves the Windows Server 2003 operating-system configuration. It saves the system state, system services, and the operating system components, but it does not back up any user data files. ASR then gives administrators the ability to quickly reinstall Windows Server 2003 by doing a ASR restore operation from a full system backup. If you use the Backup utility to back up the contents of the mounted drives, it will only back up the files on each mounted drive, not the system configuration and the current dynamic disk configuration. In addition, the system state does not include the dynamic disk configuration. Answer B is incorrect because it will not back up the system state. Answer C is incorrect because it will not back up other key files, such as system services and operating system components. Answers D and E will only copy individual files and folders, which is not a very efficient way to back up a drive.

Question 21

Answers B and E are correct. Both the Domain Name System and TCP/IP are network components that you must install to install Active Directory. Answer A is incorrect because Windows 2000 domains use DNS not WINS for the domain name-resolution protocol, so it does not have to be present to install Active Directory. Answer C is incorrect. Kerberos is the default protocol for logon authentication in Active Directory, but you do not install it. It becomes part of the Active Directory installation, but it does not have to be present before you can install Active Directory. Answer D is incorrect because Remote Procedure Call (RPC) does not need to be present before you can install Active Directory. Answer F is incorrect because NetBIOS does not need to be present to install Active Directory.

Question 22

Answers D and F are correct. To raise the function level for your forest to Server 2003, you must have all the DCs running Windows 2003 Server and all domains in the forest must be at least in Windows 2000 native mode. Answer A is incorrect because the workstation operating system is not a factor in raising the function level of the forest. Answer B is incorrect because you do not need to upgrade your servers, just the DCs. Answer C is incorrect because there is no Windows 2000 native mode for forests. Answer E is incorrect because there is no Windows 2003 domain native mode in a Windows Server 2003 Active Directory forest, only the interim and Windows 2003 levels.

Question 23

Answers D and F are correct. You prestage computer accounts in Active Directory to have more control over which computers will be able to contact a Remote Installation Services (RIS) server to download the operating system for each computer. You identify that computer using its GUID or UUID. Answer A is incorrect. Although a computer's fully qualified domain name (FQDN) must be unique within the forest, it is not used for prestaging computer accounts. Answer C is incorrect because the TCP/IP address is not used for prestaging computer accounts. Answer C is incorrect because computer names are not used for prestaging computer accounts. Answer E is incorrect because security identifiers (SIDs) are not used for prestaging computer accounts.

Question 24

Answer B is correct. Computer accounts in Active Directory must have a password to communicate with Active Directory. If the password on the computer gets out of sync with the password in Active Directory, the computer can no longer be authenticated by Active Directory. To fix this problem, you must reset the computer account and then rejoin the computer to the domain. Answer A is incorrect because the user account password has nothing to do with the computer account. Answer C is incorrect because rebooting the computer does not rejoin the computer to the domain. Answer D is incorrect because SIDs are what Active Directory uses to identify an object's permission level; they do not allow the user to log back on to the network in this situation.

Question 25

Answer A is correct. A one-way trust must be in place between a Windows NT 4.0 domain and a Windows Server 2003 domain before users who are running

Windows 98 on their computers can access resources in the Active Directory domain. Answer B is incorrect because you only use `dsclient.exe` for Windows 98 computers that need to access Active Directory features, such as querying Active Directory objects, within the same domain. Answer C is incorrect because although Kerberos is the authentication protocol for Active Directory, it is not used by Window 98 computers. Answer D is incorrect because DNS is used for locating computers, not for authentication.

Question 26

Answer B is correct. Domain local groups can contain user accounts and global groups from any domain in the forest. Answer A is incorrect because universal groups are not available in a domain set at the Windows 2000 mixed level. Answer C is incorrect because security groups refer to a type of group where you can apply permissions to the members in the group; it is not a group scope. Answer D is incorrect because in a Windows 2000 mixed-mode domain, global groups can only contain accounts from the same domain.

Question 27

Answer D is correct. In the Active Directory Users and Computers console, when you right-click any user and select All Tasks, you find the Resultant Set of Policy (Logging) option. This option lets you view policy settings for a particular computer. Answer A is incorrect because although you might be able to determine the problem by going through the Group Policy Object Editor, you have to search through all the nodes to find the one that might be causing the problem. Answer B is incorrect because you use `dsquery` for searching for computers, groups, and organizational units (OUs)—not for group policies. Answer C is incorrect because you use `dsget` for displaying the properties of computers, servers, and OUs—not for displaying group policy.

Question 28

Answers B and C are correct because the syntax of the `/user` option should be in the form of USER@DOMAIN or DOMAIN\USER. Answers A, D, and E are incorrect because these answers do not provide domain administrative credentials when running the Computer Management console.

Question 29

Answers A and C are correct. The default setting is for a Remote Assistance (RA) invitation to remain active for one hour. If the invitation expires, you cannot make a connection to the requesting computer. Also, if TCP port 3389 is blocked at the firewall, you cannot make a connection either. Answer B is incorrect because an RA invitation could not have been generated if RA were disabled. Answer D is incorrect because RA listens on TCP port 3389, not UDP port 3389. Answer E is incorrect because user permissions are not considered during an invitation response—which is why it is imperative that you fully trust the person from whom you are requesting assistance.

Question 30

Answers B and D are correct because Terminal Services (TS) stops accepting connection requests after 120 days if it does not find a TS License Server with the correct number of Terminal Server Client Access Licenses (TSCALs). Answer A is incorrect because the client operating-system version is irrelevant in this case. Answer C is incorrect because rebooting the server does not reset the 120-day period. Answer E is incorrect because the Terminal Server in this case is not corrupted.

Question 31

Answer D is the correct choice because TS listens on TCP port 3389 by default. Answers A, B, and C are incorrect because the question states that the Terminal Server is listening on the default port.

Question 32

Answer A is correct because the Terminal Services Manager provides the ability to disconnect or log off Terminal Server sessions from any Windows Server 2003 or Windows XP computer. Answer B is incorrect because you cannot terminate sessions from Terminal Services Configuration. Answer C is incorrect because you cannot terminate sessions from TS Licensing. Answer D is incorrect because there is no such TS tool.

Question 33

Answer C is correct. There you find options to view user statistics, session information, processes held by individual users, and processes held by the server. You can disconnect users as well as remotely control their sessions. Answer A is incorrect because Active Directory Users and Computers is for doing general user tasks (adding, deleting, moving, and so on) in Active Directory. Answer B is incorrect because Terminal Services Configuration allows you to set or modify Terminal Server configuration settings. Answer D is incorrect because

Terminal Services Licensing is for adding TSCALs and activating or deactivating the license servers.

Question 34

Answer A is correct because by launching the Help and Support Center and selecting the View Invitation Status option, you can force the invitation to expire immediately. Answers B and C are incorrect because you will not find the Expire or Delete button within the Invite Someone to Help You option. Answer D is incorrect because the Control Panel does not contain any options for RA.

Question 35

Answer B is correct because the RA configuration settings are stored in the Computer Configuration\Administrative Templates\System\Remote Assistance Registry subkey. Answers A, C, and D are incorrect because those Registry keys do not exist.

Question 36

Answers B and C are correct. Because all drive letters have hidden administrative shares created automatically, you can retrieve the unmodified document from a previous version using the Shadow Copies of Shared Folders feature. In this case, you have to specify the network UNC path of \\server1\e$\ specialdocs to access the previous versions; up to 64 previous versions are retained. Because you made the modification on Monday, Sunday's full backup was the last time the unmodified document was backed up onto backup media. Answer A is not correct because you modified the document on Monday. On Monday night, the modified document, minus the information you need, was backed up during the incremental backup. Answer D is not correct because you need to connect to the file over the network to work with shadow copies.

Question 37

Answers A, C, and D are correct. These three files are necessary for any 32-bit Windows Server 2003 computer to boot. You also need to make sure that the boot.ini file is correct for the computer that you are using the disk on. Answer B is not correct because it is an MS-DOS file, and you do not need it to start Windows Server 2003. Answer E is not correct because this file, although it might exist, is not a Windows Server 2003 system or boot file at all. Answer F is not correct because, although it might be needed on some Windows Server 2003 boot disks, it is not one of the required files for all installations.

Question 38

Answers B, C, and F are correct. These options all appear when you enter the advanced startup menu. Answer A is not correct because the Recovery Console is not part of Safe Mode. Answer D is not correct because you cannot launch the Recovery Console from this menu. Answer E is not correct because you start Automated System Recovery (ASR) by booting from the Windows Server 2003 CD-ROM and choosing the appropriate option.

Question 39

Answers A and C are correct. You need to boot into the Recovery Console; even if you have it installed, you cannot get to the boot menu in this case, so booting off the CD-ROM is the only practical method to launch the Recovery Console. Once in the Recovery Console, the `fixboot` command repairs the boot sector. Answer B is not correct because the question stated that you are unable to boot into Windows Server 2003 in the first place. Answer D is not correct because it creates an MS-DOS master boot record and boot sector on the hard drive, which does not allow booting Windows Server 2003. Answer E is not correct because an ASR overwrites the entire computer instead of fixing this one problem.

Question 40

Answer D is correct. You can make an ASR backup to any media supported by the Windows Server 2003 backup program, which includes files on hard drives, tapes, and other removable media. When performing the restore, however, bear in mind that Windows Server 2003 needs to be able to access the device that the backup was made on. If that device requires a third-party driver, that driver must be installed for the ASR to restore the server successfully. Answer A is not correct because part of the ASR recovery is to format the boot volume, which destroys the ASR backup. Answers B and C are not correct because the need for the manufacturer's device driver software presents an added step that other solutions do not require.

Question 41

Answer A is correct. Serial Port Console Redirection (SPCR) is a standard that must be supported by the hardware vendor for Windows Server 2003 to use it. SPCR redirects video output and accepts keyboard input using the serial port. Answer B is not correct because it is not a standard. Answer C is not correct because NTFS deals with storage on hard drives, not emergency management of the server. Answer D is not correct because Emergency Management Services (EMS) gets access to a server specifically because it is not accessible via the network.

Question 42

Answers A, B, and E are correct. The Recovery Console gives you the ability to enable and disable services using a command line. If you can get into Safe Mode or Safe Mode with Networking Support, you can easily go into the Services snap-in and disable the service that you believe is causing the problem. Answer C is not correct because ASR totally restores your server, wiping out data on the system volume in the process. Answer D is not correct because the EMS Special Administration Console (SAC) does not allow you to disable services directly. Answer F is incorrect because Directory Services Restore Mode is not a recovery tool for troubleshooting operating system services; it is used for restoring the Active Directory database on DCs.

Question 43

Answer B is correct because Safe Mode works, but enabling networking components causes the computer to stop working. Therefore, some component in the network subsystem is probably causing the problem. Answer A is not correct because if it were a video driver issue, Safe Mode itself might not function, but you would not see the different behavior in the two Safe Mode options. Answer C is not correct because although some type of corruption in networking components is likely causing the problem, the best assumption is that it is at a lower level than shared folders. Answer D is not correct because a corrupted boot sector would not allow the computer to boot even into Safe Mode.

Question 44

Answers A and E are correct. All editions of Windows Server 2003 have the capability to create shadow copies, as long as the volumes configured for shadow copies are running NTFS. In fact, if they are running FAT or FAT32, the Shadow Copies tab does not even appear. Answer B is not correct because the computer is running FAT32. Answers C and D are not correct because shadow copies are not available for creation on any edition of Windows 2000 Server. Also, the Previous Versions client has nothing to do with the creation of shadow copies, only with their restoration, and the Previous Versions client that comes with Windows Server 2003 will not install on Windows 2000. Note as well that even if Windows 2000 Server did support shadow copies, the server is running FAT32, which does not support shadow copies.

Question 45

Answer E is correct. The differential backup backs up only those files that have their archive bits set, indicating they have been modified since the last normal or incremental backup. Additionally, the archive bits are not cleared after the files are backed up during a differential backup. Answer A is incorrect because the archive bits are cleared after an incremental backup. Answer B is incorrect because a copy backup backs up all files and leaves the archive bits just as they are. Answer C is incorrect because the archive bits are cleared during a normal backup. Answer D is incorrect because a daily backup only backs up those files created or modified on the day when the backup takes place, and it does not modify the archive-bit settings on the backed-up files.

Question 46

Answer A is correct. A normal backup (also known as a full backup) copies all selected files and clears the archive bit. An incremental backup backs up files that have their archive bits set, which indicates they have been modified since the last normal or incremental backup. Once an incremental backup is performed, those files' archive bits are cleared. If you are performing a combination of normal and incremental backups, the last normal backup as well as all the incremental backups since the last normal backup are needed for the restore. Answer B is incorrect because you would not have the files and folders modified on Friday available to be restored. Answers C, D, and E are incorrect because with incremental backups, you need each incremental backup tape leading up to the most recent normal backup tape.

Question 47

Answer C is correct. Because a differential backup backs up those files that have changed since the last normal backup and it does not clear the archive bits, you need only the Sunday (normal) and the Thursday (differential) tapes. Answer A is incorrect because the Monday, Tuesday, and Wednesday backups contain the same backed-up files as the Thursday backup tape. Answer D is incorrect because you generally want to start a restore with a normal or full backup, not with a differential backup.

Question 48

Answer A is correct. With this backup routine, you need the Sunday normal; the Tuesday, Thursday, and Friday incremental; and Saturday's differential backups to restore from. It is important to remember that differential backups do *not* clear the archive bits, but the incremental backups do. Therefore, Answer B is incorrect because you do not need any differential backups except for Saturday's. The Tuesday, Thursday, and Friday incremental backups contain all the data stored on the Monday and Wednesday differential backups. Answer C is incorrect because the Sunday backup does not contain any data from Monday through Friday and the Saturday backup is only a differential backup. Answer D is incorrect because again, not enough data is being restored. Answer E is incorrect because you don't need the differential backups from Monday or Wednesday. The data from the Monday and Wednesday differential backups is contained on the incremental backups that follow those differentials.

Question 49

Answer E is correct. As with all normal backups, you only need to restore from one backup tape, which in this case is the Friday tape. Answer A is incorrect because you need to restore from two tapes—the Sunday and Friday tapes. Answer B is incorrect because you need to restore from six tapes. Answers C and D are incorrect because a daily backup backs up only the data that is new or has been changed on the same day that the backup is performed. You need to start with a normal backup to guarantee that all data is restored.

Question 50

Answers A, C, and F are correct. By default, these groups have the proper permissions to back up and restore files and folders. Answers B, D, and E are incorrect because they do not have the proper permissions to back up and restore files.

Question 51

Answer C is correct. The /V:yes switch verifies the backup, the /R:yes switch only allows access to the owner and the administrator, and the /M normal switch specifies a normal backup. Answers A, B, and D are incorrect because they don't specify the correct switch settings.

Question 52

Answers C and E are correct. The files included in a System State backup include the Windows Registry, the COM+ class registration database, boot and system files, the Certificate Services database (if Certificate Services is installed), the Active Directory database, the SYSVOL folder (if the computer is a DC), operating-system files protected by Windows File Protection (WFP), the Internet Information Services (IIS) metabase (if IIS is installed), and cluster service information (if the server is part of a cluster). Answer A is incorrect because the C$ administrative share is not included in a System State backup. Answer B is incorrect because the `%systemroot%\system32` folder is not included in a System State backup. Answer D is incorrect because the `%systemdrive%` folder is not included in a System State backup.

Question 53

Answers B and C are correct. When a Windows 2003 Server is promoted to a DC, the Directory Service and the File Replication Service event logs are automatically added to help monitor critical services that deal with Active Directory. Answer A is incorrect because system performance is not available through the Event Viewer. Answer D and E are incorrect because these logs are installed automatically with the default installation of Windows Server 2003. Answer F is incorrect because the DNS Server event log is not necessarily added when a server is promoted to a DC. The DNS Server event log appears only if the DNS service is installed on the DC. DNS might be hosted on other Windows servers or on UNIX servers.

Question 54

Answer B is correct. You can save log files in several different formats in Event Viewer, such as `.evt`, `.csv`, and `.txt`. But only log files saved as `.evt` can be viewed using Event Viewer. Answer A is incorrect because you cannot save Event Viewer log files as a Word document. Answer C is incorrect because you cannot open `.csv` files with Event Viewer. You have to use a program such as Excel to open the file. Answer D is incorrect because you can open a log file saved as `.txt` only with a program such as Notepad. Answer E is incorrect because Event Viewer cannot save a log as a `.pdf` file.

Question 55

Answer C is correct. Hard page faults occur when a process requests a page from random access memory (RAM) and the system cannot find it, so it must then be retrieved from the hard drive. As long as the value remains between 0 and 20, performance on the server should not suffer. Answer A is incorrect because this metric is too low. As long as the metric stays below 20, you will still have good performance on your server. Answers B and D are incorrect because these metrics indicate too many page faults; therefore, performance might suffer.

Question 56

Answer D is correct. Because the performance monitoring tool requires system resources to run, if you run the tool locally, the readings will not be as accurate as they could be. The readings would include not only the server's performance as a result of its workload, but also the load on the system's resources from the monitoring tool. Answers A and B are incorrect because although you use both Task Manager and System Manager for monitoring performance, the question asks how you get the most accurate results. Answer C is incorrect because you need to log the information so that it can be viewed and evaluated later; this fact does not answer the question of how to obtain the most accurate results.

Question 57

Answer C is correct. Performance Log Users group is a new group created by default that allows members to manage performance counters, logs, and alerts. Answer A is incorrect because members of the Performance Monitor Users group only have permissions to *monitor* performance counters. Answer B is incorrect because members of the Power Users group would not have the proper level of permissions to manage performance information on servers. Answer D is incorrect because members of the local Administrators group do not have permission to monitor other servers remotely.

Question 58

Answer C is correct. Events are recorded into log files by the Event Log service, which is configured to run at system startup by default. You use Event Viewer to view these log files. Answer A is incorrect because you use the Networking tab in Task Manager to view networking performance. Answer B is incorrect because you use Performance Monitor and Task Manager to view computer performance data. Answer D is incorrect because you use Event Viewer to view events that have already occurred, not events as they happen in real time.

Question 59

Answer D is correct. When an alert is triggered based on its settings, it can perform several actions, including creating an entry in the application event log, sending a network message to someone, initiating logging for a specific performance log, and running an application program. Answer A is incorrect because Performance Monitor is the monitoring program, but in the Alert log you can set up an action to be triggered based on a condition or event. Answers B and C are incorrect because neither of these types of logs can be configured to perform the action required.

Question 60

Answer B is correct. To be able to document what changes might have occurred to degrade system and network performance, you need to establish a performance baseline. In this way, you can compare the baseline-performance history with the current performance measurements to diagnose the problem. Answer A is incorrect because the Event Viewer does not show information that deals with server performance. Answer C is incorrect because to establish a baseline, you need to monitor server performance during normal usage workloads, not during high-usage workloads. Answer D is incorrect because you do not use trace logs to measure server performance.

23

C H A P T E R T W E N T Y - T H R E E

Practice Exam 2

1. How can you allow users to have their unique desktop settings follow them no matter which workstation they log on to but not save whatever changes they make to their desktop settings?

   ○ **A.** On each workstation in the domain, delete the `%systemdrive%\ Documents and Settings\Default User` folder.

   ○ **B.** Rename the file named `system` in the `%systemroot%\system32\ config\system` folder to `system.man`.

   ○ **C.** Configure a roaming profile for each user in the domain. Create a shared profile folder on a server, such as `\\server1\profiles\`. On server1, rename the `ntuser.dat` file within each user's profile to `ntuser.man`.

   ○ **D.** Create a GPO named RoamProfile. Assign the RoamProfile GPO to the domain. Configure the RoamProfile GPO to delete the local copy of each user's profile when each user logs off.

2. You have RIS running so that you can easily install the operating system for your domain. What can you do to prevent users from installing the operating system on unauthorized computers?

   ○ **A.** Upgrade all Windows 98 and Windows NT 4.0 workstation computers to Windows 2000 or Windows XP Professional so that users can log on using only the Kerberos authentication protocol.

   ○ **B.** In the ADUC console, add new computers to the RIS default container.

   ○ **C.** Create a group called Remote Installation Users and add only those users whom you want to grant permission to add computer accounts to the domain.

   ○ **D.** Specify that only prestaged computer accounts can be installed by RIS.

3. Ellen, a network administrator in your New York office, has just added a child OU named Specialties to the existing Sales OU. The Sales OU is a child OU within the Northeast OU. John, a network administrator in Chicago, has just accidentally deleted the Sales OU, after Ellen added the Specialties OU. The organization has only one Active Directory domain, and there are DCs at each physical location. You go to recover the Specialties OU in the Lost and Found container. You check the ADUC console and cannot see any Lost and Found container. What must you do to fix this?

   ○ **A.** Add yourself to the Enterprise Admins group.

   ○ **B.** Click the View menu and select Advanced Features.

   ○ **C.** Go to Control Panel, click Add or Remove Programs, and then click Add Windows Components.

   ○ **D.** Go to the ADUC console, right-click the domain name, and then click the Show Hidden Container option.

4. For which of the following domain functional levels can administrators nest groups within other groups and change the scope of groups? (Choose two.)

   ○ **A.** Windows 2000 native

   ○ **B.** Windows 2000 mixed

   ○ **C.** Windows Server 2003

   ○ **D.** Windows Server 2003 interim

   ○ **E.** Windows Server 2003 mixed

5. A user reports that she cannot log on to her Windows 2000 Professional computer because she gets the following error message: "NETLOGON Event ID 3210: Failed to authenticate with \\DC07, a Windows NT domain controller for domain CORPSALES." What must you do so that the user can log on?

   ○ **A.** Reset the computer account.

   ○ **B.** Reset the user account's password.

   ○ **C.** Delete and then re-create the user account.

   ○ **D.** Move the computer account into the Computers container and press the F5 function key to refresh the account.

6. Which of the following dsadd.exe commands creates a universal distribution group called Sales Reps in the Sales OU that is within the East Coast OU within the Windows2003.local domain?

   ○ **A.** dsadd group cn=sales reps,ou=sales,ou=east
        coast,dc=windows2003,dc=local –secgrp no -scope l

   ○ **B.** dsadd group "cn=sales reps ou=sales ou=east coast
        dc=windows2003 dc=local" –secgrp -scope u

   ○ **C.** dsadd group "cn=sales reps,ou=sales,ou=east
        coast,dc=windows2003,dc=local" –secgrp no -scope u

   ○ **D.** dsadd group "cn=sales reps,ou=sales,ou=east
        coast,dc=windows2003,dc=local" –secgrp yes -scope u

7. You have all the account information for 148 new users in an Excel worksheet. Which command-line utility can you use to import all these users into Active Directory?

   ○ **A.** dsadd.exe

   ○ **B.** ldifde.exe

   ○ **C.** dsget.exe

   ○ **D.** csvde.exe

8. In the Windows 2000 mixed domain functional level, which group can contain global groups from any domain in the forest?

  ○ **A.** Universal groups

  ○ **B.** Security groups

  ○ **C.** Global groups

  ○ **D.** Domain local groups

9. Windows Server 2003, like Windows XP, implements much stricter permissions by default. What are the default permissions for an NTFS boot partition or boot volume for the Everyone group?

  ○ **A.** Allow Full Control

  ○ **B.** Deny Full Control and Allow Read

  ○ **C.** Allow Read and Execute without inheritance

  ○ **D.** Allow Read and Execute with inheritance

10. Jean has a legacy application on the D: drive that her department relies on to complete its daily tasks. The application does not function correctly with the NTFS file system. Unfortunately, during the upgrade of the departmental server to Windows Server 2003, the central IT department converted all disks to dynamic disks and all volumes to NTFS. Jean must convert the D: drive back to FAT. What steps must she take to ensure the conversion happens without losing any data? (Choose three.)

  ○ **A.** Run the command `convert D: /fs:fat32`.

  ○ **B.** Run the command `convert D: /fs:fat`.

  ○ **C.** Back up all data to another location.

  ○ **D.** Reformat the D: drive using the Disk Management console.

  ○ **E.** Reformat the D: drive using Windows Explorer.

  ○ **F.** Convert the disk to a basic disk.

  ○ **G.** Restore the data to the reformatted volume.

11. Shadow Copies relies on the Previous Versions client software that comes with Windows Server 2003. Where is this client located?

  ○ **A.** In the `\support\tools` folder of the Windows Server 2003 CD-ROM

  ○ **B.** In the `%systemroot%\system32\clients\twclient` directory on the Windows Server 2003 computer

  ○ **C.** In the `%systemroot%\system32\clients\tsclient` directory on the Windows Server 2003 computer

  ○ **D.** In the default shared folder named `PVClient` on the Windows Server 2003 computer

12. Which of the following statements are true regarding NTFS data compression? (Choose three.)

- ○ **A.** NTFS compression is vital when using quotas because it allows a user to store more physical data than the quota allows.

- ○ **B.** Compressing a volume compresses all new files and folders created on that volume.

- ○ **C.** NTFS compression allows individual files and folders to be compressed as an attribute of the file or folder.

- ○ **D.** If a folder is compressed, all the files created or copied into the folder are compressed as well.

- ○ **E.** You must be a member of the Administrators group to have your files or folders compressed.

- ○ **F.** You must be a member of the Power Users group to have your files or folders compressed.

13. Jane wants to be able to administer her Windows Server 2003 member server using Remote Desktop for Administration. She does not want to log on to the computer as the administrator for security reasons. What must she do to ensure that her user account can log on to the server using the Remote Desktop Connection client? (Choose three.)

- ○ **A.** Mark the Allow Users to Connect Remotely to This Computer check box on the Remote tab of the System Properties window.

- ○ **B.** Mark the Turn on Remote Assistance and Allow Invitations to Be Sent from This Computer check box on the Remote tab of the System Properties window.

- ○ **C.** Ensure that her user account does not have a blank password.

- ○ **D.** Make sure that she is a member of the Terminal Services Users group.

- ○ **E.** Make sure that she is a member of the Remote Desktop Users group.

- ○ **F.** Ensure that her password is at least 12 characters long.

14. Harvey has decided to implement NTFS disk quotas on the data volume of his Windows Server 2003 computer. He enables quotas in the properties of the data drive volume. He wants to set the limit for all members of the Research group to 50MB each but no limits for anyone else currently. How can he accomplish this goal?

- ○ **A.** By setting the quotas for each user individually to 50MB

- ○ **B.** By setting the quotas for the Research group to 50MB

○   **C.** By choosing each user in ADUC and selecting Quotas from the All Tasks menu

○   **D.** By executing the command `fsutil quota modify d: 0 50 research` at a command prompt

15. What are the benefits of using FAT32 as a file system in Windows Server 2003? (Choose two.)

○   **A.** You ensure security for the Windows system files.

○   **B.** You retain the ability to access files with an MS-DOS–based boot disk.

○   **C.** You gain the ability to create fault-tolerant volumes.

○   **D.** You retain compatibility with previous operating systems that might coexist on the server.

○   **E.** You have the ability to compress files and folders at the file-system level.

16. Which applications let you publish a shared folder to Active Directory? (Choose two.)

○   **A.** The `net share` command from the command line

○   **B.** The Shared Folders console in Computer Management

○   **C.** The Sharing tab in the properties of a folder

○   **D.** Windows Explorer

○   **E.** The ADUC console

17. Arthur receives a frantic call at 2 a.m. from the auditing department of his company. They need to access files that are stored in the `E:\reports` folder on the server, but the folder is currently not shared. Arthur's computer at his home runs Windows 95 and does not have a Remote Desktop Connection client installed on it. The server at the office temporarily has the Telnet service enabled, and the firewall is forwarding all Telnet traffic to the server. How can Arthur share the `E:\reports` directory for the auditing department without having to go in to the office?

○   **A.** Dial in directly to the server and use the Windows Server 2003 shared folder snap-in over the dial-up connection.

○   **B.** Connect to the server using Telnet and run the command `net share reports=e:\reports`.

○   **C.** Connect to the server using Telnet and use the Windows Server 2003 shared folder snap-in.

○   **D.** Dial in directly to the server and run the command `net view \\ server\reports add`.

18. Max is trying to modify a file stored on a share on his Windows Server 2003 computer. He is a member of the Users and Accounting groups. The permissions that are currently in effect are as follows:

- ▶ Share permissions—Everyone:Allow Full Control
- ▶ Max's NTFS permissions—Allow Read and Execute
- ▶ Users group NTFS permissions—Allow Modify
- ▶ Accounting group NTFS permissions—Deny Write

Why isn't Max able to save his changes to the file?

- ○ **A.** The share permissions are too restrictive.
- ○ **B.** The combination of share permissions and the User group's permissions is causing the problem.
- ○ **C.** The combination of Max's and the User group's permissions is too restrictive.
- ○ **D.** Max's membership in the Accounting group is causing the problem.

19. Uma has read about Shadow Copies of Shared Folders in Windows Server 2003 and wants to enable this feature on her server. She currently has two physical disks with two volumes each. Drive D:, on physical disk 1, has four shares, but only one share needs Shadow Copies enabled. Drives E: and F:, on physical disk 2, have several shares each, but only the shares on drive E: need Shadow Copies enabled. Where should Uma enable shadow copies for these shares? (Choose two.)

- ○ **A.** On physical disk 1
- ○ **B.** On physical disk 2
- ○ **C.** On drive D:
- ○ **D.** On drive E:
- ○ **E.** On drive F:
- ○ **F.** Only on the shares that need the Shadow Copies service

20. A user who is no longer with your company encrypted some important files that you now need to access. How can you gain access to these files?

- ○ **A.** Copy the files from the NTFS volume to a FAT32 volume. They will be unencrypted by virtue of the fact that FAT32 does not support encryption.
- ○ **B.** Back up the files to tape as an administrator and restore them to another server.
- ○ **C.** Use the designated data recovery agent (DRA) to decrypt the files.
- ○ **D.** Disable encryption using group policies to force all encrypted files to become unencrypted.

21. Alison is a user in the NorthAmerica Active Directory domain, and she is a member of several different groups. As the network administrator, you need to give her access permissions to read and write to files in the `E:\Common\Sales\VPs` shared folder. You believe that by making Alison a member of the VP Assistants group, she should have the proper access permissions to the VPs folder, but she reports that she can't save documents in that folder. In diagnosing the problem, you narrow it down to an NTFS permissions issue. How can you quickly troubleshoot this problem so that you can solve it?

   ❍ **A.** Make Alison a member of the Administrators group.

   ❍ **B.** Grant Alison's user account the Allow:Modify permission for this folder only.

   ❍ **C.** Grant Alison's user account the Allow:Full Control permission for this folder only.

   ❍ **D.** Check the NTFS Effective Permissions for Alison.

22. When viewing the Effective Permissions dialog box to find the effective permissions that actually apply to a user, what are you actually looking at?

   ❍ **A.** Permissions granted explicitly to the user

   ❍ **B.** Permissions combined from the user and the groups that the user is a member of

   ❍ **C.** Permissions combined from the user and groups that the user is a member of, as well as permissions inherited from the parent object

   ❍ **D.** Permissions granted to the Everyone group

23. You notice that your E: drive, which stores all your company's data files, is starting to fill up rapidly. You want to implement disk quotas on the drive, limiting all users to 100MB of space. You will then make individual changes as necessary. You enable quotas on the E: drive, you set the default quota limit to 100MB, and then you deny space to users exceeding that limit. One of your users, Amy, compresses her folder using NTFS compression in the hope that she'll be able to store more data on drive E: and get around the disk space quota. What happens when Amy has used 97MB of disk space on drive E: and she then attempts to copy a 5MB file into her compressed folder?

   ❍ **A.** Windows Server 2003 allows the file to be copied into that folder because NTFS compression is enabled.

   ❍ **B.** Windows Server 2003 displays a warning message box to Amy regarding her disk-quota limit, but it allows her to copy the file into the compressed folder.

   ❍ **C.** Windows Server 2003 allows the file to be copied, but it will not allow any more files to be stored on drive E: for Amy unless she moves or deletes her existing files to comply with her disk quota.

   ❍ **D.** Windows Server 2003 does not allow the file to be copied into the folder because Amy would then be exceeding her disk-quota limit.

24. Which of the following are features of the NTFS file system? (Choose three.)

    ○ **A.** NTFS compresses files and folders by creating a special file to fill the drive and mounting it as a virtual drive.

    ○ **B.** NTFS offers the ability to encrypt files.

    ○ **C.** NTFS offers the ability to apply permissions to files and folders.

    ○ **D.** You can use NTFS on floppy disks.

    ○ **E.** NTFS has a disk-quota system built in that lets you implement disk-space restrictions.

    ○ **F.** You can format CD-R, CD/RW, DVD+R, DVD-R, DVD+RW, and DVD-RW media as NTFS.

25. Henrietta wants to use permissions to ensure that users' access to resources is consistent, whether they are sitting locally at the server or accessing resources remotely over the network. What permissions should Henrietta use to achieve this goal in the easiest manner possible?

    ○ **A.** NTFS permissions, setting share permissions to Everyone:Allow Full Control

    ○ **B.** NTFS permissions, leaving share permissions at their default values

    ○ **C.** Share permissions, settings NTFS permissions to Everyone:Allow Full Control

    ○ **D.** Share permissions, leaving NTFS permissions at their default values

26. What are the default share permissions in Windows Server 2003?

    ○ **A.** Users:Allow Full Control

    ○ **B.** Everyone:Allow Full Control

    ○ **C.** Users:Allow Read and Execute

    ○ **D.** Everyone:Allow Read

27. After successfully migrating your Windows 2000 Server IIS 5.0 web server to Windows Server 2003 and IIS 6.0, your CIO asks you what mode the website is currently running. Perplexed, you use Remote Access to access your IIS server to find out. Where should you look to determine the mode in which the website is running, and what answer will you give to your CIO? (Choose two.)

○ **A.** In the IIS Manager snap-in, expand the web server node that you want to work with and right-click the Web Site subnode. Select Properties and click the Services tab. There you find the Isolation Mode option.

○ **B.** In the IIS Manager snap-in, expand the web server node that you want to work with and right-click the Web Site subnode. Select Properties and click the Web Site tab. There you find the Isolation Mode option.

○ **C.** In the IIS Manager snap-in, expand the Web server node that you want to work with and right-click the Web Site subnode. Select Properties and click the Directory Security tab. There you find the Isolation Mode option.

○ **D.** You will inform your CIO that the website is running in IIS 5.0 Isolation Mode.

○ **E.** You will inform your CIO that the website is running in Worker Process Isolation Mode.

28. You have installed the default components of IIS 6.0 on server02, a Windows Server 2003 computer. You open IE 6.0 on server02 and type `https://server02:8098` in the address box. You receive a Page Cannot Be Displayed error message. What is the most likely reason that you are receiving this error?

○ **A.** The firewall is blocking TCP port 8098.

○ **B.** You did not select the Remote Administration option when installing IIS 6.0.

○ **C.** You must start the Internet services on server02.

○ **D.** You do not have administrative permissions on the domain.

29. You are a Windows 2003 Server administrator. You want to be able to browse the Web without receiving an Internet Explorer Enhanced Security Configuration alert message. However, you only want this option disabled for administrators. What must you do to disable this feature for administrators only?

○ **A.** In Internet Explorer 6.0, click Tools, Internet Options, and click the Advanced Tab. Scroll down to the Security settings and clear the Warn If Changing Between Secure and Not Secure Mode check box.

○ **B.** Open Control Panel, double-click Add or Remove Programs, click Add/Remove Windows Components, select Internet Explorer Enhanced Security Configuration, click the Details button, and make sure that both check boxes are marked.

    ◯ **C.** In Internet Explorer 6.0, click Tools, Internet Options, and click the Security tab. Click the Internet Zone and set the slider for the Security Level for This Zone to Low.

    ◯ **D.** Open Control Panel, double-click Add or Remove Programs, click Add/Remove Windows Components, select Internet Explorer Enhanced Security Configuration, click the Details button, and clear the appropriate check box.

30. Which utility allows you to change the way users are authenticated or granted access to a website? (Choose two.)

    ◯ **A.** Active Directory Users and Computers

    ◯ **B.** Internet Information Services (IIS) Manager

    ◯ **C.** IIS 6.0 Remote Administration (HTML)

    ◯ **D.** Internet Authentication Service

    ◯ **E.** Component Services

31. Which default user allows anonymous access to a website on the web server named SERVER-WEB1?

    ◯ **A.** IUSR_ANONYMOUS

    ◯ **B.** IWAM_SERVER-WEB1

    ◯ **C.** IUSR_SERVER-WEB1

    ◯ **D.** IIS_WPG

    ◯ **E.** ASPNET

32. You are a network administrator managing an internal Windows Server 2003 intranet web server. You want to give your developers the ability to modify the various scripts stored on the web server and save those modifications back to the web server. What permissions must you enable? (Choose three.)

    ◯ **A.** Write permission

    ◯ **B.** Read permission

    ◯ **C.** Directory browsing

    ◯ **D.** Index this resource

    ◯ **E.** Log visits

    ◯ **F.** Script source access

33. You need to configure a Windows Server 2003 web server's permissions that would allow users to view the files for one website only. Which steps allow you to do such a task?

○ **A.** Open Internet Information Services Manager. Right-click the website and select Properties. Click the Home Directory tab and mark the Directory Browsing check box.

○ **B.** Open Internet Information Services Manager. Right-click the website and click Properties. Click the Home Directory tab and remove all permissions to enable Directory browsing.

○ **C.** Open Internet Information Services Manager. Right-click the website and click Properties. Click the Web Site tab and mark the Directory Browsing check box.

○ **D.** Open Internet Information Services Manager. Right-click the Web Sites subnode and click Properties. Click the Home Directory tab and mark the check box for Directory Browsing.

34. Your Windows Server 2003 web server suffers a catastrophic failure. Part of the solution is to reinstall the operating system and reinstall IIS 6.0. You have reliable backups of the `metabase.xml` and `mbschema.xml` files. You decide to import the entire IIS 6.0 metabase using the scripts provided. Which two scripts provide for this functionality? (Choose two.)

○ **A.** `iisback.vbs`

○ **B.** `iisext.vbs`

○ **C.** `iiscnfg.vbs`

○ **D.** `iisapp.vbs`

○ **E.** `iisweb.vbs`

35. While working on a critical CAD drawing, a user accidentally deletes a major section of the drawing and saves the file. After realizing the mistake, he contacts you asking whether you can get the file back to its previous state. The file is stored in D:\CADD, which is shared as \\SERVER\CADD. You know that you had a successful differential backup last night and a successful full backup two nights ago. You also configured Shadow Copies of Shared Folders for the drive hosting the CADD share to run every two hours. You are currently working on the console of the server. What is the fastest way to recover the drawing for the user?

○ **A.** Restore the server from the full backup and then perform a restore from the differential backup.

○ **B.** In Windows Explorer, navigate to D:\CADD; right-click on the file; choose Properties, Previous Versions; and restore the most recent shadow copy.

    ⭘ **C.** Restore the file from the differential backup or from the full backup if it isn't on the differential.

    ⭘ **D.** In Windows Explorer, navigate to \\SERVER\CADD, right-click the file, choose Properties, click the Previous Versions tab, and restore the most recent shadow copy.

36. After installing a new RAID array driver on your Windows Server 2003 computer, you experience a STOP error and you have to reboot the computer. The server does not start successfully, so you want to remove the driver you just installed. Unfortunately, the manufacturer has a program that you must run to revert back to the previous driver, and it is stored on a remote computer. Your server does not have a floppy drive or any other type of removable storage that you can use to load the program. All drives on the server are using NTFS. What can you do?

    ⭘ **A.** Boot the computer using the Safe Mode with Networking option and then copy the previous driver from the remote computer and run the driver reversion program.

    ⭘ **B.** Boot the computer with an MS-DOS network boot disk and copy the file from the remote computer first; then, boot into Safe Mode.

    ⭘ **C.** Boot the computer with the Windows Server 2003 CD-ROM and choose Automated System Recovery.

    ⭘ **D.** Boot the computer with the Recovery Console and roll back the driver.

37. How do you install the Recovery Console so that it becomes an option that you can select while booting your server?

    ⭘ **A.** Choose Recovery Console from the Add Windows Components section of Add or Remove Programs in the Control Panel.

    ⭘ **B.** Boot from the Windows Server 2003 CD-ROM and choose the Install Recovery Console option from the Repair menu.

    ⭘ **C.** Execute the command \i386\winnt32.exe /cmdcons from the Windows Server 2003 CD-ROM.

    ⭘ **D.** Download and install it from the Windows Update website.

38. When you create an Automated System Recovery (ASR) backup set, what components are backed up? (Choose two.)

    ⭘ **A.** User data

    ⭘ **B.** Shadow copies of all shares

    ⭘ **C.** System State

    ⭘ **D.** Operating-system files

    ⭘ **E.** Data that you specify stored on the boot volume

39. Gina needs to launch an ASR of her Windows Server 2003 computer. How does she begin the restore phase of an ASR?

- ○ **A.** By booting from the Windows Server 2003 CD-ROM and pressing the F2 key when prompted
- ○ **B.** By running `NTBackup.exe` and choosing Automated System Recovery under the Restore tab
- ○ **C.** By booting from the Windows Server 2003 CD-ROM and pressing the F6 key when prompted
- ○ **D.** By booting into the Recovery Console and typing `ASRRESTORE` at the Recovery Console prompt

40. Jane has connected to an unresponsive Windows Server 2003 computer via Emergency Management Services. She wants to execute a command using the Special Administration Console to cause the server to write the contents of memory to a file on the hard disk. Which command should she execute?

- ○ **A.** `writemem`
- ○ **B.** `!sac`
- ○ **C.** `crashdump`
- ○ **D.** `dumpmem`

41. Which of the following statements is not true regarding Windows Server 2003's Emergency Management Services?

- ○ **A.** It allows you to manage a server via a serial port.
- ○ **B.** It gives you the ability to reboot a server immediately.
- ○ **C.** It requires no special hardware support.
- ○ **D.** It uses a process known as out-of-band management.

42. Norma is upgrading drivers on her new Windows Server 2003 computer, preparing it for production use in the marketing department of her company. As part of the update process, she is rebooting after every driver installation. After she installs the updated network card driver, the server crashes immediately after presenting the logon dialog box. What is the quickest method of undoing the changes Norma just made?

- ○ **A.** Boot using the Last Known Good Configuration.
- ○ **B.** Initiate an ASR restore.
- ○ **C.** Boot using Safe Mode and perform a driver rollback.
- ○ **D.** Boot into the Recovery Console and disable the Workstation service.

43. You are the administrator for eight Windows 2003 Server computers. You are creating a backup scheme that will use the Windows Server 2003 Backup Utility. You want to make sure that the backup scheme includes the Registry, the SYSVOL folder, the Active Directory database, and the boot and system files. You are not concerned about the COM+ components being backed up. Which solution presents the best choice?

    ○ **A.** From the command prompt, execute the Windows 2003 Backup Utility in System State Restore mode.

    ○ **B.** Reboot the server, press the F8 key at the boot loader prompt, and select the Backup System State option.

    ○ **C.** Run the Windows Server 2003 Backup Utility and expand the System State node. Select all System State components but deselect the COM+ component.

    ○ **D.** Run the Windows Server 2003 Backup Utility and select the option to back up the System State data.

44. Pete, a network administrator on your domain, accidentally deleted the Sales OU. You need to recover this OU as quickly as possible so that your Sales staff can perform their duties. You check the backup logs and see that the System State was backed up on each domain controller (DC) the previous night. On a randomly selected DC, you restore the System State. You breathe a sigh of relief to see the OU reappear on the DC on which you performed the restore. Thirty minutes later, you inspect another DC and see that the OU does not appear there. Concerned, you go back to the DC that you restored the system state onto and you see that the OU does not appear there either.

Why did this happen, and what should you do to ensure the permanent recovery of the Sales OU?

    ○ **A.** You can only perform System State restores on the DC that holds the Flexible Single Master Operation (FSMO) role of Schema Master. You must repeat the restore operation on this DC.

    ○ **B.** You did not perform an authoritative restore. Restart the server, press the F8 key at the boot loader menu, select Directory Services Restore Mode, perform the restore operation again, and then run the NTDSUtil.exe utility to mark the restored Sales OU as authoritative.

    ○ **C.** Only members of the Administrators, Backup Operators, and Server Operators groups can restore the System State. Log back on with an account that belongs to one of these groups.

    ○ **D.** When you restored the System State, the backed-up data was more than 60 days old. Find a newer backup set and repeat the System State restore.

45. You are attempting to perform an authoritative restore. You restart a DC, press the F8 key when prompted, and select Directory Services Restore Mode. When prompted for the administrator's password, you enter it, but you immediately receive an error. You know that you are entering the domain administrator's password correctly. What is the most likely reason for your problem?

- ○ **A.** You have not performed a System State restore on a DC yet. Restore the System State and then perform the authoritative restore.

- ○ **B.** To perform this function, the DC must be the PDC Emulator. Locate the DC that holds the PDC Emulator role and then perform the authoritative restore.

- ○ **C.** You must log on with the Directory Services Restore Mode administrator's password. Locate that password and log on again.

- ○ **D.** A domain-level GPO setting is disabling the Administrator account. Modify the GPO setting to enable the Administrator account and log on again.

46. You are a network administrator responsible for the three DCs that host a single domain. All DCs were lost when a water main broke over the server room. Given this scenario of having to rebuild the entire domain, which restore method is most recommended for the first DC?

- ○ **A.** Authoritative restore

- ○ **B.** Nonauthoritative restore

- ○ **C.** Primary restore

- ○ **D.** Normal restore

47. You are a senior network administrator for a large medical-appliance distributor. James, your junior administrator, informed you that he accidentally deleted the OU that contains the user accounts for 12 senior-level management staff. In his attempt to fix the problem, he performed a System State restore from last night's DC System State backup. He was relieved to see the OU restored on the DC. However, that relief was short-lived. James realized that he needed to seek your help immediately. After giving him a thorough reprimand about the dangers of deleting Active Directory objects and swimming within an hour of eating, you verify that the complete set of backup tapes and the ASR set are in hand. Your task is to immediately restore the OU and the senior-level management user accounts.

Which of the following do you not need in the procedure to restore the OU and user accounts? (Choose two.)

- ○ **A.** ASR set

- ○ **B.** The backup tapes

- ○ **C.** The NTDSUtil utility

- ○ **D.** An authoritative restore

- ○ **E.** A user who is a member of the Enterprise Admins group

48. William, your number-one network administrator, accidentally deletes the OU for the Marketing department. He immediately realizes what he has done and decides to pull the DC offline before it has a chance to replicate with other DCs. What two steps must William perform to restore the OU to its original state? (Choose two.)

○ **A.** Perform a System State restore on all the DCs in the forest.

○ **B.** The restore must be nonauthoritative.

○ **C.** Perform a System State restore on the DC from which the OU was deleted.

○ **D.** Perform a System State restore on all DCs in the domain.

○ **E.** The restore must be authoritative.

○ **F.** Perform a primary restore on the PDC Emulator and then bring the affected DC back online.

49. You are having a discussion with a co-worker about the default settings for the Windows Server 2003 Backup Utility. Stacey, your co-worker, makes the following list and presents it to you as fact. Being the astute systems administrator you are, you politely point out her errors. Which answers on Stacey's list are not correct? (Choose two.)

○ **A.** Default setting—Backup type is Normal.

○ **B.** Default setting—Verify Data After Backup is enabled.

○ **C.** Default setting—Information reported in the backup log is summarized.

○ **D.** Default setting—Replace the File on Disk Only If the File on Disk Is Older.

○ **E.** Default setting—Files to be restored to their original locations.

50. You are a senior network administrator performing a security audit on the corporate servers. Part of your audit leads you to determine how files are restored and who can restore them. In your investigation, you find that any backup operator can restore extremely sensitive corporate Merger and Acquisition information. The corporate policy is that only those members of the Administrators group and the owner of the files must be able to restore this information. What recommendations will you give to those who are responsible for administering the tape backups for these servers?

○ **A.** Delete the Backup Operators group.

○ **B.** Recommend that the Administrators account take ownership of the Merger and Acquisition folders and files and remove all users from the Backup Operators group.

○ **C.** Enable the Allow Only the Owner and the Administrator Access to the Backup Data option.

○ **D.** After you create the backup, add the Backup Operators to the NTFS security permissions for the folders and mark the Deny option for Full Control.

51. You are getting error message 202 stating that your Windows Server 2003 computer is out of licenses. When you go to the Licensing tool in the Administrative Tools folder on the Start menu, the information does not appear. What must you do to view this information?

- ○ **A.** Start the License Logging service.
- ○ **B.** Enable licensing on the DC.
- ○ **C.** Look in the default licensing group.
- ○ **D.** Enable licensing in the Active Directory Sites and Services console.

52. You are running out of room on the drive volume that contains the server's print spooler. You move the print spooler to a different drive volume with more disk space. The users tell you that nothing will print. What do you need to do to correct the problem?

- ○ **A.** Reinstall the drivers on the print server computer.
- ○ **B.** Stop and restart the spooler service.
- ○ **C.** Make sure that the users have full control permissions.
- ○ **D.** Stop and restart the printer service.

53. The Accounting department is printing large documents that are monopolizing the printers, and no one else can print. What is the best solution to this problem?

- ○ **A.** Get the Accounting department its own printer.
- ○ **B.** Change the Accounting department's print-queue priority to 99.
- ○ **C.** Set up a logical printer for the Accounting department and tell the accountants to use it for large print jobs.
- ○ **D.** Change the Accounting department print-queue priority to 2.

54. Management tells you that users are complaining that printing takes too long. You need to gather statistics about the company's printers and print jobs. How will you gather this information?

- ○ **A.** Use System Monitor.
- ○ **B.** Save the system log files from the Event Viewer.
- ○ **C.** Use the advanced properties of the print server.
- ○ **D.** Use Performance Logs and Alerts.

55. Your company has decided to start using SUS. You are chosen to head the project. You do a clean install of Windows Server 2003 on a Pentium 700Mhz computer with 1GB of RAM installed. After installing the SUS version 1.0 with Service Pack 1 (SP1) on the computer, you test the service and it does not work. What must you do to fix the problem?

- ○ **A.** Make sure that you have at least 3GB of disk space available.
- ○ **B.** Upgrade to Internet Explorer 6.0.
- ○ **C.** Install IIS 6.0.
- ○ **D.** Enable Remote Procedure Calls (RPCs).

56. Which of the following Microsoft operating systems and service-pack levels are not capable of using SUS? (Choose three.)

- ○ **A.** Windows NT 4.0 Workstation with SP5
- ○ **B.** Windows 2000 Professional
- ○ **C.** Windows 2000 Server with SP3
- ○ **D.** Windows XP Professional
- ○ **E.** Windows XP Home with SP1
- ○ **F.** Windows Server 2003

57. While looking through the Event Viewer, you see an entry in the System log: Disk Event ID 36. What does this signify?

- ○ **A.** The server is running out of space for the paging file.
- ○ **B.** Disk space is running low on the drive volume.
- ○ **C.** %Disk Time is greater than 50%.
- ○ **D.** A user has exceeded his or her disk quota.

58. In monitoring your server, you notice a steady increase in nonpaged bytes without a corresponding increase in server load. What is the probable cause of this performance decrease?

- ○ **A.** One of the RAM modules on the motherboard is going bad.
- ○ **B.** A program is causing a memory leak.
- ○ **C.** A process is causing excessive paging.
- ○ **D.** A process is using a disproportional amount of RAM.

59. How can you perform an ASR restore operation if you have lost the ASR floppy disk?

  ○ **A.** Make your own Windows Server 2003 boot disk.

  ○ **B.** Use an ASR floppy disk created on a different computer that runs Windows XP Professional.

  ○ **C.** Use the Backup Utility on a different Windows Server 2003 computer to restore the `asr.sif` and `asrpnp.sif` files from the ASR media backup set onto a blank floppy disk. Use the floppy disk as the ASR floppy disk during the ASR restore operation.

  ○ **D.** You cannot perform an ASR restore without the original ASR floppy disk.

60. What is the easiest and fastest way that you can restore a previously installed video driver after you install a new video driver, restart the computer, and see that the video display is completed garbled and you cannot log on to the computer?

  ○ **A.** Do not log on, restart the computer again, press the F8 key during startup, and choose the Last Known Good Configuration startup option.

  ○ **B.** Do not log on, restart the computer again, press the F8 key during startup, and choose the Safe Mode startup option.

  ○ **C.** Do not log on, restart the computer again, press the F8 key during startup, and choose the Recovery Console startup option.

  ○ **D.** Do not log on, restart the computer again, press the F8 key during startup, and choose the Enable VGA Mode startup option.

24

Answers to Practice Exam 2

1. C	**21.** D	**41.** C
2. D	**22.** C	**42.** A
3. B	**23.** D	**43.** D
4. A, C	**24.** B, C, E	**44.** B
5. A	**25.** A	**45.** C
6. C	**26.** D	**46.** C
7. D	**27.** A, D	**47.** A, E
8. D	**28.** B	**48.** C, E
9. C	**29.** D	**49.** B, D
10. C, E, G	**30.** B, C	**50.** C
11. B	**31.** C	**51.** A
12. B, C, D	**32.** A, B, F	**52.** B
13. A, C, E	**33.** A	**53.** C
14. A	**34.** A, C	**54.** D
15. B, D	**35.** D	**55.** C
16. B, E	**36.** A	**56.** A, B, E
17. B	**37.** C	**57.** D
18. D	**38.** C, D	**58.** B
19. C, D	**39.** A	**59.** C
20. C	**40.** C	**60.** A

Question 1

Answer C is correct. For users to be able to log on to any computer in the domain and have their desktop settings follow them, you need to configure each user with a roaming user profile. Configure the user account's profile setting to point to a network path that will contain the user settings. As each user logs on to any workstation in the domain, the user profile is downloaded from the server that stores the roaming user profiles. If you rename the `ntuser.dat` to `ntuser.man`, the user profile does not allow any changes to be saved to it. Answer A is incorrect because deleting the local default profile only makes it such that when a new user logs on to the computer, there is no default profile to load. Answer B is incorrect because the system file has nothing to do with the user profile. Answer D is incorrect because deleting the local profile does not allow the user's desktop settings to follow him from workstation to workstation.

Question 2

Answer D is correct. A prestaged computer account is one that has been created in advance. By specifying under Remote Installation Services (RIS) to only accept prestaged requests, you prevent any unauthorized installations. Answer A is incorrect because although Kerberos is a more secure authentication protocol than what was used by NT 4.0, it is does not control who can connect to a RIS server. Answer B is incorrect because there is no default RIS container. Answer C is incorrect. Even though you restrict which users can install with RIS, any of those users still have the ability to install unauthorized operating systems.

Question 3

Answer B is correct. By clicking the View menu and selecting Advanced Features, you can view the Lost and Found Container along with the NTDS Quotas, Program Data, and System containers. Answer A is incorrect because adding yourself to the Enterprise Admins group does not bring the Lost and Found container into view. Answer C is incorrect because the Lost and Found container is not a Windows component that you can add. Answer D is incorrect because there is no option named Show Hidden Containers in the Active Directory Users and Computers (ADUC) console.

Question 4

Answers A and C are correct. Administrators can nest groups and change the scope of groups for the Windows 2000 native and the Windows Server 2003 domain functional levels. Answer B is incorrect because administrators cannot nest groups nor change the scope of groups under the Windows 2000 mixed domain functional level. Answer D is incorrect because administrators cannot nest groups nor change the scope of groups under the Windows Server 2003 interim domain functional level. Answer E is incorrect because the Windows Server 2003 mixed level does not exist.

Question 5

Answer A is correct. Computers that are members of a domain communicate with a domain controller (DC) computer using a secure channel and a password that is automatically generated. This password is changed every 30 days. If the password stored on the DC is not synchronized with the password on the member computer, you get the error message. To fix this problem, you need to reset the computer account. Answer B is incorrect because the error is a computer password problem, not a user password problem. Answer C is incorrect as well because the error is not a user account problem. Answer D is incorrect because the F5 function key refreshes only the screen display, not the computer account.

Question 6

Answer C is correct. This command line creates a distribution group called Sales Reps in the Sales organizational unit (OU) within the East Coast OU in the Windows2003.local domain. Answer A is incorrect because there are no quotes around the LDAP distinguished name, which you need for names with embedded spaces such as "East Coast." Answer B is incorrect because the command-line option "secgrp" does not specify "no." Answer D is incorrect because it creates a security group, not a distribution group.

Question 7

Answer D is correct. Programs such as Microsoft Excel can read and write to .csv files. The csvde.exe command-line tool is Microsoft's preferred method for bulk-importing users into Active Directory. Answer A is incorrect; you use the dsadd.exe command for creating a single user at a time, not for importing and exporting .csv files. Answer B is incorrect because you use ldifde.exe for importing and exporting data in the LDAP format, not the comma-separated values format. Answer C is incorrect because you use the dsget.exe command for displaying the properties of computers, OUs, and other objects within Active Directory; it is not used for importing or exporting data.

Question 8

Answer D is correct. In the Windows 2000 mixed domain mode, domain local groups can contain global groups from any domain in the forest. Answer A is incorrect because universal groups are not available in a Windows 2000 mixed mode domain. Answer B is incorrect because there are two types of Active Directory groups—security and distribution. However, there are no groups that have a group scope of "Security" in an Active Directory domain. Answer C is also incorrect. In a Windows 2000 mixed domain, global groups can contain only user accounts from the same domain.

Question 9

Answer C is correct. Microsoft has started locking down its operating systems by default, which is drastically different from earlier products. Instead of expecting end users to understand how to secure everything, Microsoft now expects the end users to *unlock* those resources they need to use. Answer A is not correct because Full Control is not what is granted to the Everyone group under Windows Server 2003, unlike previous operating systems. Answer B is not correct because deny permissions override allow permissions, meaning that the Everyone group would have *no* permissions at all on the boot partition or volume. Answer D is not correct because the default permissions do not inherit to lower levels in the boot drive volume folder structure—which ensures that someone who misconfigures the root drive volume does not affect other critical system folders, such as the \Windows folder.

Question 10

Answers C, E, and G are correct. There is no direct path to convert from NTFS back to FAT. You must reformat the volume, and if there was any data on it, you must restore it from backup. Of course, that assumes that you backed up the data before reformatting the volume. Answer A is not correct because there is no command-line utility for converting from NTFS to FAT32 or FAT (FAT16). The same is true for Answer B. In fact, the convert command requires the /FS switch but only accepts NTFS as a valid parameter. Answer D is not correct because the Disk Management console does not let you format a volume with the FAT file system if the disk is dynamic. Answer F is not correct because there is no requirement for the drive to be basic.

Question 11

Answer B is correct. Answer A is incorrect because the client software does not reside in the \support\tools folder on the Windows Server 2003 CD-ROM.

Answer C does exist, but it is the Remote Desktop client included with Windows Server 2003, not the Previous Versions client. Answer D is incorrect because there is no default shared folder named PVClient under Windows Server 2003.

Question 12

Answers B, C, and D are correct. Compression is an attribute of the volume and the files and folders stored on that volume. If an entire volume is compressed, all new files and folders created on it are compressed as well. The same can be said for folders that are compressed. And compression is simply a check box in the attributes of a file. Even on a compressed volume, you can choose to not compress a file by turning compression off for that file. Answer A is not correct because compression is not a workaround for exceeding quota limits. The quota engine looks at the actual file size, not the amount of disk space it is using. Answers E and F are not correct because as long as you have the ability to write files to a compressed volume, your files are compressed regardless of your group membership.

Question 13

Answers A, C, and E are correct. By default, Remote Desktop for Administration is not enabled and must be turned on. Once it is on, the default restrictions stop anyone with a blank password from connecting. Users must also be a member of the Remote Desktop Users group to connect. Answer B is not correct because that option is for Remote Assistance, not Remote Desktop connections. Answer D is not correct because it is not the group that she needs to be a member of. Answer F is not correct because although you cannot have a blank password, there is no other default restriction on the type of password required to connect via Remote Desktop connections.

Question 14

Answer A is correct because you must set the quotas individually if you do not want to affect all users equally. Answer B is not correct because you cannot set a quota on a group. Answer C is not correct because quotas are not available through the ADUC console. Answer D is not correct because, again, quotas cannot be set on groups, and in addition, the 50 should be actually be 50000000 to approximate 50MB.

Question 15

Answers B and D are correct because FAT32 is accessible by most previous Microsoft operating systems and many other non-Microsoft operating systems as well. Answer A is not correct because FAT32 has no native method of applying permissions to files and folders. Answer C is not correct because NTFS gives you this ability and is a better choice for fault tolerance than FAT32. Answer E is not correct because NTFS, not FAT32, gives you the ability to compress files at the file-system level.

Question 16

Answers B and E are correct. The Shared Folders console allows you to publish a shared folder into Active Directory, either while the share is being created or after the fact from the properties of the share. ADUC allows you to create a shared-folder object that points to a physical shared folder on a server. Answer A is not correct because the net share command does not let you publish to Active Directory. Answer C is not correct because the standard properties of the folder, accessed from the Windows Explorer, offer nothing in terms of publishing to Active Directory. Only the properties accessed from the Shared Folders snap-in have the elusive Publishing tab. Answer D is not correct because Windows Explorer does not offer that option, as previously discussed.

Question 17

Answer B is correct because Telnet lets you execute only command-line programs. The correct command line to run is the net share command as specified; however, leaving the Telnet port open on a firewall is not a recommended practice because of the security vulnerability that it creates. Answer A is not correct because the question does not state that dialing into the server is an option, and Windows 95 cannot support the Windows Server 2003 administration tools. Answer C is not correct because a Telnet session does not let you run GUI utilities. Answer D is not correct because the command line listed is wrong.

Question 18

Answer D is correct because the Accounting group has been denied the write permission to the folder. Answer A is not correct because the share permissions are wide open. Answer B is not correct because the User group allows modify, which includes write. Answer C is not correct because the combination of just Max and the User group allows modify, which also includes write.

Question 19

Answers C and D are correct because Shadow Copies of Shared Folders is enabled at the drive volume (or drive letter) level. Answers A and B are not correct because you do not work with Shadow Copies at the disk level. Answer E is not correct because drive F: does not need shadow copies. Answer F is not correct because you cannot enable Shadow Copies only for specific shares.

Question 20

Answer C is correct because the designated data recovery agent (DRA) is the user whose encryption certificate is allowed to decrypt files. Answer A is not correct because you are not allowed to copy the encrypted files unless you have access to them. Answer B is not correct because the file is backed up in an encrypted state and restored in an encrypted state. Answer D is not correct because once a file is encrypted, it can only be unencrypted by the owner of the file or by the DRA.

Question 21

Answer D is correct. By right-clicking the `E:\Common\Sales\VPs` folder, you can select the Security tab, click the Advanced button, and then click the Effective Permissions tab to determine Alison's effective NTFS permissions for the folder. Answer A is not correct because if you make Alison a member of the Administrators group, you are giving her far more permission than she needs. Answers B and C are not correct because you should not assign NTFS permissions directly to user accounts; you should add users to the appropriate groups and then grant those groups the proper permissions.

Question 22

Answer C is correct because the Effective Permissions dialog box takes into account all user permissions and group permissions, both for the local computer and for the domain, as it calculates the effective permissions granted to a user. Answer A is not correct because it is only a subset of the actual effective permissions. Answer B is not correct because it does not include inherited permissions in the list. Answer D is not correct because it does not take user and other group permissions into account.

Question 23

Answer D is correct because NTFS disk quotas apply only to the uncompressed disk-space sizes of files. When Amy attempts to copy a 5MB file onto drive E: when her used quota amount is already 97MB, she would exceed her disk quota, so the file copy operation is not allowed and a message box appears. Answer A is not correct because disk quotas disregard NTFS compressed file sizes. Answer

C is not correct because NTFS disk quotas are enforced by not allowing users to exceed their disk-quota limits, even by just a little bit; there are no "grace periods." Answer D is not correct because you cannot implement disk quotas on groups.

Question 24

Answers B, C, and E are correct because they are all features of NTFS and some of the most compelling reasons to use it over FAT or FAT32. Answer A is not correct because this behavior describes the method used to compress a drive in earlier versions of MS-DOS. NTFS compresses on a file-by-file basis, giving better performance and functionality. Answer D is not correct because you cannot format floppy disks with the NTFS file system. Answer F is incorrect because you cannot format DVD recordable/rewritable or CD recordable/rewritable media as NTFS. CD media generally use the CD-ROM File System (CDFS) format and DVD media generally use the UDFS format.

Question 25

Answer A is correct because this option allows one set of permissions to essentially take effect for everyone, whether they log on locally or remotely. By setting share permissions to allow full control, they allow wide-open access, meaning that NTFS permissions are what actually enforces any restrictions. Because NTFS permissions take effect whether a user is local or remote, it is exactly what Henrietta has in mind. Answer B is not correct because the default share permissions allow only read access to a share, which could be more restrictive than NTFS permissions—which is not consistent with local file access. Answer C is not correct because share permissions affect only remote file access. Answer D is not correct because share permissions affect only remote file access—which means that someone sitting locally at the server is not affected by share permissions at all!

Question 26

Answer D is the correct choice because Windows Server 2003 tightened the defaults. First introduced in Windows XP, Everyone:Allow Read is the default permission for all new shares. Answer A is not correct because that is not the default permission. Answer B is not correct because the Everyone group is not granted Allow Full Control by default. Answer C is incorrect because it actually lists an NTFS permission rather than a share permission.

Question 27

Answers A and D are correct. Answer A is correct because you will find the setting for Isolation Mode under the Services tab for the website's properties. Answer D is correct because this server was upgraded from Windows 2000 Server and IIS 5.0. Because it was an upgrade from IIS 5.0, it operates in IIS 5.0 Isolation Mode to maintain compatibility with existing applications. Answers B and C are incorrect because you configure Isolation Mode under the Services tab on the website properties window. Answer E is incorrect because when you upgrade to IIS 6.0 from IIS 5.0, IIS maintains IIS 5.0 Isolation Mode.

Question 28

Answer B is correct. By default, no components or services are installed when IIS 6.0 is installed. Under a default installation, you must manually select the Remote Administration (HTML) option if you want remote-administration capabilities. Answer A is incorrect because you are opening IE 6.0 locally on server02; no firewall is involved. Answer C is incorrect because you do not need to restart the Internet services when you add components. Answer D is incorrect because you have not yet logged on to the Remote Administration website.

Question 29

Answer D is correct. For only the administrator to not receive the Explorer Enhanced Security Configuration error message, you must clear the For Administrator Groups check box in the Internet Explorer Enhanced Security Configuration option in Add/Remove Windows Components. Answers A and C are incorrect because the option to disable this feature is in Add/Remove Windows Components on the server. Answer B is incorrect because having both options selected enables this feature for all groups who can browse from the server.

Question 30

Answers B and C are both correct. You can set authentication requirements and you can specify the users to be granted access with both of these utilities. Answers A, D, and E are incorrect because you do not use these utilities to configure settings for IIS.

Question 31

Answer C is correct. IUSR_*ServerName* is the name of the local or domain account, depending on whether the web server is a member of a domain. This user account gives website users the ability to access the website without having to enter a valid username and password. Answer A is incorrect because there is no such user account by default. Answer B is incorrect because this user account grants the Log On as a Batch Job user right and is used for web applications. Answer D is incorrect because it is actually a group that contains the IWAM_*ServerName* and various other groups for running web applications.

Question 32

Answers A, B, and F are correct. You must have write permissions to save the changes back to the web server. You must have read permissions to "read" the file, and you must have script source access to modify, delete, or add to the script files in the virtual directory. Answer C is incorrect because Directory Browsing is not required for modifying scripts. Answer D is incorrect because the Index This Resource permission is not required for modifying scripts. Answer E is incorrect because the Log Visits permission is not required for modifying scripts.

Question 33

Answer A is correct. You can only enable Directory Browsing for an entire website. Answer B is incorrect because removing all permissions disables anyone from reading, writing, or browsing the website. Answer C is incorrect because the Web Site tab does not contain the Directory Browsing option. Answer D is incorrect because this option enables Directory Browsing for all the websites that this server is hosting.

Question 34

Answers A and C are correct. Answer B is incorrect because `iisext.vbs` enables and lists applications; adds and removes application dependencies; enables, disables, and lists web service extensions; and adds, removes, enables, disables, and lists individual files. Answer D is incorrect because `iisapp.vbs` lists applications that are running. Answer E is incorrect because `iisweb.vbs` creates, deletes, and lists websites that are being hosted on servers running Windows Server 2003. The `iisweb.vbs` script starts, stops, and pauses a website as well.

Question 35

Answer D is correct. To use the Shadow Copies capability, you must connect to the file using a network path. Answer A is not correct because restoring the server from tape is definitely not the fastest way to recover this drawing. Answer B is not correct because you cannot use Shadow Copies by connecting to a physical drive path. Answer C is not correct because restoring the file from tape is not as fast as restoring the shadow copy that was created no longer than two hours ago.

Question 36

Answer A is correct because you need networking support to copy the file from the remote computer. Safe Mode should enable the computer to start well enough to run the reversion program and get the server working again. Answer B is not correct because not only does the server not have a floppy disk, but all drives are NTFS, so MS-DOS cannot access them. Answer C is not correct because ASR is meant to restore a server quickly from bare metal, not simply recover from one driver problem. Answer D is not correct because the Recovery Console does not give you network support or the ability to roll back a driver.

Question 37

Answer C is correct because you must execute `winnt32 /cmdcons` to install the Recovery Console as a boot option. Answer A is not correct because there is no choice to install the Recovery Console from Add or Remove Programs. Answer B is not correct because you can launch the Recovery Console when you boot from the Windows Server 2003 CD-ROM, but you cannot install the Recovery Console from the CD-ROM. Answer D is not correct because you will not find the Recovery Console on the Windows Update website.

Question 38

Answers C and D are correct. The ASR process backs up the system state, the operating-system files, the drive configuration, the service configuration, and other critical information about the configuration of the operating system. Answer A is incorrect because ASR does not back up user data. Answer B is incorrect because ASR does not back up the shadow copies of all shared folders. Answer E is not correct because you cannot specify any extra data to back up during an ASR backup.

Question 39

Answer A is correct. F2 is the correct key to press when booting from the Windows Server 2003 CD-ROM. Answer B is not correct because you launch an ASR restore when you cannot boot into Windows Server 2003, which means you could not run `NTBackup.exe`. Answer C is not correct because pressing the F6 key prompts you to install a mass storage device driver; it does not launch ASR. Answer D is incorrect because that command does not exist in the Recovery Console, and you cannot launch an ASR restore from the Recovery Console.

Question 40

Answer C is correct. *Crashdump* is the term Microsoft uses to refer to the process of writing memory to a file when a STOP error occurs on your server. It chose to use this same term in reference to forcing a crashdump to happen. Answers A and D provide commands that do not exist. Answer B refers to the special administration console that you can access if all other avenues of gaining control of your server fail.

Question 41

Answer C is correct because there is a requirement for hardware support. Serial Port Console Redirection (SPCR) must be supported by the hardware before Emergency Management Services (EMS) can function. Answer A is not correct because it does give you the ability to manage basic tasks via the serial port. Answer B is not correct because you can reboot a server if necessary. Answer D is not correct because the service does utilize out-of-band management, which means managing the server through non-normal channels.

Question 42

Answer A is correct because Norma's last boot and logon before installing the new network card driver was successful. That configuration was saved as the last known good. She can boot into the Last Known Good Configuration and be at a point right before she installed the bad network card driver. Answer B is not correct because ASR restores the state of the operating system on the server to the point when an ASR backup was made. Answer C is not correct because, although it might get the server back to a stable operating state, it is not the quickest method of undoing Norma's changes. Answer D is not correct because disabling the Workstation service does not undo the problems caused by the new network card driver.

Question 43

Answer D is correct. You simply need to choose the System State check box in the Backup Utility to ensure that all System State components are backed up. Answer A is incorrect because there is no ability to restore from the command prompt; besides, the question asks how to create a backup scheme. Answer B is incorrect because the boot loader menu does not offer an option named Backup System State. Answer C is incorrect because you cannot selectively choose which System State components are to be backed up.

Question 44

Answer B is correct. You did not perform an authoritative restore. You must use the NTDSUtil.exe utility to perform the authoritative restore. Answer A is incorrect because you can restore the system state on any DC in the domain. Answer C is incorrect because Pete had the required permissions to restore the system state. However, Pete did not perform an authoritative restore. Answer D is incorrect because the age of the backup set is not relevant.

Question 45

Answer C is correct. You must know the Directory Services Restore Mode administrator's password that was created when the server was promoted using dcpromo to a DC. It is a separate account from the domain administrator's account. Answer A is incorrect because it is not the cause of the administrator not being able to log on. Answer B is incorrect because you can do an authoritative restore on any DC in the domain. Answer D is incorrect because a Group Policy Object (GPO) setting has no effect on the administrative logon under Directory Services Restore Mode.

Question 46

Answer C is correct. You want to use a primary restore on the first DC and a normal (nonauthoritative) restore on the other DCs. Answers A, B, and D are incorrect because a primary restore should be the restore method on the first DC.

Question 47

Answers A and E are not needed. The ASR set is not needed for an Active Directory authoritative restore, and the person performing the restore must know the password for the Directory Services Restore Mode administrator. Answers B, C, and D are needed to resolve this problem.

Question 48

Answers C and E are correct. You can do the restore from this DC; however, it must be an authoritative restore. Answers A and D are incorrect because you need to perform the restore only on the DC that had the OU deleted. Answer B is incorrect because it must be an authoritative restore for the restored data to replicate. Answer F is incorrect because performing a primary restore will not solve the problem.

Question 49

Answers B and D are correct. Data is not verified and "Do not replace the file on my computer (recommended)" are both the defaults. Answers A, C, and E are all correctly defined as defaults.

Question 50

Answer C is correct. You want to enable this option to prevent unauthorized access to these files and folders. Answer A is incorrect because it would unnecessarily affect other backup operators from performing their jobs. Answer B is incorrect because of the sensitive nature of these files. It would be inappropriate for the administrator to arbitrarily take ownership of those folders and files. Also, if you remove all users from the Backup Operators group, only administrators could back up those files. Answer D is incorrect because if you performed this step, only the administrators would be able to back up the files and folders.

Question 51

Answer A is correct. The License Logging service is installed by default but not started. To work with licensing, you must start the Licensing Logging service. Answer B is incorrect because you do not enable licensing on a DC. Answer C is incorrect because there is no default licensing group. Answer D is incorrect because although you can view the license site settings in Active Directory Sites and Services, you cannot see any information on the actual licenses themselves.

Question 52

Answer B is correct. When you move the print spooler to a different drive volume, you need to stop and restart the spooler service before the change to the new spooler folder takes effect. Answer A is incorrect because reinstalling the printer drivers does not make the print-spooler service restart. Answer C is incorrect because the problem is not a permissions issue. Answer D is incorrect because there is no printer service in the Services snap-in.

Question 53

Answer C is correct. By setting up a logical printer for the Accounting department, you can have large print jobs print after hours and not tie up the printer for all the other users. Answer A is incorrect because although it provides a solution, it is a costly one, so it is not the best solution to the problem. Answer B is incorrect because changing the priority to 99 gives the Accounting department's print jobs a lower priority, but when it prints large jobs, it still ties up the printer for the other users. Answer D is incorrect because setting the priority of 2 gives the Accounting department's print jobs a higher priority and ties up the printer, which is opposite of what you are trying to do.

Question 54

Answer D is correct. Performance Logs and Alerts allow you to monitor many aspects of printing and printer performance, including job errors, not-ready errors, and out-of-paper errors. Answer A is incorrect because System Monitor does not allow you to gather information on printing. Answer B is incorrect because system log in the Event Viewer does not contain information on printer performance. Answer C is incorrect because the advanced print server properties contain no information on printer performance.

Question 55

Answer C is correct. For Software Update Services (SUS) to work correctly, IIS 5.0 or higher must be installed. With Windows Server 2003, IIS 6.0 is not installed by default, so in this instance, you must install it separately. Answer A is incorrect because you need to have at least 6GB of disk space available. Answer B is incorrect because the Internet Explorer version on Windows 2003 is already IE 6.0. Answer D is incorrect because enabling Remote Procedure Calls (RPCs) is not part of the procedure to enable SUS.

Question 56

Answers A, B, and E are correct. For computers to be able to receive automatic updates through WSUS, they must have the Automatic Updates software installed. Windows NT 4.0 does not have Automatic Updates installed and neither does Windows 2000 Professional without Service Pack 3. Windows XP Home cannot be a member of a domain, so it cannot use SUS. Answers C, D, and F are incorrect because all the computers mentioned have the Automatic Updates service installed and therefore could use SUS.

Question 57

Answer D is correct. The Event ID 36 indicates that a user who is being monitored for disk-storage space has exceeded his or her allowable amount, which shows up in the System log. Answer A is incorrect because this Event ID refers to disk quotas, not the paging file. Answer B is incorrect because Event ID 36 does not refer to a low disk-space warning. Answer C is incorrect because the Event ID 36 deals with disk quotas, not disk time for performance monitoring.

Question 58

Answer B is correct. An increase in nonpaged bytes without a corresponding increase in server load indicates that one or many programs have not released their allocated memory back to the server's memory pool—which is referred to as a memory leak. Answer A is incorrect because the stated problem is not an indication of a RAM module going bad. Answer C is incorrect because excessive paging is measured in page faults, not in nonpaged bytes. Answer D is incorrect because nonpaged bytes have nothing to do with a process using a disproportional amount of RAM.

Question 59

Answer C is correct. Both the `asr.sif` file and the `asrpnp.sif` file are stored in the `%systemroot%\repair` folder by default. By restoring these files from the ASR backup media set, you can copy these files onto a floppy disk to use as the ASR floppy disk. Answer A is incorrect because you cannot use a Windows Server 2003 boot disk in place of the ASR floppy disk. Answer B is incorrect because using an ASR floppy disk that was created on another computer is not supported, especially if the other computer is not running Windows Server 2003. Answer D is incorrect because you can perform an ASR restore without the original ASR floppy disk, if you restore both the `asr.sif` file and the `asrpnp.sif` files from backup to a new floppy disk.

Question 60

Answer A is correct. Selecting the Last Known Good Configuration startup option is the fastest and easiest way to roll back the video driver to the previous version. Answer B is incorrect because the new video driver would not necessarily work under the Safe Mode option, and even if it did, you'd still have to go to the Display Properties and change the driver. Answer C is incorrect because you cannot select the Recovery Console by pressing the F8 key, and it is a more involved procedure than simply using the Last Known Good Configuration. Answer D is incorrect because you need to log on under VGA Mode, change the video driver, and then restart the computer again before you resolve the problem; the Last Known Good Configuration option is faster and easier to implement.

Suggested Readings and Resources

Because *Exam Cram* books focus entirely on Microsoft certification exam objectives, you can broaden your knowledge of Windows Server 2003 by taking advantage of the plethora of technical material that's available. Books, websites, and even the Windows Server 2003 built-in help system offer a wealth of technical insight for network and system administrators. In the following pages, we present a list of valuable resources that you can check out at your leisure.

Microsoft Windows Server 2003 Help and Support

Your first source for help with any aspect of Microsoft Windows Server 2003 should be the user-assistance features that Microsoft ships with its server products:

▶ *Help and Support*—This option is available within the Manage Your Server interface, as well as through the Start menu, and provides access to the Help and Support Center, where you can search through the online help files installed with your server.

▶ *List of Common Administrative Tasks*—This option is available within the Manage Your Server interface and provides access to a list of the more common administrative tasks you might be expected to use, along with examples of each task.

You should also check out

- *Microsoft Windows Server 2003 Resource Kit*, Redmond, Washington, Microsoft Press, 2005.

- *Microsoft Windows Security Resource Kit, Second Edition*, Redmond, Washington, Microsoft Press, 2005.

Books

The following are some useful books on Windows Server 2003:

- Boswell, William. *Inside Microsoft Windows Server 2003*. Boston, Massachusetts: Addison-Wesley Professional, 2003.

- Honeycutt, Jerry. *Introducing Microsoft Windows Server 2003*. Redmond, Washington: Microsoft Press, 2003.

- Minasi, Mark, et al. *Mastering Windows Server 2003*. Alameda, California: Sybex, 2003.

- Morimoto, Rand, et al. *Microsoft Windows Server 2003 Unleashed*. Indianapolis, Indiana: Sams Publishing, 2003.

- Regan, Patrick. *Networking with Windows 2000 and 2003*. Upper Saddle River, New Jersey: Prentice Hall, 2004.

- Scales, Lee, and John Michell. *MCSA/MCSE 70-290 Training Guide: Managing and Maintaining a Windows Server 2003 Environment*. Indianapolis, Indiana: Que Publishing, 2003.

- Stanek, William R. *Microsoft Windows Server 2003 Administrator's Pocket Consultant*. Redmond, Washington: Microsoft Press, 2003.

- Stanek, William R. *Windows Server 2003*. Redmond, Washington: Microsoft Press, 2003.

Websites

The following are useful Internet resources for Windows Server 2003:

- The Microsoft Windows Server 2003 site (many documents and technical references for this product line)—http://www.microsoft.com/windowsserver2003/

- ▶ The Microsoft Server 2003 MSDN site (access to any technical references and downloads)—`http://msdn.microsoft.com/library/ default.asp?url=/nhp/default.asp?contentid=28001691`

- ▶ The MSDN Windows Script site (extensive information on scripting)— `http://msdn.microsoft.com/library/default.asp?url=/nhp/ Default.asp?contentid=28001169`

- ▶ The Microsoft download site for the Group Policy Management Console (GPMC), including additional details on this free download (gpmc.msi)—`http://www.microsoft.com/downloads/ details.aspx?FamilyID=0a6d4c24-8cbd-4b35-9272- dd3cbfc81887&DisplayLang=en`

- ▶ The Microsoft download site for the Remote Control add-in to the Windows Server 2003 Active Directory Users and Computers MMC— `http://www.microsoft.com/downloads/details.aspx?FamilyID=0a9 1d2e7-7594-4abb-8239-7a7eca6a6cb1&DisplayLang=en`

- ▶ The Windows Server 2003 Terminal Services Technology site— `http://support.microsoft.com/default.aspx?scid=fh; EN-US;winsvr2003term`

- ▶ The Windows Software Update Service home page— `http://www. microsoft.com/downloads/details.aspx?FamilyID=9e89e4ef- 00a8-4193-8997-fe4e92215a57&DisplayLang=en`

- ▶ The Automatic Update Client for the SUS service, along with additional information on the Automatic Update process—`http://www. microsoft.com/windows2000/downloads/recommended/susclient/`

- ▶ The Windows Update site, which allows an automated evaluation of hotfixes and service packs—`http://windowsupdate.microsoft.com`

- ▶ What's New in Internet Information Services 6.0—`http://www. microsoft.com/windowsserver2003/evaluation/overview/ technologies/iis.mspx`

- ▶ *MCP Magazine*—IIS 6.0 Mature at Last: Microsoft's Internet Information Server—`http://mcpmag.com/features/article.asp? editorialsid=330`

- ▶ Microsoft TechNet Windows Server 2003 TechCenter—`http://www. microsoft.com/technet/windowsserver/default.mspx`

- ▶ Microsoft Training and Certifications site—`http://www.microsoft. com/traincert/`

- Microsoft Preparation Guide for Exam 70-290— `http://www.microsoft.com/traincert/exams/70-290.asp`

- The Shadow Copies of Shared Folders client—`http://www.microsoft.com/windowsserver2003/downloads/shadowcopyclient.mspx`

- Technical Overview of Windows Server 2003—`http://www.microsoft.com/windowsserver2003/techinfo/overview/`

- Introduction to Shadow Copies of Shared Folders—`http://www.microsoft.com/windowsserver2003/techinfo/overview/scr.mspx`

- White paper: Windows Server 2003 security guide— `http://microsoft.com/downloads/details.aspx?FamilyId=8A2643C1-0685-4D89-B655-521EA6C7B4DB&displaylang=en`

Accessing Your Free MeasureUp Practice Test—Including Networking Simulations!

This Exam Cram book features exclusive access to MeasureUp's practice questions, including networking simulations! These simulations are yet another excellent study tool to help you assess your readiness for the 70-290 exam. MeasureUp is a Microsoft Certified Practice Test Provider, so these simulations validate your hands-on skills by modeling real-life networking scenarios—requiring you to perform tasks on simulated networking devices. MeasureUp's simulations also assess your ability to troubleshoot and solve realistic networking problems. If you are planning to take the certification exam for 70-290, you should expect to see performance-based simulations on the exam. MeasureUp's Microsoft simulations will ensure you are prepared.

To access your free practice questions and simulations:

1. Retrieve your unique product ID number on the inside of the back cover of this book.

2. Go to www.measureup.com.

3. Create a free MeasureUp login account.

4. In your Personal Test Locker, on the Personal Test Locker Toolbar, click Register Test.

5. Read and accept the License Agreement by checking the check box below the License Agreement.

6. Type your key number in the text box. Do not remove any dashes or substitute any numbers.

590

Appendix B: Accessing Your Free MeasureUp Practice Test—Including Networking Simulations!

7. Click Register.

8. Click the Test Launcher link to display your Personal Test Locker.

9. Click the Practice Test link, and follow the instructions to start your test.

For more details about MeasureUp's product features, see Appendix C, "MeasureUp's Product Features."

APPENDIX C

MeasureUp's Product Features

Since 1997, MeasureUp has helped more than one million IT professionals achieve certifications from the industry's leading vendors. Created by content developers certified in their areas and with real-world experience, MeasureUp practice tests feature comprehensive questions (some with performance-based simulations), detailed explanations, and complete score reporting. As a Microsoft Certified Practice Test Provider, MeasureUp's practice tests are the closest you can get to the certification exams!

Multiple Testing Modes

MeasureUp practice tests are available in Study, Certification, Custom, Missed Question, and Non-Duplicate question modes.

Study Mode

Tests administered in Study Mode allow you to request the correct answer(s) and explanation for each question during the test. These tests are not timed. You can modify the testing environment *during* the test by clicking the Options button.

Certification Mode

Tests administered in Certification Mode closely simulate the actual testing environment you will encounter when taking a certification exam. These tests do not allow you to request the answer(s) or explanation for each question until after the exam.

Custom Mode

Custom Mode allows you to specify your preferred testing environment. Use this mode to specify the objectives you want to include in your test, the timer length, and other test properties. You can also modify the testing environment *during* the test by clicking the Options button.

Missed Question Mode

Missed Question Mode allows you to take a test containing only the questions you missed previously.

Non-Duplicate Mode

Non-Duplicate Mode allows you to take a test containing only questions not displayed previously.

Question Types

The practice question types simulate the real exam experience, and include

- ▶ Create a tree
- ▶ Select and place
- ▶ Drop and connect
- ▶ Build list
- ▶ Reorder list
- ▶ Build and reorder list
- ▶ Single hotspot
- ▶ Multiple hotspots
- ▶ Live screen
- ▶ Command line
- ▶ Hot area
- ▶ Fill in the blank

Random Questions and Order of Answers

This feature helps you learn the material without memorizing questions and answers. Each time you take a practice test, the questions and answers appear in a different randomized order.

Detailed Explanations of Correct and Incorrect Answers

You'll receive automatic feedback on all correct and incorrect answers. The detailed answer explanations are a superb learning tool in their own right.

Attention to Exam Objectives

MeasureUp practice tests are designed to appropriately balance the questions over each technical area covered by a specific exam.

Technical Support

If you encounter problems with the MeasureUp test engine on the CD-ROM, you can contact MeasureUp at 678-356-5050 or email support@measureup.com. Technical support hours are from 8 a.m. to 5 p.m. EST Monday through Friday. Additionally, you'll find Frequently Asked Questions (FAQs) at www. measureup.com.

If you'd like to purchase additional MeasureUp products, telephone 678-356-5050 or 800-649-1MUP (1687), or visit www.measureup.com.

Glossary

A

A (address) resource record A resource record that is used to map a Domain Name System (DNS) domain name to a host Internet Protocol (IP) address on the network.

Accelerated Graphics Port (AGP) An interface specification developed by Intel that is based on peripheral connection interface (PCI), but is designed especially for the throughput demands of 3D graphics. The AGP channel is 32 bits wide and runs at 66MHz, which translates into a total bandwidth of 266Mbps, as opposed to the PCI bandwidth of 133Mbps. AGP also supports two optional faster modes, with throughputs of 533Mbps and 1.07Gbps.

access control entry (ACE) An entry in an access control list (ACL). An ACE contains a set of access rights and a security identifier (SID) that identifies a user or group for whom the rights are allowed, denied, or audited.

access control list (ACL) A list of each user who has access to an object, such as an Active Directory object or an NTFS file or folder, and the type of access they have to the object.

account lockout   A Windows Server 2003 security feature that locks a user account if a certain number of failed logon attempts occur within a specified amount of time, based on security-policy lockout settings. Locked accounts cannot log on.

Active Directory   The directory service that is included with Windows Server 2003. Active Directory is based on the X.500 standards and those of its predecessor, Lightweight Directory Access Protocol (LDAP). It stores information about objects on a network and makes this information available to applications, users, and network administrators. Active Directory is also used for authentication to network resources, using a single logon process. It provides network administrators a hierarchical view of the network and a single point of administration for all network objects.

Active Directory Users and Computers (ADUC) snap-in (console)   An administrative tool designed to perform daily Active Directory administration tasks, including creating, deleting, modifying, moving, and setting permissions on objects stored in the Active Directory database. These objects include organizational units (OUs), users, contacts, groups, computers, printers, and shared file objects.

Address Resolution Protocol (ARP)   A protocol that translates an IP address into a physical address, such as a Media Access Control (MAC) address (hardware address).

administrative template   A setting found within group policies that provide the primary means of administering the user environment and defining the end-user computing experience. For example, you can define most options found when configuring the Start menu, taskbar, Desktop, Control Panel, printers, network options, system settings, and Internet Explorer.

Advanced Configuration and Power Interface (ACPI)   A power-management specification developed by Intel, Microsoft, and Toshiba that enables Windows Server 2003 to control the amount of power given to each device attached to the computer.

Advanced Power Management (APM)   An application programming interface (API) developed by Intel and Microsoft that allows developers to include power management in the Basic Input/Output System (BIOS). APM defines a layer between the hardware and the operating system that effectively shields programmers from hardware details. ACPI has replaced APM.

AGP   See *Accelerated Graphics Port*.

ARP   See *Address Resolution Protocol*.

Asynchronous Transfer Mode (ATM)   A networking technology that transfers data in cells (that is, data packets of a fixed size). Cells used with ATM are small compared to packets used with older technologies. Current implementations of ATM support data transfer rates from 25Mbps to 622Mbps. Most Ethernet-based networks run at 100Mbps or below.

attribute   A single property that describes an object, such as the make, model, or color that describes a car. In the context of directories, an attribute is the main component of an entry in a directory, such as an email address.

auditing   The process that tracks the activities of users by recording selected types of events in the security log of a server or workstation.

authoritative restore   A type of restore for Active Directory objects on a domain controller (DC) that updates the objects' update sequence numbers (USNs) to indicate that those objects should be replicated to other DCs throughout the forest. You must use the ntdsutil.exe utility to mark Active Directory objects as "authoritative."

Auto Private IP Addressing (APIPA)
A client-side feature of Windows 98 and 2000 DHCP clients. If the client's attempt to negotiate with a DHCP server fails, the client computer automatically selects an IP address from the 169.254.0.0 Class B range.

Automated System Recovery (ASR)
A feature in Windows Server 2003 and Windows XP Professional that allows you to create a recovery

backup set using the Windows Backup Utility that consists of a media backup of the system and boot drive volumes and the System State along with a backup ASR floppy disk.

Automatic Update   A service that checks with the Windows Update website for critical updates and automates the process of downloading and installing the critical updates.

B

backup domain controller (BDC)   In Windows NT 4 Server/domains, a server that receives a copy of the domain's directory database (which contains all the account and security policy information for the domain). BDCs can continue to participate in an Active Directory domain when the domain is configured in mixed mode.

Backup Utility   A Windows Server 2003 utility that helps you plan for and recover from data loss by allowing you to create backup copies of data as well as restore files, folders, and System State data (which includes the Registry) manually or on a schedule. The Windows Server 2003 Backup Utility allows you to back up data to a variety of media types besides tape. You can also run backups from the command line using ntbackup.exe and specifying the appropriate command-line options.

baselining   The process of measuring system performance so that you can ascertain a standard or expected level of performance.

basic disk   A term that indicates a physical disk, which can have primary and extended partitions. A basic disk can contain up to three primary partitions and one extended partition, or it can have up to four primary partitions. A basic disk can also have a single extended partition with logical drives.

BDC   See *backup domain controller*.

BIOS (Basic Input/Output System)   Built-in software that determines what a computer can do without accessing programs from a disk. On PCs, the BIOS contains all the code required to control the keyboard, display screen, disk drives, serial communications, and a number of miscellaneous functions.

boot partition   The partition that contains the Windows Server 2003 operating system and its support files.

C

Challenge Handshake Authentication Protocol (CHAP)   An authentication protocol used by Microsoft remote access as well as network and dial-up connections. By using CHAP, a remote access client can send its authentication credentials to a remote access server in a secure form. Microsoft has modified the original CHAP, as specified in RFC 1334. These versions are Windows specific, such as Microsoft CHAP (MS-CHAP) and MS-CHAP 2.

CLI (command-line interface)   A software tool or utility that runs from the command line rather than from the graphical user interface (GUI).

client-side caching (CSC)   See *offline files*.

compression   The process of making individual files and folders occupy less physical disk space. You can compress data using NT File System (NTFS) compression or through third-party utilities. See also *NTFS data compression*.

computer account   An account that a domain administrator creates and that uniquely identifies the computer on the domain. The Windows Server 2003 computer account matches the name of the computer that joins the domain.

Computer Management console   An MMC that allows you to manage your server. It includes device manager, event viewer, shared folders, local users and groups, disk defragmenter, disk management, and services console.

container   An object in a directory that contains other objects.

convert.exe   A Windows Server 2003 command-line utility that turns a FAT or FAT32 drive volume into an NTFS drive volume without having to reformat or delete any data that is stored on the drive. The command-line syntax is `convert.exe X: /FS:NTFS`, where *X:* represents the drive letter that you want to convert to NTFS. There is no equivalent command to convert from NTFS to FAT or FAT32.

copy backup   A backup type that backs up all selected files, but each backed up file's archive bit is not changed.

counter   A metric that provides information about particular aspects of system performance.

D

DACL   See *discretionary access control list*.

daily backup   A backup of files that have changed today which does not mark them as being backed up.

data compression   The process of making individual files and folders occupy less physical disk space. You can compress data using NTFS compression or through third-party utilities. See also *NTFS data compression*.

data recovery agent (DRA)   A Windows Server 2003 administrator who has been issued a public-key certificate for the express purpose of recovering user-encrypted data files that have been encrypted with Encrypting File System (EFS). *Data recovery* refers to the process of

decrypting a file without having the private key of the user who encrypted the file.

default gateway   An address that serves an important role in Transmission Control Protocol/Internet Protocol (TCP/IP) networking by providing a default route for TCP/IP hosts to use when communicating with other hosts on remote networks.

defense-in-depth model   A layered approach that includes securing the network infrastructure, the communication protocols, servers, applications that run on the server, and the file system. It should also require some form of user authentication. When you configure a strong layered defense, an intruder has to break through several layers to reach his or her objects.

Delegate Administrative Control   A method to give sufficient permission to an Active Directory container so that the user or group will have administrative control for the OU and the objects in it.

Device Manager   The primary tool used in Windows Server 2003 to configure and manage hardware devices and their settings.

DHCP server   See *Dynamic Host Configuration Protocol server*.

dial-up access   A type of access in which a remote client uses a public telephone line or Integrated Services Digital Network (ISDN) line to create a connection to a Windows Server 2003 remote access server.

differential backup   A backup that copies files created or changed since the last normal or incremental backup. A differential backup does *not* mark files as having been backed up. (In other words, the archive attribute is not cleared.) If you are performing a combination of normal and differential backups, when you restore files and folders, you need the last normal backup as well as the last differential backup.

digital signature   Public-key cryptography that authenticates the integrity and originator of a communication.

Direct Memory Access (DMA)   A technique for transferring data from main memory to a device without passing it through the CPU. Computers that have DMA channels can transfer data to and from devices more quickly than can computers without DMA channels. It is useful for making quick backups and for real-time applications.

Directory Services Restore Mode   A startup option for DCs only. When restoring the System State and Active Directory objects from backup, you must restart the server under Directory Services Restore Mode.

discretionary access control list (DACL)   A list of ACEs that lets administrators set permissions for users and groups at the object and attribute levels. This list represents part of an object's security descriptor that allows or denies permissions to specific users and groups.

disk group   In Windows Server 2003, a collection of multiple dynamic disks that are managed together. All dynamic disks in a computer are members of the same disk group. Each disk in a disk group stores replicas of the same configuration data, and this configuration data is stored in a 1MB region at the end of each dynamic disk.

Disk Management   A Windows Server 2003 Microsoft Management Console (MMC) snap-in that you use to perform all disk maintenance tasks, such as formatting, creating partitions, deleting partitions, and converting a basic disk to a dynamic disk.

disk quota   A control that you use in Windows Server 2003 to limit the amount of hard-disk space available for all users or an individual user. You can apply a quota on a per-user, per-volume basis only.

diskpart.exe   A command-line utility that you use for managing disk storage, including creating and deleting partitions and volumes and formatting partitions and volumes.

distribution group   A group that can contain users and other groups which cannot be assigned an access control list (ACL); no security permissions may be assigned to a distribution group. It is used as a distribution list for email purposes.

DMA   See *Direct Memory Access.*

DNS   See *Domain Name System.*

domain   The fundamental administrative unit of Active Directory. A domain stores information about objects in the domain's partition of Active Directory. You can give user and group accounts in a domain privileges and permissions to resources on any system that belongs to the domain.

domain controller (DC)   A computer running Windows Server 2003 that hosts Active Directory and manages user access to a network, including logons, authentication, and access to the directory and shared resources.

domain forest   A collection of one or more Active Directory domains in a noncontiguous DNS namespace that share a common schema, configuration, and global catalog and that are linked with two-way transitive trusts.

domain functional level   The level at which a Windows Server 2003 Active Directory domain is operating— Windows 2000 mixed, Windows 2000 native, Windows Server 2003 interim, or Windows Server 2003.

domain local group   A group within Active Directory that you can only use to specify permissions on resources within a single domain.

Domain Name System (DNS)   DNS is used primarily to resolve fully qualified domain names (FQDNs) to IP addresses. DNS is the standard naming convention for hosts on the Internet, which have both domain names (such as blastthroughlearning.com) and numeric IP addresses (such as 192.168.2.8).

domain tree   A set of domains that form a contiguous DNS namespace through a set of hierarchical relationships.

DRA   See *data recovery agent.*

driver rollback   A feature in Windows Server 2003 and Windows XP that allows a user to revert back to a previous device driver when a newly installed device driver does not work properly.

driver signing   A method for marking or identifying driver files that meet certain specifications or standards. Windows Server 2003 uses a driver signing process to make sure drivers are certified to work correctly with the Windows Driver Model (WDM) in Windows Server 2003.

dynamic disk   A physical disk in a Windows Server 2003 computer that does not use partitions or logical drives. It has dynamic volumes that you create by using the Disk Management console. A dynamic disk can contain any of five types of volumes. In addition, you can extend a volume on a dynamic disk. A dynamic disk can contain an unlimited number of volumes, so you are not restricted to four volumes per disk as you are with a basic disk.

Dynamic Host Configuration Protocol (DHCP) server A computer that dynamically assigns IP addresses to clients. The DHCP server can also provide direction toward routers, Windows Internet Name Service (WINS) servers, and DNS servers.

Dynamic Update Works with Windows Update to download critical fixes and drivers needed during the setup process. Dynamic Update provides important updates to files required to minimize difficulties during setup.

dynamic volume The only type of volume you can create on dynamic disks. There are five types of dynamic volumes: simple, spanned, mirrored, striped, and Redundant Array of Independent Disks (RAID)-5.

E

effective permissions The overall permissions that a user has over an object. Because a user can be a member of multiple groups, it is possible that a user can be assigned permissions that are assigned to the user and permissions assigned to the groups that the user is a member of for the same Active Directory object or objects. If they are permissions that have been allowed, the permissions are cumulative.

EFS See *Encrypting File System.*

Emergency Management Services (EMS) Services that can be performed on headless servers and on servers whose network connections are not currently functioning. These services offer out-of-band management through a modem or a serial port connection using the Special Administration Console or the !Special Administration Console.

emergency repair disk (ERD) A disk created by the Windows Backup utility, for Windows 2000 and earlier operating systems, that contains information about the current Windows system settings. You can use this disk to attempt to repair a computer if it does not start or if the system files are damaged or erased.

emergency repair process A process that helps you repair problems with system files, the startup environment (in a dual-boot or multiple-boot system), and the partition boot sector on a boot volume.

Encrypting File System (EFS) A subsystem of NTFS that uses public keys and private keys to provide encryption for files and folders on computers using Windows Server 2003. Only the user who initially encrypted the file and a DRA can decrypt encrypted files and folders.

Event Viewer An MMC snap-in that displays the Windows Server 2003 event logs for system, application, security, directory services, DNS server, and File Replication Service log files.

Explicit permissions   Permissions are those specifically given to the object when the object is created or assigned by another user.

F

FAT (file allocation table) or FAT16
An older file system that has a 16-bit table that many operating systems use to locate files on a disk. The FAT keeps track of all the pieces of a file. FAT retains larger cluster sizes and is unable to scale to larger volume sizes. The FAT file system has no local security.

FAT32   A 32-bit version of FAT available in Windows 95 OSR 2 and Windows 98. FAT32 increases the number of bits used to address clusters and reduces the size of each cluster. The result is that FAT32 can support larger disks (up to 2TB) and better storage efficiency (less slack space) than the earlier version of FAT. The FAT32 file system has no local security. Windows Server 2003 can use and format partitions as FAT, FAT32, or NTFS.

fault tolerance   The capability of a computer or an operating system to ensure data integrity when hardware failures occur. Within the Windows 2000 Server and Windows Server 2003 product lines, mirrored volumes and RAID-5 volumes are fault tolerant.

fax service management console
An MMC snap-in that allows you to administer the settings for sending and receiving faxes using the fax service.

firewall   A system designed to prevent unauthorized access to or from a private network. Firewalls can be implemented in both hardware and software, or a combination of both.

FireWire or IEEE (Institute of Electrical and Electronics Engineers) 1394   A newer, very fast external bus standard that supports data transfer rates of up to 800Mbps.

folder redirection   When you redirect folders, you change the storage location of folders (My Documents, Desktop, Application Data, and Start Menu) from the local hard disk on the user's computer to a shared folder on a network file server.

forest functional level   The level at which an Active Directory forest running under Windows Server 2003 is operating—Windows 2000, Windows Server 2003 interim, or Windows Server 2003.

forward lookup   In DNS, a query process in which the friendly DNS domain name of a host computer is searched to find its IP address.

forward lookup zone   A DNS zone that provides hostname-to-TCP/IP address resolution. In DNS Manager, forward lookup zones are based on DNS domain names and typically hold host (A) address resource records.

G

global group   A group that can be granted rights and permissions and can become a member of domain local groups in its own domain and trusting domains. However, a global group can contain user accounts from its own domain only. Global groups provide a way to create sets of users from inside the domain that are available for use both in and out of the domain.

globally unique identifier (GUID)   A 16-byte value generated from the unique identifier on a device, the current data and time, and a sequence number. A GUID identifies a specific device or component.

group policy   A mechanism for managing change and configuration of systems, security, applications, and user environments in an Active Directory domain.

Group Policy Editor (GPE)   A Windows Server 2003 snap-in that allows customers to create custom profiles for groups of users and computers.

Group Policy Management Console (GPMC)   A downloadable tool from Microsoft for Windows Server 2003 that lets administrators manage group policy for multiple domains and sites within one or more forests, all in a simplified user interface with drag-and-drop support.

group policy object (GPO)   An object that is created by the GPE snap-in to hold information about a specific group's association with selected directory objects, such as sites, domains, or OUs.

GUID   See *globally unique identifier*.

GUID partition table (GPT)   GPT disks are available only on computers equipped with Intel Itanium-based processors. Itanium-based computers use the Extensible Firmware Interface (EFI) instead of using a Basic Input/Output System (BIOS) as the interface between the computer's hardware devices, its firmware, and the operating system.

H

hardening   The process of closing or reducing any possible security holes in an operating system, application, device, or infrastructure.

Hardware Abstraction Layer (HAL) A component of an operating system that functions something like an API. In strict technical architecture, HALs reside at the device level, a layer below the standard API level. HAL allows programmers to write applications and game titles with all the device-independent advantages of writing to an API but without the large processing overhead that APIs normally demand.

hardware profile   A profile that stores configuration settings for a collection of devices and services. Windows Server 2003 can store different hardware profiles so that users' needs can be met even though their computers might frequently require different device and service settings, depending on circumstances.

Hash Message Authentication Code Message Digest 5 (HMAC-MD5)   A hash algorithm that produces a 128-bit hash of the authenticated payload.

headless server   A server that has no local mouse, keyboard, or video monitor directly connected to it.

hibernation   A power option in Windows, hibernation is a complete power-down while maintaining the state of open programs and connected hardware. When you bring the computer out of hibernation, the desktop is restored exactly as you left it, in less time than it takes for a complete system restart.

hidden shares   Shares that do not show up in the network browse list. Shared folders have a dollar sign ($) appended to their share names, such as admin$, c$, d$, and so on.

home directory   A location for a user or group of users to store files on a network server. The home directory provides a central location for files that users can access and back up.

HOSTS file   A local text file in the same format as the 4.3 Berkeley Software Distribution (BSD) Unix /etc/hosts file. This file maps hostnames to IP addresses. In Windows Server 2003, this file is stored in the \%SystemRoot%\ System32\Drivers\Etc folder.

I

IIS metabase   The database that holds all the configuration settings for Internet Information Services (IIS), stored in the XML file format—metabase.xml. See also *Internet Information Services*.

in-band management   Access to a server via a regular network connection as opposed to a modem or serial port connection.

incremental backup   A backup that backs up only files created or changed since the last normal or incremental backup. It marks files as having been backed up. (In other words, the archive attribute is cleared.) If you use a combination of normal and incremental backups, you need to have the last normal backup set, as well as all incremental backup sets to restore data.

Infrared Data Association (IrDA) device   A device that exchanges data over infrared waves. Infrared technology lets devices "beam" information to each other in the same way that a remote control tells a TV to change the channel.

inheritance Those permissions that flow down are known as inherited permissions. By default, when you assign explicit permissions to a container such as a domain or organizational unit that holds other objects, permissions flow down to its child objects. By using inherited permissions, you can manage them more easily and can ensure consistency of permissions among all objects within a given container.

input locale The specification of the language in which you want to type.

integrated zone storage Storage of DNS zone information in an Active Directory database rather than in a text file.

Internet Connection Firewall (ICF) A built-in service that monitors all aspects of the traffic that crosses the network interface, which includes inspecting the source and destination addresses, for further control.

Internet Connection Sharing (ICS) A feature intended for use in a small office or home office in which the network configuration and the Internet connection are managed by the computer running Windows Server 2003, where the shared connection resides. ICS can use a dial-up connection, such as a modem or an ISDN connection to the Internet, or it can use a dedicated connection such as a cable modem or Digital Subscriber Line (DSL) connection. It is assumed that the ICS computer is the only Internet connection—the only gateway to the Internet—and that it sets up all internal network addresses.

Internet Information Services (IIS) A group of services that host Internet and intranet-related features on Windows Server 2003 computers such as File Transfer Protocol (FTP) and the World Wide Web (WWW) service under IIS version 6.0. Each of these services must be installed individually; none of these features are installed by default.

Internet Printing Protocol (IPP) A standard that allows network clients the option of entering a uniform resource locator (URL) to connect to network printers and manage their network print jobs, using a Hypertext Transfer Protocol (HTTP) connection in a web browser. Windows Server 2003 fully supports IPP. The print server is either a Windows Server 2003 computer or a Windows XP Professional computer running IIS 5, or it can be a Windows 2000 Professional system running Personal Web Server (PWS). PWS is the "junior" version of IIS. You can view all shared IPP printers at `http://servername/printers` (for example, `http://Server2/printers`).

Interrupt Request (IRQ) A hardware line over which a device or devices can send interrupt signals to the microprocessor. When you add a new device to a PC, you sometimes need to set its IRQ number. IRQ conflicts used to be a common problem when you were adding expansion boards, but the Plug and Play and ACPI specifications have helped remove this headache in many cases.

I/O (input/output) port   Any socket in the back, front, or side of a computer that you use to connect to another piece of hardware.

IP (Internet Protocol)   One of the protocols of the TCP/IP suite. IP is responsible for determining whether a packet is for the local network or a remote network. If the packet is for a remote network, IP finds a route for it.

IP (Internet Protocol) address   A 32-bit binary address that identifies a host's network and host ID. The network portion can contain either a network ID or a network ID and a subnet ID.

`ipconfig`   A command that allows you to view, renegotiate, and configure IP address information for a Windows NT or 2000 computer.

IPSec (Internet Protocol Security)
A TCP/IP security mechanism that provides machine-level authentication, as well as data encryption, for virtual private network (VPN) connections that use Layer 2 Tunneling Protocol (L2TP). IPSec negotiates between a computer and its remote tunnel server before an L2TP connection is established, which secures both passwords and data.

ISDN (Integrated Services Digital Network)   An international communications standard for sending voice, video, and data over digital telephone lines or normal telephone wires. ISDN supports data transfer rates of 64Kbps. Most ISDN lines offered by telephone companies provide two lines at once, called B channels. You can use one line for voice and the other for data, or you can use both lines for data, giving you data rates of 128Kbps.

J–L

Kerberos version 5   A distributed authentication and privacy protocol that protects information on a network between devices and enables single sign-on (SSO). Kerberos version 5 is used in the Windows Server 2003 security model.

language group   A Regional Options configuration that allows you to type and read documents composed in languages of that group (for example, Western Europe, United States, Japanese, and Hebrew).

Last Known Good Configuration   A setting that starts Windows Server 2003 by using the Registry information that Windows saved at the last successful logon. You should use this setting only in cases when you have incorrectly configured a device or driver. Last Known Good Configuration does not solve problems caused by corrupted or missing drivers or files. Also, when you use this setting, you lose any changes made since the last successful logon.

Layer 2 Tunneling Protocol (L2TP)

An industry-standard Internet tunneling protocol that provides the same functionality as Point-to-Point Tunneling Protocol (PPTP). Unlike PPTP, L2TP does not require IP connectivity between the client workstation and the server. L2TP requires only that the tunnel medium provide packet-oriented point-to-point connectivity. You can use L2TP over media such as ATM, Frame Relay, and X.25.

Line Printer Remote (LPT)
A protocol used to print documents to LPD printer, usually associated with UNIX.

Line Protocol Daemon (LPD)
A protocol that provides printing on a TCP/IP network, usually associated with UNIX.

local group
A group account that is stored in the Security Accounts Manager (SAM) of a single system. You can give a local group access to resources only on that system.

local printer
Printer that is directly attached to a computer.

local user
A user account that is stored in the SAM of a single system. A local user can belong only to local groups on the same system and can be given access to resources only on that system.

logical drive
A simple volume or partition indicated by a drive letter that resides on a Windows Server 2003 basic disk.

logoff script
A file that you can assign to one or more user accounts. Typically a batch file, a logon script runs automatically every time the user logs off.

logon script
A file that you can assign to one or more user accounts. Typically a batch file, a logon script runs automatically every time the user logs on. You can use it to configure a user's working environment at every logon, and it allows an administrator to influence a user's environment without managing all aspects of it.

M

Master Boot Record partitions

Traditional partitions found on x86 and x64 computers based on the master boot record (MBR). The MBR is a small program that is executed when a computer boots up. Typically, the MBR resides on the first sector of the hard disk. The program begins the boot process by looking up the partition table to determine which partition to use for booting. It then transfers program control to the boot sector of that partition, which continues the boot process. In DOS and Windows systems, you can create the MBR with the FDISK /MBR command. MBR disks support volume sizes up to two terabytes (TB) and allow up to four primary partitions per disk. Alternatively, MBR disks support three primary partitions, one extended partition, and an unlimited number of logical drive letters.

metabase See *IIS metabase.*

Microsoft Baseline Security Analyzer (MBSA) A tool that identifies common security misconfigurations including missing security patches, blank passwords and other forms of weak passwords, as well as unnecessary services.

Microsoft Challenge Handshake Authentication Protocol (MS-CHAP) A special version of CHAP that Microsoft uses. The encryption in MS-CHAP is two-way and consists of a challenge from the server to the client that consists of a session ID. The client uses a Message Digest 4 (MD4) hash to return the username to the server.

Microsoft Management Console (MMC) A set of Windows Server 2003 utilities that allow authorized administrators to manage the directory remotely. The MMC provides a framework for hosting administrative tools, called consoles.

mirrored volume A fault-tolerant set of two physical disks that contain an exact replica of each other's data within the mirrored portion of each disk. Mirrored volumes are supported only on Windows Server computer versions.

mixed-mode domain A migration concept that provides maximum backward compatibility with earlier versions of Windows NT. In mixed-mode domain, DCs that have been upgraded to Active Directory services allow servers running Windows NT versions 4 and earlier to exist within the domain.

mounted drive, mount point, or mounted volume A pointer from one partition to another. Mounted drives are useful for increasing a drive's size without disturbing it. For example, you could create a mount point to drive E: as C:\CompanyData. Doing so makes it seem as if you have increased the size available on the C: partition, specifically allowing you to store more data in C:\CompanyData than you would otherwise be able to.

Multilink An extension to Point-to-Point Protocol (PPP) that allows you to combine multiple physical connections between two points into a single logical connection. For example, you can combine two 33.6Kbps modems into one logical 67.2Kbps connection. The combined connections, called *bundles,* provide greater bandwidth than a single connection.

Multiple Processor Support (MPS) compliant Compatible with Windows Server 2003 Symmetric Multiprocessing (SMP). Windows Server 2003 provides support for single or multiple CPUs. If you originally installed Windows Server

2003 on a computer with a single CPU, you must update the HAL on the computer so that it can recognize and use multiple CPUs. Windows XP Professional and Windows 2000 Professional both support up to a maximum of two processors.

N

name resolution   The process of mapping a computer name—either a FQDN or a NetBIOS name—to an IP address.

namespace   The hierarchical structure of objects in a group of cooperating directories or databases.

native-mode domain   A migration concept in which all DCs are running Windows Server 2003 and Windows 2000 Server Active Directory. A native-mode domain uses only Active Directory services multimaster replication between DCs, and no Windows NT DCs can participate in the domain through single-master replication.

network directory   A file or database where users or applications can get reference information about objects on the network.

network interface card (NIC), network adapter, or adapter card   A piece of computer hardware that physically connects a computer to a network cable.

network printer   A printer connected directly to the network. In a

business environment, client computers often print to a centralized print server that forwards the print jobs to a print device. Network printing or print sharing allows several people to send documents to a centrally located printer or similar device in an office so that you do not have to connect expensive printers to every single computer in the office.

normal backup   A backup that copies all files and marks those files as having been backed up (in other words, clears the archive attribute). A normal backup is the most complete form of backup.

NTBackup or NTBackup.exe   See *Backup Utility*.

ntdsutil.exe   A command-line utility for managing Active Directory, including marking Active Directory objects as "authoritative" after restoring them from backup.

NTFS (NT File System) 5   An advanced file system designed for use specifically within the Windows Server 2003 operating system. It supports file-system recovery, extremely large storage media, and long filenames.

NTFS data compression   The process of making individual files and folders occupy less disk space with the NTFS version 5.0 file system in Windows Server 2003. Compressed files can be read and written to over the network by any Windows- or DOS-based program *without* having to be decompressed first. Files decompress when opened and recompress when closed. The NTFS 5 file system handles this entire process. Compression is simply a file attribute that you can apply to any file or folder stored on an NTFS 5 drive volume.

NTFS data encryption   See *Encrypting File System*.

NTFS disk quota   See *disk quota*.

NTFS permission   A rule associated with a folder, file, or printer that regulates which users can gain access to the object and in what manner. The object's owner allows or denies permissions. The most restrictive permissions take precedence if conflicting permissions exist between share permissions and NTFS permissions on an object.

O

object   In the context of performance monitoring and optimization, a system component that has numerous counters associated with it. For example, objects include processor, memory, system, logical disk, and paging file.

offline files   A feature in Windows Server 2003, Windows XP, and Windows 2000 that allows users to continue to work with network files and programs even when they are not connected to the network. When a network connection is restored or when users dock their mobile computers, any changes made while users were working offline are updated to the network. When more than one user on the network has made changes to the same file, users are given the option of saving their specific version of the file to the network, keeping the other version, or saving both. Also known as client-side caching (CSC).

optimization   The process of tuning performance for a particular system component.

organizational unit (OU)   A type of container object used within the LDAP/X.500 information model to group other objects and classes together for easier administration.

OSI (Open Systems Interconnect) model   A layer architecture developed by the International Organization for Standardization (ISO) that standardizes levels of service and types of interaction for computers exchanging information through a communications network. The OSI model separates computer-to-computer communications into seven layers, or levels—each of which builds on the standards contained in the levels below it.

out-of-band management   Terminal-emulation support via modem or serial port for the Special Administration Console and the Special Administration Console for EMS.

owner The person who ultimately controls who can access an object and what type of an access they have.

P

pagefile See *paging file*.

paging file A system file that is an extension of random access memory which is stored on the disk drive as a kind of virtual memory.

partition A section on a basic disk created from free space so that data can be stored on it. On a basic disk, you can create up to four primary partitions or up to three primary partitions and one extended partition.

Password Authentication Protocol (PAP) A protocol that allows clear-text authentication.

password policy A group policy that determines the password settings for domain and local user accounts. It includes minimum and maximum password age, complexity of password, length of password and the number of password history.

performance bottleneck A delay in processing or transmission of data through the circuits of a computer's microprocessor or over a TCP/IP network. The delay typically occurs when a system's bandwidth cannot support the amount of information being relayed at the speed it is being processed. However, many factors can create a bottleneck in a system. Common system performance bottleneck categories include processor, memory, disk, and network.

performance counters Data items that direct the System Monitor about which areas of performance to track and display. Each performance object has several performance counters associated with it. Pages/sec, Available Bytes, and %Committed Bytes in Use are all examples of counters for the Memory performance object.

Performance Logs and Alerts A tool in Windows Server 2003 is the other half of the Performance snap-in.

Performance MMC snap-in A utility for monitoring, tracking, and displaying a computer's performance statistics, both in real time and over an extended period for establishing a system baseline. This console includes the System Monitor node and the Performance Logs and Alerts node.

performance object instances Terms that provide a method of identifying multiple performance objects of the same type. If a computer has more than one processor installed, its processor performance object displays multiple distinct instances of this object to monitor each individual processor separately.

performance objects Logical collections of performance metrics associated with a computer resource

(CPU, disk, memory) or service that you can monitor. Processor, Memory, PhysicalDisk, and Paging File are all examples of performance objects.

permission A permission defines the type of access that is granted to an object or object attribute. Users, printers, and organizational units are all examples of objects within Active Directory. Every object in Active Directory has an owner who controls how permissions are set on an object and to whom permissions are assigned. To keep track of these permissions, each object will have an access control list (ACL), which will list each user who has access to the object and the type of access they have to the object. The list of user access permissions is called the discretionary access control list (DACL).

ping (packet Internet groper) utility A utility that determines whether a specific IP address for a network device is reachable from an individual computer. ping works by sending a data packet to the specified address and waiting for a reply. You can use ping to troubleshoot network connections in the TCP/IP network protocol.

Plug and Play A standard developed by Microsoft, Intel, and other industry leaders to simplify the process of adding hardware to PCs by having the operating system automatically detect devices.

Point-to-Point Protocol (PPP) A method of connecting a computer to a network or to the Internet. PPP is more stable than the older Serial Line Internet Protocol (SLIP) and provides error-checking features. Windows XP Professional and Windows 2000 Professional are both PPP clients when dialing in to any network.

Point-to-Point Tunneling Protocol (PPTP) A communication protocol that tunnels through another connection, encapsulating PPP packets. The encapsulated packets are IP datagrams that can be transmitted over IP-based networks, such as the Internet.

policy A configuration or setting specified for one or more systems or users. Policies are refreshed at startup, at logon, and after a refresh interval, so if a setting is manually changed, the policy refreshes the setting automatically. Policies provide for centralized management of change and configuration.

prestaging computer accounts A method for creating computer accounts within Active Directory in advance of installing the computers and then joining them to the domain using RIS.

primary domain controller (PDC) In a Windows NT Server 4 or earlier domain, the computer running Windows NT Server that authenticates domain logons and maintains the directory database for a domain. The PDC tracks changes made to accounts of all computers on a domain. It is the only computer to receive these changes directly. A domain has only one PDC.

primary master   An authoritative DNS server for a zone that you can use as a point of update for the zone. Only primary masters can be updated directly to process zone updates, which include adding, removing, and modifying resource records stored as zone data. Primary masters are also used as the first sources for replicating the zone to other DNS servers.

primary monitor   The monitor designated as the one that displays the logon dialog box when you start a computer. Most programs display their windows on the primary monitor when you first open them. A Windows Server 2003 computer can support multiple monitors or displays.

primary restore   A type of restore for Active Directory objects that you should perform when there is only one DC in the domain or when you need to rebuild an entire domain from backup because all DCs have been lost.

print driver   A program designed to allow other programs to work with a particular printer without concerning themselves with the specifics of the printer's hardware and internal language.

print priority   By having multiple printers print to a single print

device, you can set up a high priority to one printer and a low priority to the other printer. The print jobs sent to the printer with the high priority will print before the printer with the lower priority. Priority 1 printers are of the lowest priority. You then assign some users to one printer and other people to the other printer. You would use permission to control who can print to which printers.

print queue   A storage area or buffer that holds print jobs until a print device is ready to print them. The printer then pulls the documents off the queue one at a time.

print scheduling   Specifying when printers can and cannot print to a printer device. By default, when you create a printer in Windows, it prints immediately when it receives a print job. In some situations, you might choose to print during certain times, such as at night or when the printer is not being used as much.

print spooler   In Windows, an executable file that manages the printing process including retrieving the location of the correct printer driver, loading the driver, creating the individual print jobs, and scheduling the print jobs for printing.

printer   In Windows, the software interface between a print device and the print clients or applications. A logical representation of a printer device in Windows has an assigned printer name and software that controls a printer device. When you print to the printer device, you print to the printer, which will then print to the printer device.

printer device   In Windows, the physical print device such as a printer, copy machine, or plotter.

printer pool   Associates two or more identical printer devices to the same printer. Although this allows for redundancy, it is most intended when you have a high volume of printing that can be evenly distributed between print devices. When a document is sent to the printer pool, the first available printer receives and prints it. If one device within a pool stops printing, the current document is still held at that device. Other print jobs will be sent to the other print devices.

privilege or user right   The capability to perform a system behavior, such as changing the system time, backing up or restoring files, or formatting the hard drive.

public-key cryptography   An asymmetric encryption scheme that uses a pair of keys to code data. The public key encrypts data, and a corresponding secret (private) key decrypts it. For digital signatures, the sender uses the private key to create a unique electronic number that can be read by anyone who has the corresponding public key, thus verifying that the message is truly from the sender.

Q–R

RADIUS (Remote Authentication Dial-in User Service)   A protocol used by Internet Authentication Services (IAS) to enable the communication of authentication, authorization, and accounting to the homogeneous and heterogeneous dial-up or VPN equipment in the enterprise.

RAID (Redundant Array of Independent Disks)-5 volume or striped set with parity volume   A fault-tolerant collection of equal-sized partitions on at least three physical disks, in which the data is striped and includes parity data. The parity data helps recover a member of the striped set if the member fails. Neither Windows XP Professional nor Windows 2000 Professional can host a RAID-5 volume, but Windows Server 2003 and Windows 2000 Server computers can.

Recovery Console   A command-line interface (CLI) that provides a limited set of administrative commands useful for repairing a computer. For example, you can use the Recovery Console to start and stop services, read and write data on a local drive (including drives formatted to use NTFS), repair a master boot record (MBR), and format drives. You can start the Recovery Console from the Windows Server 2003 CD-ROM, or you can install the Recovery Console on the computer using the `winnt32.exe` command with the `/cmdcons` switch.

Remote Assistance (RA)   A built-in service that enables another user, typically a help-desk or IT employee, to remotely help the end user with an issue that she is experiencing on her Windows XP Professional or Windows Server 2003 computer.

Remote Desktop Connection   Client software that enables you to access a Terminal Services session running on a remote computer while you are sitting at another computer in a different location. This process is extremely useful for employees who want to work from home but need to access their computers at work.

Remote Desktops MMC snap-in   An MMC snap-in that allows administrators to log on to multiple Remote Desktop sessions simultaneously from a single management console.

remote assistance (RA)   Software component designed primarily for help-desk personnel (or other trusted computer technicians) to assist users with general computer usage questions and to troubleshoot system problems for Windows XP Professional desktop computers.

remote desktop connections (RDC)   A tool/interface that uses terminal services to remotely connect to and control a PC using the Windows GUI interface.

remote desktops snap-in   A MMC snap-in allows you to view multiple Remote Desktop Connections (RDC) sessions that can all be running simultaneously within one MMC window. This tool is great for centralizing remote administration using one utility for accessing multiple servers at the same time.

Remote Installation Services (RIS)   A server that provides Windows Server 2003, Windows XP Professional, and Windows 2000 Professional operating-system images that can be downloaded and installed by network clients using network adapters that comply with the preboot execution environment (PXE) boot read-only memory (ROM) specifications. RIS requires Active Directory, DHCP, and DNS to serve clients.

remote server management   The ability to manage a server remotely (connected to the server through the network).

Removable Storage   Allows applications to access and share the same media resources. This service is used for managing removable media. Different types of media include floppy disks, Zip disks, CD-ROMs, CD-Rs, CD-RWs, DVD media, and tape backup devices. Some include removable hard drives as removable storage.

restricted groups   A groups policy that defines which members can belong to a group. Users who have been added to a group and are not specified in the restricted group policy will be removed when the group policy is refreshed.

Resultant Set of Policy (RSoP)   A term for the resulting (effective) group policies applied to a computer and user. With multiple group policies at sites, domains, and OUs, it is very complex to determine the final, resulting policies that are applied and how those policies affect the user and the computer.

reverse lookup zone   A DNS zone that provides TCP/IP address-to-hostname resolution.

route   A Windows Server 2003 command-line utility that manipulates TCP/IP routing tables for the local computer.

runas   A Windows Server 2003 GUI and command-line tool that allows a user or an administrator to run a program or to open a file under a different user's security credentials using the appropriate user account name and password.

S

Safe Mode startup options   The options you get at startup when you press the F8 function key while in Safe Mode. Safe Mode helps you diagnose problems. When started in Safe Mode, Windows Server 2003 uses only basic files and drivers (mouse, monitor, keyboard, mass storage, base video, and default system services but no network connections).

sampling interval or update interval   The frequency with which a performance counter is logged. A shorter interval provides more detailed information but generates a larger log.

scalability   A measure of how well a computer, a service, or an application can grow to meet increasing performance demands.

scheduled tasks   A system folder that stores scheduled jobs which run at predefined times. Administrators can create scheduled jobs.

Scheduled Tasks Wizard   A series of dialog boxes that simplify the process of creating scheduled task jobs.

security   Techniques for ensuring that data stored in a computer cannot be read or compromised by any individuals without authorization. Most security measures involve data encryption and passwords.

Security Accounts Manager (SAM)   The database of local user and local group accounts on a Windows Server 2003 member server, Windows XP Professional, or Windows 2000 Professional computer.

Security Configuration and Analysis tool   A popular tool you can use to analyze computer security. This tool compares the security configuration of a local computer with a template file and stored in a separate database (an .sdb file). You can then browse the security settings in the console tree to see the results.

security group A group that can contain users and other groups that can be assigned an ACL with ACEs to define security permissions on objects for the members of the group.

security identifier (SID) A unique number that represents a security principal such as a user or group. You can change the name of a user or group account without affecting the account's permissions and privileges because the SID is granted user rights and resource access.

security logs Logs that contain security events.

security policy A combination of security settings that affect the security on a computer or domain. With a local security policy, you can control account policies, local policies, public key policy, software restriction policy, and IP Security policies.

Security Principals Any object within the operating system that can be authenticated by the operating system. Examples of these objects (or entities) include user accounts, computer accounts, and security groups. A security principal can also be a thread or a process that runs within the security context of a user account or a computer account.

security template A template that provides a single place where all system security can be viewed, analyzed, changed, and applied to a single machine or to a Group Policy

object. Security templates do not introduce new security parameters: They simply organize all existing security attributes into one place to ease security administration. Security templates can also be used as base configuration for security analysis, when used with the Security Configuration and Analysis snap-in.

security updates Updates or patches that relate to security.

Serial Line Internet Protocol (SLIP) An older remote access communication protocol used in Windows Server 2003 for outbound communication only. This protocol is commonly used for connecting to Unix servers.

Server Update Services (SUS) An old service loaded on a Windows server that provides a central point for client computers and servers to acquire Windows updates.

service packs Updates bundled together to a software version that fixes or patches existing problems, such as a bugs, or provides enhancements to the product that will appear in the next version of the product.

Setup Manager A utility program that ships on the Windows Server 2003 CD-ROM and that is used to create answer files for unattended installations. Setup Manager can create answer files for unattended, sysprep, or RIS installations.

Shadow Copies of Shared Folders A new feature in Windows Server 2003 that creates "snapshots," or copies, of original data volumes at various scheduled intervals and during data backup operations. You can retrieve previous versions of files and folders from Shadow Copies by installing the Previous Versions Client software on Windows XP workstations and by installing the Shadow Copy Client software on Windows 2000 and previous operating systems.

share permission A rule associated with a folder to regulate which users can gain access to the object over the network and in what manner.

shared folder A folder that is shared for use by remote users over the network.

Shared Folder snap-in A MMC console/snap-in (also found within the Computer Management console) that provides a central location for managing all shared folders on a server.

Shiva Password Authentication Protocol (SPAP) A protocol that third-party clients and servers typically use. The encryption for SPAP is two-way, but it is not as good as that for CHAP.

simple volume In Windows Server 2003, the disk space on a single physical disk. A simple volume can consist of a single area on a disk or multiple areas on the same disk that are linked together. You can extend a simple volume within the same disk or among multiple disks. If you extend a simple volume across multiple disks, it becomes a spanned volume.

slipstreaming The process of integrating a Windows Server 2003 service pack (SP) into an existing Windows Server 2003 installation share. Subsequent installations of Windows Server 2003 do not require separate SP installation because the updated SP files are included (slipstreamed) into the installation share.

smart card A credit-card–sized device used to securely store public and private keys, passwords, and other types of personal information. To use a smart card, you need a smart card reader attached to the computer and a personal identification number (PIN) for the smart card. In Windows Server 2003, you can use smart cards to enable certificate-based authentication and SSO to the enterprise.

Software Update Services (SUS) An add-on program you can download from Microsoft's website that allows an organization to centrally manage and deploy software patches and updates for Microsoft operating systems. It works in a similar fashion to the Microsoft Windows Update website.

spanned volume In Windows Server 2003, the disk space on more than one physical disk. You can add more space to a spanned volume by extending it at any time. In NT 4 and earlier operating systems, a spanned volume is called a volume set.

Special Identity Groups Built-in groups that the operating system uses internally. No user can change the membership of these groups; membership is situational, and the membership of these groups is determined by what activities users are currently involved in on the server and on the network. Group scopes do not apply to special identity groups. However, you can apply user rights and assign security permissions to SI groups for specific resources. Special identity groups include the authenticated users and the everyone group.

spooler service The primary Windows Server 2003 service that controls printing functionality.

SRV (service) record A resource record used in a zone to register and locate well-known TCP/IP services. The SRV resource record is specified in Request for Comments (RFC) 2052 and is used in Windows Server 2003 or later to locate DCs for Active Directory service.

standard permission Standard permissions are the most common and frequently assigned permissions that apply to the entire object. Assigning standard permissions is sufficient for most administrative tasks.

standard zone storage Storage of zone information in a text file rather than in an Active Directory database.

standby mode A power-saving option in Windows Server 2003, Windows XP, and Windows 2000 computers in which a computer switches to a low-power state where devices, such as the monitor and hard disks, turn off and the computer uses less power. When you want to use the computer again, it comes out of standby quickly, and the desktop is restored exactly as you left it. Standby is useful for conserving battery power in portable computers. Standby does not save the desktop state to disk; if you experience a power failure while in standby mode, you can lose unsaved information. If there is an interruption in power, information in memory is lost.

stateful firewall A firewall that keeps track of connections so that it knows what traffic it lets in.

static pool A range of IP addresses configured on the remote access server that allows the server to allocate IP addresses to the remote access clients.

striped volume A volume that stores data in stripes on two or more physical disks. Data in a striped volume is allocated alternately and evenly (in stripes) to the disks of the striped volume. Striped volumes are not fault tolerant. Striped volumes can substantially improve the speed of access to the data on disk. You can create them on Windows Server 2003, Windows XP Professional, Windows 2000 Professional, and Windows 2000 Server computers. Striped volumes with parity, also known as RAID-5 volumes, can be created only on Windows Server 2003 and Windows 2000 Server computers.

strong password   A password that is difficult to detect by both humans and computer programs, effectively protecting data from unauthorized access. A strong password consists of at least six characters (and the more characters, the stronger the password) that are a combination of letters, numbers and symbols (@, #, $, %, and so on) if allowed. Strong passwords should not contain words that can be found in a dictionary or parts of the user's own name.

subnet mask   A filter used to determine which network segment, or subnet, an IP address belongs to. An IP address has two components: the network address and the host (computer name) address. For example, if the IP address 209.15.17.8 is part of a Class C network, the first three numbers (209.15.17) represent the Class C network address, and the last number (8) identifies a specific host (computer) on that network. By implementing subnetting, network administrators can further divide the host part of the address into two or more subnets.

suspend mode   A deep-sleep power-saving option that does use some power.

symmetric multiprocessing (SMP)   A computer architecture that provides fast performance by making multiple CPUs available to complete individual processes simultaneously (that is, multiprocessing). Unlike with asymmetric processing, with SMP you can assign any idle processor any task as well as add additional CPUs to improve performance and handle increased loads. A variety of specialized operating systems and hardware arrangements support SMP. Specific applications can benefit from SMP if their code allows multithreading. SMP uses a single operating system and shares common memory and disk I/O resources. Windows Server 2003 supports SMP.

sysprep   A tool that prepares a Windows Server 2003, Windows XP Professional, or a Windows 2000 Professional computer to be imaged by using third-party disk image software. It does so by removing unique identifiers such as computer name and SIDs. sysprep modifies the target operating system's Registry so that a unique local domain SID is created when the computer boots for the first time after the disk image is applied.

System Access Control List (SACL)
An ACL that specifies the security events to be audited for a user or group.

System Monitor   A node in the Performance MMC snap-in for monitoring and logging computer performance statistics using performance objects, counters, and instances.

System State   In the Windows Backup utility, a collection of system-specific data that you can back up and restore. For all Windows Server 2003, Windows XP, and Windows 2000 operating systems, the System State data includes the Registry, the Component Object Model (COM)+ Class Registration database, and the system boot files. For Windows Server 2003 and Windows 2000 Server, the System State data also includes the Certificate Services database (if the server is operating as a certificate server). If the server is a DC, the System State data also includes the Active Directory database and the `sysvol` directory.

sysvol   A shared directory that stores the server copy of the domain's public files, which are replicated among all DCs in the domain.

T

Task Manager   A utility program that displays the current application programs and processes that are running on the computer. It also monitors the system's recent processor usage, recent memory usage,

current network utilization, and currently logged on users.

Terminal Server   A computer that is running Terminal Services. A Windows Server 2003 computer installs Terminal Services in Remote Desktop for Administration mode by default. You must set up Terminal Services in Application Server mode separately.

Terminal Services   A built-in service that enables you to use the Remote Desktop Connection software to connect to a session running on a remote computer while you are sitting at another computer in a different location. This process is extremely useful for employees who want to work from home but need to access their computers at work.

Terminal Services Remote Administration   Tools that allow you to manage the terminal services remote connections and settings.

ticket   A feature of the Kerberos security model by which clients are granted access to objects and resources only indirectly, through services. Application servers use the service ticket to impersonate the client and look up its user or group SIDs.

tracert   A Windows Server 2003 command-line utility that follows the path of a data packet from a local computer to a host (computer) somewhere on the network (or internetwork). It shows how many hops the packet requires to reach the host and how long each hop takes. You can use `tracert` to figure out where the longest delays are occurring for connecting to various computers.

U–V

universal group A security or distribution group that you can use anywhere in a domain tree or forest; universal groups are only available when the domain's functional level is set at Windows 2000 native or Windows Server 2003. A universal group can have members from any Active Directory domain in the domain tree or forest. It can also include other universal groups, global groups, and accounts from any domain in the domain tree or forest. Universal groups can be members of domain local groups and other universal groups but cannot be members of global groups. Universal groups appear in the global catalog and should contain primarily global groups.

USB (universal serial bus) An external bus standard (released in 1996) that supports data transfer rates of 12Mbps. You can use a single USB port to connect up to 127 peripheral devices, such as mice, modems, and keyboards. USB also supports Plug and Play installation and hot plugging. It is expected to completely replace serial and parallel ports.

user account An object within Active Directory that contains information about a user, including the user logon name, password, and group memberships. Also, an object with a local computer's SAM database that contains information about a user, including the user logon name, password, and group memberships.

User Datagram Protocol (UDP) A connectionless protocol that runs on top of IP networks. Unlike TCP/IP, UDP provides very few error-recovery services and does not guarantee delivery of data. UDP is a direct way to send and receive datagrams over an IP network. It's used primarily for sending broadcast messages over an IP network.

user locale A group of settings that control the date, time, currency, and numbers on a per-user basis. All applications use these settings, and you can configure them via the Regional and Language Options applet in the Control Panel.

user profile A collection of desktop and environmental settings that define the work area of a local computer.

user right See *privilege*.

User State Migration Tool (USMT) A CLI set of tools that stores user data and settings for an upgrade or reinstallation of the computer. The tools include `scanstate` and `loadstate`, which extract the information and restore the information, respectively.

universally unique identifier (UUID)
See *globally unique identifier*.

video adapter The electronic component that generates the video signal sent through a cable to a video display. The video adapter is usually located on the computer's main system board or on an expansion board.

virtual private network (VPN) A private network of computers that is at least partially connected using public channels or lines, such as the Internet. A good example of a VPN is a private-office local area network (LAN) that allows users to log in remotely over the Internet (an open, public system). VPNs use encryption and secure protocols such as PPTP and L2TP to ensure that unauthorized parties do not intercept data transmissions.

volume A section on a dynamic disk that is created from unallocated space so that data can be stored on it. You can only create simple volumes, striped volumes, spanned volumes, mirrored volumes, and RAID-5 volumes on dynamic disks.

Volume Shadow Copy Service (VSS)
A service in Windows Server 2003 and Windows XP that creates "snapshots," or copies, of original data volumes at various scheduled intervals and during data backup operations. Under Windows Server 2003, you can retrieve previous versions of files and folders from Shadow Copies; under Windows XP, Shadow Copies are used only for taking snapshots of data for backup operations.

W

WDM (Windows or Win32 Driver Model) A 32-bit layered architecture for device drivers that allows for drivers that Windows Server 2003, Windows XP, Windows 2000, Windows NT, and Windows 98 computers can use. It provides common I/O services that all operating systems understand. It also supports Plug and Play; USB; IEEE 1394; and various devices, including input, communication, imaging, and DVD.

Wi-Fi Protected Access (WPA) A Wi-Fi standard designed to improve upon the security features of WEP. The technology is designed to work with existing Wi-Fi products that have been enabled with WEP (that is, as a software upgrade to existing hardware), but the technology includes improved data encryption through the temporal key integrity protocol (TKIP) and user authentication.

Windows Installer Service package
A file with the `.msi` extension that installs applications. Such files contain summary and installation instructions, as well as the actual installation files. You can install Windows Installer Service packages locally or remotely through Windows Server 2003 group policies.

Windows Internet Name Service (WINS) A service that dynamically maps NetBIOS names to IP addresses.

Windows Management Instrumentation (WMI) An initiative supported in Windows Server 2003 that establishes architecture to support the management of an enterprise across the Internet. WMI offers universal access to management information for enterprises by providing a consistent view of the managed environment. This management uniformity allows you to manage the entire business rather than just its components. You can obtain more detailed information regarding the WMI Software Development Kit (SDK) from the Microsoft Developer Network (MSDN).

Windows Messenger The new application built into the operating system that allows for chatting, notifications, voice communication, file transfer, and sharing of applications.

Windows Update Offers device-driver support that supplements the extensive library of drivers available on the installation CD. Windows Update is an online extension, providing a central location for product enhancements.

Windows Server Update Services (WSUS) A service loaded on a Windows server that provides a central point for client computers and servers to acquire updates. With

WSUS, you can also update Microsoft Office, Microsoft SQL, Microsoft Exchange and other Microsoft applications.

winnt32 /cmdcons The command and switch used to install the Recovery Console on a Windows Server 2003 computer. This command uses `winnt32` on the installation media or in the distribution source.

Wired Equivalent Privacy (WEP) A security protocol for wireless local area networks (WLANs) defined in the 802.11b standard. WEP is designed to provide the same level of security as that of a wired LAN. WEP aims to provide security by encrypting data over radio waves so that it is protected as it is transmitted from one end point to another. However, it has been found that WEP is not as secure as once believed. WEP is used at the two lowest layers of the OSI model—the data link and physical layers. Therefore, it does not offer end-to-end security.

Wireless Internet service provider (WISP) An Internet service provider (ISP) that offers Internet connection services to subscribers using a wireless connection.

Wireless Provisioning Services (WPS) Services that facilitate the use of wireless hotspots while enhancing wireless security. WPS with Windows Server 2003 Service Pack 1 (and with R2), along with Microsoft Internet Authentication

Service (IAS), allows users' computers to more easily detect, connect, and move between wireless hotspots with stronger security.

workgroup   A peer-to-peer network in which user accounts are decentralized and stored on each individual system.

written security policy   A document or set of documents that outlines the rules, laws, and practices for computer network access. This document regulates how an organization will manage, protect, and distribute its sensitive information (both corporate and client information) and lays the framework for the computer-network–oriented security of the organization.

X–Z

.ZAP file   A file that you use to allow applications without an `.msi` file to be deployed via Active Directory group policy.

zone   In DNS standards, the namespace partition formed by each domain within the global namespace or within an enterprise namespace. Each zone is controlled by an authoritative DNS server, or in the case of Active Directory services, by a group of DCs.

zone transfer   Copying DNS database information from one DNS server to another.

Index

M

T

X – Y – Z

Safari
BOOKS ONLINE
ENABLED

THIS BOOK IS SAFARI ENABLED

INCLUDES FREE 45-DAY ACCESS TO THE ONLINE EDITION

The Safari® Enabled icon on the cover of your favorite technology book means the book is available through Safari Bookshelf. When you buy this book, you get free access to the online edition for 45 days.

Safari Bookshelf is an electronic reference library that lets you easily search thousands of technical books, find code samples, download chapters, and access technical information whenever and wherever you need it.

TO GAIN 45-DAY SAFARI ENABLED ACCESS TO THIS BOOK:

- Go to **www.examcram.com/safarienabled**
- Complete the brief registration form
- Enter the coupon code found in the front of this book on the "Copyright" page

If you have difficulty registering on Safari Bookshelf or accessing the online edition, please e-mail customer-service@safaribooksonline.com.

MCSE titles from Exam Cram

Prepare for the MCSE, MCSA, and other Microsoft Certifications with Exam Cram

Exam Cram has the resources you are looking for to prepare for your MCSE certification. These proven and popular Exam Cram series match the different learning needs of different certification candidates, providing expert authors, proven practice tools, and valuable learning and exam readiness feedback.

Look to Exam Cram for

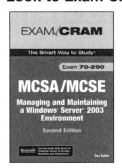

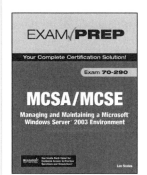

EXAM✓CRAM

QUICK Exam Crams provide strong foundational knowledge review, test-taking tips, exam practice, and readiness feedback. Exam Crams provide you with a succinct way to hone your knowledge for test day to ensure you maximize your score.

EXAM✓PREP

COMPREHENSIVE
Exam Preps are the whole package. You get in-depth tutorial learning on the test topics, practice testing on both individual test sections as well as simulating the complete exam, test-taking strategies, and feedback on areas requiring further preparation.

MCSE Titles

ISBN	TITLE	ISBN	TITLE
0-7897-3617-9	MCSA/MCSE 70-290 Exam Cram	0-7897-3650-0	MCSE 70-293 Exam Prep
0-7897-3648-9	MCSA/MCSE 70-290 Exam Prep	0-7897-3620-9	MCSE 70-294 Exam Cram
0-7897-3618-7	MCSA/MCSE 70-291 Exam Cram	0-7897-3651-9	MCSE 70-294 Exam Prep
0-7897-3649-7	MCSA/MCSE 70-291 Exam Prep	0-7897-3360-9	MCSA/MCSE 70-270 Exam Cram
0-7897-3619-5	MCSE 70-293 Exam Cram	0-7897-3363-3	MCSA/MCSE 70-270 Exam Prep

Visit www.examcram.com for more information on these and other Exam Cram products.